"Verwisch die Spuren!"
Bertolt Brecht's Work
and Legacy
A Reassessment

AMSTERDAMER BEITRÄGE ZUR NEUEREN GERMANISTIK

66 2008

Herausgegeben von

Norbert Otto Eke
Martha B. Helfer
Gerhard P. Knapp
Gerd Labroisse

"Verwisch die Spuren!"
Bertolt Brecht's Work and Legacy

A Reassessment

Edited by

Robert Gillett and Godela Weiss-Sussex

Amsterdam - New York, NY 2008

Die 1972 gegründete Reihe erscheint seit 1977 in zwangloser Folge in der
Form von Thema-Bänden mit jeweils verantwortlichem Herausgeber.

Reihen-Herausgeber:

Prof. Dr. Norbert Otto Eke
Universität Paderborn
Fakultät für Kulturwissenschaften, Warburger Str. 100, D - 33098 Paderborn,
Deutschland, E-Mail: norbert.eke@upb.de

Prof. Dr. Martha B. Helfer
Rutgers University
172 College Avenue, New Brunswick, NJ 08901
Tel.: (732) 932-7201, Fax: (732) 932-1111, E-mail: mhelfer@rci.rutgers.edu

Prof. Dr. Gerhard P. Knapp
University of Utah
Dept. of Languages and Literature, 255 S. Central Campus Dr. Rm. 1400
Salt Lake City, UT 84112, USA
Tel.: (1)801 581 7561, Fax (1)801 581 7581 (dienstl.)
bzw. Tel./Fax: (1)801 474 0869 (privat) E-Mail: gerhard.knapp@m.cc.utah.edu

Prof. Dr. Gerd Labroisse
Sylter Str. 13A, 14199 Berlin, Deutschland
Tel./Fax: (49)30 89724235 E-Mail: Labroisse@t-online.de

Cover:
Linoleum block print of Bertolt Brecht by John Sokol

All titles in the Amsterdamer Beiträge zur neueren Germanistik
(from 1999 onwards) are available online: See www.rodopi.nl
Electronic access is included in print subscriptions.

The paper on which this book is printed meets the requirements of "ISO
9706:1994, Information and documentation - Paper for documents -
Requirements for permanence".

This book is published simultaneously as Volume 92 in the series
PUBLICATIONS OF THE INSTITUTE OF GERMANIC STUDIES
(Institute of Germanic & Romance Studies
School of Advanced Study, University of London)
ISBN 978 0 85457 218 2

ISBN: 978-90-420-2432-8
©Editions Rodopi B.V., Amsterdam – New York, NY 2008
Printed in The Netherlands

Contents

6

Acknowledgements

This volume originated in a conference held at the University of London Institute of Germanic & Romance Studies in February 2006. Thanks are due to Jane Lewin, whose work in the preparation and organization of this conference was invaluable, and to all who attended the conference for the animated and fruitful discussions which have fed into several of the essays presented here.

The editors also wish to thank Michael Minden for his helpful comments and Marielle Sutherland for her thorough and efficient proofreading. Both have helped in important ways to bring about the final shape of the book.

For permission to print material from the Bertolt Brecht Archive we thank the Bertolt Brecht Erben and the Suhrkamp Verlag.

Abbreviations

BBA   Bertolt Brecht Archiv

BFA   Bertolt Brecht: *Werke. Große kommentierte Berliner und Frankfurter Ausgabe*. Hg. von Werner Hecht, Jan Knopf, Werner Mittenzwei und Klaus-Detlef Müller. 30 Bde. Berlin – Weimar: Aufbau / Frankfurt am Main: Suhrkamp 1988–2000.

WBGB   Walter Benjamin: *Gesammelte Briefe*. Hg. von Christoph Gödde und Henri Lonitz. 6 Bde. Frankfurt am Main: Suhrkamp 1995–2000.

WBGS   Walter Benjamin: *Gesammelte Schriften*. Hg. von Rolf Tiedemann und Hermann Schweppenhäuser. 7 Bde; in 14 Teilbänden. Frankfurt am Main: Suhrkamp 1972–1989.

Introductory Note

Even fifty years after Brecht's death, the complexity of his personality and the sheer richness of his work have lost none of their power to fascinate. In the intervening period, though, his influence has been pervasive. This semicentenary volume of essays has been carefully designed to reflect both facets of the "Brecht phenomenon". It covers the whole of Brecht's career, from the early one-acter *Kleinbürgerhochzeit* of 1919 (which is the subject of Marielle Sutherland's piece), to the *Sinn und Form* years immediately preceding his death (which Stephen Parker examines), while also paying careful attention to his predecessors (notably in the contribution of Frank Krause), his use of tradition, and his legacy. By way of redressing a tendency in Brecht reception to regard him mainly as a dramatist, the volume covers novels, poetry, film, photography, journalism and theory as well as plays. The approaches adopted are equally multifarious, ranging from detailed exegesis to cultural criticism in the broadest sense and illuminating Brecht's work from a wide variety of different perspectives.

At the same time, much thought has gone into ensuring that the volume constitutes a coherent whole. After a trio of essays underlining the essence of Brecht's achievement in the major genres, including new insights from Martin Swales on exactly what it is that makes his theatre so special, the thrust of the book is roughly chronological, following Brecht's career from its lyric beginnings through his encounter with Expressionism, his move to the city, and his experience of exile and the GDR, to his death and afterlife. Within this broad sweep, there are also tighter clusters. With regard to each of the major genres, for example, questions of tradition, achievement and legacy are addressed. Thus the contribution of Ernest Schonfield details Brecht's debt to the picaresque. Klaus-Detlef Müller gives a careful account of Brecht's anti-Aristotelian novels. And Martin Brady explains how one such novel became an extremely influential film. Peter Hutchinson explores Brecht's break with the mellifluous and reassuring tradition of bourgeois verse. Ron Speirs offers a detailed analysis of the *Svendborger Gedichte*. And Karen Leeder follows the traces of Brecht as a person and a writer in contemporary poetry. Equally, Michael Patterson revisits the question of Brecht's debt to Expressionism and hence of the roots of his theatre. Hans-Harald Müller re-examincs the *Leben des Galilei*. And Robert Gillett discusses an avatar of that play in Grass's *Die Plebejer proben den Aufstand*. Again, in Steve Giles's contribution, Brecht's theory of realism is read in relation both to his predecessors and to influential older and younger contemporaries. At the same time, the deliberate juxtaposition of different genres, which is such a feature of Brecht's dramatic theory, is shown to pertain in

12

other contexts also. Thus Tom Kuhn addresses the relationship between poetry and photography in the *Kriegsfibel*. And John and Ann White explore the relationship between poetry and dramatic enactment in the *Furcht und Elend* complex.

Thematically, there is a concentration on two particular constellations: the city and mortality. The former is here enriched, in the contribution of Erdmut Wizisla, by snapshots of an investigation into the relationship between Brecht and *the* theorist of the modern city, Walter Benjamin. But it is also painstakingly contextualized in Ulrike Zitzlsperger's essay and seen from a postmodern, theoretical perspective in that of Andrew Webber. The theme of Brecht and mortality is the subject of David Midgley's contribution. It also constitutes a *locus classicus* where issues of tradition and legacy meet – here expressed in the typical Brechtian paradox of encompassing in the traditional guarantor of posterity the injunction "Verwisch die Spuren!". It is therefore no accident that the relevant poem is discussed in no fewer than three of the essays in this volume. And these "Spuren" themselves are the hotly debated subject of Godela Weiss-Sussex's essay, in which she uses judgements about translations in order precisely to reassess Brecht's work and its legacy.

Klaus-Detlef Müller

Der antiaristotelische Roman: Brechts Beitrag zum Roman der klassischen Moderne

It was not only the drama of the twentieth century that Brecht changed fundamentally with his Epic Theatre. He also effected innovations in the area of prose fiction that have so far been rather neglected. Here too the word he used to describe his procedure was "anti-Aristotelian". The aim is to counter empathetic reception and to develop narrative possibilities that do not depend on individual characters. The Dreigroschenroman *and* Die Geschäfte des Herrn Julius Caesar *will be used here to show how this is feasible in theory and fruitful in practice.*

1

Zu den auffälligsten Eigenarten der satirischen Erzählweise Brechts in seinem *Dreigroschenroman* (BFA 16) gehört es, daß die Figuren bisweilen gar nicht verantwortlich sind für das, was ihnen als ihr Denken zugeschrieben wird. So reflektiert der Kriegsinvalide Fewkoombey aus gegebenem Anlaß darüber, daß Abtreibungen vernünftigerweise verboten und folglich glücklicherweise unerschwinglich teuer sind, weil sonst keine Frau so unmütterlich wäre, ihrem Kind die Existenz in einer Welt des in seiner Perspektive allgegenwärtigen und unaufhebbaren Elends zuzumuten. Die Pointe dieser im objektiven Horizont der Figur so sachgerechten wie schlüssigen Überlegungen ist freilich, daß das gar nicht seine Gedanken sind, denn es heißt anschließend: "So ungefähr hätte der Soldat wohl gedacht, wenn er gedacht hätte. Aber er dachte nicht: er war zur Disziplin erzogen" (BFA 16. S. 74). In ähnlicher Weise wird dem Bettlerkönig Peachum angesichts eines fehlgeschlagenen Geschäfts eine hochpathetische Rede zugeschrieben, in der er sein Unglück mit dem der tragischsten Helden der griechischen Antike vergleicht, allerdings mit dem Hinweis, daß er so hätte reden können, wenn er "gebildet gewesen wäre" (BFA 16. S. 97), was er eben nicht ist, so daß er sich jedenfalls nicht in der ihm hier zugeschriebenen Weise äußert. Wer also redet hier mit der Stimme der Figuren, die sich nicht in der für den Erzählkontext geeigneten Weise artikulieren können? Offenbar ist das die (satirische) Erzählinstanz, die sich aber nicht von der Figur distanziert, sondern in deren eingeschränktem und durch die Erzählkonstellation durchaus kritisiertem Horizont verbleibt und deshalb ihre Stimme benutzt. Im weiteren Sinne ist es damit die erzählte Situation und ihre zugleich subjektiv befangene und objektiv erhellende Wahrnehmung, die hier buchstäblich zur Rede wird.

Beide Monologe sind im Romantext durch Kursivdruck hervorgehoben. Die Verwendung dieser typographischen Auszeichnung für die Wiedergabe von Gedanken, Reflexionen, Reden und auch Träumen der Romanfiguren, von Teilen dessen, was ihnen an sprachlicher Artikulation zugeschrieben wird oder auch nur zugeschrieben werden könnte, ist eines der wichtigsten und das wohl auffälligste Stilmittel des Romans. Es dient keineswegs einfach der Hervorhebung von Passagen im Sinne einer didaktischen Leserlenkung, denn gelegentlich ist das Kursivierte auch beiläufig und belanglos, während umgekehrt für den Gehalt besonders wichtige Stellen nicht kursiviert sind. Das ist kein Versehen Brechts, wie Bernd Auerochs annimmt,[1] sondern ein Hinweis auf die Funktion dieser Verfahrensweise.

Walter Benjamin hat die kursiv gedruckten Passagen als "eine Sammlung von Ansprachen und Sentenzen, Bekenntnissen und Plädoyers" bezeichnet, "die einzig zu nennen ist. Sie allein würde dem Werk seine Dauer sichern. Was da steht, hat noch nie jemand ausgesprochen, und doch reden sie alle so".[2] Brecht hat seine Mitarbeiterin Margarete Steffin, die die Verfahrensweise nicht verstanden hatte, auf deren Bedeutung nachdrücklich hingewiesen: "Das Herausfallen, Künstliche, Übergangslose der Moralischen Betrachtungen ist gewollt".[3] Und er hat dem Verlag für die technische Herstellung des Drucks präzise Anweisungen gegeben und begründet: Es komme auf den Eindruck an, "daß hier etwas *zitiert* wird, daß hier bestimmte Sprüche und Redereien *ausgestellt* werden".[4] "Die Kursivstellen müssen Zitatcharakter haben, das heißt der Leser muß die Assoziation 'Zitat' haben. [...] Der Leser muß denken: warum plötzlich eine andere Schrift?".[5] Eine vorläufige und unvollständige Antwort auf der Grundlage der bisher eingeführten Befunde könnte lauten: Brecht arbeitet mit einer neuartigen Engführung von Figur, erzählter Situation, Erzählinstanz und Erzählweise sowie Orientierung auf das Wirklichkeitsbewußtsein des Rezipienten. Wenn das mehr ist als ein singuläres Formexperiment, impliziert die Verfahrensweise eine neue und andere Ästhetik des Romans.

---

[1] Bernd Auerochs: *Erzählte Gesellschaft. Theorie und Praxis des Gesellschaftsromans bei Balzac, Brecht und Johnson*. München: Fink 1994. S. 153 (Anm. 55).

[2] Walter Benjamin: Brechts *Dreigroschenroman*. WBGS III. S. 440–449. Hier S. 445–446. Vgl. auch Klaus-Detlef Müller: *Brecht-Kommentar zur erzählenden Prosa*. München: Winkler 1980. S. 184–185; Auerochs: *Erzählte Gesellschaft* (Anm. 1). S. 153–158; Wolfgang Jeske: Dreigroschenroman. Entstehung. In: BFA 16. S. 396–414. Hier S. 403–404; Klaus-Detlef Müller: Die Aktualität von Brechts *Dreigroschenroman*. In: *Bertolt Brecht und das moderne Theater. Jahrbuch der Koreanischen Brecht-Gesellschaft* 5 (1998). S. 51–72. Hier S. 69–71.

[3] Bertolt Brecht: Brief an Margarete Steffin 19.8.1933. BFA 28. S. 379.

[4] Bertolt Brecht: Brief an den Verlag Allert de Lange 26.8.1934. BFA 28. S. 433 (Hervorhebungen im Text).

[5] Bertolt Brecht: Brief an den Verlag Allert de Lange 1.9.1934. BFA 28. S. 435.

Und in der Tat bezieht Brecht von Anfang an, schon in den zwanziger Jahren, eine dezidierte Frontstellung zum bürgerlichen realistischen Roman, auch zum bürgerlichen Roman der klassischen Moderne, den er als historisch überholt ablehnt, genau so wie die bürgerliche Dramatik. Beide sind nach seiner Einschätzung in der aristotelischen Poetik begründet, die Epos und Tragödie ja in der Tat als parallele Formen dichterischer Nachahmung versteht. Die aristotelische Verfahrensweise verlangt nach Brecht vom Rezipienten Einfühlung und Identifikation[6] sowie kritiklose Hingabe an illusionierende Mimesis. Eine ihrer wichtigsten Voraussetzungen ist die Darstellung " 'freier' Einzelpersönlichkeiten" als handelnder Subjekte.[7] Das ist in besonderer Weise nicht mehr zeitgemäß: "Den Individuen kann in den Büchern nicht viel mehr Platz eingeräumt und vor allem kein anderer Platz eingeräumt werden als in der Wirklichkeit".[8]

Eine solche Sichtweise ist freilich nicht so neu, sondern bezeichnet zunächst eine Grundtendenz des Romans der klassischen Moderne, der im Zeichen der "Krise des Erzählens" in Deutschland Gestalt gewann. Er beruht auf der Erfahrung, daß sich die Romanwelt, das heißt die Wahrnehmung der Welt im Roman, nicht von einer zentralen Figur, nicht einmal von einem Ensemble selbständiger Figuren her aufbauen läßt, weil in der zunehmend verdinglichten und abstrakt gewordenen Wirklichkeit eine auch nur annähernd selbstbestimmte Identität gar nicht mehr möglich und individuelles Handeln bedeutungslos geworden ist.[9] Brecht befindet sich mit dem Widerspruch gegen eine

---

[6] Vgl. hierzu etwa Bertolt Brecht: *[Kritik der "Poetik" des Aristoteles]*. BFA 22.1. S. 171–172, wo die Einfühlung auch als eine Form der Religiosität und als solche als überholt bezeichnet wird.

[7] Vgl. hierzu Bertolt Brecht: *Thesen über die Aufgabe der Einfühlung in den theatralischen Künsten*. BFA 22.1. S. 175–76. Hier S. 175.

[8] Bertolt Brecht: *[Über Georg Lukács]*. BFA 22.1. S. 483–487. Hier S. 485. Die Polemik richtet sich hier gegen das Realismusverständnis von Georg Lukács.

[9] Selbst der von Brecht verabscheute Thomas Mann konfrontiert im *Zauberberg* einen ausdrücklich als "mittelmäßig" bezeichneten Protagonisten, Hans Castorp, mit einer essayistisch entfalteten Bestandsaufnahme nicht vermittelbarer Zeittendenzen, denen er intellektuell nicht gewachsen ist und die er in der abgehobenen künstlichen Welt eines Schweizer Lungensanatoriums ebenso fasziniert wie befremdet zur Kenntnis nimmt. Hermann Broch zeigt in den *Schlafwandlern,* wie die erzählten Subjekte Opfer unbegriffener Kulturfiktionen werden, die als Setzungen ein den Figuren nicht bewußtes Eigenleben entwickeln und deren Verhalten bestimmen. Alfred Döblin hat in *Berlin Alexanderplatz* die Großstadt Berlin zum Protagonisten des Romans gemacht und die Geschichte des Franz Biberkopf nur als eine Hilfskonstruktion verwendet, die auf die Gattungskonventionen gerade nicht eingeht und sie durch den moritatenhaften Gestus zugleich entwertet. Robert Musil konzipiert die Zentralgestalt seines Romans ausdrücklich als eigenschaftslos und verweigert ihr damit jene Identität, die den "ewigen Kunstgriff der Epik" ermöglicht, eine Geschichte am Lebensfaden einer Figur zu erzählen (Robert Musil: *Der Mann ohne Eigenschaften*. Hamburg: Rowohlt 1952. S. 649–650). Und Franz Kafka zeigt im *Schloß,* daß die alles bestimmende verdinglichte Ordnung so ungreifbar geworden ist, daß sie jeden Subjektentwurf von vornherein unmöglich macht.

romanhafte Darstellung auf der Grundlage autonomer Individualität also in einem gattungsgeschichtlichen "mainstream", den er allerdings, wie zu zeigen ist, auf radikalisierte Weise fortschreibt und zu neuen Lösungen führt. Als aristotelisch und mithin zu einfühlender und identifikatorischer Lektüre bestimmt versteht Brecht auch den herkömmlichen Aufbau der epischen Welt:

> Der bürgerliche Roman gestaltet heute noch jeweils "eine Welt". Er tut dies rein idealistisch aus einer Weltanschauung heraus, der mehr oder weniger privaten, jedenfalls aber individuellen Anschauung seines "Schöpfers". Innerhalb dieser Welt stimmen dann alle Einzelheiten natürlich genau, die, aus dem Zusammenhang gerissen, den "Details" der Realität gegenüber keinen Augenblick waschecht wirken könnten. Man erfährt über die wirkliche Welt nur so viel, als man über den Autor erfährt, den Schöpfer der unwirklichen, um nicht sagen zu müssen, man erfahre nur etwas über den Autor und nichts über die Welt.[10]

Die scheinbare Stimmigkeit solcher fiktionalen Konstrukte ergibt sich daraus, daß deren Elemente gleichmäßig verzeichnet sind, so daß durch "allseitige Verkürzung und Verkrüppelung […] der Eindruck von Logik" entsteht.[11] Das setzt freilich ein bestimmtes Rezeptionsverhalten voraus, auf das hin die "eigene Welt" des Dichters, "die sich mit der andern nicht zu decken braucht", entworfen ist: "die auf Basis der Suggestion hergestellte Einfühlung […] in den Künstler und über ihn in die Personen und Vorgänge".[12]

Vom Standpunkt des Individuums und im Horizont seiner Erlebnismöglichkeiten als der Grundlage der Einfühlungstechnik ist die Wirklichkeit, der "gesamte soziale Kausalkomplex", wie Brecht präzisiert,[13] nicht mehr darstellbar, schon gar nicht als eine veränderbare und beherrschbare, als die sie für Brecht Gegenstand einer operativen und eingreifenden Kunst sein sollte. Hegels Definition des Epos und des weiteren des epischen Kunstwerks als Darstellung des Ganzen einer Welt, in der eine individuelle Handlung geschieht, ist mit Brechts Literaturverständnis durchaus vereinbar, wenn man das Weltganze als außerästhetische Wirklichkeit versteht, die in einer besonderen und insoweit individuellen Handlungsfolge, also organisiert in einer Fabel, Gestalt gewinnt. Die Figuren sind dann exemplarische Repräsentanten des gesellschaftlichen Gesamtkomplexes, wenn auch keineswegs autonome Individuen. Eigentlicher Gegenstand ist die als Totalität verstandene Wirklichkeit, und zwar als solche,

---

[10] Bertolt Brecht: *Der Dreigroschenprozeß. Ein soziologisches Experiment*. BFA 21. S. 448–514. Hier S. 465.
[11] Bertolt Brecht: *Notizen über realistische Schreibweise*. BFA 22.2. S. 620–640. Hier S. 627.
[12] Bertolt Brecht: *Über experimentelles Theater*. BFA 22.1. S. 540–557. Hier S. 551.
[13] Bertolt Brecht: *Übergang vom bürgerlichen zum sozialistischen Realismus*. BFA 22.1. S. 460–462. Hier S. 461.

das heißt nicht eingeschränkt durch ästhetische Zwänge, sondern in historischer Konkretheit. Und das gilt nicht nur für den Roman, sondern in gleicher Weise für die Dramatik, weshalb Brecht sein Theater als ein episches, das heißt dem epischen Totalitätsgesichtpunkt verpflichtetes bezeichnet hat. Darum sind die Prinzipien der Theatertheorie auch für sein Romanschaffen weitgehend verbindlich. Das gilt auch und insbesondere für die antiaristotelische Wendung. Die Wirklichkeit, wie Brecht sie in den ersten Jahrzehnten des 20. Jahrhunderts erfährt, ist durch die universelle "Verdinglichung der menschlichen Beziehungen" bestimmt, so daß auch die Kunst nicht mehr vom Erlebnis her organisiert und im Horizont des Individuums gestaltet werden kann: "Wer von der Realität nur das von ihr Erlebbare gibt, gibt sie selbst nicht wieder".[14] Vor allem aber behindert der überholte subjekt- und erlebnisorientierte Darstellungstypus die Wahl repräsentativer Gegenstände. Brecht hat das ironisch am Beispiel eines eifersüchtigen Fliegers erläutert: Ein fliegender Eifersüchtiger ist zwar zur Thematisierung der Eifersucht geeignet, kaum aber zu der der Fliegerei.[15] Auf die neuen "großen Gegenstände" kommt es aber an. Genannt sind beispielhaft "Krieg, Geld, Öl, Eisenbahnen, Parlament, Lohnarbeit, Boden",[16] von denen einige Brechts Romane bestimmen. In den "großen Seelengemälden" der herkömmlichen Romanproduktion kommen sie allenfalls als Hintergrund vor, als "Naturkräfte, schicksalshafte Mächte, die den Menschen geschlossen gegenübertreten".[17] Sie gelten als unpoetisch, wobei Brecht aber sehr wohl weiß, daß sie nur im Rahmen figurenbezogener Handlungen, also als besondere Abschattungen des mit ihnen gemeinten Allgemeinen, zum Gegenstand der Dichtung werden können.

Wie nun die herkömmliche Erzählweise mit den neuen Gegenständen verfahren würde, hat Brecht am Beispiel des Rechtswesens in einer kurzen, aber wichtigen Notiz mit dem Titel *Über den aristotelischen Roman* erläutert:

> Nehmen wir an, er [der aristotelische Roman] baut sich auf auf dem Satz:
> Die Justiz ist ungerecht (1),
> so wird daraus sofort – der Romanform wegen:
> Ein Richter ist ungerecht (2),
> und in einer Fabel wird – der Romanform wegen – daraus:
> Ein Richter tut etwas Ungerechtes (3).[18]

Das Problem für den an den neuen Gegenständen interessierten Autor liegt nun darin, daß die für die Romanform notwendige Konkretisierung des allgemeinen Satzes (1), auf den es ihm ankommt, diesen nicht veranschaulicht. Denn wenn

---

[14] Brecht: *Dreigroschenprozeß* (Anm. 10). S. 469.
[15] Bertolt Brecht: *[Benutzung der Wissenschaften für Kunstwerke]*. BFA 22.1. S. 479–480.
[16] Bertolt Brecht: *Die großen Gegenstände*. BFA 22.1. S. 480–481. Hier S. 480.
[17] Ebd. S. 481.
[18] Bertolt Brecht: *Über den aristotelischen Roman*. BFA 21. S. 538–539.

"alle Richter justiztreu [sind] und, indem sie justiztreu sind, ungerecht [handeln]", dann sind sie keine individuell Handelnden. Sind sie aber nicht justiztreu, dann wird der Satz, daß die Justiz ungerecht ist, durch ihr Handeln zumindest punktuell widerlegt. "Sind die Richter ungerecht und nicht justiztreu und soll die Justiz ungerecht sein, so kann *dieser* Totalsatz vom aristotelischen Roman mit einer Fabel nicht bewältigt werden".

Die Konsequenz dieser syllogistischen Widerlegung der aristotelischen Romanform ist die Forderung eines "nichtaristotelischen Romanschreibens",[19] das nun allerdings nicht nur als eine Darstellungstechnik zu begreifen ist, sondern auch eine Funktionsänderung des Literarischen bezeichnet. Denn es soll darum gehen, "solche Aussagen über Erscheinungen zu machen, welche Operationen mit diesen Erscheinungen gestatten, praktische Aussagen, also operative Sätze aufzustellen". Wie das epische Theater soll auch die Lektüre des antiaristotelischen Romans Wirklichkeit nicht nur wiedergeben, sondern durch Einsicht in ihre Gesetzmäßigkeiten praktisches, weltveränderndes Handeln ermöglichen und provozieren. Das klingt nach Didaktik, aber Brecht hat (fast) immer betont, daß Belehrung im ästhetischen Medium unterhaltsam sein muß und insofern höchste ästhetische Ansprüche stellt. Nach diesen Grundsätzen verfährt er im *Dreigroschenroman*, wie im folgenden zu zeigen ist.

2

Gegenstand des Romans ist die kapitalistische Ökonomie, die zwar im Sinne der Marxschen Lehre verstanden ist, mit dieser aber sehr frei umgeht. In der *Dreigroschenoper* war diese Thematik nur sehr marginal angelegt, und zwar in der von Brecht zur Gayschen Vorlage weitgehend hinzuerfundenen Peachum-Handlung, war aber in den weiteren Bearbeitungen des Stoffes immer stärker in den Vordergrund getreten. Der Gegenstand ist also groß und zeitgemäß und äußerst prosaisch, aber er wird mit hohem Kunstverstand vermittelt. Das wird vor allem möglich durch die satirische Schreibweise und die erzählerische Ironie. Als Satiriker orientiert Brecht sich ausdrücklich an Jonathan Swift und insbesondere an dessen *Modest Proposal* (1729), das er folgendermaßen referiert:

> Jonathan Swift schlug in einer Broschüre vor, man solle, damit das Land zu Wohlstand gelange, die Kinder der Armen einpökeln und als Fleisch verkaufen. Er stellte genaue Berechnungen auf, die bewiesen, daß man viel einsparen kann, wenn man vor nichts zurückschreckt. Swift stellte sich dumm. Er verteidigte eine bestimmte, ihm verhaßte Denkungsart mit vielem Feuer und vieler Gründlichkeit in einer Frage, wo ihre ganze Gemeinheit jedermann erkennbar zu Tage trat.[20]

[19] Bertolt Brecht: *Über ein nichtaristotelisches Romanschreiben*. BFA 21. S. 541.
[20] Bertolt Brecht: *Fünf Schwierigkeiten beim Schreiben der Wahrheit*. BFA 22.1. S. 74–89. Hier S. 85.

Wie bei Swift handelt es sich auch im *Dreigroschenroman* nicht um Personensatire, die angesichts der unterstellten Bedeutungslosigkeit des Individuums und seiner Handlungsweisen zu unbedeutend wäre, sondern – mit einem von Bernd Auerochs eingeführten treffenden Terminus – um Systemsatire.[21] Für die Narration stellt sie ein Problem dar, das sich aus dem für die Satire bestimmenden Prinzip von Norm und Abweichung ergibt. Die Personensatire als geläufiges literarisches Muster zeigt ein Verhalten, das nach den für die Erzählinstanz und die Rezipienten gleichermaßen verbindlichen, in der Regel ethisch begründeten Maßstäben fragwürdig und falsch ist und den Handelnden kritisiert und durch Lächerlichkeit moralisch vernichtet – Satire ist nach der allgemein akzeptierten Definition von Jürgen Brummack "ästhetisch sozialisierte Aggression".[22] Ein solcher normativer Orientierungspunkt fehlt im *Dreigroschenroman* scheinbar, auch wenn er für die Konstruktion der Romanwelt nach dem marxistischen Gesellschaftsmodell durchaus vorhanden ist. Aber die Erzählinstanz vermittelt ihn nicht als Wissen, und für die Lebenswelt des Lesers hat er keine oder noch keine Bedeutung und kann deshalb zur Erzielung von Einverständnis nicht abgerufen werden. Dabei gibt es durchaus Normenkonflikte, aber die sind nur scheinhaft. Vorstellungen von Moral und Rechtsinstanzen sind vorhanden, allerdings erscheinen sie nur als Produkte eines Systems, das sich durch sie legitimiert und so den Schein von Ordnung produziert, der sein Überleben garantiert. Und das bedeutet, daß sie im Konfliktfall wirkungslos sind und selbstverständlich geopfert werden. Sie haben Alibifunktion und wirken affirmativ. Deshalb will der Roman auch kein Einverständnis mit ihnen erreichen, sondern ist im Gegenteil dazu bestimmt, sie zu kritisieren.

Als "DEMONSTRANDUM EINES DREIGROSCHENROMANS", also als Erzählintention des Buches, hat Brecht festgehalten: "die kleinen verbrecher sind ebenso bürgerlich wie die kleinen bürger, die grossen bürger sind ebenso verbrecherisch wie die kleinen verbrecher".[23] Mit der Kategorie des Verbrecherischen ist hier scheinbar eine besonders verbindliche Norm eingeführt. Sie ist aber zugleich aufgehoben, weil sie keine Differenz bezeichnet. Im Sinne der Systemsatire sind die Geschäfte der Kapitalisten verbrecherisch und die Aktivitäten der kleinen Verbrecher zugleich systemkonform, also gar nicht abweichend oder anders, sondern vernünftig und im System sogar notwendig,

---

[21] Auerochs: *Erzählte Gesellschaft* (Anm. 1). S. 170.

[22] Jürgen Brummack: Zu Begriff und Theorie der Satire. In: *Deutsche Vierteljahrsschrift für Literaturwissenschaft und Geistesgeschichte* 45 (1971). Sonderheft Forschungsreferate. S. 275–377. Hier S. 282.

[23] BBA 295/11. Vgl. hierzu Dieter Schlenstadt: Das Demonstrandum des *Dreigroschenromans*. In: *Brechts Tui-Kritik. Aufsätze, Rezensionen, Geschichten.* Hg. von Herbert Claas und Wolfgang Fritz Haug. Berlin: Argument 1976. S. 150–175 (Argument Sonderband 11); Müller: *Brecht-Kommentar* (Anm. 2). S. 134–185.

genauer überlebensnotwendig. Als These ist die Gleichsetzung von Geschäft und Verbrechen plakativ wie vulgärmarxistische Propaganda. Brecht war sich dessen wohl bewußt und hat die erwarteten Einsprüche der Kritik satirisch ins Leere laufen lassen, indem er im Roman eine Apologie des "plumpen Denkens" formuliert, das "der Wirklichkeit sehr nahe" komme und eben deshalb in schlechtem Ruf stehe (BFA 16. S. 173).[24] Entscheidend ist aber, wie diese These romanhaft zur Anschauung gelangt.

Erzählt werden drei Geschäftshandlungen von unterschiedlicher Qualität, die im Romanverlauf ineinandergreifen und am Schluß zu einer einzigen werden: 1. das völlig legale Bettlergeschäft Jonathan Peachums, der das schlechte Gewissen der Besitzenden gegenüber den Besitzlosen ausbeutet, indem er zu Bettlern kostümierte Profis, gewissermaßen eine Art Schauspieler des aristotelischen Theaters, so ausstattet und schult, daß sie mit Erfolg an das Mitleid derjenigen appellieren, die insgeheim wissen, daß sie Verursacher des Unglücks sind;[25] 2. das Schiffegeschäft des Maklers Coax, das Brecht aus der Darstellung "des bedeutendsten kaufmännischen Piraten und kommerziellen Gauners seiner Zeit" Cornelius Vanderbilt in Gustavus Myers' *Geschichte der großen amerikanischen Vermögen* übernimmt[26] und als ein typisches Beispiel von Wirtschaftskriminalität in den Roman integriert; und 3. der Aufstieg des Kleinkriminellen Macheath, alias Mackie Messer, zum Bankdirektor und Chef eines Einzelhandelssyndikats. Die dritte Handlung ist die wichtigste, in ihr sind die beiden anderen aufgehoben.

In der *Dreigroschenoper* hatte sich Mackie Messer unter dem Galgen mit der Einsicht verabschiedet:

> Meine Damen und Herren. Sie sehen den untergehenden Vertreter eines untergehenden Standes. Wir kleinen bürgerlichen Handwerker, die wir mit dem biederen Brecheisen an den Nickelkassen der kleinen Ladenbesitzer arbeiten, werden von den Großunternehmern verschlungen, hinter denen die Banken stehen. Was ist ein Dietrich gegen eine Aktie? Was ist der Einbruch in eine Bank gegen die Gründung einer Bank? Was ist die Ermordung eines Mannes gegen die Anstellung eines Mannes?[27]

Der neue Macheath des *Dreigroschenromans* geht genau den hier bezeichneten Weg, der die Kriminalität nicht nur gefahrloser macht, weil er nicht zum Galgen

---

[24] Hierzu auch Benjamin: Brechts *Dreigroschenroman* (Anm. 2). S. 445–447.

[25] Vgl. BFA 16. S. 23: "Um der zunehmenden Verhärtung der Menschen zu begegnen, hatte der Geschäftsmann J. J. Peachum einen Laden eröffnet, in dem die Elendsten der Elenden sich jenes Aussehen erwerben konnten, das zu den immer verstockteren Herzen sprach".

[26] Gustavus Myers: *Geschichte der großen amerikanischen Vermögen*. Berlin: S. Fischer 1926. S. 269. Brecht lobt die deutsche Übersetzung als eines der besten Bücher des Jahres 1926: *[Die besten Bücher des Jahres 1926]*. BFA 21. S. 176.

[27] Bertolt Brecht: *Die Dreigroschenoper*. BFA 2. S. 229–322. Hier S. 305.

führt, sondern auch ungleich profitabler ist. Er gründet zwar keine Bank, aber steigt vom Einbrecher zum Bankdirektor auf, und er ist in vielfältiger Weise ein Mann, der andere anstellt und vom Mehrwert ihrer Arbeit lebt. Als der kriminellste der drei Geschäftsleute, die die Romanhandlung zusammenführt, erweist er sich als der cleverste: Der Makler Coax hat den Bogen überspannt, indem er die Partner seiner Geschäfte zu betrügen und zu ruinieren, also gleichsam geschäftlich zu ermorden versuchte. Macheath, Polly und Peachum sehen sich deshalb je für sich gezwungen, ihn wirklich umzubringen, so daß er von seinesgleichen zum Tode befördert wird und nicht, wie er es für logisch hielt[28] und wie es dann auch als offizielle Version verbreitet wird, von den eigentlichen Opfern seiner verbrecherischen Geschäfte. Und Peachum ist zwar fähig, das lukrative Schiffegeschäft von Coax zu seinem Vorteil zu Ende zu führen, hat aber für "napoleonische Pläne" (BFA 16. S. 152), wie sie Macheath zugeschrieben werden, nicht das nötige Format, weil er pessimistisch und ängstlich ist. Er muß sich dem Schwiegersohn geschlagen geben. Der hat sich an die Empfehlung seines Freundes, des Polizeichefs Brown, gehalten: "Warum unrechte Wege gehen? [...] Das soll man nicht. Ein Kaufmann bricht nicht ein. Ein Kaufmann kauft und verkauft. Damit erreicht er das gleiche. [...] Arbeite mit den Banken, wie alle andern Geschäftsleute! Das ist doch eine andere Sache!" (BFA 16. S.146/47). Aber was heißt hier Format, und was hat es mit den "napoleonischen Plänen" auf sich? Am Ende des Romans wird Macheath von allen Seiten als große Persönlichkeit und als weitblickender Wirtschaftslenker gepriesen, woraufhin er sich ein bemerkenswertes Bekenntnis erlauben kann:

Ich mache kein [sic] Hehl daraus: ich stamme von unten. [...] Ich habe meine Tätigkeit klein begonnen, in einem anderen Milieu. Sie blieb aber im großen und ganzen immer die gleiche. Man schreibt im allgemeinen den Aufstieg eines Mannes seinem Ehrgeiz oder einem großen, verwickelten Plan zu. Offen gestanden, hatte ich keinen so großen Plan. Ich wollte nur immer dem Armenhaus entgehen (BFA 16. S. 374).

Der Roman ist so erzählt, daß der Leser das als eine zwar beschönigende, aber im ganzen zutreffende Aussage bestätigen kann. Macheath' Handeln war folgerichtig und im Hinblick auf die Gesetzmäßigkeiten der Wirtschaftsordnung vernünftig. Er hat in jeder Situation mit der Bereitschaft zum Risiko das Richtige getan, ohne aber dabei einem großen Plan zu folgen. Der Roman ist also nicht die Geschichte eines Aufsteigers, nicht einmal die satirische Enthüllung einer bemerkenswerten Karriere. Und Macheath ist nicht ein großes Individuum, sondern ein gut funktionierender Agent des Wirtschaftssystems: Der eigentliche Protagonist des Romans ist die Ökonomie. Ihre Gesetze bestimmen

---

[28] "'Eigentlich ist es auch unbegreiflich', dachte er, 'daß man uns nicht einfach niederschlägt, wo man uns trifft. Schließlich sind wir gar nicht so viele'" (BFA 16. S. 301).

die Handlungsmöglichkeiten und die ganz und gar nicht autonomen Handlungsweisen der Figuren. Schon in seiner Gegenstandswahl wird der Roman damit antiaristotelisch.[29]

Die satirische Pointe liegt nun darin, daß es ein kleiner Verbrecher ist, der hier zum Wirtschaftsboß aufsteigt. Damit kommt das Formmuster des Kriminalromans als des für eine solche Gegenständlichkeit "zuständigen" Genres ins Spiel. Brecht schreibt zwar einen Dreigroschenroman und keinen Groschenroman, er bekennt sich aber zu einer Erzähltradition, die in ihrer ironischen Pointierung nicht durch psychologisierende Verfahrensweisen und einfühlende Rezeption ihren ästhetischen Standard beansprucht, sondern Forderungen an den Intellekt stellt, auch wenn sie als trivial gelten. Den Vorzug des Kriminalromans sieht er in seinem "gesunden" Schema:

> Entscheidend ist, daß nicht die Handlungen aus den Charakteren, sondern die Charaktere aus den Handlungen entwickelt werden. Man sieht die Leute agieren, in Bruchstücken. Ihre Motive sind im dunkeln und müssen logisch erschlossen werden. Als ausschlaggebend für ihre Handlungen werden ihre Interessen angenommen, und zwar beinahe ausschließlich ihre materiellen Interessen. Nach ihnen wird gesucht.[30]

Dabei ist "die Konzeptionsweise der Kriminalromanschreiber von der Wissenschaft beeinflußt" und verschafft nur Vergnügen, wenn "die Kausalität befriedigend funktioniert".[31] Die Aufdeckung der Zusammenhänge ist Sache des Detektivs, zugleich aber des Lesers. Das Genre fordert also eine aktive Rezeption.

Abweichend vom Schema des Detektivromans liegen nun aber die kriminellen Handlungen der Protagonisten hier nicht im Verborgenen, müssen also nicht aus Indizien erschlossen werden. Daraus hat Ulf Eisele gefolgert, daß der *Dreigroschenroman*, entgegen dem Forschungskonsens, der ihn als eine Sonderform dieses Genres versteht, überhaupt kein Kriminalroman ist.[32] Es bedarf keines Detektivs, weil hier gar nichts aufzudecken ist und weil die Rechtsordnung gar kein Interesse daran hat, die kriminellen Handlungen, durch die das System

---

[29] Ironisch hat Brecht das in einer Glosse kommentiert: *Über die Darstellung von Geschäften im Drama.* BFA 21. S. 376–377: "Schreibt ein Schriftsteller heute ein dramatisches (oder auch belletristisches) Werk, in dem Geschäfte vorkommen, so muß er damit rechnen, daß jene, die vom Inhalt seines Stückes (oder Buches) etwas verstehen würden, es nicht lesen und jene, die es lesen würden, vom Inhalt nichts verstehen. [...] Ein Hauptargument [...] gegen die Darstellung von Geschäften in der Kunst [...] ist [...]: die Kunst ist zu ernst, als daß sie sich mit etwas so Niedrigem wie Geschäften befassen dürfte".
[30] Bertolt Brecht: *Über die Popularität des Kriminalromans.* BFA 22.1. S. 504–510. Hier S. 505.
[31] Ebd. S. 506 und 507.
[32] Vgl. Ulf Eisele: *Die Struktur des modernen Romans.* Tübingen: Niemeyer 1984. S. 210–256. Hier: S. 219ff.

funktioniert, zu bestrafen. Das ist richtig, schließt aber die Verwendung der Technik des Detektivromans, und nur darum handelt es sich, gar nicht aus. Denn das Verbrecherische sind nicht primär die kriminellen Handlungen der Protagonisten, sondern vielmehr, im Sinne der Systemsatire, die Verhältnisse, die sie ermöglichen und begründen. Mit der berühmten Formulierung Brechts im *Dreigroschenprozeß* ist auch hier die "eigentliche Realität in die Funktionale gerutscht" (BFA 21. S. 469). Die Erkenntnis der wirklichen Zusammenhänge hinter den offensichtlichen ist damit Aufgabe des Lesers, dem im Roman kein Detektiv zur Seite steht. Er muß gewissermaßen auf eigene Faust zum Detektiv werden. Allerdings gibt es auch romanimmanent ein detektivisches Prinzip, insofern als die konkurrierenden Protagonisten ständig versuchen müssen, sich gegenseitig auf die Schliche zu kommen, um handeln zu können und damit die verdeckte Kausalität aufdecken.

Für den satirischen Biß des Erzählens ist es zudem entscheidend, daß die Protagonisten sich wechselseitig als Verbrecher durchschauen. Peachums Nachforschungen über Macheath ergeben: "Irgendwie verlief dieses Leben nach rückwärts unten in die Unterwelt. Zu irgendeiner nicht allzu fern liegenden Zeit waren die Methoden dieses erfolgreichen Herrn noch nackter, gröber und den Gerichten greifbarer gewesen" (BFA 16. S. 112). Entsprechend zweideutig ist auch seine Erscheinung, wie der Konkurrent seiner Ladenkette, der Kaufmann Aaron, bemerkt: "Für einen Räuber war er ziemlich gut bürgerlich, aber für einen Bürger war er ziemlich räuberisch" (BFA 16. S. 178). Umgekehrt erkennt Macheath, daß er bei seinen Verhandlungen mit den Geschäftsleuten unter die Räuber gefallen ist:

Man versucht mich zu betrügen? Ich tue alles, um solide zu werden, ich verzichte auf jede Gewaltanwendung und halte mich sklavisch oder doch jedenfalls ziemlich genau an die Gesetze, ich verleugne meine Herkunft [...] und das erste, was ich in dieser höheren Sphäre erleben muß, ist, daß man mich bestiehlt! Das soll sittlich höher stehen, als was ich immer gemacht habe? Das steht niedriger! Diesen Leuten sind wir einfachen Verbrecher nicht gewachsen (BFA 16. S. 140).

Bei seinen Verhandlungen mit den Großkaufleuten hat er den Eindruck, "er sei unter Wegelagerer gefallen" (BFA 16. S. 181), und bringt deren Praktiken auf den Begriff: "Also erst Raub und dann Mord. Auf der Landstraße ist es umgekehrt. Da kommt zuerst der Mord" (BFA 16. S. 238). Und als er am Ziel ist und als Bankdirektor mit den anderen Bankern verhandelt, erkennt er:

Sie warten nur darauf, Verträge machen zu können. [...] Dabei ekelt mich, den einstigen Straßenräuber, dieses Gefeilsche wirklich an! Da sitze ich dann und schlage mich um Prozente herum. Warum nehme ich nicht einfach mein Messer und renne es ihnen nicht in den Leib, wenn sie mir nicht das ablassen wollen, was ich haben will? [...] Immer dieses unwürdige Sichverschanzen hinter Richtern und Gerichtsvollziehern! Das erniedrigt einen doch vor sich selber. Freilich ist mit der einfachen, schlichten und natürlichen Straßenräuberei heute nichts mehr zu machen. Sie verhält sich zu der Kaufmannspraxis wie die Segelschiffahrt zur Dampfschiffahrt (BFA 16. S. 358).

Folglich muß er einsehen, daß er zum Bürger werden muß, um größere Beute machen zu können, was zwar keine Absage an die Kriminalität ist, ihm aber in der Unterwerfung unter die Gesetze der ökonomischen Rationalität weitere Spielräume eröffnet:

> Ein wahrer Durst nach Solidität befiel ihn. Ein gewisses Maß von Ehrlichkeit und Vertragstreue, einfach von menschlicher Verläßlichkeit, war eben doch unentbehrlich, wenn es sich um größere Geschäfte handelte! Warum wäre sonst Ehrlichkeit, fragte er sich, überhaupt so geschätzt, wenn es auch ohne sie ginge? Das ganze Bürgertum war ja doch darauf schließlich begründet (BFA 16. S. 222).

Damit kommt dann doch so etwas wie eine Norm oder ein Maßstab für die Systemsatire ins Spiel, allerdings in Gestalt einer nützlichen Ideologie, die das Handeln keineswegs bestimmt und auch die Polizei, die Gerichte und die Kirche zu nichts verpflichtet. Es ist aber vor allem ein ingeniöser Kunstgriff Brechts, daß er zum Protagonisten eines Romans, der die Identität von Geschäft und Verbrechen, von Bürger und Räuber thematisiert, einen Verbrecher wählt, der zu seiner Verwunderung die Erfahrung machen muß, daß sich mit dem Entschluß zur Verlagerung seiner Tätigkeit in den Bereich des Legalen gar nichts ändert. Sein Erkenntnisprozeß erlaubt es, die Kriminalität des Geschäftslebens satirisch auszustellen, denn für das Verbrecherische ist er Spezialist. Die damit gewonnene Sichtweise verfremdet die Vorgänge und macht zugleich deutlich, daß ein Handeln nach den Maßstäben individueller und gesellschaftlicher bürgerlicher Moralität unter den gegebenen Bedingungen unzweckmäßig wäre. Nur wer unmoralisch und kriminell agiert, verhält sich hier vernünftig, indem er nichts anderes tut, als sich den gegebenen Spielräumen anzupassen.

Was damit in satirischer Affirmation sichtbar gemacht wird, sind die Gesetzmäßigkeiten der Mehrwertproduktion. Sie werden ideologisch gerechtfertigt durch das biblische Gleichnis vom Pfund, mit dem gewuchert werden soll.[33] Wer das nicht tut, wird bestraft. Das Gleichnis wird durch den Roman bestätigt und nur außerhalb des Romans, im Epilog, durch einen Traum des Soldaten Fewkoombey, ahnungsweise widerlegt.[34] Dieser Träumende ist das detektivische Erkenntnismedium des Kriminalromans. Fewkoombey verfügt aus existentieller Not zwar über den Willen, die Verhältnisse zu durchschauen, nicht aber über die intellektuellen und mentalen Fähigkeiten. So träumt er gewissermaßen über seine Verhältnisse und deshalb folgenlos. Und ausgerechnet

---

[33] Lukas 19, 12–28; auch Matthäus 25, 14–30.
[34] Vgl. hierzu Klaus-Detlef Müller: Die Fewkoombey-Handlung als Erkenntnismedium. In: *Bertolt Brecht. Epoche – Werk – Wirkung.* Hg. von Klaus-Detlef Müller. München: Beck 1985. S. 195–197.

er wird dann als stellvertretendes Opfer für die zum Skandal gewordenen Verbrechen der erfolgreich mit dem Pfund Wuchernden "zum Tode verurteilt und aufgehängt, in Anwesenheit und unter dem Beifall einer großen Menge von Kleingewerbetreibenden, Nähmädchen, invaliden Soldaten und Bettlern" (BFA 16. S. 391). Beifall für das Urteil einer korrupten Justiz spenden also paradoxerweise gerade die Opfer des Systems.

Wie die Aussagen in den kursiv gedruckten Stellen ist auch der Traum nicht der Person zuzurechnen, der er von der Erzählinstanz zugeschrieben wird. Es ist vielmehr der objektive Gehalt der Situation, der hier zur Sprache wird. In der verdinglichten Wirklichkeit sind die Personen funktionale Medien für die Reflexion der erzählten Sachverhalte, die durch sie objektiv gedeutet werden, ohne daß das Gesagte durch ihre Subjektivität eingeholt wäre. Auf diese Weise löst der antiaristotelische Roman das Problem, daß es in der modernen, abstrakt gewordenen Welt keine Charaktere für den Romanschriftsteller mehr gibt,[35] daß aber der Roman gleichwohl handelnde Figuren braucht. Sie sind bei Brecht keine selbständigen Individuen, die zu Identifikation und Einfühlung einladen und durch Introspektion zugänglich wären. Handlungsfähig sind sie bestenfalls als Charaktermasken, die über die Realität Auskunft geben, ohne das verantworten zu müssen. Die Erzählinstanz, die ihnen das zuschreibt, muß sich ihnen anpassen: Sie zeigt die Benutzung und souveräne Mißachtung der nützlichen Gesellschaftsideologie durch die Geschäftsleute, die Justiz und die Kirche, die selbstzerstörerische Ideologiegläubigkeit der Kleinbürger und das verblendete Fehlverhalten der Unterschichten, die bejahen, was sie vernichtet – der Erzählgestus ist also Mimikry an das Verkehrte, die aber durch Ironie und Satire aufgehoben ist.

3

Ob die satirische Darstellung für den antiaristotelischen Roman zwingend ist,[36] läßt sich nicht entscheiden – auf jeden Fall bestimmt sie aber auch die beiden weiteren Romanprojekte Brechts, den fragmentarischen Roman *Die Geschäfte des Herrn Julius Caesar* (BFA 17. S. 163–390) und die Entwürfe zum *Tui-Roman* (BFA 17. S. 9–161). Sie ermöglicht eine Schreibweise, die sich auf die Gegenständlichkeit einläßt, zugleich aber eine verfremdende Distanz einbezieht und damit der für Brechts funktionales Literaturverständnis grundlegenden

---

[35] Vgl. Bertolt Brecht: *Gibt es noch Charaktere für den modernen Romanschriftsteller?* BFA 21. S. 132–133.

[36] Im Zusammenhang der sog. Realismusdebatte wendet Brecht sich anläßlich einer für ihn undiskutablen Kritik Alfred Kantorowiczs am *Dreigroschenroman*, der hier als "idealistisches Buch" eingeschätzt wird, in einem Brief von Anfang/Mitte Januar 1935 an Johannes R. Becher mit dem Einspruch gegen die für ihn völlig abwegige These, daß für den Realismus "die ganze Gattung der Satire ausfällt, weil nicht realistisch" (BFA 28. S. 478). Für ihn sind Swift und Cervantes realistische Autoren, ebenso auch Hašek.

Kommentarfunktion den Gestus einer direkten Belehrung zugunsten einer unterhaltenden Vorgehensweise nimmt.

Mit dem *Caesar*-Roman begibt er sich auf das bei den Exilautoren hochgeschätzte Gebiet des historischen Romans. Das Projekt geht auf einen Stückplan zurück, dessen Stoff er in einem Brief an Karl Korsch als eine "Dreigroschenhistorie" bezeichnet.[37] Zugleich hält er aber fest, daß er im Gegensatz zur geläufigen Praxis nicht auf Aktualisierbarkeit zielt: "Ich will nicht ein Anspielungsstück machen, die Verhältnisse liegen so sehr anders in der Antike. [...] Die Schwierigkeit: Caesar bedeutet immerhin einen Fortschritt und die Anführungszeichen zu Fortschritt sind riesig schwer zu dramatisieren".[38]

Auf das durchaus bemerkenswerte Bild der römischen Geschichte, das der Roman entwickelt, kann ich nur am Rande und nur so weit eingehen, wie es das Erzählverfahren begründet und bestimmt oder umgekehrt aus ihm hervorgeht. Dabei ist die Praxis des antiaristotelischen Romans eine andere als im *Dreigroschenroman*. Und die Begründung ist in den überlieferten Paratexten expliziter, weil Brecht in der sogenannten Realismusdebatte mit seinem Romanverständnis in die Defensive geraten war – unsinnigerweise, weil er gegenüber dem Dogmatismus von Georg Lukács und dessen Adepten den viel moderneren Standpunkt vertrat.

In diesem Zusammenhang reflektiert er über den "Begriff des Kunstakts":

> Wähle ich eine bestimmte Erzählerhaltung (vielleicht besser gesagt: sehe ich mich veranlaßt, eine bestimmte Erzählerhaltung einzunehmen), so sind mir nur ganz bestimmte Wirkungen zugänglich, mein Stoff ordnet sich selber in der Perspektive, mein Wortmaterial und Bildmaterial liegt in einer ganz bestimmten Linie, holt sich aus einem ganz bestimmten Fundus, von der Fantasie meines Hörers steht mir soundso viel (und nicht mehr) zur Verfügung, von seinen Erfahrungen kann ich soundso weit Gebrauch machen, seine Emotionen werden auf derundder Linie ausgelöst usw. Die Haltung ist natürlich nichts Einheitliches, Gleichbleibendes, Widerspruchsloses.[39]

---

[37] Bertolt Brecht: Brief an Karl Korsch, Ende Oktober/Anfang November 1937. BFA 29. S. 58. Der Wechsel des Genres und des Mediums ist eine für Brecht unproblematische Praxis, da dramatische Darstellung und Erzählen im epischen Theater vorgängig vermittelt sind. Ähnliches gilt (im gleichen Stoffbereich) auch für die epische Narration und für den Film: Aus einem Filmexposé für den Regisseur William Dieterle (vgl. Bertolt Brecht: *Journal* 8.4.1942. BFA 27. S. 80–81) wird ohne große Änderungen eine der faszinierendsten Kalendergeschichten: *Cäsar und sein Legionär* (BFA 18. S. 389–404). Vgl. dazu Müller: *Brecht-Kommentar* (Anm. 2). S. 343–346. In beiden Fällen ist die epische Form zwar durch erschwerte oder fehlende Realisierungschancen in Theater und Film bedingt, ist deswegen aber kein Kompromiß.

[38] BFA 29. S. 57. In einem Brief an Karl Korsch von April 1938 hat er diese Einschätzung als Ergebnis der Arbeit am Roman widerrufen: "Die gewisse 'positive' Seite Caesars, die ich zunächst nicht als Vorurteil einfach übersehen wollte, ist bei fortgesetztem Studium bald in Rauch aufgegangen. Die Frage 'für wen positiv?' hat alles geklärt" (BFA 29. S. 92).

[39] Brecht: *Journal* 7.12.1939. BFA 26. S. 349.

Im *Caesar*-Roman ist die Erzählerhaltung schon als solche keine einheitliche wie im *Dreigroschenroman*, sondern es wird von verschiedenen Personen mit unterschiedlichen Interessen und dementsprechend aus unterschiedlichen Perspektiven erzählt, wobei die Satire aus dem Gegeneinander der Sichtweisen in einer gewissermaßen objektiven Form entsteht, eher auf der Ebene der *histoire* als auf der des *discours*.

Die übergeordnete Erzählinstanz ist durch den jungen Historiker bezeichnet, der zwanzig Jahre nach Caesars Tod dessen Biographie schreiben will und dafür Recherchen anstellt und Material sammelt. Er geht von einem bereits verfestigten Bild des Gründers des Imperiums als einer welthistorischen Persönlichkeit aus, auch wenn er weiß, daß sein "Idol" (BFA 17. S. 171) selbst systematisch an seinem Bild für die Nachwelt gearbeitet hat und dieses folglich nicht die historische Wahrheit repräsentiert. Die geplante Biographie erweist sich jedoch als unrealisierbar, weil die Quellen und die Auskünfte der Zeitgenossen nicht nur den Erwartungen, also der Forschungshypothese, widersprechen, sondern sogar die Möglichkeit einer biographischen Geschichtsschreibung als solche in Frage stellen. Der Roman ist so der Bericht über einen scheiternden Versuch, indem er die ermittelten Dokumente selbst vorlegt. Brecht folgt damit einer frühen romantheoretischen Überlegung, die er unter dem Titel *Kleiner Rat, Dokumente anzufertigen* veröffentlicht hat und in der er die Selbstbiographie des "ungeheuren Lügners" und Snobs Frank Harris als "viel interessanter" bezeichnet "als fast alles, was gegenwärtig an Romanhaftem produziert wird" (BFA 21. S. 163–165. Hier S. 163).

Die Verlagerung des Erzählens auf die Wiedergabe von Dokumenten führt im *Caesar*-Roman dazu, daß der Historiker als Erzählinstanz an den Rand tritt, im wesentlichen nur noch eine, allerdings wichtige, Vermittlungsfunktion hat. Das zentrale fiktive Dokument sind vor allem die Tagebücher von Caesars Sekretär Rarus, die im Besitz des Bankiers Mummlius Spicer sind. Einsicht in die Tagebücher gewährt Spicer aber erst, als der Historiker eher spielerisch als ernsthaft einräumt, daß Ökonomisches, wie etwa die Notierung der Kornpreise, Aufschlüsse über geschichtliche Sachverhalte geben könne. Die Aufzeichnungen sind vor allem in dieser Perspektive materialreich, denn "dieser Rarus hatte mit der geschäftlichen Seite der Unternehmungen zu tun und Sie wissen, daß diese Seite die Historiker wenig interessiert. Sie wissen keinen Deut, was Kurzverkaufen ist".[40] Spicer verkauft [!] die Informationen nur unter der Bedingung, daß er mit Erläuterungen, die sich schon vom dritten Buch an immer mehr von Rarus' Aufzeichnungen entfernen, zu Rate gezogen wird. Er erwärmt sich zunehmend für das Projekt. Und in den späteren unausgeführten Büchern, die den Gallischen Krieg behandeln sollten, wären seine Erinnerungen zur wichtigsten Quelle geworden. Ironischerweise ist es aber gerade das zuerst

---

[40] Bertolt Brecht: *Die Geschäfte des Herrn Julius* Caesar. BFA 17. S. 169.

nur vorgespielte Interesse für die Geschäfte des Herrn Julius Caesar, das die geplante Biographie verhindert und in Spicers sarkastisches Referat der römischen Ökonomie in den letzten Jahren der Republik aufhebt. Außerdem verlagert sich der Erzählgegenstand auf Probleme der Geschichtsschreibung, in deren Zeichen der Roman zunehmend selbstreflexiv wird.

Damit kommen zwei weitere Perspektivfiguren ins Spiel. Der Staatsrechtler Afranius Carbo, der als Syndikus für einen Trust arbeitet, begeistert sich für das Vorhaben: "Der Gedanke des Imperiums! Die Demokratie! Die Ideen des Fortschritts! Endlich ein auf wissenschaftlicher Grundlage geschriebenes Buch, das der kleine Mann lesen kann *und* der Mann der City" (BFA 17. S. 192). Er klagt über einen Mangel an historischem Sinn, wodurch es versäumt wurde, "den Handel selbst, seine Ideale ins rechte Licht zu setzen. Die großen, demokratischen Ideale!" (Ebd.). "Wir haben vergessen, daß wir Plebejer sind. Sie sind es, Spicer ist es, und ich bin es. Sagen Sie nicht, daß das heute nichts mehr ausmacht. Gerade das ist es, was erreicht wurde: daß es heute nichts mehr ausmacht. Das ist eben Caesar." (BFA 17. S. 196). Es ist wiederum Ironie, daß damit ein Geschichtswerk ins Auge gefaßt wird, das der Historiker gerade nicht schreiben will, denn er verfolgt einen "literarischen Plan" (BFA 17. S. 192), das aber am Ende in dem romanhaften Bericht über das gescheiterte Vorhaben doch vorliegt, wenn auch in Gestalt der Dokumente mit einer ganz anderen Aussage, als Carbo sie erwartet hat.

Einen nochmals unterschiedlichen Gesichtspunkt entwickelt der Dichter Vastius Alder, der selbst als ein geschwätziger Schöngeist eingeführt wird und seinerseits Caesar in das Licht einer forciert sarkastischen Satire rückt:

> Ein großer Mann, [...] eine Figur, wie die Historiker sie brauchen. Der Mann des Volkes und der Mann des Senats. Diese Art Leute wird abgemalt von einem Buch ins andere, durch die Jahrtausende. [...] Ich zweifle, [...] ob ein Dichter, geneigt, über ihn zu schreiben, mehr als zwei Zeilen zu Papier brächte. [...] Für die Dichtung ist der Mann, von dem wir sprechen, etwas, in das Brutus sein Schwert steckte. Sie können tausend Mal sagen: der Gründer des Imperiums, eine Usance im Weltmaßstab! Sie setzt nicht Patina an, diese Usance (BFA 17. S. 303–304).

Der aufgeschriebene Monolog Alders umfaßt ein Vielfaches der zwei Zeilen, die er dem Dichter über die "Usance" zugestehen wollte, und es drängt ihn, wie Spicer verächtlich bemerkt, "sein Geschwätz sogleich aufzuschreiben" (BFA 17. S. 306).

Enttäuschend ist auch die Begegnung mit einem früheren Legionär Caesars, von dem der Historiker etwas über die "abgöttische Verehrung für den großen Feldherrn" (BFA 17. S. 188) zu erfahren hofft, nachdem ihm Spicers Ausführungen dem "wirklichen Caesar" nicht gerecht zu werden scheinen. Die lakonischen Auskünfte des Veteranen, der den Feldherrn in Gallien nur zweimal aus großer Ferne gesehen hat, bringen ihn nicht weiter. Auf die Frage, wie Caesar denn ausgesehen habe, äußert der Legionär nur: "Verlebt" (BFA 17.

S. 191). So kann der Erzähler nur über "die menschliche Unfähigkeit" klagen, "Größe da zu sehen, wo sie ist" (ebd.). Was er nicht bemerkt, ist die Tatsache, daß die widerwilligen Auskünfte des Legionärs über seine Lebensumstände in einem exemplarischen Plebejerschicksal schon vorab vollständig enthalten sind und so bestätigen, was die im folgenden wiedergegebenen Dokumente als historische Wahrheit bezeugen.

Die Dokumente und die Auskünfte der Zeitzeugen liefern also kein Material für die Biographie eines welthistorischen Individuums, wohl aber für die Darstellung einer wichtigen Phase der römischen Geschichte, die die Vorurteile der zeitgenössischen und der späteren Geschichtsschreibung widerlegt und dies zusätzlich thematisiert. Caesar ist zwar der Protagonist des Romans, aber er ist es nicht als Subjekt, von dem aus und auf den hin die Romanwelt entworfen wird. Er erscheint in konsequenter Außenschau, in einer Sichtweise, die Brecht filmisch genannt hat: "Jede Motivierung aus dem Charakter unterbleibt, das Innenleben der Personen gibt niemals die Hauptursache und ist selten das hauptsächliche Resultat der Handlung, die Person wird von außen gesehen".[41] Die Erzählinstanzen stehen Caesar gegenüber, es gibt keinerlei Introspektion, keine Gelegenheit zur Einfühlung und keinen Versuch einer Rechtfertigung seines Verhaltens aus der Eigenart seiner Persönlichkeit oder aus subjektiver Motivation. In diesem Sinne sind *Die Geschäfte des Herrn Julius Caesar* als antiaristotelischer Roman zu bezeichnen. Brecht hat das Prinzip der Entsubjektivierung, das in einem modernen Wirklichkeitsverständnis begründet ist, auf den historischen Stoff übertragen und diesen zum Gegenstand eines materialistischen Geschichtsverständnisses gemacht. Damit ist dann freilich ein Rezeptionsproblem entstanden. Selbst Walter Benjamin und Fritz Sternberg, "sehr hochqualifizierte Intellektuelle", die doch mit Brechts Intentionen und seiner Schreibweise vertraut waren, haben, wie er im *Journal* festhält, das Buch "nicht verstanden und dringend vorgeschlagen, doch mehr menschliches Interesse hineinzubringen, mehr vom alten Roman!".[42] Obwohl er das als widersinnig und der gewählten Romanform widersprechend auffassen mußte, hat er in einer Arbeitsnotiz festgehalten: "Die Personen müssen also deutlicher werden, und zwar beinahe alle. Rarus muß Stadtklatsch beisteuern" (BFA 17. S. 364).

Das würde allerdings an der Gesamtkonzeption nichts ändern. In einem Fragment zum 4. Buch wird Rarus bedeutet, daß er der geeignete Verfasser einer "Biographie des gefeierten Julius" wäre, eines ganz eigenen Typus der "Biographie von Geschäftsleuten und [...] ihrer Beauftragten". Rarus' Einwand, daß damit keine Gestalt entstünde, wird mit der Feststellung entkräftet: "Aus diesem

[41] Brecht: *Dreigroschenprozeß* (Anm. 10). S. 465. Vgl. hierzu auch: Bertolt Brecht: *Glossen zu Stevenson*. BFA 21. S. 107–108.
[42] Brecht: *Journal* 26.2.1939. BFA 26. S. 331.

deinem Julius würde auch kein anderer Bericht eine Gestalt machen können. […] Dein Herr [ist] keine Einzelperson, sondern nur der sichtbarste Teil eines kräftigen, bösartigen, sein Aussehen übrigens immerfort wechselnden Wesens" (BFA 17. S. 371–372).

Brecht hat sich über die damit bezeichneten Schwierigkeiten des Romanprojekts Rechenschaft abgelegt. Im *Journal* hält er fest: "Die ganze 'Caesar'-Konzeption ist unmenschlich. Andererseits kann Unmenschlichkeit nicht dargestellt werden, ohne daß eine Vorstellung von Menschlichkeit da ist", und zwar nicht erst in einer gegenwärtigen Perspektive, sondern schon in der historischen Zeit, in der das Erzählte allerdings faktisch "eine kalte Welt" ist und deshalb nur in einem "kalten Werk" Gestalt gewinnen kann.[43] Dabei ist der Eindruck zu vermeiden, "daß es so kommen mußte, wie es kam", eine gängige Vorstellung, die die "Geschichtsschreiber zu Fatalisten" gemacht hat.[44]

Die Lösung des Darstellungsproblems sei die satirische Schreibart,[45] die "natürlich amüsant" sein müsse.[46] Das erfordere stilistische Konsequenzen:

> Die Raruspartien erheischen einen schlechten Stil, wenn man darunter Uneleganz, Schlampigkeit, Unplastik versteht. Die "Schönheiten" liegen auf der architektonischen Linie. […] Die Spicerpartien erlauben bessere Reflexionen, und das Satirische wird direkter, dagegen verarmt das architektonische Element.[47]

Wenn Spicer ebenso wie Carbo und Alder satirische Instanz ist, so ist er es nicht im Sinne der Orientierung an einer vom Leser akzeptierten Norm, etwa der von Brecht ins Spiel gebrachten "Menschlichkeit". Er ist vielmehr ein Anwalt der Geschäftsinteressen der City. Als Sohn eines Freigelassenen war er zunächst der für Caesar zuständige Gerichtsvollzieher – schon das ist eine für die Satire ergiebige Konstellation –, und als dessen Schulden gigantische Ausmaße angenommen haben, wird er als Banker zu deren Verwalter und im Gallischen Krieg zu seinem Aufpasser, so daß Alder berechtigt ist, Caesar als Spicers "Angestellten" zu bezeichnen (BFA 17. S. 306). Spicer ist auch der Lektor und Zensor von Caesars *De bello Gallico*: "Ich habe das Manuskript damals sehr genau durchgegangen. […] Ich glaube nicht, daß irgend etwas Interessantes darin stehen geblieben ist" (BFA 17. S. 376).

---

[43] Brecht: *Journal.* 25.7.1938 BFA 26. S. 314–315.
[44] Brecht: *Journal.* Ebd. 23.7.1938 Ebd. S. 312. Vgl. hierzu auch Brechts Arbeitsnotiz *Fatalismus der Deterministen.* BFA 17. S. 386–387.
[45] In einem Brief an die American Guild for German Cultural Freedom spricht Brecht von einem "satirischen Roman […] auf streng historischer Grundlage" (BFA 29. S. 110–111. Hier S. 111). In einer Notiz heißt es über den *Caesar*-Roman: Er "ist ein historischer, er benötigt umfangreiche Studien, die römische Geschichte betreffend. Er ist satirisch" (Bertolt Brecht: *Über den formalistischen Charakter der Realismustheorie.* BFA 22.1. S. 437–445. Hier S. 437).
[46] Bertolt Brecht: Brief an Martin Domke 19.11.1937. BFA 29. S. 61–64. Hier S. 63
[47] Brecht: *Journal* 21.9.1939. BFA 26. S. 349–350.

Die Satire ergibt sich folglich aus dem Kontrast des verklärten Caesar-Bildes zur erlebten Realität. Spicer gesteht Caesar zwar Format zu, aber was er darunter versteht, hat eine sehr eigene Qualität:

> Denken Sie nicht, […] daß ich ihn nicht für einen großen Mann halte. […] Ich halte ihn für einen großen Mann, für einen der größten. So wie er sind große Männer. […] Wenn man ihn auf die richtige Spur setzte, machte er alles sehr tüchtig. […] Sie sagten, er habe keinen Charakter, aber wer hat Charakter in der Politik? […] Mir ist immer als das großartigste an Caesar erschienen, daß er absolut keine Meinungen hatte (BFA 17. S. 384).

Die romanimmanente satirische Instanz bezieht also nicht Standpunkt gegen Caesar und gegen das Unmenschliche der "kalten Welt", sondern begründet beide aus der Perspektive der von ihnen vertretenen Interessen. Die Satire ist damit objektiv, wie im *Dreigroschenroman* und wie in Swifts *Modest Proposal*. Sie provoziert den Leser, der aber keineswegs aufgefordert wird, gegen Spicers destruktiven Sarkasmus für Caesar Partei zu ergreifen, sondern zu beiden auf Distanz gehen muß, indem er begreift, daß durch sie zwei Seiten der gleichen Sache bezeichnet sind. Ähnlich wie im *Dreigroschenroman* ist im *Caesar*-Roman der Erfolg des Protagonisten nicht das Ergebnis eines "großen Plans", sondern die Konsequenz einer Konstellation, in der Caesar sogar viel abhängiger und unfreier ist als Macheath. Er ist nicht Subjekt, sondern weitgehend unselbständiges Medium der Romanvorgänge.

4

Es mag zweifelhaft sein, auf dem Befund zweier literarischer Texte und einer Reihe theoretischer Äußerungen ein eigenes Genre begründet zu sehen. Ein drittes Beispiel ist Brecht schuldig geblieben: Der (zu) groß konzipierte und über einen langen Zeitraum geplante *Tui-Roman* ist nicht über die Sammlung ausformulierter Materialien hinaus gediehen. Die "formalen Schwierigkeiten" (BFA 22.1. S. 438) blieben ungelöst, die entworfenen Modelle erwiesen sich offenbar als ungeeignet oder nicht realisierbar. Die erhaltenen Entwürfe sind eine brillante satirische Verfremdung der Geschichte der Weimarer Republik, allerdings ohne spezifischen Erkenntnisgehalt und ohne ästhetischen Eigenwert. Es fehlt noch eine tragende Handlung, und es fehlen besondere Figuren. Obwohl deren Autonomie und selbständige Bedeutung vom antiaristotelischen Roman gerade programmatisch bestritten wird, sind sie offenbar für seine Erzählbarkeit weiterhin unverzichtbar.

Wenn ich an dem von Brecht eher beiläufig eingeführten Terminus "antiaristotelischer Roman" festhalte, so ist das durch das eigenartige Profil des *Dreigroschenromans* und der *Geschäfte des Herrn Julius Caesar* in der Gattungsgeschichte des Romans der klassischen Moderne begründet. Zwar ist die Infragestellung des autonomen Individuums als Romansubjekt, wie gesagt, nicht originell – fast alle wichtigen Autoren gehen davon aus –, aber sie ist bei Brecht nicht Gegenstand der Reflexion und Selbstreflexion wie bei ihnen, sondern Darstellungsprinzip für die Romanwelt. Das hat allerdings zur Konsequenz, daß die Erzählinstanz an Bedeutung gewinnt, nicht als Figur, sondern als Gestaltungsprinzip und als impliziter Kommentator. Hier überträgt Brecht den epischen Gestus seiner Theatertheorie auf die epische Gattung und bezieht zugleich in der Kontroverse mit Georg Lukács einen "avantgardistischen" Standpunkt. Mit diesem spezifischen Profil scheint mir der antiaristotelische Roman in der Tat ein wichtiger Beitrag zum Roman der klassischen Moderne zu sein.

Peter Hutchinson

Uncomfortable, Unsettling, Alienating: Brecht's Poetry of the Unexpected

What makes Brecht's poetry distinctive is its consistent combination of disruptive techniques and its element of surprise. Although much attention has been given to the anti-traditional handling of rhythm and subject-matter, more needs to be devoted to the combination of these features with unorthodox use of rhyme, language, and context. Poems from all stages of his career – with the exception of the eulogies on aspects of socialism – reveal the aim of unsettling and engaging the reader in an intellectual exercise.

In much verse, what is suggested, or half-said, or obviously omitted, may be just as significant as what is actually stated. Indeed, the poet's naming, or guiding, detracts from the reader's intellectual pleasure of logical deduction, or of insight. Bertolt Brecht provides a prime example of the understating author, and, furthermore, in a predominantly intellectual mode. His verse regularly makes its impact through what might be termed "economy" – the poet's omission of a full context, of clear stages in progression, or of an appropriate attitude towards his subject-matter. He consistently works in the conviction that the active reader wants to supply the ideas that the poet has "suppressed" – be they in individual words, lines, or even stanzas. His best-known poetic example of this is probably "Ulm 1592",[1] in which the reader's awareness of historical progression demands that a "missing" final stanza be provided. Had Brecht himself included that stanza, he would have denied the reader's *participation* in the process of reasoning, something which he consistently tries to promote. This poet does not want to tell, but to show. He does not want to conclude, but to enable his reader to do so. The very title "Ulm 1592" creates a context which the historically-minded reader will immediately question: what is the significance of the minor town of Ulm exactly one hundred years after the discovery of America? The point is made in a very different way in the poem on Empedocles' shoe (BFA 12. Pp. 30–32): a clever teacher can create a complex learning opportunity even out of his own demise. Brecht's focus on Empedocles' decision to die without leaving any trace but his sandal is, as has been nicely suggested,

---

[1] BFA 12. Pp. 19–20. Significantly, Brecht suggested that this poem would be appropriate for inclusion in the GDR primary school syllabus, as an alternative to "Legende von der Entstehung des Buches Taoteking…". (see Bertolt Brecht: Brief an Rudolf Engel 3.1.1952. BFA 30. Pp. 102–103.) For a good general introduction to the poem, see the entry by Heinrich Kaulen in: *Brecht Handbuch in fünf Bänden*. Ed. by Jan Knopf. Stuttgart – Weimar: Metzler 2001–2003. Vol. 2. Pp. 261–264.

an instance of "creative misdirection" for the reader.[2] False trails may actually be productive. And although by no means all of Brecht's poems provide ambiguous directions of this kind, his best certainly do. They drive us onwards as we sift through – often mutually exclusive – possibilities. Indeed the minimalist style of the late poetry, which teases through its brevity, is a natural culmination of this art of the unstated, an art which ensures definitive interpretation remains impossible.[3] In Brecht this is deliberate, because his aim is not a simple depiction of the world. As he emphasized in a response to a poem by Wordsworth, poetry involves far more than simple representation, and reading this genre is therefore a taxing exercise:

> Lyrik ist niemals bloßer Ausdruck. Die lyrische Rezeption ist eine Operation so gut wie etwa das Sehen oder Hören, d.h. viel mehr aktiv. Das Dichten muß als menschliche Tätigkeit angesehen werden, als gesellschaftliche Praxis mit aller Widersprüchlichkeit, Veränderlichkeit, als geschichtsbedingt und geschichte-machend. Der Unterschied liegt zwischen "widerspiegeln" und "den Spiegel vorhalten".[4]

The claims may be slightly grandiose, but the final play on words is illuminating. "Holding up a mirror" for the reader is quite different from "mirroring". The difference between the two is that the reader must complete the second stage of the process.

This business of engaging us to see the world differently and draw our own conclusions is, however, often made uncomfortable. Readers may be encouraged to predict a certain development and then find they are "wrong" – Brecht's "logic" sometimes runs contrary to expectation. Further, it is not only the progression of ideas on which Brecht relies to disturb us and prompt a reaction: his choice of unexpected language and unsettling rhythms are another important plank for the creation of a reactive, mentally creative mood. At numerous points this language seems out of place, for it can be colloquial, or hard, or unpleasant, or even ridiculous – Brecht will go to the limits of banality, even beyond. The lines too, despite their syntactic simplicity and often laconic style, regularly contain some disruptive element. This may range from a rhythmic "irregularity" (suggesting casualness, uncertainty, insecurity, or apparent lack of direction), to prose seemingly forced into verse, or to potential verse forced out of an expected pattern into something akin to prose. Rhyme

---

[2] See Ray Ockenden: Empedocles in Buckow: a Sketch Map of Misreading in Brecht's Poetry. In: *Empedocles' Shoe: Essays on Brecht's Poetry*. Ed. by Tom Kuhn and Karen Leeder. London: Methuen 2002. Pp. 178–205 (see in particular p. 189).

[3] For an example of how Brecht's succinctness can continue to inspire fresh readings, even of his earlier works, see the lively analysis of "Vom armen B.B." by Ronald Speirs: Of Poor B.B. – and Others. In: Kuhn and Leeder (eds.): *Empedocles' Shoe* (n. 2). Pp. 37–52.

[4] Bertolt Brecht: *Journal* 24.8.1940. BFA 26. Pp. 417–418. Here p. 418. Brecht is reacting to Wordsworth's "She was a phantom of delight".

also takes on a changed purpose in Brecht, its aim often being quite different from that of his predecessors. In "Legende vom toten Soldaten", for example, (BFA 11. Pp. 112–115), the rhyme of lines two and four of each stanza, often strong, may be crude or simplistic or ridiculously forced, and thus comically unsuited to the lugubrious content (e.g. "Marsch"/"Arsch"; "rot"/"Kot"; "her"/"militär-[ische]"). This too is what might be termed another principle of "disruption", and in the following essay I should like to show how such principles can be seen at all stages of Brecht's work. Themes may change, the occasionally scandalizing elements may disappear, and the *degree* of disturbance may diminish; but the unsettling interplay of subject-matter and its context, unexpected language, rhyme and rhythm remains a distinctive feature of Brecht's verse technique. And the drive to instruct is increasingly consolidated by numerous rhetorical devices, as we would expect in the work of any intellectual moralist – direct address to his readers, sometimes use of the imperative to them, and above all, regular questioning. (The tacit "warum?" of the earlier works becomes explicit in the later ones.) It is significant that Brecht's least successful work arises when he fails to follow these principles. And that occurs when he is dealing with something against which he decides not to react.

It is surprising that Brecht took so long to formulate his views on the *Verfremdungseffekt*, since from his very first poems he had employed techniques geared to make us look at poetry in a new way. From the beginning he delights in the surprising, and sometimes the shocking. This is part of the young man's desire to upset his audience by reacting sharply against the values of a traditional readership, and it is evident throughout the first, unpublished collection, the *Lieder zur Klampfe* (1918), which opens on a "song" celebrating sexual promiscuity. The next item begins with a parody of Goethe, the next contains a sarcastic dismissal of the harmful effects of alcohol, and the next is inspired by Villon.[5] In every poem of his first published collection, the *Hauspostille* (1927), decorum is likewise rejected in favour of a subject-matter which is distasteful or distressing (such as girls who have been seduced, girls who have drowned and rot away in the water, child murderers, penitent prostitutes, or those about to be hanged).[6] Such determination to avoid the traditional realms of nineteenth-century poetry, already opened up by the social and political cabaret songs of Wedekind (as well as the Expressionists), is unceasing, and even when Brecht writes of such apparently harmless or potentially idyllic occasions as swimming in lakes or climbing in trees, his experience of these events is quite different from what we expect. At his more aggressive, Brecht is anti-sentimental and embarrassing, deliberately offending society with his anti-religious and anti-military poems, with blasphemy and sometimes with

[5] BFA 11. Pp. 7–14.
[6] BFA 11. Pp. 37–120.

vulgarity. References in a title to a "Märtyrer", or to the "Seligen", or a "Hymne" or a "Psalm" are always ironic.[7] Yet this preference for the offensive has a creative, intellectual purpose. Anything confrontational, or destructive, or parodic, is part of the poet's attempt to engage intellectually, and although he does not posit an intellectual reader, he does at least assume a mind which can be stimulated. In this connection Tom Kuhn has recently drawn attention to a letter by Brecht to Wieland Herzfelde, in which the poet points out that the attitude he adopts in his poems can only be employed by someone who can reckon with "alert readers".[8] In the early work, though, he sometimes goes too far and his vulgarity can be simply gratuitous. An example from one of his most famous poems, "Vom armen B.B." (BFA 11. Pp. 119–120), is the crude metaphor "pissen die Tannen". This is not the way in which fir trees drip rainwater – Brecht simply wants to cause offence. The same applies to the suppression of the verb in the fourth line of "Über die Anstrengung" (BFA 11. Pp. 70–71), in which smoking, something else, and writing poetry are paralleled: "Man raucht. Man geht k... Man macht ein Gedicht". Three dots simply indicate suppression, but some later editions have six, designed, clearly, to prompt us into selecting a specific, offensive possibility. However, such moments are unusual, and rudeness is usually linked to a higher purpose. Brecht chose not to publish one of his most vulgar poems, "Sonett über einen durchschnittlichen Beischlaf" (1926), but his changing the title from "guten" to "durchschnittlichen"[9] reveals something for which his work is seldom explored: the playful side of his creativity. The context which "durchschnittlich" provides is much more intriguing than would have been "guten". The urge to play is also obvious in his including defecation as an important element of "Anstrengung". This sense of humour, sometimes wry, is to be found in early and late poems; rarely, however, in those of the middle period.

Brecht's intellectual challenge is constantly linked with rhythmic flexibility, with lines of uneven length, and lines which do not scan in the expected manner. And in the early work especially, rhyme too is exploited to particular advantage. It may seem surprising that rhyme is a regular feature of these early anti-traditional works; yet in the *Hauspostille* there are only two poems which do not rhyme. But the rhymes are regularly there to unsettle us, and are often monosyllabic and banal. In the opening poem, for example, "Vom Brot und den

---

[7]Cf. Bertolt Brecht: *Psalmen*. BFA 11. Pp. 15–35.
[8]Tom Kuhn: Introduction. In: Kuhn and Leeder (eds.), *Empedocles' Shoe* (n. 2). Pp. 8–36. Here p. 24, referring to a letter of May 1950 (BFA 30. P. 26): "In der Tat sind sie in einer Haltung geschrieben, die jemand nur einnimmt, wenn er mit aufmerksamen Lesern rechnet". Brecht was praising Herzfelde's selection of one hundred of his poems. Kuhn also draws attention to related ideas in the essay "Lyrik und Logik". BFA 22.1. Pp. 188–190.
[9]See the commentary by Ana Kugli in: Knopf (ed.): *Brecht Handbuch* (n. 1). Vol. 2. Pp. 133–135. Here p. 133.

Kindlein" (BFA 11. Pp. 41–42), we find "Schrein"/"Stein", "will"/"still", "Brot"/"Not", etc. Brecht will even "rhyme" identical words, such as the awkward "gegessen"/"essen", in the first stanza or, on the other hand, employ imperfect rhyme as in "Vieh"/"sie", or, by total contrast, strong rhymes ("stürzen"/"Gewürzen"), with the choice of words from different lexical categories providing clear potential for laughter. The avoidance of harmony – followed by the opposite – may arouse amusement, but through the absence of traditional "security" in either rhythm or rhyme, it also creates a mood of uncertainty. Take the first stanza of "Vom Brot und den Kindlein":

> Sie haben nicht gegessen
> Das Brot im hölzernen Schrein
> Sie riefen, sie wollten essen
> Lieber die kalten Stein.

Traditionalists may be offended by such basic "failings" as the grammatically incorrect title, the absence of commas (or a full stop), and the absence of an apostrophe in the final word to denote the omission of plural "e". Further, no two lines scan similarly, and as noted above, the "rhyme" of "gegessen" to "essen" offends the ear. (There is the comparable example of "entzwei"/"zwei" in the following "Ballade von der Freundschaft". BFA 11. Pp. 95–97. Here p. 96). The subject-matter too is odd: the title has referred to "Kindlein", suggesting something delicate, but why are they refusing bread and declaring they would rather eat stones? This is a clear example of a missing context which compels us to muse. The reader's experience of this stanza is unsettling, and our mood is heightened in the following one. The first stanza has set up an expectation of the common rhyme scheme, abab; the second works against this, with the final words of lines one and three being "verschimmelt" and "Himmel". Now "Schimmel" could easily have been worked into that first line, but Brecht has avoided it; he plays instead on our sense of a rhyme being missed, lost within a verb. But in the following stanza the scheme is re-established, abab, with especially strong rhymes. This return to traditional expectations leaves us disoriented. The poet is playing with us, working against what he would later denounce as "die Glätte und Harmonie des konventionellen Verses".[10]

Brecht suggested, in fact, that his approach to versification was a natural, instinctive one, which actually captured the dissonances of the age without his being aware of their true character: "Es handelte sich, wie man aus den Texten sehen kann, nicht nur um ein 'Gegen-den-Strom-Schwimmen' in formaler Hinsicht, einen Protest gegen die Glätte und Harmonie des konventionellen Verses, sondern immer doch schon um den Versuch, die Vorgänge

---

[10] Bertolt Brecht: *Über reimlose Lyrik mit unregelmäßigen Rhythmen.* BFA 22.1. Pp. 357–364. Here p. 359.

zwischen den Menschen als widerspruchsvolle, kampfdurchtobte, gewalttätige zu zeigen".[11] The final adjectives here are powerful, overstated, and written, of course, in retrospect. Brecht's thrust was not quite as politically engaged as he wanted us to believe. And that this poet, like so many others, was not the best judge of his own intentions is clear from other comments made here on the *Hauspostille*. He suggests, quite wrongly, that "die Versformen sind verhältnismäßig regelmäßig" (BFA 22.1. P. 358), and goes on to note: "Reimlos war nur ein einziges Gedicht, das regelmäßig rhythmisiert war" (ibid.). In fact, however, neither of the *two* poems which do not rhyme is in a regular rhythm. Where one can wholeheartedly agree, however, is that his rejection of smoothness and harmony is indeed a "Protest". It is a rejection of the nineteenth century and of standard forms of representation. It is unlikely that it encouraged its first readers to recognize "die Vorgänge zwischen den Menschen als widerspruchsvolle, kampfdurchtobte, gewalttätige", but it certainly led to questioning – and also, of course, widespread rejection.

Another *Hauspostille* example of rhyme, rhythm, content, language, and context combining to disturb is the anti-Goethe tirade of the "Liturgie vom Hauch".[12] The title itself suggests an unreal situation: a "liturgy" suggests formal religious worship, a "breath" suggests something trivial, insubstantial; this seems almost meaningless until we recognize its source in the poem's refrain. The sudden act of intertextualization here is dramatic, and the tension between the refrain and what has preceded it is the basis of the entire poem: Brecht sets against his own story of political violence one of the best known poems of the German canon to celebrate peace, smoothness and harmony, Goethe's "Über allen Gipfeln". We have the antithesis of stanza and refrain, Brecht and Goethe, reality and false idyll, but also horror and complicity, politics and "poetry". This conflict is reinforced by the rough language of Brecht's lines (in contrast to the complete avoidance of everything rough in Goethe), by rhyme and by rhythm. Each of Brecht's lines is, puzzlingly, numbered, as if it were a stanza in itself, and the expectation of the title's two concepts, something liturgical and soft, is immediately shattered by the opening lines.

1
Einst kam ein altes Weib einher
2
Die hatte kein Brot zum Essen mehr

[11] Ibid.
[12] BFA 11. Pp. 49–53. This is taken from the first section of the *Hauspostille*, which, Brecht suggested in his introduction, contained poems directed at "das Gefühl des Lesers", in contrast to those of the second section, which were aimed "mehr an den Verstand" (BFA 11. P. 39). The best interpretation of the poem probably remains that by Klaus Schuhmann in his book *Der Lyriker Bertolt Brecht 1913–1933*. 3. Aufl. [Ost] Berlin: Rütten und Loening 1971. Pp. 187–192.

3
Das Brot, das fraß das Militär
4
Da fiel sie in die Goss' die war kalte
5
Da hatte sie keinen Hunger mehr.
6
Darauf schwiegen die Vöglein im Walde
Über allen Wipfeln ist Ruh
In allen Gipfeln spürest du
Kaum einen Hauch.

The first five lines are, by traditional standards, unpoetic in content and form: they are all brief, simple statements, with bad grammar (no congruence in "ein altes Weib...die"), and wrong word order ("die hatte"), colloquialism ("zum Essen"), "fraß" suggesting vulgarity, the apocope of spoken language ("Goss") where one is not concerned with the niceties of speech, and the final, almost sarcastic, euphemism informing us that the old woman has died. Brecht then confounds us by the move into the most classical celebration of peace in the German language, which we immediately recognize as an escapist retreat into Nature. Brecht mocks the Goethean idyll even further by inverting the order of motifs in his source, notably by placing the "Wipfel" before the "Gipfel"; he also "crams" Goethe's five lines into three. The "confusion" of the treetops and the mountain-tops is another indication of Brecht's scorn for the original, but the compression of Goethe's lines is important on rhythmical grounds: it forces the pace (the omission of Goethe's comma plays a part in this too), suggesting the impatience of the poet with the silence there, and this sense of frustration rises as the relationship between the following stanzas and the classical refrain becomes increasingly ironic.

Part of the grotesque humour of this poem lies in the tension between what might be termed "poetic" and "colloquial" features. Not just between stanza and refrain, but between elements in the main stanzas themselves. There is a rhyme scheme – that is, a traditional element of poetry – alongside unconventional elements, such as colloquialism and slang, but that rhyme scheme is potentially comic because it is so strong and so inappropriate to the grim scene. We have here, then, a powerful form of the *Verfremdungseffekt*, as the poet forces us to stand back from what we read.[13] Take, for example, the lines

---

[13] For the first serious study of Brecht's verse as a reflection of some of his theatrical methods, see Clemens Heselhaus: Brechts Verfremdung der Lyrik. In: *Immanente Ästhetik – Ästhetische Reflexion: Lyrik als Paradigma der Moderne*. Ed. by Wolfgang Iser. München: W. Fink 1966. Pp. 307–326. Heselhaus includes "Liturgie vom Hauch" as one of his examples and draws attention to what he considers the importance of "Witz" in Brecht's formulations.

20
Der hatte einen Gummiknüppel dabei
21
Und zerklopfte dem Mann seinen Hinterkopf zu Brei.

Here social protest is incorporated within a form of verse which flaunts its elevation of rhyme above concern for metre and also, provocatively, above gruesome circumstance.

"Liturgie vom Hauch" seems to end positively. Although the subject-matter moves despondently from one violation of human rights to another, the refrain remains largely constant (the only changes being to the word or words which introduce it); the final refrain, however, shows a complete change. As soon as there has been an attack on the "little birds" themselves – by which point the significance of the context has been fully established and we have grasped that these apparently harmless "Vöglein" are the impassive, unconcerned, morally culpable classical poets – the "birds" take action. The cynicism of preceding refrains is continued with the idea that these creatures only respond when they themselves are threatened:

Da schwiegen die Vöglein nicht mehr
Über allen Wipfeln ist Unruh
In allen Gipfeln spürest du
Jetzt einen Hauch.

Is this a positive resolution, as even the bastions of the establishment react? Or is their response undercut by a (potentially comic) recreation of the fluttering of the agitated birds in the changed sound and rhythmic structure of the first two lines? And by the recognition that their activity is nothing more than a "Hauch", that is, something meek and insubstantial? As usual, Brecht's unsettled reader is faced with choices, not least by the breadth of reference which his "Vöglein" embody. The latter could be seen as any writers, or intellectuals, or even readers, who resort to Weimar Classicism whenever their social conscience is pricked. This multi-pronged attack on the irrelevance of classical poetry in a modern world bristles with unexpected ideas and emotions.

In his best poems, Brecht always provokes a response; that response can vary considerably, for this is a poet with an extremely broad range and feelings that are not always clear. Indeed, these feelings are regularly concealed behind a mask. The early works reveal a great mixture of styles and attitudes, nihilistic or anarchical pieces, those displaying an acute social conscience, some revealing heavy influence from other poets, but also parody, travesty and sometimes even wholesale plagiarism. Throughout his life Brecht was experimenting, and he never settled for long in any one style. His next volume, *Aus einem Lesebuch für Städtebewohner*, expresses the poet's unease with Big City life in a way that is almost the complete opposite of his early works. This collection is quite unlike anything which had preceded (or indeed, which follows) it, and displays distrust, pessimism, helplessness, and isolation in a hostile, rapacious world. Rhyme is abandoned, rhythm is uneven, the language is colloquial, the sentences are short, all to reflect the urgency and seriousness of the message, on how to survive in the City. The final poem of this sequence contains the address:

> Wenn ich mit dir rede
> Kalt und allgemein
> Mit den trockensten Worten
> Ohne dich anzublicken (BFA 11. P. 165).

The final line of this famous exhortation deserves more emphasis than it usually gets – indeed, sometimes only the first three lines are quoted. The point here is that no sense of communion is intended between speaker and listener, no emotional rapport established between the two. And yet it is obvious that these poems do have an emotional effect. They achieve it through their calculated understatement, from the clear attempts of the speaker to adopt masks and to avoid facing his reader, and lastly, of course, through the subject-matter. There is a shifting persona behind these poems and, as has only recently been noticed, the context is often only supplied in the last line (which typically appears in brackets).[14] But the major change here is that this verse is much more openly didactic, and the dismal message is presented within a discourse of the unsentimental, if not the cynical.

One of Brecht's favourite means of stimulating a reaction is simply by moving to an opposite perspective. In the later works this is often achieved by a simple "warum", but from the very beginning it is more commonly signalled by an "aber". In one of his earliest poems, "Prototyp eines Bösen" (BFA 11. Pp. 53–54), one of the (numbered) stanzas consists of this single word: "Aber". Such a change to an alternative approach is never again highlighted in such a pronounced manner, but the principle of stimulating the reader, either gently or forcefully, is a constant, and that pivotal conjunction is seen in many other poems. "Die Nachtlager" (BFA 14. Pp. 137–138) is a useful example, since we are here twice encouraged to revise our views as the poet unexpectedly inverts our reading of the situation. Written in the early thirties, and inspired by a chapter in Theodore Dreiser's *Sister Carrie*, it describes a situation in which a man in New York badgers passers-by for money so that the homeless can be found a

---

[14] See David Midgley: The Poet in Berlin: Brecht's City Poetry of the 1920s. In: Kuhn and Leeder (eds.), *Empedocles' Shoe* (n. 2). Pp. 91–106. Here p. 99. Midgley's essay provides a good exploration of Brecht's subject-matter and technique in this period.

bed for the night. The poem initially seems as direct and unsentimental as those of the *Städtebewohner* cycle, yet with a difference: things are being done, it seems, some of the poor are being helped. But Brecht then embarks on a double inversion of our expectations:

> Die Welt wird dadurch nicht anders
> Die Beziehungen zwischen den Menschen bessern sich nicht
> Das Zeitalter der Ausbeutung wird dadurch nicht verkürzt
> Aber einige Männer haben ein Nachtlager
> Der Wind wird von ihnen eine Nacht lang abgehalten
> Der ihnen zugedachte Schnee fällt auf die Straße.

The first three lines of this second stanza seem to negate the optimistic opening of the first, diminishing the achievement of the good Samaritan; but the second three lines restore some balance. The most important word rhythmically here is "aber". Brecht now changes to direct address, totally in the spirit of the "Städtebewohner", creating a stanza out of a single line and showing how he knows he is being uncomfortable:

> Leg das Buch nicht nieder, der du das liesest, Mensch.

> Einige Männer haben ein Nachtlager
> Der Wind wird von ihnen eine Nacht lang abgehalten
> Der ihnen zugedachte Schnee fällt auf die Straße.
> Aber die Welt wird dadurch nicht anders
> Die Beziehungen zwischen den Menschen bessern sich nicht
> Das Zeitalter der Ausbeutung wird dadurch nicht verkürzt.

Brecht is here engaging in something which becomes more common in his later poems, inverted repetition: he repeats the second stanza word for word, but he plays with the original order of the lines, with the last three of the second stanza now becoming the first. The critical "aber" retains its position. Whereas the second stanza began gloomily but ended more hopefully, in the final one the progression is away from hope to gloom, leaving the reader on this note. Brecht challenges us more directly and invites us to recognize that although small acts are good, the real need is to change society fundamentally.

The titles of Brecht's poems, as well as the sequence in which they are placed, often suggest an important context against which we may need to react. They can raise surprise, doubt, disbelief, curiosity, annoyance, or even amusement. One obviously provocative one is "Schlechte Zeit fur Lyrik" (1939: BFA 14. P. 432). In what way can the times be bad for poetry when here is one poem obviously made out of them? The poem opens in a typically oblique way, for the topic dealt with in the first stanza seems quite unrelated to the title. And we may, indeed, find ourselves in broad agreement with its initial claim, simple and relatively uncontentious as it is:[15]

Ich weiß doch: nur der Glückliche
Ist beliebt. Seine Stimme
Hört man gern. Sein Gesicht ist schön.

Der verkrüppelte Baum im Hof
Zeigt auf den schlechten Boden, aber
Die Vorübergehenden schimpfen ihn einen Krüppel
Doch mit Recht.

Die grünen Boote und die lustigen Segel des Sundes
Sehe ich nicht. Von allem
Sehe ich nur der Fischer rissiges Garnnetz.
Warum rede ich nur davon
Daß die vierzigjährige Häuslerin gekrümmt geht?
Die Brüste der Mädchen
Sind warm wie ehedem.

In meinem Lied ein Reim
Käme mir fast vor wie Übermut.

In mir streiten sich
Die Begeisterung über den blühenden Apfelbaum
Und das Entsetzen über die Reden des Anstreichers.
Aber nur das zweite
Drängt mich zum Schreibtisch.

The poem comprises a sequence of Brechtian "lateral thinking", that is, the poet does not approach a problem directly, but from the side, or from the opposite, and especially through the unexpected concrete example. From what is admired, in stanza one, the poet turns in the second stanza to what is scorned, using negative analogy to force us into recognizing the contrary. Here we are presented with the stunted tree, whose growth is explained away in terms of its bad location; but our expectations are confounded by the following "aber", itself succeeded by a completely unexpected "mit Recht". Here, clearly, we are forced into sharp disagreement with the poet: the people are surely not justified in condemning the tree, because its ugliness is undoubtedly attributable to the bad soil. From this second, everyday example, Brecht shifts back into the first person and slowly begins to suggest the relevance of what has preceded to the

[15] Typically, this statement has produced other reactions. For a different view, see Philip Thomson: *The Poetry of Brecht: Seven Studies*. Chapel Hill – London: University of North Carolina Press 1989. P. 104. Thomson's reading, as of all texts he tackles, is remarkably sensitive.

nature of his own work. The first line of this third stanza may begin on a hopeful note, and with pleasing alliteration in its second part: "die grünen Boote und die lustigen Segel des Sundes"; but the next line shatters this optimism, as we realize the poet has inverted the standard sequence of subject-verb-object (a common feature of the later verse), and is here telling us what he does not see. And then we proceed to what he does see, he, the poet with the social conscience: the torn nets of the fishermen. The point of the poem is now more or less made, but Brecht chooses to reinforce it, albeit again obliquely. Here too he relies on the intellectual co-operation of the reader. His question in stanza four is rhetorical: the reader now knows why the poet speaks of the oppressed, and the use of "gekrümmt" here takes us back to the "verkrüppelten Baum". We also now know why he cannot write of the warm breasts of the girls, that is, we assume, on "love", a standard subject of lyric poetry. And so the significance of the title now emerges fully: it is a bad time for poetry because pleasurable subjects are no longer possible in it. Nor are the techniques of poetry admissible in such an age, as he makes clear in the next two lines. The "technical" beauty of rhyme must also be discarded. The final stanza re-states the point of the whole poem, but in a specific historical context. The poet has not forgotten the objects of beauty, but it is the threats of the demagogue Hitler – "der Anstreicher" – which spur him into action.

The poem reflects the motto to the second part of the *Svendborger Gedichte*, which raises the question of whether it is possible to "sing" in dark times. This motto provides a context for that part of the cycle: "In den finsteren Zeiten / Wird da auch gesungen werden? / Da wird auch gesungen werden. / Von den finsteren Zeiten" (BFA 12. P. 16). This simple, witty, characteristic inversion – and note the unexpected, delaying full stop at the end of the third line – provides the basis for "Schlechte Zeit für Lyrik". Brecht laments what he "cannot" write of simply by naming it: that is, attractive people, relaxing activities, warm breasts, rhymes, nature in bloom; and he balances this with what the political poet should address: that which is condemned to ugliness by its underprivileged background, destitute fishermen, women worn out through hard work, fascism. The latter must displace the lyrical, but as Joyce Crick, among many others, has pointed out: "the poet [...] resolves the conflict, behind his own back, as it were, by celebrating the beauty of the world in the very act of rejection".[16]

From its title onward, this poem unsettles. It was written in the year after the essay on "reimlose Lyrik", and as we would expect, the rhythms are certainly irregular – in fact no two lines are the same. The first stanza follows a speech pattern; it is actually prose, divided into abrupt statements, and each new line

---

[16] Joyce Crick: The Fourth Door: Difficulties with the Truth in the *Svendborg Poems*. In: *Brecht's Poetry of Political Exile*. Ed. by Ronald Speirs. Cambridge: Cambridge University Press 2000. Pp. 114–134. p.116.

contains an element of surprise. A slow reading is ensured by the arresting words/concepts, as well as a "logic" we must struggle to follow; as we progress we realize that we need to pause regularly for fear of missing an idea: there is no pattern of expectations, and any word could be a crucial one. This is very much a poem of anticipation, for we are constantly looking forward to how the issues of the title will be resolved – and yet is hard to predict what will follow. Moreover ideas frequently run across the line boundaries. This "enjambment of idea" does not, however, produce anything which can be read in a flowing manner: the poem is arranged in jerky sequences of two or three lines, and our reading is therefore apprehensive. As Brecht explains: "Es ist […] zuzugeben, daß das Lesen unregelmäßiger Rhythmen zunächst einige Schwierigkeiten bereitet".[17] It is surprising that Brecht feels the need to "concede" this point, only then to justify it in a slightly half-hearted manner: "Das scheint mir aber nicht gegen sie zu sprechen" (ibid.). "Schwierigkeiten", not just in matters of rhythm, are central to his didacticism.

There are other "difficulties" and anomalies within this poem, and one of them strikes at the very heart of political poetry. Those lines devoted to subjects which are perceived as "attractive" are mellifluous. Rhythmically, and in terms of their sound values, they are pleasing on the ear. Those concerning the more troubling aspects of living are harsher, less satisfying in terms of sound, rhythm, and cadence. The most striking contrast occurs in the comparison of the stooping forty year-old and the breasts of the young girls. Perhaps surprisingly, Brecht does not extend the "gekrümmt geht" on to the next line – as might be our expectation, for that would reflect the idea of being "bent". Instead the line stands out by its length and its difficulty of articulation. It thus contrasts notably with the two brief, smooth ones that follow, which are among the shortest in the poem and in which some critics detect a hint of assonance. Equally unsettling here is the use of "Brüste" and "warm" (the latter carrying the strongest rhythmic weight in this couplet). Tom Kuhn suggests the topic in these lines is "pretty girls", while Jan Knopf suggests it is "Liebe".[18] But is it as simple as this? The choice of "Brüste" is unexpected (why not the inoffensive "Küsse"?), as is the choice of "warm".

That adjective suggests either female desire, or projected male sexual pleasure. At all events, it complicates our reading, as does the slightly archaic "ehedem". The poet is revealing that deep physical feelings lurk below his claims of a political conscience. To the sensitive reader, this is clearly unsettling. It is succeeded by the trochees of the following line, which draws attention to the attraction of technical beauty, and the awkward prose of the next, which rejects it.

---

[17] Brecht: *Über reimlose Lyrik* (n. 10). P. 363.
[18] Kuhn: Introduction (n. 8). P. 22; Jan Knopf: Schlechte Zeit für Lyrik. In: Knopf (ed.): *Brecht Handbuch.* (n.1). Vol. 2. Pp. 322–324. Here p. 324.

As a final example, I should like to draw attention to a poem which actually predates "Schlechte Zeit" but which, in mood and construction, is comparable to many of the post-war period. Unusually for Brecht, it carries no title. Now untitled poems are usually quoted by their first line, but in my experience this is not the case with the following, an apparently modest proposal concerning an epitaph. The final word, crucial to the poet's pattern of thinking, is usually omitted when the poem is cited:

> Ich benötige keinen Grabstein, aber
> Wenn ihr einen für mich benötigt
> Wünschte ich, es stünde darauf:
> Er hat Vorschläge gemacht. Wir
> Haben sie angenommen.
> Durch eine solche Inschrift wären
> Wir alle geehrt.[19]

If one were to restructure this poem according to its natural units of sense, then the final "aber" of line 1 would become the first word of line 2; the "Wir" of line 4 would also advance to the following line; and "wären" of line 6 would likewise either become the first word of line 7 or, more appropriately, lines 6 and 7 would be a single line. Brecht breaks away from this for various reasons. Even in the earliest work the end of a line often does not coincide with a break in the meaning, on the contrary, we are driven on in search of the subject or the idea. This animates a poem, while also making it unsettling. With the exception of line 5, all the lines in this poem point forward, and the sense modifiers "aber", "Er", "Wir", "Wir alle" drive us firmly onwards. They also gain emphasis by being put into rhythmic relief through natural stress. As a result, these lines are jerky; and the alternate lines in particular read very uneasily. On first reading, in particular, we may struggle to find which word in the second line should carry stress (exacerbated by the surprise over the contents of this line). We now realize that each word, each line, needs to be taken slowly. There are only three nouns in whole poem, and the shifts are essentially between the pronouns (nine of them), especially "ich" and "wir". The pivot of the poem is the simple "Er hat Vorschläge gemacht", an exceptionally modest, if slightly vague (under)statement, and the idea of "our" adopting them is mirrored in this action being dragged over into the following line. The subject-matter may be positive,

---

[19] Brecht's changes to the first version of this poem reveal an attempt to sharpen the element of surprise. One relevant modification is the change to "aber" (in the first line) in place of "wenn [/ Ihr keinen benötigt"]. See BFA 14. Pp. 191–192 for the final poem; ibid. p. 537 for the first two versions. Philip Thomson's discussion is especially valuable, emphasizing that the poet manages to convey "alongside the surface message of the poem at least as strongly the opposite message" (Thomson: *The Poetry of Brecht* (n. 15). Pp. 181–182 and 187–189. Here p. 187).

but there is no smoothness or harmony here, and the very understatement encourages a reaction: perhaps of respect for this apparent humility, or more likely, given the knowledge that the poet was not renowned for his unassuming nature, of laughter at the prominent self-underestimation. But some form of reaction is assured. This is the perfect Brechtian epitaph in that it unites didacticism, unsettling form, ambiguity, irony, and also, as we read, unpredictability. And like "Schlechte Zeit für Lyrik", it inverts its contextualizing "title" by actually providing what the poet claims he does not need.

Even in his love poetry, Brecht was different. But then, of course, the very designation "love" poetry might be challenged: the emotions betrayed in these poems are often those of lust, especially in the *Augsburger Sonette* (BFA 11. Pp. 121–130) or the famous "Die Ballade von der sexuellen Hörigkeit" (BFA 14. Pp. 13–14) – famously not sung (for reasons of propriety) at the première of *Die Dreigroschenoper*. Brecht's subject-matter is male sexual pleasure, a sense of mutual enjoyment is rare, relations between the sexes seem more animal than human, the speaker is irresponsible, egocentric, hedonistic. How better to upset many readers? And even in those poems reckoned amongst the most tender, emotions are presented in a questionable manner. "Erinnerung an die Marie A.", for example (BFA 11. Pp. 92–93), undermines the concept of love by suggesting that a cloud which the poet saw at the time he kissed someone was more memorable than the kiss or the woman herself. And "Terzinen über die Liebe" (BFA 14. Pp. 15–16) depicts love by the wholly unexpected metaphor of two *cranes* flying in the sky. The situation here is further undermined by the fact that although this is a duet which is shared between two lovers, the context is grotesque: one of the singers is a prostitute whose next customers are waiting outside. In both these poems – as indeed in most of Brecht's often sexually explicit works – the harmony of strong rhymes (especially the *terza rima*) seems at odds with the cynically depicted content. It is hard for any sensitive reader not to feel ill at ease. This was, clearly, Brecht's expectation.

So even in poetry regarded as the most intimate, Brecht aims to provoke. He is again proving his need to be different, to be completely independent, to play with ideas and reader expectations. This is the obvious reason why he could not write true "love" poetry, and also why his poetry of praise is in general unsatisfying, indeed sometimes bland and trite. So, for example, when we find him endorsing Soviet Communism or aspects of the GDR, he has abandoned his natural urge to invert, to ironize, or to parody. Poems of praise are simply not Brecht's natural home (unless that "praise" is intended ironically, of course, or the subject of praise is totally unexpected),[20] and the "context" provided by

---

[20] Notable examples would be "Lob der Vergesslichkeit" (BFA 14. P. 422) or "Lob des Zweifels" (BFA 14. Pp. 459–461). For a lively reassessment of Brecht's poems of

their uncontroversial titles is uncharacteristic, for it is unproblematic and predictable: "Inbesitznahme der großen Metro durch die Moskauer Arbeiterschaft am 27. April 1935" for example (BFA 12. Pp. 43–45), or the plain "Aufbaulied der F.D.J." of 1948 (BFA 15. Pp. 196–197). Philip Thomson suggests that Brecht's "failures" after his return from exile are largely attributable to the new public with which he is faced.[21] This may indeed be part of the explanation, but the principal reason for weak poems lies with the poet rather than his readers, with Brecht's inability to change his natural way of thinking to a subject-matter which demanded a different approach. The best works of the late period remain the problematic ones with titles that establish an intriguing context: "Beim Lesen des Horaz", for example (BFA 12. P. 315), or "Der Radwechsel" (BFA 12. P. 310). These, in that laconic mode which underlies the *Buckower Elegien*, continued Brecht's natural predilection for uncertainty: he was only confident as a critic and a questioner, when he was being cynical or exploratory. His best poetry is that of confrontation, in which the reader must not fear that which is potentially upsetting. As the poet himself grudgingly conceded about Baudelaire, "er verkauft eben Schocks".[22] By engaging with these, though, Brecht clearly hopes we may learn.

praise, see Elizabeth Boa: The Eulogistic Mode in Brecht's Poetry. In: Kuhn and Leeder (eds.), *Empedocles' Shoe* (n. 2). Pp. 107–129. Professor Boa distinguishes carefully between different forms of "eulogy".

[21] Thomson: *The Poetry of Brecht* (n. 15). P. 171. Thomson's chapter devoted to this period is significantly entitled "Problems with his readership: Brecht's bad poetry".

[22] BFA 22. P. 452, part of a series of notes on Baudelaire, especially his *Les fleurs du mal*.

Martin Swales

"Theatre that shows…"? Reflections on Brecht's Importance as a Dramatist

This paper begins by acknowledging some of the "totalizing" simplifications of Brecht's dramatic theories. Yet, in spite of these shortcomings, Brecht creates a dramaturgy that, in both theory and practice, allows the play itself to be a site of cognition in excess of what the characters themselves know. In Brecht's hands, the play acquires the kind of voice that is present in the lyric "I" of poetry and in the narrative persona of "epic" writing.

Interviewed by Sue Lawley on the popular BBC radio programme *Desert Island Discs*, the English actor Jeremy Irons said at one point that the whole thrust of his work as an actor had been to get away from "theatre that shows". With this remark he was repudiating artificial theatre, theatre where the audience knows that they are in the theatre. I think it is fair to say that, if Brecht had been listening, he would have been furious. He believed above all in theatre that shows – in both senses of the word: he believed in theatre that consistently presents itself as theatre, and he believed in theatre that has expository force, in theatre that shows something.

I want to examine these beliefs by first considering Brecht's theory of theatrical practice. This may seem a shade quixotic – if for no other reason than that he himself constantly urged that his theory was secondary to his practice, and that it was more important to attend to the play-in-performance than to discursive commentary on that performance. This is undeniably true. Even so, the fact remains that Brecht produced a sizeable body of theory throughout his creative life. That theory may have been secondary; but there was – and is – a great deal of it about. Moreover the theory has had considerable impact; it is constantly referred to and (it has to be said) constantly misunderstood. In any event, it simply will not go away.

Let me start off playing Devil's advocate, and stressing the limitations and imperfections of Brecht's theory. Firstly, it tends, as a body of work, to be very schematic. Indeed, one of his most famous theoretical statements is, precisely, a scheme – the contrasting columns of the *Mahagonny* notes – where two (as it seems) diametrically opposed modes of theatre are played off against each other (and one – the "epic" – is approved, while the other – the "dramatic" – is disparaged).[1] The chief aspect that needs to be stressed here is that Brecht is

---

[1] Bertolt Brecht: *Anmerkungen zur Oper "Aufstieg und Fall der Stadt Mahagonny"*. BFA 24. Pp. 74–85. Here p. 85.

arguing not dialectically but (as it were) adversarially. John J. White, in his excellent study of Brecht's theatrical theory, stresses Brecht's fondness for the "nicht A sondern B" pattern of thought.[2] That pattern is omnipresent and seems to govern the argument even when Brecht is not being overtly schematic. Brecht seems frequently reluctant to argue in the "on the one hand, on the other" mode. And this tendency towards false dichotomization can on occasion degenerate into conceptual crudity.

In part because of this stridency, Brecht's theory has lent itself to terrible simplifications. Brecht constantly found himself having to re-state, to refine, to correct and re-emphasize his theoretical position in order to deal with misunderstandings for which, it has to be said, he was in large measure responsible. One difficulty, though, that he was powerless to prevent lies in the fact that many of the terms he employs do not translate easily into English. "Verfremdung" is not particularly well served by "estrangement", "alienation", "disillusionment", or "distantiation". A similar problem arises with "epic", "epicizing", "historicizing", "culinary" or even "non-Aristotelian". The problem is not that these terms are meaningless; but somehow they do not sit easily in English, they seem reluctant to yield up their meanings. One might almost say that they are, in some strange way, counter-intuitive. Indeed, the issue of problematic mediation from German into a foreign culture is never far from Brecht's theoretical project. As White reminds us, much of the theory was written when Brecht was in exile, when, in other words, he needed to explain his purposes to a world that (both literally and metaphorically) did not speak the same language as he did. That being the case, it is hardly to be wondered at if misrepresentation and misunderstanding are the order of the day.

Quite apart from these formal and linguistic difficulties, though, certain tenets of the theory are, surely, highly questionable. The notion, for example, that once the audience is informed of the outcome of a scene, it will thereby feel little tension, expectation, or involvement is misguided. Taken to its logical conclusion, it would mean that one can never go to a play twice without feeling detached the second time round. I suspect I am not the only theatregoer who finds *King Lear* terrifying every time (even in an indifferent production). Similarly, some of the Brechtian claim that if the mechanics of theatre performance (the lights, the supports for flats, the fly bars) are not hidden, the audience will find its capacity for empathy diminished seems to me problematic. Any visit to (say) an English pantomime at Christmas will demonstrate that an audience (even a very young one) can cope with multiple statements whereby an illusion is both powerfully established and firmly undermined, only then to be re-instated – all in a matter of minutes.

[2] John J. White: *Bertolt Brecht's Dramatic Theory.* Rochester – Woodbridge: Camden House 2004. P. 111.

At the heart of Brecht's theory is the polemical totalizing claim that all drama previous to his was in some way Aristotelian-cathartic-identificatory. In his *"Kritik der Poetik des Aristoteles"* he defines this kind of theatre as follows:

> Als aristotelische Dramatik (…) wird da alle Dramatik bezeichnet, auf welche die aristotelische Definition der Tragödie in der *Poetik* in dem, was wir für ihren Hauptpunkt halten, paßt. Die bekannte Forderung der drei Einheiten betrachten wir nicht als diesen Hauptpunkt, sie wird vom Aristoteles auch gar nicht erhoben, wie die neuere Forschung festgestellt hat. Uns erscheint von größtem gesellschaftlichem Interesse, was Aristoteles der Tragödie als Zweck setzt, nämlich die "Katharsis", die Reinigung des Zuschauers von Furcht und Mitleid durch die Nachahmung von furcht- und mitleiderregenden Handlungen. Diese Reinigung erfolgt auf Grund eines eigentümlichen psychischen Aktes, der "Einfühlung" des Zuschauers in die handelnden Personen, die von den Schauspielern nachgeahmt werden. Wir bezeichnen eine Dramatik als aristotelisch, wenn diese Einfühlung von ihr herbeigeführt wird, ganz gleichgültig, ob unter Benutzung der vom Aristoteles dafür angeführten Regeln oder ohne deren Benutzung. Der eigentümliche psychische Akt der Einfühlung wird im Laufe der Jahrhunderte auf ganz verschiedene Art vollzogen (BFA 22.1. Pp. 171–172. Here p. 171).

And in one of the fragments of *Der Messingkauf* Brecht insists that this is the essence of theatre itself:

> Das Theater hat sich, seit Aristoteles dies schrieb, oft gewandelt, aber kaum in diesem Punkt. Man muß annehmen, daß es, wandelte es sich in diesem Punkt, nicht mehr Theater wäre.[3]

Thus, however often Brecht re-stated his theoretical position, however much his theory was shifting, dynamic, self-interrogatory, his aversion to what he took to be the prevailing Aristotelian-tragic-cathartic-culinary mode remained a constant. This is, in other words, the immovable "not A" off which the variable "but B" is bounced.

One way of at least redeeming part of Brecht's totalizing tendency is to hear it in its historical context. For much of his creative life Brecht was acutely aware of the battle being fought between two totalitarian (and, by that token, totalizing) ideologies and regimes: National Socialism and Communism. The former particularly, in terms of its aesthetics, favoured the as it were Aristotelian mode of cathartic identification. Its aim was to achieve the self-surrender of the spectator to feelings of solidarity with the mass, of oceanic oneness; and Brecht, not dishonourably, one might feel, answers with a totalizing programme of aesthetic self-reflectivity, with the programme of a drama where the theory was omnipresent as a kind of meta-statement, as the interrogation that at every turn questions the theatrical statement being made. And, as

---

[3] Bertolt Brecht: *Der Messingkauf.* BFA 22.2. Pp. 695–869. Here p. 779.

Brecht made clear in a note of 1949, that critical, interrogative stance should also be passionate:

> Es ist nicht der Fall – wiewohl es mitunter vorgebracht wurde – daß episches Theater, das übrigens – wie ebenfalls mitunter vorgebracht – nicht etwa einfach undramatisches Theater ist, den Kampfruf "Hie Vernunft – hie Emotion (Gefühl)" erschallen läßt. Es verzichtet in keiner Weise auf Emotionen. (…) die "kritische Haltung", in die es sein Publikum zu bringen trachtet, kann ihm nicht leiden-schaftlich genug sein.[4]

Here Brecht seeks to challenge the notion that his battle with Aristotelian orthodoxy entails a theatre of bloodless, cerebral didacticism. This argument may go some way towards nuancing Brecht's propensity for lock, stock, and barrel thinking. But it does not get us very far. Let us take another look at Brecht's disparagement of a "cathartic", identificatory theatre in the name of a more lucid and overtly argumentative mode of writing and performing theatre. Perhaps one could put the matter another way and say that Brecht believed in a kind of unashamedly expository theatre. To say that is to be reminded of a particular problem that has confronted many dramatists over the centuries – how to write a plausible exposition, how to tell the audience things they need to know which antedate the beginning of the play's action proper. Within the (broadly speaking) realistic mode, conversations or soliloquies have to be engineered which can put us in the picture (so to speak). Brecht's solution is frequently to dispense with psychological and social realism, is not to put us in the picture but simply to give us the picture wholesale – as a picture. Let me take two examples, from the openings of *Die Mutter* and *Der gute Mensch von Sezuan*. *Die Mutter* begins as follows:

> DIE MUTTER PELAGEA WLASSOWA Fast schäme ich mich, meinem Sohn diese Suppe hinzustellen. Aber ich kann kein Fett mehr hineintun, nicht einen halben Löffel voll. Denn erst vorige Woche ist ihm von seinem Lohn eine Kopeke pro Stunde abgezogen worden, und das kann ich durch keine Mühe mehr hineinbringen. Ich weiß, daß er bei seiner langen, schweren Arbeit kräftigeres Essen braucht. Es ist schlimm, daß ich meinem einzigen Sohn keine bessere Suppe vorsetzen kann; er ist jung und beinahe noch im Wachsen. Er ist ganz anders als sein Vater war. Er liest dauernd Bücher und das Essen war ihm nie gut genug. Jetzt ist die Suppe noch schlechter geworden. So wird er immer unzufriedener.
> *(Sie gießt die Suppe in ein Traggeschirr und trägt es ihrem Sohn hinüber. Wenn sie an den Herd zurückgekehrt ist, sieht sie, wie der Sohn, ohne von seinem Buch aufzusehen, den Deckel eines Geschirrs abnimmt und an der Suppe schnuppert, dann den Deckel wieder hinauftut und das Geschirr wegschiebt.)*
> Jetzt schnuppert er wieder an der Suppe. Ich kann ihm keine bessere herschaffen. Er wird auch bald merken, daß ich ihm keine Hilfe mehr bin, sondern eine Last.

[4] Friedrich Wolff and Bertolt Brecht: Formprobleme des Theaters aus neuem Inhalt. Ein Zwiegespräch. BFA 23. Pp. 109–113. Here p. 110.

Wofür esse ich mit, wohne in seiner Stube und kleide mich von seinem Verdienst? Er wird noch weggehen. Was kann ich, Pelagea Wlassowa, 42 Jahre alt, Witwe eines Arbeiters und Mutter eines Arbeiters, tun? Ich drehe jede Kopeke dreimal um. Ich versuche es so und versuche es so. Ich spare einmal am Holz und einmal an der Kleidung. Aber es langt nicht. Ich sehe keinen Ausweg.[5]

The opening of *Der gute Mensch von Sezuan* reads:

WANG Ich bin Wasserverkäufer hier in der Hauptstadt von Sezuan. Mein Geschäft ist mühselig. Wenn es wenig Wasser gibt, muß ich weit danach laufen. Und gibt es viel, bin ich ohne Verdienst. Aber in unserer Prozinz herrscht überhaupt große Armut. Es heißt allgemein, daß uns nur noch die Götter helfen können. Zu meiner unaussprechlichen Freude erfahre ich von einem Vieheinkäufer, der viel herumkommt, daß einige der höchsten Götter schon unterwegs sind und auch hier in Sezuan erwartet werden dürfen. Der Himmel soll sehr beunruhigt sein wegen der vielen Klagen, die zu ihm aufsteigen. Seit drei Tagen warte ich hier am Eingang der Stadt, besonders gegen Abend, damit ich sie als erster begrüßen kann.[6]

I venture to suggest that there are two things that immediately strike one about both speeches. One is the urgency with which the psychology of both characters, their inner life, is shown to derive from their social and economic circumstances. The other is that the aesthetic of both statements is anti-realistic: that is to say, neither soliloquy corresponds to what we "realistically" expect a soliloquy to be – a moment of intense reflectivity where a character feels impelled to explain him or herself to him or herself, and we the audience eavesdrop on that moment of inwardness. In the examples just quoted we are listening not so much to the character as to the actor playing the character who speaks through the situation of that character on the play's behalf. It is worth noting at this point that, when *Die Mutter* was performed by the Theatre Union in New York in 1935, its aesthetic was normalized; it was transposed out of the Brechtian expository mode into a realistic one. The audience, in other words, eavesdropped on Pelagea's distress. It may seem that this is only a modest re-configuration of the theatrical statement. But it is not modest. What the New York modifications did was profoundly to change the theatre from a site of expository knowledge to a place of detailed mimesis. At the risk of overstatement, one might say that the New York production waited for the characters to do the knowing; whereas Brecht's play does not have to wait for the characters to do the knowing; it can do it for them.

All this may seem to make heavy weather of a simple distinction. And I do not want to fall into the Brechtian trap of totalizing. Of course Western European drama has long known of the possibility of non-realistic expositions. Greek

[5] Bertolt Brecht: *Die Mutter*. BFA 3. Pp. 261–324. Here p. 263.
[6] Bertolt Brecht: *Der gute Mensch von Sezuan*. BFA 6. Pp. 175–279. Here p. 177.

tragedy, that most Aristotelian of forms, could call on the Chorus to set the scene. Shakespeare opens *Romeo and Juliet* with a resolutely expository Chorus figure (wittily updated in Baz Luhrmann's film version of the play to a television reporter) who tells us of the enmity between the Capulets and the Montagues. What Brecht does is to capitalize fully on the device to the point where it becomes more than a device; it becomes a consistent strand within the theatrical statement. In other words, at frequent junctures, Brechtian drama allows itself to know on behalf of, and in excess of, the characters' own social and psychological specificity.

Brecht's theatre, then, does more than represent; it also knows. That knowingness can, as we have just registered, express itself through soliloquies. Sometimes the soliloquies become stylized – into poetry and song. Brecht once observed that, at such moments, the actors speak on behalf of the characters and on behalf of the dramatist himself; they become "Mitwisser des Stückeschreibers".[7] The point, then, of such moments of heightened utterance – heightened because the realistic condition of prose gives way to the meta-statement that is verse or song – is not to lift the emotional temperature to achieve cathartic release, but rather to make possible a kind of privileged knowing beyond the parameters of quotidian experience. In Scene 4 of *Mutter Courage*, Courage, waiting to make a complaint to a senior officer, sings the "Lied der großen Kapitulation". In it she, or, more accurately perhaps, the voice speaking on her behalf, explains how life grinds people down to the point where they do not complain. At the end of the song, the arrival of the officer is announced. Courage, re-entering the realistic condition, decides not to complain. But the song, on her behalf, on the play's behalf, on Brecht's behalf, does complain. In the midst of the hideous attrition of the Thirty Years War to which *Mutter Courage* bears eloquent witness there are also instances of privileged knowing.

This notion of privileged knowing brings us centrally into the territory of (Aristotelian) tragedy. Brecht, as we have already noted, objected to theatre that was centrally grounded in processes of catharsis, in the identificatory intensity of shared, cultic experience. He also distrusted the implied metaphysic of Greek tragedy whereby the suffering of the protagonist produces a moment of anagnorisis, the attainment of higher, finer, more truthful knowing than is available to and in the quotidian condition. Hence Brecht's distrust of heroism (both as a social virtue and as a form of aesthetic grandeur invested in the protagonists of high drama), of notions of inevitability, of tragic necessity, of the Immutability of the World Order (as opposed to the historical specificity – and therefore changeability – of a particular world). At one point Brecht found himself wondering how to get beyond the various categories of Aristotelian

[7] Bertolt Brecht: *Die Gesänge*. BFA 12. P. 330.

tragedy – fear, pity, catharsis (linked to the higher knowing of anagnorisis). He tentatively suggested "Wissensbegierde anstelle der Furcht vor dem Schicksal" and "Hilfsbereitschaft anstelle des Mitleids".[8] Above all, he wanted his plays to make possible the kind of knowledge that might lead not to catharsis but to interventionist critique. Hence, he was prepared to dramatize both the characters' realistic unknowingness and inarticulacy and to assert a (meta-realistic) knowingness and articulacy on their behalf. (Consider, for example, the Sänger's comments of the "hört was sie dachte, nicht sagte" kind in *Der kaukasische Kreidekreis*.[9]) Brecht was, in other words, a master both of realism and of meta-realistic stylization – not so much in the spirit of "nicht A sondern B" but of "einerseits A andererseits B". (Accordingly, John and Ann White, in their detailed discussion of *Furcht und Elend* in this volume, highlight the coexistence in that play of intense realism on the one hand and of distancing stylization on the other.)

This dramaturgy represents, I believe, an extraordinary achievement. And the crucial point is that it relates not only to Brecht's theatre but to possibilities that have always been latent in theatre itself. At the risk of succumbing to the totalizing mode for which I have criticized Brecht, there is an energy that flows from his theatre which can touch Greek tragedy, Shakespearean tragedy, French neo-classical tragedy, modern tragedy (Schiller, Kleist, Büchner, Ibsen, Chekhov, Lorca, Eugene O'Neill, Arthur Miller, Tennessee Williams). In so many of the dramas within this tradition there is, seen through Brechtian eyes, the acute problem of anagnorisis. How may the entrapped and suffering creatures struggle free of their determined condition and know better? How may the plays in question bear witness not only to the difficulty but also to the possibility of historical and cognitive change? Perhaps, in the tradition of European tragedy, there are moments of commentary and self-reflection that are given not only to the characters but also to the plays themselves on their behalf. If so, Brechtian dramaturgy can help by demanding of us that complex seeing which is engendered when cathartic theatre rubs shoulders with the possibility of (as Brecht liked to think of it) interventionist thinking. Brecht's achievement is to understand that the play-in-performance is both a simulacrum of the characters' feeling and knowing and also an agency of feeling and knowing in its own right.

Within the context of the traditional tripartite division of literary modes into epic, lyric, and dramatic, the dramatic mode finds itself in the peculiar situation of (as it were) not having a voice. That is to say: epic works have a narrator (whether third person or first person), poems have a lyrical subject that says "I" or "we", but drama eavesdrops on a plurality of voices. What Brecht does – unforgettably – is to empower it by giving it a voice.

[8] Bertolt Brecht: *Über experimentelles Theater*. BFA 22.1. Pp. 540–557. Here p. 554.
[9] Bertolt Brecht: *Der kaukasische Kreidekreis*. BFA 8. Pp. 92–185. Here p. 149.

Ernest Schonfield

Brecht and the Modern Picaresque

This essay analyzes Brecht's engagement with the picaresque genre, which derives from his reading of Hašek and Grimmelshausen. Proceeding chronologically, the discussion begins with the subversive cabaret humour of Mann ist Mann (1926), which Brecht rediscovered in a different form when he read Hašek's Švejk in 1927. The poems Aus dem Lesebuch für Städtebewohner (1926/27) are considered as an example of the transposition of picaresque elements into lyric poetry. Brecht's involvement with Piscator's Schwejk (1927/28) is shown to be an important phase in his development of Epic Theatre, since three key features of Epic Theatre – episodic structure, exposition and Verfremdung – have structural affinities with the picaresque genre. The essay concludes with an examination of the picaresque in the later plays Mutter Courage und ihre Kinder and Schweyk.

Let us begin with some definitions. The picaresque novel, or "Schelmenroman" in German, is an extremely rich narrative genre which originated in sixteenth century Spain and which soon spread throughout Europe. The first picaresque novel, *La Vida de Lazarillo de Tormes*, was published anonymously in 1554. Major exponents of the genre include Quevedo, Grimmelshausen, Lesage, Defoe, Smollett, and Fielding. Having petered out by the late eighteenth century, the picaresque novel enjoyed a remarkable comeback in the twentieth century, and especially in German literature, as Wilfried van der Will has shown.[1] The term derives from the "pícaro", meaning wily trickster or rogue; the precise etymology of the term is unknown, but it may derive from the verb "pizcar", meaning "to pinch". The most celebrated examples of the modern picaresque novel include: Jaroslav Hašek, *Osudy dobrého vojáka Švejka za světové války* (*The Adventures of the Good Soldier Švejk in the World War*, 1921/23); Louis-Ferdinand Céline, *Voyage au bout de la nuit* (1932); Saul Bellow, *The Adventures of Augie March* (1953); Thomas Mann, *Bekenntnisse des Hochstaplers Felix Krull* (1954); Günter Grass, *Die Blechtrommel* (1959); and Joseph Heller, *Catch-22* (1961).[2]

---

[1] Wilfried van der Will: *Pikaro heute: Metamorphosen des Schelms bei Thomas Mann, Döblin, Brecht, Grass.* Stuttgart: Kohlhammer 1967.

[2] For recent studies on the modern picaresque, see Claudia Erhart-Wandschneider: *Das Gelächter des Schelmen. Spielfunktion als Wirklichkeitskonzeption der literarischen Schelmenfigur. Untersuchungen zum modernen Schelmenroman.* Frankfurt am Main: Peter Lang 1995; Tonia Haan: *Postérité du picaresque au XXe siècle. Sa réécriture par quelques écrivains de la crise de sens.* Assen: Van Gorcum 1995.

In his seminal essay *Toward a Definition of the Picaresque* (1971), Claudio Guillén identifies eight distinguishing features of the genre.[3] These may be summarized as follows: (1) the pícaro is a victim of circumstance, a deracinated "half-outsider" who can "neither join nor actually reject his fellow men";[4] (2) the narrative is first-person and pseudo-autobiographical; (3) the narrative viewpoint is partial and prejudiced; (4) the narrative contains moral, philosophical and religious reflections; (5) there is an emphasis on the sordid aspects of material existence; (6) the pícaro encounters diverse characters from a number of different social groups; (7) the pícaro moves horizontally through space and vertically through society; and (8) the structure of the narrative is episodic. It is important to stress that a novel does not need to satisfy all eight of these conditions in order to be regarded as picaresque. Fielding's *Tom Jones*, for example, is narrated in the third person, but is nonetheless picaresque, since it meets the other conditions.

Another important aspect of the picaresque, according to Matthias Bauer, is the way in which it conveys disenchantment or disillusionment with the world (in Spanish, "desengaño").[5] The pícaro has what might be called a worm's eye view: he views society from below, or, as Gero von Wilpert puts it, "aus der Perspektive von unten her".[6] The pícaro's sceptical gaze, his "Blick von unten her" is highly effective when it comes to unmasking the hypocrisy and pretensions of ruling elites. But, as Richard Bjornson points out, picaresque "desengaño" is also related to the socio-historical uncertainties of the baroque period, which saw "the disintegration of traditional value systems".[7] According to Alexander Blackburn, the distrust of the "illusory quality of observed reality" is an essential aspect of the genre.[8]

In this essay I will argue that the theatre of Bertolt Brecht has a number of important affinities with picaresque narratives. This of course raises the problem of genre. I do *not* wish to claim that Brecht's prose narratives are picaresque, and I certainly do not regard *Der Dreigroschenroman* as a picaresque

---

[3] Claudio Guillén: *Toward a Definition of the Picaresque*. In: Claudio Guillén: *Literature as System. Essays Toward the Theory of Literary History*. Princeton: Princeton University Press 1971. Pp. 71–106.

[4] Ibid. p. 80.

[5] Matthias Bauer: *Der Schelmenroman*. Stuttgart – Weimar: Metzler 1994. P. 34. On "desengaño", cf. also Claudio Guillén: *The Anatomies of Roguery*. New York – London: Garland 1987. P. 318.

[6] Quoted in Wilfried van der Will: *Pikaro heute* (n. 1). Pp. 11–12.

[7] Richard Bjornson: *The Picaresque Hero in European Fiction*. Madison (WI): University of Wisconsin Press 1977. P. 19.

[8] Alexander Blackburn: *The Myth of the Picaro: Continuity and Transformation of the Picaresque Novel 1554–1954*. Chapel Hill: University of North Carolina Press 1979. P. 15. For a general overview, see also Ellen Turner Gutierrez: *The Reception of the Picaresque in the French, English and German Traditions*. New York: Peter Lang 1995.

novel. Instead, I wish to suggest that certain aspects in some of Brecht's *dramas* and in some of his *lyrics* might be termed "picaresque". For it is important to note that the pícaro can cross genres too, and that the pícaro can be put on the stage: the washerwoman Frau Wolff, the central character of Gerhart Hauptmann's play *Der Biberpelz* (1893), is unmistakeably a pícaro, or rather pícara. Indeed, the fact that Brecht used two picaresque novels, Grimmelshausen's *Courasche* and Hašek's *Švejk* as the basis of two of his mature plays – *Mutter Courage und ihre Kinder* (written 1938–39, first performed 1941) and *Schweyk* (written 1941–43, first performed 1957) – indicates that Brecht himself thought that he could transpose picaresque narrative into drama. As Hans Wagener puts it, it would be too simplistic to claim that Brecht is developing a form of "picaresque theatre".[9] It is legitimate, though, to analyze Brecht's work in the light of his adaptations of Grimmelshausen and Hašek, in order to see whether it contains any elements which might be called picaresque.

This essay will focus on picaresque elements in the following three works: the poem-cycle *Aus dem Lesebuch für Städtebewohner* (written 1926/27; published 1930) and the plays *Mutter Courage und ihre Kinder* and *Schweyk*. My analysis will be based on the assumption that although the picaresque is a narrative genre, it is nonetheless possible to invoke aspects of the picaresque in other literary genres such as drama and lyric poetry. Moreover, I wish to argue that Brechtian drama has not only thematic, but also important *formal* affinities with the picaresque. The pícaro is a non-tragic hero, and this emphasis on the non-tragic hero ("der untragische Held") is a principal feature of Brecht's Epic Theatre, as Walter Benjamin points out.[10] In particular, I have identified three structural features of the picaresque novel which could potentially be related to the development of Epic Theatre: (1) the episodic structure; (2) the importance of commentary and exposition; and (3) the use of disillusionment or "desengaño". In my view, the "desengaño" of the picaresque novel bears a remarkable affinity to Brechtian *Verfremdung*. Indeed Matthias Bauer implicitly equates "desengaño" with *Verfremdung* when in his discussion of Quevedo's *Vida del Buscón*, he writes: "Erzählperspektive und Sprachgestus stehen dabei gemeinsam im Dienst der Verfremdung, die wiederum auf die 'desengaño'-Problematik bezogen werden kann".[11]

Now, I am not trying to suggest that Brecht had any profound acquaintance with the Spanish picaresque novel, or that he was even aware of the term "desengaño". Neither do I wish to claim that the picaresque was a decisive

[9] Hans Wagener: Die Renaissance des Schelms im modernen Drama. In: *Der moderne deutsche Schelmenroman. Interpretationen.* Ed. by Gerhart Hoffmeister. Amsterdam: Rodopi 1985/86. Pp. 53–77. Here p. 53.
[10] Walter Benjamin: *Was ist das epische Theater? (1). Eine Studie zu Brecht.* WBGS II.2. Pp. 519–531. Here p. 523.
[11] Bauer: *Schelmenroman* (n. 5). P. 52.

factor in the development of Epic Theatre. However, it may be worth consider-
ing the picaresque alongside the more widely-acknowledged influences on
Epic Theatre, such as the political theatre of Erwin Piscator and agit-prop,
Frank Wedekind, cabaret, Chinese theatre, Soviet theatre and the comedy of
Charlie Chaplin and Karl Valentin.[12]

How and when does Brecht become acquainted with the picaresque? Not,
apparently, through the Spanish tradition, but principally via his interest in
Jaroslav Hašek and Grimmelshausen. The prelude to the engagement with
Hašek in 1927 is Brecht's liking for the Bavarian comedian Karl Valentin.
Valentin, whom Brecht met in 1919, is a crucial figure in the development of
Epic Theatre. Indeed, Brecht later claimed (in conversation with Walter
Benjamin) that the invention of Epic Theatre took place as early as 1924, during a production of *Edward II*. Brecht did not know which directions to give the
soldiers for the battle scene and asked Valentin what to do. Valentin replied that
the soldiers were pale, and so it was agreed to paint the soldiers' faces white.[13]
This event could arguably be called the first *Verfremdungseffekt*. Valentin's
influence may be observed in the play *Mann ist Mann*, written between 1924
and 1926. The opening of the play begins, like Grimmelshausen's *Simplicissimus*
(and like Hašek's *Švejk*, which Brecht was to read the following year) with the
protagonist being forced to join the army. Once he is in the army, a number of
comic episodes ensue. The comedy here owes much to Valentin. Indeed,
some of the gags in *Mann ist Mann* may be considered as prototypical
Verfremdungseffekte under the influence of Valentin. Valentin's humour, like
Hašek's, is based on semantic misunderstandings. The cabaret clown (like the
Švejkian pícaro) follows orders in an exaggerated or confused manner. In doing
so, he sends up the whole system. In *Mann ist Mann*, the confused sincerity of
Galy Gay means that when he enters the army and follows his orders to the
point of absurdity, the army itself appears in a different light. The same thing
occurs when Widow Begbick fools Galy Gay into buying a gherkin, or when
Galy Gay buys a fake elephant: economic exchange is made to seem strange,
even absurd. In this play, for the first time, Brecht has his characters speak what
Hans Mayer has called a "Sklavensprache", a "slave language" or coded

---

[12] Cf. Peter Brooker: Key Words in Brecht's Theory and Practice of Theatre. In: *The
Cambridge Companion to Brecht*. Ed. by Peter Thomson and Glendyr Sacks.
Cambridge: Cambridge University Press 1994. Pp. 185–200. Here p. 187.
[13] Walter Benjamin: Tagebuchnotizen 1938. WBGS VI. P. 535.
[14] Hans Mayer: *Brecht in der Geschichte. Drei Versuche*. Frankfurt am Main: Suhrkamp
1971. Pp. 104–115. Mayer draws attention here to a tension within "Sklavensprache":
to the extent that it complies with the dominant discourse, the slave language perpetu-
ates oppressive structures. Only if the slave language is dialectical, only if it articulates
"Nichteinverständnis" as well as "Einverständnis", is it truly effective as a force for
resistance (p. 113).

vocabulary of resistance to authority figures which sounds like obedience.[14] Brecht seems to have learned this subversive use of language from Valentin. As Werner Hecht points out: "Für Valentin war keine Gelegenheit, kein Vorgang eindeutig und sicher".[15] And Hecht quotes Eugen Gerster, a contemporary commentator on Valentin:

> Das uns so vertraute Beziehungssystem dieser äußeren Welt […] ist für Karl Valentin nirgends dicht genug, um nicht einem Zweifel Raum zu geben, ob nicht vielleicht doch noch andere Verbindungen zwischen den Dingen möglich sind als die, die uns geläufig geworden sind.[16]

Valentin's multi-dimensional humour subverted habitual associations by presenting everyday occurrences in unexpected ways, and this is precisely what Brecht does in *Mann ist Mann*. *Mann ist Mann* (1926) is thus a first step towards *Verfremdung* under the influence of Valentin. It is more comic than picaresque. Even so, Brecht's ideas on the subversion of everyday associations could only have been confirmed by his reading of *Švejk* in 1927, for in this novel Brecht found a destabilizing humour which was closely akin to Valentin's. In my view, it could well have been Brecht's interest in Valentin which made him so acutely receptive to Hašek.

Before I explore the connection between Hašek and *Verfremdung* in detail, however, I wish to consider whether the poem-cycle *Aus dem Lesebuch für Städtebewohner*, which Brecht wrote around 1927, might not be another key moment in Brecht's reception of the picaresque. Is it possible to discern elements of the picaresque in these poems? I believe so. The poems have been associated with the genre of *Gebrauchslyrik* or functional poetry, even though the term was first coined by Kurt Tucholsky in 1928, a year after they were written.[17] These functional poems, related to *Neue Sachlichkeit*, offered advice and instructions to their readers. According to John J. White, *Gebrauchslyrik* at its best represented "a cross-fertilization between literature and other forms of culture" including cabaret and popular songs.[18] Brecht's *Lesebuch* poems express a complex series of attitudes and are distinguished by what Walter Benjamin calls an extreme sensitivity for "die spezifischen Reaktionsweisen des Städters".[19] The poems, and especially the first poem of the collection,

---

[15] Werner Hecht: *Brechts Weg zum epischen Theater. Beitrag zur Entwicklung des epischen Theaters 1918 bis 1933*. Berlin: Henschel 1962. P. 66.
[16] Cited in: Ibid. p. 66.
[17] John J. White: The Cult of "Functional Poetry" during the Weimar Period. In: *Weimar Germany: Writers and Politics*. Ed. by Alan Bance. Edinburgh: Scottish Academic Press 1982. Pp. 91–109. Here p. 95.
[18] Ibid. p. 107.
[19] Walter Benjamin: *Zu dem "Lesebuch für Städtebewohner"*. WBGS II.2. Pp. 555–560. Here p. 557.

"Verwisch die Spuren!", have been interpreted in a number of different ways. Benjamin regards "Verwisch die Spuren!" as portraying the experience of the political activist.[20] Béla Balász views it in Nietzschean terms as a Dionysian frenzy of self-denial;[21] Franco Buono as providing instructions for urban guerillas.[22] P.V. Brady investigates the complex rhetorical structure of the poems.[23] Helmut Lethen interprets the poems as expressing a behavioral doctrine.[24] (However as David Midgley points out, Lethen's argument has some serious methodological flaws.[25]) Midgley's own reading examines the poems in terms of public idioms, as "articulating the tactical responses of individuals to particular conditions of urban life";[26] and sees the poems emerging from the cabaret verses of Walter Mehring which confront the bustle of Weimar Germany with "the debunking street wisdom of the Berlin vernacular".[27] Now, this "street wisdom", with its accompanying disillusioned gaze, is a principal feature of the picaresque genre. And just as the pícaro often has to behave like a chameleon, so the *Lesebuch* poems do not disclose a single attitude, but rather shift through a number of different moods and personae. A number of these might legitimately be termed picaresque. Indeed, these poems meet several of the eight conditions which Claudio Guillén uses to define the picaresque and which I listed at the beginning of this essay: many of the poetic voices here, and especially the female voice of poem four, appear to be the victims of circumstance; the poems adopt a partial, first-person perspective (they are addressed to an implied "du"); they contain philosophical reflections; and they certainly emphasize the sordid aspects of material existence. These poems suggest that the modern city is a dangerous place, and even mention a number of potential dangers by name: poverty, starvation, cocaine addiction, syphilis, and of course being made into mincemeat ("Hackfleisch"). Moreover, the

---

[20] Ibid. p. 80.

[21] Béla Balász: Sachlichkeit und Sozialismus. In: *Die Weltbühne* 18.12.1928.

[22] Franco Buono: Nachwort. In: Bertolt Brecht: *Gedichte für Städtebewohner*. Ed. by Franco Buono. Frankfurt am Main: Suhrkamp 1980. Pp. 145–157. Here p. 153.

[23] Philip Brady: *Aus einem Lesebuch für Städtebewohner*: On a Brecht Essay in Obliqueness. In: *German Life and Letters* 26 (1972). Pp. 160–172.

[24] Helmut Lethen: *Verhaltenslehre der Kälte. Lebensversuche zwischen den Kriegen*. Frankfurt am Main: Suhrkamp 1994. Pp. 170–181.

[25] David Midgley: Vom Lebenswandel in der mechanisierten Gesellschaft. Zu neueren Tendenzen in der Theoretisierung der kulturellen Entwicklung im Zeitraum der Weimarer Republik. In: *Schwellen. Germanistische Erkundungen einer Metapher*. Ed. by Nicholas Saul, Daniel Steuer, Frank Möbus and Birgit Illner. Würzburg: Königshausen & Neumann 1999. Pp. 177–184.

[26] David Midgley: The Poet in Berlin: Brecht's City Poetry of the 1920s. In: *Empedocles' Shoe. Essays on Brecht's Poetry*. Ed. by Tom Kuhn and Karen Leeder. London: Methuen 2002. Pp. 91–106. Here p. 96.

[27] Ibid. p. 94.

poems also display the semantic instability and pragmatism often associated with the picaresque.

The first poem, "Verwisch die Spuren!", advises readers to keep a low profile if they wish to survive (BFA 11. P. 157). The first line of the poem: "Trenne dich von deinen Kameraden auf dem Bahnhof", recommends trusting nobody – an attitude which is germane to the picaresque. In a world of swindlers, the pícaro can move faster, and is less conspicuous, if he is alone. The poem urges readers that in the struggle for existence it will be better for them if they are not weighed down by any ties of allegiance; indeed, it suggests that the chaos of the "Großstadt" even renders familial ties null and void. One may take shelter in a house briefly, if it is raining, but one should not stay there too long, in case one wears out one's welcome: "Bleibe nicht sitzen! Und vergiß deinen Hut nicht!" (ibid.). And the poem concludes with a hyperbolic irony, urging readers not to leave a gravestone after their death. As Hans-Thies Lehmann points out, there is a baroque, *memento mori*-like aspect to this final stanza, recalling the baroque Spanish tradition of "desengaño", which regarded death as the ultimate disenchantment with reality.[28] The harsh doctrine of "Verwisch die Spuren!" seems motivated by a crisis, some unnamed historical catastrophe. The advice can be seen as a set of instructions to be given in the case of direst emergency, – and yet the poem seems to insinuate that emergency is the usual, normal state of affairs. Now, for a person who has nothing, for a pícaro, emergency *is* the normal state of affairs: the pícaro cannot even afford the luxury of memory because he is continually on the move, in search of the next meal. And yet the hyperbolic overstatement of the poem invites the reader's mistrust. The final line "(Das wurde mir gelehrt.)", added when the poem was published in 1930, highlights the lyric "I" as a picaresque persona, a self which has been hardened by experience. But it also alerts the reader that this lyric voice is itself partial, prejudiced and even unreliable.

Poem five (BFA 11. Pp. 160–162) gives, in the first person, what might be termed a classical description of the pícaro: "Ich bin ein Dreck". The lyric "I" here is a sort of pícara, perhaps a prostitute. She admits that she is unreliable, but proceeds to justify herself: "Leider mußte ich / Rein um mich am Leben zu erhalten, viel / Tun, was mir schadete; ich habe / Gift gefressen" (ibid. p. 161). In other words, this self has had no choice: the concern for survival must override all other concerns. A pícara must swallow her poisonous medicine with a good grace, must take the rough with the smooth. But one day, perhaps, she will achieve upward social mobility: "Ich bin ein Dreck; aber […] ich / Komme herauf, ich bin/Unvermeidlich, das Geschlecht von morgen" (ibid. p. 162). This may well be linked to the vertical movement through the social hierarchy

---

[28] Hans-Thies Lehmann: Schlaglichter auf den anderen Brecht. In: *The Other Brecht*. Ed. by Marc Silberman et als. Madison (WI): University of Wisconsin Press 1992. Pp. 1–13 (The Brecht Yearbook 17). Here p. 10; also in: Midgley: The Poet in Berlin (n. 26). P. 102.

which, according to Claudio Guillén, is characteristic of the pícaro. Poem seven reaffirms the picaresque wisdom of keeping a low profile: "In einem Tank kommen Sie nicht durch ein Kanalgitter: / Sie müssen schon aussteigen" (BFA 11. P. 162). Like Herr Keuner, the picaresque urbanite must learn to bend like a reed in a storm in order to survive: "So überstand er den Sturm in seiner kleinsten Größe".[29] In brief, then, the *Lesebuch* poems accost readers with a variety of social idioms which invite critical reflection. The complexity of these poems is not only due to their plurality of voices, but also to the plurality of genres which they invoke. Indeed, these poems are rich precisely because of the juxtaposition of different genres including *Gebrauchslyrik*, dramatic mono-logue and cabaret song. This protean quality could be programmatically assim-ilated to the condition of the pícaro himself. And one of the voices which undoubtedly makes itself heard in the collection is indeed that of the pícaro.

This is not at all surprising, since around the time Brecht was composing these poems, he was also assiduously reading what is generally regarded as one of the most important examples of the modern picaresque: Hašek. In order to assess the impact of the picaresque on Brecht's work, we must therefore focus on an examination of Brecht's reception of Hašek's masterpiece, *Osudy dobrého vojáka Švejka za světové války* (*The Adventures of the Good Soldier Švejk in the World War*). Švejk is a bumbling anti-hero: a certified imbecile who is conscripted into the Austro-Hungarian army during World War One and who survives the war due to his own superb incompetence. According to Rolf-Peter Janz, *Švejk* is a key instance of the modern picaresque, ranking alongside Thomas Mann's *Felix Krull* and Robert Walser's *Jakob von Gunten*.[30] *Švejk* first appeared in Czech in 1923 and was translated into German by Grete Reiner as *Die Abenteuer des braven Soldaten Schwejk während des Weltkrieges*. The translation appeared in four volumes between 1926 and 1927.[31] Brecht read it in 1927, and it had a lasting influence on his work, as Pavel Petr has shown.[32] Brecht called Hašek's novel "die einzige große volkstümliche Erzählung der Zeit",[33] and Walter Benjamin recalls that Brecht ranked Hašek much higher than Dostoyevsky: "Dabei konnte Dostojewski sich neben Hašek nicht sehen lassen".[34] Brecht seems to have been fascinated by Hašek's novel for a number

[29] Bertolt Brecht: *Geschichten vom Herrn Keuner*. BFA 18. Pp. 11–43. Here p. 28.
[30] Rolf-Peter Janz: Schwindelnde Männer oder die Liebe zum Betrug. Krull, Schwejk, Gunten, "Rotpeter". In: *Schwindelerfahrungen. Zur kulturhistorischen Diagnose eines vieldeutigen Symptoms*. Ed. by Rolf-Peter Janz, Fabian Stoermer and Andreas Hiepko. Amsterdam: Rodopi 2003. Pp. 99–116.
[31] Jaroslav Hašek: *Die Abenteuer des braven Soldaten Schwejk während des Weltkrieges*. 4 vols. Trans. by Grete Reiner. Prague: Synek 1926–27.
[32] Pavel Petr: *Hašeks "Schwejk" in Deutschland*. Berlin: Rütten & Loening 1963.
[33] Bertolt Brecht: *Journal* 18.8.1938. BFA 26. Pp. 321–322.
[34] Walter Benjamin: Notizen Svendborg Sommer 1934. WBGS VI. P. 532.

of reasons. Firstly there was the figure of Švejk himself, who confounds interpretation: Švejk appears to be an idiot, but he is adept at extricating himself
from the most dangerous situations. Švejk is an enduring mystery to his com-
manding officers. Lieutenant Lukáš tells him: "I still don't know whether
you're just pretending to be a mule or whether you are a born one",[35] while
Lieutenant Dub is convinced that Švejk is a fraud: "This man, sir [...] pretends
to be a half-wit for the sole purpose of concealing his rascality under the mask
of imbecility".[36] Secondly, there was the quality of the translation itself.
Hašek's original was written in idiomatic Czech with syntactical and lexical
borrowings from German and Russian. Grete Reiner's translation transposed
this Czech idiom into the Czech-influenced German dialect spoken by the
bilingual Prague petite-bourgeoisie at the turn of the century.[37] Brecht's interest in this Prague-German dialect is clear from the linguistic borrowings in his
later work identified by Petr.[38] Thirdly, as I will seek to demonstrate, Brecht's
reading of Švejk and his experience of adapting it for the stage in 1927 may
well have contributed to his development of the techniques of Epic Theatre.

Brecht's involvement with Švejk (or rather, Schwejk, as the novel is called in
German) has been well documented by Herbert Knust and is as follows.[39] In
late 1927, Brecht helped to adapt it for the stage as part of a team of writers
working for Erwin Piscator, working from a first draft by Max Brod. Later, in
Danish exile in 1936, Brecht prepared the exposé for a film version of the
novel. In Sweden between 1937 and 1939 he organized readings of Schwejk
among the circle of German literary emigrés. Then, in 1943, Brecht reworked
the story again, producing the play Schweyk (also known as Schweyk im zweiten
Weltkrieg), transposing the figure into the context of the Second World War.

In my view, Brecht's encounter with the picaresque through Hašek – his
reading of Schwejk in 1927 and his work on adapting it with Piscator – was a
formative experience for him, and a key phase in the development of Epic
Theatre. The premiere of Piscator's production of Schwejk was on 23 January
1928, with backdrops by George Grosz. Both Brecht and Piscator claimed credit
for the text, but it is likely that much of the adaptation was in fact written by
Piscator's principal dramaturge Felix Gasbarra.[40] In any case, the result was a

[35] Jaroslav Hašek: The Good Soldier Švejk and his Fortunes in the World War. Trans. by
Cecil Parrott. Harmondsworth: Penguin 1987. P. 219.
[36] Ibid. p. 722.
[37] Vladimir Ulrich: Zur Rezeption Hašeks im deutschen Sprachraum. In: Jaroslav
Hašek 1883–1983. Proceedings of the International Hašek-Symposium Bamberg June
24–27, 1983. Ed. by Walter Schamschula. Frankfurt am Main: Peter Lang 1989. Pp.
530–544. Here p. 531.
[38] Petr: Hašeks "Schwejk" in Deutschland (n. 32). P. 153.
[39] Materialien zu Bertolt Brechts "Schweyk im zweiten Weltkrieg". Ed. by Herbert
Knust. Frankfurt am Main: Suhrkamp 1974.
[40] See ibid. pp. 21–22.

memorable production which captured the epic movement of the novel by having Max Pallenberg, the actor playing Schwejk, walking continuously on a moving conveyor belt. The conveyor belt was significant because it emphasized the instability and insecurity of Schwejk's own position, but also because it portrayed Schwejk as being confronted by an ever-changing, constantly unfolding reality: the reality of the First World War. The epic, episodic picaresque structure of Hašek's novel required an epic staging, and was therefore, in my view, conducive to a new type of theatre. Indeed, the novel has a number of profound structural affinities with Brechtian Epic Theatre, as Radko Pytlík pointed out in 1983:

> The principles of the Epic theatre as formulated by Brecht are similar to the epic principles of Hašek's novel. There too there is no room for parading "emotions" [...] Hašek deliberately creates an impression of reality unfolding by itself, as if it were being merely demonstrated and explicated in epic form.[41]

I wish to take Pytlík's argument a step further and suggest that Hašek's picaresque novel helped to contribute to the development of Epic Theatre.

In my view, there are three principal features of Epic Theatre that are closely related to the picaresque genre, and which may have been influenced, at least partly, by Hašek's *Švejk*. These three features are: (1) the use of episodic structure; (2) the emphasis on commentary and exposition rather than "character"; (3) the use of estrangement effects, *Verfremdungseffekte*, in order to provoke the audience to reflect. Let us examine each of these three features in turn.

1. Episodic Structure

The disjointed, episodic structure which is so typical of the picaresque novel is integral to Epic Theatre as well. Brecht liked to quote a remark of Alfred Döblin's, "Epik könne man im Gegensatz zur Dramatik sozusagen mit der Schere in einzelne Stücke schneiden".[42] Rather than following the logic of character development which predominates in classical theatre, Epic Theatre, like the picaresque novel, offers a string of isolated episodes whose principal connecting feature is the same wandering hero. Events in Epic Theatre, as in the picaresque novel, are not motivated by character, but instead are continually referred back to a socio-historical background, which is revealed as the true basis of the action. The result is a mosaic of shorter episodes in the manner of a revue or cabaret.

---

[41] Radko Pytlík: *Jaroslav Hašek and the Good Soldier Schweik*. Trans. by David Short. Prague: Panorama 1983. P. 88.
[42] Bertolt Brecht: *Vergnügungstheater oder Lehrtheater*. BFA 22.1. Pp. 106–118. Here pp. 107–108.

2. Commentary and Exposition rather than "Character"

Picaresque novels are usually narrated in the first person. The pícaro introduces himself and explains his life to the reader. As Matthias Bauer points out, the pícaro as narrator describes a world full of cheats and frauds, but may be a fraud himself. Thus the unreliable narration of the pícaro formally conveys the instability of the picaresque world, and provokes readers to reflect upon the narrator's own intentions.[43] Thus the structure of the picaresque novel issues a direct interpretative challenge to the reader. This is analogous to the expository mode of delivery in Epic Theatre, in which the performers often address their words directly to the members of the audience. Being confronted by these expositions, the audience is invited to reflect upon whether the actors' claims are justified or not. In this way, as Brecht puts it, the individual becomes the object of a debate: "Der Mensch ist Gegenstand der Untersuchung".[44] In Epic Theatre, this emphasis on commentary serves to displace the very notion of a fixed "character". Instead, Epic Theatre focuses on the behaviour of "Der veränderliche und verändernde Mensch".[45] In so doing it shows "character" and attitudes to be dependent upon context. In picaresque novels too, and especially in Hašek's Švejk, character is also shown to be mutable, inconsistent and subject to debate.[46] For example, Švejk is only too happy to explain and comment on his actions when his superiors order him to do so, but his commentaries often serve to bewilder and confuse his fictional audience. The critic Lubomír Doležel points out that Švejk lacks character because his actions are completely erratic: he continually shifts between acting like an idiot and acting like a wise man (with several stages in between).[47] He survives by acting like a loyal soldier, but this behaviour may well be a form of imitation designed to give him room to manoeuvre ("Spielraum") in an otherwise impossible situation.[48] Thus Švejk's actions cannot be judged in terms of psychology or "character", but only in terms of the context in which they are carried out. As Radko Pytlík puts it, the figure of Švejk resists interpretation because he is "merely the epical mediator of the events of the world war".[49]

---

[43] Bauer: *Schelmenroman* (n. 5). P. 1.
[44] Brecht: *Vergnügungstheater oder Lehrtheater* (n. 42). P. 109.
[45] Ibid.
[46] It is true that Hašek's *Švejk* is narrated in the third person rather than the first, as is usually the case in picaresque novels. However, in Hašek's novel, Švejk himself often intervenes as a storyteller. He is highly talkative, loves to comment on events, and has an anecdote for every occasion – for him, exposition is a way of life.
[47] Lubomír Doležel: Der Weg der Geschichte und die Umwege des braven Soldaten. In: Schamschula (ed.): *Jaroslav Hašek 1883–1983* (n. 37). Pp. 166–178. Here p. 166.
[48] Ibid. pp. 167–168.
[49] Pytlík: *Hašek and Schweik* (n. 41). P. 88.

3. *Verfremdung*

In *Über experimentelles Theater* (1939) Brecht defines *Verfremdung* as follows: "Einen Vorgang oder einen Charakter verfremden heißt zunächst einfach, dem Vorgang oder dem Charakter das Selbstverständliche, Bekannte, Einleuchtende zu nehmen und über ihn Staunen und Neugier zu erzeugen".[50] For Brecht, then, *Verfremdung* is based on his conviction that theatre should be about exposing, showing, and drawing attention to things, rather than creating an illusion of reality.[51] He uses the term in order to describe a large number of linguistic and technical effects which he had been using consciously at least since his first significant formulation of Epic Theatre in 1930 (in his notes on *Mahagonny*).[52] Indeed, as we have seen, it can be argued that, thanks to his interest in comedians such as Karl Valentin and Charlie Chaplin, Brecht was already well on the way towards *Verfremdung* in the mid-1920s. However, he first uses the word *Verfremdung* in 1935 after seeing the acting style of Mei Lan-fang in Moscow.[53] Now, if Brecht's concept of *Verfremdung* becomes crystallized around his experience of Chinese theatre, then it is important to note that this Chinese theatre reminds Brecht of Piscator's production of *Schwejk*. In his essay *Verfremdungseffekte in der chinesischen Schauspielkunst* (1936), Brecht writes:

> Dieses Gefühl des Zuschauers wird hervorgerufen durch die Haltung des Artisten: sie ist es, die diese Fahrt berühmt macht. Die Szene erinnerte uns an den Marsch nach Budweis in der Piscatorschen Aufführung des "Braven Soldaten Schwejk". Der Dreitagemarsch des Schwejk unter Sonne und Mond an die Front, die er merkwürdigerweise nie erreicht, war ganz und gar historisch gesehen, als eine Begebenheit, nicht weniger denkwürdig als etwa Napoleons Zug nach Rußland 1812.[54]

It is thus clear that Brecht associates *Verfremdung* with *Schwejk*. Why? Because Schwejk (or Švejk) has a decentering, destabilizing effect. In Švejk's presence, humble everyday actions take on huge significance; conversely, Švejk makes the most grandiose ideals seem petty and small. Švejk's relentlessly levelling transformative function is, in my view, closely related to the

---

[50] BFA 22.1. Pp. 540–557. Here p. 554.
[51] For a summary of the reception of the term *Verfremdung* in the secondary literature, see John J. White: *Bertolt Brecht's Dramatic Theory*. Rochester (NY): Camden House 2004. Pp. 121–126.
[52] Bertolt Brecht: *Anmerkungen zur Oper "Aufstieg und Fall der Stadt Mahagonny"*. BFA 24. Pp. 74–85.
[53] Brooker: Key Words in Brecht (n. 12). P. 192.
[54] BFA 22.1. Pp. 200–210. Here p. 202. Brecht is referring to the march to Budějovice in Piscator's *Schwejk*, known in Hašek's novel as the Budějovice (Budweiser) anabasis. When Schwejk is ordered to join his company at the front line at Budějovice, he promptly marches off in the wrong direction, and manages to wander in a complete circle. In Piscator's staging, this march takes on epic proportions.

disillusionment or "desengaño" of the Spanish picaresque novels, and it is the clue to the affinity between picaresque "desengaño" and Brechtian *Verfremdung*. In Hašek's novel, Švejk's apparent innocence has a highly subversive power. When his landlady tells him of the death of Ferdinand at the beginning of the novel, he asks whether she means the Ferdinand who works as a delivery man for the local chemist's and who drank a bottle of hair oil by mistake, or the Ferdinand who collects dog manure. Švejk's innocent response has a satirical force, instantly deflating the aura surrounding the name of Archduke Ferdinand through the juxtaposition with two menial labourers. One of the standard features of the picaresque is the way in which official ideology and morality are constantly besmirched and demeaned by being exposed to mundane reality. As Mikhail Bakhtin has shown in his work on Rabelais, grotesque bodily imagery is often used in a satirical way by popular discourse in order to unmask the ideology of the dominant social class.[55] Grotesque humour is, however, only one of the strategies adopted by Hašek's Švejk. Even more subversive is the way in which Švejk's bumbling obedience serves to undermine the orders he has been given. Ordered to join his company at the front line at Budějovice, he heads off in the wrong direction. Ordered by Lieutenant Lukáš to get a dog, he steals the stable pinscher of General Friedrich Kraus von Zillergut and disaster ensues. Ordered by the chaplain Otto Katz to find oil consecrated by a bishop, he returns with a bottle of hempseed oil number three, used for varnishing.

Erwin Piscator, in *Das politische Theater*, recalls the intense debate among his team as to whether Schwejk really was a complete idiot or whether he only pretended to be so. In the end they decided that Schwejk was a grand sceptic whose tireless affirmation of the prevailing order only serves to undermine it (*reductio ad absurdum*):

> Schwejk [ist] der große Skeptiker, der durch seine starre, unermüdliche Bejahung in Wirklichkeit alles verneint. Schwejk, so argumentierten wir, ist ein zutiefst asoziales Element, kein Revolutionär, der eine neue Ordnung will, sondern ein Typus ohne gesellschaftliche Bedingungen, der auch in einer kommunistischen Gesellschaft zersetzend und auflösend wirken würde.[56]

Thus, according to Piscator, Schwejk is highly disruptive, almost anarchic figure: he threatens the existing order by affirming it in such a way that it is shaken to its foundations. As Lieutenant Lukáš tells Švejk in the novel: "You have raised your idiocy to the degree of infinity until everything has burst catastrophically".[57] Švejk bewilders and confuses his superiors by obeying their

---

[55] Mikhail Bakhtin: *Rabelais and His World*. Trans. by Hélène Iswolsky. Bloomington: Indiana University Press 1984.
[56] Erwin Piscator: *Das politische Theater*. Hamburg: Rowohlt 1963. P. 193.
[57] Hašek: *Švejk* (n. 35). P. 286.

orders in unexpected ways, and thereby presenting those orders in a new and disturbing light. In my view, it is clear that this Švejkian method is an important precursor of Brecht's *Verfremdung*. The specifically Švejkian form of *Verfremdung* consists in obeying, or following through, the principles of an ideology in such a way that they are revealed to be false. Brecht uses this technique in Scene 13 of *Die Mutter*, where Pelagea Wlassowa speaks out in favour of the war and urges the other women to donate copper so that more bullets can be manufactured. In this way, she says, the war will last longer, and her son will be promoted to the rank of "Feldwebel". The scene does not derive from the novel by Maxim Gorky, but is Brecht's own addition.[58]

Put simply, then, *Verfremdung* in the Švejkian sense is not the critique of ideology from a point outside the system, but from within the ideological system itself. In this respect, any ideology could prove vulnerable to Švejkian absurdity. Brecht's own view of Švejk, when working on his own dramatization of *Schweyk* in 1943, was remarkably similar to Piscator's view: rather than being the bearer of a revolutionary ideology, the figure of Švejk expresses a wisdom which is potentially disruptive ("umwerfend") of all ideology:

> Auf keinen Fall darf Schweyk ein listiger hinterfotziger Saboteur werden. Er ist lediglich der Opportunist der winzigen Opportunitäten, die ihm geblieben sind. […] Seine Weisheit ist umwerfend. Seine Unzerstörbarkeit macht ihn zum unerschöpflichen Objekt des Mißbrauchs und zugleich zum Nährboden der Befreiung.[59]

Švejk deflates ideologies because his thinking is relentlessly small-scale – a phenomenon Brecht apparently relates to Hašek's own technique as a novelist: "Hašek baut ohne Spannung und mit sehr kleinen Konflikten".[60] In this respect too the picaresque point of view embodied in Hašek's work was conducive to the development of Brechtian *Verfremdung*.

At the same time, there is a fourth, structural, element of Epic Theatre which may also be linked to *Švejk*: the importance of circularity. As Lubomír Doležel and Freddie Rokem have shown, the circle is a crucial figure in the work of both Hašek and Brecht.[61] The circle is also a key aspect of Spanish picaresque novels, which often allude to the goddess Fortuna and her wheel. Now, this

---

[58] See Petr: *Hašeks "Schwejk" in Deutschland* (n. 32). P. 155.
[59] Brecht: *Journal* 27.5.1943. BFA 27. P. 151.
[60] Bertolt Brecht: *Weite und Vielfalt der realistischen Schreibweise*. BFA 22.1. Pp. 424–433. Here p. 433.
[61] Lubomír Doležel: Circular Patterns: Hašek and *The Good Soldier Švejk*. In: *Studies in Honour of Zbigniew Folejewski*. Ed. by J.D. Clayton and G. Schaarschmidt. Ottawa: University of Ottawa Press 1981. Pp. 21–28; Freddie Rokem: The Meaning of the Circle in Brecht's Theatre. In: *Bertolt Brecht. Centenary Essays*. Ed. by Steve Giles and Rodney Livingstone. Amsterdam: Rodopi 1998. Pp. 109–120.

metaphor also crops up in a number of Brecht's works, as Reinhold Grimm has demonstrated.[62] The picaresque genre deals with circular and crooked motion because it is rooted in a world in which it is literally impossible for individuals to move in a straight line. In Hašek's novel, Švejk survives because his Budějovice anabasis takes him in a complete circle, and he thus miraculously avoids the front. Brecht himself points out in the *Buch der Wendungen*, in an allusion to relativity theory which states that space is bent by gravity: "[Der] Weg [der Materie] nun ist gekrümmt, denn gerade Bewegungen können von Materie nicht ausgeführt werden, wie die Erfahrung zeigt".[63] As experience – the school of hard knocks – demonstrates, the best way to move between two points may not be a straight line after all. Indeed, as a piece of humble matter, the pícaro is forced to move in a highly restricted space: threatened on all sides, he is reduced to performing "krumme Bewegungen", often in ever-decreasing circles.

Comparable vicious circles are laid out for the heroine of Brecht's most famous dramatic treatment of the picaresque, *Mutter Courage und ihre Kinder*. Although the framework of this play comes nominally from Grimmelshausen, Brecht's Mutter Courage is very different from Grimmelshausen's Courasche: she is a trader and mother rather than a prostitute. As Hans Wagener points out, the Courasche of Grimmelshausen's tale seeks to marry for money, and in this she resembles Yvette Pottier, the camp whore of Brecht's play, rather than Mutter Courage herself.[64] Indeed, Brecht's journal suggests that *Mutter Courage und ihre Kinder* owes much more to Hašek than it does to Grimmelshausen. After completing *Herr Puntila und sein Knecht Matti*, Brecht wrote: "den *Puntila* fertiggemacht. […] der ton ist nicht original, es ist Hašek's ton im schwejk, den ich auch schon in der *Courage* benutzte".[65] Hašek's influence on *Mutter Courage und ihre Kinder* is thus not in terms of character, but in terms of tone. This tone is evident whenever individuals accept the war, but in doing so, show it to be absurd. Švejk does not resist authority, but survives by being submissive, by subverting the commands which he is given; Mutter Courage responds in a similar way when the Finnish regiment which she is following is captured by the Catholic army. As the Imperial forces

---

[62] Reinhold Grimm: Brecht's Rad der Fortuna. In: Reinhold Grimm: *Brecht und Nietzsche oder Geständnisse eines Dichters. Fünf Essays und ein Bruchstück*. Frankfurt am Main: Suhrkamp 1979. Pp. 138–155.

[63] 'Bertolt Brecht: *Buch der Wendungen*.' BFA 18. Pp. 45–194. Here p. 182.

[64] Wagener: Die Renaissance des Schelms (n. 9). P. 69.

[65] Brecht: *Journal* 19.9.1940. BFA 26. Pp. 424–425. Mutter Courage may also be compared to Hauptmann's Mutter Wolff. See Herbert W. Reichert: Hauptmanns Frau Wolff und Brechts Mutter Courage. In: *The German Quarterly* 34 (1961). Pp. 439–448.

arrive, she quickly hides the regimental flag and pretends to be Catholic. Later, she describes her interrogation by her captors as follows:

> Ich hab ihnen gesagt, daß ich gegen den Antichrist bin, den Schweden, wo Hörner aufhat, und daß ichs gesehn hab, das linke Horn ist ein bissel abgeschabt. Mitten im Verhör habe ich gefragt, wo ich Weihkerzen einkaufen kann, nicht zu teuer.[66]

In other words, her attitude combines exaggerated acquiescence (implied parody) with the promise of a bribe (her interest in buying devotional candles). It is at moments like this – in which she is clearly the underdog – that Mutter Courage's picaresque resourcefulness comes most clearly to the fore. After all, the pícaro is the victim of circumstance, someone who lacks power, but who makes effective use of the opportunities left to them. Such scenes demonstrate that it is the dangers of Mutter Courage's position which make her crooked. For her, crookedness is a means to survive, as she points out, using trees as a metaphor: "Das ist wie mit die Bäum, die graden, luftigen werden abgehaun für Dachbalken, und die krummen dürfen sich ihres Lebens freun" (BFA 6. P. 60). And Mutter Courage is at her best when she perceives the huge gulf between those in power and those who actually fight wars on their behalf. Thus, the death of Field Marshal Tilly prompts her to remark that the grand plans of Kaisers and generals always fail because of the small-mindedness of the rank and file:

> dann scheiterts am gemeinen Volk, was vielleicht ein Krug Bier will und ein bissel Gesellschaft, nix Höheres. Die schönsten Pläne sind schon zuschanden geworden durch die Kleinlichkeit von denen, wo sie ausführen sollten (BFA 6. P. 54).

In this Švejkian comment, the megalomania of the warmongers is ironically satirized. However, Courage's own attitude to war is also deeply problematic. While she is aware that rulers declare war for personal profit, she still believes that she too can profit from the war: "die Großkopfigen […] führn den Krieg für Gewinn. Und anders würden die kleinen Leut wie ich auch nicht mitmachen" (BFA 6. P. 31–32). And despite her recognition that "Die Sieg und Niederlagen der Großkopfigen oben und der von unten fallen nämlich nicht immer zusammen" (BFA 6. P. 35), she still thinks that she can turn the war to her own advantage. This is a form of hubris which is lacking in Švejk, and Courage pays dearly for it. Only when her daughter Kattrin is maimed at the end of Scene 6 does she momentarily curse the war: "Der Krieg soll verflucht sein" (BFA 6. P. 61). But this denunciation is all too brief, and she soon goes back to trading from the war. Thus, despite her picaresque ingenuity, Mutter Courage learns nothing; she goes along with the system that destroys her and her children. She becomes a victim of her own individualism, an individualism

---

[66] Bertolt Brecht: *Mutter Courage und ihre Kinder.* BFA 6. Pp. 7–86. Here p. 35.

which spells ruin for those closest to her. But Brecht is more interested in whether the audience learns than whether Mutter Courage learns: "Dem Stückeschreiber obliegt es nicht, die Courage am Ende sehend zu machen [...] ihm kommt es darauf an, daß der Zuschauer sieht".[67] Thus, in much the same way as the picaresque novel sets up a combination of admiration, censure and skepticism in the reader, the stage pícaro can provoke ambivalent reactions from audiences and may potentially incite them to criticize the social system within which the pícaro operates.

Brecht's other most picaresque play, written later on, is *Schweyk* (1943). The play transplants the character from the Austro-Hungary of the First World War into the Czech "protectorate" of the Third Reich during the Second World War. When Brecht completed *Schweyk* on 24 June 1943, he wrote in his journal that he considered it to be "ein gegenstück zur *Mutter Courage*" (BFA 27. P. 152). A counterpart it may be, but *Schweyk* has never enjoyed a level of success comparable to that of *Mutter Courage und ihre Kinder*. It was first performed in Polish in Warsaw in 1957; the German premiere was in Erfurt in 1958, and it was not performed at the Berliner Ensemble until 1962. Several critics of the play have felt that the transposition of Hašek's novel into the early forties does not work because of the incommensurable differences between the Nazi regime and the Austro-Hungarian monarchy of the original. Thus Pavel Petr argues that while Hašek's Švejk preserves a significant degree of autonomy, Brecht's Schweyk is forced to capitulate to the Nazis simply in order to survive; faced with a threat of this seriousness, Schweyk becomes a "hinterfotziger sabotör" – precisely what Brecht did not want.[68] Petr also claims that Brecht's figure is more *kleinbürgerlich* than Hašek's: whereas Švejk sells dogs occasionally to get by, Brecht's Schweyk is "ein regelrechter Hundehändler, ein Geschäftsmann".[69] Cecil Parrott agrees, saying: "with Hašek's *Švejk* it is Švejk's innocence which triumphs. He appears not to be consciously undermining authority, whereas Brecht's *Schweyk* presents a Švejk who is boastfully conscious of his demoralizing influence".[70] It is certainly the case that Brecht's Schweyk is more political than the original, for example when he exclaims: "Am Hitler sind die schuld, wo ihm in München die Tschechoslowakei zun Pressent gemacht ham";[71] or when he shouts "Hoch Benesch!" into the ear of a sleeping SS-man

[67] Bertolt Brecht: *Notate zur Aufführung Berlin 1949*. Quoted from: *Brechts Mutter Courage und ihre Kinder. Materialien*. Ed. by Klaus-Detlef Müller. Frankfurt am Main: Suhrkamp 1982. Pp. 67–69. Here p. 68.

[68] Petr: *Hašeks "Schwejk" in Deutschland* (n. 32). P. 174.

[69] Ibid. p. 167.

[70] Cecil Parrott: *Jaroslav Hašek: A Study of "Švejk" and the Short Stories*. Cambridge: Cambridge University Press 1982. P. 187.

[71] Bertolt Brecht: *Schweyk*. BFA 7. Pp. 181–257. Here p. 242.

(BFA 7. S. 190). Indeed, Brecht's Schweyk is more heroic than Hašek's, to the extent that he is willing to risk his life in order to save his gluttonous friend Baloun. It is almost as if the experience of fascism has radicalized Schweyk, making him more cunning. Like Mutter Courage, he is "gefangen, aber so wie die Laus im Pelz" (BFA 6. P. 35). Even though Brecht's Schweyk lacks the sovereign indeterminacy of the original, it is still highly satisfying to see him undermine the Nazi regime from below, like a termite. It is also important to stress that Schweyk's opposition to the Nazis does not have a fixed ideological basis, but still suggests the anarchic nature of the pícaro.

Brecht's *Schweyk* may not be the equal of Hašek's novel, but is still a very enjoyable play. As in *Mutter Courage und ihre Kinder*, Brecht makes full use of the idea that the schemes of "great men" are doomed to failure because of the mediocrity of those they command. The Hitler of Brecht's play is desperate to know what the man in the street thinks of him: "Wie […] steht eigentlich *der kleine Mann* zu mir?" (BFA 7. P. 183). Schweyk's offhand remark indirectly provides the answer to Hitler's question:

> Die großen Männer sind immer schlecht angeschrieben beim gewöhnlichen Volk […] Warum, es versteht sie nicht und hält alles für überflüssig, sogar das Heldentum. Der kleine Mann scheißt sich was auf eine große Zeit, er will bissel ins Wirtshaus gehn und Gulasch auf die Nacht (BFA 7. P. 191–192).

In other words, inhuman projects fail because they rely on human beings to carry them out. And when Schweyk does meet Hitler at the end of the play, it is in order to lead him to his defeat at Stalingrad, and to explain the three reasons for his downfall: "ich hier, der Winter und der Bolschewik" (BFA 7. P. 250). According to Keith A. Dickson, Schweyk represents the unheroic resiliency of humanity itself – a stubbornness which helps to frustrate Hitler's grandiose ambitions.[72] This is also implied by the "Lied von der Moldau" which is sung at the end of the play:

> Es wechseln die Zeiten. Die riesigen Pläne
> Der Mächtigen kommen am Ende zum Halt.
> […] Das Große bleibt groß nicht und klein nicht das kleine.
> Die Nacht hat zwölf Stunden, dann kommt schon der Tag (BFA 7. P. 251–152).

The "Lied von der Moldau" is a song of universal change, and it could be regarded as an allusion to Chinese philosophy, to the *I Ching* or *Book of Changes*. However, in my view the song is also related to a fundamental category of the picaresque, as defined by Claudio Guillén: the fact that the pícaro

---

[72] Keith A. Dickson: *Towards Utopia. A Study of Brecht*. Oxford: Oxford University Press 1978. Pp. 188–189.

is always on the move, moving *horizontally* through space and *vertically* through society ("Das Große bleibt groß nicht und klein nicht das kleine"). The constant motion of the pícaro not only threatens social hierarchies; it also has a destabilizing effect on ideology. Schweyk is *not* a hero, but his indeterminacy is disruptive and potentially liberating.

Schweyk is not Brecht's final pícaro. I would like to conclude by mentioning Azdak in *Der kaukasische Kreidekreis* (1944/45).[73] Unlike most judges, Azdak is a judge who is partial rather than impartial, one who admits he is corrupt. But that is Brecht's point: in order for justice to be done, the judges themselves must be put on trial – and potentially condemned. The judgment of the Caucasian chalk circle is miraculously fair because it is pronounced in a moment of interregnum: a moment in which the social hierarchy has collapsed, vested interests are suspended, and a pícaro is made into a judge. By means of Azdak, justice itself is made to seem questionable and strange. Azdak is crooked, but his indeterminate, half-outsider status means that he is momentarily capable of pronouncing a fair judgment: he is "der gute schlechte Richter" (BFA 8. P. 166).[74] It is perhaps a fitting title for all of Brecht's pícaros: they are the good and bad judges of the world.

[73] Brecht's final pícara is Frau Wolff in: Bertolt Brecht: *Gerhart Hauptmann. Biberpelz und roter Hahn* (1950) (BFA 8. Pp. 373–446).
[74] Bertolt Brecht: *Der kaukasische Kreidekreis*. BFA 8. Pp. 93–185. Here p. 166.

Marielle Sutherland

Brecht's *Die Kleinbürgerhochzeit*: A Stück Coming Unstuck?

Brecht's Die Kleinbürgerhochzeit, *a one-act play, was written in 1919. The play has received scant attention from critics, although it has seen performances at the Berliner Ensemble and film and television adaptations. It presents a petit bourgeois family awkwardly trying to keep up appearances at a wedding feast. As they extol the virtues of middle class life and take pride in what they have built with their own hands, their home and relationships begin to collapse around them. They represent the remnants of the German empire, the last remaining members of a crumbling Wilhelmine society who refuse to accept that their values are no longer sustainable and that their illusional worldview can no longer be propped up. In this essay I explain why I think the language "experience" this play offers is one that can sensitize performers and audience to Brecht's social commentary and his interest in language as theatre. I consider some staging issues related to my own productions of this play, and I describe how, in the two student productions of this play that I have directed, the actual practice of production reflected the themes of the play and Brecht's use of self-conscious theatre to comment on society.*

Introduction

In *Schwarzauge in Deutschland,* Emine Sevgi Özdamar amusingly describes a fraught production of her play *Karagöz in Alamania* (1982).[1] Under the pressure of the production her actors reproduced the racial and cultural tensions between Turks and Germans that are the subject of the play. She tells tales of in-fighting (between both her human and animal actors!), egos and jealousy, and draws a parallel between the restless life of the *Gastarbeiter* and the near-pandemonium on stage during rehearsals, bringing home the banalities of real theatrical work. The story of her play's production is clearly part of the play itself to her – the author and director – and is by no means banal. Özdamar demonstrates how her production formed a parallel microcosm of the social situation she was trying to depict in her play.

Here I wish to make a similar case for the relationship between the play and the production process of Brecht's *Die Kleinbürgerhochzeit*. I have directed student productions of this play at both University College London (2001) and Oxford Brookes University (2005). The Oxford Brookes production was also performed at the University of Bristol as part of the British and Irish Universities' German Language Drama Festival 2005. In both productions the

---

[1] Emine Sevgi Özdamar: *Schwarzauge in Deutschland*. In: Emine Sevgi Özdamar: *Der Hof im Spiegel. Erzählungen*. Köln 2001. Pp. 47–53. My thanks to Rachel Goddard for drawing this text to my attention.

tensions we had during rehearsals seemed to replicate the theme of bourgeois façade and repression. Firstly, I will draw out the thematic aspects of the play, then I will turn to its theatrical aesthetics, and finally I will come back to reflecting both of these through my experiences of directing and producing the play.

Die Hochzeit is one of five one-act plays written by Brecht in 1919, and was published as *Die Kleinbürgerhochzeit* in 1961. It was performed in 1926 for the first time at the Frankfurter Schauspielhaus in a production by Melchior Vischer. Brecht also adapted the play for an episode in the film *Kuhle Wampe*. More recently it has seen many productions, including Philip Tiedemann's at the Berliner Ensemble, premiered in 2000. A translation by Rory Bremner was staged at The Young Vic in 2007, directed by Joe Hill-Gibbins. The scene is a wedding celebration in the new apartment of the newlyweds. The furniture is also new – the bridegroom has made it all himself, he boasts, contemptuous of modern mass production ("Auf das Lumpenzeug in den Läden kann man sich ja nicht verlassen!").[2] He has even made the glue that holds it all together. Of course, the different items of furniture break one by one, and the tension rises amid the bickering of the wedding guests: a matrimonially-worn couple, a flirtatious sister, a mischievous semi-impostor, a father with interminable reels of anecdote, and a troublesome friend – all types rather than characters, speaking and acting according to predictable patterns. The celebration is not going well. The less than inspiring conversation keeps drying up, and so those present have to keep coming up with other things they can do (card games, dancing, inspecting the rest of the house and furniture). The Mother scolds The Bridegroom repeatedly for his table manners, whilst he and his friend rub each other up the wrong way. Nobody can remember the words to the songs they decide to sing, the bride is awkwardly trying to conceal her pregnancy, and one of the guests has too much to drink and then swears he will punish his wife for treating him like an animal all these years. The guests leave on account of having nowhere left to sit, and the bride and groom argue bitterly. The last thing to break is the bed, as the couple fall onto it in drunken lustfulness.

"Kleinbürgerlichkeit" in its Social and Psychological Aspects

Brecht presents a family wedding party around 1919 still clinging to the ideals of pre-war Germany. These include patriotism, and references to a family history and tradition that seem outdated, not to mention unpalatably bound up with death. The father's anecdote on the death of uncle August from dropsy in the huge wooden bed is intended as a narrative of inheritance, for he wants his daughter to have the bed: "DER VATER: Das sind sogar Erbstücke!" (BFA 1. P. 247); "Darin ist nicht nur ein Glied unserer Familie gestorben, Maria" (ibid.).

---

[2] Bertolt Brecht: *Die Kleinbürgerhochzeit*. BFA 1. Pp. 241–267. Here p. 245. References in brackets in the text are to this play.

But of course the image of uncle August's elephantine legs and of him groaning and swearing on the bed distorts the gravity of "Altertumswert" (ibid.) and is enough to put anyone off that inheritance and that sense of tradition.

Associated with these values are the solidity and self-sufficiency of the family unit, the individual aura and authenticity of the hard-working, achieving man and the self-made home ("DIE BRAUT: Er ist jeden Tag um 5 Uhr aufgestanden. Und hat gearbeitet". BFA 1. P. 245). Deluding themselves that these past values are still intact, they are contemptuous of the new, capitalist society, its mode of mass production and the division of labour.[3] In his analysis of Germany's "Mittelstand", Hermann Lebovics states:

"Even if the concept of a middle estate with its implications of a pre-industrial society organized in Stände, or corporate bodies, could represent no economic or social reality after the middle of the nineteenth century, it could, and did, represent the unity of aspiration and of fear for the future".[4]

He argues that the fear of economic irrelevance and the loss of status plagued the middle classes.[5] Dirk Jung describes how the petite bourgeoisie saw themselves: they believed they were the centre of society, that they set its moral standards, that they were hardworking pillars of the community, that their interest represented the common good, and that they were the defenders of decency, good citizenship and tradition.[6] Klaus M. Schmidt has already related this description to the depiction of the petite bourgeoisie in Brecht's later works.[7] They refused to acknowledge modern mass society in which they would be relegated from "the heart, or better, the soul of the social body"[8] to anonymous, indistinct entities in the crowd. By heroically building the furniture themselves Brecht's "Kleinbürger" insist on a form of non-alienated labour which they proudly believe marks them out as pre-modern and underscores the stability and continuation of German values and society. It is as if they are trying to get back to a prior, coherent, harmonious condition amidst the ruins of their world. But the glue that used to hold together the metaphorical furniture

[3] See Roland Jost: Die Einakter von 1919. In: *Brecht Handbuch in fünf Bänden*. Ed. by Jan Knopf. Stuttgart – Weimar: Metzler 2001–2003. Pp. 100–113. Here p. 104.
[4] Herman Lebovics: *Social Conservatism and the German Middle Classes 1914–1933*. Princeton: Princeton University Press 1968. P. 5.
[5] Ibid.
[6] Dirk Jung: *Vom Kleinbürgertum zur deutschen Mittelschicht. Analyse einer Sozialmentalität*. Saarbrücken: Die Mitte 1982. P. 41.
[7] See Klaus M. Schmidt: The "Little House in Louisiana": The Role of the Petite Bourgeoisie in Brecht's Concept of Nazism. In: *Brecht Unbound. Presented at the International Bertolt Brecht Symposium Held at the University of Delaware February 1992*. Ed. by James K. Lyon and Hans-Peter Breuer. Newark – London 1995. Pp. 63–75. Here p. 67.
[8] Lebovics: *Social Conservatism* (n. 4). P. 9.

of that world has failed, and the insistence on these values is undermined by the groom's anxiety that his chairs and tables will collapse, a fear he tries to mask with a forced joviality and carefree attitude. As the bed breaks, the petit bourgeois scenery of marital solidity and the intactness of family life comes crashing down, reflecting the devastation of the German empire and Wilhelmine society, the socio-economic decline of the bourgeoisie, and the exposure and subsequent wrecking of bourgeois morals and fictions. The characters give the impression of exhausted, battered marionettes who keep on with their performance even though the stage has collapsed.

Moreover, the petit bourgeois wedding is the respectable veneer under which the anarchic nature of sexuality is denied and suppressed in this play. A repressed salaciousness is evident in the undercurrent of sexual innuendo throughout the script, such as in the *double entendre* "Darin ist nicht nur ein Glied unserer Familie gestorben, Maria" (BFA 1. P. 247), and the preoccupation with "Eier", which causes The Friend to giggle uncontrollably (BFA 1. P. 246). Brecht references his own play, *Baal* (another early play that attacks middle-class morality), in order to bring out the anti-modernity, repressiveness and intolerance that characterize the responses of contemporary "Kleinbürger" to his own plays. When The Young Man asks The Man if he has seen the play *Baal*, the latter replies "Ja, es ist eine Sauerei" (BFA 1. P. 258), and The Father agrees: "Bei den Modernen wird das Familienleben so in den Schmutz gezogen. Und das ist doch das Beste, was wir Deutsche haben" (ibid.). As has been argued elsewhere,[9] The Man distances himself from this "Sauerei", the offensive Baal, just as sexuality and lasciviousness are suppressed by a bourgeois morality of decency, politeness, diligence, thrift, conformism and patriotism. The irony is, of course, that all efforts to uphold this moral veneer are undermined by the bride's obvious pregnancy, making the wedding and the white wedding dress pure performance and pretence. Furthermore, the bride and The Friend dance together provocatively, whilst the bridegroom flirts with The Woman. Such hypocrisy becomes the theme of the sexually explicit and offensive "Keuschheitsballade in Dur", sung by The Friend to get back at the bridegroom after one of the groom's chairs gives him a splinter in his trousers.[10] After the bride and groom have argued at length about how each embarrassed the other at the wedding, the sexual union that takes place is neither reconciliatory nor fulfilling. Both are drunk, and their wedding night no longer holds any mystery or ritual significance. With their new home already in ruins and themselves in a state of inebriated cynicism, they now have only the prospect of sexual gratification, and the stage directions indicate the groom's brutality towards the

---

[9] See Knopf (ed.): *Brecht Handbuch* (n. 3). P. 102.
[10] BFA 1. P. 255. The song text is not given in the edition from which I am quoting. It can be found in: Bertolt Brecht: *Gesammelte Werke*. Ed. by Suhrkamp Verlag in cooperation with Elisabeth Hauptmann. Vol. 7. Frankfurt am Main 1967. Pp. 2729–2730.

bride at this point. The breaking of the bed signifies of course the violent eruption of repressed sexuality and the collapse of the bourgeois theatre of marriage.

It might be useful here to compare this wedding to other wedding scenes in
Brecht's portfolio. In *Die Dreigroschenoper*, Polly Peachum marries Mackie
Messer, and in this wedding too furniture and accessories are used as a mask
for a world that is not at all beautiful or morally cohesive. The wedding takes
place in a stable, and Mackie Messer's thieves have been out robbing and mur-
dering the upper and upper middle classes in order to provide the wedding furniture, tableware, carpets, and presents.

The makeshift wedding venue is further emphasized by the gangsters cutting
off the legs of the harpsichord in order to turn it into a bench because there are no
chairs. The wedding performed is a cruder version of a petit bourgeois wedding.
Each time a slip of the tongue threatens to reveal that Mac is already married,
he throws withering looks, and when one of the guests makes dirty jokes he
throws a punch. Mac shouts at the guests until they agree to sing a song to provide
some entertainment, but they do so begrudgingly, and, furthermore, the song
they choose is offensive, for it is about a couple who get married without knowing
one another, and it implies that the woman is sleeping with other men. When
Mac's men unveil the stolen bed and leave the couple alone, the scene takes
such a turn that one might even begin to hear again the sound of the offstage
bed in *Die Kleinbürgerhochzeit* collapsing under the newlyweds' sexual activity.

In *Der kaukasische Kreidekreis* a marriage of convenience, contracted for
the sake of the child and carried out by a drunken monk who is not above making obscene speeches, becomes an intolerable inconvenience. Married life
reproduces the patterns of exploitation we see in Brecht's married couples generally. Gruscha must scrub her husband's back in the bath while he tells her
what he expects of a wife: "Die Frau jätet das Feld und macht die Beine auf, so
heißt es im Kalender bei uns".[11] The farmer now treats his wife as his possession. Similarly, in *Der gute Mensch von Sezuan*, Shen Te's status as a vulnerable
female is underlined by various attempts to marry her, and similar confusion
surrounds the issue of love matches and marriages of convenience. The wedding is set in a cheap restaurant and the groom is refusing to proceed until the
money turns up. The bridegroom's mother is concerned that the guests are guz-
zling the wine and that it will run out before the celebration is over. Finally, the
official leaves, by which time the groom is drunk and Widow Shin is full of
schadenfreude: "Das nenne ich eine Blamage!".[12]

A comparable "Blamage" occurs in *Die Kleinbürgerhochzeit* when the
bridegroom's implicit claim to have forged an authentic, stable and coherent
domestic world is exposed as a misplaced attention to accessories and furnishings

---

[11] Bertolt Brecht: *Der kaukasische Kreidekreis*. BFA 8. Pp. 7–191. Here p. 54.
[12] Bertolt Brecht: *Der gute Mensch von Sezuan*. BFA 7. Pp. 175–279. Here p. 239.

as the furniture collapses and the guests fall out. The petit bourgeois world is presented as precarious and superficial, sustained by outworn and meaningless conventions and manners. The Mother and The Bride repeatedly scold members of the family for not adhering to the apparently senseless rules of the table: "DIE BRAUT: Ina, tu das Messer weg bei Fisch!" (BFA 1. P. 244); "DIE MUT-TER: Jakob, schneid das Gebäck nicht!" (BFA 1. P. 250). The play also shows how the pseudo-educated petite bourgeoisie like to show the rest of society they are cultured, whilst remaining in essence anti-intellectual. The reference to *Baal*, for example, is The Young Man's attempt to represent himself as a theatregoer. As a self-conscious literary moment in the text it demonstrates middle class self-consciousness around "Bildung".

Language

Just as the furniture comes apart, the artificiality of the conversation bares its empty centre. The play dramatizes the failure of social glue and the non-adhesive nature of bourgeois discourse as language comes apart at the seams. The external forms of good manners and delicate speech are eroded as the characters resort to cliché, anecdote and puerile conversation in order to keep the conversation going.

The Father represents a sentimental and nostalgic language of the past. He emphasizes the value of antiques and inherited furniture, and he tells stories about the past rather than engaging with the present or with living people. He regresses into extended, unappetizing anecdotes about toilets and tumescent illnesses, a formulaic language of *divertissement* designed to substitute for any real interaction and relationship whilst leaving the impression that there is a communal experience. The sentimental wedding speech, made by The Young Man, is taken directly from a book – he has no words of his own to offer the couple. When the characters are at a loss for language they often resort to primitive and unfunny insinuations and innuendos such as the term "Eier". This linguistic inertia both stems from and contributes to the disconnection between the characters. Their inability to communicate is reflected in the broken, lazy, alienated, dialogues that allow them to remain snugly confined to their private selves, essentially uninterested in anyone else.

The dialogue is built on ignorance and small talk: "Sind Sie für das Romantische?"/"Ja. Sehr. Besonders für Heine. Der hat so ein süßes Profil" (BFA 1. P. 244). It is propelled by cliché: "Ja, früher wußte man, was man tat" (BFA 1. P. 247); "Wir haben doch unsere eigenen Sachen, es klebt Schweiß daran und Liebe zu den Sachen" (BFA 1. P. 251). Flattery ("Die Beleuchtung finde ich großartig!". BFA 1. P. 250; "So gut wie du, Mutter, kann sie doch nie kochen!". BFA 1. P. 246) and boastfulness ("Mein Mann hat es entworfen, gezeichnet, die Bretter gekauft, gehobelt, alles, und dann geleimt, also alles, und es sieht doch ganz gut aus". BFA 1. P. 245) come automatically. Backhanded criticisms are also common: "Diese Einlagen hat man jetzt doch gar nimmer, jetzt hat man Glas mit bunten Vorhängen" (BFA 1. P. 251). The characters repeatedly tell lies. When The Young Man and The Sister leave the room for a romantic interlude they return saying they have been helping mother make the cream; and the bride complains to her husband in private that she had been planning to say that her child was premature rather than conceived out of wedlock. When it comes to sex, the characters manage to say without saying: "Das Kleid ist sehr gut gemacht, daß man nicht einmal sieht, daß du..." (BFA 1. P. 261). Each of these modes of speech is designed to mask the truth and suppress the emptiness and resentment at the heart of the characters' interactions and lives.

The dominance of language for language's sake, language with no real commitment, content or communicative and relational – adhesive – power is finally acknowledged by the father as he is taking his leave after the celebration has deteriorated into a slanging match. Referring to his anecdotes, he suggests that he was trying to keep everyone distracted from their mutual alienation, from their own incapability of real human dialogue: "Ich dachte immer, wenn man etwas erzählt, was niemand angeht, wird's besser. Sie vertragen es so schlecht, wenn man sie sich selbst überläßt" (BFA 1. P. 264).

Each contribution to the dialogue is of minimal length, unless the characters are recounting or whingeing, and this perpetual, non-connective, dizzying transfer between speakers shows up the dialogue in its inability to anchor or spark. The very false and superficial methods the characters use to establish some kind of coherence in their group communication appear to the audience as dialogues only strenuously and tenuously kept going (for example, whenever there is an uncomfortable silence, a character might forcibly introduce a new topic or raise a toast so that everybody is propelled into communality again in the joint action of raising glasses and the chorusing of "Prost!"). The audience hear words and see people, but they are given no sense that this noise is any more than surface and disguise. The father's anecdotes take their cues at random. They are derived from word-association rather than from a connection with any communal, meaningful discourse. The exchange about how many eggs the mother has put into the cream, for instance, triggers another unrelated reminiscence by the father, but he eventually gets cut off: "Ja, Eier. Mir gab deine selige Mutter mal eins mit auf die Reise..." (BFA 1. P. 246).

The text consists of non-talk, word association, spiralling round an empty centre that has undercurrents of sex, defecation, disease and death. The artificiality of the bourgeois discourse springs from this sense of nihilism. The central lie is that the bride is not pregnant, and to preserve this appearance the lie must be propped up by discursive pretences, by a range of linguistic furniture that obscures a core privation. Bourgeois life is furnished and accessorized with a discourse of authenticity and coherence, but its language is pure theatre, as it struggles to conceal the fact it has no fixed centre of referentiality and is unreliable, open to misinterpretation and innuendo.

Hypocrisy, Façade and Theatre

The recurring motif of breaking furniture in *Die Kleinbürgerhochzeit* plays out on stage the breaking up of a material reality, and it represents Brecht's intellectual attitude, which is one of dismantling and defamiliarizing our experience and perceptions of reality in order to be able to assess them more adequately. As one critic has observed: "Our experience is broken down into components which we see laid bare, stripped of our habitual harmonization. It is left to us to reconstruct the relation of the work of art to empirical reality, at the same time discovering the criticism we can apply to our previous view of that reality".[13] In *Die Kleinbürgerhochzeit* the bourgeois world with all its furnishings comes apart because it is being intellectually dismantled, diagnosed and dislodged. The self-perception of the middle classes as a centred, unchanging and harmonious unit is a frozen image that is broken down, examined from a distance and exposed as sham. Brecht defamiliarizes and destabilizes this apparently fixed reality and shows it to be capable of change. This exposure and breakdown are translated into the aesthetic of the piece.

Brecht presents in this play the façade and hypocrisy of the bourgeois wedding as an extension of the differences between theatre and reality. The self-conscious references to theatre break and expose the pretences of the petit bourgeois wedding, and on another level they deconstruct theatrical experience as part of Brecht's anti-illusional aesthetic. Breakdown has meaning on three different levels in this play. It means (1) the breakdown of middle class ideals; (2) the breakdown of illusional, static images of reality, images that have become so familiar and ingrained that they are no longer questioned or regarded as changeable; (3) the breakdown of illusional theatre.

Although this play predates Brecht's theory and practice of Epic Theatre, there is much in *Die Kleinbürgerhochzeit* that points to the future distancing, dis-illusioning techniques in Brechtian theatre. Because this deliberately self-conscious theatre is held up as a mirror for society, the theatrical spectacle of the bourgeois life is set up in the play to lose its scenery and props. In his writings on Epic Theatre, Brecht says that illusionism in décor is done away with, allowing the décor to tell the spectator that s/he is in a theatre by exposing its machinery.[14] In *Die Kleinbürgerhochzeit* the breakdown of furniture is an image of the theatrical machinery, of a set glued together to give the illusion of reality – it is a theatrical image coming unstuck. There are many references to

[13] Alfred D. White: *Bertolt Brecht's Great Plays*. Basingstoke – London: Macmillan 1978. P. 30.
[14] "Es ist heute wichtiger, daß die Dekoration dem Zuschauer sagt, daß er im Theater ist, als daß er etwa in Aulis ist [...] Am besten ist es, die Maschinerie zu zeigen [...] Die Dekoration muß so aussehen, als sei sie, wenn sie etwa eine Stadt darstellt, eine Stadt, die nur für zwei Stunden erbaut wurde" (Bertolt Brecht: *Dekoration*. BFA 21. Pp. 283–284).

the staging of the bourgeois world which overlap with the staging of the play and turn the apparatus of theatre into a theme in its own right.

In addition to the furniture collapsing, the guests talk at length about individual pieces of furniture[15] and, encouraged by the bride, they go off to offstage rooms to view the rest of the set, i.e. the other furniture the groom has made. There is repeated discussion of the lamp, a reference to theatrical lighting.[16] The play references its own props by having the characters continually offer, or ask to be passed the objects on the dinner table, i.e. the cream, the fish, etc., and knives and forks are also frequently referred to. In addition, a vase is accidentally smashed as The Man takes a swipe at his wife. Costume is thematized in The Woman's insinuation that the bride's dress has been made well enough to conceal her pregnancy, but also when the groom spills wine onto his shirt and is scolded by his mother, when The Friend makes a fuss about getting a splinter in his best trousers, and when the groom changes into such an unattractive house-jacket that his bride feels compelled to tell him how ugly he looks in it.

The guests repeatedly ask for some kind of entertainment (as does Mackie Messer in *Die Dreigroschenoper*), and this could also be read as a reference to theatre. They dance while The Friend plays the guitar, and The Woman goads her husband into playing the guitar and singing a song. Interestingly, the song does not come to fruition because The Man has forgotten the words – in other words, his lines – and this (as well as the exposing of the Young Man's speech as "auswendig gelernt". BFA 1. P. 249) may also be intended as a nod towards the role of script. One piece of entertainment is the offensive song about prostitution performed by The Friend, "Die Keuschheitsballade in Dur". Hans-Peter Bayerdörfer has argued that this song stands apart from the dramatic plot, remaining void of any realistic motivation, and therefore has the cabaretistic quality of the "Choral" in *Baal*.[17] In this play, then, the Greek tragedy's Chorus has become a dirty, comedic song that holds a mirror up to the hypocrisy of sexual morality in bourgeois relations. It is a set-piece parody, and as such, a demonstrative device that has been taken from the tradition of comic theatre. It is a moment of *Verfremdung*, when the action is interrupted and the audience hears a narration relating to and commenting in some way on the action from a different angle.

---

[15] "DIE FRAU: Von außen ist der Schrank ja nun wirklich nicht so überwältigend, diese Einlagen hat man jetzt doch gar nimmer, jetzt hat man Glas mit bunten Vorhängen" (BFA 1. P. 251).
[16] "Die rote Laterne brennt.
DIE FRAU: Ist die Lampe eigentlich nicht fertig geworden?
DER FREUND: Das ist das richtige Licht für einen Kabeljau" (BFA 1. P. 244).
[17] Hans-Peter Bayerdörfer: Die Einakter – Gehversuche auf schwankhaftem Boden. In: *Brechts Dramen. Neue Interpretationen*. Ed. by Walter Hinderer. Stuttgart: Reclam 1984. Pp. 245–265. Here p. 252.

Equally, when The Young Man asks The Man if he has seen the play *Baal*, this is a self-consciously theatrical moment, when the play seems to remind the audience that this is not a real wedding feast but a play with an author. The reference to *Baal* plays on the two theatrical levels. The Young Man self-consciously and theatrically raises the topic of a very specific piece of theatre that deconstructs middle-class pretence. Brecht's wink to the audience here is the irony of the intertextual promotion of one of his plays within another, an indulgence in cultural reference that is potentially as smug and self-promotional as that of a "Kleinbürger" at a social gathering. Here there are layers of theatre on theatre.

When The Father admits that he has used anecdotes to distract people from silence, he effectively admits that he has used a theatrical device to mask an unbearable reality. Because this is a play about the theatricalities of bourgeois life and language, the performing of the play takes on thematic relevance. Its language should be indulged, performed in its empty verbiage rather than confined to the page, and this *performance* of language anticipates the self-conscious language-in-quotation-marks of Brecht's later epic theatre. As part of Brecht's self-conscious theatre of social comment, the play exposes how language conspires to produce a seemingly intact and coherent reality that actually comes unstuck if we stop suspending our disbelief in it. The serious narrative of authenticity that the characters struggle to hold together throughout the play is gradually broken down into its component parts by humour and ridicule. The rhythmic non-drama of this social chattering is best heard as words bouncing, dispassionate and directionless, back and forth between the characters. The staging reinforces the dialogue's tendency to restlessly shift focus, for the different voices perpetually come from different ends of the table. The overall impression is of fragments struggling but failing to unite into a whole. Continuous, uncommitted, uninterested dialogue is best spoken and heard for the sake of its theatrical noise, showing up its own failure to seal up the cracks. Brecht wants us to hear the theatre here.

The sentimental wedding speech by The Young Man is a set-piece that emphasizes the dearth of engagement at the heart of this human interaction. It is the vehicle through which the over-sophisticated, ceremonious language indulged in at weddings is ridiculed, i.e. shown to be comically unrelated to the reality of marriage, which Brecht depicts again and again in his plays as a contract for exploitation of one sort or another. The Young Man's use of an extended participial phrase is unnatural in speech and therefore heavily stylized: "Wenn zwei junge Menschen in die Ehe treten, die reine Braut, und der in den Stürmen des Lebens gereifte Mann, dann singen, heißt es, die Engel im Himmel!" (BFA 1. P. 248). It is language recited, and it should *sound* recited, faked, stolen, "auswendig gelernt". It should be performed with exaggeration, made to sound like noise rather than anything that has anything real to say, for as such it operates as a *Verfremdungseffekt*, i.e. it breaks the identification with the character and denaturalizes and defamiliarizes the words.

The comic mode is suited to the play's critical purpose because the ridicule to which the wedding party is subjected is a form of distancing that enables an analytical frame. In Brechtian comedy, amusement and instruction always go together, for the drama is a productive tool in the criticism of the existing order. With reference to *Herr Puntila und sein Knecht Matti*, for example, "Theaterarbeit" is said to deal with "Das Gesellschaftlich-Komische", with the actors described as drawing "die Komik aus der heutigen Klassensituation", i.e. class division.[18] As critics have noted, Marx wrote in *Zur Kritik der Hegelschen Rechtsphilosophie* that the comic treatment of the bourgeoisie is the last stage in its critical undoing, for the progression to the comical signals that the subject has already been undermined by serious analysis.[19] In line with this, the characters in *Die Kleinbürgerhochzeit* are laughed off the stage.

The play's comedic moments may also be moments when the audience becomes aware of the play as an artificial construct. The audience's laughter cuts through the characters' pretensions and their empty rituals,[20] perceiving the deterioration of the sincere, bourgeois family idyll into pure comedy.[21] Giese argues that the audience is not allowed to regret the passing of such precious values, nor even to be outraged by the advent of a more alienated and sexualized individualism, because this fall from a delusional and theatrical state of grace is just too funny.[22] It is the comedy that exposes the pretence and the pretensions, and although this is not one of Brecht's "epic" plays, the Epic Theatre is certainly germinating within it. The play repeatedly asks to be seen as comic send-up and play, e.g. in its reference to comic theatre in the performance of the "Keuschheitsballade". At times I felt that because the audience's laughter was a vocal sound, it was also becoming part of the script, and is perhaps meant to be re-heard by the audience itself, listening to and becoming aware of itself in the theatre and its participation in the theatrical event. On hearing its own laughter the audience hears itself consenting to be played to and entertained. In its laughter it may well hear the double-sided relationship between theatre and reality. Its laughter says both "this is real", for it is a real, individual response to a set of events, and "this is not real", for it also hears itself as a collective laughter engendered artificially in a theatrical space and encouraging the play to go on producing its image and producing laughter. The production of

---

[18] *Theaterarbeit. 6 Aufführungen des Berliner Ensembles.* Ed. by Berliner Ensemble and Helene Weigel. Berlin n.d. P. 42.

[19] Peter Giese: *Das Gesellschaftlich-Komische. Zu Komik und Komödie am Beispiel der Stücke und Bearbeitungen Brechts.* Stuttgart: Metzler 1974. P. 16. White: *Bertolt Brecht's Great Plays* (n. 13). P. 33.

[20] Giese: *Das Gesellschaftlich-Komische* (n. 19). P. 29.

[21] Ibid. p. 30. Hill-Gibbins's production played up the farcical elements of the play, which kept the audience in a state of constant laughter.

[22] Giese: *Das Gesellschaftlich-Komische* (n. 19). P. 37.

laughter becomes part of how the play breaks the mould of a bourgeois theatre that believes in its own illusion.

Brechtian Theatre in Practice

The principal aim of this article has been to examine the central theme of the *Die Kleinbürgerhochzeit* – the polite bourgeois façade – and to argue that in the play Brecht employs self-consciously theatrical techniques to underscore the bourgeoisie as a world of pretence and performance. These aspects of the play become especially clear when it is actually experienced in the theatre. For example, the constrained, claustrophobic quality of the petit bourgeois world was conveyed by Tiedemann's production at the Berliner Ensemble by occupying only a corner of the stage with the set and placing the table in a cramped box. In Hill-Gibbins's production the action was played on a scaffold that looked like an enlarged doll's house, with the audience looking in on two cramped rooms. In both our productions the performance space was extremely small, and we crammed into it as much furniture as we could.

The play offers a comment on bourgeois and theatrical illusion both on the page and in production, and in so doing it foreshadows Brecht's later epic theatre both in its theatrics and its productional aspects. Accordingly, the impulse behind Tiedemann's production from 2000 seemed to be that of a theatrical heightening, self-consciously staging, and thereby exposing, the theatricalities that prevail unconsciously and uncritically in bourgeois life. In conversation I have heard the play criticized for its simple, slapstick humour, and Tiedemann's production certainly had the budget and the stage resources to indulge in some serious undermining of set and character. The characters were almost set up as skittles to be knocked down. They sat stiff and painted, unnaturally facing the audience instead of each other, along one side of a long table, which was suspended by wires in a cramped box defining a stage within a stage. Their heavily made-up faces and exaggeratedly styled hair heightened them into illusions and caricatures, and the stage presented a theatrical façade that suggested from the beginning an imminent structural accident. The scene was set for a slapstick show of the most merciless proportions. Not content with realistic breakages and collapsings, this production saw the whole inner stage collapse and sink diagonally like a ship below the main stage, taking the table and its guests with it, as the music played them out. The overly indulgent staging of calamities fitted well with the play's comedic and theatrical intentions. It was part of the director's defamiliarization of the scene and its characters.

In our productions the final image was that of a domestic wasteland left behind the couple who have charged into the offstage bedroom. We used an exaggerated sound effect to emphasize the ripping of the dress as an act of sexual frenzy, and a collapsing bed sound effect accompanied by a light and sound effect of a lamp blowing a fuse. Our intention was to show that by the end of the play, sexual appetite has outgrown the theatre of decorum, moral decency and self-sacrifice for the family, and has asserted itself as the only remaining possible satisfaction. We used loud, cartoonish sound effects, for they drew attention to the staged, unreal quality of the theatrical illusion and constituted a *Verfremdungseffekt*.

The bourgeois norm of illusion or "keeping up appearances", the play's central theme, seemed to apply directly to the practical aspects of the play's rehearsal in both the productions with which I was involved. By the end of the performance run our nerves were as shot as those of the characters in our play, and just as the characters had to keep up the illusion of respect and politeness (with varying degrees of success!), each of us had experienced the pressure of projecting the theatrical edifice. More than has been the case in any other play I have directed, we had to keep together, trust and elicit trust, force belief in the production out of ourselves. In essence, we had to artificially impose cooperation and patience on ourselves in order to produce the perfected art piece. The Brechtian dynamic between actor and character, illusion and reality is underpinned in this play not just by a theatrical gesturing towards it (e.g. in the intertext with Brecht's *Baal*, or in the *Verfremdungseffekt* of the song) but also in the experience of its process of production, in which the status of the play as an artificial thing, glued together, kept up by will and imagination only, is felt again and again.

The social context of post-war collapse and the bourgeois determination to continue as before was reflected in our production in this sense of having to keep the play's illusion going under difficult conditions. The anxiety around upholding the illusion of the solid family home and unit passed into the production itself, for we were perpetually afraid our home-made set might collapse at the wrong moment or *not* collapse at the right moment. The claustrophobic aspect of the petit bourgeois world, its awkward manoeuvrings within its own theatre, was conveyed onstage but was also understood by the production team from the point of view of the production of theatre – aware as we were of the loosely screwed table legs and the lightly bound chair backs, every move we made had to be careful and controlled in order to preserve the furniture piece until its scripted destruction. Right behind an actor at the table was a structurally unsafe cupboard; by the feet of The Father was a *chaise longue* with its back precariously balanced on a pole; and the table with all its crockery and glassware had to be hastily moved around the stage at one point whilst still held together only by loose catches. The uncomfortable feeling prevailed that we could never move our limbs as quickly or extend them as far as would seem natural. The restraint and self-awareness, the self-conscious theatre of the "Kleinbürgerwelt" – world had physically entered our production.

The wedding guests' struggle to keep the conversation going was mirrored in the effort on our part as a theatrical company to sustain the immaculate theatrical image in the dialogue. We had to keep a very difficult script, consisting of a nine-way dialogue of mainly one-liners, going. The script contains the occasional monologue, but on the whole the dialogue jumps around between characters. Because each line takes its cue from the previous line, one slip-up and we would find ourselves jumping or jumbling lines, losing our place and destroying the coherence. This perilous script proved quite exhausting for us. It was imperative to simply keep the momentum. A slight change in text or rhythm or a hesitation could potentially destabilize the very tight dialogue. In general, our productions had the air of precarious Kleistian structures throughout, imbued with our anxiety that we could not hold them together. We were striving to uphold the text and the illusion in the same way Brecht's "Kleinbürger" were desperately perpetuating their own fictions.

Just as the façade of the "Kleinbürger" is in constant danger of succumbing to laughter, so we had one odd moment in one performance when laughter seemed to run off with the show altogether. We were supposed to be performing an "epic freeze". We were trying to demonstrate how the characters had mentally switched off whilst The Father was telling them one of his lengthier anecdotes. He kept talking whilst the other actors froze in their positions with bored expressions on their faces. But the actors got the giggles, breaking the freeze and therefore this "epic" moment. I am not entirely sure how many layers of illusion came laughing down at that point, but I have the feeling that Brecht would not really have minded.

Furthermore, the nature of the script made it impossible to rehearse the play in individual scenes with individual actors or different groups of actors. This meant that the whole cast had to attend every rehearsal, and of course if one actor's lines were weaker, there had to be extra rehearsals with the whole cast to allow that actor to practice more. The nausea, boredom, and resentment behind the play's dialogue translated into a general rehearsal-malaise among the actors. They were over-rehearsed, tired, and a little sick of the sight of one another at times – rather like Brecht's "Kleinbürger" themselves.

The tensions described above led to outbursts from actors in both productions that seemed to replicate the patterns of repression and eruption in the language of the play. They threatened to abandon the production because the set was diabolical, the dialogue still uncoordinated, and certain other actors could not be relied upon to have learned their lines. As tempers flared, I as the director maintained a veneer of politeness and calm through the gritted teeth of the "Kleinbürgerin". Suddenly I was the petit bourgeois bridegroom in the play itself, trying to hold his house together, play down underlying resentment and conflict, and encourage his guests to enjoy themselves: "So. Jetzt seid aber mal lustig! Ich habe nicht alle Tage Hochzeit. Trinkt und sitzt nicht so steif da" (BFA 1. P. 258).

Conclusion

I have tried to show how the pronounced disunity of appearance and reality in these productions seems pertinent to the play itself. Of course, Brecht did not deliberately write the productional difficulties described above into the play, and such problems can occur in the preparation of any dramatic piece (indeed, the correlation between the play and my two productions of the play might simply be down to my own weaknesses as a director!). But in this case these problems formed theoretical and practical parallels with the subject matter, thus giving further insight into Brecht's theory of theatre in practice.

1926 saw the emergence of Brecht's *Lehrstücke* after his conversion to Marxism-Leninism. These plays combined a political, moral and aesthetic education for their actors, conceived as training for the real world and the role of socialism in it:

> Das Lehrstück lehrt dadurch, daß es gespielt, nicht dadurch, daß es gesehen wird. Prinzipiell ist für das Lehrstück kein Zuschauer nötig, jedoch kann er natürlich verwertet werden. Es liegt dem Lehrstück die Erwartung zugrunde, daß der Spielende durch die Durchführung bestimmter Handlungsweisen, Einnahme bestimmter Handlungen, Wiedergabe bestimmter Reden usw. gesellschaftlich beeinflußt werden kann.[23]

Brecht's conversion to Marxism and the introduction of the *Lehrstück* did not in any way mark a caesura in his work. There are many thematic and stylistic continuities between the *Lehrstücke* and those plays that were written before and after. In the case of our play, the actors were learning not only from the experience of embodying certain socially relevant actions and language, but also from the claims of the production in practice. Not only were actors learning to read the content of the play and its theatrical presentation critically, via that curious dialectic of didacticism and amusement, but another *Lehrstück* was playing from the productional point of view. As the production team, we attained a new level of theatrical and social awareness: that we were trying to make a piece of art stick together in spite of the fact "daß der Leim schlecht war" (BFA 1. P. 265).

---

[23] Bertolt Brecht: *Zur Theorie des Lehrstücks*. BFA 22.1. Pp. 351–352. Here p. 351.

Michael Patterson

Brecht's Debt to Theatrical Expressionism

It would appear at first sight that much of Brecht's theatrical practice stands in direct opposition to theatrical Expressionism, his sober, ironic view of life seeming totally opposed to the emotionalism of the Expressionists.

But in fact, Brecht owed a considerable debt to the Expressionists. This article discusses their engagement in a debate about contemporary events, the so-called Stationendrama structure, the interest in representative types rather than psychologically nuanced individuals, the introduction of "telegraphese" and the Expressionists' exploitation of the resources of the theatre in this context. It furthermore contends that although Expressionist theatre tended to cast collectives in a negative light (the opposite of Marxist thought), Brecht too tended to have at best an ambiguous response to collective action.

Der Expressionismus der Nachkriegsepoche hatte die Welt als Wille und Vorstellung dargestellt und einen eigentümlichen Solipsismus gebracht. [...] Er war eine Revolte der Kunst gegen das Leben, und die Welt existierte bei ihm nur als Vision, seltsam zerstört, eine Ausgeburt geängsteter Gemüter. Der Expressionismus [...] zeigte sich ganz außerstande, die Welt als Objekt menschlicher Praxis zu erklären.[1]

So wrote Brecht in his essay *Über experimentelles Theater* of 1939, and at first sight it would seem that Brecht was diametrically opposed to Expressionist thought. His sober, ironic view of life contrasts strongly with the emotionalism of the Expressionists. The Expressionists' inward-turning neo-Romantic view of the artist is poles apart from Brecht's self-deprecating view of himself not as a creative genius but simply as a "Stückeschreiber". He created the amoral and wonderfully gross figure of Baal to some extent as a riposte to Hanns Johst's sentimental depiction of Grabbe as an idealized suffering artist in *Der Einsame*. His review of Ernst Toller's *Die Wandlung*, when Brecht was writing as a theatre critic in Augsburg, was similarly dismissive: "Gedichtete Zeitung, bestenfalls. Flache Visionen, sofort zu vergessen. Kosmos dünn. Der Mensch als Objekt, Proklamation statt: als Mensch. Der abstrahierte Mensch, der Singular von Menschheit".[2]

Indeed Brecht's *Trommeln in der Nacht* can be usefully compared with *Die Wandlung*. (Brecht's play cannot have been influenced by Toller's, since Brecht had completed *Spartakus*, his first version of *Trommeln in der Nacht*, by the end of February 1919, over half a year before the premiere of *Die Wandlung*.) Both protagonists, Friedrich and Andreas Kragler, are "Heimkehrer" figures

---

[1] Bertolt Brecht: *Über experimentelles Theater*. BFA 22.1. Pp. 540–557. Here p. 546.
[2] Bertolt Brecht: *Dramatisches Papier und anderes*. BFA 21. Pp. 88–89. Here p. 89.

who find themselves involved in a revolution, but while Friedrich's revolution is pure, idealized, and depends on his personal leadership, the Spartacus revolt as portrayed in Brecht's play is confused, real, and develops its own impetus. In *Die Wandlung* the birth of a child will herald the New Man, while in *Trommeln in der Nacht* Kragler goes off to bed with his fiancée, who is pregnant not with the New Man but with a child conceived with someone else.

Brecht jeered at the ecstatic utterances of Expressionism and despised the arrogant individualism of these self-proclaimed prophets of rebirth. It is impossible to imagine Brecht appealing in a law court, as Kaiser famously did: "Tut dem Geiste nicht weh!". And yet in the essay quoted at the start, Brecht conceded that Expressionism "die Ausdrucksmittel des Theaters sehr bereicherte".[3] Significantly, he consistently excluded Kaiser from his attacks on Expressionism, was appreciative of *Von morgens bis mitternachts*, noting its technical modernity: "Kaiser macht eine Filmaufnahme!",[4] and, similarly, after seeing *Himmel, Weg, Erde* wrote: "Die Entwicklung, unaufhaltsam, läuft zum Film hin" (BFA 21. P. 89). While having strong reservations about *Gas*, he nevertheless recognized that the Milliardärsohn, despite his confused ideology, was to be respected for relentlessly trying to change the industrial system: "[…] Schlechtlaufen [ist] besser als Garnichtlaufen […]".[5]

In this paper I shall make some fairly predictable points about Brecht's debt to Expressionism as a model for a new theatre (consideration of form) and conclude with the more contentious assertion that Brecht's ideology is not as opposed to Expressionist thought as Brecht and his Marxist apologists would prefer to believe (consideration of content).

In terms of dramatic construction it is clear that Brecht's dictum "Jede Szene für sich"[6] is derived from the Expressionist "Stationendrama", which in turn, of course, owed a debt to the dramaturgy of the *Sturm und Drang* and to Georg Büchner, whose plays were recently being rediscovered. The well-made play, in which each scene led smoothly into the next, had been replaced by the leaps in the construction of Expressionist plays. Thus, *Von morgens bis mitternachts* begins in a bank, jumps forward to a hotel room, and, by way of a snow-covered field, takes us to the Cashier's modest home, then suddenly changes location from the provinces to a big city, where we visit in turn a sports stadium, a nightclub, and a Salvation Army hall. Almost the only element that links these seven "stations" is the figure of the Cashier. In a similar way Brecht emulates the leaps he recognizes in the natural world, at once laying claim to be a realist and

---

[3] Brecht: *Über experimentelles Theater* (n. 1). P. 546.
[4] Bertolt Brecht: *Tagebuch* 17.6.1921. BFA 26. P. 230.
[5] Bertolt Brecht: *Georg Kaisers "Gas" im Stadttheater*. BFA 21. Pp. 58–59. Here p. 59.
[6] Bertolt Brecht: *Anmerkungen zur Oper "Aufstieg und Fall der Stadt Mahagonny"*. BFA 24. Pp. 74–86. Here p. 79.

also implying in a way that was definitely not part of the Expressionist agenda that in each gap between these leaps there is the possibility of change. Set against the so-called "dramatic form of theatre", which emphasizes the necessity of the outcome ("evolutionäre Zwangsläufigkeit"[7]), Brecht sets his new "epic form", whose "montage" urges the audience to reflect on whether the outcome is indeed necessary or could be steered in a new direction.

With regard to the creation of character, Brecht again followed the Expressionists in their abandonment of psychology in favour of creating generalized representatives of humanity. As Paul Kornfeld argued: "Die Psychologie sagt vom Wesen des Menschen ebensowenig aus, wie die Anatomie".[8] Kaiser's unnamed Cashier serves as a model for the Carpenter and the Policeman of *Der gute Mensch von Sezuan*. However, it must be conceded that, except in his *Lehrstücke*, Brecht did not create unnamed protagonists, as the Expressionists often did. Indeed, as a materialist, Brecht would have forcefully rejected any notion that, for example, Galileo could stand as a generalized representative of humanity instead of a man conditioned by the particular historical and social situation in which he finds himself.

In terms of dialogue, Brecht's sober diction contrasts with the ecstatic outpourings of much Expressionist drama. However, the terse communication of some Expressionist writers, seen at its most extreme in the single word exchanges of August Stramm's plays, characterized as "Telegrammstil", rejected the everyday clutter of Naturalist speech, and so again served as a model for Brecht's own economical dialogue.

Above all, the Expressionists exploited the resources of the theatre to the full, restoring boldness and poetry to the stage. Brecht noted in the mid-1920s, "daß es für das Theater unendlich schwieriger ist, sich radikal umzustellen, als es dies für die Dramatik war. […] Das Theater entwickelt sich viel langsamer, es hinkt mühsam hinterher".[9]

The recognition that the theatre needed revolutionizing in order to do justice to Expressionist works like those of Kaiser, which presented enormous challenges to the stage, served as an essential impetus to Brecht to initiate his own theatre reforms. With regard to acting, Brecht was also attracted to the boldness (if not the emotional indulgence) of Expressionist performance, challenging the actor, as in Kornfeld's words: "Er wage es, groß die Arme auszubreiten und […] so zu sprechen, wie er niemals im Leben täte".[10] The Expressionists rejected

---

[7] Ibid.
[8] Paul Kornfeld: Kunst, Theater und anderes. In: *Literatur-Revolution 1910–1925*. Ed. by Paul Pörtner. Darmstadt: Luchterhand 1960. Vol. 1. Pp. 364–368. Here p. 365.
[9] Bertolt Brecht: *Das neuere Theater und die neuere Dramatik*. BFA 21.1. Pp. 276–277.
[10] Paul Kornfeld: Nachwort an den Schauspieler. In: Pörtner (ed.): *Literatur-Revolution* (n. 9). Vol. 1. Pp. 350–352. Here p. 350.

the "hands-in-the-pocket-style" of Naturalistic acting and re-established the theatricality of theatre. The fast-paced and colourful plays of Brecht, often incorporating songs, owed an obvious debt to the theatrical revolution of the Expressionists.

In terms of content, Brecht's ideology seems apparently positioned at the opposite end of the spectrum from that of the Expressionists. But here we have to be cautious, for it is anyway impossible to assert that the Expressionists shared a consistent ideology. In his *Spiegelmensch* of 1920 Franz Werfel characterized the ideological confusion of the Expressionists:

> Eucharistisch und tomistisch,
> Doch daneben auch marxistisch,
> Theosophisch, kommunistisch,
> Gotisch kleinstadt-dombau-mystisch,
> Aktivistisch, erzbuddhistisch,
> Überöstlich-taoistisch,
> Rettung aus der Zeit-Schlamastik
> Suchend in der Negerplastik,
> Wort- und Barrikaden wälzend,
> Gott und Foxtrott fesch verschmelzend –
> …
> Also lautet spät und früh
> Unser seelisches Menu.[11]

Both the Catholic mystic Sorge and the left-wing activist Toller could be regarded as Expressionists. The lack of a coherent ideology is also reflected in their subsequent political alignments: thus Benn and Johst became Fascists, while Becher and Bronnen joined the Communist Party. What is significant, however, is that, whatever their political stance, nearly all the Expressionist playwrights engaged with social themes. Brecht may have dismissed *Die Wandlung* as "[g]edichtete Zeitung", but at least it *was* newspaper rather than the imagined universe of the plays of the Symbolists and the *Neuromantik*.

What most separates the later Brecht from his Expressionist forebears would appear to be his commitment to a Marxist belief in a collective social revolution contrasted with the Expressionist belief that such change can come about only through the renewal of the individual. Certainly, the collectives represented in Expressionist drama tend to be viewed negatively, anonymous masses easily swayed by self-interest. The cycle-race crowds in *Von morgens bis mitternachts* become frenzied with the mounting prizes provided by the Cashier but fall obediently silent when the monarch arrives. Later in the same play, the Salvation Army congregation immediately abandon their Christian posturing when money is thrown into their midst. The workers of Kaiser's *Gas I* reject the

[11] Franz Werfel: *Spiegelmensch*. München: Kurt Wolff Verlag 1920. P. 130.

Milliardärsohn's ideal vision of rural bliss and demand to return to the drudgery and dangers of factory life. The Worker/Prisoners of *Die Wandlung* can be led to freedom only by following the strong individual, Ferdinand. In Hasenclever's *Die Menschen*, humankind is seen as grotesque gamblers, prurient onlookers in the courtroom, or as inmates of a madhouse. In Toller's *Masse Mensch* the idealism of Sonja, the "Mensch", is set against the unprincipled actions of the masses, and in his *Maschinenstürmer* the mob destroys the idealist leader, Jimmy Cobbett.

These manifestations of humanity in a collective are unflattering but make a colossal impact. Who, having seen a production of Kaiser's *Gas I* would remember clearly the abstract appeals of the Milliardärsohn compared with the powerful presence of the assembled workers? Which scenes from Fritz Lang's *Metropolis* (1926), inspired by Kaiser's play, linger in the mind? Surely, above all, the scenes in the factory, with the workers arriving for their shift or tending their massive machines. Whether in Expressionist theatre or cinema, the collective, however much we are meant to view it negatively, provides the major focus of interest.

Significantly, Brecht's main quarrel with the Expressionists is not that they concentrated too much on the individual, but that their representation of the individual lacked substance. In a note dating from 1920 he observes:

Expressionismus bedeutet: Vergröberung. [...] Heraus- oder Übertreibung des Geistes, des Ideellen, [...] die Freude an der Idee, aber keine Ideen [...]; d.h., statt Leiber mit Geist zu füllen, kaufte man (möglichst bunte) Häute für Geister auf, und statt in den Leibern die (wie man argwöhnte: verkannte) Seelen aufzuzeigen, machte man die Seelen zu Leibern, vergröberte sie, materialisierte sogar noch den Geist.[12]

Here Brecht succeeds in hitting the Expressionists where it hurt them most. If there was one thing that the Expressionists were concerned with, it was refinement, to penetrate to the essence behind the world of coarse surface reality, "was in Fabriken göttlich, was in Huren menschlich ist",[13] as Edschmid had said. Brecht attacked them for doing exactly the reverse. His concern for "Geist" and "Seele" is curious, and it may be that the materialist Brecht was merely scoring points off the Expressionists by using their terminology. However, this note was not intended for publication and may in fact point to a genuine concern with the essence of the individual. He appears to resent the way that the refinement pursued by Expressionist writers in fact often resulted in crude simplification; abstracting the individual took from him all the wonderful complexities that distinguished his individuality and in so doing rendered him an automaton.

---

[12] Bertolt Brecht: *Über den Expressionismus*. BFA 21. Pp. 48–49.
[13] Kasimir Edschmid: *Über den dichterischen Expressionismus*. In: Kasimir Edschmid: *Frühe Manifeste*. Darmstadt: Luchterhand 1960. Pp. 26–43. Here p. 33.

What Brecht was trying to achieve was a representation of the individual that related recognizably to the realities of life (in a way that the Expressionists did not attempt to do) while eschewing the psychological clutter that limited the figures created by the Naturalists. In a revealing note of 10 February 1922, Brecht outlines a prototype of the "V-Effekt" with reference to two of his early plays: "Einen großen Fehler sonstiger Kunst hoffe ich im *Baal* und *Dickicht* vermieden zu haben: ihre Bemühung mitzureißen. Instinktiv lasse ich hier Abstände [...] Die 'splendid isolation' des Zuschauers wird nicht angetastet". Instead of the emotional engagement encouraged by both Naturalist and Expressionist theatre, Brecht hoped to encourage a higher kind of interest: "das am Gleichnis, das am Andern, Unübersehbaren, Verwunderlichen".[14] Once again the use of metaphysical language comes unexpectedly from Brecht's pen. It is evidence, however, that, in the early 1920s at least, Brecht's major complaint about Expressionism was not that it supported the individual against the collective, but rather that their writers did not do justice to the potential richness of the individual protagonist.

It is predictable perhaps that, prior to his conversion to Marxism, Brecht would champion the individual and offer at best ambivalent support for the collective. His early plays, none of which he ever disowned, show collectives in a negative light. The Spartacists in *Trommeln in der Nacht* are shadowy figures and offer no real prospect of a better future. In *Mann ist Mann,* there is no suggestion of a porters' union, some positive collective to which Galy Gay might belong. Instead, there is only the collective of the British army, which transforms Galy Gay into a fighting machine, a transformation that he could resist only by holding on determinedly to his own individuality.

After Brecht embraced Marxism, one might expect that he would regard the collective more positively. However, this is questionable. In *Die heilige Johanna der Schlachthöfe* the Black Straw Hats treacherously compromise their religious beliefs to promote capitalism; on the other hand, the Communists, ill-defined and threatening violence, do not offer a welcome alternative. As Christopher McCullough observes: "Indeed it is the very focus on the individual plight of Joan that almost robs the play of any effective dialectical alternative to the efforts of The Black Straw Hats to alleviate misery".[15]

In *Mutter Courage* we may disapprove of Courage's short-sighted involvement with the war, but she remains the focus of our interest, not the men who are fighting and dying in this war. Similarly, in his thought-provoking book, *Vladimir's Carrot*, the critic John Peter points to the weak depiction of society

[14] Brecht: *Tagebuch* 10.2.1922. BFA 26. P. 271.
[15] Christopher McCullough: Saint Joan of the Stockyards. In: *The Cambridge Companion to Brecht*. Ed. by Peter Thomson and Glendyr Sacks. Cambridge: Cambridge University Press 1994. Pp. 69–103. Here p. 102.

in *Der gute Mensch von Sezuan*. Complaining of the *faux-naïveté* of Brecht's settings, John Peter asserts that

> *The Good Person of Setzuan* is weakened by its lack of a sense of community. […] Setzuan never comes across as a village where life has its ways and people have their habits and social functions. The population is no more than a backdrop, and this fatally weakens the play's argument which is about the survival or otherwise of personal integrity in a community founded on greed.[16]

In *Der kaukasische Kreidekreis* Grusche stands out as an individual resisting the herd mentality of her fellow servants, saving little Michael at great cost to herself. Even more obviously, Azdak is a unique figure, resisting common notions of the law with his own irrepressible sense of justice. A similar maverick, who engages our sympathies, is Galileo, the great individual who opposes the collective authority of the Catholic Church.

Again and again, Brecht draws our sympathies towards the individual, and one recalls how his unease at mass demonstrations led to his unwillingness to become involved with the revolt in the GDR of 17 June 1951, fictionalized in Günter Grass's play, *Die Plebejer proben den Aufstand*. Indeed, it is only in a *Lehrstück* like *Die Maßnahme* that the collective, in this case the Communist Party, is valued more highly and is given as much prominence through the Control Chorus as the individual. However, I for one find it hard to believe that *Die Maßnahme* should be taken entirely at its face value; it may be that Brecht is here deliberately setting up a dialectic between the harsh but necessary means of the Party and our own outraged sense of humanity.

Whatever our view of *Die Maßnahme*, I would argue that Brecht's debt to Expressionism was not only to the theatrical elements, that of structure, characterization and dialogue. His major interest as a playwright remained, as did that of the Expressionists, with the relation of the individual to the world about him or her.

In asserting this, I am not attempting to revive the silliness of Martin Esslin in his book *Brecht: a Choice of Evils*, where in Maro Germanou's words, Esslin argued that "Brecht's plays are good, despite Brecht, his theory and his politics".[17] Clearly there is a vast difference between the treatment of the individual by the Expressionists and by Brecht, but it would be a mistake to deny that here too Brecht owes a significant debt to his theatrical forebears.

[16] John Peter: *Vladimir's Carrot*. London: André Deutsch 1987. P. 308.
[17] Maro Germanou: Brecht and the English Theatre. In: *Brecht in Perspective*. Ed. by Graham Bartram and Anthony Waine. London: Longman 1982. Pp. 208–224. Here p. 213.

Frank Krause

Von Kaiser zu Brecht: Drama und Prosa

Georg Kaiser's Expressionist plays are often said to anticipate Bertolt Brecht's Epic Theatre; but as Kaiser's influence is not manifest in inter-textual connections, the actual importance of his drama for Brecht is difficult to ascertain. A reassessment of Brecht's literary-critical comments on Kaiser and an analysis of Brecht's much-neglected appropriation in short prose of Kaiser's play Gas *will shed new light on this problem. Brecht's exploration of the degree to which Kaiser's forms and themes are suited to the concerns of Epic Theatre leads to conflicting results: whilst Kaiser's concerns and techniques often run counter to the principles of Brecht's drama, they can occasionally be integrated into a kind of short prose which anticipates or entails salient features of non-Aristotelian literature. Brecht's critical exploration of the usability of Kaiser's plays thus contributes to his understanding of the challenge posed by the quest for an Epic Theatre: the need for a synthesis between drama and the techniques of advanced prose.*

Im Jahre 1928 hatte Bertolt Brecht in einem Rundfunkgespräch und in einer Notiz das expressionistische Drama Georg Kaisers als Vorläufer des epischen Theaters gewürdigt. Die gewiß veränderungsbedürftige Technik dieses Dramas erziele, indem sie sich an die Ratio wende, bereits vorbildliche Wirkungen.[1] Welchen Beitrag die Dramen Kaisers zur Entstehung des epischen Theaters ab etwa 1926 leisten, wird in der Forschung indessen kontrovers diskutiert.

Brechts literaturkritische Anmerkungen zu Kaiser, die vorwiegend aus den frühen 1920er Jahren stammen, geben – wie sich zeigen wird – auf diese Frage keine eindeutige Antwort. Für Brecht sind Kaisers Techniken positiv, sofern sie Einsichten in unanschauliche soziale Zusammenhänge vermitteln; die konkreten Ausprägungen dieser Techniken kritisiert er aber derart umfassend, daß er ihre adressierten Effekte nicht zur Nachahmung empfehlen kann. Dennoch bewertet Brecht, indem er Kaisers Dramen teils gegen den Strich liest, auch deren Wirkung selbst als vorbildlich; Brechts Zeitgenossen hingegen bezweifeln zum Teil, daß Kaisers Drama für das epische Theater von formprägender Bedeutung ist.[2]

---

[1] Bertolt Brecht: *[Neue Dramatik]*. BFA 21. S. 270–275. Hier S. 274: Bertolt Brecht: *[Theater als geistige Angelegenheit]*. BFA 21. S. 252–253. Vgl. auch Bertolt Brecht: *[Dem fünfzigjährigen Georg Kaiser]*. BFA 21. S. 252.

[2] So fragt Herbert Ihering im Kölner Rundfunkgespräch (*[Neue Dramatik]*. BFA 21. S. 274): "Das verstehe ich aber nicht ganz. Gerade Georg Kaiser scheint mir die letzte Entwicklung des individualistischen Dramas zu bedeuten, also eines Dramas, das im äußersten Gegensatz zum epischen Theater steht. [...] Er hat seine Themen durch Stil aufgebraucht, die Wirklichkeit durch Stil überholt. Was ist verwertbar von diesem Stil?

Die Forschung der 1970er Jahre hat die Frage nach Brechts Nähe zu Kaiser wieder aufgegriffen; Ernst Schürer, Klaus Kändler und James M. Ritchie haben Ähnlichkeiten von Stoffen bzw. Techniken und Traditionsbrüchen bei Kaiser und Brecht herausgearbeitet,[3] und sie haben damit die – seither verbreitete – These gestützt, Brechts Bezüge auf Kaiser markierten eine wichtige Wirkungslinie im Prozeß der literarischen Moderne;[4] diesen Studien zufolge scheint vor allem Brechts Einsatz episierender Techniken in sozialkritischer Absicht in erheblichem Ausmaß durch Kaisers expressionistische Dramen inspiriert zu sein.[5] Seit Mitte der 1990er Jahre betont die Forschung hingegen, jene Ähnlichkeiten seien nicht spezifisch genug, um interauktoriale Bezüge zwischen Kaiser und Brecht belegen zu können;[6] der Nachweis solcher Bezüge muß, so die jüngste These zum Thema von Marcus Sander, vielmehr schon im Ansatz

Kaisers Stil ist eine persönliche Handschrift, ist ein privater Stil". Iherings Position bis in die Wortwahl hinein zurückweisend, betont Brecht: "Gefragt [...], ob ich die Dramatik Georg Kaisers für entscheidend wichtig, die Situation des europäischen Theaters für durch ihn verändert halte, habe ich mit Ja zu antworten. *Ohne die Kenntnis seiner Neuerungen ist die Bemühung um ein Drama fruchtlos, sein 'Stil' ist keineswegs nur 'Handschrift' [...], und vor allem muß seine durchaus kühne Grundthese, der Idealismus, unbedingt diskutiert und die Diskussion darüber zur Entscheidung geführt werden"* (Bertolt Brecht: *[Dem fünfzigjährigen Georg Kaiser]*. BFA 21. S. 252).
[3] Ernst Schürer: *Georg Kaiser und Bertolt Brecht. Über Leben und Werk.* Frankfurt am Main: Athenäum 1971: Klaus Kändler: "Die Sinnlichkeit des Gedankens". Zur Dramaturgie Georg Kaisers. In: *Weimarer Beiträge* 24 (1978). H. 9. S. 5–23: James M. Ritchie: Georg Kaiser und das Drama des Expressionismus. In: *Handbuch des deutschen Dramas.* Hg. von Walter Hinck. Düsseldorf: Bagel 1980. S. 386–400.
[4] So urteilt Silvio Vietta: "Wie auch immer modifiziert sie verlief, die Sozialkritik des frühen Eugene O'Neill und Bert Brechts wären ohne Georg Kaiser nicht denkbar". Silvio Vietta und Hans-Georg Kemper: *Expressionismus* [1975]. München: UTB Fink 1997. S. 85. Vgl. auch *Bertolt Brecht. Epoche – Werk – Wirkung.* Hg. von Klaus-Detlef Müller. München: Beck 1985. S. 131: Helmuth Kiesel: *Geschichte der literarischen Moderne.* München: Beck 2004. S. 373: Peter Sprengel: *Geschichte der deutschsprachigen Literatur 1900–1918.* München: Beck 2004. S. 546.
[5] Zu Recht betont Marcus Sander mit einem Zitat von Schürer, daß Brecht die Verfahren seines Anregers erheblich modifiziere: "Von Anfang an ist Brechts Beziehung zum Expressionismus dialektisch. Er wird von ihm tief beeinflußt, aber nicht zur Nachahmung, sondern zur Gegnerschaft, zum Bessermachen herausgefordert. Im Widerspruch gegen die Expressionisten findet er sich selber, als Dramendichter, als Dramenkritiker und als Dramaturg". Zitiert in: Marcus Sander: *Strukturwandel in den Dramen Georg Kaisers 1910–1945.* Frankfurt am Main: Lang 2004. S. 74. Vgl. Ernst Schürer: *Georg Kaiser.* New York: Twayne 1971. S. 211–212.
[6] "The claim that Kaiser is a precursor of epic theater has not yet been sufficiently substantiated. Ritchie's and Kändler's general discussions and Schürer's identification of thematic parallels between Kaiser and Brecht need to be followed by thorough analysis of epic features in Kaiser's dramas. Citation of Kaiser's theoretical statements or even of Brecht's identification of Kaiser as a forerunner are not enough to make the case" (Audrone B. Willeke: *Georg Kaiser and the Critics. A Profile of Expressionism's Leading*

scheitern, denn Brecht kritisiert Kaisers Formensprache so umfassend, daß mit intertextuellen Bezügen ihrer literarischen Werke kaum zu rechnen ist. Kaiser habe Brecht Anstöße gegeben, spiele bei der Entstehung des epischen Theaters aber keine traditionsstiftende Rolle; einen erkennbaren Einfluß nehme Kaiser in erster Linie auf Brechts theoretische Selbstverständigung.[7]

Sander problematisiert einschlägige Einschätzungen des literarhistorischen Gewichts von Kaiser für Brecht, läßt aber die Signatur von Kaisers Wirkung auf Brechts literaturkritische Selbstverständigung unterbestimmt und faßt deren Bedeutung für das epische Theater erst gar nicht genauer ins Auge – und zwar aus gutem Grund, denn seine Studie streift Kaisers Wirkung auf Brecht nur am Rande. Im folgenden sei diese – bislang vernachlässigte Signatur in drei Schritten genauer herausgearbeitet; in literaturkritischen Anmerkungen (1.), die zum ersten Mal bei Sander umfassend ausgewertet wurden, sowie in einer literarischen Aneignung (2.), die in der Forschung selten berücksichtigt wird,[8] lotet Brecht das Potential von Kaisers Drama aus divergenten Blickwinkeln aus; seine Ergebnisse tragen, wie abschließend zu zeigen ist, zur Bestimmung der Problematik bei, die Brecht mit seinem epischen Drama löst (3.).

1. Brechts Anmerkungen über Kaiser

Brechts Anmerkungen über Kaiser entwerfen keine kohärente Theorie, sondern harren in einer ambivalenten, zwischen Respekt und Polemik schwankenden Perspektive aus und folgen der Suche nach praktisch verwertbaren Ansätzen; der oft affektiv geladene Ton der kritischen Bemerkungen von Brecht belegt, daß diese Suchbewegungen durchaus von Gewicht sind.[9] Diese Bewegungen gehen in drei verschiedene Richtungen.

Erstens: Brecht würdigt Kaisers Dramen, weil sie das Publikum zur reflektierenden Distanz gegenüber den handelnden Figuren anleiten, und er hebt dabei

---

Playwright. Columbia (SC): Camden House 1995. S. 112–113). "Das Weltverständnis beider Autoren war so gegensätzlich, daß etwa Schürers Untersuchung *Georg Kaiser und Bertolt Brecht* (1971), die primär darauf abzielt, Analogien zwischen beiden Autorenoeuvres darzustellen, zwangsläufig an Grenzen stoßen muß. Schürer hat die traditionsbildende Funktion von Kaisers Dramaturgie des Zeitraumes 1910–1920 für das epische Theater nachdrücklich unterstrichen. Sein Ansatz überzeugt allerdings deshalb nicht vollends, weil sich intertextuelle Bezüge, die über lose thematische Entsprechungen hinausgehen, an den Autorenoeuvres nicht nachweisen lassen". Sander: *Strukturwandel* (Anm. 5). S. 69–70.

[7] Sander: *Strukturwandel* (Anm. 5). S. 69–70 u. S. 74.

[8] Eine Ausnahme stellt Viettas Besprechung dar (Silvio Vietta: *Die literarische Moderne. Eine problemgeschichtliche Darstellung der deutschsprachigen Literatur von Hölderlin bis Thomas Bernhard*. Stuttgart: Metzler 1992. S. 260–261).

[9] Siehe Fußnote 13. Vgl. auch die folgende Bemerkung: "Ihr könnt mich steinigen, aber ich sage doch nicht, daß Georg Kaiser das Unterhaltungsdrama, das ihm vorschwebt,

vor allem *Gas* und *Der gerettete Alkibiades* als positive Beispiele hervor.[10] Diese Stücke stellen Figuren dar, deren widersprüchliches Handeln sich aus der Perspektive ihres Selbstverständnisses nicht zureichend verstehen läßt und durch ein in der empirischen Realität unanschauliches Gesetz bedingt wird. Brecht erblickt die zentrale Leistung Kaisers also in Verfremdungen, die der Erkenntnis einer durch unanschauliche Gründe determinierten Praxis dienen. Indem solche Verfremdungen abstraktes Wissen vermitteln, appellieren sie an den Verstand oder – mit Brechts Worten – an die Ratio (BFA 21. S. 274).

Zweitens: Den allegorischen Ansatz dieser Verfremdungen lehnt Brecht ab. Kaisers verfremdete Figuren personifizieren abstrakte Zusammenhänge, indem sie die unanschaulichen Kräfte, die ihr eigenes Handeln bestimmen, sinnfällig verkörpern. Das Gesetz, unter dem ihr Handeln steht, ist in ihrem abstrakt verfremdeten Gestus gleichsam inkarniert und stellt die allgemeine Tendenz des besonderen Sinns dar, der jenem Gestus innewohnt. Das epische Theater Brechts hingegen möchte Einsichten in solche Gesetzmäßigkeiten vermitteln, deren Tendenz im inkarnierten Sinn des sinnfälligen Gestus gerade nicht bruchlos aufgeht, und auch der frühe Brecht führt in diesem Sinne aus:

> Es gilt also nicht, große, ideelle Prinzipiendramen zu schaffen, die das Getriebe der Welt und die Gewohnheiten des Schicksals darstellen, sondern einfache Stücke, die die Schicksale von Menschen schildern, Menschen, die die Gewinne der Stücke sein sollen. Beispiel: Daß Burschen von einer gewissen, eigentümlichen Struktur die Schaufel aufs Genick kriegen, ist nicht das, was das Stück zeigen soll. Sondern: Wie sie sich dabei benehmen, was sie dazu sagen und was für ein Gesicht sie dabei machen.[11]

Aus diesem Grund weist Brecht das Ideendrama des Expressionismus als gedichtete Zeitung – oder als einen "durch Dramatisierung verdorbene[n] Essay" – zurück; da dieses Ideendrama seine Einsichten in abstrakte soziale Zusammenhänge – wie übrigens auch seinen Glauben an eine metaphysische Substanz des Menschen – nur sinnenhaft einkleidet, bleiben die Figuren leblose Träger einer allzu konstruiert erscheinenden Tendenz.[12] Das Ideendrama selbst würdigt Brecht zwar als prinzipiell ehrwürdige Gattung – der Versuch, das

gestalten konnte. [...] z. B. G. Kaisers Stücke sind (sehr schlechte) Stücke einer sehr hohen Gattung. Sie entsprechen der (fast uninteressierten) Freude an der reinen Dialektik, an der Eleganz der Kurve und dem Spieltrieb. Leider ist Kaisers dichterische Potenz zu schwach, um den Ideen, an denen er sich sozusagen angeilt, leibhaftige Kinder zu machen" (Bertolt Brecht: *Über das Unterhaltungsdrama*. BFA 21. S. 47–48).

[10] Bertolt Brecht: *Über den Expressionismus*. BFA 21. S. 48–49. Hier S. 48. Brecht: *[Theater als geistige Angelegenheit]*. BFA 21. S. 253.

[11] Bertolt Brecht: *Tagebuch 21.8.1920*. BFA 26. S. 138.

[12] Bertolt Brecht: *Dramatisches Papier und anderes*. BFA 21. S. 88–89. Hier S. 88.

Allgemeine am Besonderen sinnfällig herauszuarbeiten, sei nicht grundsätzlich abzulehnen (BFA 21. S. 47–48). Kaiser versuche sich in dieser Gattung aber auf eine schlechte Weise. Brecht schätzt Kaisers Nähe zum Kino, wenn dessen Drama (wie in *Hölle Weg Erde*) die sichtbare Gestalt des verfremdeten Gestus betont (auch wenn dieses Stück einer für Brecht nicht überzeugenden Ethik dient) (BFA. 21. S. 89); aber wenn Kaiser (wie in *Von morgens bis mitternachts*) Wort und Bild nicht in eine spannungsreiche Beziehung bringt, sondern wie der Stummfilm um den gesteigerten Ausdruck unmittelbar sinnfälliger Bedeutungen bemüht ist, verliert Brecht die Geduld.[13] Brecht lotet das Potential von Kaisers Technik aus, die das Handeln der Figuren zu Zeichen empirisch unanschaulicher Kräfte stilisiert, und er stößt dabei immer wieder auf das Problem, daß in dessen Allegorien das Allgemeine im Besonderen allzu bruchlos aufgeht – und damit der spezifische Charakter jenes Allgemeinen verfehlt wird.

Die lehrreichen Effekte der Stücke Kaisers lassen sich also nur dann in den Horizont von Brechts Theater einholen, wenn ihre ursprünglichen Formen und Stoffe weitgehend aufgelöst werden: Die Figuren, ihre Sprache, ihre Beziehung zur abstrahierten Idee und die durch diese Ideen vermittelte Problemsicht weist Brecht zurück. Damit wird verständlich, warum Brechts Versuche, sich positive Effekte der Dramen Kaisers produktiv anzueignen, in den Formen und Stoffen des epischen Theaters keine eindeutigen Spuren hinterlassen. Kaiser stellt Brecht eine anregende Aufgabe, fordert aber zu Lösungen heraus, zu denen Kaisers Formen und Stoffe nicht fähig sind. So lassen sich zwar manche Parallelen wie etwa zwischen der Stationentechnik bei Kaiser und der Betonung struktureller Diskontinuitäten bei Brecht beobachten;[14] diese

---

[13] Bertolt Brecht: *Tagebuch* 17.6.1921. BFA 26. S. 230. Vgl. Bertolt Brecht: *Über das Rhetorische*. BFA 21. S. 49–50: "G. Kaiser lernt gegenwärtig öffentlich das Reden. Er ist der redselige Wilhelm des deutschen Dramas. Er hat dessen Pathos, dessen Gedankenarmut, dessen Geschmacklosigkeit, dessen Sinn für Prägnanz, dessen Liebe am Theatralischen und dessen Freude daran, das was 'klappt'. […] Er sagt, er hat bei Platon gelernt, daß Reden schön ist. Bei sich könnte er das Gegenteil lernen. (Aber er hat keine Zeit, das Schreiben zu lernen, da er zu sehr mit Stückeschreiben beschäftigt ist)".
[14] Sander zufolge sind für Kaisers Drama *Von morgens bis mitternachts* […] die folgenden episierenden Verfahren kennzeichnend […]: (1) Aufhebung der Finalität: offene Form des Dramas, (2) Aufhebung der Absolutheit: auktoriale Episierung des Nebentextes, z.B. in der Schneefeld-Szene, (3) Verweigerung einer aristotelischen, auf die Erregung von Affekten (phobos und eleos) abzielenden Wirkungspoetik, (4) Spannungserzeugung: Konzeption einer 'Wie-Spannung' im zweiten Teil des Stationendramas, (5) Außersprachliche Episierung (Bloßlegen des theatralischen Apparates am Schluß des Stückes), (6) Rollendistanz; Gestus des Zeigens (in der Figur des Kassierers angelegt), (7) Sentenz-Dramaturgie" (Sander: *Strukturwandel* (Anm. 5). S. 69. Fn. 182).

Parallelen mögen sich aber ebenso – wie neuerdings Helmuth Kiesel betont – auch den Anregungen Döblins oder des Dadaismus verdanken.[15]

Drittens: Brechts Urteil über Kaiser wird dadurch kompliziert, daß er – bei aller grundlegenden Distanz zu den konkreten Mitteln Kaisers – das epische Theater im ästhetisch-idealistischen Denken seines Vorgängers bereits angelegt sieht; dieses Denken gilt ihm nicht, wie zu vermuten wäre, als der obsolete Überbau von verbesserungsbedürftigen Mitteln, sondern als Bedingung einer Technik, die schon bei einer zureichend kritischen Rezeption von Kaisers Stücken kognitiv maßgebende Effekte zeitigt. So notiert Brecht im Jahre 1928:

> Ich weiß: Ein Teil unserer jungen Leute wird Georg Kaisers entscheidende Leistung, seinen Idealismus, erstaunt ablehnen. Sie werden sagen, daß hier eine Generation (Klasse, Schule) jene technischen Mittel ausgebildet habe, welche die ihr folgende für ihre (anderen) Zwecke brauchen wird. Für diese (anderen) Zwecke werde jene Technik noch besser geeignet sein. Tatsächlich wurde das Theater durch Kaiser schon einem neuen Zwecke zugeführt: indem er es zu einer geistigen Angelegenheit machte, Kontrolle ermöglichte, ja sogar benützte und selbst dort, wo er vom Zuschauer noch Erlebnisse verlangt, doch schon bloßes Interesse gestattet (BFA 21. S. 252–253).

Brecht bezieht seine Anregungen von Kaiser also aus der häretischen Lektüre; im Unterschied zur analytischen Kritik der immanenten Konzeption von Kaisers Stücken stößt diese Lektüre auf ästhetisch maßgebende Ansätze. Der Prozeß einer solchen produktiven Aneignung, der über Richtung und Ausmaß der Wirkung von Kaiser auf Brecht Auskunft geben könnte, ist dem Zugriff der Forschung damit weitgehend entzogen – mit einer Ausnahme, die ich im folgenden analysieren möchte.

2. Brechts Anschlüsse an Kaiser

Eine im Jahre 1920 verfaßte kritische Würdigung von Kaisers Drama *Gas* erlaubt es nämlich, Brecht gleichsam bei der Arbeit zuzusehen. Brecht faßt den Inhalt des Stücks hier mithilfe einer kurzen Erzählung zusammen, und zwar in der Form einer Parabel, die sich an Kaisers allegorische Figuren anlehnt, deren Gestus aber grundlegend umgestaltet. Im Anschluß an eine Skizze der Problematik von *Gas* sei Brechts produktive Aneignung von Kaisers Technik genauer analysiert.

In Kaisers Stück bringt eine Explosion die industrielle Erzeugung des Rohstoffs Gas zum Stillstand – ein Stoff, der für die Wirtschaft des Landes zentral und unersetzlich ist. Die Gasexplosion in der Fabrik geht nicht auf falsche Berechnungen oder Fehler bei ihrer technischen Umsetzung zurück, sondern entspringt einem grundlegenden Mißverhältnis zwischen wissenschaftlicher

---

[15] Vgl. Kiesel: *Geschichte* (Anm. 4). S. 373–376 (zum Einfluß Döblins und des Dadaismus auf den Montage-Charakter des epischen Dramas) u. S. 430 (zum nach- bzw. nebenexpressionistischen Charakter des Montageprinzips).

Erkenntnis und der essentiellen, jenseits der objektivierbaren Welt liegenden Ordnung der Dinge. Die Arbeiter der Fabrik, in der sich die Explosion ereignet, sind am Gewinn beteiligt, der – gestaffelt nach Altersgruppen – gleichmäßig unter den Beschäftigten ausgeschüttet wird. Auch der Besitzer des Betriebs ist nur ein einfacher Mann unter vielen; als Eigner von geerbtem Kapital bleibt er freilich Milliardärsohn. Die Gewinnbeteiligung hatte die Arbeiter zur Höchstleistung angestachelt; ihre Lebensform, ganz an den Imperativen der Produktionssteigerung ausgerichtet, verlor so jeden Kontakt mit den Fragen des guten Lebens. Die Unterbrechung der Produktion bringt den Arbeitern diese Entfremdung zu Bewußtsein; zudem suchen sie nach einem Schuldigen für die Explosion im Werk. Erst wenn der Ingenieur entlassen ist, wollen sie die Arbeit wiederaufnehmen. Die Position der Arbeiter ist widersprüchlich, und sie verkennen die Ursache der Explosion. Sie erkennen, daß die Industriearbeit der menschlichen Bedürfnisnatur entfremdet ist, wollen ihre bisherige Lebensform aber letztlich nicht ändern; und daß die industrielle Produktionsweise der metaphysischen Substanz der äußeren Natur entfremdet ist, entgeht ihnen. Der Milliardärsohn glaubt, an einem historischen Wendepunkt zu stehen: der Mensch, der zur zielgerichteten Verausgabung seiner Energien tendiere, habe die sinnstiftende Funktion der Industriearbeit erschöpfend ausgelotet – und stehe nun an der Schwelle zur Versöhnung von innerer und äußerer Natur in der selbstbestimmten Landarbeit.

Die Arbeiter lehnen die Pläne des Milliardärsohns, auf dem Grundstück des zerstörten Gaswerks landwirtschaftliche Siedlungen für sie zu errichten, aber ab. Als der Ingenieur, der für die Wiedererrichtung des Werks plädiert, sich bereit erklärt, um der Gasproduktion willen der Forderung nach seiner Entlassung nachzukommen, akzeptieren die Arbeiter ihn als Führer. Der Milliardärsohn versucht, die Arbeiter an der Rückkehr ins Werk zu hindern; doch da Gas kriegswichtig ist, wird das Werk unter staatliche Kontrolle gestellt und wiederaufgebaut. Die metaphysische Substanz der entfremdeten Arbeiter, die sich für einen kurzen Augenblick erkannt hatten, ist wieder verschüttet; der Milliardärsohn richtet seine Hoffnung auf die kommende Generation. Kaiser arbeitet mit einem apokalyptischen Geschichtsmodell: der innere Antrieb zur Leistungssteigerung muß bis zum unumkehrbaren Zusammenbruch der Ordnung, in der die Menschen sich verausgaben, ausgelebt werden; aber mit der literarisch zu befördernden Vorwegnahme des umfassenden Sinnverlusts der Verausgabung öffnen sich vielleicht die Augen für das wahre Wesen der Gattung. Jedenfalls erklären sich die Widersprüche im Verhalten der Arbeiter aus antagonistischen Prozessen; der eine wird von den Imperativen der sozialen Selbstbehauptung gesteuert, der andere aus essentiellen Bedürfnissen gespeist.[16]

---

[16] Georg Kaiser: *Gas*. In: Georg Kaiser: *Werke*. Hg. von Walther Huder. Frankfurt am Main u.a.: Propyläen 1970–1972. Bd. 2. S. 9–58.

Dieses Stück faßt Brecht nun in der folgenden Parabel zusammen:

Das Stück ist visionär. Es stellt dar die soziale Entwicklung der Menschheit oder wenigstens die geistigen Gesetze, nach denen sie sich vollzieht. Der Sinn des Stückes ist vielleicht der: Ein Mann läuft. Er läuft wundervoll. Er ist ein Kunstläufer. Ein Turnlehrer hat ihm das Laufen beigebracht. Wenn der Mann eine Stunde gelaufen hat, fällt er um und schnappt nach Luft. Er schnappt durchaus kunstgerecht nach Luft, er fällt durchaus einwandfrei zu Boden. Der Turnlehrer hat es ihm beigebracht. Da kommt ein dritter Mann und sagt: 'Sie haben ein Herzleiden. Sie müßten stillsitzen, statt laufen. Sie sehen doch: Sie leiden unter Luftmangel und Atemnot!' Da erhebt sich der Mann und gibt seinem Turnlehrer eine Ohrfeige. Weil ihm der nicht das richtige Laufen beigebracht hat. Da verteidigt der zweite Mann den Turnlehrer. Da sagt der Turnlehrer: 'Geben Sie mir noch eine Ohrfeige, laufen Sie anders, aber laufen Sie.' Da sieht der Mann, daß der Turnlehrer sein Mann ist und Schlechtlaufen besser als Garnichtlaufen ist, und läuft wieder. Das Stück ist sehr interessant. Merz inszenierte es für Augsburg. Es war eine sehr gute Leistung, die geistiges Format hatte [...]. Kritisch wurde die Situation nur, wo er sich von Kaiser zu sehr beeinflussen ließ, etwa im dritten Akt. (Völlig verfehlt der letzte Akt, der ganz unklar blieb, noch unklarer als im Buch!) [...] Die Aufführung des Stückes bedeutet eine wirkliche Tat für Augsburg. Das Publikum und ein Teil der Presse fiel durch.[17]

Die Parabel aus dem Bereich des Sports beansprucht, den Sinn eines Stücks über Probleme der industriellen Produktion zu erhellen. Damit sind die Leser aufgefordert, Parallelen zwischen Erzählung und Drama nachzugehen; ohne Bezug zum Stück wäre gar nicht ersichtlich, auf welchen Praxisbereich die Erzählung zu beziehen wäre. Überdies sind die Motive der Figuren Brechts nicht unmittelbar verständlich; auf der Ebene der Erzählung bleibt das Handeln sprunghaft und muß im Rahmen der Problematik, die Kaiser behandelt, erst interpretiert werden. Die Lücken, die Brecht in seine Parabel einarbeitet, verfremden den traditionellen Gestus der gleichnishaften Erzählung, die vom Leser in der Regel nur verlangt, die symbolische Bedeutung einer schlüssigen Handlung zu finden.

In Brechts Parabel fungiert der Läufer als Symbol der Industriearbeiter; der Prozeß des Laufens, durch Atemnot unterbrochen, symbolisiert die Produktion, die von zyklisch eintretenden Überlastungen der Arbeiter begleitet wird. Der Turnlehrer personifiziert die Träger des Wissens, das die Industrieproduktion ermöglicht; dieses Wissen schließt auch Techniken ein, mit deren Hilfe jene gelegentlichen Überlastungen bewältigt werden können, die zu Produktionspausen führen. Der dritte Mann vertritt die systemkritische Ansicht, daß diese Überlastungen gegen die bisherige Form der Arbeit sprächen; die Arbeiter hingegen wollen die Träger des Wissens für ihre Probleme bei der Arbeit bestrafen. Als die wissenschaftliche Leitung der Industriearbeit diese Strafe akzeptiert,

---

[17]Bertolt Brecht: *Georg Kaisers "Gas" im Stadttheater*. BFA 21. S. 58–59.

erkennen die Arbeiter, daß sie vor der Wahl stehen, die Industrie als unvollkommen zu akzeptieren oder aber als ganze abzulehnen – und sie entscheiden sich für die Industriearbeit. Brecht möchte sich mit dieser Parabel dem Sinn von Kaisers Stück annähern, doch er denkt mit Kaiser gegen Kaiser, tilgt jeden Bezug sozialer Probleme auf metaphysische Sinngebung – und spitzt die Problematik des Stücks auf die Alternative von Arbeiten und Nichtarbeiten zu; Brecht zeigt, daß die bloße Kritik der Produktionsweise gegenüber den unausweichlichen Imperativen der Arbeit machtlos bleibt. Während die soziale Praxis bei Kaiser als fehlgeleitete Kanalisierung spiritueller Antriebe kritisiert wird, gründet sie bei Brecht in einem einsichtigen Lernprozeß über materielle Verhältnisse. Daß die wissenschaftlich-technische Leitung ihr Bestes gibt und eine ungerechte Strafe akzeptiert, wenn dies denn dem Fortbestand der Produktion dient, zeigt den Arbeitern, wer ihren materiellen Interessen zuarbeitet. Die Krise der Produktion verliert bei Brecht damit jede endzeitliche Intensität; die abstrakte Systemkritik bleibt für die Eigendynamik der kritisierten Praxis vielmehr blind.

Auch formal knüpft Brecht an Kaiser an, ohne dem metaphysischen Denken zu folgen; die Figur des weißen Herrn, die in Kaisers Stück essentielle Kräfte der Zerstörung personifiziert und sich in Halluzinationen einer Figur offenbart, die auch dem Publikum unmittelbar zugänglich sind,[18] läßt Brecht ebenso fallen wie die am Schluß vom Milliardärsohn gehegte (und im verklärten Körper seiner schwangeren Tochter verheißene) Erlösungshoffnung. Statt dessen steigert er den Abstraktionsgrad der Figuren Kaisers; er bezieht sich mit der Symbolik aus dem Bereich des Sports nur indirekt auf die ökonomische Praxis und repräsentiert das Kollektiv der Arbeiter in nur einer Figur. Die Personifizierung eines Prozeßmerkmals fällt bei Brecht also nicht mehr unmittelbar mit der Darstellung der betroffenen Personen zusammen, ja nicht einmal mehr durchgängig mit der Darstellung *einzelner* realer Personen. Der Gestus der widersprüchlichen Figuren Kaisers macht die Prozesse, die deren Handeln bestimmen, sinnfällig; in Brechts Erzählung wird das Handeln der Figuren zum ursprünglich rätselhaften Anzeichen eines erst reflexiv erkennbaren Prozesses, dessen Tendenz mit der sinnfälligen Bedeutung des Figurengestus mithin nicht kongruiert. Zwar hält es Brecht für lehrreich, daß Kaiser widersprüchliche Handlungen als Symbole der sie steuernden Prozesse darstellt, die den Betroffenen gleichsam im Rücken liegen, und die Figuren bleiben bei Brecht allegorisch; ihr Handeln verliert aber seine unmittelbare symbolische Transparenz.

Brechts *Gas*-Kritik verweist auf ein grundsätzliches Problem, das er bei der produktiven Aneignung von Kaisers Figuren bewältigen muß. In Kaisers

---

[18] Kaiser: *Gas* (n. 16). S. 11–13 u. 19.

Drama verweisen Widersprüche des Handelns auf die Antithetik positiver und negativer Kräfte; der Gestus der Figuren wird in unversöhnte Anteile gespalten, bleibt aber mit seinem immanenten Sinn für diese Kräfte transparent. Die Umwandlung dieses zeichenhaften Gestus von einer Allegorie in einen für Brechts Ansatz interessanten Index löst die ursprüngliche Anlage der Figur nur dann nicht völlig auf, wenn der Eigensinn dieses Gestus die angezeigten Tendenzen nicht prinzipiell verdeckt. So sind Kaisers Figuren für Brecht nur dann geeignet, wenn sie zeigen, wie Akteure auf eine immanent nachvollziehbare Weise in Widersprüchen ausharren; sie taugen für Texte, in denen widersprüchlich gefügte Akte exemplarischer Figuren auf ihre subjektiv einsichtige Motivation zurückgeführt werden. Da eine solche Transparenz aus Brechts Sicht nur episodisch möglich ist, eignet sich zu ihrer isolierten Gestaltung eher die Kurzprosa als das Drama (auch Brechts Versuch aus den 1930er Jahren, den Stoff von Kaisers *Der gerettete Alkibiades* für die Prosa zu erschließen, geht in diese Richtung).[19] Freilich spricht im Fall der *Gas*-Kritik auch ein anderer Grund für diese Wahl der Gattung, denn Brecht will den Zusammenhang mit den konkreten Formen Kaisers wahren; angesichts seines Abstands zum Vorbild kann er dies aber nur im Rahmen einer metasprachlichen Parabel leisten, die in der Reflexionsprosa an den Kommentar zu Kaisers Stück angeschlossen werden muß, damit der Bezug zum Vorbild sichtbar wird. Jedenfalls wird Brecht von Kaiser zu einem Formexperiment angeregt, in dem sich – zunächst im Medium der Prosa – einige Züge des für Brechts Drama später maßgebenden Verfremdungseffekts schon 1920 abzeichnen. Die Verwendung episierender Mittel; die Auffassung vom Rezipienten als Beobachter eines wandelbaren, nicht als selbstverständlich hinzunehmenden Menschen in einem sprunghaften sozialen Prozeß; die Vermittlung von Einsichten in die soziale Determination der Praxis, die durch einen fremdartig wirkenden Gestus angezeigt wird, ohne sich völlig in ihm zu verkörpern; die Auffassung vom Rezipienten als Zuschauer eines gleichsam sportlichen Ereignisses: all dies weist bereits auf wichtige Merkmale des epischen Theaters voraus[20] – wenn

---

[19] Vgl. Frank D. Wagner: Der verwundete Sokrates. In: *Brecht-Handbuch in fünf Bänden*. Hg. von Jan Knopf. Stuttgart – Weimar: Metzler 2001–2003. Bd. 2. S. 313–319: ders.: Tapferkeit. Brechts verwundeter Sokrates. In: *Heinrich-Mann-Jahrbuch* 16 (1998). S. 115–132. Die Systemironie, die Klaus-Detlef Müller im vorliegenden Band als charakteristisches Merkmal der nicht-aristotelischen Prosa herausarbeitet, findet sich in Brechts Sokrates-Geschichte, nicht jedoch schon in der *Gas*-Kritik. Während Kaisers Sokrates Hermen produziert, ist Brechts Sokrates im Zivilberuf ein Schuhmacher, tritt sich aber im Krieg einen Stachel in den Fuß, weil er von der Armee mit minderwertigem Schuhwerk ausgerüstet wird; in der *Gas*-Kritik trägt zwar die Rede vom wundervollen Kunstcharakter des Laufens und Luftschnappens ironische Züge, doch das soziale System selbst erscheint nicht in ironischer Brechung.

[20] Vgl. Bertolt Brecht: *Anmerkungen zur Oper "Aufstieg und Fall der Stadt Mahagonny"*. BFA 24. S. 74–84. Hier S. 78–79.

auch im werkgeschichtlichen Ausnahmefall, der zudem die radikal distanzierenden Wirkungen des späteren V-Effekts noch nicht erreicht. In den frühen 1920er Jahren hängt Brecht nämlich noch einem nachmetaphysischen Vitalismus an, der sich zwar zur Entwertung sakralisierter Gesten des Expressionismus eignet; die sozial- und ideologiekritische Perspektive des epischen Theaters ist darin aber keinesfalls schon angelegt.

3. Der "Umschlag" von Kaiser zu Brecht

Brecht schätzt Kaisers Verfremdung des leiblichen Gestus zu einem Zeichen heteronomer Prozesse, die das sichtbare Handeln steuern; Kaisers idealistisches Denken deutet den Leib indessen als akzidentielle Hülle eines substantiellen Allgemeinen und bevorzugt daher den allegorischen Körper, der empirisch unanschauliche Kräfte mit der handelnden Figur sinnfällig abbildet.[21] Brecht deutet den Leib aus materialistischer Perspektive als Medium einer regelhaften Praxis, deren faktische Tendenzen sich mit der sinnfälligen Bedeutung des Gestus nicht decken. Er erprobt zwei Ansätze, um Kaisers Verfremdung des fremdbestimmten Leibes in den Horizont des nachmetaphysischen Denkens einzuholen (wobei er Anfang der 1920er Jahre freilich einem vitalistischen Materialismus huldigt und noch nicht zu einem marxistischen Verständnis der Praxis gelangt ist).[22] Brechts *analytische Kritik* geht dem Potential der Technik nach, mit deren Hilfe Kaiser wünschenswerte Distanzierungseffekte erzielt, und kommt zu dem Schluß, daß diese Technik nur um den Preis der Auflösung ihrer ursprünglichen Formen und Stoffe zu haben ist. Brechts *produktive Aneignung* beschränkt sich auf Figuren, deren Handeln durch Widersprüche markiert ist, die sich in der Prosa als lehrreiches Exempel auch subjektiv einsichtiger Handlungsweisen retten lassen. Für den frühen Brecht sind die instruktiven Figuren Kaisers mithin ambivalente Vexierbilder: als Anzeichen eines subjektiv unbegriffenen sozialen Kräftespiels sind die Figuren zwar interessant, doch ihre konkrete Gestalt überzeugt nicht; in ihrer konkreten Gestalt hingegen arbeiten sie der Kurzprosa zu, sofern diese eine aus materialistischer Sicht exemplarische, auch den Betroffenen einsichtige Praxis gestaltet.

[21] Zwar betont die Forschung seit den 1970er Jahren (vgl. Vietta und Kemper: *Expressionismus* (Anm. 4)), die zivilisations- und kulturkritische Formensprache des Expressionismus diene oftmals nicht dem Ausdruck metaphysischer Evidenzen, sondern der kritischen Darstellung unanschaulich-innerweltlicher Prozesse. Als destruktive Ausdrucksformen des unverstandenen Eigensinns substantieller Energien von innerer und äußerer Natur haben freilich auch die entfremdenden Kräfte in *Gas* einen metaphysischen Ursprung.
[22] Zum Verhältnis von Metaphysik, Vitalismus und Expressionismus vgl. auch Frank Krause: *Klangbewußter Expressionismus. Moderne Techniken des rituellen Ausdrucks.* Berlin: Weidler 2006. S. 57–63.

Rückblickend kann Brecht Ende der 1920er Jahre im epischen Theater die Synthese jener beiden – analytisch bzw. literarisch ausgeloteten – Anregungen der Stücke Kaisers erkennen, denn der im epischen Theater verfremdete Gestus ist oftmals gerade beides, Ausdruck eines falschen Bewußtseins und Anzeichen materialistisch verstandener Bedingungen sozialer Praxis. Das epische Theater *resultiert* nicht aus der Aufhebung der von Kaiser empfangenen Impulse: Wenn Brecht, der Literaturkritik in praktischer Absicht betreibt,[23] sich an Kaiser abarbeitet, gelangt er zwar zu Ergebnissen, die zunächst auf eine irritierende Weise in praktisch unversöhnliche Momente auseinandertreten, während das epische Theater die Resultate der kritischen Würdigung von Kaisers Drama auf einer ästhetisch komplexeren Stufe schließlich zusammenführt – aber nicht etwa aufgrund einer dialektischen Entwicklungslogik der Werkgeschichte, deren Telos sich bereits beim frühen Brecht abzeichnete. Vielmehr begreift Brecht seinen Weg zum epischen Theater als Lösung des Problems, Impulse aus der Prosa in eine neue Formensprache für die Bühne zu übersetzen.[24] Das praktische Problem besteht darin, die Ausschlußbeziehungen der anregenden Gehalte von tradierten Techniken, Inhalten und Gattungen zu überwinden.[25] Indem sich das maßgebende Potential der Dramen Kaisers gegen produktive Aneignungen für die Bühne auf eine Weise sträubt, deren Bedingungen Brecht mit seinen Formexperimenten zu überwinden trachtet, spielen diese Dramen für Brecht eine maßgebende, nämlich problemdefinierende Rolle. Die Richtung der Lösung ist in dieser Problemdefinition freilich nicht angelegt; auch stellt sich

[23] "Es hat keinen Sinn, eine Kritik aufzubauen, die wie das Subjekt dem Objekt gegenübersteht, eine Legislative, zu der die Kunst dann die Exekutive abgibt. […] Die Kritik […] kann insofern künstlerischer werden, als sie faktisch der Produktion hilft. ([…] Es könnte die Kunst sein, die Formen, Schreibweisen u.s.w. zur Verfügung stellt, und die Kritik, die sie benutzt.)" (Bertolt Brecht: *[Kunst und Kritik]*. BFA 22.1. S. 434–435. Hier S. 434).

[24] "Es handelt sich doch wirklich nur darum, eine Form zu finden, die für die Bühne dasselbe möglich macht, was den Unterschied zwischen Ihren und Thomas Manns Romanen bildet! […] Ich weiß nicht, ob dieses Bestreben bei dem sehr widerspenstigen Schauspielapparat deutlich genug herauskommt, meist löst es im Zuschauer ja nur dumpfe Angst aus. Ich weiß also nicht, ob Sie selber z.B. schon sagen könnten, diese Art Theater müßte etwa den 'Wang-lun' […] schon eher spielen können als das bisherige?" (Bertolt Brecht: Brief an Alfred Döblin Oktober 1928. BFA 28. S. 316).

[25] "Die naturalistische Dramatik übernahm vom französischen Roman das Stoffliche und zugleich die epische Form. Diese letztere (schwächste Seite der naturalistischen Dramatik!) übernahm die neuere Dramatik unter Verzicht auf die Stoffe – als rein formales Prinzip. Mit dieser epischen Darstellungsweise übernahm sie jenes lehrhafte Element, das in der naturalistischen Dramatik, einer Erlebnisdramatik, doch schon steckte, brachte dieses Element selber aber erst einigermaßen rein zur Geltung, als sie die neue epische Form nach einer Reihe rein konstruktivistischer Versuche im leeren Raum nunmehr auf die Realität anwandte, worauf sie die Dialektik der Realität entdeckte (und sich ihrer eigenen Dialektik bewußt wurde). Die Versuche im luftleeren

das Problem selbst in den einzelnen Phasen von Brechts Werk nicht in einheitlicher Form. Dieser Befund rechtfertigt, wie mir scheint, nach wie vor die These, daß Kaiser für Brecht in einem wichtigen Prozeß der literarischen Moderne eine maßgebende Rolle spielt – bei aller berechtigten Skepsis der jüngeren Kaiser-Forschung gegenüber der Aussagekraft älterer Thesen über Wege von Kaiser zu Brecht.

Raum waren aber nicht einfacher Umweg gewesen. Sie hatten zur Entdeckung der Rolle des Gestischen geführt. Das Gestische war für sie eben das Dialektische, das im Dramatisch-Theatralischen steckt" (Bertolt Brecht: *Die dialektische Dramatik*. BFA 21. S. 431–443. Hier S. 435). Die Authentizität des aus diesen Notizen konstruierten Argumentationsgangs ist umstritten (vgl. Knopf (Hg.): *Brecht-Handbuch* (Anm. 19). Bd. 4. S. 44). Der Inhalt einzelner Abschnitte bleibt von dieser Debatte aber unberührt. Vgl. auch das Kölner Rundfunkgespräch (BFA 21. S. 273–274): "Die Anfänge des Naturalismus waren die Anfänge des epischen Dramas in Europa. [...] Die Naturalisten, Ibsen, Hauptmann, suchten die neuen Stoffe der neuen Romane auf die Bühne zu bringen und fanden keine andere Form dafür als eben die dieser Romane: eine epische". Brecht würdigt dies als "Vorstoß in die epische Form". Günter Berg und Wolfgang Jeske betonen, daß sich Brecht bei allem phasenspezifischen Mangel an Sitzfleisch, das für die Arbeit an Langformen des Erzählens nötig ist, auf der Suche nach Formen für die Behandlung von Stoffen von Anfang immer wieder auch an der Prosa bedient hat (Günter Berg und Wolfgang Jeske: *Bertolt Brecht*. Stuttgart – Weimar: Metzler 1998. S. 158). Zu Anregungen, die Brecht dem Kriminalroman für das Theater abgewinnt, siehe Bertolt Brecht: *Glossen über Kriminalromane*. BFA 21. S. 130–132. Als Beispiel für ein Drama nach einem Roman wäre *Die Mutter* zu nennen.

Steve Giles

Photography and Representation in Kracauer, Brecht and Benjamin[1]

The debate about the nature and purpose of representation in photography and other art forms which took place in Germany from the 1920s onwards was part of a larger discussion which began with the opposed positions of Realism and Symbolism and was continued in a slightly altered form in the work of the Russian Formalists and Futurists and the German Expressionists. This essay sketches out that debate and its antecedents with special reference to Kracauer, Brecht and Benjamin. In the process it sheds particular light on the Brechtian notion of Verfremdung *and on the intellectual relationship between Brecht and Benjamin.*

1

One of the most striking aspects of Thomas Levin's recent translation of Siegfried Kracauer's Weimar essays is its inclusion of photographic material from the 1920s and early 1930s which typifies the "new photography" associated with the *Neue Sachlichkeit* movement.[2] Disappointingly perhaps, Kracauer's 1927 essay on photography, published in the *Frankfurter Zeitung* some four months after *Das Ornament der Masse*, does not present us with a systematic, dialectical critique of this "new photography" and its functions in the culture of distraction.[3] However, it does embody certain modernist discursive presuppositions that invite explication. These presuppositions offer an intriguing parallel with two other Marxist aesthetic theorists who were exercized by problems

---

[1] This crucial contextualization of Brecht is an abridged and pointed version of Steve Giles: Limits of the Visible: Kracauer's Photographic Dystopia. In: *Counter-Cultures in Germany and Central Europe. From Sturm und Drang to Baader-Meinhof.* Ed. by Steve Giles and Maike Oergel. Berne: Lang 2003. Pp. 213–239.

[2] Siegfried Kracauer: *The Mass Ornament. Weimar Essays.* Ed. and trans. by Thomas Levin. Cambridge (MA): Harvard University Press 1995. On the "new photography", see: *Germany – The New Photography 1927–33.* Ed. by David Mellor. London: Arts Council of Great Britain 1978, and Hans G. Vierhuff: *Die Neue Sachlichkeit. Malerei und Fotografie.* Köln: Dumont 1980.

[3] Siegfried Kracauer: *Die Photographie.* In: Siegfried Kracauer: *Schriften.* Ed. by Inka Mülder-Bach. Frankfurt am Main: Suhrkamp 1990. Vol. 5.2: *Aufsätze (1927–1931)* Pp. 83–98. Referenced henceforth in main text as *Die Photographie.* Unlike *Das Ornament der Masse* (in: Ibid. pp. 57–67), *Die Photographie* has generally not received detailed and sustained critical attention, notwithstanding the major upsurge in Kracauer scholarship since his centenary year of 1989. The only exception is Inka Mülder: *Siegfried*

of photographic representation after modernism, namely Bertolt Brecht and Walter Benjamin. A careful exploration of them therefore will not only help to situate Brecht's aesthetic theory within the context of its time. It will also provide some much-needed historical background to the notion of *Verfremdung*. And it will offer a chance to touch briefly on one concrete outcome of the intellectual companionship between Brecht and Benjamin.

2

By the early 1920s – in Western Europe and the USA, at any rate – there had developed two clearly articulated but polarized discourses on photography, namely the documentary and the fetishistic, the scientific and the magical, which betray their roots in the aesthetic theories of the 1880s and 1890s.[4] On the one hand, we have the photographer as witness, producing images of reportage which ostensibly provide empirically verified and verifiable information. On the other hand, we find the photographer as seer, using imagination to transcend empirical reality and express inner truths. In other words, artistic discourses on photography in the early years of the twentieth century were dominated by Realism/Naturalism and Romanticism/Symbolism. With the emergence of Cubism, however, both of these positions were undercut. Instead of being construed as a mediator of a prior or pre-existing reality, whether external or internal, the visible surface of the painting came to be seen as an autonomous entity in its own right. The dispute between Realism/Naturalism and Romanticism/

Kracauer – Grenzgänger zwischen Theorie und Literatur. Seine frühen Schriften 1913–1933. Stuttgart: Metzler 1985. Pp. 72–77 and 96–101, which does not engage with the aesthetic presuppositions that underpin *Die Photographie*. Brief discussions may also be found in Dagmar Barnouw: *Critical Realism. History, Photography, and the Work of Siegfried Kracauer*. Baltimore: The Johns Hopkins University Press 1994. Pp. 27, 29–30 and 60–62; David Frisby: *Fragments of Modernity. Theories of Modernity in the Work of Simmel, Kracauer and Benjamin*. Cambridge: Polity 1985. Pp. 127 and 153–155; Miriam Hansen: Decentric Perspectives. Kracauer's Early Writings on Film and Mass Culture. In: *New German Critique* 54 (1991). Pp. 54–55; Thomas Levin: Introduction. In: Kracauer: *Weimar Essays* (n. 2). Pp. 21–22; Inka Mülder-Bach: Der Umschlag der Negativität. Zur Verschränkung von Phänomenologie, Geschichtsphilosophie und Filmästhetik in Siegfried Kracauers Metaphorik der "Oberfläche". In: *Deutsche Vierteljahrsschrift für Literaturwissenschaft und Geistesgeschichte* 61 (1987). Pp. 370–373; Johanna Rosenberg: Nachwort. In: Siegfried Kracauer: *Der verbotene Blick. Beobachtungen – Analysen – Kritiken*. Leipzig: Reclam 1992. Pp. 361 and 363; Heide Schlüpmann: Phenomenology of Film: On Siegfried Kracauer's Writings of the 1920s. In: *New German Critique* 40 (1987). Pp. 102–105.

[4] See Allan Sekula: On the Invention of Photographic Meaning. In: *Thinking Photography*. Ed. by Victor Burgin. London: Macmillan 1982. Pp. 84–109. On the rather different approaches to photography in the Soviet Union, see Simon Watney: Making Strange: The Shattered Mirror. In: Ibid. pp. 154–176.

Symbolism, which had turned on the nature of the truths that art should mediate, was thereby transmuted into a more radical confrontation concerning the very essence and possibility of representation as such. At one extreme we find the fundamentalist Naturalism of Arno Holz, according to which art has a tendency "wieder die Natur zu sein";[5] at the other, the non-objective Suprematism of Kasimir Malevich, whereby art must utterly abandon subject matter and objects in favour of the sheer superficiality of artefacts such as *White on White*.[6]

The Holz/Malevich axis is, however, intersected by an alternate modernist perspective, which certainly rejects the representational ideology of Naturalism, yet also wishes to retain a determinate relationship to "nature", whether human or otherwise. Russian Futurist/Formalist and German Expressionist aesthetics are fully aware of the Holz/Malevich concern with the adequacy of artistic representation, but they integrate that concern with more general reflections on a crisis of consciousness (which itself, ironically, has Romantic/Symbolist antecedents).[7] In order to illustrate this point, let us consider some instances from Viktor Shklovski and Kasimir Edschmid.[8]

Shklovski and Edschmid both inhabit a world where everyday perception has been deadened, and authentic seeing has been eroded, if not rendered impossible. Shklovski implicitly relates this loss of vision to a process of rationalization and disenchantment, in consequence of which we never "see" beyond the surface of things. Edschmid distinguishes between the authentic visionary space of the Expressionist artist and mere photography, bound up no doubt with the surface actualities of social facts. But there are also crucial, if subtle differences between Shklovski and Edschmid, and Futurism/Formalism and Expressionism. While Shklovski wants art to make things visible by making them look strange, Edschmid suggests that art can achieve the same strategic aim of restoring authentic vision by making visible essential relationships

---

[5]Arno Holz: Die Kunst. Ihr Wesen und ihre Gesetze. In: *Theorie des Naturalismus*. Ed. by Theo Meyer. Stuttgart: Reclam 1974. Pp. 168–174. Here p. 174.
[6]Reproduced in: Camilla Gray: *The Russian Experiment in Art 1863–1922*. London: Thames and Hudson 1990. P. 242. As the facing page in Gray suggests, the only answer to *White on White* is Alexander Rodchenko's *Black on Black* (ibid. p. 243). On Malevich's aesthetic theory, see *Russian Art of the Avant-Garde. Theory and Criticism*. Ed. by John E. Bowlt. London: Thames and Hudson 1991. Pp. 116–135.
[7]See Watney: Making Strange (n. 4). Pp. 154–156.
[8]On the Futurist antecedents of Formalism, see Victor Ehrlich: *Russischer Formalismus*. Frankfurt am Main: Suhrkamp 1973. Pp. 46–57. The Futurist roots of Shklovski's Formalism are clearly indicated by the fact that the conception of language deployed in *Kunst als Verfahren* is first developed in his Futurist essay of 1914: The Resurrection of the Word. In: *Russian Formalism*. Ed. by Stephen Bann and John E. Bowlt. Edinburgh: Scottish Academic Press 1973. Pp. 41–47.

which are otherwise inaccessible to everyday perception. Edschmid therefore requires the artist to *break through* the surface of actuality in order to grasp and mediate its otherwise non-visible essence, whereas Shklovski advocates *intensification* of our perception of objects by making them more palpable. Hence Shklovski wants the stone to be *more* stony:

> Und gerade, um das Empfinden des Lebens wiederherzustellen, um die Dinge zu fühlen, um den Stein steinern zu machen, existiert das, was man Kunst nennt. Ziel der Kunst ist es, ein Empfinden des Gegenstandes zu vermitteln, als Sehen, und nicht als Wiedererkennen; das Verfahren der Kunst ist das Verfahren der "Verfremdung" der Dinge und das Verfahren der erschwerten Form, ein Verfahren, das die Schwierigkeit und Länge der Wahrnehmung steigert.[9]

Edschmid on the other hand wants the building to *transcend* its stony objectivity:

> Ein Haus ist nicht mehr Gegenstand, nicht mehr nur Stein, nur Anblick, nur ein Viereck mit Attributen des Schön- oder Häßlichseins. Es steigt darüber hinaus.[10]

3

Certain aspects of these artistic discourses are particularly relevant to Siegfried Kracauer's critique of photography, as expounded in an essay published in 1927 in the *Frankfurter Zeitung*. For much of *Die Photographie*, Kracauer characterizes photography in Realist/Naturalist terms, in such a way as to disqualify photography from attaining artistic status. He even suggests that photographs are the representational counterpart of historicism, in that they merely record the detritus of History rather than its authentic truth-content. The mediation of truth is the prerogative of Art, but Kracauer's conception of Art is radically anti-mimetic. Although he concedes that since the Renaissance, Art has entertained a close relationship with nature, he contends nonetheless that Art has always sought to achieve higher aims, by presenting knowledge in the medium of colour and contour. Art-works do not strive to resemble the objects they depict, nor is their configuration governed by an object's spatial appearance. Instead, Art grasps the significance of an object and mediates that significance spatially. As a result, Art is fundamentally anti-photographic, so that if History is to be represented in Art, then the surface context associated with photography must be destroyed.

[9] Viktor Shklovski: Die Kunst als Verfahren. In: *Russischer Formalismus. Texte zur allgemeinen Literaturtheorie und zur Theorie der Prosa.* Ed. by J. Striedter. München: Fink 1981. Pp. 3–35. Here P. 15.
[10] K. Edschmid: Über den dichterischen Expressionismus. In: *Theorie des Expressionismus.* Ed. by Otto F. Best. Stuttgart: Reclam 1976. Pp. 55–67. Here p. 58.

Kracauer's account of the photographic turn in contemporary media culture is thus for the most part unremittingly negative. In the final section of the photography essay, however, he suddenly changes direction, as he insinuates that even photography may be redeemable in artistic and historical terms. He first reminds us that a consciousness entrapped in nature is incapable of catching sight of its own foundation – the prerequisite for the emergence of liberated consciousness. But he then produces the astonishing assertion that it is the task of photography to display this as yet unexamined foundation: astonishing because hitherto, photography had been seen as a mere reflector of surface appearance, whereas now it is suddenly invested with the power to make visible the as yet unseen. Kracauer justifies this seemingly preposterous claim – preposterous in terms of his argumentation thus far, at any rate – by drawing our attention to a more spatially ambitious photographic genre:

Sie zeigt die Städte in Flugbildern, holt die Krabben und Figuren von den gotischen Kathedralen herunter; alle räumlichen Konfigurationen werden in ungewohnten Überschneidungen, die sie aus der menschlichen Nähe entfernen, dem Hauptarchiv einverleibt (*Die Photographie*. P. 96).

This alternative mode of photography is preferred because it supposedly enables us to see the world of objects in its independence from human beings, and because it preserves images of alienated nature. Moreover, the *dis*-order of the detritus reflected in photography is, he suggests, best represented by suspending normal or usual relationships between the elements of nature. In other words, one might conclude, the utopian dimension of avant-garde photography consists in its ability to mirror the sheer negativity of contemporary life. In the contemporary world, Art has reached a turning-point. Kracauer notes that the epoch of nature-based Art inaugurated by the Renaissance may be coming to an end, and he refers to three categories of contemporary Art that seek to reject natural verisimilitude. First, he mentions modern painters – presumably Cubists, Constructivists or Dadaists – who put their pictures together from photographic fragments in order to underline spatially the simultaneous coexistence of the reified appearances they represent (*Die Photographie*. P. 88). Secondly, the works of Franz Kafka are said to be imbued by a liberated consciousness which has demolished natural realities and has disarranged or displaced the resulting fragments against one another (*Die Photographie*. P. 97). Finally, film is credited with the capacity to transcend "normal" or usual relationships between elements of nature by assembling strange or alien configurations through cutting and editing (ibid.). And whereas the muddle and jumble of illustrated newspapers is merely chaotic, the defamiliarized representation of natural elements and relationships is said to be redolent of the confusion of daily residues in dreams. For Kracauer, "das freigesetzte Bewußtsein zerschlägt die natürliche Realität und verstellt die Bruchstücke gegeneinander", a possibility which film "verwirklicht überall dort, wo er Teile und Ausschnitte zu fremden Gebilden assoziiert" (ibid.). The implication would seem to be that in the contemporary world, Art can only fulfil its epistemological role by adopting the radically anti-Naturalistic representational techniques of the modernist avant-garde.

Kracauer's critique of photography is thus grounded in a series of presuppositions about aesthetics and modernity that can be traced back to his earliest published essays on artistic themes from 1920 and 1921.[11] His brilliantly succinct account of German Expressionism commends the Expressionist artist's rejection of Naturalism and Impressionism in favour of an art form that dismisses the ontological claims of the actual world as it presents itself to us, in order instead to express directly the world's innermost being. Kracauer takes the view that Expressionism shatters "normality" and proclaims its visions in art forms which hardly refer to the world of the senses, suspending familiar spatial relationships and embedding fragments of our perceptions into a matrix of lines and shapes, whose structure is determined by the innermost needs of the artist. Even when recognizable objects and people do seem to emerge, their external configuration is but an empty mask that the artist removes in order to reveal the true visage. Contemporary actuality turns out to be shadowy and insubstantial, a chaos without soul or meaning, whose absurdity can only be represented in a distorted image.

When he reviews Kafka's *Das Schloß*, Kracauer's vision is significantly darker. The world of *Das Schloß* is infused by the absence of truth, plunging that world into a state of *Angst* which is the antithesis of the fairy tale. Kafka's novel is said to mediate the *non*-realization of truth in human history and display the *distortion* of a mundane life bereft of truth. Its representational techniques thus involve the suspension of normal or usual interconnections (as we also saw in the photography essay), together with the displacement of objects isolated by that process so that they show their obverse to the viewer, thereby demonstrating the inadequacy of the full-frontal perspective that had seemed to be true. Put more positively, Kafka's novel replaces "normal" everyday images and surface relationships with a mosaic of facts and reasons that utterly suppresses the cosy familiarity of actuality as given to us. *Das Schloß*, in other words, seems to combine a Formalist strategy of defamiliarization with the representational tactics of Cubism.

It should be evident even from this brief discussion that Kracauer's representational requirements for contemporary art forms involve a Futurist/Formalist emphasis on defamiliarization of "normal" interconnections and

---

[11] See, for example, Siegfried Kracauer: *Schicksalswende der Kunst*. In: Kracauer: *Schriften* 5.2 (n. 3). Pp. 72–78, and Siegfried Kracauer: *Georg von Lukács' Romantheorie*. In: Ibid. pp. 117–123.

relationships which is to be achieved by adopting distorted or distorting perspectives. At the same time, his critique of mimetic depiction presupposes the categories of Expressionist aesthetics. Thus although his "positive" alternative to that tradition in photographic theory which legitimizes photography in mimetic or naturalistic terms has some affinity with the notion of the photographer as seer, the key to his re-evaluation of the photographic lies ultimately in his attempt to synthesize the aesthetics of "making visible" and "making strange", bringing together the insights of Russian Futurism/Formalism and German Expressionism in the context of a general advocacy of modernist art-forms.

The point at issue is the discrepancy we noted earlier between intensification and transcendence of perception. Applied to photography, these contradictory positions would lead to two contrasting representational practices: on the one hand, the adoption of bizarre perspective and point of view associated with the more radical exponents of *Neue Sachlichkeit*, and on the other the "painting with light" associated with, say, Christian Schad or Man Ray. In both cases, the documentary and evidential force of photography would appear to have been forsaken, and realist art forms modelled on the traditional truth claims of photography would appear to be in need of revision. Hence Adorno will insist with regard to the novel: "Will der Roman seinem realistischen Erbe treu bleiben und sagen, wie es wirklich ist, so muß er auf einen Realismus verzichten, der, indem er die Fassade reproduziert, nur dieser bei ihrem Täuschungsgeschäfte hilft".[12]

Adorno advocates a mode of novelistic composition whose fundamental aim is realist and demystificatory, lifting the veil of reification so as to reveal those essential societal relations that would otherwise remain hidden from view. This aim is to be achieved by breaking through the façade of surface deception in true Expressionist fashion. But if the façade is *not* to be reproduced, how is the novel's real object – an alienated social order – to be represented? Kracauer's famous answer, which applies as much to sociology as it does to aesthetics, is encapsulated in his methodological remarks in *Die Angestellten*:

> Hundert Berichte aus einer Fabrik lassen sich nicht zur Wirklichkeit der Fabrik addieren, sondern bleiben bis in alle Ewigkeit hundert Fabrikansichten. Die Wirklichkeit ist eine Konstruktion. Gewiss muss das Leben beobachtet werden, damit sie erstehe. Keineswegs jedoch ist sie in der mehr oder minder zufälligen Beobachtungsfolge der Reportage enthalten, vielmehr steckt sie einzig und allein in dem Mosaik, das aus den einzelnen Beobachtungen auf Grund der Erkenntnis ihres Gehalts zusammengestiftet wird. Die Reportage photographiert das Leben; ein solches Mosaik wäre sein Bild.[13]

[12] Theodor W. Adorno: *Standort des Erzählers im zeitgenössischen Roman*. In: Theodor W. Adorno: *Gesammelte Schriften*. Frankfurt am Main: Suhrkamp 1974. Bd. 11: *Noten zur Literatur*. Pp. 41–48. Here p. 43.
[13] Siegfried Kracauer: *Die Angestellten. Aus dem neuesten Deutschland*. Frankfurt am Main: Suhrkamp 1971. P. 16.

Although he dismisses the façade of photographic reportage, Kracauer insists on the need to *construct* – from empirical impressions, observations and reports – a mosaic that will constitute a valid image of socio-economic realities. Crucially, whilst Kracauer endorses the modernist/Expressionist critique of Naturalistic representation, his aesthetic and epistemological alternative to "mere photography" also questions Expressionist transcendence. Even in 1920, Kracauer had noted that although Expressionism was necessary, its mission had been completed, and he concludes his essay *Schicksalswende der Kunst* by rejecting Expressionist abstraction. We might infer that, like Adorno, Kracauer wishes to establish a mode of realism whose underlying metaphysic draws on Expressionism, but whose representational strategies owe more to Futurism/ Formalism and avant-garde montage.[14]

4

Kracauer's critique of photographic reportage as a basis for analyzing industrial relations uncannily anticipates Brecht's musings on this topic. The *locus classicus* here is the critique of photographic realism in *Der Dreigroschenprozeß*:

> Die Lage wird dadurch so kompliziert, daß weniger denn je eine einfache "Wiedergabe der Realität" etwas über die Realität aussagt. Eine Fotografie der Kruppwerke oder der AEG ergibt beinahe nichts über diese Institute. Die eigentliche Realität ist in die Funktionale gerutscht. Die Verdinglichung der menschlichen Beziehungen, also etwa die Fabrik, gibt die letzteren nicht mehr heraus. Es ist also tatsächlich "etwas aufzubauen", etwas "Künstliches", "Gestelltes". Es ist also ebenso tatsächlich Kunst nötig. Aber der alte Begriff der Kunst, vom Erlebnis her, fällt eben aus. Denn auch wer von der Realität nur das von ihr Erlebbare gibt, gibt sie selbst nicht wieder. Sie ist längst nicht mehr im Totalen erlebbar. [...] Aber wir reden, so redend, von einer Kunst mit ganz anderer Funktion im gesellschaftlichen Leben, nämlich der, Wirklichkeit zu geben.[15]

Like Kracauer, Brecht suggests that the "reality" of a factory cannot be conveyed by a "merely photographic" reproduction of the immediately visible surfaces of social life. In Brecht's view, this is because socio-economic realities have become functional and human relationships have become reified in such a way that they are not immediately given in experience, visual or otherwise. Brecht, too, argues that a new type of art is needed, which (re-)constructs fundamental societal relationships. His argumentation here, as he himself notes, was strongly influenced by his discussions with the Marxist sociologist Fritz

---

[14] On montage as a core aesthetic feature of avant-garde texts, see Peter Bürger: *Theorie der Avantgarde*. Frankfurt am Main: Suhrkamp 1982. Pp. 97–108.

[15] Bertolt Brecht: *Der Dreigroschenprozeß. Ein soziologisches Experiment*. BFA 21. Pp. 448–514. Here p. 469.

Sternberg.[16] Sternberg had suggested that there was a fundamental difference between the late medieval/early modern era, and contemporary industrial society. Whereas in the sixteenth century, key societal relationships were visible to the naked eye and thus amenable to photographic representation, in the twentieth century such relationships have to be rationally reconstructed, thus rendering their photographic representation inadequate or impossible.[17]

This line of argument – together with Marx's account of commodity fetishism and Korsch's critique of naïve realism – underpins Brecht's advocacy of a cognitive or abstract type of realism from 1932 onwards.[18] Nevertheless, Brecht also insists on the importance of making societal realities *visible*. This is a recurrent theme in *Der Dreigroschenprozeß*, where the process of making visible is even likened to producing a photographic print from a negative.[19] At the same time, Brecht's emphasis on visibility must be grasped in relation to the aesthetic co-ordinates that frame Futurism/Formalism and Expressionism. At one level, "Brecht the post-Expressionist" is committed to "making visible" socioeconomic structures and relationships which are not immediately given in sense perception. At another level, however, "Brecht the post-Formalist" advocates an aesthetic of estrangement that heightens our perception of aspects of social behaviour which are literally embodied in the *Gestus*. As he writes around 1940,

> Es ist der Zweck des V-Effekts, den allen Vorgängen unterliegenden gesellschaftlichen Gestus zu verfremden. Unter sozialem Gestus ist der mimische und gestische Ausdruck der gesellschaftlichen Beziehungen zu verstehen, in denen die Menschen einer bestimmten Epoche zueinander stehen.[20]

This "making strange", whereby the *V-Effekt* seeks to defamiliarize and thereby reveal the societal *Gestus* that underlies interactive processes has its counterpart in a "making visible", whereby otherwise abstract societal relations are to be displayed to the audience in the palpable form of observable, physical behaviour. As Brecht observes with reference to Shakespeare's *King Lear*:

> Wenn König Lear (1. Akt, 1. Szene), sein Reich unter die Töchter verteilend, eine Landkarte zerreißt, so wird der Teilungsakt verfremdet. Es wird so nicht nur der

[16] See Bertolt Brecht: *Durch Fotografie keine Einsicht*. BFA 21. Pp. 443–444.

[17] See Sternberg's account of comments which he made in conversations with Brecht in ca. 1928/29, in: Fritz Sternberg: *Der Dichter und die Ratio. Erinnerungen an Bertolt Brecht*. Göttingen: Sachse und Pohl 1963. Pp. 14–15.

[18] For further discussion, see Steve Giles: *Bertolt Brecht and Critical Theory. Marxism, Modernity and the "Threepenny" Lawsuit*. Berne: Peter Lang 1998. Pp. 175–177.

[19] See Brecht: *Der Dreigroschenprozeß* (n. 15). P. 460, and Giles: *Bertolt Brecht and Critical Theory* (n. 18). P. 74.

[20] Bertolt Brecht: *Kurze Beschreibung einer neuen Technik der Schauspielkunst, die einen Verfremdungseffekt hervorbringt*. BFA 22. Pp. 641–659. Here p. 646.

Blick auf das Reich gelenkt, sondern, indem er das Reich so deutlich als Privateigentum behandelt, wirft er einiges Licht auf die Grundlage der feudalen Familienideologie.[21]

5

Brecht's considerations on the medium had a demonstrable influence on the thought of his friend and intellectual sparring partner Walter Benjamin. Benjamin's critique of photographic representation in his *Kleine Geschichte der Photographie* takes as its starting point Brecht's commentary on Krupp and AEG,[22] and cites both Brecht and Kracauer's photography essay in its account of contemporary photographic theory and practice. By the time Benjamin's essay appeared in 1931, the "new photography" had fully established itself, and his perspective on photography differs from Kracauer's in two main ways: he is prepared to concede a greater positive potential to the "new photography",[23] and he is much more sceptical of the aesthetic categories within which photography had traditionally been located. In particular, Benjamin follows Brecht in criticizing the auratic view of art adhered to by photographic theorists and pays much more attention to issues of photographic technology. His positive strategy – and his more positive response to the "new photography" – involves assimilating Brecht's critique of photographic realism to the artistic practices of Surrealism and Constructivism. Benjamin also rejects photographic reportage in favour of an aesthetic of "making strange": the camera has the potential to produce images which *shock* the viewer and interrupt his/her mechanisms of association, creating a space for the incorporation of photography into what Brecht had referred to as the literarization of all aspects of life.

6

This brings photography into that realm of "complex seeing" which all three – Kracauer, Brecht and Benjamin – by the late 1920s and early 1930s consider to be the way forward for a socially critical, avant-garde aesthetic practice, whose prime exemplar is film.[24] It is far from self-evident, however, that simply

---

[21] Ibid. p. 653.

[22] Walter Benjamin: *Kleine Geschichte der Photographie*. WBGS II.1. Pp. 368–385. In some quarters this essay is best known for its Brechtian critique (deriving directly from *Der Dreigroschenprozeß*) of the photography of *Neue Sachlichkeit* (ibid. pp. 383–384), a critique which also plays a crucial role in Benjamin's theory of the avant-garde in: *Der Autor als Produzent*. WBGS II.2. Pp. 683–701. For further discussion of Benjamin's indebtedness to Brecht in this regard, see Giles: *Bertolt Brecht and Critical Theory* (n. 18). Pp. 133–136.

[23] See Benjamin: *Kleine Geschichte der Photographie* (n. 22). Pp. 382–383.

adopting filmic modes of representation can resolve the theoretical dilemmas that confronted Brecht and Kracauer in particular, and the following crucial questions remain open. How can the relative merits of two ostensibly incompatible aesthetic strategies – making visible and making strange – be combined in such a way as to take full account of the modernist/Expressionist critique of naïve realism as manifested in Naturalistic representation, without losing sight of the need to make social realities perceptible in a way that avoids the pitfalls of Expressionist abstraction and transcendence? If social realities are to be made perceptible for a mass audience, how can the "new media" of photography and film be harnessed to that project – or must they simply be dismissed as irredeemably mystificatory or ideological? Is there, ultimately, a third way between Adorno's elitist but melancholic modernism and Lukács's fetish for a pre-modernist realism?

[24] For further discussion of these issues in relation to Brecht and Benjamin, see Giles: *Bertolt Brecht and Critical Theory* (n. 18). Pp. 140–158.

Erdmut Wizisla

Walter Benjamin und Bertolt Brecht: Bericht über eine Konstellation[1]

The relationship between Walter Benjamin and Bertolt Brecht is one of the most important friendships between artists of the last century. Their influence in literature, theatre and political thinking remains important to this day. Benjamin's friends, especially Adorno and Scholem, didn't appreciate his meetings with Brecht. This paper presents material from the author's book Benjamin und Brecht *(Suhrkamp 2004/Libris 2007). several episodes illustrate the cooperation between Benjamin and Brecht: the project* Krise und Kritik: *Benjamin's Paris speech on German Avantgarde from 1934; chess in Danish exile; and the impact of Brecht's poem "Legende von der Entstehung des Buches Taoteking auf dem Weg des Laotse in die Emigration".*

Im Februar 1937 sandte Walter Benjamin Margarete Steffin einen Auszug aus Chestertons Dickens-Buch. Mit dieser Passage sei "das beste über den Dreigroschenroman gesagt [...], was man nur sagen kann".[2] Worum geht es? Dickens, schreibt Chesterton, habe die tollsten satirischen Ausgeburten auf einer Londoner Hauptstraße oder in einer Anwaltskanzlei auftreten lassen. Er sei ein maßloser Spaßmacher gewesen, weil er Mäßigung im Denken besaß. Seine zügellose Phantasie entsprang seiner maßvollen, vernünftigen Denkweise.

London gehört zur Topographie der Beziehungen zwischen Benjamin und Brecht. Erst kürzlich, im Frühjahr 2005, ist in Moskau der Entwurf eines Telegramms aufgetaucht, das Benjamin im Juni oder Juli 1936 an Brecht, Hampstead, Abbey Road, richtete: "Drahtet wann bestimmt Svendborg seid/ Benjamin".[3]

Aus London hatte Brecht im April 1936 Benjamins Sammelreferat "Probleme der Sprachsoziologie" mit den Worten gerühmt: "So könnte man durchaus eine neue Enzyklopädie schreiben". Der Brief – einer der wenigen erhaltenen – endet mit einer Einladung nach Svendborg: "Also wie ist es mit dem Sommer? Im Juni bin ich zurück. Werden wir uns sehen? Allzu viele Sommer werden wir kaum noch unter den Apfelbäumen schachspielen können".[4]

---

[1] Dieser Essay präsentiert Thesen und Materialien meines Buches *Benjamin und Brecht. Die Geschichte einer Freundschaft.* Frankfurt am Main: Suhrkamp 1994, dessen englische Fassung bei Libris, London, in Vorbereitung ist. – Mein Dank gilt Godela Weiss-Sussex, Robert Gillett und Hamish Ritchie für die ausgezeichnete Londoner Tagung.

[2] Walter Benjamin: Brief an Margarete Steffin 26.4.1937. WBGB V. S. 521.

[3] Russisches Staatliches Militärarchiv ("Sonderarchiv"), Bestand Walter Benjamin, Mappe 48. Vgl. dazu Reinhard Müller und Erdmut Wizisla: "Kritik der freien Intelligenz". Walter-Benjamin-Funde im Moskauer "Sonderarchiv". In: *Mittelweg 36.* 14 (2005). H. 5. S. 61–76.

[4] Bertolt Brecht: Brief an Walter Benjamin April 1936. BFA 28. S. 550–551.

Abb. 1: Benjamin und Brecht beim Schach, Skovsbostrand, Sommer 1934, Bertolt-Brecht-Archiv, Fotograf unbekannt.

Wenn die hier zur Rede stehende Beziehung als *Konstellation* bezeichnet wird, so ist damit zunächst nicht zum Ausdruck gebracht, daß die Begegnung zwischen Benjamin und Brecht mehr als eine Tatsache ihrer Biographien war. Diese Formulierung paraphrasiert den Beginn von Max Kommerells Aufsatz "Jean Paul in Weimar". Der Aufenthalt Jean Pauls in Weimar sei nicht anders zu umschreiben als mit dem Wort *Konstellation*, schreibt Kommerell. Zufälliges und Gesetzliches seien dabei kaum zu unterscheiden. Der Begriff drücke aus, "wo jeder steht, wie zu jedem und wie alle zu allen" – "in dieser Zeit hoher Bewußtheit und schärfster Spiegelung".[5] Gemeinsamkeiten zur Stellung der Gestirne liegen im Zusammentreffen nicht zufälliger, spezifischer – hier: günstiger – Umstände, in der Verbindung von Einzigartigkeit und Gesetz und in der Erwartung, daß die daraus resultierenden besonderen Erfahrungen und Haltungen nicht auf das Wollen und Handeln von Individuen beschränkt sind.

In Benjamin und Brecht begegneten sich divergierende Erfahrungen, Interessen, politische und kunsttheoretische Positionen. In der Begegnung lösten sich die Differenzen nicht auf, aber es kam zu einer fruchtbaren, gleichwohl spannungsgeladenen Beziehung, die merkwürdigerweise viele in Unruhe versetzte. "Du bist in eine falsche Gesellschaft geraten: Brecht plus Benjamin", warnte Johannes R. Becher Asja Lacis.[6]

Als ich vor vielen Jahren begann, mich mit dieser Beziehung zu beschäftigen, war ich überrascht, wie viele Zeugnisse bis dahin unberücksichtigt geblieben oder bewußt falsch gedeutet worden waren. In erster Linie ist das die Folge der Abwehr, mit der Benjamins Umfeld auf die Freundschaft reagierte. Theodor W. Adornos Vorbehalte gegen "Berta [d. i. Brecht] und ihr Kollektiv" sind ebenso einschlägig wie seine Behauptung, Benjamin habe den "Kunstwerk"-Aufsatz geschrieben, "um Brecht, vor dem er sich fürchtete, an Radikalismus zu überbieten".[7] Wie Adorno kritisierte Gershom Scholem die Beziehung: "Ich würde eher sagen, daß ich diesen Einfluß Brechts auf die Produktion Benjamins in den dreißiger Jahren für unheilvoll, in manchem auch für katastrophal halte".[8] Es ist schon erstaunlich, welche Wirkung diese Vorurteile hatten. Das geht bis in die Edition der *Gesammelten Schriften* Benjamins, die – vor allem was die Brecht-Arbeiten angeht – voller Fehler sind.

---

[5] Max Kommerell: Jean Paul in Weimar. In: Max Kommerell: *Dichterische Welterfahrung*. Essays. Frankfurt am Main: Klostermann 1952. S. 53–82. Hier S. 53 und S. 55.
[6] Asja Lacis: *Revolutionär im Beruf. Berichte über proletarisches Theater, über Meyerhold, Brecht, Benjamin und Piscator*. Hg. von Hildegard Brenner. München: Rogner & Bernhard 1971. S. 59.
[7] Rolf Tiedemann: *Studien zur Philosophie Walter Benjamins* [1965]. Frankfurt am Main: Suhrkamp 1973. S. 112.
[8] Gershom Scholem: *Walter Benjamin* [1965]. In: Gershom Scholem: *Walter Benjamin und sein Engel*. Vierzehn Aufsätze und kleine Beiträge. Hg. von Rolf Tiedemann. Frankfurt am Main: Suhrkamp 1983. S. 9–34. Hier S. 26.

Unter den positiven Gegenstimmen – zu denen u. a. Günter Anders, Elisabeth Hauptmann, Ruth Berlau gehören – sei hier nur die emphatischste zitiert: Hannah Arendt. Die Beziehung zu Brecht sei ein "Glücksfall" für Benjamin, Brecht sei ihm "in dem letzten Jahrzehnt seines Lebens, vor allem in der Pariser Emigration, der wichtigste Mensch" gewesen. Und weiter:

> Die Freundschaft Benjamin-Brecht ist einzigartig, weil in ihr der größte lebende deutsche Dichter mit dem bedeutendsten Kritiker der Zeit zusammentraf. [...] [E]s ist seltsam und traurig, daß die Einzigartigkeit dieser Begegnung den alten Freunden niemals, auch als beide, Brecht und Benjamin, längst tot waren, eingeleuchtet hat.[9]

Elisabeth Hauptmann äußerte sich 1972 in einem Gespräch zu dieser Freundschaft. Ihre Stimme ist hier zu zitieren, weil sie den Überschwang Hannah Arendts ein wenig dämpft. Zugleich ist ihr Urteil – als das einer unmittelbar Beteiligten – von besonderem Gewicht. Benjamin und Brecht hätten ihre Haltungen nicht an einer gemeinsamen Arbeit ausprobiert, sagt sie – nicht ganz zutreffend. Die gegenseitige Einwirkung sei jedoch enorm gewesen. Benjamin als Partner für Brecht sei "mit das Beste, was es gab", gewesen.[10]

Der Begriff *Konstellation* spielt in Benjamins Reaktion auf das Mißtrauen eine zentrale Rolle. Im Mai 1934 schrieb ihm Gretel Karplus, die spätere Ehefrau Adornos, sie sehe seiner Übersiedlung nach Dänemark "mit etwas Ängstlichkeit entgegen", weil sie gegen Brecht sehr große Vorbehalte habe. Manchmal habe sie das Gefühl, Benjamin stehe irgendwie unter Brechts Einfluß, der für ihn eine große Gefahr bedeute (vgl. WBGB IV. S. 442–443).

Benjamins Antwort verweist auf eine entscheidende Eigenschaft seines Denkens:

> Was Du da über seinen Einfluß auf mich sagst, das ruft mir eine bedeutende und immer wiederkehrende Konstellation in meinem Leben ins Gedächtnis. [...] In der Ökonomie meines Daseins spielen in der Tat einige wenige gezählte Beziehungen eine Rolle, die es mir ermöglichen, einen, dem Pol meines ursprünglichen Seins entgegengesetzten zu behaupten. [...] In solchem Falle kann ich wenig mehr tun, als das Vertrauen meiner Freunde dafür erbitten, daß diese Bindungen, deren Gefahren auf der Hand liegen, ihre Fruchtbarkeit zu erkennen geben werden. Gerade Dir ist es ja keineswegs undeutlich, daß mein Leben so gut wie mein Denken sich in extremen Positionen bewegt (WBGB IV. S. 440–441).

Im folgenden werden einige Elemente der Konstellation bezeichnet. Es sind Zeugnisse, Bruchstücke, die stellvertretend für das Ganze stehen sollen.

---

[9] Hannah Arendt: Walter Benjamin. In: Hannah Arendt: *Walter Benjamin, Bertolt Brecht. Zwei Essays.* München: Piper 1971. S. 7–62. Hier S. 21.

[10] Elisabeth Hauptmann im Gespräch mit Wolfgang Gersch, Rolf Liebmann und Karlheinz Mund für den Film *Die Mit-Arbeiterin* (1972), Archiv der Akademie der Künste, Elisabeth-Hauptmann-Archiv (CD-Auswahl von Karlheinz Mund 2003, CD 2). – Diese Äußerung ist mir erst nach Erscheinen meines Buches *Benjamin und Brecht* zugänglich geworden.

Methodisch darf hier vielleicht eine Fühlungnahme mit Brechts Montagetechnik und Benjamins Allegorieverständnis reklamiert werden. Der Allegoriker, sagt Benjamin, fügt das Zerschlagene zusammen.

Krise und Kritik

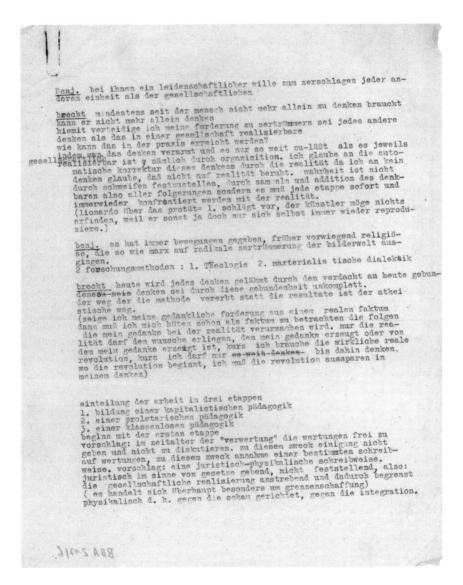

Abb. 2: Auszug aus einem Protokoll zum Zeitschriftenprojekt *Krise und Kritik*, etwa September 1930, Bertolt-Brecht-Archiv 217/06.

Wesentlicher Bestandteil meines Buches sind die Protokolle von Gesprächen zur Gründung der Zeitschrift *Krise und Kritik*, die Benjamin und Brecht, zusammen mit Bernard von Brentano und Herbert Ihering und unter Mitarbeit von Bloch, Kracauer, Kurella und Lukács, 1930/31 im Rowohlt Verlag herausgeben wollten. Gedacht war an ein Organ, "in dem die bürgerliche Intelligenz sich Rechenschaft von den Forderungen und den Einsichten gibt, die einzig und allein ihr unter den heutigen Umständen eine eingreifende, von Folgen begleitete Produktion im Gegensatz zu der üblichen willkürlichen und folgenlosen gestatten".[11]

Die Gesprächsprotokolle dokumentieren eine ungewöhnliche Vielfalt an Themen und methodischen Zugängen. Im Zentrum stehen Reflexionen über den Standort des Künstlers und Intellektuellen und über das Verhältnis von Inhalt und Form in der Kunst. Auf einen besonders gehaltreichen Wortwechsel, der auf etwa September 1930 zu datieren ist, sei hier exemplarisch hingewiesen. Die an dem Projekt Beteiligten sind Intellektuelle und Künstler, denen die Funktion des Denkens ein Thema ist. Brecht schlägt – in seiner Pragmatik durchaus typisch – vor: "zu zertrümmern sei jedes andere denken als das in einer gesellschaft realisierbare".[12] Benjamin reagiert darauf mit einem gewichtigen Gesprächsbeitrag. Es ist einer jener Splitter, die mehr in sich bergen als manch ausgeführtes Gedankensystem: "es hat immer bewegungen gegeben, früher vorwiegend religiöse, die so wie marx auf radikale zertrümmerung der bilderwelt ausgingen./2 forschungsmethoden: 1. Theologie 2. materialistische dialektik".[13]

Benjamin verstand theologische und materialistische Methoden als Ergänzungen, weil ihm Kriterium für die Beurteilung eines Ansatzes nicht dessen Tradition oder weltanschaulicher Ort, sondern seine "Brauchbarkeit" war. So mochte er in der theologischen historisch-kritischen Forschung philologische Potenzen entdecken, die er in den Geisteswissenschaften vermißte. Seine 1931, in der Rezension "Literaturgeschichte und Literaturwissenschaft" formulierte Anregung, Kunstwerke "in der Zeit, da sie entstanden" darzustellen, um auf diese Weise die "Zeit, die sie erkennt – das ist die unsere – zur Darstellung zu bringen" (WBGS III. S. 290), verdankte der historisch-kritischen Forschung Anregungen, auch wenn keine unmittelbare Berührung nachzuweisen ist. Vor allem aber interessierte ihn theologisches Denken in Methode und Anspruch, weil es die Totalität in den Blick nahm, während jede andere Betrachtung von den Gegebenheiten ausging. Die Aufgeschlossenheit für scheinbar konträre Positionen ergab sich aus dem Versuch, eingefahrene Problemstellungen aufzubrechen und der gesellschaftlichen Wirklichkeit radikal zu begegnen.

---

[11] Walter Benjamin: *Memorandum zu der Zeitschrift "Krisis [sic] und Kritik"*. WBGS VI. S. 619.
[12] BBA 217/06.
[13] Ebd.

Die Begegnung von Theologie und materialistischer Dialektik, von Messianismus und Marxismus in Benjamins Denken ist freilich nicht auf methodische Fragen zu reduzieren. Die Theologie hatte für ihn, wie Adorno es über Benjamins Marxismus gesagt hat, *Experimentalcharakter*. Benjamins Interesse, die Richtung seines Denkens "auf diejenigen Gegenstände zu lenken, in denen jeweils die Wahrheit am dichtesten vorkommt" (WBGB IV. S. 19), führte zu einer originären Verschmelzung von scheinbar antinomischen Denktraditionen.

Zur Zeit von *Krise und Kritik* findet sich die Spannweite ausgedrückt in dem programmatischen Brief an Max Rychner vom 7. März 1931: Hier bat Benjamin darum, in ihm nicht "einen Vertreter des dialektischen Materialismus als eines Dogmas, sondern einen Forscher zu sehen, dem die *Haltung* des Materialisten wissenschaftlich und menschlich in allen uns bewegenden Dingen fruchtbarer scheint als die idealistische" (WBGB IV. S. 19–20). Beinahe eine Dekade später sollte diese ungewöhnliche Konfrontation philosophischer Modelle in den Thesen "Über den Begriff der Geschichte" ihren authentischen Niederschlag finden. Über diesen Text hat Brecht gesagt, er sei "klar und entwirrend (trotz aller Metaphorik und Judaismen)".[14]

Avantgarde

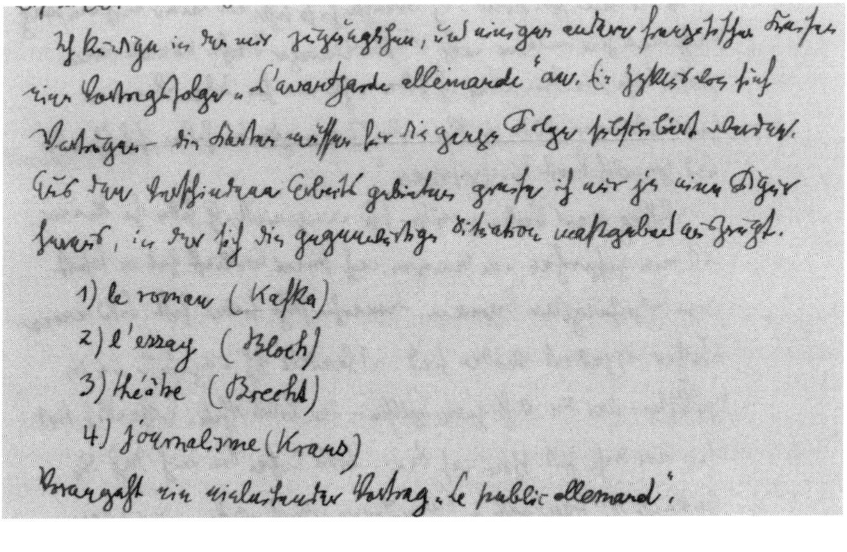

Abb. 3: Benjamin an Brecht, 5. März 1934, Bertolt-Brecht-Archiv 478/16.

[14] Bertolt Brecht: *Journal* 9.8.1941. BFA 27. S. 12.

Die Initialzündung zur umfassenden Auseinandersetzung mit Brechts Werk ging vom ersten Heft der *Versuche* aus, das im April 1930 vorlag. Benjamin ist der erste mit theoretischem Anspruch arbeitende Kritiker Brechts gewesen. Der Einfluß seiner Lesarten ist bis heute zu erkennen; man denke nur an Heiner Müllers Blick auf Brecht.

Benjamin begriff Brechts Werk als Weg aus einer Sackgasse, die er 1932 als "sture Gegenüberstellung von Schriftstellerei und Dichtung" beschrieb. Keine große Dichtung lasse sich ohne das Moment des Technischen verstehen, das ein Schriftstellerisches sei.[15] Die alte Polarität, die den "echten" Dichter und seine ingeniösen, nicht rational erfaßbaren Schöpfungen vom Schriftsteller oder Literaten und seinen profanen, unkünstlerischen Mitteilungen absetzte, erschien Benjamin fragwürdig. Auch Brecht wendete sich im Zusammenhang mit dem Zeitschriftenprojekt gegen die "Abtrennung der sogenannten 'schönen Literatur' und ihre gesonderte Behandlung als 'eigentliche Literatur' ", sie habe "die Literaturgeschichte zu einem Tummelplatz der Geschmäcker gemacht".[16]

Unter den völlig veränderten Bedingungen des Exils blieb die exemplarische Bedeutung Brechts für Benjamin konstant. Das zeigte sich in dem Plan von Vorträgen, die Benjamin im April 1934 bei dem Pariser Arzt Jean Dalsace halten wollte. Er unterrichtete Brecht am 5. März 1934:

> Ich kündige in den mir zugänglichen, und einigen andern französischen Kreisen eine Vortragsfolge "L'avantgarde allemande" an. Ein Zyklus von fünf Vorträgen – die Karten müssen für die ganze Folge subscribiert werden. Aus den verschiednen Arbeitsgebieten greife ich nur je eine Figur heraus, in der sich die gegenwärtige Situation maßgebend ausprägt.
>
> 1) le roman (Kafka)
> 2) l'essay (Bloch)
> 3) théâtre (Brecht)
> 4) journalisme (Kraus)
>
> Vorangeht ein einleitender Vortrag "Le public allemand" (WBGB IV. S. 362).

Benjamin schuf sich mit bemerkenswerter Urteilssicherheit für seine Vortragszwecke eine Gruppe, die tatsächlich nicht existierte. Detlev Schöttker rekonstruiert, da nur Stichworte überliefert sind, den Zusammenhang als einen Beitrag zu einer "Theorie des literarischen Konstruktivismus". Benjamins Äußerungen zu Kraus, Kafka, Bloch und Brecht treffen sich in einem Interesse an Konstruktionen und künstlerischen Techniken, an Verknappungen des Stils und Reduktionen auf das Wesentliche, wie sie in dem Begriff "Erfahrungsarmut" aus dem Kraus-Aufsatz gebündelt sind.

---

[15] Walter Benjamin: *Jemand meint.* WBGS. S. 360–363. Hier S. 362.
[16] Bertolt Brecht: *Über neue Kritik.* BFA 21. S. 402–404. Hier S. 402.

Außer im Falle Brechts können die Beziehungen zwischen den Figuren und ihren Arbeitsgebieten wohl nur mit einer gehörigen Portion Verfremdung erklärt werden: Kafka – Roman/Bloch – Essay/Kraus – Journalismus, das sind alles eher Verhältnisse, die gegen den Strich gesetzt sind. Methodisch ist das eine Fortsetzung des Zeitschriftenprojekts *Krise und Kritik*: Der Schlüssel zu Benjamins Lesart ist der Begriff *Kritik*; die von ihm aufgenommenen Vertreter der Avantgarde begegneten ihren Gattungen kritisch – sie wälzten sie um.

Abb. 4: Jean-Baptiste Siméon Chardin: *Le Château de cartes* / Benjamin an Brecht, etwa 13. Januar 1934, Bertolt-Brecht-Archiv 478/20.

Kartenhäuser und Schach

Kartenhäuser im Exil: Im Januar 1934 schickt Benjamin Brecht die Reproduktion eines Gemäldes aus dem Louvre: *Le Château de Cartes* des französischen Malers Jean-Baptiste Siméon Chardin. Das Bild ist Mitte des 18. Jahrhunderts entstanden. "Lieber Brecht", begann er, "hier schicke ich Ihnen eine Bauvorlage, um Ihr Training, an dem ich als Meister wohlwollend interessiert bin, zu unterstützen".

Das Gemälde gibt Anlaß, die im Exil gewachsene besondere Nähe zwischen Benjamin und Brecht zu illustrieren. Im Spätherbst 1933 lud Brecht Benjamin zum ersten Mal nach Dänemark ein; auch später verzichteten er, Steffin und Weigel in ihren Briefen selten auf eine Einladung. Unmittelbar nachdem er aus Paris angekommen war, am 22. Dezember 1933, warb Brecht mit den Vorzügen der Insel:

> Es ist hier angenehm. Gar nicht kalt, viel wärmer als in Paris. Sie kämen nach Ansicht Hellis mit 100 Kr (60 Reichsmark, 360 Fr) im Monat aus. Außerdem verschafft die Svendborger Bibliothek *jedes* Buch. – Wir haben Radio, Zeitungen, Spielkarten, bald Ihre Bücher, Öfen, kleine Kaffeehäuser, eine ungemein leichte Sprache, und die Welt geht hier *stiller* unter (BFA 28. S. 395).

Auch Benjamin genoß es, daß das Haus am Sund wie aus den Kämpfen herausgenommen wirkte. Von seinem zweiten Aufenthalt, im Sommer 1936, schrieb er: "Es ist ein sehr wohltätiges Leben und ein so freundliches, daß man sich täglich die Frage vorlegt, wie lange es das in diesem Europa noch geben wird".[17] Und zwei Jahre später, mit deutlicher Korrespondenz zu Brechts Formulierung, die Welt gehe hier stiller unter: "Die Zeitungen kommen hierher mit so großer Verspätung, daß man sich etwas eher das Herz nimmt, sie aufzuschlagen".[18]

Die gemeinsame Zeit in Skovsbostrand in den Sommermonaten 1934, 1936 und 1938 war geprägt von einer "Atmosphäre der Vertrautheit", um eine Beschreibung von Ruth Berlau aufzunehmen.[19] Zu den Tätigkeiten, die Nähe stifteten, gehörten Gespräche, die Arbeit im Garten, Zeitungslektüre und die Information am Rundfunkempfänger, gelegentliche Ausfahrten in das nahe gelegene Svendborg. Mit Leidenschaft verlegte sich die kleine Exilgemeinschaft auf Brett- und Kartenspiele. Man spielte vor allem Schach, aber auch Würfelspiele wie das 1935 lizensierte Monopoly, Tischbillard, Poker und Sechsundsechzig. "eisler

---

[17] Walter Benjamin: Brief an Bryher [?] ca. Mitte August 1936. Entwurf. WBGB V. S. 362.
[18] Walter Benjamin: Brief an Kitty Marx-Steinschneider 20.7.1938. WBGB VI. S. 142.
[19] *Brechts Lai-tu. Erinnerungen und Notate von Ruth Berlau.* Hg. von Hans Bunge. Darmstadt – Neuwied: Luchterhand 1985. S. 105.

ist ungekrönter könig in '66' ",[20] vermeldete Margarete Steffin, und Helene Weigel schrieb Benjamin:

Ich will gerne wissen, wie es Ihnen gesundheitlich geht und ob Sie mit jemanden [*sic*] 66 spielen können, mit allen Ihren unfreundlichen Eigenheiten die ich etwas vermisse. Ich habe angefangen Schach spielen zu lernen und es gäbe also die Möglichkeit für Sie mich tot zu ärgern. Wann haben Sie Lust dazu?[21]

"Sein Verhalten beim Pokerspiel", notierte Benjamin über Brecht: (WBGS II.3. S. 1371). Es wurden Turniere veranstaltet und Preise ausgelobt – einmal ging es um einen "Doppelwhisky" im Schach, wobei Eisler mit 2 : 3 verlor, ein anderes Mal wurde erbittert um ein Stück Lebkuchen gepokert, das Brecht nicht hergeben wollte. Neue Spiele waren gefragt: "Kennen Sie Go?", erkundigte sich Benjamin am 21. Mai 1934, noch vor seiner ersten Reise, bei Brecht, "ein sehr altes chinesisches Brettspiel. Es ist mindestens so interessant wie Schach – wir müßten es in Svendborg einführen. Beim Go werden Steine nie bewegt, nur auf das, anfänglich leere, Brett gesetzt" (WBGB IV. S. 427).

Der Langeweile vorzubeugen, regte Brecht nach einem Schachspiel im Juli 1934 die Entwicklung eines neuen Spiels an; Benjamin hat den Vorschlag protokolliert:

Also, wenn der Korsch kommt, dann müßten wir mit ihm ja ein neues Spiel ausarbeiten. Ein Spiel, wo sich die Stellungen nicht immer gleich bleiben; wo die Funktion der Figuren sich ändert, wenn sie eine Weile auf ein und derselben Stelle gestanden haben: sie werden dann entweder wirksamer oder auch schwächer. So entwickelt sich das ja nicht; das bleibt sich zu lange gleich (WBGS IV. S. 526).

Besonders das Schachspiel wurde zum Inbegriff für die ruhige und vertraute Kommunikation in Skovsbostrand, es sollte Benjamin motivieren, eine "Nordlandfahrt" anzutreten: "Das Schachbrett liegt verwaist, alle halben Stunden geht ein Zittern der Erinnerung durch es: da wurde immer von Ihnen gezogen". In den Spielen reflektierte sich Benjamins Stimmung, die ihrerseits vom Fortgang der Arbeit abhängig war: "Ein oder zwei Partien Schach, die etwas Abwechslung in das Leben bringen sollten, nehmen ihrerseits die Farbe des grauen Sundes und der Gleichförmigkeit an: denn ich gewinne sie nur sehr selten".[22] Als die Familie

---

[20] Margarete Steffin: Brief an Walter Benjamin 20.7.1937. In: Margarete Steffin: *Briefe an berühmte Männer. Walter Benjamin, Bertolt Brecht, Arnold Zweig.* Hg., mit einem Vorwort und mit Anmerkungen versehen von Stefan Hauck. Hamburg: Europäische Verlagsanstalt 1999. S. 247.
[21] Helene Weigel: Brief an Walter Benjamin 20.1.1935. In: *"Wir sind zu berühmt, um überall hinzugehen". Helene Weigel. Briefwechsel 1935–1971.* Hg. von Stefan Mahlke. Berlin: Theater der Zeit/Literaturforum im Brecht-Haus Berlin 2000. S. 12.
[22] Walter Benjamin: Brief an Gretel Adorno 20.7.1938. WBGB VI. S. 139.

aus Dänemark geflohen war, bedauerte Benjamin den Verlust in einem Brief vom 18. April 1939 an Margarete Steffin nach Skovbostrand: "Die Schachpartien im Garten sind nun auch dahin" (WBGB VI. S. 267).

Tatsächlich ist das Schachspiel nicht nur Teil, sondern auch Modell der Kommunikation oder Konstellation: Schachfiguren werden gesetzt und bewegt, das heißt es gibt eine Gesetzlichkeit (Feld, Figuren mit definierten Möglichkeiten,

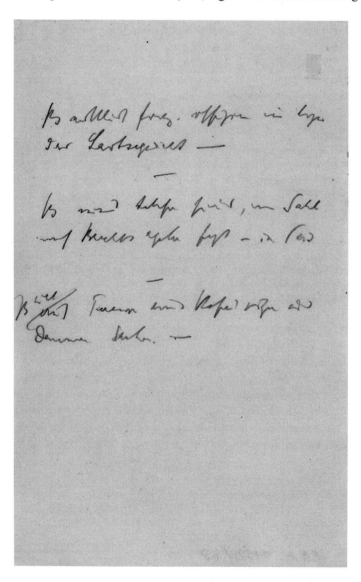

Abb. 5: Notiz Brechts, New York, 1945, Bertolt-Brecht-Archiv 1157/68.

Regeln) und Variabilität (jedes Spiel ist anders). Gelassenheit und Geistesgegenwart sind die Quellen für eine wirkungsvolle Strategie. Die spielerische Gegnerschaft kann sich ohne den Partner nicht entfalten. Konkurrenz fordert den Vergleich heraus. Dem Besiegten bleibt die Chance zu einem neuen Spiel. Nähe und Distanz, Einvernehmen und Unabhängigkeit korrespondieren in fruchtbarem Wechsel. Es ist kein Zufall, daß die erste von Benjamins Thesen "Über den Begriff der Geschichte" das Schachspiel modellhaft auf eine philosophische Konstellation übertragen hat.

Talisman Laotsegedicht

Das letzte hier vorzuführende Bruchstück ist eine Notiz Brechts nach einem Gespräch mit Hans Sahl, 1945 in New York:

> B erklärt franz. offizieren im lager das Laotsegedicht –
> B nimmt telefon heraus, wenn Sahl nach Brechts ergehen fragt – in Paris
> B will auf Terrasse eines Kafés sitzen und Daumen drehen. – [23]

Daß Brecht mit dem Initial B keinen anderen als Benjamin meinen kann, ergibt sich daraus, daß der auf die Caféterrasse bezogene Wunsch als Ausspruch Benjamins in dem Roman *Die Wenigen und die Vielen* und in einem Tagebuch von Hans Sahl überliefert ist. In der Fassung des Tagebuchs sagte Benjamin: "Wenn ich hier lebend herauskommen sollte, will ich nichts anderes mehr verlangen, als auf einer Caféterrasse sitzen – in der Sonne – und die Daumen drehen!".[24]

Das "Laotsegedicht" ist Brechts "Legende von der Entstehung des Buches Taoteking auf dem Weg des Laotse in die Emigration", der Benjamin einen seiner "Kommentare zu Gedichten von Brecht" gewidmet hat. Dieser Kommentar hat Hoffnung und Freundlichkeit zu seiner Sache gemacht. Er behandelt das "Minimalprogramm der Humanität", es begegne im Gedicht wieder in dem Satz "Du verstehst, das Harte unterliegt". Das Gedicht, formulierte Benjamin, "ist zu einer Zeit geschrieben, wo dieser Satz den Menschen als eine Verheißung ans Ohr schlägt, die keiner messianischen etwas nachgibt".[25]

Benjamins Kommentar übte – wie der Verfasser es sich wünschte – eine unmittelbare Wirkung aus; der Ausgangspunkt der Wirkung waren verblüffenderweise französische Internierungslager. Gedicht und Kommentar waren am 23. April 1939 in der *Schweizer Zeitung am Sonntag* erschienen. Der Publikationsort ist brisant: Die *Schweizer Zeitung am Sonntag* verfolgte eine unverblümt antifaschistische, gegen die Appeasementpolitik gerichtete Linie und

[23] BBA 1157/68.
[24] Hans Sahl: *Tagebuch* (Deutsches Literaturarchiv Marbach a. N.).
[25] Walter Benjamin: *Zu der "Legende von der Entstehung des Buches Taoteking auf dem Weg des Laotse in die Emigration".* WBGS II.2. S. 568–572. Hier S. 572.

rief von neutralem Boden aus zum bewaffneten Widerstand auf. Der Schweizer Theologe und Barth-Schüler Fritz Lieb, der den Druck vermittelt hatte, veröffentlichte in der gleichen Nummer einen Artikel unter der Überschrift "Warum wir schießen müssen". Das Konzept einer präventiven Volksbewaffnung fand Benjamins ausdrückliche Zustimmung.

Die Nummer der Zeitung, die Gedicht und Kommentar enthielt, hatte Benjamin voller Ungeduld erwartet. Nun trug er selbst zu ihrer Verbreitung bei; er bat Lieb am 3. Mai 1939 um Belegexemplare, mit konspirativem Unterton: "Ein Hauptzweck so einer Publikation liegt darin, daß man sie den richtigen Leuten in die Hände spielen kann; das habe ich vor" (WBGB VI. S. 275).

Heinrich Blücher, Hannah Arendts Mann, setzte bei Beginn der Internierungen im September 1939 Brechts Gedicht "wie einen Talisman mit magischen Kräften" ein: "Diejenigen seiner Mitinsassen, die es lasen *und* verstanden, waren als potentielle Freunde erkannt".[26] Und Arendt erinnerte sich: "Wie ein Lauffeuer verbreitete sich das Gedicht in den Lagern, wurde von Mund zu Mund gereicht wie eine frohe Botschaft".[27]

Benjamin hatte ähnliche Erfahrungen wie Blücher. Als er im Herbst 1939 im Lager Nevers war, brachte er Brechts Gedicht und seinen Kommentar unter die Internierten und – wie sich aus Brechts Notiz ergibt – ihre Bewacher. Die Lehre vom Sieg des Wassers über den Stein, die Laotse das Exil eingetragen hatte, ermunterte jetzt die Vertriebenen. Brecht wird das Zeugnis von der Vermittlerrolle seines wichtigsten Kommentators zu Lebzeiten als Ermutigung empfunden haben. In einem erst kürzlich aufgetauchten Brief an den Theologen Karl Thieme vom April 1948 spielte er an auf das tragische Ende des Freundes im spanischen Grenzort Portbou. Dabei stellte er eine Nähe zwischen Laotse und Benjamin her, die mehr wiegt als manch ein Nachruf:

Das von Ihnen zitierte Laotsegedicht hat Benjamin, wie ich hörte, in dem französischen Lager, in dem er zuletzt war, mehrere Male aus dem Gedächtnis deklamiert. Er selber fand ja dann keinen Grenzwächter, der ihn auch nur hätte passieren lassen.[28]

[26] Elisabeth Young-Bruehl: *Hannah Arendt. Leben, Werk und Zeit.* Frankfurt am Main: S. Fischer 1986. S. 221.
[27] Hannah Arendt: Bertolt Brecht. In: Arendt: *Walter Benjamin, Bertolt Brecht* (Anm. 9). S. 63–107. Hier S. 102.
[28] Wizisla: *Benjamin und Brecht* (Anm. 1). S. 221 und 114.

Ulrike Zitzlsperger

Bertolt Brecht: Stadtraum und Architektur

It is mainly in the 1920s that Brecht considers the phenomenon of the city in a more abstract manner. After the Second World War his commentaries become considerably more precise, especially as regards the role of architecture as a socio-political challenge. While at this point his thoughts on Berlin are more focused, the reflections of his contemporaries and of later generations on his role in the city continue to provide a subjective topography of Brecht's timeless literary presence. Both this reception and his own commentaries mirror the contradiction between urban visions of the metropolis and social realities.

Das Thema "Bertolt Brecht und die Metropole" erlaubt die Entzifferung der Stadt als Text auf unterschiedlichen Ebenen: Dazu gehören die Ausführungen Brechts zu Städten im allgemeinen und Berlin im besonderen, aber auch die Wahrnehmung Brechts im Stadtraum, die in den zwanziger Jahren einsetzt und seit dem Fall der Mauer eine Renaissance erlebt.

Zitate der Brechtschen Stadt- und Berlinbilder kommentieren Innen- und Außenräume und evozieren Besonderheiten Berlins zu unterschiedlichen Zeiten. Nur Theodor Fontane hat in der wiedervereinigten Stadt eine Brecht vergleichbare Rolle inne: beide dienen der Spurensuche, die, Wohn- und Wirkungsorte mit "grundsätzlichen" Kommentaren zum Großstadtleben und bestimmten Zeiten verknüpfend, das "Neue Berlin" nachvollziehbar zu machen sucht. Das erfolgt mittels Themenwanderungen – im Brechtjahr 1998 unter anderem "Bertolt Brecht: Finale seines Lebens"; "Bertolt Brecht und das Berliner Theater" und "Buckow und der Rückzug in den stillen Winkel" –, autorenbezogener Nachforschungen in Berlin gewidmeten Publikationen oder in der literarischen Verarbeitung. Doch während "Fontanopolis" im Detail nicht zuletzt infolge der Lücken im Stadtbild recht genau nachvollziehbar wird, ist Brechts topographische Präsenz verallgemeinerbarer und trägt zu seinem Anspruch bei, daß Städte, wie es das Moskau der dreißiger Jahre vorführte, durch die verschiedensten Schriftzeichen literarisiert werden können und auf diese Weise für die Bewohner ansprechender werden.

In Martin Jankowskis *Seifenblasenmaschine, Berliner Szenen* wird, beispielsweise, Brechts Zeitlosigkeit aktualisiert. Der Protagonist einer der Kurzgeschichten ist Bertolt:

> Er lief in den Straßenschluchten von New York umher und fühlte sich. Er spürte, daß etwas im Gange war. Etwas das man nicht sehen oder umfassen konnte, das aber dennoch da war. Es war sehr sympathisch und sehr urban. Man hätte einen Rap daraus machen können. Aber weiße Männer können nicht rappen, ohne daß es gymnasiastenhaft wirkt. Bertolt wußte das. Weiße Männer besitzen eine Form von Härte,

142

die anders ist. Deshalb blieb Bertolt lakonisch. Er rappte niemals. Er schrieb nur kurze, harte Sätze nach den Regeln von Sparta. Seine Taktart ist der heilige Schuß.[1]

Jankowskis Bertolt "wohnt gleich um die Ecke vom Dorotheenstädtischen", eine Gegend, die er aus nostalgischen Gründen und, ihrer Einfachheit und Heiterkeit wegen schätzt. "Doch es gibt auch das Rauhe, die Großstadt, den Verkehr, das Geld und die Nutten. Und es gibt Bertolt".[2] Bertolt, der Handybesitzer haßt und Katzen liebt, heißt in Wirklichkeit Christian – aber das, so heißt es, spiele eigentlich keine Rolle. Der Untertitel von *Seifenblasenmaschine*, "Berliner Szenen", hebt das Doppelbödige hervor: Brecht, der die Künstlerszene der zwanziger Jahre so nachhaltig bestimmte, ist durchaus noch szenetauglich, gleichzeitig ist er wie viele der Typen, die Jankowski stilisiert, ein Großstadtphänomen neben anderen.

Eine ähnliche Relativierung nimmt Michael Rutschky in *Berlin. Die Stadt als Roman* vor. Die fotografierte Stadt wird hier genauer hinterfragt – so auch das BB, das auf dem "zentrale[n] Brechtgelände der Hauptstadt" an einer Hauswand aufgenommen wurde.[3] BB steht nicht für die Verehrung Brechts seitens der Unbekannten im Stadtraum, sondern es handelt sich um eine Anweisung an die Heizstofflieferanten, "daß hier Briketts ebenso wie Braunkohle einzukellern sind".[4] Doch der Betrachter hat sich erst einmal gern irreführen lassen; das Umfeld des Dorotheenstädtischen Friedhofs und des Berliner Ensembles provozieren Zusammenhänge, die die Stadt literarisch verankern und die Bedeutung Brechts als großstädtisch-repräsentativen Typus kenntlich machen.[5] Ein solches "Sich-Einschreiben" in die Stadt wird möglich,

[1] Martin Jankowski: *Bertolt*. In: Martin Jankowski: *Seifenblasenmaschine. Berliner Szenen*. Berlin: Schwartzkopff Buchwerke 2005. S. 190–195. Hier S. 191.
[2] Ebd. S. 195.
[3] Michael Rutschky: *Berlin. Die Stadt als Roman*. München: Quadriga 2001. S. 161.
[4] Ebd. S. 161–162.
[5] Eine weitere solche Facette des Wirkens Brechts machte die Finissage der Ausstellung *Foto im Plakat. Fotografie des Berliner Ensembles* in der Inselgalerie (1.–17. September 2005) deutlich: Der Schauspieler und Regisseur Hans-Joachim Frank verband den Vortrag der Lyrik Brechts mit einer Hommage an den kurz zuvor verstorbenen Schauspieler Ekkehard Schall, der das Berliner Ensemble von 1977 bis 1991 mit geleitet hatte und für seine Darstellung der Brechtschen Antihelden berühmt geworden war. Die Verbindung des Ausstellungsthemas, das einem bestimmten Ort gewidmet ist, mit der Lesung, die den Ort mit einem ihn bestimmenden Autor verknüpft und schließlich der Verweis darauf, daß mit Schall einer der Hüter Brechtscher Theatertradition verloren worden war, ist ein weiterer Mosaikstein in der die Stadt vernetzenden Kontinuität des Zitats Brechts. Ausführlich zu einer solchen vergegenwärtigenden Spurensuche: Nicolas Whybrow: *Streetscenes: Brecht, Benjamin & Berlin*. Bristol: Intellect 2005. Das Bild der zwanziger Jahre mit Brecht als Medium in Bezug zu den neunziger Jahren findet sich beispielsweise auch in Wolf von Eckardt und Sander L. Gilman: *Bertolt Brecht's Berlin. A Scrapbook of the Twenties*. Lincoln (NE): University of Nebraska Press 1993 und Alexandra Ludewig: Zu Dresens *Nachtgestalten*: Die

weil Brechts Bezug zu Berlin von Anfang an vielfältig ist; die sich dabei abzeich-
nende Entwicklung soll im folgenden chronologisch veranschaulicht werden.

In der Korrespondenz zwischen Arnold Zweig und Walter Benjamin heißt
es, Brechts literarische Verarbeitung der Stadterfahrung der zwanziger Jahre
nehme die Erfahrung der Emigration vorweg.[6] Die Stadt ist ein mühsam
erstrittener und dann poetisierter Lebensraum, in dem man sich über Präsenz
Geltung verschafft. Brechts Berlin der zwanziger Jahre ist kaum vom Wissen
um seine Biographie und die jeweiligen Wirkungsorte zu trennen: die
Freundschaften mit Bronnen und Zuckmayer, Begegnungen mit Canetti, die
kritische Zusammenarbeit mit Grosz gehören ebenso dazu wie die Ateliers,
Wohnungen oder Cafés. Brecht ist vor allem auch in der Kulturkritik allgegen-
wärtig: Kurt Tucholsky bescheinigt ihm herausragende Bedeutung; nur die
Songs, das Land Mahagonny, bleiben dem Berliner fremd.[7] In der Kritik an der
Dreigroschenoper verdichtet sich das, weil sie für Tucholsky an der Berliner
Realität vorbeigeht:

> Mir will scheinen, als ob der Lärm um diese Stücke zur Bedeutung der opera operata
> Brechts, der trotz allem eine große Begabung bleibt, in keinem rechten Verhältnis
> steht. Diese Dreigroschen-Philosophie: "Wie man sich bettet, so liegt man", diese
> sorgsam panierte Rohheit, diese messerscharf berechneten Goldgräberflüche… so
> ist das Leben ja gar nicht. […] … auch die Beziehung zu Deutschland 1930 bleibt
> flau. Es ist stilisiertes Bayern.[8]

Der Vergleich mit Bayern steht bei Tucholsky für übersteigerte und konservative
Provinz – ist die Politik nicht dezidiert genug, so bleibt der Ort der Handlung
für Tucholsky Chiffre, ohne Authentizität.

Geht für Tucholsky Brecht am politischen und realen Berliner Thema vorbei,
wird er bei Canetti der Mittelpunkt einer hektischen und auf Spektakel
bedachten Berliner Scheinauthentizität. Das Kapitel "Im Gedränge der Namen,
Berlin 1928" seiner Autobiographie widmet Canetti den Gebrüdern Herzfelde,

---

Berliner Republik als Mahagonny. Brechtsche Impressionen im zeitgenössischen
deutschen Film und Theater. In: *New German Review* 20 (2005). S. 183–205. Zu Brecht
als Stadtführer im zeitgenössischen Berlin einerseits und der historischen Spurensuche
andererseits: Michael Bienert: *Mit Brecht durch Berlin. Ein literarischer Reiseführer.*
Frankfurt am Main Insel Verlag 1998.
[6] Vgl. Erdmut Wizisla: *Benjamin und Brecht. Die Geschichte einer Freundschaft.*
Frankfurt am Main: Suhrkamp 2004. S. 214.
[7] Kurt Tucholsky: *Bert Brechts Hauspostille.* In: Kurt Tucholsky: *Gesammelte Werke.*
Hg. von Mary Gerold-Tucholsky und Fritz J. Raddatz. Reinbek bei Hamburg: Rowohlt
1975. Bd. 6. S. 60–63. Hier S. 63.
[8] Kurt Tucholsky: *Proteste gegen die Dreigroschenoper.* In: Tucholsky: *Gesammelte
Werke* (Anm. 7). Bd. 8. S. 105–106. Hier S. 106.

Grosz, Isaak Babel, Ludwig Hardt und Brecht detaillierte Beschreibungen. Er erinnert an eines seiner Streitgespräche mit Brecht:

> Brecht sagte, er habe das Telefon immer auf dem Tisch und könne nur schreiben, wenn es oft läute. Eine große Weltkarte hänge vor ihm an der Wand, auf die schaue er hin, um nie aus der Welt zu sein. [...] Ich hielt mich über Reklamen auf, von denen Berlin verseucht war. Ihn störten sie nicht, im Gegenteil, Reklame habe ihr Gutes. Er habe ein Gedicht über Steyr-Autos geschrieben und dafür ein Auto bekommen.[9]

In Canettis Beschreibung verkörpert Brecht das sachliche, moderne, unruhige Berlin. *Die Dreigroschenoper*, der "genaueste Ausdruck dieses Berlin", der "gemeinsame Nenner" der Zeit,[10] ist schließlich für Canetti der stilisierte Auslöser für die Rückkehr nach Wien, während sie für Brecht stadtgesellschaftliche Prozesse auf den Punkt bringt.

Brechts Wahrnehmung des Großstadtphänomens Berlin bleibt bis zu seiner erzwungenen Emigration eher allgemein: sei es die rasende Autofahrt durch die nächtliche Stadt in Richtung Grunewald in *Barbara* (BFA19. S. 280–283), sei es, daß er mit Hilfe griffiger Formulierungen im Dickicht der Städte das Wunschbild Metropole ausmacht. Die Stadt ist für Brecht aus Zeit und Raum gelöst, Mythos zwischen Schöpfung und Endzeit, eine Montage metropolitaner Assoziationen. Daneben nimmt er jedoch auch gezielt zur Stadt als sozialen Raum Stellung.

Berlin, das zu erobern sich Brecht nach dem Ersten Weltkrieg aufgemacht hatte, war von grundsätzlichen Veränderungen geprägt, die sich unter anderem im sogenannten "Neuen Bauen" spiegelten; die Stadt wurde nun als technischer Organismus begriffen, und ihre Gestaltung geriet für manche zum bloßen Formproblem. "Berlin hat Tempo, hat Betrieb, noch aber fehlt die Form", stellte beispielsweise der Architekt Walter Curt Behrend fest.[11] Vor allem der Verkehr wurde als Zeichen des Fortschritts angesehen und war, wenn auch nicht unumstritten, in den Planungen für die Stadtmitte zusammen mit den Zweckbauten der Industrie strukturbildendes Element. Solche städtebaulichen Entwicklungen und Ambitionen gingen allerdings an der Tatsache vorbei, daß Berlin in den Nachkriegsjahren akut an Wohnungsmangel litt. Gegen Ende der zwanziger Jahre rückte dann die Utopie, die, wie etwa unter dem sozialdemokratischen Stadtbaurat Martin Wagner, in der Stadtplanung und Architektur das demokratische Gesicht der Republik in Form eines neuen Wohnungsbaus verwirklicht sehen wollte, in den Vordergrund.

Dem an der Realität ungeprüften utopischen Design der Stadt stand Brecht von Anfang an kritisch gegenüber, so in seiner Erzählung *"Nordseekrabben"*

---

[9] Elias Canetti: *Die Fackel im Ohr*. Frankfurt am Main: Fischer (1982). S. 257.
[10] Ebd. S. 286.
[11] Walter Curt Behrend: Berlin wird Weltstadt – Metropole im Herzen Europas. In: *Das Neue Berlin* (1929). H. 5. (1929). S. 98–101. Hier S. 98.

oder Die moderne Bauhaus-Wohnung (BFA 19. S. 267–275), die sich mit den Vorstellungen der Bauhaus-Bewegung und einer auf die Spitze getriebenen Funktionalität – zumal im privaten Wohnraum – auseinandersetzt. Architektur als die Gesellschaft formende Kraft richtet sich hier für Brecht in erster Linie gegen die Befindlichkeit des Einzelnen.

In dem Film *Kuhle Wampe*, an dem Brecht zusammen mit Ernst Ottwald und Hanns Eisler unter der Regie Slatan Dudows mitwirkte, steht den Bauszenarien der Berliner Innenstadt das Wohnungselend der Armen und Arbeitslosen gegenüber.[12] Die Eingangsszenen präsentieren die Stadt als trostloses Industriegebiet. Diese Disposition wird in Form montierter Schlagzeilen, die auf Arbeits- und Obdachlosigkeit im Berlin der Zwischenkriegszeit verweisen, bestätigt; ein Eingriff in die bestehenden Verhältnisse bleibt jedoch auf die kritische Darstellung gesellschaftlicher Zwänge beschränkt. In *Kuhle Wampe* werden die Schrebergärten am Rand der Stadt als Fluchtpunkt für jene gezeigt, die in der Metropole keine Chance mehr haben; die innerstädtischen Utopien werden gegen den Stadtrand und die sich hier entfaltenden gesellschaftspolitischen Träume ausgespielt. Während in Fritz Langs Film *Metropolis* das soziale Gefüge der Gesellschaft als Ober- und Unterwelt einander gegenübergestellt werden, bleibt bei Brecht, Ottwald und Dudow in einer an den realen Umständen orientierten Hierarchie, die das Zentrum dem Stadtrand gegenüberstellt, den Armen die Vorstadt vorbehalten, während dem Kapital die Innenstadt gehört.[13]

Dieses Interesse Brechts an Fragen des Stadtbaus im Kontext sozialer Problemstellungen verstärkte sich weniger als ein Jahrzehnt später unter politischen Vorzeichen angesichts der Zerstörung der Städte im Verlauf des Zweiten Weltkriegs. Am 21. September 1940 notiert Brecht in der Emigration in seinem Journal: "Die *Berliner Illustrirte* ist immer sehr interessant. In der Nr. 38 finde ich auf einander folgenden Seiten das Bild des gebombten London und dann *Deutsche Baumeister*".[14] Brecht montiert die in der *Berliner Illustrirten* ursprünglich nicht zusammenhängenden Bilder nebeneinander; auf das Bild des zerstörten London folgt nun unmittelbar der Entwurf einer nationalsozialistischen Idealstadt, die Brecht um das Foto seines Sohnes ergänzt. Dieses Nebeneinander verschärft den Kontrast zwischen der fabrikmäßig geplanten, geometrischen Stadt und den zerstörten Stadtteilen Londons; beide

---

[12] *Kuhle Wampe oder: Wem gehört die Welt?* (1931). Regie: Slatan Dudow; Drehbuch: Bertolt Brecht und Ernst Ottwald. Dudow hatte sich des Schicksals der Arbeiter schon 1930 in dem Film *Zeitprobleme: Wie der Arbeiter wohnt* angenommen.

[13] Vgl. David L. Pike: "Kaliko-Welt": The *Großstädte* of Lang's *Metropolis* and Brecht's *Dreigroschenoper*. In: *Modern Language Notes* 119 (2004). S. 274–305.

[14] BFA 26. S. 425 und S. 426–427. Vgl. auch den Kommentar auf S. 664. Weitere Beispiele zur Stadt im Krieg finden sich in der *Kriegsfibel*. BFA 12. S. 163, 173 und 259. Brecht interessiert sich für Luftfotografien von Städten, die das Ausmaß der Zerstörung besonders klar machen.

Fotografien zeigen nur die Bausubstanz, keine Menschen. Eine solche Gegenüberstellung entspricht dem Montage-Prinzip John Heartfields, denn erst die Konfrontation der Ausschnitte entfaltet die auf Entlarvung der Zeit gerichtete schockierende Wirkung und weckt die entsprechenden Emotionen. Die Montage spiegelt zudem Brechts Interesse an der fotografierten Stadt. So hatte er schon 1926 den Bildband *Amerika. Bilderbuch eines Architekten* von Erich Mendelsohn unter die besten Bücher des Jahres gereiht und über die technische Qualität hinaus angemerkt, die Bilder vermittelten den täuschenden Eindruck, die großen Städte seien bewohnbar.[15]

Der Text, der das Bild der zerstörten Stadt in der Ausgabe der *Berliner Illustrirten Zeitung* begleitet, stilisiert die Bombardierung – die flächendeckende Zerstörung – seitens der Deutschen als Antwort auf eine vorausgegangene Provokation. Die Ziele in London werden in der deutschen Propaganda auf die Industrie reduziert. Ebenso erschreckend wie die zerstörte Stadt ist aber die stadträumliche Homogenisierung, die die von Brecht dazumontierte Modellstadt der nationalsozialistischen Baumeister der Zukunft vornimmt. Im Vordergrund steht hier der Prozeß der Stadtschöpfung mit einer Planmäßigkeit, die sich für Brecht von der menschlicheren Zufälligkeit der Stadtentwicklung nachteilig unterscheidet. Der dazu gehörende Bildtext der nationalsozialistischen Presse erklärt:

Es ist in der Geschichte selten, daß große Städte nach einheitlichem Willen in wenigen Jahren entstehen. Meist wachsen Siedlungen und Städte aus kleinem Kern in Jahrzehnten oder Jahrhunderten. Heute wachsen vor unseren Augen große Wohnviertel und Arbeiterstädte in kurzer Zeit empor. Die größte Neuanlage wird die Stadt der Hermann-Göring-Werke in Mitteldeutschland sein, die unter Leitung von Regierungsbaumeister Rimpl gebaut wird (BFA 26. S. 664).

Nicht nur die Konzentration auf diese Produktionsstätten ist bemerkenswert, sondern die Unterscheidung zwischen den gewachsenen Städten der Vergangenheit und der technischen Errungenschaft der zukünftigen Planstädte. Die neue Stadt entbehrt als durchkomponierter Wohn- und Wirkungsort der Arbeiter des menschlichen Charakters.

Brechts Montage zeigt nicht nur die Wirklichkeit des Krieges und totalitären Gedankenguts, sondern impliziert eine Dichotomie, die sich durch seine Wahrnehmung der Ballungsräume zieht: Aufstieg und Fall, Schöpfung und Zerstörung der großen Städte, sei es Babylon, Karthago, Mahagonny, London oder Berlin. Das Gebaute ist keine Garantie für Bestand, weil es sich letztlich

---

[15] Brecht verweist auf "eine Fotografie vom Eingang des Broadway in New York (das Tor dieser Zementschlucht, über dem 'Danger' steht)" (Bertolt Brecht: *Das Theater der großen Städte*. BFA. 21. S. 187–188).

immer als Ausdruck der Zeit und der Situation des 20. Jahrhunderts, in dem die Städte komplexer und die Maschinen dominanter werden, erweist.

Die "Stadt der Hermann-Göring-Werke" ist nur *ein* Beispiel für die macht- und prestigeorientierte Baupolitik der Nationalsozialisten. Seit den dreißiger Jahren hatten Hitler und Speer auch die Ersetzung Berlins durch Germania vorangetrieben, ein Plan, der zahlreiche Abrisse im Stadtzentrum erforderlich machte. Die Allgewalt des Staates wird deutlich, wenn man sich an Hitlers megalomane Träume über die Zukunft Germanias erinnert: eine Architektur, die sich an der Einschüchterung und Überwältigung ihres Betrachters orientiert – zum Beispiel die Reichskanzlei und die Plan gebliebene Halle des Volkes –, nicht aber an der Bewohnbarkeit der Stadt.[16]

Das zerbombte London neben dem Titel "Deutsche Baumeister" und die Musterstadt der nationalsozialistischen Moderne als technischer Schöpfungsakt sind gleichermaßen beunruhigend. Brecht ironisiert den Begriff des Baumeisters, doch Bauen ist für ihn immer relativ: Sei es, daß die Zerstörung vorangeht oder zwangsläufig folgt und meist in der Hand der selben Kräfte steht, sei es, daß die eigentliche Ausführung der Arbeit über das Design immer neuer Glanzleistungen vergessen wird, oder aber, daß Kompromisse geschlossen werden müssen, die den Erwartungen nicht entsprechen.[17]

Nach der Kriegserfahrung rückten für Brecht konkrete Schwerpunkte der Stadtgestaltung in den Vordergrund. Unter dem Titel *Brecht und die Architektur. Wovon unsere Architekten Kenntnis nehmen müssen* veranstaltete das Architekturmuseum Schwaben 1998 eine Ausstellung, die Brechts Werk auf die topographischen – insbesondere architektonisch motivierten – Konstanten hin durchleuchtete.[18] Die Ausstellung wurde in drei Bereiche untergliedert: das Haus als Raum persönlicher Inszenierung zwischen Verblüffung der Besucher, reduzierter Wohnform und Verlustraum im Exil; die "heroische Landschaft"[19] der Stadt als Ort gesellschaftlicher Verdichtung; und schließlich der Staat, der an die Architektur politisch motivierte Fragen richtet. Nach dem Zweiten

---

[16] Vgl. Alan Balfour: *Berlin. The Politics of Order 1737–1989*. New York: Rizzoli 1989. Hier S. 69–106: "Hitler".

[17] Vgl. z.B. Bertolt Brecht: Fragen eines lesenden Arbeiters. BFA 18. S. 409.

[18] Architekturmuseum Schwaben: *Brecht und die Architektur. Wovon unsere Architekten Kenntnis nehmen müssen*. 2. Juli 1998 – 30. August 1998. Unter dem gleichen Titel erschien die Publikation (Heft 7), hg. vom Architekturmuseum Schwaben. Ausstellung und Katalog berücksichtigen den Einfluß der Augsburger Herkunft und die Auseinandersetzungen über Architektur mit Max Frisch 1948. Zu Brecht und Architektur vgl. auch Erdmut Wizisla: Berliner Thema: Brecht und Frisch: Theater und Architektur. In: *Brecht 100<=>2000*. Ed. by Marc Silberman et als. Madison (WI): University of Wisconsin Press 1999. S. 39 (The Brecht Yearbook 24). Zum Disput über die Architektur zwischen Frisch und Brecht, besonders S. 28–30. Brecht bemängelt angesichts der Schweizer Wohnungen für Arbeiter deren geringe Größe; die Begegnung mit Frisch geriet zur Enttäuschung.

[19] Bertolt Brecht: *[Autobiographische Notizen]* Ende Juli 1925. BFA 26. S. 282.

Weltkrieg stehen die Gestaltung des privaten wie des staatlich gelenkten Raumes, die beide neu entworfen werden müssen, im Vordergrund. Der unmittelbare Bedarf an Wohnraum geht mit den Ansprüchen gerade der Regierung der Deutschen Demokratischen Republik an ein fortschrittlicheres Deutschland einher und erlaubte Brecht die greifbare Praxis des Neubaus unter zu Beginn scheinbar idealen Bedingungen.

Brecht war erst einige Jahre nach dem Krieg in die Wahlheimat zurückgekommen und hatte sich für Ost-Berlin entschieden. Hatte ihn in "Vom armen B.B." die Mutter aus den schwarzen Wäldern in die Städte getragen, ist die Stadt, der er sich zu Fuß von Lichterfelde nähert, nun ein Ruinenfeld. Bestätigt hat sich die 8. Strophe des Gedichts: "Von diesen Städten wird bleiben: der durch sie hindurchging, der Wind!" (BFA 11. S. 120). Die Großstadtlyrik der zwanziger Jahre, insbesondere *Aus dem Lesebuch für Städtebewohner*, ist von der Wirklichkeit eingeholt worden: Die Zeit der Riesenstädte ist vorbei, statt des Hurrikans, der Mahagonny bedrohte, statt des Bankrotts, der den "Ruhm der Riesenstadt New York"[20] negierte und des Kommerzes, den Brecht in den Hollywood-Elegien als unterminierende Kraft beschreibt, hat sich in Berlin die menschliche Bedrohung in Form der Politik und der ihr zur Verfügung stehenden Technik als die tatsächliche Herausforderung erwiesen.

In einem Journaleintrag vom Oktober 1948 wird die Zerstörung Berlins mit konkreten Namen verbunden, während sich die Ruinenstadt selbst angesichts des sie umgebenden vieldeutigen Dunkels wieder der Natur annähert; die Reste der Asphaltstadt eignen sich nicht für metropolitane Assoziationen:

> Berlin, eine Radierung Churchills nach einer Idee Hitlers.
> Berlin, der Schutthaufen bei Potsdam.
> Über den völlig verstummten Ruinenstraßen dröhnen in den Nächten
> die Lastaeroplane der Luftbrücke.
> Das Licht ist so schwach, daß der Gestirnhimmel wieder von der Straße aus
> sichtbar geworden ist.[21]

Statt des sozialen Spektakels Metropole, der Montage des großstädtischen Pandämoniums, das Brecht in den 20er Jahren entfaltet hatte, dominiert nun die Einbettung Berlins in die Zeitgeschichte. Der veränderte Blickwinkel spiegelt auch Brechts veränderte Lebenssituation: Die Inszenierung menschlichen Scheiterns, das in der Zerstörung Berlins und anderer Städte im Zweiten Weltkrieg seine Bestätigung fand, wird für den Heimkehrer Brecht von der Auseinandersetzung mit dem Wiederaufbau abgelöst. Die Kenntnisnahme der Architektur, die er nun einfordert, steht für den Neuanfang schlechthin. Das Nachkriegsberlin, das weitaus schlimmer verwüstet ist als London im Jahre

---

[20] Bertolt Brecht: *Verschollener Ruhm der Riesenstadt New York*. BFA 11. S. 243–250.
[21] Bertolt Brecht: *Journal* 27.10.1948. BFA 27. S. 281–282.

1940 und für Beobachter allenfalls den Vergleich mit Karthago und Babylon, Wüsten und Mondlandschaften nahelegt, nimmt Brecht wie in den zwanziger Jahren auch schreibend wahr. Die widersprüchliche Atmosphäre eines sozialistischen Neuanfangs spiegelt sich in seiner persönlichen Arbeitssituation ebenso wie in seinen Kommentaren zu den Aufgaben der Architektur, die jetzt erfüllt werden können.

Die erste Phase der Baupolitik der DDR wird vom Architekturkritiker Bruno Flierl wie folgt beschrieben:

> In den 50er Jahren war mit der Orientierung auf den Wiederaufbau und eine Architektur der nationalen Tradition – nicht zuletzt gerade wegen des im Krieg eingetretenen Verlustes an historischer Bausubstanz – bei allem Streben nach selbstbewußter Setzung des Neuen, die Sorge um die Stadt noch lebendig.[22]

Das Muster- und Vorzeigeprojekt *Stalinallee* (heute: Karl Marx-Allee), das unter solchen Gesichtspunkten und nach dem Vorbild der Sowjetunion entstand, ist noch heute eine der wenigen großstädtischen Achsen Berlins und wurde von einem Kollektiv entworfen und gebaut. Als Beispiel des real existierenden Sozialismus ist sie ein Unikum und kennzeichnet die Gründerphase des Staates. In den von der Regierung konzipierten und auch für die Stalinallee gültigen *16 Grundsätzen* hieß es 1950 unter anderem optimistisch, daß die Stadt "wirtschaftlichste und kulturreichste Siedlungsform für das Gemeinschaftsleben der Menschen" und "Ausdruck des politischen Lebens und nationalen Bewußtseins des Volkes" sei; Ziel des Städtebaus sei die "harmonische Befriedigung des menschlichen Anspruchs auf Arbeit, Wohnung, Kultur und Erholung".[23] Ein Mitarbeiter des Planungskollektivs der Stalinallee, die im Zuge dieser Aufbruchstimmung entworfen wurde, war Hermann Henselmann (1905–1995), einer der wenigen bekannten Architekten der DDR. Flierl beschreibt Henselmanns Anspruch wie folgt:

> Selbst fasziniert vom Aufbau einer sozialistischen Gesellschaft, an die er als sozial engagierter Architekt glaubte, wollte er – gerade nach den sinnlosen Zerstörungen des Krieges – mit Architektur als baulich-räumlicher Form des Lebens faszinierende Bilder für den Aufbruch in eine neue, dem Frieden zugewandte gesellschaftliche Zukunft schaffen.[24]

---

[22] Bruno Flierl: Blindes Fortschrittsdenken und böses Erwachen. In: *Gebaute DDR. Über Stadtplaner, Architekten und die Macht. Kritische Reflexionen 1990–97*. Berlin: Verlag für Bauwesen. 1998. S. 9–12. Hier S. 9.
[23] Bruno Flierl: Hermann Henselmann – Bauen in Bildern und Worten. In: *Gebaute DDR*. (Anm. 22) S. 172–207. Hier S. 174.
[24] Ebd. Zu Henselmanns Leitlinien vgl. Hermann Henselmann: *Vom Himmel an das Reißbrett ziehen: Baukünstler im Sozialismus. Ausgewählte Aufsätze 1936–1981*. Hg. von Marie-Jose Seipelt und Jürgen Eckhardt. Berlin (West): Verlag der Beeken 1982.

Henselmann tat sich mit dem staatlichen Diktat, dem funktionalistischen Modernismus abzusagen und stattdessen traditionalistische Bauformen zu wählen, schwer. An diesem Punkt kommt Brecht ins Spiel, mit dem ihn die gemeinsame Prägung durch die kulturelle Szene der zwanziger Jahre und der Glaube an die Verknüpfung des kulturellen Auftrags mit dem gesellschaftlichen Engagement verband. In einer Reihe von Diskussionen überzeugte Brecht Henselmann von der Notwendigkeit der Rückkehr zu traditionellen Bauformen und bestimmte auf diese Weise langfristig dessen Bauphilosophie. Der Architekt zitierte Brecht noch 1992 in der Ankündigung eines Buches mit dem Untertitel *Lob denen, die den undurchführbaren Plan vergessen* und erneut in einer Publikation, die auf Brechts uneingelöste Grabinschrift zurückgeht: "Ich habe Vorschläge gemacht". Henselmann verstand Brecht als eines von "drei Ichs", die ihn – neben dem Architekten Le Corbusier und dem Physiker Hans-Jürgen Treder – geprägt hatten: Brecht habe ihm den Marxismus vermittelt, aber auch Einsicht in die Notwendigkeit der Berücksichtigung der wahren Bedürfnisse der Bevölkerung. Ein Brecht-Zitat ziert folgerichtig das Hochhaus an der Weberwiese in Berlin: "Friede in unserem Land, Friede in unserer Stadt. Daß sie den gut behause, der sie gebauet hat". Tatsächlich lag eine Auswahl von Entwürfen solcher Zitate vor: das Behagen der Bewohner steht immer im Vordergrund.[25] Dieses Zitat wird allerdings durch eine der *Geschichten vom Herrn Keuner*, die ebenfalls um 1953 entstanden ist, relativiert. Hier hinterfragt Keuner die Permanenz des Bauens: Verzierungen, die auf klein-bürgerliche Kunstauffassungen zurückgingen, könnten mit der Spitzhacke entfernt

---

[25]Brecht war sich des Werts seiner Zitate bewußt. Pragmatisch stellte er Gegenforderungen, die nicht nur die schwierige Alltagssituation in den fünfziger Jahren unterstreichen, sondern Sinn und Unsinn der Architektur und des Denkmalschutzes angriffen. So schreibt er an Henselmann am 15. Dezember 1953, wenige Monate nach der Einweihung der durch den Aufstand der Arbeiter in die Schlagzeilen geratenen Stalinallee (BFA 30. S. 225):

Nun könnt ihr ja nicht verhindern, daß Spatzen oder Leute auf Denkmäler scheißen. Aber die Klosettlosigkeit braucht in denkwürdigen Gebäuden doch nicht geschützt zu werden. Kurz, als Gegenleistung für gewisse Verse über besseres Leben, die Du gele-gentlich in Deine Häuser einmeißelst, erbitte ich ein WC in Schumannstrasse 14b.

herzlich
Dein Brecht.

Vgl. Bertolt Brecht: *Inschriften für das Hochhaus an der Weberwiese*. BFA 23. S. 202–203. Zur Literarisierung des Straßenbildes vgl. *Bertolt Brecht. 22 Versuche, eine Arbeit zu beschreiben* (Ausstellungskatalog). Zusammengestellt und kommentiert von Erdmut Wizisla. Berlin: Akademie der Künste 1998. Hier S. 113–122: Was sind schon Städte, gebaut ohne Weisheit des Volkes.

werden, Bauten seien angesichts der "gewaltigen Entwicklung der Zerstörungs-
mittel" nichts als "Versuche, wenig verbindliche Vorschläge, Anschauungs-
material für Diskussionen der Bevölkerung". Bestand hat hier nur die "schnelle
Entwicklung", sprich: Änderung von Einstellungen der Menschen.[26]
Während die nach menschlichen Ansprüchen durchdachte Stadt im Prinzip
wünschenswert ist, warnte Brecht frühzeitig vor "scheußlichen Plänen", wie er
sie dann vor allem während des Krieges in Deutschland beobachtete. Die
Gestaltung der Städte muß im Einklang mit den dort lebenden Menschen stehen.[27] Das Vorbild der Maschine erweist sich als unzureichend, denn, so die
unzufriedenen Arbeiter: "Wir haben einen Abscheu vor dem nur Nützlichen".[28]
1952 formulierte Brecht elf Punkte unter dem Titel *Wovon unsere Architekten
Kenntnis nehmen müssen* (BFA 23. S. 203–204). Hier werden die Kritik am
Bauhaus seit den zwanziger Jahren, das bestimmte Aspekte der Funktionalität
auf die Spitze getrieben hatte, die Diskussionen mit Henselmann und die
Ansprüche der neuen Regierung, die Brecht weitgehend unterstützte, miteinan-
der verbunden. Unter dem zweiten Punkt stellt Brecht im Sinne der Regierung
der DDR fest, "daß [die neue führende Klasse] [...] bauen *muß* und daher den
Architekten nicht allzuviel Zeit für die Umstellung lassen kann". Die neue
Zeit, so der dritte Punkt, mache auch eine neue Architektur erforderlich, die sich
als ideologische Ausdrucksform unter vielen erweise, denn "das letzte Wort der
bürgerlichen Architektur [könne] nicht das letzte Wort der proletarischen sein".
Brecht unterstützt den Bau von Wohnpalästen im Gegensatz zu Einfamilien-
häusern und vergleicht die Notwendigkeit mit der Priorität der Schwerindustrie
als Grundlage gegenüber der untergeordneten Gebrauchsmittelindustrie. Die
Vorbilder in der Sowjetunion und Polen schließlich seien auf ihr sozialistisches
Element hin zu betrachten, wobei es aber auf Dauer möglich sei, "in Deutschland
die deutsche Tradition der großartigsten Epochen zu benutzen".
Das kriegszerstörte Berlin wird zum Schaffensraum, zu der "Küche", auf
die Brecht in einer seiner *Geschichten vom Herrn Keuner* im Vergleich zu
Augsburg, das ihn nur zu Tisch gebeten hatte, anspielt.[29] Brechts "Baumeister"
verfügen nun über die Möglichkeit, politische Vorstellungen in Form zu gießen –
womit die Anforderungen für die Architekten der DDR angesichts der
Erfahrungen der vorangegangenen Jahre umso präziser werden.

Brechts mittelbarer Zugriff auf das Thema Architektur, sei es über seine in
Augsburg vorgeprägten Beiträge in den zwanziger Jahren oder beispielsweise

[26] Bertolt Brecht: *Architektur*. BFA 18. S. 42.
[27] Bertolt Brecht: *Ihr müsst euer Leben bauen*. BFA 18. S. 96.
[28] Bertolt Brecht: *Was ist schön*. BFA 18. S. 147–148. Hier S. 148.
[29] Bertolt Brecht: *Zwei Städte*. BFA 18. S. 27.

sein Einfluß auf Henselmann in den fünfziger Jahren, ist kontinuierlich. Die entscheidende Veränderung in diesen drei Jahrzehnten sind die politischen Vorgaben und Möglichkeiten. Die von der Regierung der DDR in der Aufbauphase des Staates geplanten Wohnpaläste in der Stadtmitte sind für Brecht – in Erinnerung an die Kritik in *Kuhle Wampe* – zwangsläufig eine vielversprechende Umkehrung der Verhältnisse und zu Beginn die Annäherung an ein gesellschaftspolitisches Ideal. Eine Stadt bauen verlangt zu allen Zeiten vor allem nach menschlichem Maß: Dieses von Brecht angemahnte Maß hatte er unter anderem in seinem Journaleintrag des Jahres 1941 mit dem montierten Bild seines Sohnes angesichts der nationalsozialistischen Planstadt in Erinnerung gebracht.

Die Stadt als Lebensraum im Sinne Brechts ist von konkreten Vorstellungen geprägt, während die Metropole als Wahrnehmungsraum, die bei der Vergegenwärtigung Brechts vordergründig ist, den sinnfälligen Gegensatz der mythischen Metropolis als Erfüllungsraum von Wünschen einerseits und der Konzentration von Ängsten andererseits wiederholt.

Andrew Webber

"Unbewohnbar und doch unverlaßbar": Brecht in and through Berlin

This essay considers Brecht's relationship to, and representations of, Berlin. Drawing on a range of examples from across his works, it revises the assumption that Berlin is merely one city amongst many for Brecht, suggesting that it also has a more specific and focal role among his more or less abstracted catalogue of "Städte". More detailed cases of Berlin settings are taken from four of his works, covering a wide scope in both historic and generic terms: the poem "Vom armen B. B." from his Hauspostille *collection; the texts he wrote for Weill's* Berliner Requiem; *the* Vorspiel *to his adaptation of Sophocles'* Antigone; *and the film for which he wrote the screenplay,* Kuhle Wampe. *It is argued that these Berlin settings are given an allegorical form, following the terms developed by Walter Benjamin. On the one hand, this enables a way of speaking otherwise of and through the city, achieving forms of ideological critique through engagement with its architectures and topographies. But the allegorical function is also attached to the melancholic figures of the ruin and the corpse, which are as haunting for the constructive-destructive character of Brecht's project as they are for Benjamin's.*

> *Lücke, irgendetwas dazwischen, dann:*
> *Auch du, vielstädtiges Berlin*
> *Unter und über dem Asphalt geschäftig*[1]

The quotation in the title comes from the 1934 poem "Untergang der Städte Sodom und Gomorra". It appeals to one of the discursive commonplaces of Berlin in the Weimar period: the fleshpot city as latter-day Sodom: "unbewohnbar / Und doch unverlaßbar, ganz wie London / Und Berlin war Sodom und Gomorra" (BFA 14. P. 247). The adversative couple "unbewohnbar und doch unverlaßbar" are thus put in series with two other couples, the one – "Sodom und Gomorra" – an archetypal urban collocation, the other – "London und Berlin" – less routine and yet deemed completely comparable in these terms to the cities of the plain. This is characteristic for Brecht's mobilization of Berlin: its attractions and its impossibilities are at once singular and in series, linked to other cities both ancient and modern. As if to mark this combination of singularity and plurality, Sodom and Gomorra are yoked together in the singular verb. The internal rhyme-word "war" resonates both with Gomorra, artificially drawing out its final syllable and thereby subjecting the poetic diction to an act of *Verfremdung*, and with the repetition of the suffix of functionality – "bar" – turned here into two forms of urban dysfunction. Ultimately, the city of Berlin is

---

[1] Verses from Brecht's poem "Über Deutschland", as remembered in lacunary form by Kalle in the migrant text *Flüchtlingsgespräche* (BFA 18. Pp. 195–327. Here p. 258).

included by implication in the prognosis of "Untergang der Städte". It is "unbewohnbar" in varying degrees, for the unemployed, for political dissidents, for
the evicted and deported, and for the remaining population, those for whom the
city remains "unverlaßbar", when the latter-day city of the plain is bombed into
its virtual "Untergang".

The relationship between Brecht and Berlin is something of a curiosity. The
unlivable but unleavable city is the key location for his life, writing, and theatre
work, and yet its role is also abstracted or effaced. We might consider the short
Herr Keuner text *Zwei Städte*, where the cities in question are marked by the
letters A and B (BFA 18. P. 27). On one level, it may be tempting to read the letters
as initials standing for the principal cities in Brecht's life, Augsburg and Berlin.
This would follow the *à clef* principle of a signature text like the poem "Vom
armen B. B." and thereby also inscribe Berlin into the writer's monogram as his
signature city. But the letters are more evidently understandable of course as
pure ciphers for model cities, and Brecht's Berlin constantly tends in that direction.
The resistance to individualist identification that informs Brecht's project extends
to the city as model rather than as individual and identificatory. The model or
methodical Berlin is the city of the *Straßenszene* essay, where typical urban
experience comes together "an irgendeiner Straßenecke" in an ensemble of
topographical location, personal and group action, and demonstration.[2] Brecht's
Berlin serves, therefore, as a site of experiment and engagement between the specific and the transferable, between the individual and the ensemble: a person and
a population, a house and housing, a street and the streets, a city and cities.

As Michael Bienert notes of Brecht's writing in his literary travelogue *Mit
Brecht durch Berlin*: "Selten fällt der Name Berlin".[3] And when it does occur,
he says, it tends to be "verallgemeinert und verfremdet",[4] as indeed we saw in
"Untergang der Städte Sodom und Gomorra". *Verfremdung* is here understandable as a technical showing of alienation, of the city's character as "unbewohnbar". In the light of this, it might seem, to adapt a well-known formulation from
Brecht's urban poetry, that what persists of the city as experiential site is that
which has passed through it, the wind, rather than any settled sense of habitation or inhabitation. This would be to follow Marie Neumüllers in her account
of Brecht's city-texts as aligned with Augé's dialectic of "place" and "non-
place",[5] where any sense of location is only understandable as a function of

---

[2] Bertolt Brecht: *Die Straßenszene. Grundmodell einer Szene des epischen Theaters.*
BFA 22.1. Pp. 370–381. Here p. 371.
[3] Michael Bienert: *Mit Brecht durch Berlin: Ein literarischer Reiseführer.* Frankfurt am
Main – Leipzig: Insel 1998. P. 11.
[4] Ibid. p. 17.
[5] Marie Neumüllers: Mahagonny, das ist kein Ort. In: *Mahagonny.com.* Ed. by Marc
Silberman and Florian Vassen. Madison (WI): University of Wisconsin Press 2004. Pp.
42–53. Here p. 42 (The Brecht Yearbook 29).

passage. The wind that serves as a key element in Brecht's construction of the city is at once an effect of place and of non-place, always also in transition or migration: elsewhere. The wind that blows through Berlin is also the wind of the proverbially windy city Chicago, or that which Brecht imagines blowing the ruins of wartime Berlin over to California and reassembling them in Santa Monica.[6]

If Berlin is to be viewed as having singular status among Brecht's "Städte", then paradoxically, it seems, by virtue of the special changeability of its identity. As Brecht writes in 1928: "Es gibt einen Grund, warum man Berlin anderen Städten vorziehen kann: weil es sich ständig verändert. Was heute schlecht ist, kann morgen gebessert werden".[7] It is perhaps just this principle of changeability that makes Berlin available as a template for transformation into the city or cities *per se*. But the transformations of what the poem "Über Deutschland" calls "vielstädtiges Berlin" (BFA 14. P. 453) are as much on the side of loss, abjection, or melancholia as on the side of activist betterment. It is perhaps appropriate that an urbanist, the GDR architect Henselmann, should see in his friend and collaborator Brecht not an "Aktionist" but a "melancholischer Revolutionär".[8] Brecht's treatments and transmutations of Berlin are typically cast between these models of political actionism or activism and left melancholy.

This ambivalence can be traced in some of the key transformations that Berlin undergoes in Brecht's works. The Berlin-Chicago of *Arturo Ui* as allegory of the modern metropolis might serve as an example here. This is allegory as, following its etymology, an other (*allos*) place or marketplace (*agora*) to speak (*euein*): an other place for trading words and, equally, a place of exchange for speaking otherwise. The "Speicherbrandprozeß" of *Arturo Ui*, inevitably understandable as a transposition or migration to another place of the "Reichstagsbrandprozeß", represents just such a site for speaking otherwise. It is an allegorical treatment of a historical process of public speaking, of propagandistic rhetoric and corrupt juridical pronouncement, transposed from the burnt-out Berlin parliament to the burnt-out architecture of the Chicago marketplace. Berlin is a foundation for transposition, seen and spoken otherwise and used as a site for seeing and speaking otherwise. This principle should alert us to the dangers of making ready assumptions about the city's role in Brecht's work, where it will often appear in modes of disguise – in allegorical form. The principle of allegory here implies both the element of speaking otherwise that inheres in the project for change, but, following Benjamin in the

---

[6] See Bertolt Brecht: *[Wo ich wohne]*. BFA 23. Pp. 48–51. Here p. 48.
[7] Bertolt Brecht: *Silvester 1928*. BFA 21. P. 267.
[8] Quoted in Susanne von Götz: "Ich habe der Arbeiterklasse ins Antlitz geschaut": Ein Gespräch mit Hermann Henselmann, Architekt der Stalinallee, über Brecht und den 17. Juni 1953. In: *Der Tagesspiegel* 17.6.1993.

specification of allegory in his *Ursprung des deutschen Trauerspiels*, it also bespeaks the catastrophic conception of history that he famously emblematizes in the angel of history, subverting that project in the direction of melancholia.

It was Benjamin's contention that Brecht displayed "Fühllosigkeit für den städtischen Dekor, verbunden mit einer äußersten Feinfühligkeit für die spezifischen Reaktionsweisen des Städters".[9] While his account supports the idea of Brecht the sociologist, analysing the "specific modes of reaction" of the city-dweller, as if in psycho-technical laboratory conditions, as so often with Brecht, there are contradictions at play here. His early responses to the city, as recorded in letters from the 1920s, recurrently focus on the powerful effects of the urban environment, the impact of its traffic and architecture. Thus, he describes Berlin in a letter to Arnolt Bronnen of 1923 as what might be called, after Eisenstein, a montage of attractions, both generic and site-specific:

> Baden, schreien, Kakao trinken
> Friedrichstraße, Aschinger, Charité
> Gleisdreieck, UFA, Wannsee.[10]

The Charité, where Brecht was treated for malnutrition in 1922, introduces a wry *memento mori* into the enthusiastic ensemble of urban activity, consumption and attraction. And Marieluise Fleißer gives an account of the writer as semiologist of this urban ensemble: "Brecht war aufgeschlossen für die Zeichen der Großstadt".[11] He is seen in her description as *flâneur* and *bricoleur*, reading the streets and collecting their signage: "Er lief gern in entfernten Stadtvierteln zu Fuß, er stieg einfach irgendwo aus, spazierte die Straßen auf und ab und gebrauchte die Augen".[12]

These signs can be configured as street performance and hence function as models transferable to the stage.[13] Fleißer relates how, on his wandering through Berlin, Brecht witnessed a street-scene between a prostitute and a "dicklicher Zuhälter", who was giving her directions in how to comport herself: "Erika, die Tasche halte flotter!".[14] Social *Gestus* in its most express form – the body demonstrating itself in order to sell itself – is thus a kind of street-theatre, subject

---

[9] Walter Benjamin: *Kommentare zu Gedichten von Brecht*. WBGS II.2. Pp. 539–572. Here p. 557.

[10] Bertolt Brecht: Letter to Arnolt Bronnen end February/beginning March 1923. BFA 28. Pp. 191–193. Here p. 192.

[11] Marieluise Fleißer: Der frühe Brecht. In: *Materialien zum Leben und Schreiben der Marieluise Fleißer*. Ed. by Günther Rühle. Frankfurt am Main: Suhrkamp 1973. Pp. 153–157. Here p. 156.

[12] Ibid. p. 153.

[13] For discussion of Brecht's street–theatre, see Nicholas Whybrow: *Street Scenes: Brecht, Benjamin and Berlin*. Bristol: Intellect 2005.

[14] Fleißer: Der frühe Brecht (n. 11). P. 153.

to directorial styling. And the signs that Brecht reads are not just those of human reaction, but also of the material landscape that elicits and frames reaction. Thus, in one of his short prose pieces in the *feuilleton* or reportage style from the mid-1920s, *Kritik*, he describes a theatrical encounter with a girl standing alone beneath a "Torbogen" in the Münzstraße. While she is found in the site of prostitution, she offers another kind of service: gratuitous fashion advice, and this through an elaborately gestic performance of showing. " '*Lang* ist modern! Nicht kurz!! Bitte!!!' Bei den Worten: *Lang* ist modern! vollführte sie mit der rechten Hand eine lange, zunächst abwärts und dann dem Trottoir parallel streichende Geste" (BFA 19. Pp. 279–280. Here p. 279).[15] It is the prostitute who now plays the role of actor-director. The pavement is appropriated as a teaching-stage here, one that is set, as it were, before the proscenium arch of the "Torbogen". It is used to give the measure of what is appropriate everyday behaviour on that same stage. The street-scene of fashion criticism can work as a model for the methods of critical theatre.

Fleißer describes Brecht as seeking to immerse himself in the stimulation of the city: "Leidenschaftlich gern fuhr er Autobus [...] in gleicher Augenhöhe mit der Reklame".[16] When he goes out to study modes of social reaction, he is also eye-to-eye with what Janet Ward has called Weimar surfaces, the culture of illumination and façade that galvanized Berlin in the 1920s.[17] It is at once the city of mass entertainment, focused for Brecht especially on the institution of the Sportpalast, which finds its way into his writing in various forms, and the city of mass movement on the streets. While Brecht took in the city with the methodology of the *flâneur*, he was no self-effacing observer. Or rather, if he was self-effacing, it was only in as far as he constructed himself as part of the Berlin spectacle. Portraits from the 1920s attest to this. His trademark shiny leather jacket was fashioned, it seems, as another kind of specular Weimar surface, as seen most famously in Rudolf Schlichter's portrait in the *Neue Sachlichkeit* style.

If this suggests that the fashion victim of *Kritik* has become a self-fashioning man who is at home – or at least a proficient visitor – in the city and its cultural, media, consumption and transport networks, another of the *feuilleton* pieces from 1926 presents a different picture. In *Meine längste Reise* (BFA 19. Pp. 283–285), the narrator, describing a time when he had none of his present "Großspurigkeit", is at a loss in his negotiation of Berlin's public transport system. Fleißer describes Brecht as being disinclined towards the underground,[18]

---

[15] I have corrected a mistranscription in the *Werkausgabe* here. In the manuscript (BBA 51/50) "Nicht kurz" is followed by two exclamation marks rather than one, thus forming part of a mounting series.

[16] Fleißer: Der frühe Brecht (n. 11). P. 153.

[17] Janet Ward: *Weimar Surfaces: Urban Visual Culture in 1920s Germany*. Berkeley: University of California Press 2001.

[18] Fleißer: Der frühe Brecht (n. 11). P. 153.

and this text gives an account of the anomie and anxiety that is paradoxically induced by the regulated system. The narrator takes the U-Bahn from the Kaiserhof station to Nollendorfplatz, but finds himself transported on an allegorical journey well beyond his nominal goal. He has reached the end of his credit, has forfeited his meal ticket for Aschinger's restaurant, and been given to understand "daß man auf mein Vorhandensein in dieser Stadt keinen direkten Wert legte" (BFA 19. P. 284). The first version in the manuscript of the piece had a nice slip, with "keinen direkten Weg", hand-corrected to "[…] Wert" (BBA 457/10), and his lack of personal or cultural capital is indeed transferred into a lack of direction in getting round the city. In the full carriage he feels only an "eigentümlich leere Stelle" in his head, and this empty place is duly transported with him, depriving him of the "Selbstbewußtsein" necessary to get out at Nollendorfplatz (BFA 19. P. 284). As he travels on further down the line, the idea of the "Ziel" that he thought he had becomes in its turn an empty place. He gets out at the terminus, Reichskanzlerplatz, and returns on foot to Nollendorfplatz, still arriving too early at a place where nothing much awaits him. The text ends with the change of fortunes that soon came along, but also with the thought that these might change back at any time. The "außerordentlich lange Reise" (BFA 19. P. 285) remains as a spectre of the sort of disorder, the lack of agency and orientation, that might return on the Berlin network.

It is not only the U-Bahn that can lead to disorientation, notwithstanding its fixed topological scheme. One of Brecht's late poems provides an image that can serve as emblematic for the negotiation of urban topography in his work:

"HIER IST DIE KARTE, da ist die Straße
Sieh hier die Biegung, sieh da das Gefäll!"
"Gib mir die Karte, da will ich gehen.
Nach der Karte
Geht es sich schnell" (BFA 15. P. 286).

The map provides an image of the street, a form as it were of "Stadtbild" or "Straßenbild", apparently offering facility of negotiation. Its two-dimensionality, however, means that it is incommensurate with its object: the map duly represents turns ("Sieh hier die Biegung"), while the street also displays vertical contours ("sieh da das Gefäll"). The second voice in the poem is made to fixate on the abstraction of the map as alternative urban space, as exposed in the double meanings that emerge in the response. The "da" in "da will ich gehen" becomes readable as the site of the map itself, substituted for the "da" that was the street, and "Nach der Karte" readable as "to the map", rather than according to it. This is indeed a self-reflexive journey ("Geht es sich"), a topographical short-circuit avoiding the gradients of the streets and quickly completed. The map stands here for maps of all kinds: for a map of Berlin, certainly, but also for other modes of abstracted representation. Brecht's project is constantly caught in the tension between the demands of real space and time and the guiding medium of their negotiation: the map, the image, or the formula. And this tension in the orientation and mediation of his project is especially in evidence in its allegorical turns, for which the map in the poem might be seen to stand.

This allegorical turn in Brecht's work will be illustrated here through four examples, set in a form of critical montage, all of them linked by what is an emblematic assembly of figures for Brecht's mapping of Berlin: the particularly allegorical figures of the gate, door, or arch as threshold structures. These are in turn seen – following Benjamin – in their relationship to the ruin and, by extension, to another key allegorical figure: the ruined body or corpse.[19] All are concerned with disorientation in the places and spaces of the city, with experience between place and non-place.

The first example is "Vom armen B. B" (BFA 11. Pp. 119–120), which will be read here as mediated by Benjamin's commentary.[20] Benjamin's reading of the *Hauspostille* collection is allegorically disposed. Following the model of architectural and topographical representation in the poems, caught between memorialization and oblivion, Benjamin adopts the ruined gate as a figure for "Vom armen B. B.". It is indicative that the first version of the poem was written on the night train heading south after Brecht's unsuccessful attempt at establishing himself in the capital in the winter of 1921/22. The infelicitous speech act "In der Asphaltstadt bin ich daheim" (BFA 11. P. 119), yoking the "Asphaltstadt" Berlin to the vernacular "daheim" of his Bavarian origins, betrays the immigrant. This is poetry in the transitional mode, on the move between locations. The gate figures this transitional moment in the mock-martyric stations of the poem.

The subject's place as he passes through the stations of the poem is interstitial, at once inside and outside of any habitable structures. He imitates the habits of the city-dweller, but remains unhabituated, inviting others into his home, but without offering firm foundations: "In mir habt ihr einen, auf den könnt ihr nicht bauen" (BFA 11. P. 120). As a specimen of his species – "ein leichtes Geschlechte" (BFA 11. P. 120) – the poetic subject identifies with the builders of cities and their medial networks, but here too the foundations are not firm: the "indestructible" cities of Manhattan or Berlin are built not to last, or only to last in what passes through them: the wind. Benjamin's suggestion that the city might find a new habitation in the wind, redeeming the negation in a dialectical *Aufhebung* (WBGS II.2. P. 553), remains uncertain, haunted by the possibility that the *Aufhebung* will collapse back into the moment of abolition or erasure.

---

[19] Walter Benjamin: *Ursprung des deutschen Trauerspiels*. WBGS I.1. Pp. 203–430. Here p. 391.
[20] Walter Benjamin: *Zu dem Gedicht "Vom armen B. B."*. WBGS II.2. Pp. 551–554.

Against this nihilistic framework, the Babylonian city is emptied out: "Fröhlich machet das Haus den Esser: er leert es" and vandalized by a generation of "Vorläufige" (BFA 11. P. 120) who, however, are not followed by anything of account.

As a representative of a provisional generation without meaningful successors, the destructive character of Brecht's "Ich" is caught in a condition of fundamental displacement.[21] Benjamin notes the "Häufung von Präpositionen der Ortsbestimmung" (WBGS II.2. P. 554), a heaping that also extends to temporal siting: "Ich, Bertolt Brecht, in die Asphaltstädte verschlagen/Aus den schwarzen Wäldern in meiner Mutter in früher Zeit" (BFA 11. P. 120). The predicted ruination of the city is imitated by this archaeological heaping of incompatible habitations; if the sequence is, as Benjamin comments, "ungewöhnlich beirrend", then it resonates with the loss of orientation through *habitus*, the sense of habitual living-space that goes with the "gewöhnlich".[22]

The poet is constructed in Benjamin's commentary as a topographical figure, one that combines the wind-blown door of the poem "Gegen Verführung" (BFA II. P. 116) and the "Hundestein" as abject memorial for the poet's passing in "Von den Sündern in der Hölle" (BFA II. Pp. 118–119). He thus becomes a metaphorical gate through which the reader might pass and bearing "in verwitterter Schrift ein B. B" (WBGS II.2. P. 554). It is a monogram that we might again double-read as identifying Brecht with Berlin. It seems most appropriate to construe this as the city-gate through which the "armer B. B." passes but without achieving a settled place inside. It stands as a signature structure of entry for the reader as "Passant", but like the dead figures of "Von den Sündern", it seems that the reader, in following the poet through the gate that carries his monogram, is also made to identify with it as a memorial for lost selfhood. Out of this figure of self-effacement and passing over, Benjamin constructs the possibility of a more active kind of gate, one that resists mere passage of its own efforts and of the reader through it. In order to block such access, it seems that the gate has to fall, but only thereby does it come to stand in a meaningful way: "Am besten wird der zu seiner Sache stehn, der den Anfang damit gemacht hat, sich selbst fallen zu lassen" (WBGS II.2. P. 554).

---

[21] Brecht is a model for the destructive character, clearing ground for historical change, as theorized by Benjamin in "Der destruktive Charakter" (WBGS IV.1. Pp. 396–398. Here p. 396).

[22] Ron Speirs has argued that "Aus den schwarzen Wäldern" can be read as made out of the woods, thus preparing for the identificatory figures of trees that run through Brecht's poetry. In that case, the tree-poet is here transplanted from the woods into the asphalt of Berlin, from one cold habitat not properly his to another. See Ron Speirs: "Vom armen B. B.". In: *Brecht Handbuch in fünf Bänden*. Ed. by Jan Knopf. Stuttgart – Weimar: Metzler 2001–2003. Vol. 2. Pp. 104–109. Here pp. 106–107.

The uncertainty of Benjamin's recuperative move in the mode of a dialectical *Aufhebung*, taking the ruin as "vorläufig", a necessary prelude to the engagement of the later poetry, is nicely caught in this figure of standing through falling. It provides a suitably ambivalent shape for the gate through, or past, which to pass to Brecht's later city poetry, as the writer who is resident, but also vagrant, in Berlin turns from the genre of the home breviary to that of the city-primer in *Aus dem Lesebuch für Städtebewohner* (BFA 11. Pp. 155–176), a reader of city life in poems, but also a guide to the reading of the city and its modes of habitation. Benjamin's dramatization of the implications of the ballad "Vom armen B. B." through the allegorical figure of the fallen gate implies a removal of personal trace, as in the already partially effaced memorial monogram. And the removal of traces becomes the prime *Gestus* of the *Lesebuch*, as instanced in the refrain of its opening poem: "Verwisch die Spuren!" (BFA 11. P. 157). It is in this context that Benjamin makes his claim that Brecht is unfeeling for the décor of the city, but without suspecting that this is in itself might be an effect of the strategic removal of traces on the part of the city-dweller.

The configuration of the ruined gate and traces of passage recurs in the second example of the allegorical turn, the 1948 *Vorspiel* to *Die Antigone des Sophokles*. Antigone has come to serve as a key embodiment for the working through of the crimes of the Nazi period in post-war Germany, a figure of active mourning in resistance to the postulation of a national "Unfähigkeit zu trauern".[23] She has also been embraced as a model agent in many contemporary theories of ethics. For post-war Berlin she stands for the possibility of mourning for the victims of war and of the death camps, for those that have lain unburied and unmourned both inside and outside the city walls. In the aftermath of the war, Brecht felt that in order to be represented Berlin had to undergo another allegorical transformation, to become another Thebes as framing site for his *Antigone*. While the collapse of the great city comes at the end of Sophocles' *Antigone*, here it is also set before it in an act of proleptic memorialization. This scene from the latter-day "Trümmerstadt" becomes the ruined gate through or past which the viewer passes into the mythical terrain of the gated city of Thebes, the city that in the course of the play will become in its turn "die stürzende Stadt".[24]

The *Vorspiel* is outside, not yet in the space and time of the drama proper, but it is also internally split. The set is riven by a crack that marks this condition, and the title board, reading "BERLIN. APRIL 1945. TAGESANBRUCH" introduces a break into the temporality of the scene by splitting off the "BRUCH".

---

[23] See Alexander Mitscherlich and Margarete Mitscherlich: *Die Unfähigkeit zu trauern: Grundlagen kollektiven Verhaltens*. München: Piper 1977.
[24] Bertolt Brecht: *Die Antigone des Sophokles*. BFA 8. Pp. 193–242. Here p. 241.

Both the place and the time of this *Vorspiel* are thus breached. It is cast between inside and out, before and after, in a condition of spatial and temporal liminality. Brecht employs here his signature epic method of splitting the action between drama in the present tense and narration in the past, between the present site of the action and a perspective outside it. The two sisters come up out of the air-raid cellar into their apartment and find the door open, taking it to have been blown open by the fire-storm outside. The evidence, however, is of another cause:

> DIE ZWEITE Schwester, woher kommt da im Staub die Spur?
> DIE ERSTE Von einem, der hinauflief, ist es nur (BFA 8. P. 195).

The trace of what has been here becomes profoundly ambiguous in the manuscript versions of the *Vorspiel*. In the original version, the second part of the first line read as "ein Staub die Spur?" (BBA 1071/12).[25] That is, in the original version, dust – the key material for *Antigone* as for the ruined city – is, whether by accident or design, the minimal stuff of the trace rather than the material in which it is left. The variants collapse figure and ground into the anti-material of which they are made: dust to dust. The dust, which in *Antigone* is both the corporeal material of death and that which is used by Antigone, with her epithet of "Staubaufsammelnde" (BFA 8. P. 200), in her work of mourning in covering the dead, modulates here between a sign of life and a sign of death. And the following line is also at variance with the manuscript version, where "hinauflief" is corrected to read "hinauslief" (BBA 593). The intruder who has come from without and run upstairs is counterbalanced here with one who has run out of the house.

Inside and out are thus confounded in the textual adjustments, and the trace is doubly uncertain. If the dust is really the sign of the brother inside the family home, along with his uniform and the food he has brought, then this is undermined by the line "Er hat sich aus dem Staub gemacht" (BFA 8. P. 197). His desertion seems ready also to mean that he has left the house, left the dust trace in the house or the trace in the dust of the house, indeed – at limit – made himself of or into dust.[26] Dust, as the allegorical substance of destruction and death configures the ruin with the body. The dust-trace points towards the corpse in the ruins outside, and the sisters fail to identify and follow it in time. While the first sister seems to want to adopt the role of latter-day Antigone, the dissident who goes outside the city to challenge the power within, both are caught inside, and the possibility of intervention after the event and at pain of death remains suspended. Cast

---

[25] This is hand-corrected in BBA 593.
[26] This limit reading follows the logic of Ron Speirs's account of "Vom armen B.B." (See n. 22 above).

between the possibilities of killing her brother's killer, of going outside to cut his body down for appropriate mourning, or of staying inside and in silence, this latterday Antigone represents the ethical as a fraught and broken project for post-war Berlin. She is a figure in an allegorical constellation, caught at the threshold to the agonistic space of Berlin-Thebes behind the "Vorspielwand", with the open door as city-gate and frame for the hidden corpse.[27]

The Antigone figure leads to the third example to be considered here, the *Berliner Requiem*. As an alternative to the Berlin *Vorspiel* for *Antigone*, a "Tafel mit der Darstellung einer modernen Trümmerstadt" was considered.[28] The implication is that Berlin-Thebes, the archetype of the city in ruins, can be represented by an image of any "Trümmerstadt" of modernity. The ruined city is also a city without recognizable identity, one that has lost its topographical bearings and so become interchangeable. This is the city as corollary of one of its iconic inhabitants, and one for whom subsequent processes of mourning have followed the Antigone model: Rosa Luxemburg. The *Berliner Requiem* is constructed over the body of Luxemburg as allegorical figure of loss in the city. Its texts are bound to the past, to the darker days following the First World War, and suggest an attachment to death, and the political causes of death, that subsists in the Berlin of the late 1920s. The requiem that takes its base in Berlin and mourns individual Berliners becomes understandable as a requiem for what will come to have been: the city as a whole.

The mourning of Rosa Luxemburg is enacted in several different versions within the *Requiem*. In the texts to the songs "Vom ertrunkenen Mädchen" and the "Marterl", "Hier ruht die Jungfrau", Luxemburg becomes identified with the sort of epitaphic inscription that is characteristic of the *Hauspostille* collection. She becomes a figure of allegory for lost life in the city, her memorial designed to be a site of breakage and discomfort, intrinsically divided from where she lies. As the poem "Grabschrift 1919" has it: "Die rote Rosa nun auch verschwand. / Wo sie liegt, ist unbekannt" (BFA 11. P. 205). The version of this that appears as an alternative text for the "Marterl" song from the *Requiem* in Weill's *Song-Album* for voice and piano of 1929 is varied, as follows:

Die rote Rosa schon lang verschwand.
Die ist tot, ihr Aufenthaltsort ist unbekannt.

[27] For Benjamin in *Ursprung des deutschen Trauerspiels*, Hölderlin's Sophocles translations, attributed to his "baroque" late style, are evidence of the way in which the Classical is dismembered and reassembled around the allegorical principle (WBGS I.1. Pp. 364–365). In Brecht's refunctioning of Hölderlin's version, that baroque style is at once incorporated and defamiliarized. To adopt terms from Benjamin's account of baroque drama, the *Vorspiel* can be understood as an allegorical mask for the play, a Hippocratic face (WBGS I.1 P. 343) and ruined façade, put before it as a historicizing device.
[28] Bertolt Brecht: *Antigonemodell 1948*. BFA 25. Pp. 71–168. Here p. 78.

"Lokalkolorit" is used in conventional theatre, Brecht says, to be determined "wie bei der Auswahl einer Ansichtspostkarte auf einer Reise".[33] The film's establishing image is concerned not with local colour, but with the framing of a process of understanding. The proffering of the incomplete postcard image subjects the standard opening *Gestus* to an effect of *Verfremdung*, equivalent to that of the incomplete set in epic theatre, as in the *Vorspiel* to *Antigone*. It is a strategically false start for a work that will resist the generic standards of the postcard film, creating a basis for a montage of city images at a critical remove from the standard picture.

The postcard shot of the gate without a base to stand on marks out the Brandenburg Gate, this parading landmark of German history, as a ruin-in-waiting masquerading as total. It is appropriated for a project of change, but one that remains afflicted by a more melancholy sense of the limits of historical changeability – in particular possibilities of change in what Brecht had called the city of change, Berlin. The postcard might be understood as one of the cards that Brecht assembles in the allegorical house of cards identified by Benjamin when he sends Brecht a reproduction of Chardin's *Château de cartes* from his Paris exile in 1934. Benjamin glosses this work of art in the age of its technical reproducibility with the ironic commentary: "hier schicke ich Ihnen eine Bauvorlage, um Ihr Training an dem ich mich als Meister wohlwollend interessiert bin, zu unterstützen" (WBGB IV. P. 335). This card demonstrating a card-game serves as a playful *mise-en-abyme* for the relationship between Brecht and Benjamin, players of cards, chess, and ideas.[34] The two men, master-builders both, construct their allegorical houses of cards, each according to their method. The postcard and its text provide a wry commentary on their models for living in unlivable times, and in particular their respective attempts to make livable the unleavable city that both had already left by 1934.[35]

Their houses of cards, not least cards representing ruins, also correspond to another allegorical image, another postcard design for the alternative building project, that Brecht considers in his writings on *Verfremdung*: Brueghel's *The Tower of Babel*. The image is described as representing the tower as "schief gebaut" and always provisional: "oben scheint ein neuer Plan in Ausführung, der das anfänglich gigantisch geplante Unternehmen reduziert".[36] The commentary might be construed as Brecht's contribution to the discourse, especially

[33] Bertolt Brecht: *Über den Bühnenbau der nichtaristotelischen Dramatik*. BFA 22.1. Pp. 227–234. Here p. 229.
[34] See Erdmut Wizisla's essay in this volume.
[35] Benjamin continues that project in the reconstructive work in exile on his *Berliner Kindheit um Neunzehnhundert*.
[36] Bertolt Brecht: *V-Effekte in einigen Bildern des älteren Breughel*. BFA 22.1. Pp. 271–273. Here p. 273.

prevalent in the Weimar years, of Berlin-Babylon, suggesting a sequence of plans and counter-plans for the city that have catastrophe at their base. Babylon thus enters the network of ruined cities around Berlin, joining Sodom and Gomorra and Thebes. While the poem "Über Deutschland" builds Berlin up as deserving to remain – "Auch du, vielstädtiges Berlin / Unter und über dem Asphalt geschäftig, kannst bleiben" (BFA 14. P. 453) – the multi-city's powers of resistance to adverse winds of change remain uncertain. Even as Brecht's building projects, his houses of cards, are mediated by effects of *Verfremdung*, showing critical awareness of their own constructedness, they are always also haunted by the liability of collapse into ruin, if not for internal reasons, then through the intervention of Benjamin's catastrophic wind of history,[37] which may always be all that will remain of them.

[37] This is the gale-force wind that assails the angel of history in Benjamin's *Über den Begriff der Geschichte*, while the ruins pile up inexorably before him (WBGS I.2. Pp. 691–704. Here pp. 697–698).

Tom Kuhn

Poetry and Photography: Mastering Reality in the *Kriegsfibel*[1]

The critical literature is notably reticent or uncertain about Brecht's Kriegsfibel *and its importance. This article seeks to reassess the collection, both by close analysis of selected pages and, above all, by reading the work against two contexts: Brecht's long-standing interest in photography and the pictorial, and his preoccupations of the war years: realism and the lyric. The work emerges as a very considered and carefully constructed cycle with a crucial place in Brecht's ongoing reflections about a cognitive, even interventionist realism.*

Brecht's collection of press cuttings and accompanying epigrams, the *Kriegsfibel*, has suffered a rather peculiarly, not to say scandalously, delayed and attenuated reception. The work is perhaps familiar enough to readers now, even in Britain (especially since the publication of an English translation in 1998), but it is still surprisingly little discussed in the secondary literature, and its place in Brecht's oeuvre is not so much disputed as simply passed over, in confusion over its generic status and its whole import. So I shall start with a descriptive account of a couple of pages from the work. The location of the conference at which this paper originated, not so very far from the City of London, gives me the excuse for my choice of examples: images of the bombing raids over Britain.

The first picture in this short sequence from about a quarter of the way through the work (Nr. 15)[2] is provided with a caption – possibly by Brecht or Ruth Berlau, or, more likely, by the designer (Peter Palitzsch) and editors (Günter

---

[1] This essay originated in a paper given at a conference initiated by the Institute of Germanic and Romance Studies at the University of London. It takes up material and issues also discussed in my two articles published recently in *The Brecht Yearbook*: "Was besagt eine Fotografie?". Early Brechtian Perspectives on Photography. In: *Young Mr. Brecht Becomes a Writer.* Ed. by Jürgen Hillesheim. Madison (WI): University of Wisconsin Press 2006. Pp. 261–283 (The Brecht Yearbook 31). and Beyond Death: Brecht's *Kriegsfibel* and the Uses of Tradition. In: *Brecht and Death.* Ed. by Jürgen Hillesheim, Mathias Meyer and Stephen Brockmann. Madison (WI): University of Wisconsin Press 2007. Pp. 67–90 (The Brecht Yearbook 32). In fact it attempts something of a bridge between those two articles, to pose the question how Brecht got from those early sceptical reflections on the medium of photography to arrive at the daring experiment of the *Kriegsfibel*. I am grateful for the encouragement and critiques provided by my discussants both in London and in Augsburg (where the second of the above articles was born) and by my most critical reader on this occasion, Simon Korner.
[2] Bertolt Brecht: *Kriegsfibel.* BFA 12. Pp. 127–283. Here p. 159. This follows the sequence of the second, extended German edition (Berlin: Eulenspiegel 1994). In the first GDR edition (Eulenspiegel 1955) and the West German imprint (Frankfurt am Main: Zweitausendeins 1978) both the pages and the images are unnumbered.

Wir sind's, die über deine Stadt gekommen
O Frau, die du um deine Kinder bangst!
Wir haben dich und sie aufs Ziel genommen
Und fragst du uns warum, so wiss': aus Angst.

Kunert and Heinz Seydel) of the first book publication in 1955: "Besatzung eines deutschen Bombers". Brecht's four-line verse beneath the photograph reads as follows:

Wir sind's, die über deine Stadt gekommen
O Frau, die du um deine Kinder bangst!
Wir haben dich und sie aufs Ziel genommen
Und fragst du uns warum, so wiss': aus Angst.

The 1994 edition includes material which it was deemed impolitic to publish in the GDR in the 1950s. The order and numbering of the images in the English edition, *War Primer*, translated and edited by John Willett (London: Libris 1998) differs substantially and includes some pieces which, although they are photo-epigrams, were never part of the original *Kriegsfibel* (there is quite a detailed account of the genesis of the work and a concordance at the back).

The whole book is constructed like this: with a black page on the right providing a frame and context for the newspaper photographs, which take up markedly
different amounts of the space on the page; and with a white page on the left,
either blank, or with these minimal captions and translations into German of
any foreign text included on the newspaper cuttings themselves (mostly from
the English or Swedish). The Swedish text above and below the next image (16)
reads in English translation: "The City of today. In the course of the air raids
the central districts of London have acquired the character of a ruined quarter.
This view over the City was taken from St Paul's Cathedral". The verse reads:

So seh ich aus. Nur weil gewisse Leute
Tückisch in andre Richtung flogen als

Ich plante; so wurd ich statt Hehler Beute
Und Opfer eines, ach, Berufsunfalls.

The next (17) is an aerial photograph of the docks in Liverpool, with fires
smoking in the background.

Noch bin ich eine Stadt, doch nicht mehr lange.
Fünfzig Geschlechter haben mich bewohnt
Wenn ich die Todesvögel jetzt empfange:
In tausend Jahr erbaut, verheert in einem Mond.

And then (18) another German airman: "'Die hat hingehauen!'", reads what
is this time a German newspaper text, "Der Beobachter, der soeben die
Abwurfvorrichtung ausgelöst hat, freut sich über den Erfolg seiner Bombenreihe".

Hamnen i Liverpool, Englands näststörsta, har som bekant varit föremål för flera tyska bombräder och
härvid blivit utsatt för många träffar. Här se vi en vacker bild från hamnen och eldsvådorna i bakgrun-
den utvisa, att hamnanläggningarna nyligen haft känning av de tyska bomberna.

Noch bin ich eine Stadt, doch nicht mehr lange.
Fünfzig Geschlechter haben mich bewohnt
Wenn ich die Todesvögel jetzt empfange:
In tausend Jahr erbaut, verheert in einem Mond.

Seht einen Teufel hier, doch einen armen!
"Ich lache, weil ich andre weinen weiß.
Ich bin ein Wäschereisender aus Barmen
Wenn ich auch jetzt in Tod und Elend reis".

This short sequence already makes a number of things very clear. First of all, this is a cycle. The alternation of ruined cityscapes and very individualized bombers is important. The relationships are not always quite as easy to explicate as that. More often we have to contend with jerky, Brechtian discontinuities and cross-associations, which demand work and imagination from his readers. Nevertheless, even though over the years between its conception and

„Die hat hingehauen!" Der Beobachter, der soeben die Abwurfvorrichtung ausgelöst hat, freut sich über den Erfolg seiner Bombenreihe.

Seht einen Teufel hier, doch einen armen!
„Ich lache, weil ich andre weinen weiß.
Ich bin ein Wäschereisender aus Barmen
Wenn ich auch jetzt in Tod und Elend reis'."

its first publication the order was tinkered with, it was clearly always an important part of the composition. Secondly, the order also tracks the chronological course of the war, or of those parts of it which seemed important to Brecht at the time. It is often impossible to date these little poems precisely, but the first and the last of these were furnished with dates by Brecht himself: the first was written on 26 September 1940 and the last on 6 November the same year, a span of just six weeks. The first air raids on London had begun on 13 August. The first major bombardment of Liverpool took place on 11 October. Brecht was tracking these events with horror, as they unfolded, with newspapers and radio broadcasts his primary sources. Even before the Blitz began, he had noted in his *Journal* (10.8.1940): "Der eiserne Ring schließt sich um England. Das Flugzeug, die neue Waffe, zeigt sich um so schrecklicher neu, als sie schon im letzten Krieg angewendet wurde". And a month later, on 10 September:

Es ist zwölf Uhr zwanzig. Ich hörte eben den Ansager in dem bombardierten London. Er sitzt im Luftschutzkeller, die deutschen Bomber sind wieder über der "Hauptstadt der Welt". Das Feuer wütet noch von den gestrigen und vorgestrigen Bombardements, es ist "beinahe in jedem Fall under control". Über einem zerstörten Geschäft in der City habe der Inhaber heut früh die Aufschrift angebracht "Gegründet 1628, immer noch in Betrieb".
Die Slums an den Docks stehen in Brand.[3]

Several of the themes and preoccupations of the cycle are also evident in these four examples. Time and again Brecht returns to the fates of mothers and their children in this war, as he often had when writing about the First World War as well: "O Frau, die du um deine Kinder bangst!". Time and again he insists that the ordinary soldiers on both sides are the victims: "arme Teufel" who are driven, above all, by fear of their superiors, and later by hunger and desperation. And, as if his social and political sympathies were not clear enough, in that second poem, which is not immediately so simple to comprehend, the direction in which the London financial centre might more logically, according to Brecht, have planned its offensive is, it is implied, against the Soviet Union.

The very fact that some of these poems seem obscure or difficult to understand – and there are plenty of more extreme examples of this in the cycle[4] – is itself also worthy of note. Brecht's syntax is sometimes complex, his main clauses interrupted, his word order inverted. He seems to be aiming here at a quite elevated diction, with frequent apostrophe and exclamations, "O" and "ach". Amongst his models – and others have written in persuasive detail about this – was a collection of classical Greek epigrams in German translations,

---

[3] Bertolt Brecht: *Journal.* BFA 26–27. Henceforth entries will be identified by date only.
[4] I have, for example, read no convincing explanatory commentary on Nr. 58.

which he had recently acquired.[5] The sense of the cycle is further complicated by the voices of these poems. Brecht puts words – as in my examples – into the mouths of soldiers, addressed directly to their victims, and he lets the ruined cities speak up for themselves, in the first person. He also gives voices to nations and classes, and to the dead. The different sources of his newspaper cuttings (and the anonymity of the photographers) permit him to combine and juxtapose perspectives from different countries and different sides in the conflict. In the poems he employs direct speech marks too; some of the poems are little dialogues, one between industrial workers preparing the war effort, another between Göring and Goebbels themselves. But as well as all this, he also speaks as the poet, in the first person again, and addresses his readers in the second person plural. The cycle is a complex weave of voices and perspectives.

Finally, some commentators have written about these poems, perhaps seduced by the direct speech and the concrete and occasionally very direct vocabulary, as if they were in some popular, vernacular verse form. The editors of the *Berliner und Frankfurter Ausgabe* even talk of "Knittelverse".[6] Nothing could be further from the truth. These fourliners are, almost without exception, in impressively regular iambic pentameters, with alternating rhymes, and with just the occasional inversion of stress at the start of a line, or an irregular foot at the end. By its very regularity, the metre sometimes struggles a little with the natural speech rhythms of a clause – that second poem (16) is a good example – thus underlining the formality and, again, elevated register of the whole enterprise. This was the same metre as employed in those German versions of Greek elegiac distichs which Brecht had been reading. And the whole impression of a "high" literary form is also underpinned by the frequent internal rhymes, assonances and repetitions which the verses employ, as well as by, amongst the more down-to-earth expressions, the occasional antiquated lexeme, biblical-sounding formulation, or direct literary quotation.

Even this brief introduction must dispel any impression that this might be a somehow casual composition, a scrapbook of random images and hastily composed captions. On the contrary, the *Kriegsfibel* is a very considered and carefully constructed cycle of crafted poems, designed both to tell the story of the war and to disclose its larger context and purposes.

---

[5] *Der Kranz des Meleagros von Gadara*. Selected and translated by August Oehler (pseud. of August Mayer). Berlin: Propyläen 1920. It is mentioned in the *Journal* 25.7.1940. See also Marion Lausberg: Brechts Lyrik und die Antike. In: *Brechts Lyrik. Neue Deutungen*. Ed. by Helmut Koopmann. Würzburg: Königshausen & Neumann 1999. Pp. 163- 198; and Anya Feddersen's piece on the *Kriegsfibel* in: *Brecht Handbuch in fünf Bänden*. Ed. by Jan Knopf. Stuttgart: Metzler 2001–2003. Vol. 2. Pp. 382–397, to which I am in general much indebted.

[6] BFA 12. P. 414. On this point compare Feddersen: Kriegsfibel (n. 5). P. 393.

These aspects of the text – literary and visual sources, form and register, narrative stance and cyclical structure – are discussed in more detail in my piece in *The Brecht Yearbook* (2007).[7] What I intend to do here is to trace some of the roots of this work in Brecht's intellectual and artistic development, in the earlier exile and in the 1920s, and to argue for a more central place for it in Brecht's oeuvre than it has usually been accorded. First, a very brief note about the genesis and publication history of the work. Brecht called this combination of newspaper cutting and fourline poem a "Fotoepigramm", and the very first attested examples of the new form date from the summer of 1940. In October of that year a couple of these compositions appear amongst the pages of the *Journal*. It was not, however, until February to June 1944 that Brecht first published such photo-epigrams, in the New York journal *Austro American Tribune*. There they were introduced as extracts from a longer work by Brecht given, at this point, the perhaps revealingly biblical title, "Und siehe, es war sehr schlecht" (an inversion of Genesis). At the end of 1944 Ruth Berlau, whose technical assistance was essential to the work, put together a whole series of sixty-six photo-epigrams, now under the title *Kriegsfibel*, and a copy, which is now in Harvard University Library, was sent to Karl Korsch. After this, for the time being, very little was done to the cycle. However, as soon as they were back in Europe, Berlau was instructed to try to find a publisher. After the Munich publisher Kurt Desch rejected the work, it seemed for a time that the East Berlin Verlag Volk und Welt would provide a home. Then, in March 1950, the "Kultureller Beirat für Verlagswesen" stepped in, and the GDR "Ministerpräsident" himself, Otto Grotewohl, judged the volume "völlig ungeeignet" for publication, because of its generally pacifist tendency and supposedly inadequate analysis of the imperial warmongers.[8] All of this was accompanied by detailed wrangles over individual images and poems – the total number of which had now grown to over seventy, some of which had been newly put together, and others of which were re-written and included or excluded from the selection at various points. It was only in November 1955 that the *Kriegsfibel* (now comprising sixty-nine photo-epigrams) was finally published, by the Eulenspiegel Verlag in East Berlin. The West German edition, by Zweitausendeins, did not appear until 1978. An extended edition by the Eulenspiegel Verlag appeared in 1994, and the first English edition as late as 1998. So it is a work that has been slow in reaching a public.

Yet it is an extraordinary composition, critics agree on that, strikingly innovative in its form and still remarkably powerful in its anti-war protest. It is

---

[7] Kuhn: Beyond Death (n. 1).
[8] Compare BFA 12. P. 409; Feddersen: Kriegsfibel (n. 5). P. 385; Willett: *War Primer* (n. 2). P. xiii.

exceptional within Brecht's own oeuvre, and in this post-war period, in its juxtaposition of materials. Indeed, there are few works like it anywhere. When the
English edition came out, a critic in the *Guardian* compared it to Goya's
famous *Disasters of War*, which was indeed almost certainly an inspiration for
Brecht.[9] All the same, despite this sort of high praise, there has been comparatively little informed criticism, and it has often been treated as somewhat marginal to Brecht's output, neither taken very seriously as a cycle of poems nor
easily categorized as anything else. Most of the important commentaries have
approached the work, very reasonably, from Brecht's own genre description of
the "Fotoepigramm", and there has been a degree of discussion of the relationship between image and text. Much of the early debate was dominated by
Reinhold Grimm's notion of a "Marxistische Emblematik", developed on the
basis of the baroque model.[10] This was not a very fruitful approach. As my
examples show, the images here are very different from the kind of memorable
symbol we associate with the baroque emblem, nor are they at all consistently
tripartite (*pictura, inscriptio, subscriptio*) in their structure. Indeed, part of the
principle is that they are all structured slightly differently, again demanding
input from the reader. Besides, their source, in the contemporary news media,
is quite evidently important. Several of them, but by no means all, have their
own original captions or other textual material, as well as Brecht's epigrams.
One is a cutting of newspaper-text only, with no picture. Other critics have
invoked the idea of the documentary. Of course, this has some force. These are
pictures from the world of the real, derived from documentary sources. What
they show, however, is precisely that that surface of reality is insufficient for
comprehension and must be explicated by commentary, and high-literary commentary at that. If this is a work of documentary, it expands our notions of what
that term can mean.

My own point of approach is somewhat different. For one thing my view of
the work is informed by a study of Brecht's long-standing interest in photography. This is a medium he has thought about before, and those thoughts are pertinent. What is more, throughout his creative life, Brecht made enormous use
of pictures and the pictorial, from Neher to Breughel and from Grosz to *Life*
magazine, as potentially powerful instruments in the cognitive process.

---

[9] Cited from the cover of the paperback edition.

[10] Reinhold Grimm: Marxistische Emblematik. Zu Bertolt Brechts *Kriegsfibel*. In:
Wissenschaft als Dialog. Studien zur Literatur und Kunst seit der Jahrhundertwende.
Ed. by Renate von Heydebrand and Klaus Günther Just. Stuttgart: Metzler 1969. Pp.
351–379 and 518–524. A version of the baroque model is still occasionally asserted,
e.g. by Theo Stammen: Brechts *Kriegsfibel*. Politische Emblematik und zeitgeschichtliche
Aussage. In: Koopman (ed.): *Brechts Lyrik* (n. 5). Pp. 101–141 (especially p. 124), but
the approach has been roundly denounced by Feddersen.

(He thought of his theatre too as a succession of tableaux.) Secondly, I shall try to contextualize the *Kriegsfibel* in relation to Brecht's ongoing reflections, especially in the exile period, on the lyric and on realism. These two contexts do not necessarily contradict the previous literature; they are rather an adjustment and expansion of our view of the work and help to establish that more central place for it in Brecht's oeuvre.[11]

This is not the place to reprise the history of Brecht's early interest in photography,[12] but let's go back a little. Brecht's most famous remark about photography is from the writings of the *Dreigroschenprozeß* from about 1930: "Eine Fotografie der Kruppwerke oder der AEG ergibt beinahe nichts über diese Institute. Die eigentliche Realität ist in die Funktionale gerutscht".[13] Here photography stands in for the sort of surface realism which permits no analysis. Elsewhere he remarks: "Die Fotografie ist die Möglichkeit einer *Wieder*gabe, die den Zusammenhang wegschminkt".[14] This account of photography as little more than a model of impotent and context-less mimetic realism is not, however, just the throwaway opinion of someone not much interested in the medium; rather it is a concerted reaction against some of the developments of the more "artistic" photography which was then enjoying such a boom in the popular print media, the so-called "neue Photographie" of the 1920s and early 30s. It is a resistance on two fronts: both to the aestheticized images of such trendy practitioners as Albert Renger-Patzsch, and also to the naive documentary claims of some photographic reportage. Back in 1928, in a short sketch unpublished at

---

[11] Of course I am not the first to attempt this sort of historical sweep through Brecht's approaches to photography and the visual. Amongst those who have made some similar points to what follows and in whose writing the *Kriegsfibel* looms large are Philip Brady: From Cave-Painting to "Fotogramm": Brecht, Photography and the *Arbeitsjournal*. In: *Forum for Modern Language Studies* XIV (1978). Pp. 270–281; Dieter Wöhrle: Von der Notwendigkeit einer "Kunst der Betrachtung": Bertolt Brechts *Kriegsfibel* und die Gestaltung von Text-Bild-Beziehungen. In: *alles was Brecht ist... Fakten – Kommentare – Meinungen – Bilder*. Ed. by Werner Hecht. Frankfurt am Main: Suhrkamp 1997. Pp. 232–244; and Philippe Invernel: L'oeil de Brecht. À propos du rapport entre texte et image dans le *Journal de travail* et l'*ABC de la guerre*. In: *Brecht 98. Poétique et Politique/Poetik und Politik*. Ed. by Michel Vanoosthuyse. Montpellier: Bibliothèque d'Etudes Germaniques et Centre-Européennes 1999. Pp. 217–231.

[12] That is the subject of my article in *The Brecht Yearbook* (2006) (n. 1). See also Philip Brady: Die "zweite Betrachtung": photography and the political message, 1925–1933. In: *Text und Bild, Bild und Text: DFG-Symposion 1988*. Ed. by Wolfgang Harms. Stuttgart: Metzler 1990. Pp. 329–338, and the article by Steve Giles.

[13] Bertolt Brecht: *Der Dreigroschenprozeß. Ein soziologisches Experiment*. BFA 21. Pp. 448–514. Here p. 468.

[14] Bertolt Brecht: *[Durch Fotografie keine Einsicht]*. BFA 21. Pp. 443–444. Here p. 443.

the time, Brecht observed that the time when a photograph had had true documentary force had passed:

> Ich meine nicht nur die Auswahl der Objekte, obwohl ich auch die meine, sondern vor allem jenen Ausdruck von Einmaligkeit, Besonderheit in der Zeit, den Künstler ihren Bildern verleihen können, die wissen, was ein Dokument ist. Aber dazu gehört Interesse für die Dinge und genügt nicht Interesse für die Beleuchtung.[15]

And in 1931 he wrote a very short piece for the celebration of the ten-year anniversary of the *Arbeiter-Illustrierte-Zeitung*. As well as providing more evidence that Brecht had been watching the development of modern photography with rather more alert and critical eyes than that passing remark about the Kruppwerke might imply, his piece gives us some sense of the resistance which he felt in the face of the bourgeois fetishism of the "truths" which could supposedly be revealed by placing objects before a camera lens.

> Die ungeheure Entwicklung der Bildreportage ist für die *Wahrheit* über die Zustände, die auf der Welt herrschen, kaum ein Gewinn gewesen: die Photographie ist in den Händen der Bourgeoisie zu einer furchtbaren Waffe *gegen* die Wahrheit geworden. Das riesige Bildmaterial, das tagtäglich von den Druckerpressen ausgespien wird und das doch den Charakter der Wahrheit zu haben scheint, dient in Wirklichkeit nur der Verdunkelung der Tatbestände.[16]

Brecht's more familiar early remarks on photography seem at first sight, out of context, just an expression of his repudiation of mimetic literalism, where the medium is made to stand in, almost lazily, for the "mirror" aesthetic. To a certain extent, photography does indeed have that function in Brecht's critique of realism in the later 1920s. Considered against this background, however – and in close dialogue with the work of Walter Benjamin certainly and probably Siegfried Kracauer – his scattered comments begin to coalesce as a more sophisticated critique, not of the medium for itself, but of a particular set of assumptions about photography and photographic reportage and of a particular fashionable practice of photographic art. Ruth Berlau, in her prefatory note to the first edition of the *Kriegsfibel*, makes a comment which almost eerily echoes Brecht's remarks of some twenty-five years earlier:

> Die große Unwissenheit über gesellschaftliche Zusammenhänge, die der Kapitalismus sorgsam und brutal aufrechterhält, macht die Tausende von Fotos in den Illustrierten zu wahren Hieroglyphentafeln, unentzifferbar dem nichtsahnenden Leser.[17]

[15] Bertolt Brecht: *[Über Fotografie]*. BFA 21. Pp. 264–265.
[16] Bertolt Brecht :*[Zum zehnjährigen Bestehen der A–I–Z]*. In: *A–I–Z*. No. 41. October 1931 (BFA 21. P. 515). This comment is very similar to more or less contemporary remarks by Kracauer.
[17] Ruth Berlau: In: *Kriegsfibel* (1955) (n. 2).

There is, however, one other earlier text where Brecht mentions photography, and this time – this will become important in the long run – it is in the context of reflections on poetry. In his 1927 *Kurzer Bericht über 400 (vierhundert) junge Lyriker* Brecht makes another passing, disparaging remark about the uselessness of photographs as a tool of enlightenment, and in the very same text exhorts that poems – almost, it would seem, in the place of photographs – should aspire to documentary force: "Alle großen Gedichte haben den Wert von Dokumenten".[18]

Given Brecht's interest in the pictorial, given his fascination with photography – as with all new technologies, and given his inclination to generic experiment, it seems astonishing that he didn't produce something like the *Kriegsfibel* earlier. Perhaps we should recognize that Brecht's critique of the naive documentary and his repudiation of the unpolitical avant-garde left him with some rather awkward territory to negotiate if he was to incorporate photographs into his own artistic practice. The point was to develop a form which might avoid both naturalist realism and context-less abstraction.

It perhaps took time to work that out. It has been suggested that there were other models for the *Kriegsfibel* in the late Weimar Republic: Ernst Friedrich's shocking collection of documentary photographs of the First World War, *Krieg dem Kriege* (Berlin 1926), which Brecht recommended when it first came out; Kurt Tucholsky and John Heartfield's satirical volume, *Deutschland, Deutschland über alles* (Berlin 1929); and the combinations of photographs and commentaries, even poems, in the *A-I-Z*.[19] It seems pretty plain that these did indeed all stimulate Brecht's interest. It is, however, equally clear that none of them comes very close to the actual practice of the *Kriegsfibel*. What they all have in common is just some degree of experiment in the relationship between photograph and text or caption, an issue in which both Benjamin and Brecht were particularly interested, both at the time and later.

It is not quite clear when Brecht himself started collecting newspaper cuttings; it must have been sometime in the 1920s. The first editions of both *Mann ist Mann* and *Im Dickicht der Städte* (Berlin: Propyläen 1926 and 1927) include (unattributed) photographs on the cover, endpapers and, in the latter, a series of four plates, to support their radically *verfremdet* views of modern society.[20]

---

[18] Bertolt Brecht: *Kurzer Bericht über 400 (vierhundert) junge Lyriker*. BFA 21. Pp. 191–193. Here p. 191.

[19] These are variously discussed in my article in *The Brecht Yearbook* (2007) (n. 1); Feddersen: Kriegsfibel (n. 5). Pp. 394–395; and in BFA 12. P. 410.

[20] "Fotografische Belege, nicht Buchschmuck, Sachdarstellung, nicht Illustration", commented Herbert Ihering in his review of *Im Dickicht*. See Herbert Ihering: *Von Reinhardt bis Brecht. Vier Jahrzehnte Theater und Film*. Berlin: Aufbau 1958. P. 247.

There are already substantial collections of cuttings amongst the working materials for *Die heilige Johanna der Schlachthöfe* and for *Die Rundköpfe und die Spitzköpfe*. The practice continued and probably intensified through the 1930s. An entry in the *Journal* from 1939 mentions "eine Mappe mit Fotos" (8.12.1939) amongst a list of Brecht's (more valuable) possessions. Besides, by this time he had already started the practice of sticking photos and cuttings into this work journal, which he maintained from July 1938 into the 1950s.

No one has undertaken a proper analysis of the function of the illustrations in the *Journal*, nearly all of which are photographs from the news media, or of the relationship between the images and the text. Philip Brady has made an extremely useful start. He speaks, in general terms, of the "unintended ambiguities and ironies" provoked by some of the banal and hardly newsworthy pictures, and comments that the purpose is not documentary, rather the interest for Brecht is "the camera's ability to capture assumptions about authority and the social order and unwittingly to expose those assumptions as vulnerable".[21] The very first photographs included are of Brecht himself and his family, and of the house at Skovsbostrand – as if he were first fixing an identity and locality, a perspective for the subsequent entries. Even here, the very first photograph (a rather anxious-looking portrait of Brecht) is situated between an entry about reading Shelley and one ridiculing Lukács's view of realism (16.8.–18.8.1938). It is these sorts of preoccupations of the *Journal*, and these juxtapositions which will become important for my argument. The first photograph which is *not* of family, friends or their homes is from a Swedish newspaper, and it shows a man in a gas-mask (5.9.1939). This is a full year later, amidst talk of the "phoney war" in the West and the inadequacy of preparations for war. Then, just a couple of days later (10.9.1939) comes a comment on the "Hirtengesänge" in Goethe's fragmentary *Pandora*, and on the close encounter in that work of the refined and the primitive: "Immer wieder taucht die Hand da in die Tiefe, etwas nach oben hebend, von dem einiges herabtropft, andres bleibt, völlig verfremdet in der neuen Gesellschaft". It is striking that reflections on the lyric, on the aesthetics of realism, and on politics here rub shoulders extremely closely, and are interspersed with photographs. To suggest that these were simply Brecht's unconnected preoccupations at the time, and that he was unaware of their proximity in the *Journal*, would be daft. After all, he

---

[21] Philip Brady: From Cave-Painting to "Fotogramm" (n. 11). P. 274. Grischa Meyer is currently undertaking a detailed study of the pictures of the *Journal* and the *Kriegsfibel* and their sources, and in particular he is looking at the context of the images that would have been available to Brecht as he scanned the news media of the time. This work, which establishes once and for all just how odd Brecht's "selection" was, is unpublished and I am grateful to the author for giving me the benefit of some of his preliminary findings.

typed, cut and pasted most of the pages himself. Rather, I would contend, he is beginning to try something out which will connect all these things.[22] The comment on *Pandora* provides a first clue: for he seems to be remarking how productive the "verfremdet" relationship (and that is scarcely a chance choice of word) can be between the high literary (or here, reversing the metaphor, "deep") and the primitive, surface, comparatively "real" world: "Die Glätte des Stroms zeigt seine Tiefe an". Throughout 1940 the photographs become much more frequent interruptions to the text of the *Journal*. Then, on 24 June 1940, he comments on his first sight of Picasso's *Guernica*: "Es macht starken Eindruck auf mich, und ich nehme mir vor, in dieser Richtung einmal etwas zu machen". Now I have no wish to imply that this has anything very intimately to do with the aesthetics of the *Kriegsfibel*, but it is most certainly a symptom of Brecht's interest in the power of the pictorial to intervene in this political world: "Interessante romantische V-Effekte, dabei klassizistische Form". One month later (25.7.1940) he writes about August Oehler's translations of Greek epigrams, and starts himself to write epigrams.

It is, finally, a series of entries in the last week of August 1940 which fully establishes the connections I want to make. Before discussing these, though, let me just say a word about the great essays on realism of the later 1930s, which also contribute to the intellectual context for these thoughts. From about the time of the *Dreigroschenprozess* onwards, Brecht is clearly and increasingly less interested in the representation of reality, than in what he calls the "Meisterung der Realität".[23] There is a shift towards explanatory or cognitive realism. The main arguments are set out in detail in *Volkstümlichkeit und Realismus* (BFA 22.1. Pp. 405–413) and *Weite und Vielfalt der realistischen Schreibweise* (BFA 22.1. Pp. 424–433) both from the summer of 1938, and *Notizen über realistische Schreibweise* of 1940 (BFA 22.2. Pp. 520–640). In the first of these Brecht defines his, or rather "unser Realismusbegriff" as follows:

> *Realistisch* heißt: den gesellschaftlichen Kausalkomplex aufdeckend/die herrschenden Gesichtspunkte als die Gesichtspunkte der Herrschenden entlarvend/vom Standpunkt der Klasse aus schreibend, welche für die dringendsten Schwierigkeiten, in denen die menschliche Gesellschaft steckt, die breitesten Lösungen bereit hält/das Moment der Entwicklung betonend/konkret und das Abstrahieren ermöglichend (BFA 22.1. P. 409).

---

[22] Brady makes a similar point, about "disparate worlds" not joined neatly (Philip Brady: From Cave-Painting to "Fotogramm" (n. 11). P. 279). And Invernel speaks thus of the relationships between the parts of the *Journal*: "convergences, décalages, distorsions, le jeu des éloignements et des rapprochements oblige à d'incessants rétablissements, pour une pensée qui entend relever le défi de la pratique" (Philippe Invernel: L'oeil de Brecht (n. 11). Pp. 224–225).

[23] Bertolt Brecht: *[Über die eigene Arbeit]*. BFA 22. 1. Pp. 445–449. Here p. 446.

Notice how the capacity for abstraction has now become a part of his definition of realism. In *Weite und Vielfalt* he goes on to subject his notion of realism to what might seem to be the ultimate test, lyric poetry: he argues that the politically useful poet may be a realist, just as much as any novelist – specifically, that Shelley is as great a realist as Balzac. Here Brecht's argument for a greatly expanded sense of what counts as realism proceeds not just through a defence of Shelley's poetic imagination, but also, by implication, through a defence of Shelley's own great aesthetic essay, *Defence of Poetry*, in which he, in turn, argues that every line of real poetry proceeds by erasing or negating the given or everyday understanding of things as they are.[24]

Two years later, in August 1940, Brecht revisited these questions in his *Journal*:

> Zur Frage des *Realismus*: Die gewöhnliche Anschauung ist, daß ein Kunstwerk desto realistischer ist, je leichter die Realität in ihm zu erkennen ist. Dem stelle ich die Definition entgegen, daß ein Kunstwerk desto realistischer ist, je erkennbarer in ihm die Realität gemeistert wird. Das pure Wiedererkennen der Realität wird oft durch eine solche Darstellung erschwert, die sie meistern lehrt (6.8.1940).

Realism too proceeds by, first of all, making the recognition of reality more difficult or by contradicting our everyday assumptions. Let us recall that the very first example of a photo-epigram in the form of the *Kriegsfibel* also dates from August 1940, in fact it bears the date 4 August.[25] At the end of that same month, at the height of the Battle of Britain (when one might have expected him to have very different things on his mind) he returned to the idea of the potentially "realist" (in his sense) function of lyric poetry and, in a note in the *Journal* (24.8.1940), he enlisted the even more unlikely figure of Wordsworth for his argument.

> Ich traf auf "She was a phantom of delight" und dachte über diesem uns so entfernten Stück, wie vielfach die Funktion der Kunst ist und wie achtsam man sein muß beim Aufstellen von Vorschriften. [...] Der Kleinbürger, der heute mit Jagdflinte und Dynamitflasche [...] Englands Felder durchpatrouilliert, mag seinen Wordsworths einige Schuld geben können, aber gerade in dieser entmenschten Situation kann
>
> > "a lovely apparition, sent
> > to be a moment's ornament"
>
> die Erinnerung wachrufen an menschenwürdigere Situationen. [...] Die Kunst *ist* ein autonomer Bezirk, wenn auch unter keinen Umständen ein autarker.

---

[24] In this sentence I am paraphrasing and part-quoting sentences from Robert Kaufman's unpublished paper presented to the MLA (San Diego, December 2003).
[25] "Fliegende Haie nannten wir uns prahlend". See BFA 12. P. 411.

These reflections on the social practice of lyric poetry, which Brecht now sees as directly interventionist ("geschichtsbedingt und geschichtemachend"), end with this thought: "Der Unterschied liegt zwischen 'widerspiegeln' und 'den Spiegel vorhalten' ". In that last phrase, the metaphor of the mirror aesthetic is transformed from the relatively passive notion of reflection (familiar from aesthetic commentators from Plato to Alberti to Johnson to Abrams) to a much more specific active choice. The phrase, "jemandem den Spiegel vorhalten", means not just "holding the mirror up to someone", but "revealing, disclosing their true nature, which hitherto had been concealed". In the first published version of *Volkstümlichkeit und Realismus* Brecht uses the metaphor in a similarly active sense, when he writes that the oppressors have "viele Methoden, sich dem Spiegel, der vorgehalten wird, zu entziehen".[26] So one forms the image, not of Plato's great reflector of nature set up in the landscape, but of a hand-mirror, apt for swift and unexpected interventions in the hands of the wily political artist – the sort of mirror you could hit someone over the head with if the need arose.

Now it so happens that there is a photograph stuck into the *Journal* at exactly this moment, on the sheet with this one day's entry and immediately after that phrase about holding up the mirror.[27] It shows a group of people doing drill in gas masks – they are in fact British civilians preparing for the possibility of German invasion. The illustration was taken from the *Berliner Illustrirte Zeitung*, but it originated from the London *Picture Post*.[28] The connection between Brecht's thoughts on the lyric and this somewhat bizarre document of contemporary reality is at first unclear. But it must be this: inspired, as it were, by Wordsworth's image of "menschenwürdigere Situationen", the English petty bourgeoisie is preparing to repulse a German invasion. The commentary on the poem and the photographic document conspire in a mutually *verfremdend* dialectic to make us re-assess our assumptions and to get Brecht's message across.[29]

This last week in August has some other relevant fragments to add to the emerging picture. The next entry sees a mention of the graphic artist Hans Tombrock and of Breughel; and the one after includes a remark about Greek epigrams as a poetry of objects, "Gebrauchsgegenstände", including specifically weapons; then there are three attempts at adaptations from Oehler's translations, and

---

[26] Bertolt Brecht: *Volkstümlichkeit und Realismus*. In: *Sinn und Form* 10 (1958). P. 499.
[27] The relevant archive sheet (BBA 277/37) makes it entirely clear that this photograph belongs with this particular day's journal entry. The German edition of the *Journal* includes the photograph at this point (24.8.1940. BFA 26. P. 418), but it is missing from the English edition (*Journals*. Ed. by John Willett, trans. by Hugh Rorrison. London: Methuen 1993. Pp. 90–91).
[28] See note at BFA 26. P. 661.
[29] Brady (n. 11) makes much the same point (p. 279).

photographs of the interior of a bomber and of hand-grenades (BFA 26. Pp. 418–421). The close interweaving of all of these concerns is remarkable. And the first steps towards the photo-epigram form come at exactly this same point in the *Journal*. All of this antedates by only one month the sequence of pages from the *Kriegsfibel* with which I opened this essay.

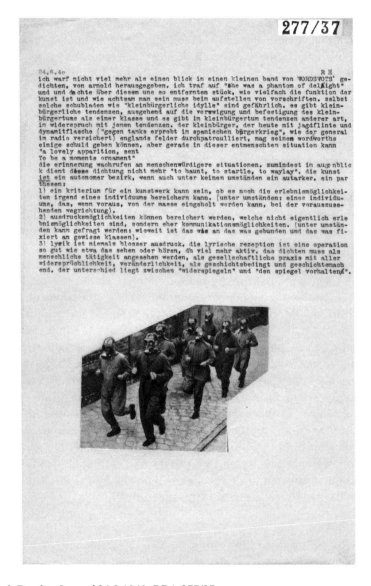

Bertolt Brecht: *Journal* 24.8.1940. BBA 277/37.

Two years later, in April 1942, at another low point for the Allies (in the face of rapid Japanese advances and the fall of Singapore), we encounter another *Journal* entry devoted to the problem of lyric poetry. This one ends with the seemingly desperate assertion, "Die Schlacht um Smolensk geht auch um die Lyrik" – the point being, again, that this is a war for the sake of "menschen-würdigere Situationen" in which it will no longer be a "schlechte Zeit für Lyrik" (BFA 14. P. 432). Again there is a photograph, this time a cutting from *Life* magazine, which shows a woman sitting amidst the devastation of a bombed-out Singapore, apparently bewailing the destruction of her own child, whose corpse lies nearby.[30] As many readers will recognize, it is an image which Brecht takes up and uses again in the *Kriegsfibel* (Nr. 39), where it is accompanied by a notably elevated four-line poem:

O Stimme aus dem Doppeljammerchore
Der Opfer und der Opferer in Fron!
Der Sohn des Himmels, Frau, braucht Singapore
Und niemand als du selbst brauchst deinen Sohn.

An unconscious memory of the same picture, Brecht believed, may have inspired Helene Weigel for the famous silent scream, the *Gestus* with which, as Mother Courage, she greeted the corpse of her son at the end of Scene 3 of that play.[31] So it is an important and resonant image in several ways.

What I set out to do in this paper was to re-situate the *Kriegsfibel* in relation to Brecht's interest in photography and the pictorial, on the one hand, and, on the other, to his more commonly recognized central obsessions of the later exile: realism and the lyric. I hope that has been achieved, and with it a clearer idea of how important the *Kriegsfibel* is in Brecht's output. Whereas one might usually think of newspaper photography and lyric poetry at opposite ends of some aesthetic spectrum – the one base, realist, objective, scientific, dependent on the particulars of social reality, the other elevated, subjective, un-technological, shading off into abstraction or into some autonomous realm – Brecht's practice is always to upset one genre or medium by confronting it and juxtaposing it with another. It begins to seem almost a logical extension of his thoughts on realism to bring together the polished lyric and the grainy documentary photograph. The images are transformed by Brecht's difficult lyric voice; and the poems are made shockingly powerful by the insistence on the real which the photographs appear to guarantee.

---

[30] Brecht: *Journal* 5.4.1942. BFA 27. Pp. 79–80 and notes p. 412. The Battle of Smolensk (July–September 1941) was an important reversal for the German troops advancing on Moscow.
[31] Bertolt Brecht: *Couragemodell*. BFA 25. Pp. 169–398. Here pp. 203–204.

The "Singapore Lament" photo-epigram has many of the features I picked out at the outset. It is of course very overtly about mothers and sons again. It is of an elevated register, and the interrupted and slightly forced syntax have perhaps classical echoes. And it is tightly written in the standard iambic pentameters and ABAB rhyme, with repetition (Opfer/Opferer; Sohn/Sohn) and perhaps little archaic gestures in the words "Chore" and "Fron". It divides into two halves: the first two lines an exclamation, the second two a direct address by the poet to the woman. In the first half, Brecht makes that move, not unfamiliar from the rest of this work, of insisting that the perpetrators are also in their way victims of the war, forced to do this work, and so allied to their "Opfer" in a "Doppeljammerchor". So our perceptions of the reality to which the photograph refers us are immediately complicated. Our assumptions about perpetrators and victims – an intensely pathetic example of which squats in the centre of this picture – are disturbed. This is not just an empathetic lament. The significance of the picture is not that one woman is bewailing her child's death, but that the world resounds with a chorus of "Jammer", of which the event pictured here is just a symptom and a symbol. The "Sohn des Himmels" in the third line is a typically slightly obscure reference, here not to one of Brecht's individualized bombers but to the Japanese Emperor Hirohito. Hirohito is one of the many political leaders who also appear on the pages of the *Kriegsfibel*, and who are never given their own names, but referred to by a series of evasive epithets and euphemisms. In this way Brecht makes another of those briefly sketched and deft gestures towards a political analysis which are characteristic of the cycle. At the same time, the very fact of poetry recalls an alternative world of dignity and creativity that is in marked contrast to the destruction apparent in the photograph: the howl of despair is opposed to the balanced iambic cadences of Brecht's "Stimme aus dem Doppeljammerchore", and both can be taken to refer as much to his own voice, the poet observing this destruction, as to the bereft mother. In their mutually *verfremdend* interaction it becomes possible to re-read the poem as a document (of the poet's response on the occasion of this news item) and to look again at the picture as a formal construct (with qualities of balance, frame and symbolism).

The position of this photo-epigram in the cycle also serves to contextualize and relativize what seems at first one of the most pathetic images of the whole collection. The picture which precedes this one is of Churchill with a tommy gun, looking for all the world like a gangster from *Arturo Ui*; and immediately after we have an American soldier posing with a cigarette over the corpse of a Japanese soldier he's killed – "It was just like in the movies" – and, most bizarre of all the images in this work, the photograph of a "sexy carrot", sent in by a reader to the editor of *Life*. It is part of a sequence about capitalist-imperialist pillage. On this particular page, the cutting is *not* this time from *Life*; Brecht must have had another source, although we do not know what that was. In comparison with the version in the *Journal*, the picture has now been severely cropped along the top, bringing the focus down to the foreground, where the child's body has also been retouched for clarity. And it is given that huge bold banner title: "Singapore Lament", which is then directly taken up in Brecht's word, "Jammerchor". There is, I think, no suggestion that Brecht or Berlau themselves manipulated these images, but they certainly sourced and selected them very deliberately. The picture is very neatly framed by the black surround this time. Black has, throughout the *Kriegsfibel*, the potential to refer us to war, death, and lament; and in this instance the black edging seems to reflect a suggestion of mourning in the woman's clothes. The symbolism also of the broken wheels and wrecked carriage seems almost as important as the human wreckage – and is again resonant in relation to *Mutter Courage*. Yet one is discouraged from going too far in a formal reading of the photograph, firstly by the blurred quality of the image – all the photographs of the *Kriegsfibel* betray their origins in the news media, and that is obviously important here too. Moreover, in this instance there is also a small label in the bottom left corner which reads "AP WIREPHOTO". That seems both to give us that guarantee of authenticity and immediacy which are so crucial for the whole composition, and also to take up the critique of press photography and the whole politics of representation, which is equally a part of the collection.

Here indeed is a contemplative, cognitive, even interventionist realism, which eschews both passive naturalism and context-less abstraction, without missing out either on particular reality or on general reflection. Here is a genre, of what one might call *gestische* tableaux, that demands our active reading, as we move back and forth between image and verse, on this page and between pages. Instead of simply indexing "objective reality" in an attempt to uncover the real as something independent of social and political subjectivity, Brecht has developed an approach that dialogically structures reality into representation, invites a disrobing gaze, encourages understanding, and even implies the possibility of intervention. In the *Messingkauf* (these notes also written in the last years of the war) he comments: "Es müssen die Gesetze sichtbar werden, welche den Ablauf der Prozesse des Lebens beherrschen. Diese Gesetze sind nicht auf Photographien sichtbar"[32] – not, that is, on photographs alone. Photographic positivism has been replaced by a radically probing version of documentary. The *Kriegsfibel* is of course (in the terms of that note from the *Journal*) "geschichtsbedingt" and has no wish to be otherwise, but, in 1944 – and in 1955 when it was finally published, and still in 2007 – it can also aspire to be "geschichtemachend" in its project of enlightenment. That is the challenge and, I would suggest also, the achievement of this *Fibel*.

[32] Bertolt Brecht: *Messingkauf*. BFA 22. Pp. 695–869. Here p. 792.

Ronald Speirs

Poetry in Dark Times: Brecht's *Svendborger Gedichte*

The essay examines Brecht's treatment of time in the Svendborger Gedichte. *It argues that the poet's response to the "dark times" of fascism that drove him and many others into exile is to invest the ancient existential theme of transience with new political significance. The class struggle is not simply about the re-interpretation and redirection of the course of history. What is at stake, rather, is the right of each individual to enjoy the brief time that is given to him on earth. Whereas the poems of the* Hauspostille *had mainly treated time as an immutable given of the natural world, the* Svendborger Gedichte *concentrate on the role played by human attitudes, habits, actions and institutions in exacerbating the problems of mortality.*

In 1938, when Brecht and Benjamin were discussing the selection of poems from exile that eventually came to be published under the title of the *Svendborger Gedichte*, they argued about whether some of Brecht's "Kinderlieder" ought to be included in the collection. Benjamin thought not, because he felt the children's songs might diminish the contrast between the political and the private poems, which, he felt, expressed the experience of exile so powerfully. Brecht, on the other hand, insisted that these songs *must* be included in order to demonstrate, "daß das Leben, trotz Hitler, weitergeht, daß es immer wieder Kinder geben wird".[1] Brecht then elaborated on his reasons as follows:

> In dem Kampf gegen die darf nichts ausgelassen werden. Sie haben nichts Kleines im Sinn. Sie planen auf dreißigtausend Jahre hinaus Ungeheures. Ungeheure Verbrechen. Sie machen vor nichts halt. Sie schlagen auf alles ein. Jede Zelle zuckt unter ihrem Schlag zusammen. Darum darf keine von uns vergessen werden. Sie verkrümmen das Kind im Mutterleib. Wir dürfen die Kinder auf keinen Fall auslassen.[2]

Of course we cannot be certain about the accuracy of Benjamin's account of the conversation, but it has the ring of truth about it, principally because time, which features so prominently in Brecht's argument for including the children's songs, is one of the organizing principles and chief concerns of the *Svendborger Gedichte* (BFA 12. Pp. 7–92).[3]

The collection had a huge ambition. As Brecht's comment to Benjamin makes clear, it aimed at nothing less than wresting the control of history from

---

[1] Walter Benjamin: Tagebuchnotizen 1938. WBGS VI. Pp. 532–539. Here p. 538.
[2] Ibid. p. 539.
[3] For more detailed consideration of many other aspects of the collection, see: *Brecht's Poetry of Political Exile.* Ed. by Ronald Speirs. Cambridge: Cambridge University Press 2000.

the hands of the fascists. If *they* had plans for the next 30,000 years, then so did Brecht and those with whom he believed himself allied. What was at stake in that battle for history was ultimately the fragile, brief span of life given to each individual – "meine Zeit, die auf Erden mir gegeben war"[4] – the personal experience of time passing that has always been a wellspring of poetry. Brecht's sympathy with the cells of an unborn child recoiling from the violence done to humanity during the years of National Socialist dictatorship was intimately connected with the inherent sensitivity of the lyric poet to all encroachments on time as the very element of poetry and of life itself. In poetry, as in music, metre and rhythm are time made palpable. Rhyme is recurrence in time made audible. The root sense of "verse" is the turning and re-turning of words as they move through time in sensible patterns. Poetry, in other words, is a form of art that transforms our sense of time passing into a source of pleasure. For a young child, the play with time involved in chanting a nursery rhyme is still innocent and instinctive. In adults, by contrast, poetic play is rarely free from the awareness that it is we who, in the end, are the playthings of time. Once lost, the carefree sensibility of a child can never be recovered, but part of the pleasure we take in poetry is surely the distant memory of an earlier, freer way of feeling which its forms awaken in us. This, I would suggest, explains why Brecht insisted so vehemently on the inclusion of the "Kinderlieder" in the *Svendborger Gedichte*: they, more than any other part of the collection, pointed towards the ideal of free, creative play with time that had to be defended against the regimented barbarity of the fascists.

In this collection, admittedly, even the children's songs could not remain entirely untouched by an overshadowing sense not just of time passing, but of "the times", the "finsteren Zeiten" in which the happiness of childhood is made even briefer and more fragile than it need otherwise be. Here too the liberating *delectare* that is the primary effect of poetic form is contaminated by the necessity of *prodesse*, as lyric play is harnessed uncomfortably to rhetoric with a practical purpose. That purpose includes, ultimately, the defence of poetry's aspiration to play freely with time (as the younger Brecht had done when he composed many of the poems in the *Hauspostille*), but "ultimately" lies a long way off in the future. In the meantime the poet feels obliged to make his skills useful to those whom he believes capable of taking history in a just and proper direction. On the other hand, simply to abandon the forms of poetry entirely in favour of the prosy rhetoric of the political pamphlet would be to give up any claim to the patrimony of poetry, perhaps even cause it to be forgotten. The *Svendborger Gedichte* are the product and expression of precisely this conflict between the practical necessities imposed by "the times" and the poet's desire to play freely in the short time he still has to live. In other words, these poems

---

[4] Bertolt Brecht: An die Nachgeborenen. BFA 12. P. 86.

are not just *about* history, about the dark times in which they were written, but are imbued with and shaped by the pressures of contemporary events on the poetic imagination. In their forms and language the poems are stamped by the contradictions in which the poet is enmeshed, the conflict between time and the times, between existential concerns and historical obligations.

Perhaps the most obvious way in which these poems deal purposively with time is in their documentation of the "finsteren Zeiten". Following his own advice to other artists to create documents with their work,[5] Brecht's poetry documents much more fully and precisely than most some of what he considered to be the key aspects of life in the 1930s. The *Svendborger Gedichte* document, for example, not just the experience of exile, both in its personal dimensions and in relation to the larger political issues which drove so many Germans out of the country at that time, but also the preparations for war and their impact on German industry, the National Socialists' treatment of Jews, political opponents or critics, their reliance on propaganda and censorship, the deteriorating living conditions for ordinary people when "great things" are being planned by those in high places.

Far from simply recording details of those "dark times", however, this is poetry that attempts to act in its turn upon the historical and political processes affecting society and individual alike. In theme, treatment, structure and style the poems are informed by Brecht's notion of "interventionist thinking", with its requirement that each individual, when reflecting on cause and effect in society, should include him- or herself amongst the range of factors capable of making a difference, however slight, to the course of history.[6] Thus the poems employ a wide range of modes of address or *Gestus* designed to influence the reader's response to events: information, criticism, exhortation, sarcasm, variations of focus or perspective, directness, indirectness, plain style and high style, the contemporary and specific alongside the historically distant and general. To give just one small instance of the thought Brecht gave to the gestural aspect of the poetry, he changed the title of one poem from a statement ("In unserm Lande") into a question ("Und in eurem Lande?") between the first and the ultimately published version.[7] The reader is thereby addressed directly, engaged in a dialogue, and challenged to take a view on how things are in his or her country.

---

[5] See Bertolt Brecht: *Kleiner Rat, Dokumente anzufertigen*. BFA 21. Pp. 163–165. Here p. 163.
[6] See, for example Bertolt Brecht: *Das Denken als ein Verhalten*. BFA 21. Pp. 421–422. Here p. 422: "Das eingreifende Denken. Praktikable Definitionen: solche Definitionen, die die Handhabung des definierten Feldes gestatten. Unter den determinierenden Faktoren tritt immer das Verhalten des Definierenden auf".
[7] See BBA 75/86.

The poems show the poet thinking not just about the political relevance of his themes and modes of address but also about form as something with a political dimension, both in individual poems and in the structure of the whole collection and its component parts. In this collection the experience of time is considered chiefly in its shared, social aspect. In part this was a consequence of the poet's exile, an experience he shared with many others for whom life in Nazi Germany had been made intolerable or simply too dangerous. A book of poems could serve as a place to communicate with other exiles and even, so the poet hoped, with those who remained in Germany and who were still willing and able to listen to voices other than those of the "housepainter" speaking through megaphones of great times to come. As Tom Kuhn observes, "[o]ne of the major tasks, then, was to construct a sense of society and community in which the dialectical pedagogy of his poems could be heard and could make sense".[8] Thus the second section of the *Svendborger Gedichte*, for example, is united formally by the (sociable) genre of song. The types of song range from children's songs to ballads and marching songs for political rallies, but all of them, some directly, others much less obviously so, bear out the motto at the head of this section, namely that "in the dark times" there will indeed still be singing – "of the dark times" themselves (BFA 12. P. 16). In such times even to sing about a "child who wouldn't wash" implies a not-singing about so many other things (such as the well-scrubbed, drum-beating little boys beloved of Nazi propaganda) that the little song becomes charged with political significance. On the other hand, it belongs equally to Brecht's overall design that this poem resists being completely politicized, insisting as it does on the right of little children *not* to want to wash and to care not a fig about whether or not they ever see "the emperor", i.e. the world of politics.

The six sections of the *Svendborger Gedichte* are unified by three interrelated concerns. If one is to document the "dark times", the second is the poet's determination to bring the light of reason to bear on these dark times, the true nature of which the new power-holders and their financial backers are intent on keeping obscure, by engaging in a process of teaching and learning; the third is to open up a perspective on the possibility of other times, other ways of living, another course of history. For the project of enlightenment to succeed, however, the poetry – and the present state of the world – calls for a certain kind of reader. Such a reader will ask the kind of penetrating questions rehearsed in the opening poem of the "Chronicles" section ("Fragen eines lesenden Arbeiters". BFA 12. P. 29). If the world were full of sharply intelligent worker-readers with such a firm grasp of their own class interests, it is implied, the poet might not have had the unwelcome task of describing such dark times in the first place. Since the

[8] Tom Kuhn: "Visit to a Banished Poet": Brecht's Svendborg Poems and the Voices of Exile. In: Speirs (ed.): *Brecht's Poetry* (n. 3). Pp. 47–65. Here p. 58.

world is as it is, however, the poet must reckon with other, less well-informed and less alert readers who have allowed it to become like this. The inculcation in the reader of a critical attitude to the times, through the very process of reading, is therefore one of the prime tasks the poet sets himself in the *Svendborger Gedichte*.

Thus the genre chosen to open the collection is a type of book designed to teach the rudiments of reading, in this instance reading the language of war. Hence the preference throughout the "Deutsche Kriegsfibel" for the simplest forms of sentence and the predominance of paratactic structures. So determined was Brecht to keep returning to the ground-bass of this basic (but in fact very artful) pattern, that he even removed an unremarkable inversion from one poem, turning "abgeholzt / stehen die Lorbeerhaine" into "Die Lorbeerhaine stehen abgeholzt".[9] The reading skills taught in this primer are intended to be applied not just to the inconspicuous subtleties of the poems but to the unperceived or misperceived structures of the world. To achieve this, the poet combines seeming simplicity with a degree of challenge or difficulty. Nothing could be (seemingly) simpler in diction or structure than the following brief poem, one of the minor masterpieces of the "German War Primer":

AUF DER MAUER STAND MIT KREIDE:
Sie wollen den Krieg
Der es geschrieben hat
Ist schon gefallen (BFA 12. P. 12).

Time is evidently moving at a fearful pace. The slogan once "stood" on the wall; the man who wrote it there hastily, using chalk, has since "fallen". Yet "proper" war has not yet broken out. Why, then, has this man already fallen? Why has the peaceful act of writing led to a war-like death? In what circumstances could the act of writing be construed, and responded to, as an act of war? Because no answers are given, the poet's artfully elliptical verse makes us into "readers who work" and who must discover for themselves what is left unstated in the gaps between the sentences. The reading eye that makes connections between the lines of the poem (and between this poem and a later one, "Die unbesiegliche Inschrift". BFA 12. Pp. 39–40) is being trained by the careful patterning of the language, particularly the mixture of symmetry and asymmetry linking the two sentences of the stanza, to make connections in the world and thus to uncover what there too goes unsaid.

---

[9] See the archive folder BBA 75; in this early version the poem had a title: "Kriegsbeginn". All such titles disappeared during the preparations for publication. Like the "simple" syntax, the brevity on which the effectiveness of the poems in this section depends was also something that had to be worked at. Thus the poem "Mann mit der zerschlissenen Jacke" was reduced by a stanza between the first and the final, published form of the collection; see BBA 75/10.

Running through the six sections of the collection is a wave-like rhythm that moves between registering the way things are (and how they are likely to develop) in these dark times, and summoning up various forms of resistance to this state of affairs, urging individuals to commit their own brief time to the battle for the present and the times to come. The "Deutsche Kriegsfibel", for example, opens with an explanation of why the present is as it is and why the present keeps reproducing the bad features of the past. The theme of the first poem (BFA 12. P. 9) is surprising, for it is not about war as it is generally understood, but about the inequalities in society produced by the class-warfare that allows "die Oberen" to maintain their position precisely because "die Niedrigen" are not sufficiently aware that this kind of war is permanently being waged against them. The last poem in this cycle (BFA 12. Pp. 14–15), by contrast, shifts attention away from the self-reproducing structures of a bad present and towards the inception of a different future: soon "der Trommler" will begin to wage "his" war, but this will also be the moment when politically enlightened Germans will follow Lenin's injunction to transform imperialist war into civil (i.e. *class*) war, and show *their* patriotism precisely by sabotaging *his* plans for the future.

On behalf of the "Niedrigen", whose historical mission is to become the active subjects rather than the passive objects of the historical process, the poet of the *Svendborger Gedichte* re-functions an inherited way of thinking about the structure of time. Its source – "Sie werden lachen", as Brecht once observed – was the Bible.[10] As was the case in the *Hauspostille*, the overall conception of time in the *Svendborger Gedichte* is teleological and "eschatological": the present is seen in the light of a cataclysmic ending and a radically changed future. In the *Hauspostille*, however, the end of time that will come with the death of the poet was imaginatively projected onto the whole of contemporary civilisation. Like the author of Revelations,[11] the poet would dearly like to see the "Erdbeben, die kommen werden" consume the cities when the time comes for him to leave them and return to the cold of the "schwarzen Wäldern" where life began before he was carried, still in his mother's womb, into the cities. In the meantime the intensity of painful and pleasurable experience cultivated by the poet is meant to incorporate into *this* life the Heaven and the Hell which he no longer believes to lie beyond death.[12] In the *Svendborger Gedichte*, by contrast, the eschatology conforms more closely to the biblical order of events, although here too the imagined new life is again to be found in

---

[10] Asked about "der stärkste Eindruck" he had experienced, Brecht answered: "Sie werden lachen: Die Bibel" (BFA 21. P. 248).

[11] Revelations 16, 18–19.

[12] See the three poems collected under the title *Anhang: Vom armen B. B.*. BFA 12. Pp. 117–120.

this world rather than then next: first there will be Armageddon and the Last Judgement,[13] which will be followed by the transfiguration of the earth.[14] Whereas those "at the top" of the social order ("die Oberen") have always expected that the proletariat will fight their wars for them "bis zum Jüngsten Tage",[15] Brecht foretells a different future that will come about when the working class has finally won the war between the classes: "Und er blutet und zahlt bis zu seinem Siege / Der ihn für immer zum Herren macht" (BFA 12. P. 25). This victory – in what "Die Internationale" calls "das letzte Gefecht" – will bring the epoch of exploitation to an end and usher in a new age where there will be no more alienation of men from men, men from work, men from nature. To achieve this, however, the revolutionary soldiers will require a set of virtues which read like an alternative Beatitudes:

> Tapfer wird sein, wer gegen ihn kämpft.
> Klug wird sein, wer seine Pläne vereitelt.
> Nur wer ihn bekämpft, wird Deutschland helfen (BFA 12. P. 15).

The blessings to come will be the work of human hands alone. Whereas the Psalmist cried out to the Lord "from the depths",[16] Brecht prophesies that mankind's liberation will only come from those who are themselves "in tiefster Tiefe".[17] Whereas it was the Lord who fed ("speiste")[18] Israel in the desert, Brecht asserts that it will be the hungry themselves who will feed ("speisen") the hungry (BFA 12. P. 23).

Thus in both collections Brecht appropriates and "refunctions" the biblical structure of time. In both cases he urges the reader not to be tempted by the once popular theological view that a life of deprivation in this world will receive its recompense in the hereafter. But whereas the *Hauspostille* praised those who fight ruthlessly for their own enjoyment before their personal Last Day, the *Svendborger Gedichte* praise those who fight for the eventual happiness of "those below" in the world as it will be after the end of class-history.

---

[13] See also Anthony Phelan's argument about the link between Walter Benjamin's theses on the philosophy of history and Brecht's thought. Anthony Phelan: Figures of Memory in the "Chroniken". In: Speirs (ed.): *Brecht's Poetry* (n. 3). Pp. 172–189. Here pp. 177–178.

[14] The language of biblical eschatology appears to have engaged Brecht's imagination throughout his career. For example, amongst his papers in the Brecht Archiv there is a poem (possibly written by Brecht himself, although Elisabeth Hauptmann thought otherwise) entitled "Lied der neuen Erde" (BFA 15. Pp. 293–294) where the biblical vision of the "new earth" that is to be created after the Day of Judgment is equated with the victory of socialism.

[15] Bertolt Brecht: Lied gegen den Krieg. BFA 12. Pp. 24–26. Here p. 25.

[16] See Psalm 130: "Out of the depths I have cried unto thee, o Lord".

[17] Bertolt Brecht: Keiner oder alle. BFA 12. Pp. 23–24. Here p. 23.

[18] Deuteronomy 8, 16.

198

The pleasure in fighting for its own sake so relished by the pirates and adventurers of the early poetry has been transformed into a political version of the Good Fight. The inner-worldly transcendence of individual life previously sought through acts of physical identification with unconscious, long-lived nature (swimming in rivers, climbing trees)[19] has been replaced by work for the future of mankind, which rewards transient individuals for their commitment to the common cause of humanity by allowing them to survive in the memory of others, as in the case of Empedocles and the mysterious legacy of his shoe (BFA 12. Pp. 30–32), Laotse's legendary composition of the book Tao Teking on his journey into exile (BFA 12. Pp. 32–34), Lenin, now "eingeschreint / In dem großen Herzen der Arbeiterklasse",[20] or even the otherwise unknown Mike McCoy, a railwayman and comrade whose widow is still supported by the workmates who have not forgotten his solidarity with them.[21]

The *Svendborger Gedichte* propose not only a new way of thinking about the structure of historical time, but also a new approach to the recording and interpretation of history. Through the persona of the "lesender Arbeiter", astute and keenly aware of the interests of the class to which he belongs, Brecht asks why history books do not record the names of cooks or foot-soldiers, and why kings or emperors, rather than stonemasons, are credited with building cities. Those "above", he implies, have had history written in the way it always has been (as the history of "great men") to ensure that the "ruling ideas" (about history, power and "the way things are") will forever remain the ideas of the rulers,[22] thereby ensuring that it is they who remain "above" while others remain "below" in an exploitative social structure. To train the non-ruling (or rather, the not-yet-ruling) reader in the art of re-appropriating history, Brecht includes a little ballad, of the fairground type, about the tailor from Ulm, who, to the evident delight of the Bishop of Ulm, falls to his death from the church roof in an abortive attempt to fly.[23] The outcome appears to confirm the scepticism and Schadenfreude of the townspeople ("Es war eine Hatz"), an attitude the bishop seeks to reinforce by having the church bells rung, and proclaiming that, "Der Mensch ist kein Vogel / Es wird nie ein Mensch fliegen" (BFA 12. P. 20).

[19] See, for example, the poems "Vom Klettern in Bäumen" (BFA 11. Pp. 71–72) and "Vom Schwimmen in Seen und Flüssen" (BFA 11. P. 73). Echoing the Satanic promise, "Eritis sicut deus", the poet of the *Hauspostille* conjures up the pleasure of drifting down rivers on warm summer evenings: "wie der liebe Gott tut / Wenn er am Abend noch in seinen Flüssen schwimmt" (BFA 11. P. 73).
[20] Bertolt Brecht: Lob des Revolutionärs. BFA 12. Pp. 59–60. Here p. 60.
[21] Bertolt Brecht: Kohlen für Mike. BFA 12. Pp. 40–41.
[22] "Die herrschenden Ideen einer Zeit waren stets nur die Ideen der herrschenden Klasse". Karl Marx and Friedrich Engels: *Manifest der Kommunistischen Partei.* Stuttgart: Reclam 1969. P. 44.
[23] Bertolt Brecht: Ulm 1592. BFA 12. Pp. 19–20.

Thereby the bishop smugly re-asserts the supposedly God-given, natural order of things which includes, of course, the authority of the Church to tell "the people" how things are and forever must remain. Most of this, however, is deliberately left implicit in the poem, so that the reader must work back from the bishop's false prediction of the future to ask him- or herself what underlies the Church's preference for the supposed immutability of natural "law" over historical innovation. The generation of those who have taken command of the air in recent years are thus invited, by implication, to consider whether they have also taken command of *history* since the days of the little tailor's failed experiment, or whether, like the people of Ulm, they are still stuck in the view that what has "always" been the case will forever remain so. A new history and a new version of the Last Day will not come about, the poet has clearly decided, by simply *telling* readers, as the bishop once told the people, the "correct" historical facts. Instead his poem prompts *questions*, inviting readers to recognize both the fallibility of human beings and their ability to learn from experience and thereby gain confidence in their own ability to understand and judge things. History, the poem suggests, is there for the making – and the taking.

Another of the children's poems, "Der Pflaumenbaum" (BFA 12. Pp. 21–22), reinforces the point with a negative example. The little plum tree, identifiable only by its leaf, never bears fruit, not from any fault of its own but because it stands alone (so that it cannot be pollinated) and in a sunless courtyard. The potential of the future, in other words, may never be realized if the crippling conditions of the present are not challenged and changed. Only by common human action can the present, fed by an understanding of the past, flow into a radically different future. Equally unspoken, again for pedagogic reasons, is the connection between "Ulm 1592" and the preceding poem in the *Svendborger Gedichte*, the "Lied der Starenschwärme" (BFA 12. Pp. 18–19). The fate of the birds is determined in advance by their instinct to fly south when they feel the cold of winter approaching. In consequence they meet death in the nets set in the southern provinces by men who have learned to predict their annual migration. What the poet thinks, but does not say, is that this is exactly the sort of thing that happens to any life lived unthinkingly, in uncomprehending submission to the "laws of nature". If human beings lead their lives in the same, automatic way as the migrating starlings do, behaving as if social phenomena were equally predetermined, they too can expect to become victims. Conversely, however, just as the understanding of cyclical, natural time has enabled men to trap the starlings, an understanding of history as humanly directed progress could teach people to evade the intellectual and social traps set by authority, tradition and the powers that be. The Bishop of Ulm may exult, for the moment, that "man is not a bird", but precisely because this is indeed the case (in the opposite sense to that intended by the bishop), he may well find some day that he no longer has an acquiescent flock prepared to accept such "eternal" verities.

If "the people" are to take possession of history, whether on the level of events or in their recording and interpretation (historiography), they need a sharpened sense of the temporality of things, of the relations between what was, what is, and what could be, of the flux of change that is at work not just age by age, but year by year, or even, at times of crisis, day by day.[24] The awareness of time passing is just as important for the poetic organization of the politically understood world of the *Svendborger Gedichte* as it was for the poetic organization of a world governed principally by the forces of nature in the *Hauspostille*. This is readily apparent, for example, in the refrain of "An die Nachgeborenen", the last (composite) poem in the *Svendborger Gedichte*: "So verging meine Zeit / Die auf Erden mir gegeben war" (BFA 12. P. 86). Here the poet's experience of the times is given added poignancy by his simultaneous awareness of his personal transience and of the conflicts between his – curtailed – participation in nature on the one hand and the historical-political dimensions of life on the other:

Mein Essen aß ich zwischen den Schlachten
Schlafen legte ich mich unter die Mörder
Der Liebe pflegte ich achtlos
Und die Natur sah ich ohne Geduld (BFA 12. P. 86).

Less obvious, perhaps, but in fact quite pervasive are the poet's references to time when describing the lives of others. Thus in the brief opening poem of the first section of the collection (the "Deutsche Kriegsfibel"), the differences between the classes are underscored by the simple device of contrasting tenses and adverbs of time: those on top regard talk of food as "low" because they have *"already"* eaten, whereas those below will *"never"* rise to power unless they make a point of thinking about such *"low"* things as food. As things are now, the low will *"not yet"* have seen the mountains and the great sea when their time is *"already"* up; instead they must leave the earth without ever "having tasted" good meat; on "fine evenings" they are too exhausted even to reflect on where they have come from or where their lives are going. Thus the low are deprived physically, have restricted horizons, and are denied the opportunity even to think about how their time has been spent. All three deprivations, which sap the strength of body, mind and will, conspire to ensure that the future will replicate the present just as their present replicates their past. Unless the low learn to master history, and take charge of the reading and writing of history, they will never have any time to call their own. In the class struggle even time, the least tangible of possessions, is something that has to be fought for.

---

[24] Historical flux is a central preoccupation of Fredric Jameson in his: *Brecht and Method*. London – New York: Verso 1998.

In the next but one poem of the "Kriegsfibel" a single adverb of time ("noch") is deployed with consummate skill to create an eerie sense of impending catastrophe:

Der Anstreicher spricht von kommenden großen Zeiten
Die Wälder wachsen noch.
Die Äcker tragen noch.
Die Städte stehen noch.
Die Menschen atmen noch (BFA 12. P. 10).

It is as if the whole of "still breathing" humankind were waiting tensely for "still" to become "no longer". The poet seems to have no confidence that the clouds of war will simply pass over. Rather his poems give elementary instruction on the nature of war, using the dark future to illuminate an ill-understood present and what it harbours. Whereas "those at the top" claim that war and peace are made of different stuff, the poet insists that what they call peace is already a form of war, and that war will grow from it as a storm grows from the wind or a son from the womb of his mother (BFA 12. P. 10). These images are drawn (with evident irony) from nature because, in a capitalist society, men allow themselves to remain as subject to the destructive consequences of trade cycles as migrating starlings are to the cycle of the seasons. The tone is again that of the prophet (in this case: Hosea 8, 7), warning that whosoever sows the wind shall reap the whirlwind.

Such spare poems compress quite complicated messages into the brief space of an urgent communication, the poet's words made as hard and plain as the facts:

Der du zur Arbeit läufst stundenlang
In zerfetzten Schuhen: der Wagen
Der für dich gebaut wird, hat
Eine Eisenwand nötig (BFA 12. P. 12).

The worker who now travels slowly on foot will soon travel, presumably more quickly, by "car". As the car that is being built "for him" will have an iron wall, he will be protected in it. Yet, although cars cost more to build than shoes, he normally walks to work in tattered shoes which do not protect his feet. Are the car and the protection really "for him" in this case? If not, what else needs to be protected by the car with the iron wall? Why is he soon to travel more quickly? Why, indeed, does the car need an iron wall? Why has the "Volkswagen" Hitler promised the Germans been replaced by a tank? If the dangers to the car are so great, would the worker not in fact be better protected in his tattered shoes? Are not his tattered shoes a sign of the economic warfare between classes and nations which will eventually give rise to the need for cars with iron walls? It takes time to tease out these messages, more time than is required to grasp a slogan scrawled in chalk on a wall or painted on a banner.

Although the poet makes concessions to the urgency of the situation, he does not surrender to it entirely. If the war is to have a different outcome from most wars in the past (merely another victory for "those above" on the one side rather than the other), some precious time must be spared to understand its nature. Although neither he nor his readers can afford any longer the ostentatious, luxuriating time-wasting of the *Hauspostille*, the poet of the *Svendborger Gedichte* does nevertheless take the time needed to make his weapons polished and sharp. [25] Thus he equates, provocatively, usefulness with killing, and thinking with a "defect":

> General, der Mensch ist sehr brauchbar.
> Er kann fliegen und er kann töten.
> Aber er hat einen Fehler:
> Er kann denken. (BFA 12, 13–14).

The world has been topsy-turvy like this for so long that today's problems are still reflected in a Chinese poem of the 11th Century, in which the poet, whose life has been "ruined" by his intelligence, hopes that his new-born son will be ignorant and intellectually lazy enough to earn a quiet life as a minister in the cabinet.[26] Witty paradoxes of this kind provide insight and pleasure in one, rewarding the "defect" of thinking with the thrill of recognition. The elegant, athletic form adds persuasiveness to the message. Overshadowed though the times are, the aesthetic qualities of the poems signal a refusal to allow the present to be laid waste entirely by the inhuman future for which "the housepainter" is preparing. What the spare beauty of the poems offers to the present is a modest token of a quite different, more humane future, beyond the war.

Because history does not move at the same pace everywhere, Brecht (following Marx) believed that the future was already available for inspection in the present, provided one looked in the right places. Like others before him, he thought he had seen the future (during a brief visit to Russia) and that it worked. As he describes it, the marble-clad Moscow Underground is a palace of the people, built by the people, for the people. It redeems at long last the hopes of the past, for the workers who emerge from the tunnels beaming, showing off their clay-caked overalls, are presented as descendants of the prisoners in Beethoven's *Fidelio* who once shuffled, blinking, out of their dungeons into the light of freedom.

---

[25] The role and importance of aesthetic qualities in this kind of political poetry have been well described by David Constantine: The Usefulness of Poetry. In: Speirs (ed): *Brecht's Poetry* (n. 3). Pp. 29–46. See also Hans Hiebel: *Das Spektrum der modernen Poesie*. Teil I. Würzburg: Königshausen & Neumann 2005. Pp. 257–312.
[26] Bertolt Brecht: Bei der Geburt eines Sohnes. BFA 12. P. 52.

If the past, recent or distant, offers models of how to move towards a better future, there are also negative lessons to be drawn from it. There is the recent case of the widows of Ossega in Czechoslovakia, for example, whose husbands were killed in a mining disaster, and who came to Prague to ask for help from the government, only to be met with armed police, speeches from politicians, and snow which falls on them as they sit out in the streets at night.[27] The moral is plain, if unstated: a bad past is not made into a good future merely by asking for help from the powerful; it would be better by far to remove the power which makes the asking necessary. "Kleines Bettellied" (BFA 12. P. 21), another of the children's songs, makes a similar point on a smaller scale: since begging implicitly re-affirms the existing structures of power and wealth, beggars must always expect to have the door closed in their faces or find a trouser-button in the begging-box.

The poet's double perspective on history in the *Svendborger Gedichte*, both as a set of verifiable facts and as a course of events that could and should have been different, if only the common man had understood more clearly the manmade nature of history as the history of class-warfare, is not without its problems for contemporary readers. The poet's ultimate purpose of guiding his readers towards a future that will be different from the present leads at times to an unacknowledged blurring of the distinction between history and invention that is at odds with his insistence elsewhere on facts, the truth, the application of reason. The poems which describe, for example, the death of Empedocles, or how Laotse came to write the book Tao Teking, or what befell the unnamed tailor of Ulm, and a good many others besides, all invent or change facts to suit the historical "moral" being taught by the poet. Admittedly the poems dealing with the past mostly acknowledge, in one way or another, their legendary character. Brecht's poem about the opening of the Moscow underground, by contrast, claims to depict actuality when it shows only happy workers (as persistently "fröhlich" as the good folk in Goethe's classicizing epic *Hermann und Dorothea* were "froh" and "trefflich"), representatives of a society united by its common dedication to progress.[28] Yet the poem says nothing of the terrible costs exacted by this enterprise, as by so many centrally conceived and ruthlessly prosecuted collective undertakings in the Soviet Union.[29] In other words, despite Brecht's allegiance to the "scientific" method of historical materialism, and despite his insistence that it was necessary to study history in order to grasp the relativity and changeability of human societies, what a good number of the *Svendborger Gedichte* offer the reader is more fiction or myth rather than history.

[27] Bertolt Brecht: Ballade von den Osseger Witwen. BFA 12. Pp. 17–18.
[28] Bertolt Brecht: Inbesitznahme der großen Metro durch die Moskauer Arbeiterschaft am 27. April 1935. BFA 12. Pp. 43–45.
[29] See the essay by Katharine Hodgson: Exile in Danish Siberia. The Soviet Union in the *Svendborg Poems*. In: Speirs (ed.): *Brecht's Poetry* (n. 3). Pp. 66–85.

Seen in the context of the "dark times", optimistic myth-making of this kind can be justified as part of the struggle against the destructive myths of National Socialism, as the creation of "useful" fictions designed to help working men become the makers and masters of history.[30] Viewed with hindsight, however, the myths which no doubt seemed "useful" to many at the time can now be seen to have helped to reinforce a set of illusions about political institutions as they really existed in the Soviet Union and its satellites which in practice certainly did not operate with the benignity of the poet's friendly and gentle Laotse. It could perhaps be argued that the contrast between the idealized vision of Soviet life and the reality he knew to fall far short of the ideal was actually a deliberate strategy on Brecht's part, aimed at inviting criticism of all forms of totalitarianism, whether fascist or Stalinist. Taken in isolation, the legend about Laotse's journey into exile could indeed be so read, but within the *Svendborger Gedichte* there are repeated pointers to the Soviet Union as the champion of a new, practical, humane order, all of which encourage one to read Brecht's version of Laotse's story as part of the pre-history of communist society, an expression of the ancient, long subverted values that Soviet communism aims to realize, at long last, in the lives of ordinary people. Thanks to the discrepancy between actual conditions in the Soviet empire and the hopes and dreams invested in it, at the very time when Brecht was in Svendborg writing his poem about the kindliness of an exiled Chinese sage, many thousands of his own compatriots whose socialist beliefs had led them to choose the Soviet Union as their place of exile from fascism were being rounded up, imprisoned or killed under a system of institutionalized paranoia.[31] The politically engaged poet whose concern for time leads him, in dark times, to attempt to shape both the present and the future has to accept the possibility that he may get things badly wrong. Perhaps because he feared that things might turn out thus, the poet closed the collection with a poem ("An die Nachgeborenen") in which he asks future readers to bear in mind the damaging consequences of living and writing in times of profound conflict and "to remember us with understanding".

---

[30] See Elizabeth Boa's defence of post-modern history-making in her essay: Assuaging the Anxiety of Impotence. Poetic Authority and Power in the *Svendborg Poems*. In: Speirs (ed.): *Brecht's Poetry* (n. 3). Pp. 153–171.

[31] See David Pike: *German Writers in Soviet Exile 1933–1945*. Chapel Hill: University of North Carolina Press 1982.

John White and Ann White

The Songs and Poems of Brecht's *Furcht und Elend* Complex

This analysis focuses on four key "epic" features of Brecht's most important anti-fascist play: the poems written in connection with certain scenes of Furcht und Elend des Dritten Reiches; *the framing devices used in, or considered for, early productions; the replacement frame devised for* The Private Life of the Master Race; *and the song in the "Moorsoldaten" scene in* The Private Life of the Master Race. *Differences between preparatory poems and companion scenes are shown to involve changes in emphasis or* Gestus *of a genetic or potential rehearsal value. A comparison of "Die deutsche Heerschau" with the commenting devices used in* The Private Life of the Master Race *demonstrates that the former has advantages over the framing poetry used in the American adaptation. In conclusion, a consideration of the "Moorsoldaten" scene concentrates on the political significance of the embedded song "Die Moorsoldaten", arguing that it makes a greater contribution to the play's theme of resistance than has hitherto been recognized.*

Songs and poems play a different role in Brecht's *Furcht und Elend* complex from that of the songs in such canonical works as *Mutter Courage und ihre Kinder*, *Der gute Mensch von Sezuan* and *Der kaukasische Kreidekreis*. Instead of establishing a fixed corpus of spoken and sung commenting devices relatively early on, Brecht experiments at almost every stage of the play's evolution with a changing repertoire of sung prologue verses, epilogues and macroscopic framing devices. The main reason for this fluid repertoire of "episierende Elemente" is to be found in the chequered history of Brecht's repeated attempts to have the play published and staged during his years of exile.

Work on *Furcht und Elend des Dritten Reiches* spans virtually the entire period of Brecht's exile from Nazi Germany. Not long after his arrival in Denmark, he and Margarete Steffin set about assembling relevant material from press reports, eyewitness accounts and literary depictions of life under the Nazis in the work of fellow refugee writers. In July 1937 he began drafting individual scenes for an epic documentary play (working title: *Die Angst*) intended to present a picture of everyday life in Germany from 1933 to 1938, the year of the annexation of Austria. Some scenes from the work-in-progress were pre-published in France, Switzerland, Czechoslovakia and the USSR, thereby initially giving the false impression that Brecht was writing a series of disparate one-act plays. In fact, by June 1938 he had already completed a single work consisting of twenty-eight interrelated scenes, some eventually to be replaced by others written during the work's prolonged period of gestation. The play's premiere, using only eight scenes presented under the collective title *99%: Bilder aus dem Dritten Reich*, took place in Paris in May 1938. This landmark production brought to its culmination the first phase of the work's complex genesis. The second and most complicated phase covers the period of Brecht's exile in the United States (1941–1947) and the third that of the work's post-war publication and staging history. During the Second World War portions of the play were staged (1941) and filmed (1942) in the USSR and thirteen scenes from it were published in Moscow both in the original German and in English and Russian translations (1941). An adaptation comprising seventeen scenes was published in the USA in 1944 and staged the following year under the title *The Private Life of the Master Race: A Documentary Play*. The full German text was first published in New York in 1945 as *Furcht und Elend des III. Reiches: 24 Szenen*. After Brecht's return to Europe the play went on to be printed in the Soviet Zone of Germany in 1948, the year of its successful staging at the Deutsches Theater in East Berlin, and from then on it was included in all major Brecht editions. Between 1957 and 1963 it formed part of the Berliner Ensemble's repertoire and as a consequence played a role in the GDR's belated cultural attempts to come to terms with Germany's "unbewältigte Vergangenheit".

The picture that emerges from this brief survey is of a work that existed, and was mediated, in a multiplicity of – invariably epic – forms, a feature that was in part the result of Brecht's constant re-jigging and re-writing of the material to suit specific exile circumstances, his continued re-thinking of the possibilities of Epic Theatre in exile and the fact that *Furcht und Elend*'s full montage of scenes was too compendious to be staged – or sometimes even published – in its entirety.

The Preparatory Poems

One unique feature of the work's genesis is the number of scenes (seven) for which a companion poem exists. No other play by Brecht ever stood in such a systematic relationship to a series of preliminary sketches in verse-form. These poems have received little attention and there has been no consensus about their function. Edgar Marsch assigns them to the category "vermutlich für *Furcht und Elend*", not meaning that Brecht considered inserting them into the play (they would not have worked there), but instead suggesting a private exercise of essentially genetic value.[1] Notes to the relevant BFA poetry-volumes

---

[1] Edgar Marsch: *Brecht Kommentar zum lyrischen Werk*. München: Winkler 1974. P. 233. Some of the preparatory poems in the *Furcht und Elend* complex may even have been intended as "Übungsstücke für Schauspieler" by analogy with the exercises in *Der Messingkauf* (BFA 22. Pp. 830–839). The fact that "Das Kreidekreuz" was pre-published in *Die Sammlung* (August 1934). Pp. 641–642 and "Begräbnis des Hetzers im Zinksarg" was set to music by Hanns Eisler in 1937, certainly suggests that some of these poems could have been for more than private use.

repeatedly state that the poems stand "[in] keine[r] direkte[n] Verbindung zur Szenenfolge".[2] *Stücke 4*, containing the play itself, merely observes the existence of "einige Gedichte zu dieser Thematik" (BFA 4. P. 523), i.e. that of *Furcht und Elend des Dritten Reiches* as a whole. But this does little more than suggest an ill-defined status comparable to that of Brecht's *Deutsche Satiren*, once described as the Third Reich play's "lyrisches Pendant".[3] In the case of the "Kreidekreuz" scene, a more specific point is made: "Das Thema der Szene hat Brecht [...] vorher in dem Gedicht "Das Kreidekreuz" behandelt; dort ist deren Fabel schon zu erkennen" (BFA 4. P. 535). "Die 'Fabel' [...] vorwegnehmen" has also been seen as the purpose of the *Vorsprüche* that introduce the play's individual scenes (ibid. p. 22). In the light of the general importance Brecht attached to establishing "die Fabel",[4] this might well have been a conceivable task for the verses he composed before going on to write the relevant *Furcht und Elend* scenes. However, it is doubtful whether this was meant to be their main function, especially since most of them are *Rollengedichte*. According to Busch:

> Brecht liebte es, soziale Sachverhalte, die in einer Szene geschildert werden, noch einmal eigens in Rollengedichten vorzuführen, um das sozial und politisch Repräsentative bestimmter Erfahrungen herauszustellen. [...] Nicht nur die Opfer, auch die Mörder und Helfer kommen bei Brecht zu Wort.[5]

Busch's "noch einmal" implies that the poems reprise episodes already written, when in fact their composition invariably pre-dates that of the relevant scene. However, his thesis that the *Rollengedicht* genre gives selected characters in the play greater opportunity "zu Wort [zu] kommen"[6] highlights an essential difference between the first-person *Rollengedichte* and the play's kaleidoscope of scenes based on interaction between two or more characters. This can be appreciated from a comparison of the poem "Der Nachbar" (BFA 14. P. 238) with Scene 2 ("Der Verrat") (BFA 4. P. 344).

---

[2] BFA 14. P. 587.
[3] Walter Busch: *Bertolt Brecht: "Furcht und Elend des Dritten Reiches"*. Frankfurt am Main: Diesterweg 1982. P. 12: "In der Tat fällt es nicht schwer, sich manches aus den *Deutschen Satiren* szenisch ausgearbeitet als Teil des dramatischen Zyklus vorzustellen".
[4] E.g. Bertolt Brecht: *Kleines Organon für das Theater*. §12. BFA 23. Pp. 65–97. Here pp. 69–70, and Bertolt Brecht: *[Die Methode der "physischen Behandlung" am Berliner Ensemble]*. BFA 23. P. 229. On the implications of this, see John J. White: *Bertolt Brecht's Dramatic Theory*. Rochester (NY): Camden House 2004. Pp. 225–231.
[5] Busch: *Furcht und Elend* (n. 3). P. 30.
[6] In the case of the relationship between "Begräbnis des Hetzers im Zinksarg" and "Die Kiste", the scene's parallel poem presents a counter-perspective. A similar relationship has been posited between "Der Nachbar" and "Begräbnis des Hetzers im Zinksarg" on the ground that the latter depicts the "Hetzer" "von der 'anderen Seite her'" (Marsch: *Brecht Kommentar* (n.1). P. 233).

"Der Nachbar" begins with a bald statement ("Ich bin der Nachbar. Ich habe ihn angezeigt"), followed by a clumsy attempt at self-justification ("Wir wollen in unserem Haus / Keinen Hetzer haben"). This presents a different picture of the neighbour-as-informer from the one in the play, a difference already signalled in the two titles. The noun "Nachbar" in the poem's title neatly challenges the informer's façade of self-righteousness by mimicking his assumption that denouncing a "Hetzer" ensures security and order in one's tenement block and is thus the "neighbourly" action of a loyal member of the new "Volksgemeinschaft". The title of Scene 2 states that what we are about to witness is an act of "Verrat": not just denunciation, but "Klassenverrat". The third and fifth verses of the poem record a sense of discomfort on the denouncer's part. Evidently he is concerned about the brutal nature of the arrest and also about how "einige Leute" will react to having an informer in their midst. "Der Nachbar" sees things from a vantage-point some time after the arrest, whereas Scene 2 is set in its immediate aftermath. The *Rollengedicht* is as a result able to take us further into the mindset of a denouncer than the drama's equivalent scene. In both poem and play, the specific allegation – that the man taken into Gestapo custody has been illegally listening to foreign radio broadcasts – makes the denunciation look politically motivated. But in the poem's version of events a series of prior disputes is also remembered (or maliciously fabricated) by the denouncer. These include his neighbour's refusal to display the swastika flag on prescribed occasions, his criticism of the size of the informer's family (an attack that flies in the face of the National Socialist motherhood campaign) and his questioning of the man's new-found confidence in Germany's future. In the light of all this, the denunciation might seem to be more the result of personal animosity than a response to some perceived threat to Nazi Germany's security. Perhaps this is why the man tries so hard to rationalize his action: "Wir haben genug Sorgen im Kopf, da / Muß wenigstens Ruhe [im Haus] herrschen", "Die ihn abgeholt haben, sagen / Daß wir uns richtig verhalten haben". This is presumably what it is like inside the mind of a shabby opportunist out to exploit the new system to settle old scores or enhance his standing, yet clearly unable to do so without knowingly compromising himself.

Brecht's class-based interpretation of informing under the Nazi regime ensures that the issue of poverty is prominent in both versions. The play's words "sie hätten ihm nicht die Jacke zu zerreißen brauchen. So dick hat es unsereiner nicht" have their counterpart in the poem's "Sie haben ihm den Kittel zerrissen. / Das wäre nicht nötig gewesen. So viele Kittel / Hat keiner von uns". But Scene 2, explicitly set in a "Kleinbürgerwohnung", makes a differently nuanced use of the socio-economic factor. Transposing material from poem to play in this case involves externalizing the *Rollengedicht*-persona's bad conscience in a series of backbiting exchanges with his wife. The woman in "Der Verrat" may come out with the callous sentiment "Es geschieht ihnen recht. Warum sind sie

Kommunisten", but she is still anxious to attribute sole responsibility for the consequences of the denunciation to her husband. The poem offers evidence of an ongoing vendetta between two neighbours, yet even if the denunciation has a more political connotation in the play, we are still left wondering whether or not the allegation that the man has been listening illegally to foreign broadcasts is true.[7] Clearly, what Brecht achieves here is more than a simple transposition of the poem's content (or *Gestus*[8]) to another genre. He introduces subtle shifts of emphasis as well as changing various details in the episode's pre-history. But such fine-tuning would surely have been possible without recourse to a preparatory *Rollengedicht*. So why did Brecht go to such lengths? One possible reason is hinted at in his theoretical writings of the time.

His journal for 11 January 1941 notes that at rehearsal stage ("beim Kreieren der Figur") an epic actor's identification with his or her character can be extremely useful (BFA 26. Pp. 454–455). *Der Messingkauf* also stresses the tactical value of limited "Einfühlung". Having asked the Philosopher "du willst nicht sagen, daß ich eine Figur nachahmen soll, in die ich mich nicht im Geiste hineinversetzt habe?", the Actor immediately finds himself on the receiving end of a lecture on the advantages of controlled emotional identification at rehearsal stage and the need for its avoidance during performance.[9] The idea that an actor's "Sichhineinversetzen" must be followed by a "Sichhinausversetzen" is taken up again in §53 of *Kleines Organon für das Theater* (BFA 23. Pp. 85–86). In the specific context of the preparatory poems written as part of the *Furcht und Elend* project, however, the question is whether Brecht converted this view into a play-writing strategy and also whether any of the satellite *Rollengedichte* was written specifically with rehearsals in mind. In the case of the "Kreidekreuz" scene, it has been pointed out that "[Brecht] verfaßte [...] eigens ein Rollengedicht für die Figur des Dienstmädchens".[10] In other words, just as role-swapping was seen as a useful form of distanciation for actors (*Kleines Organon*. §59. BFA 23. P. 88), so being permitted, through the lens of a *Rollengedicht*, to see things temporarily with the eyes of another character could be of help to all five actors involved in Scene 2 of *Furcht und Elend*.

One striking feature of the "Kreidekreuz" poem (BFA 14. Pp. 236–237) is its focus on a subsidiary character, whereas the scene's centre of interest is the series

---

[7] This is especially so, given the proximity of this episode to Scene 1 ("Volksgemeinschaft") where two SS men recall raiding a "Marxistennest", only to discover that they had targeted a Catholic "Lehrlingsverein" (BFA 4. P. 342).

[8] On the relationship of some preparatory poems to the scenes of *Furcht und Elend* as involving changes of *Gestus* rather than the establishment of a shared *Fabel*, see Frank Dietrich Wagner: *Bertolt Brecht: Kritik des Faschismus*. Opladen: Westdeutscher Verlag 1989. P. 233.

[9] Bertolt Brecht: *Der Messingkauf*. BFA 22.2. Pp. 695–869. Here p. 822.

[10] Busch: *Furcht und Elend* (n. 3). P. 25.

of exchanges between Worker and SA Man. The lack of any reference to the Worker in the poem is revealing, for, unlike the Worker and the SA Man, the Dienstmädchen is not a political animal. Her *Rollengedicht* performance is that of uncomprehending observer, with none of the scene's undercurrent of Schweykian subversion and no mention of the Worker's cunning demolition of the SA man's cockiness. Damning evidence of her blinkered perspective can be found in the case of the trick with the chalk mark: in her recollection of how her boyfriend "zeigte [...] mir lachend, wie sie es machen", "Wir lachten darüber". As this suggests, using a *Rollengedicht* can involve more than bringing to life the unspoken thoughts of an actor's character; it can also help an epic ensemble come to terms with the challenge of depicting revealing instances of false consciousness.[11]

Brecht's preparatory poems are more diverse than there is space to go into here. For example, "Wer belehrt den Lehrer?" (BFA 14. P. 247) is remarkably generalized and comes nowhere near to fleshing out the complex predicament of the teacher and his wife in "Der Spitzel" (BFA 4. Pp. 391–400). "Der Arzt" (BFA 14. P. 237) concentrates on its scene's starting-point and merely sets the context for one of the play's less memorable episodes ("Berufskrankheit". BFA 4. Pp. 379–381), whereas "Wer belehrt den Lehrer?" prepares the ground for one of its most powerful ones. Two poems ("Der dem Tod Geweihte". BFA 14. Pp. 237–238) and "Die Untersuchung" (BFA 14. Pp. 242–243) are in any case not *Rollengedichte*, but instead assume the Olympian stance of "Mitwisser des Stückeschreibers".[12] In this, they are closer to the various framing poems and songs which are a salient feature of most versions of *Furcht und Elend*. It is to these devices that we now turn.

Framing Devices

From the outset Brecht seems to have recognized that the relatively autonomous *Furcht und Elend* scenes needed some kind of epic framing. This realization was no doubt reinforced by the gross misrepresentation of the play during the Moscow "Realismusdebatte". In 1938 a series of verses modelled on Shelley's "The Masque of Anarchy"[13] and entitled "Die deutsche Heerschau" supplied

[11] Cf. the treatment in *Der Messingkauf* (BFA 22. Pp. 710–712) of what Brecht calls "die Unwissenheit" and the account of "false consciousness" in White: *Bertolt Brecht's Dramatic Theory* (n. 4). Pp. 103–104 and 269–270.

[12] The phrase occurs in "Die Gesänge", a *Messingkauf* poem on the role of commenting songs in Epic Theatre (BFA 12. P. 330).

[13] Probably in response to Alfred Wolfenstein's translation of the final part of Shelley's "The Masque of Anarchy" (published under the title "Sie sind wenige – Ihr seid viel!" in: *Das Wort* 2. H. 6 (1937). Pp. 63–65), Brecht wrote *Der anachronistische Zug oder Freiheit und Democracy* in the following year. On Shelley's significance for Brecht's *Weite und Vielfalt der realistischen Schreibweise* (BFA 22. Pp. 424–433) and on the "Shelleynähe" of other poems generically resembling Brecht's prologue, see Hans Peter Neureuter: Steffinsche Sammlung. In: *Brecht Handbuch in fünf Bänden*. Ed. by Jan Knopf. Stuttgart – Weimar: Metzler 2001–2003. Vol. 2. Pp. 342–348. Here p. 347.

the introductory "Ballade" (BFA 29. P. 209) for the eight scenes used at the play's Paris premiere. Various other framing possibilities were either mooted or tried out in the years to come. In 1941 extracts from *Deutsche Kriegsfibel 1937* were included in the Russian-language miscellany of thirteen scenes (*Strakh i otchayanie v III. Imperii*, Moscow: Khudozhestvennaya kniga 1941), while an English translation of the latter (*Fear and Misery of the Third Reich*, Moscow: Khudozhestvennaya kniga 1942) incorporated verses 1, 2, 4 and 6 of the only *Rollengedicht* to be included in the play: "Lied einer Deutschen Mutter" (BFA 15. P. 80). The following year found Brecht casting around for a new "musikalischen Rahmen",[14] having rejected an opening proposed by Erwin Piscator which had a pianist striking up *The Star-Spangled Banner*, only to be interrupted by a pistol-toting SS man demanding that he play the *Horst-Wessel-Lied* instead.[15] "Die deutsche Heerschau" (substantial parts of which had already been translated in readiness for the planned American adaptation of the play) was in due course replaced by another purpose-written song, referred to variously as "Lied der Besatzung des Panzerkarrens", "Chor der Panzerbesatzung" and "Lied der Panzerjäger". In *The Private Life of the Master Race*, the American version of *Furcht und Elend*, the new framing song, with music by Hanns Eisler, is untitled.

Within a relatively short space of time Brecht's scenic montage had received a number of different frames, most of them based on bold presentational paradigms. The main ones are: (1) the "Heerschau", (2) the sung comments of the "Chor der Panzerbesatzung", linking individual soldiers' pasts with their present and (3) the tales of their prior civilian life in the Third Reich told by the deserting German soldiers in Pudovkin's film-version in order to justify their defection to the Soviets.[16] Sadly, a further framing metaphor with substantial

---

[14] Bertolt Brecht: Letter to Max Reinhardt. Late May 1942. BFA 29. P. 231.

[15] James K. Lyon: *Bertolt Brecht in America*. Princeton: Princeton University Press 1980. P. 135. With the end of the Second World War approaching, Berthold Viertel considered updating the material using an alternative frame whereby each of the male characters in individual scenes would be introduced by means of an interrogation which would act as an introduction to their scenes in the play. For details, see Hans Cristof Walter: *Theater im Exil*. München: Hanser 1973. Pp. 167–169, and Berthold Viertel: *Schriften zum Theater*. Berlin: Henschel 1970. Pp. 216–221.

[16] Vsevolod Pudovkin: *Ubitsy vychodyat na dorogu* (*Die Mörder machen sich auf den Weg*, 1941–42). The film's framing technique is outlined in Wolfgang Gersch: *Film bei Brecht: Bertolt Brechts praktische und theoretische Auseinandersetzung mit dem Film*. München: Hanser 1975. P. 297. Hanns Eisler's account of an American film scenario explored by Brecht, Eisler and Clifford Odets at Fritz Lang's house on 5 June 1942 suggests that a comparable frame to Pudovkin's was under consideration on this occasion: in a series of anti-illusionist flashbacks, the frame would present "die Geschichte jedes einzelnen Soldaten [...]. Das heißt: Was war notwendig, um diese Leute in den Panzerwagen gegen die Sowjetunion zu kriegen". See Hanns Eisler: *Fragen Sie mehr über Brecht: Gespräche mit Hans Bunge*. Darmstadt – Neuwied: Luchterhand 1986. P. 29. For Brecht's account of the discussion, see Bertolt Brecht: *Journal* 5.6.1942. BFA 27. P. 102.

satirical potential – that of the "private life of the master race" – remains under-exploited in the American adaptation, perhaps because one's private life was no longer a private matter in the Third Reich. As late as June 1945 Brecht remained undecided about which solution to adopt: "Natürlich ist es durchaus möglich, daß der gegenwärtige balladeske Rahmen allein nicht ausreicht", he writes to Erwin Piscator (BFA 29. P. 355).

Brecht has disappointingly little to say about his ingenious "deutsche Heerschau" metaphor, except to inform Piscator in 1941, at the time with US audiences in mind, that the play is "enorm aktuell, da es das Milieu zeigt, aus dem Hitlers Soldaten kommen" and that it offers "eine riesige Heerschau, die […] zeigt, was die Leute hier erwartet, wenn sie hier Diktatur kriegen".[17] But although he fails to elaborate on the original "Heerschau" idea, his correspondence relating to *The Private Life of the Master Race* has much to say about the new framing song, in place by 1942 and introduced in the stage-directions in the following way:

> A band plays a barbaric march. Out of the darkness appears a big signpost: TO POLAND, and near it a Panzer truck. Its wheels are turning. On it sit twelve to sixteen soldiers, steel helmeted, their faces white as chalk, their guns between their knees. […] The soldiers sing to the tune of the Horst Wessel Song: [there follow the first three stanzas of the Panzer soldiers' song].[18]

The armoured troop-carrier, Brecht informed Berthold Viertel, "würde viermal auftauchen, mit einer Ballade (auf die von Eisler variierte Melodie des Horst-Wessel-Liedes)".[19] Dessau, who had supplied the music for the Paris production, was replaced in America by Eisler, whose initial score was rejected as "Filmkitsch" and eventually replaced with a new setting (also by him) in June 1945.[20] Brecht not only swapped composers, he was often in two minds about which framing device to adopt – or whether one was needed at all. "Die deutsche Heerschau" was not used in the 1941 Soviet stage adaptation or in Pudovkin's film, presumably because the frame's liberal dose of what Brecht once called

[17] Bertolt Brecht: Letter to Erwin Piscator. Late July 1941. BFA 29. P. 210.
[18] Bertolt Brecht: *The Private Life of the Master Race: A Documentary Play*. Trans. by Eric Russell Bentley with the assistance of Elisabeth Hauptmann. New York: New Directions 1944. P. 1.
[19] Bertolt Brecht: Letter to Berthold Viertel. May/June 1942. BFA 29. P. 236.
[20] The music by "Peter Sturm" (i.e. Paul Dessau) – at the time dismissed by Helene Weigel as "fad" (BFA 4. P. 531) – was played by Dessau himself on percussion and piano. Eisler's replacement score for "Die deutsche Heerschau" had originally been considered for use in *The Private Life of the Master Race*. On Brecht's rejection of Eisler's "Horst Wessel Lied" parody as "Filmkitsch", see his journal for 20.7.1945 (BFA 27. P. 226); Eisler: *Fragen Sie mehr über Brecht* (n. 16). P. 84 and Albrecht Dümling: *Laßt euch nicht verführen: Brecht und die Musik*. München: Kindler 1985. P. 529.

"in die Augen fallende Verfremdungen" (BFA 24. P. 521) risked the play's being proscribed as formalist. Having scheduled "Die deutsche Heerschau" for Volume 3 of the abortive pre-war Malik edition and originally for the American stage adaptation, Brecht put it to one side, only resurrecting it in the 1945 Aurora edition, after which it became a firm fixture. The "Chor der Panzerbesatzung" employed in *The Private Life of the Master Race* then disappeared from use virtually for good.[21]

Such chopping and changing raises questions about the relative merits and disadvantages of the principal framing devices. Why was "Die deutsche Heerschau" at one stage jettisoned in favour of a demonstrably weaker framing song coupled with a series of bland commenting verses? Was this a matter of historical and cultural differences between a play written for the Europe of 1938 and a new adaptation for the America of 1943? If so, why did Brecht subsequently reinstate the "deutsche Heerschau" frame? In the absence of explanatory statements from the playwright himself, any answer to these questions remains speculative.

Like the play it was written to introduce, "Die deutsche Heerschau" presents the Germany of the period 1933–38 as a country single-mindedly preparing for war. "Es gibt doch nichts mehr", one of the characters says, "was nicht für den Krieg ist!" (BFA 4. P. 436). Although the metaphor of reviewing the troops elaborates on this situation, it can be read in different ways. One connotation, given that the framing song dates from 1937, is that the male figures we meet in the individual scenes are in most cases civilians soon to be drafted into Hitler's *Wehrmacht*: a pathetic ragbag of recruits-in-waiting, the very opposite of the heroic image the Third Reich's film propaganda sought to project. A more specific *Sein-und-Schein* variation on this idea posits a detailed juxtaposition of the shabby participants in the play's social panorama with familiar images from the Nuremberg Rallies, as cohorts of representative groups of citizens march in review formation – stanza-by-stanza, contingent-by-contingent – past their leaders (or, by extension, past the play's audience).[22] By the time of *The Private Life of the Master Race*, with a savage war by then being waged ruthlessly on the Eastern Front at a high cost in human lives, the extended military metaphor received a fresh twist, as the Panzer-chorus's refrain reports how

---

[21] For unclear reasons, the original German text of *The Private Life of the Master Race* was performed at the Stadttheater Basel as late as June 1947. See Joachim Lucchesi and Ronald K. Shull: *Musik bei Brecht*. Frankfurt am Main: Suhrkamp 1988. P. 657. Given that "der Fortfall chorischer Elemente" was one of the features of his play that Brecht assumed had led Lukács to underestimate the work's epic qualities (see *Anmerkungen zu "Furcht und Elend des Dritten Reiches"*. BFA 24. P. 521), the inserted "Chor der Panzerbesatzung" could be read as a deliberate counter to such a misinterpretation.

[22] See Busch: *Furcht und Elend* (n. 3). P. 16.

"out of the factories and out of the kitchens and out of the breadlines / we fetched the men for our Panzer".[23] Between 1938 and 1943, the ceremonial troop-review image had been replaced by the pessimistic one of loading onto the war-wagon the representative socio-political types the audience meets in the American version's selection of scenes. The second frame scenario nevertheless retains an allegorical dimension, for the omnivorous troop-carrier is a cross between a Moloch and a modern Ship of Fools. And whereas the earlier *Furcht und Elend* cycle ended on an inspirational note of German resistance, the "Panzerkarren" comes to a standstill: "vereist in der Gegend von Smolensk", as Brecht explained to Max Reinhardt.[24]

A variant reading sees the "army" which the audience is invited to inspect as a metaphor for an already militarized civilian society. (Brecht once presented his play as trying to capture "die seelische Verfassung der Armee des totalitären Staates, *die ja die ganze Bevölkerung umfaßt*" as well as offering "ein Bild von der Brüchigkeit dieser Kriegsmaschine".[25]) In the pre-war scenario, the work reviews a *figurative Wehrmacht*, made up of members of the cowering, capitulating society that lies in the real army's hinterland, whereas the American adaptation brings out the causality (the widespread fear, misery and moral capitulation) linking the *real historical* military debacle in Russia to the earlier period of civilian conditioning for a total war in which an entire nation was being prepared to participate. One common denominator, whichever reading one privileges, is the way the presentational scenario is repeatedly echoed in later parts of the play. In the case of the "Heerschau" the march-past metaphor is present in the repetition of the verb "kommen", from the introductory image – "Dort kommen sie herunter / Ein bleicher, kunterbunter / Haufe" (BFA 4. P. 341) – to each of the subsequent verses ("Dort kommen SS-Offiziere", "Es kommen die SA-Leute", "Dann kommen die Herren Richter", etc.). Seemingly autonomous scenes thus become part of a symbolic troop-review or, in *The Private Life of the Master Race*, part of the pattern of events leading from the progressively corrosive fear and misery of pre-war Germany via mobilization to the ultimate collapse of the German Army's ill-fated Russian offensive.

Despite the binding function of the original troop-review image, some commentators have assumed that the title "Die deutsche Heerschau" (at one stage under consideration for the entire play)[26] refers only to the four "prologue"

[23] Brecht/Bentley: *The Private Life* (n. 18). P. 25.
[24] Bertolt Brecht: Letter to Max Reinhardt. Late May 1942. BFA 29. P. 231.
[25] Bertolt Brecht: Letter to the American Guild for German Cultural Freedom, Svendborg. September 1938. BFA 29. P. 110. Our emphasis.
[26] Bertolt Brecht: Letter to Erwin Piscator. March/April 1938. BFA 29. P. 82.

verses.[27] This, however, ignores the continuation of the image from the initial verses on through all the ensuing *Vorsprüche*. Brecht once transcribed the prologue and subsequent verses as a single continuous poem, giving the manuscript the overall title "Die deutsche Heerschau" (BFA 14. P. 658). In spite of such circumstantial evidence, the chief stumbling block to a holistic reading of these verses[28] would seem to be the marked stylistic differences between the four first-person plural "prologue" verses (an example of "reimlose Lyrik mit unregelmäßigen Rhythmen") and the mocking march-beat rhythm of the *Vorsprüche*. But this is not an insuperable obstacle. In *Die Dreigroschenoper* and *Mutter Courage und ihre Kinder*, for example, one finds Brecht using songs with alternating sections in clashing styles for defamiliarizing purposes. In the case of the "deutsche Heerschau" frame in *Furcht und Elend*, comparable antithetical styles can be accounted for by reference to changes in subject-matter and mood, as we leave the reviewing rostrum to descend, figuratively speaking, to inspect the individual predicaments of those in the Third Reich whose fear and misery is about to be powerfully evoked and at the same time critically dissected. Whereas the "prologue" verses radiate an assured political omniscience (be it that of the dramatist, the acting ensemble or the audience), the *Vorsprüche* home in to belittle what is about to happen, at the same time as setting the scene.

In abandoning "Die deutsche Heerschau" in favour of a completely new frame for *The Private Life of the Master Race*, Brecht did not merely replace one *Rahmenlied* with another. The Panzer soldiers' chorus is only a part of a more complicated over-arching framework deployed at the beginning and end

---

[27] Perhaps influenced by Brecht's distinction between the introductory "Balladenstrophen" – which he hoped W. H. Auden would translate into English – and what he calls the "Zwischensprüche" which had already been translated by Ferdinand Reyher and Hans ("John") Viertel (see: BFA 29. Pp. 237–238), some commentators have concluded that only the four "prologue" verses constitute "Die deutsche Heerschau". Thus Busch (*Furcht und Elend* (n. 3). P. 22) contrasts what he refers to as the "Prolog 'Die deutsche Heerschau' " with the *Vorsprüche*, presenting them as contrasting poetic styles serving different purposes. James K. Lyon (in: *Brecht Handbuch* (n. 13). Vol. 1. P. 345) makes a similar distinction between the "Prolog Die deutsche Heerschau" and "die lyrischen Mottos" to the individual scenes. And Lucchesi and Shull (*Musik bei Brecht* (n. 21). P. 655) likewise contrast "Vorstrophen" and "Verbindungsstrophen".

[28] Jan Knopf (*Brecht-Handbuch: Theater. Eine Ästhetik der Widersprüche*. Stuttgart: Metzler 1980. P. 145) talks of the play being introduced by "Die deutsche Heerschau", "(*d. h. seine ersten vier Strophen; die folgenden 26 Strophen* […] *sind den jeweiligen Szenen vorangesetzt*)" (our emphasis). The first published version of the play to include "Die deutsche Heerschau" prints both prologue verses and *Vorsprüche* all in italics, but positions verses 2–4, which precede the play, substantially nearer the right-hand margin, thus giving them the same position as that of the *Vorsprüche* (Bertolt Brecht: *Furcht und Elend des III. Reiches: 24 Szenen*. New York: Aurora 1945. P. 7).

of the play as well as being inserted into the gaps between the three Parts. Added to which an anonymous speaker, referred to simply as the Voice, comments on individual scenes, while the "Lied einer Deutschen Mutter" (now in an English translation) supplies the work with what is essentially a second epilogue. If anyone wanted to refute Lukács's assumption that Brecht had finally returned to the Socialist Realist fold,[29] these interlocking commenting devices in three genres (cross-cut with the sound effects intermittently supplied by the "Panzerkarren") furnish ample evidence to the contrary. Such a super-abundance of epic paraphernalia arguably only made sense because of the specific conditions under which *The Private Life* was produced in America, for the new stage adaptation bears many signs of having been originally conceived "for Broadway".[30] Brecht had to court an "Aristotelian" audience largely conditioned by Stanislavskian theatre, but still needed to work with epic counter-balances, if he was going to achieve the play's documentary and political goals. This explains why he could impose a new (closed) Aristotelian structure on the American stage adaptation, while at the same time inserting a more complex epic frame than earlier versions of the play possessed. Witness his new grouping of clusters of scenes into Parts, the use at the end of each Part of emotive "curtain" silences to replace the Voice's comments, and the supplementing of the powerful "Lied einer Deutschen Mutter" (set by Eisler for solitary voice and piano to contrast with the exaggeratedly military song of the Panzer chorus) with three further historicizing verses from the chorus to produce a grand finale. Emotional scenes tend to be placed towards the end of each Part, and a strategic postponing of the

[29] In his essay "Es geht um den Realismus", published in the Moscow exile journal *Das Wort*, Georg Lukács refers to the scene "Der Spitzel", published in *Das Wort* earlier the same year, in uncharacteristically glowing terms: "Brecht hat [...] einen kleinen Einakter veröffentlicht, in welchem er den Kampf gegen die Unmenschlichkeit des Faschismus bereits in einer bei ihm neuen, vieltönigen und abgestuften realistischen Weise führt; er gibt dort ein lebendiges, durch *Menschenschicksale* vermitteltes Bild vom Schrecken des faschistischen Terrors in Deutschland" (*Das Wort* 3. H. 6 (1938). Pp. 112–138. Here p. 138). Reacting to Lukács's misguided comments, Brecht noted in his journal for 15.8.1938: "*Furcht und Elend des Dritten Reiches* ist jetzt in Druck gegangen. Lukács hat den 'Spitzel' bereits begrüßt, als sei ich ein in den Schoß der Heilsarmee eingegangener Sünder. [...] Übersehen ist die Montage von 27 Szenen und daß es eigentlich nur eine Gestentafel ist" (BFA 26. P. 319). For discussions of this misreading within the context of the Moscow "Realismusdebatte", see David Pike: *German Writers in Soviet Exile, 1933 to 1945*. Chapel Hill: University of North Carolina Press 1982. Pp. 259–306, and David Pike: *Lukács and Brecht*. Chapel Hill: University of North Carolina Press 1985. Pp. 119–155. For an exploration of the play's epic features as well as its use of covert alienation devices, see John J. White: Bertolt Brecht's *Furcht und Elend des III. Reiches* and the Moscow "Realism" Controversy. In: *Modern Language Review* 100 (2005). Pp. 138–160.

[30] See Lucchesi and Shull: *Musik bei Brecht* (n. 21). P. 656.

archetypal German mother's lament to the end creates a powerful dramatic effect. Unlike Aristotelian theatre's gratuitous emotionalism, the feelings evoked by this song represent what Brecht once termed "eine Einfühlung erlaubter Art".[31] However, there are other problematic features to the hybrid amalgam of Aristotelian and epic elements in *The Private Life*, ones Brecht was able to avoid when he eventually re-adopted the "deutsche Heerschau" frame. An uncharacteristic structural rigidity, coupled with the cumulative emotional appeal within the constituent Parts of the sequence, clearly risked the charge of making too many concessions to American audiences by reducing the number of epic features.[32]

Earlier we expressed surprise that the highly effective "deutsche Heerschau" frame had been rejected in favour of *The Private Life*'s combination of weaker *Rahmenlied* and the Voice's bland commenting verses. The Voice is at times deployed to offer retrospective comments rather than deliver pre-emptive *Vorsprüche*, while elsewhere we encounter a mixture of both and at times mere floating generalizations. Compare the following pairs of illustrations of the *Vorspruch* used in *Furcht und Elend* and the corresponding commentary spoken by the Voice in *The Private Life of the Master Race*. The first pair is taken from "Der Verrat" / "The Betrayal":

Dort kommen Verräter, sie haben
Dem Nachbarn die Grube gegraben
Sie wissen, daß man sie kennt.
Vielleicht: die Straße vergißt nicht?
Sie schlafen schlecht: noch ist nicht
Aller Tage End (BFA 4. P. 344).

Thus neighbor betrayed neighbor.
Thus the common folk devoured each other
and enmity grew in the houses and in the precincts.
And so we went forth with confidence
and shoved onto our Panzer
every man who had not been slain:
a whole nation of betrayers and betrayed
we shoved onto our iron chariot.[33]

In the above pairing the Voice's comment follows its scene, whereas in our second illustration (from "Rechtsfindung" / "In Search of Justice") the Voice's comment

---

[31] Brecht: *Journal*. 23.11.1938. BFA 26. P. 326.

[32] Lee Baxandall sees in the "quasi-naturalistic" style of *Furcht und Elend* an "adjustment" calculated to gain Brecht a more favourable American reception, although no distinction is made between *Furcht und Elend des Dritten Reiches* and *The Private Life of the Master Race* (Lee Baxandall: Brecht in America, 1935. In: *The Drama Review* 12 (1967). No. 1. Pp. 69–87. Here p. 85).

[33] Brecht/Bentley: *The Private Life* (n. 18). P. 3.

precedes it. It should be noted that the new verse in *The Private Life* forms a bridge between legal conditions in pre-war Nazi Germany and events during the German occupation of France.

Dann kommen die Herren Richter
Denen sagte das Gelichter:
Recht ist, was dem deutschen Volke nützt.
Sie sagten: wie sollen wir das wissen?
So werden sie wohl Recht sprechen müssen
Bis das ganze deutsche Volk sitzt (BFA 4. P. 363).

And there are judges also on our Panzer,
clever at taking hostages, picking out a hundred victims
accused of being Frenchmen
and convicted of loving their country,
for our judges are trained in the German Law
and know at last what is demanded of them.[34]

The framing elements in *Furcht und Elend* and those supplied by the Voice not only serve different purposes, but in the latter case appear at times to lack any clear function at all. In contrast, the *Furcht und Elend Vorsprüche* efficiently establish the specific context for their scene as well as adopting a satirical stance vis-à-vis the behaviour the audience is about to witness. Their word-plays, bold satirical rhymes and assorted one-off presentational tricks contribute substantially to the wit and humour with which *Furcht und Elend* situates its material. The Voice's portentous verses fail to contextualize or pre-emptively undermine scenes in a comparably devastating way. At most, they bridge the gap between various wartime situations and the home front. In the later parts of the play they become progressively shorter and more generalized, as critical comment gradually becomes superfluous. The Voice's words concentrate excessively on the bundling of individual scenes' characters onto the "Panzerkarren" (though many of them would have needed little persuasion!). As a result, too much attention is deflected to the Russian Front at the expense of the more important "Vorgänge hinter den Vorgängen" (BFA 22. Pp. 519–520). What is more, the Voice fails to exploit the promised private life metaphor or even to make clear just what a scene is intended to show.

The end-notes to the Suhrkamp *Werkausgabe* of Brecht's *Furcht und Elend des Dritten Reiches* do, however, contain what is presented as "eine spätere Epilogstrophe" to "Die deutsche Heerschau":

Wir haben sein Heer gesehen
Es wird ihm bleiben stehen

---

[34] Ibid. pp. 49–50.

In Sumpf und Niederlag.
Wir würden lachend drauf zeigen
Wär's nicht unser Bruder und Eigen
Was da verkommen mag.[35]

At the time this was written, Brecht was obviously still hunting around for a satisfactory epilogue.[36] He abandoned the above solution, which is just as well, given that the proposed verse's blandness compares badly even with the multi-tiered finale to *The Private Life of the Master Race*. In any case, the final scene of *Furcht und Elend* ("Volksbefragung") already contains a rousing epilogue in the shape of the condemned communist's letter to his son. It would have been foolish to try to better this by replacing powerful prose with lame verse.

Fortunately, the over-determining, all too repetitive multiplicity of counter-balancing epic strategies in *The Private Life* remains confined to the second phase of *Furcht und Elend*'s history. In preparation for his return to Europe, Brecht reverted to "Die deutsche Heerschau", a frame now expanded to combine a broader panoramic picture than was attempted in the Paris, Soviet and American productions with the advantages of a more circumscribed repertoire of commenting devices. Moreover, it returns the play to the specific pre-war "Konkretisierung" of episodes leading cumulatively up to the historical turning-point of the *Anschluss*, rather than moving the time-frame on to the Sixth Army's defeat in Russia.

"Die Moorsoldaten"

The words of one song added to *The Private Life of the Master Race* and retained in all subsequent editions of *Furcht und Elend* were not by Brecht. Because the scene in which it occurs ("Moorsoldaten") hinges on the historically crucial issue of the anti-fascist *Volks-* or *Einheitsfront*, the song ("Die Moorsoldaten", written in 1933 by Johann Esser and Wolfgang Langhoff, original score by fellow prisoner Rudi Goguel[37]) makes one of the most significant

---

[35] Bertolt Brecht: *Gesammelte Werke in 20 Bänden*. Ed. by Suhrkamp Verlag in cooperation with Elisabeth Hauptmann. Frankfurt am Main 1967. Vol. III. Anmerkungen P. 2*.
[36] Writing to Dudow in April 1938, Brecht had stressed the need for the play to end with a rousing "Schlußepilog": "Wir brauchen nicht zum Kampf aufzurufen, wir zeigen den Kampf! Das *Nein* am Schluß scheint mir nicht zu wenig" (BFA 29. P. 85). He nevertheless toys with a further possibility when writing to Max Reinhardt in May 1942: "als Epilog könnten die Schauspieler an die Rampe treten und (inhaltlich) dem Publikum sagen: Ihr aber, wenn ihr diesen Wagen aufhaltet – und haltet ihn auf, um Gottes willen, haltet ihn mit Gewalt auf! – vergeßt nicht, daß Gewalt nicht genügt in einer Welt, die so kalt ist" (BFA 29. P. 232).
[37] Brecht's primary source was Wolfgang Langhoff's published account of his Börgermoor experiences: *Die Moorsoldaten: 13 Monate Konzentrationslager. Unpolitischer*

political contributions to the play's resistance discourse. "Moorsoldaten" was added in 1942 to replace the scene "Die Internationale".[38] Like that of the Hitler Youth poem "Das Mahnwort" in the scene of the same name (BFA 4. Pp. 430–431) and the socialist revolutionary hymn "Die Internationale", the use of the song "Die Moorsoldaten" is plot-motivated, whereas most of the material we have considered so far works on a meta-diegetic level.

There were compelling reasons connected with the content and status of the embedded songs for replacing a concentration camp scene centred on "Die Internationale" with "Prisoners Mix Cement" (as "Moorsoldaten" is called in the American adaptation) and for positioning the new scene much earlier than in fourteenth place: it now becomes Scene 3 in *The Private Life* and Scene 4 in the Aurora edition of *Furcht und Elend*. Unlike "Die Internationale", the rallying song and marching hymn of world socialism, "Die Moorsoldaten" had become primarily associated with the history of the German communist underground in the early concentration camps. Originally performed as part of Langhoff's cabaret "Zirkus Konzentrazani" in Börgermoor Camp (Emsland), the song went on to become "a key song of resistance of most prisoners of the camps between 1933 and 1945".[39] Indeed, in the world beyond the camps, it

---

Tatsachenbericht. Zürich: Schweizer Spiegel 1935. Especially pp. 175–195. According to his letter to Herzfelde of July/August 1935 (BFA 28. P. 518), Brecht had read Langhoff's *Die Moorsoldaten* long before starting work on *Furcht und Elend.* See also Eric Bentley: The Real Story behind the Song "The Peat Bog Soldiers". In: *Sing Out! The Folk Song Magazine* 16 (1966). No. 4. Pp. 37–39.

[38] Ilja Fradkin (in: *Bertolt Brecht: Weg und Methode.* Leipzig: Reclam 1977. P. 176) calls "Moorsoldaten" a "thematisch analoge Szene" to "Die Internationale". This is correct, in the sense that both scenes show concentration camp prisoners moving from cowed obedience to politically motivated resistance and each takes its title from the song that serves as catalyst. Brecht's reasons for replacing the one scene with the other nevertheless have more to do with differences than similarities. The two prisoners in "Die Internationale" are not endowed with specific attributes, whereas those in "Moorsoldaten" are situated on a politically differentiated spectrum. Hence, "Moorsoldaten" is able to contribute to the Popular Front debate in a way that the scene it replaces could not. It also may not be chance that the replacement of "Die Internationale" by "Moorsoldaten" coincides with the Comintern's shift of emphasis from international anti-fascist activity to a strong emphasis on the role of national patriotism in the fight against National Socialism. On this context, see Werner Herden: Zum Beitrag Georgi Dimitroffs für die Grundlegung des Volksfrontbündnisses in der antifaschistischen Literaturbewegung. In: Werner Herden: *Wege zur Volksfront: Schriftsteller im antifaschistischen Bündnis.* Berlin: Akademie 1978. Pp. 38–52. For a detailed discussion of Brecht's complex relationship to the Popular Front campaign, see Raimund Gerz: *Bertolt Brecht und der Faschismus.* Bonn: Bouvier 1983. Pp. 76–86.

[39] Joanne McNally: "Die Moorsoldaten": From Circus-cum-Cabaret to International Anthem. In: *Words, Texts, Images.* Ed. by Katrin Kohl and Ritchie Robertson. Oxford: Peter Lang 2002. Pp. 214–230. Here p. 215 (CUTG Proceedings. Vol. 4). When Ernst

enjoyed an iconic status comparable to that of *Kuhle Wampe*'s "Solidaritätslied".[40] Eisler's 1935 score and Paul Robeson's and Ernst Busch's recordings of the song contributed greatly to its international fame, as did Langhoff's and Bredel's documentary accounts of the powerful bonding function it had had for the early political prisoners. As one inmate put it in retrospect: "Vor allem war es das Lied, das die Kameraden fest zusammenschweißte, ihnen moralischen Halt, sowie physische Kraft verlieh und in ihnen Lebenszuversicht wachhielt".[41] Although the "Solidaritätslied" made its way from the fictive context of Brecht-Dudow's *Kuhle Wampe* out into the wide world of international class struggle, "Die Moorsoldaten" remained historically more "konkretisiert" due to its continued association with organized leftwing resistance in the concentration camps. However, its actual status back in 1934, which according to the Aurora edition was when Brecht's concentration camp scene was set,[42] remained rather ambiguous: singing the song at that time could just as well have been a tacitly sanctioned activity as an act of covert resistance.

Brecht's journal for 16 February 1943 records a visit from Heinz Langerhans (an old comrade and fellow exile who at the time was working on his study *Deutsche Märtyrer in Konzentrationslagern*). He gave Brecht to understand that "Die Moorsoldaten" was "in allen Lagern verbreitet und erlaubt" (BFA 27. P. 149). But whereas Langerhans was for that reason inclined to dismiss the song as a Nazi-sanctioned "Sklavenlied", Brecht preferred to concentrate on how its last verse was clandestinely sung in the camps: "Bei der Negation im letzten Refrain '*nicht* mehr mit dem Spaten ins Moor', auf das Nein warteten immer alle geil und stampften beim Nein auf, daß die Baracke wackelte" (BFA 27. P. 149).

Toller inserts the song into Act II of *Pastor Hall* (1938), a prisoner is reluctant to sing it because the song is "verboten!" (in: Ernst Toller: *Gesammelte Werke*. Ed. by Wolfgang Frühwald and John M. Spalek. München: Hanser 1978. Vol. 3: *Politisches Theater und Dramen im Exil, 1927–1939*. Pp. 245–331. Here p. 298).

[40] On the political significance of "Die Moorsoldaten" in the 1930s, see Werner Mittenzwei: *Exil in der Schweiz*. Leipzig: Reclam 1978. Especially pp. 162–166. See also Klaus Jarmatz et al.: *Exil in der UdSSR*. Leipzig: Reclam 1979. Pp. 238–239 and p. 247.

[41] Reported by one of Heinz Hentschke's informants in: *Lieder aus den faschistischen Konzentrationslagern*. Ed. by Inge Lammel and Günter Hofmeyer. Leipzig: Friedrich Hofmeister 1962. P. 6. In the same year as Langhoff's *Die Moorsoldaten* was published, the song's origins were also documented in Anon. [Willi Bredel]: *Als sozialdemokratischer Arbeiter im Konzentrationslager Papenburg*. Moscow – Leningrad: Verlagsgenossenschaft ausländischer Arbeiter in der UdSSR 1935. Pp. 27–28. Willi Dickhut, who was in Börgermoor Camp with Langhoff and who edited the GDR reprint of Langhoff's *Die Moorsoldaten*, largely confirms the facts of Langhoff's account, but presents a more differentiated treatment of the song's status (see: Willi Dickhut: Als Moorsoldat gegen den faschistischen Terror. In: Willi Dickhut: *So war's damals...: Tatsachenbericht eines Solinger Arbeiters, 1926–1948*. Stuttgart: Neuer Weg 1979. Pp. 181–230).

[42] Brecht: *Furcht und Elend* (n. 28). P. 28.

Willi Dickhut's and Wolfgang Langhoff's own recollections of the song's status suggest that any contrast between its being *banned* or *allowed* is an over-simplification:

> Manchmal, wenn wir ins Moor marschierten, etwas abseits vom Lager, forderten auch die SS-Begleiter: "Los, das Moorlied!"
> Dann sangen wir mit Begeisterung. Im Lager selbst sangen die Genossen gedämpft oder summten vor sich hin: "Wir sind die Moorsoldaten und ziehen mit dem Spaten ins Moor". Das Lied wurde zu einem Kampflied und munterte manchen auf, der schon resignierte.[43]

> Zwei Tage darauf [after its first performance] wurde das Lied verboten. Wahrscheinlich wegen der letzten Strophe, die ja auch wirklich mehrdeutig ausgelegt werden kann. Trotzdem waren es die SS-Leute, die immer wieder und wieder das Lied zu hören verlangten und es gegen die Kommandantur durchdrückten, daß wir auf den weiten Märschen zum Arbeitsplatz das Lied sangen.[44]

Langhoff recalls numerous occasions when the song was performed, despite the Camp Commandant's injunction: " 'Jetzt singen wir als erstes das Börgermoorlied. Aber leise, daß es die Posten nicht hören' ".[45] According to Langhoff, the song was also always sung when prisoners were about to be moved on from the camp: " 'Auf Wiedersehen, Kameraden.' Leise wird das Börgermoorlied angestimmt".[46] It is clear that the singing of the last verse was particularly important to the prisoners (and even at times to their guards). McNally emphasizes the *"strategic ambiguity* inherent in the song, especially in the final verse, which could be interpreted as being released from the camp as well as from Fascism".[47] But the final stanza could on occasions also generate cathartic feelings of aggression, rather than mere pious hope for a better future. This was very clear on the occasion of the song's first performance: "Bei den Worten, 'Dann ziehn die Moorsoldaten *nicht* mehr mit dem Spaten ins Moor' stießen die sechzehn Sänger die Spaten in den Sand und marschierten aus der Arena, die Spaten zurücklassend, die nun, in der Moorerde steckend, als Grabkreuze wirkten".[48] When delivered in this way, far from being a matter of cautious ambiguity, the final refrain became an unequivocal *Gestus* of collective solidarity.

In 1934, the year when "Prisoners Mix Cement" is set, a situation existed where the song could be officially banned in the concentration camp in which

[43] Dickhut: *So war's damals* (n. 41). P. 198.
[44] Langhoff: *Die Moorsoldaten* (n. 37). P. 194.
[45] Ibid. p. 214.
[46] Ibid. p. 230.
[47] McNally: "Die Moorsoldaten" (n. 39). P. 219.
[48] Lammel and Hofmeyer (eds.): *Lieder aus den faschistischen Konzentrationslagern* (n. 41). P. 17.

it originated (and from which it was smuggled out to other camps and prisons) and yet still be requested by individual guards. But there were also occasions when the final verse was only included "when the inmates could be sure that no hostile ears were listening"[49] or when singing it was a more open act of insubordination and could represent a deliberately hostile gesture of resistance on the prisoners' part.[50] To this must be added, in order to do justice to the song's complex role in Brecht's "Moorsoldaten", the fact that in most camps from 1933 onwards prisoners were frequently forced to sing songs central to their convictions as a form of degradation.[51] This was, after all, the spirit in which the communist prisoner had been dared to sing "Die Internationale" while being savagely beaten by a fellow prisoner at the start of the play's original Scene 14 (BFA 4. P. 410). By the time he wrote the "Moorsoldaten" scene, Brecht was able to exploit a far more differentiated spectrum of possibilities than the recollections of Langhoff, Bredel or Langerhans offered him. The most compelling evidence for Brecht's not sharing either Langerhans's or Toller's diametrically opposed assumptions about the song's status lies in the way each of the verses of "Die Moorsoldaten" serves a different function in the "Prisoners Mix Cement" scene.

Near the beginning of this scene, a work-party is ordered by a guard to sing the song's first verse, a command that at this stage makes it still a "Sklavenlied" in Langerhans's sense.[52] But in the later occurrences of the song in this scene, the tables are turned. When the SS man patrols for a second time in the direction of the work-party, it is the Pastor – in the German the "Bibelforscher" – who alerts them to the danger, and it is Brühl, the Social Democrat, who sings the second verse to allay the guard's suspicions. ("Up and down the guards are marching" is appropriately the first line of the verse they sing on this occasion.[53])

---

[49] McNally: "Die Moorsoldaten" (n. 39). P. 225.
[50] According to McNally (ibid. p. 226), "the size of the audience, and number of voices joining in with the song, would depend on where [the singing took place]: these could range from 20 to 30 (sleeping quarters), 150 in the dayrooms, and 400 to 500 in the washrooms". Similar figures are given by Aleksander Kulisiewicz in: *Adresse: Sachsenhausen. Literarische Momentaufnahmen aus dem KZ*. Ed. by Claudia Westermann. Gerlingen: Bleicher 1997. P. 27. However, Kulisiewicz makes an important distinction between clandestine "illegal" performances, confined to relatively small groups, and "die offiziellen Konzerte" attended by 400 to 500 inmates. Kulisiewicz, who was in Sachsenhausen from May 1940 until 1945, recalls "die illegalen Veranstaltungen" of those years: "zuletzt sangen wir das Moorsoldatenlied, Arbeiterlieder und ganz leise die Internationale" (ibid. p. 26).
[51] For examples of concentration camp prisoners being forced to sing songs as a form of degradation or while being tortured, see Shirli Gilbert: *Music in the Holocaust: Confronting Life in the Nazi Ghettos and Camps*. Oxford: Clarendon 2005. Pp. 116–117 and p. 134.
[52] Brecht/Bentley: *The Private Life* (n. 18). P. 27.
[53] Ibid. p. 28.

His quick thinking saves the situation and the guard again moves off. Not long after, however, the political squabbling reaches a crescendo, as Brühl himself starts shouting and threatening the communist with his shovel. The Pastor once more warns his fellow prisoners of the danger of reprisals they are putting themselves in and as a diversion another figure, in *The Private Life* the Non-Political Man, begins to sing a further verse of "Die Moorsoldaten".[54] In almost all published editions of Brecht's play, Brühl is said to sing the third verse and the "Bibelforscher" the last one. But in the shorter three-verse adaptation of "Die Moorsoldaten" to be found in both Ernst Toller's *Pastor Hall* and *The Private Life*, the third and the final verse of the song are one and the same![55] What all versions of the "Moorsoldaten" scene except the authorized American adaptation refer to as the *third* verse is, in fact, the second (i.e. less contentious) one. To point this out is not pedantry. The well-documented resistance associations of the final, highly provocative verse of "Die Moorsoldaten" endow the concluding part of this scene with a particularly charged significance. In *The Private Life of the Master Race*, this dangerously subversive verse sung by the *Non-Political* Man reminds his fellow prisoners that their oppression cannot last forever ("One day we shall say rejoicing: / Home, now you are mine again!"[56]). In true *Einheitsfront* spirit, the verse is thus used to tell them that they must bury the hatchet and find common cause so that such a future can come about. Which is precisely how the scene ends: with all the prisoners refusing to point the finger of accusation at one another after singing what has once more become *their* song. The final verse plays a key part in transforming them from a collection of bickering sectarian individualists into a determined resistance cell. But it is not just the contentious nature of this verse in contrast to the preceding ones, but the specific context in which it is sung that can give

[54] Ibid. p. 29.
[55] Presumably for dramatic reasons, Toller and Brecht use a shortened version of "Die Moorsoldaten" rather than the six verses given by Langhoff in: *Die Moorsoldaten* (n. 37). Pp. 190–193. Whether Brecht was influenced by *Pastor Hall* is uncertain. The third act had been published in 1939, in a journal of which Brecht was an editor (Ernst Toller: Friedrich Halls Flucht: Dritter Akt des Dramas *Pastor Hall*. In: *Das Wort* 4. H. 1 (1939). Pp. 42–51). And Stephen Spender's and Hugh Hunt's translation of the entire work, with W. H. Auden's version of "Die Moorsoldaten", had appeared in London in the same year (*Pastor Hall: A Play in Three Acts*. London: John Lane The Bodley Head 1939). While Toller and Brecht both use the same three verses (1, 5 and 6 – Auden's middle stanza is not the same), this is not *prima facie* evidence of influence. The song had already been reduced by others: for example, Lilo Linke's translation of Langhoff (*Rubber Truncheon: Being an Account of Thirteen Months Spent in a Concentration Camp*. London: Constable 1935) had already done so in the year the original German version of *Die Moorsoldaten* had first appeared.
[56] Brecht/Bentley: *The Private Life* (n. 18). P. 29.

it a revolutionary connotation. If the complex status of "Die Moorsoldaten" and its various verses is not taken into account, it looks as if the entire group has suddenly seen the light and acted in a spirit of newfound political solidarity.

Concluding Remarks

Few plays by Brecht were preceded by such an array of parallel exercises in another genre as *Furcht und Elend des Dritten Reiches* was. The poems treated above as forerunners of specific scenes are typical of his habit of conducting parallel experiments with related anti-fascist material across a number of text-types (e.g. his prose sketch "Der Spitzel" in *Mies und Meck* (BFA 18. Pp. 331–338. Here p. 331) or the poems in the "Deutsche Satiren" dealing with other aspects of life under National Socialism (BFA 12. Pp. 61–80)). Like the short caricaturing verses which introduce scenes in *Leben des Galilei*, the *Furcht und Elend Vorsprüche* and the Voice added in the case of *The Private Life of the Master Race* function as essentially anti-illusionist forms of epic comment imposed from outside and standing above the mini-dramas that are played out in the following scene. In this they differ strikingly from the plot-motivated songs sung by characters in *Mutter Courage und ihre Kinder* and *Der gute Mensch von Sezuan*. There has been a major shift of emphasis, when compared with the pre-war version of *Furcht und Elend*, in the ratio of dramatic to distancing devices. In both *Furcht und Elend* and *The Private Life of the Master Race*, there is a new, more rigorous division between epic commenting and events unfolding in the individual scenes. Moreover, Brecht continually adjusts the balance between Aristotelian and epic elements, depending on the particular audience the material is intended for. Another important factor influencing the choice of specific commenting devices is the gravity of the chosen subject matter. Whereas in the often comic realms of *Die Dreigroschenoper* and *Der kaukasische Kreidekreis* it might be aesthetically permissible for characters to step out of their theatrical roles in order to comment with superior insight on what is happening, this would hardly be appropriate in *Furcht und Elend*. Therefore Brecht turns to the same solution as he uses in *Leben des Galilei*: that of deploying extraneous commenting material that can be either sung or spoken as a quasi-prologue or epilogue to individual scenes and to the work in its entirety.

Hans-Harald Müller

Brechts *Leben des Galilei*: Eine Interpretation zweier Dramen

Although Brecht scholarship was quick to recognize the change in the character of Galileo between the "Danish" and the American versions, it has failed to offer a satisfactory explanation of this change; and more importantly it has failed to point out that it is unacceptable for a Marxist to arrive at two contradictory explanations for the behaviour of a single and identical individual. In the accounts of the "Danish" and American versions of Brecht's Galileo which are offered here, I put forward the view that in fact they must almost be regarded as two different plays because in the American version Becht jettisons his prior conception of ethics, which was grounded in logical empiricism, and adopts instead a moralistic viewpoint.

Um nicht als Pedant zu erscheinen, möchte ich ein paar Vorbemerkungen machen. Erstens: Brechts Werk gehört der ganzen Menschheit, und es ist frei für Adaptionen und Interpretationen aller Art. Zweitens: Auch die Philologie ist frei, Brechts Werk für alle nur denkbaren Arten der Interpretation in Anspruch zu nehmen. Drittens: Ich folge in meinem Aufsatz einer spezifischen wissenschaftlichen Art der Interpretation, bei der es – wie Brecht im *Galilei* sagt – gilt, "die Meinungen den Fakten zu unterwerfen". Mir geht es um eine intentionalistische Interpretation, die an den Fakten kritisiert werden kann. Das ist eine Art der Interpretation, die in der europäischen Hermeneutik eine lange Tradition besitzt und in der jüngeren Vergangenheit durch die Analytische Philosophie, vor allem aber auch durch den *cognitive turn* in den Textwissenschaften wieder verstärkte Aufmerksamkeit erlangt hat.

Vor dem Hintergrund dieser engeren Auffassung von Philologie gibt es an der Brecht-Forschung viel zu kritisieren, und in diesem Zusammenhang möchte ich bedauern, daß das Unternehmen, das Ron Speirs mit seinem Brecht-Buch 1982 begonnen hat,[1] keine Nachfolger gefunden hat. Meine Kritik an der Brecht-Forschung möchte ich am Beispiel der Interpretation des *Leben des Galilei* darstellen, einer Interpretation, die mindestens zwei Dramen zu gelten hat.

Die umfangreiche Forschung hat herausgefunden, daß Brechts Bewertung des Galilei sich zwischen 1938/39, der Phase der Entwürfe und der Niederschrift der ersten Fassung, und 1947, dem Jahr der Aufführung der amerikanischen Fassung, die Brecht in Berlin 1955/56 noch radikalisierte, völlig verändert hat: Aus dem listigen Widerstandskämpfer ist ein sozialer Verräter geworden. So klar wie die Einsicht in diesen Sachverhalt ist, so unbefriedigend sind die Konsequenzen, die aus ihm gezogen wurden. Keiner der zahlreichen Interpreten

---

[1] Ronald Speirs: *Brecht's Early Plays*. London: Macmillan 1982.

hat darauf hingewiesen, daß es für einen Marxisten wie Brecht völlig undenkbar ist, bei der Analyse ein und desselben historischen Exemplums zu zwei einander diametral widersprechenden Ergebnissen zu gelangen; keiner hat darauf aufmerksam gemacht, daß eine komplette Reinterpretation der Galilei-Gestalt, wie Brecht sie vornahm, nur im Zuge einer umfassenderen weltanschaulichen Neuorientierung denkbar ist, die Spuren in Brechts Werk hinterlassen haben muß. Niemand hat Konsequenzen aus der Einsicht gezogen, daß komplette Umwertungen zentraler Figuren ein Strukturmerkmal der Evolution von Brechts Werk sind: Aus dem großen *Baal* wird *Der böse Baal der asoziale*, aus dem letzten Abenteurer-Verbrecher Macheath in der *Ludenoper* wird der Faschist Macheath im *Dreigroschenroman*, und aus dem listigen Widerstandskämpfer Galilei wird der verächtliche Knecht der Inquisition. Schließlich hat außer Steve Giles niemand die zahlreichen Hinweise auf Brechts Beziehung zum Logischen Empirismus ernst genommen, die auch für die erste Fassung des *Galilei* von Bedeutung ist.[2]

Ich möchte im folgenden zeigen, daß Brecht zwischen der dänischen und der amerikanischen Fassung seine Ethik-Konzeption ausgewechselt hat, die in den dreißiger Jahren zum "harten Kern" seiner Überzeugungen gehörte, die auch in seinen Stücken ihren Niederschlag fanden. Ich halte den Wandel der Ethik-Konzeption und dessen Konsequenzen für so gravierend, daß er berechtigt, von einem "Bruch" oder einer "Zäsur" in Brechts Werk zu sprechen. Die nach dem *Galilei* geschriebenen Stücke vertreten sämtlich eine apodiktische Moral, die mit der Ethik-Kozeption Brechts aus den dreißiger Jahren nicht vereinbar ist.

Für Brechts Bewertung der Galilei-Figur lassen sich 4 Stufen unterscheiden:

1. Die Phase der Entwürfe (vermutlich Frühjahr bis Herbst 1938).
2. Die nach der ersten Niederschrift erstellte erste Fassung (Februar 1939).
3. Die amerikanische Fassung (1947).
4. Die Berliner Fassung (1955/56).

1. Die Phase der Entwürfe

In der Phase der Entwürfe konzipierte Brecht die Gestalt Galileis als die "legendäre" eines "großen Widersachers gegen die Mächtigen jener Zeit",[3] er machte aus ihm, worauf John White noch einmal hingewiesen hat,[4] "einen

---

[2] Steve Giles: *Bertolt Brecht and Critical Theory. Marxism, Modernity and the "Threepenny" Lawsuit*. Berne: Peter Lang 1997.

[3] Werner Mittenzwei: *Bertolt Brecht. Von der "Maßnahme" zum "Leben des Galilei"*. Berlin – Weimar: Aufbau 1973. S. 265–266.

[4] John J. White: *Leben des Galilei*. London: Grant & Cutler 1996. S. 13 (Critical Guides to German Texts).

listigen Kämpfer gegen die Inquisition".[5] Zu den legitimen Listen des Widerstandskämpfers gehörte für Brecht auch der Widerruf Galileis. Daß er zu diesem Widerruf ursprünglich ein recht entspanntes Verhältnis besaß, geht aus einem Entwurf hervor, in dem Brecht skizziert, wie Galilei der Schwester des Andrea, einer jungen Frau, nachstellt, aber "nur in ihr schlafzimmer kommt, indem er abschwört (zwischen tür und angel)".[6] Daß er den Widerruf prinzipiell für unproblematisch hielt, geht auch aus der *Keunos*-Parabel der ersten Fassung hervor:

In die Wohnung des kretischen Philosophen Keunos, der wegen seiner freiheitlichen Gesinnung bei den Kretern sehr beliebt war, kam eines Tages während der Gewaltherrschaft ein gewisser Agent, der einen Schein vorzeigte, der von denen ausgestellt war, welche die Stadt beherrschten. Darauf stand, ihm sollte jede Wohnung gehören, in die er seinen Fuß setze; ebenso sollte ihm auch jedes Essen gehören, das er verlange; ebenso sollte ihm auch jeder Mann dienen, den er sähe. Der Agent setzte sich auf einen Stuhl, verlangte Essen, wusch sich, legte sich nieder und fragte, mit dem Gesicht zur Wand, vor dem Einschlafen: wirst du mir dienen? Keunos deckte ihn mit einer Decke zu, vertrieb die Fliegen, bewachte seinen Schlaf und wie an diesem Tage gehorchte er ihm sieben Jahre lang. Aber was immer er für ihn tat: vor einem hütete er sich wohl, das war: auch nur ein Wort zu sagen. Als nun die sieben Jahre um waren und der Agent dick geworden war vom vielen Essen, Schlafen und Befehlen, starb der Agent. Da wickelte ihn Keunos in die verdorbene Decke, schleppte ihn aus dem Haus, wusch das Lager, tünchte die Wände, atmete auf und antwortete: nein. [7]

Diese Keuner-Geschichte gehört ursprünglich in den Kontext einer Reihe von Texten, in denen Brecht sich zu Beginn der dreißiger Jahre mit Problemen der Ethik auseinandersetzte. Die erste trägt den Titel *Von den Trägern des Wissens*:

"Wer das Wissen trägt, der darf nicht kämpfen; noch die Wahrheit sagen; noch einen Dienst erweisen; noch nicht essen; noch die Ehrungen ausschlagen; noch kenntlich sein; Wer das Wissen trägt, hat von allen Tugenden nur eine: daß er das Wissen trägt", sagte Herr Keuner (BFA 18. S. 14).

---

[5] Ernst Schumacher: *Drama und Geschichte: Bertolt Brechts "Leben des Galilei" und andere Stücke*. Berlin: Henschelverlag 1965. S. 98. Schumacher dokumentierte mit umfangreichem Belegmaterial, daß diese Galilei-Gestalt im Zusammenhang mit Brechts Hoffnungen auf die Widerstandskraft der Wissenschaften im Dritten Reich zu sehen ist. Diese Darstellung verdient unbedingt den Vorzug vor der Mittenzweis, der behauptete, "daß Brecht durch die Partei auf die großen Lebensfragen der Nation und ihre Lösung hingelenkt wurde" und die Erstfassung des Galilei "ganz im Geiste der Volksfrontpolitik" konzipiert habe (Mittenzwei: *Bertolt Brecht* (Anm. 3) S. 257).
[6] BBA 648/53. Zitiert bereits bei Mittenzwei: *Bertolt Brecht* (Anm. 3). S. 271: Anm. 28.
[7] Bertolt Brecht: *Leben des Galilei* [Fassung 1938/39]. BFA 5. S. 7–115. Hier S. 72–73.

Während diese Keuner-Geschichte das Ziel des Wissens nicht nennt, läßt der zweite Verhaltenskatalog, der aus der *Maßnahme* stammt, keinen Zweifel am Ziel:

> Wer für den Kommunismus kämpft, der muß kämpfen können und nicht kämpfen; die Wahrheit sagen und die Wahrheit nicht sagen; Dienste erweisen und Dienste verweigern; Versprechen halten und Versprechen nicht halten. Sich in Gefahr begeben und die Gefahr vermeiden; kenntlich sein und unkenntlich sein. Wer für den Kommunismus kämpft, hat von allen Tugenden nur eine: daß er für den Kommunismus kämpft.[8]

Aus dem Text geht hervor, daß Gegenstand der "Tugend" nur das Ziel ist, nicht aber die zur Erreichung des Ziels angewendeten Maßnahmen. Diese "Tugendlehre" nun hängt nicht mit der marxistischen Ethik zusammen, die von Kant und dem Neukantianismus geprägt war, sondern, wie ich schon bemerkte, mit dem Logischen Empirismus. Ich werde sie kurz erläutern.

1.1 Brechts Ethik-Konzeption

Brechts marxistische Revolutionskonzeption sah, um es knapp auszudrücken, eine Allianz zwischen revolutionärer Intelligenz und revolutionärer Arbeiterklasse vor. Die Skizze einer solchen Allianz findet sich etwa in der aus dem Jahre 1935 stammenden Betrachtung *Wozu braucht das Proletariat die Intellektuellen?* (BFA 22.1. S. 150), in der den Intellektuellen außer der Ideologiekritik auch die Arbeit an der "reinen Theorie" aufgetragen wird. Unter revolutionärer Intelligenz dürfte er die dem Marxismus nahe stehenden Naturwissenschaftler und "deren" Philosophen, die Logischen Empiristen, verstanden haben. Der revolutionären Intelligenz kam die Aufgabe zu, die bürgerliche Ideologie "zu durchlöchern" (BFA 22.1. S. 150; Z. 3), der revolutionären Arbeiterklasse jene, die bürgerliche Gesellschaft zu zertrümmern.

Brechts Überlegungen zur Ethik hängen unmittelbar mit seiner Wahrheitskonzeption zusammen, als deren Abbreviatur er gern das einschlägige, aber interpretationsbedürftige Hegel-Zitat "Die Wahrheit ist konkret" verwendete. "Wahrheit" ist für Brecht immer in Bezug auf ein Handlungsmodell definiert. Handeln findet immer in spezifischen Situationen statt, und so besitzt Brechts Handlungsmodell nicht allein eine Ziel-, sondern auch eine Situationskomponente; die letztere entscheidet darüber, wann eine "Wahrheit" anwendbar oder "praktikabel" ist.[9] Faßt man nun Verhaltensnormen oder ethische

---

[8] Bertolt Brecht: *Die Maßnahme*. BFA 3. S. 73–125. Hier S. 78.

[9] Auf der Basis einer Reihe von Äußerungen Brechts haben wir gezeigt, daß Brecht dieses "Praktikabilitätskriterium" als eine Verschärfung des Relevanzkriteriums des Logischen Empirismus aufgefaßt und kritisch gegen "objektivistische" Sätze mit allgemeinem Wahrheitsanspruch geltend gemacht hat. Vgl. Lutz Danneberg und Hans-Harald Müller: Brecht und der Logische Empirismus. In: *Fiction in Science – Science in Fiction. Zum Gespräch zwischen Literatur und Wissenschaft.* Hg. von Wendelin

Maximen als "Wahrheiten" auf, so gilt nach Brechts Konzeption auch für diese, daß sie keine universelle, sondern nur eine situationsspezifische Geltung beanspruchen können. Diesen Gedankengang hat Brecht in einer Reihe von Überlegungen verdeutlicht, die in der Berliner und Frankfurter Ausgabe erstmals unter dem Titel *Verurteilung der Ethiken* im Zusammenhang publiziert wurden (BFA 18. S. 152–154). In diesem von den Herausgebern "um 1936" datierten Text (BFA 18. S. 547) findet sich nicht allein der Satz "ME-TI SAGTE: KA-MEH UND MIEN-LEH stellten keine Sittenlehre auf" (BFA 18. S. 152; Z. 4–5), sondern auch das von Brecht auch hier abgewandelte Lenin-Zitat: "MIEN-LEH SAGTE: UNSERE SITTLICHKEIT leiten wir von den Interessen unseres Kampfes gegen die Unterdrücker und Ausbeuter ab" (BFA 18. S. 152; Z. 30–32).

Vor dem Hintergrund dieser Ethik-Konzeption und der *Keunos*-Parabel kann es als sicher gelten, daß Brecht in der Phase der Entwürfe das Verhalten Galileis als das eines listigen Kämpfers gegen die Gewalt der Kirche und für die fortschrittliche Physik für angemessen hielt.[10]

2. Die nach der ersten Niederschrift erstellte erste Fassung (Februar 1939)

Obwohl die in die Fassung vom Februar 1939 übernommene *Keunos*-Parabel sich wie "eine vorweggenommene Entschuldigung für Galileis spätere Haltung" liest,[11] reicht sie allein für eine Interpretation der dänischen Fassung des *Galilei* nicht aus, denn mit ihr ist Galileis Selbstverurteilung aus der 13. Szene nicht vereinbar. Diese Selbstverurteilung ist allerdings so schwer verständlich, daß sie einer genaueren Analyse bedarf.

Kompliziert ist Galileis Analyse des eigenen Falls schon allein auf Grund der Kommunikationssituation, in der sie stattfindet. Während der Selbstanklage ist nicht nur Andrea anwesend, sondern auch Virginia, von der Galilei weiß, daß sie ihn im Auftrag der Inquisition überwacht. Galilei spricht die Selbstanklage also in einer doppelt verzerrten Kommunikationssituation: Zum einen kommuniziert er verstellt mit Virginia, zum anderen aber auch mit Andrea, der ihm zunächst kühl und distanziert gegenübertritt. Weshalb Galilei allerdings die verdeckte Kommunikation mit Andrea beibehält, nachdem Virginia den Raum verlassen hat (BFA 5. S. 103; Z. 6), bleibt unerfindlich, zumal Galilei Andrea auch vertraulich als "mein Lieber" anspricht (BFA 5. S. 104; Z. 24).

Schmidt-Dengler. Wien: Hölder–Pichler–Tempsky 1998. S. 59–70 (Wissenschaftliche Weltauffassung und Kunst. Hg. vom Institut Wiener Kreis. Band 3).

[10] Schumacher zitiert aus einem Interview Brechts mit der Zeitschrift *Berlingske Tidende* vom 6. Januar 1939: "Ich habe den heldenmütigen Kampf Galileis für seine moderne wissenschaftliche Überzeugung: Daß sich die Erde bewegt, schildern wollen" (Schumacher: *Drama und Geschichte* (Anm. 5). S. 16).

[11] Vera Böhm: *Die Früh- und Spätfassung von Bertolt Brechts "Leben des Galilei". Ein Vergleich.* Typoskript Brecht-Archiv 1958. S. 49.

In dieser Kommunikationssituation erfolgt nun die berühmte Selbstanklage Galileis, die zahlreiche Interpretationsprobleme aufwirft. Ich werde mich im folgenden auf die wichtigsten Argumente konzentrieren. Die Wissenschaft kann, so Galilei, sich nicht damit begnügen, "daß ihre Mitglieder an sie eine bestimmte Anzahl von Sätzen abliefern" (BFA 5. S. 101; Z. 29 – S. 102; Z. 1); sie ist "bei Gefahr der Vernichtung" nicht imstande, "ihren Mitgliedern alle weitergehenden Verpflichtungen zu erlassen". Zum "Beispiel die Verpflichtung, an der Aufrechterhaltung ihrer selbst als Wissenschaft mitzuarbeiten" (BFA 5. S. 102; Z. 4–8). Diese Verpflichtungen gelten kategorisch: Ein Wissenschaftler kann "logischerweise nicht auf seine etwaigen Verdienste als Forscher verweisen, wenn er versäumt hat, seinen Beruf als solchen zu ehren und zu verteidigen gegen alle Gewalt" (BFA 5. S. 102; Z. 12–15). Daß dies ein "umfangreiches Geschäft" darstellt, exemplifiziert Galilei an den grundlegenden Aufgaben der Wissenschaft selbst: "Denn die Wissenschaft beruht darauf, daß man die Fakten nicht den Meinungen unterwerfen darf, sondern die Meinungen den Fakten unterwerfen muß" (BFA 5. S. 102; Z. 16–18). Die Aufgabe der Geltungsprüfung der "Meinungen" an "Fakten" ist eine universelle; sie darf nicht eingeschränkt werden. Um ihr gerecht werden zu können, muß die Wissenschaft zwei Imperative erfüllen: Sie muß zum einen "dafür kämpfen", daß die Sätze über die Geltungsprüfung "auf allen Gebieten geachtet werden", und sie muß "Menschen, die es versäumen, für die Vernunft einzutreten", mit "Schande davonjagen" (BFA 5. S. 102; Z. 28). Aus diesen allgemeinen Maximen mit kategorischer Geltung deduziert nun Galilei, der sich "von der Denkweise der Wissenschaft ausgeschlossen hat" (BFA 5. S. 102; Z. 4), die Beurteilung seines Falls: "Das ist der Grund, warum die Wissenschaft einen Menschen wie mich nicht in ihren Reihen dulden kann" (BFA 5. S. 102; Z. 32–34).

Diese Selbstanklage Galileis enthält einen umfangreichen Katalog wissenschaftsethischer Gebote, die ausnahmslos gelten und nicht mit Brechts Ethik-Konzeption in Übereinstimmung zu bringen sind. Bevor ich jedoch auf dieses Problem eingehe, möchte ich darauf hinweisen, daß bislang ausschließlich die Argumente erwähnt worden sind, die Galilei selbst in der internen Kommunikation mit Andrea zur Beurteilung seines Falls angeführt hat. Brecht arbeitet in dieser Szene aber mit dem Mittel der diskrepanten Information von Mitspielern und Zuschauern, das heißt die Zuschauer sind im Besitz zahlreicher Argumente, die zu einer ganz anderen Beurteilung des Falls führen könnten. Ich nenne nur die wichtigsten vom Beginn der Szene 13:

a) Aus dem Eingang der 13. Szene weiß der Zuschauer, daß es Galilei, obgleich er von der Inquisition und Virginia überwacht wird, in der Vergangenheit gelungen ist, die Dialoge über die zwei größten Weltsysteme nach Holland hinauszuschmuggeln (BFA 5. S. 95; Z. 4–6).

b) Aus dem Gespräch mit dem Hafner erfährt der Zuschauer, daß Galilei ein separates Exemplar der *Discorsi* fertiggestellt und konspirativ mit dem Hafner herauszuschmuggeln versucht hat, bislang allerdings ergebnislos.

c) Dem Gespräch mit dem Arzt kann der Zuschauer entnehmen, daß es Galilei gelungen ist, die Inquisition und Virginia über den Zustand seiner Augen zu täuschen.

Die planmäßige Fortführung der wissenschaftlichen Arbeit, die strategische Täuschung der Bewacher, die konspirative Zusammenarbeit mit dem Hafner und schließlich das gelungene Hinausschmuggeln seiner Arbeiten haben bei Lesern, Zuschauern und in der Forschung[12] zu einer anderen Beurteilung des Widerrufs geführt, als Galilei sie in seiner Selbstanklage vornimmt. Die Szene 13 ist aber mit Galileis Selbstanklage noch nicht beendet, und ihr Schluß bietet weitere Argumente zur Beurteilung seines Verhaltens. Zwar bleibt Galilei, wie erwähnt, auch nach Virginias Abgang bei seiner Art der uneigentlichen Kommunikation mit Andrea, aber seine Verstellung wird doch durchsichtiger, er sagt nämlich in der Regel genau das Gegenteil von dem, was er denkt.[13]

Zunächst wiederholt Galilei eine Information, die der Zuschauer schon aus dem Gespräch mit dem Hafner besitzt, nämlich die, daß er die *Discorsi* abgeschlossen hat. Sodann behauptet er, daß er dieses Buch nur für sich geschrieben habe. Diese Behauptung ist, wie der Zuschauer aus dem Gespräch mit den Hafner weiß, falsch. Ebenso falsch ist wahrscheinlich die folgende Aussage, Galileis Versicherung: "Auch was ich darüber dachte, daß es nötig sei, nicht nur in seinem eigenen Kopf, sondern auch in den Köpfen anderer zu denken, war ja, wie ich höre, ein völliger Irrtum, ungefähr diesem kopernikanischen Irrtum vergleichbar, den die Kirche widerlegt hat. Ein gefährlicher Irrtum!".[14] Diese uneigentlich gemeinte Distanzierung enthält auf durchsichtige Weise zwei Bekenntnisse: Zum einen bekennt sich Galilei – in einer von Brecht bekanntlich gern verwendeten Formulierung – zur Verbreitung des Wissens, zum anderen bekennt er sich zur kopernikanischen Lehre.

Am Ende der Szene 13 besitzt Andrea den Informationsstand über Galileis Verhalten, den der Zuschauer schon vor der Selbstanklage Galileis hatte, und er

---

[12] Vgl. z.B. Böhm: *Früh- und Spätfassung* (Anm. 10). S. 49: "Er [scil. Galilei] widerruft beinahe, um das Buch [scil. die *Discorsi*] schreiben zu können".

[13] In einer Anmerkung zu *Galilei, 13* aus dem Jahre 1947 erläutert Brecht dieses Verfahren selbst. Die von Galilei geäußerte Furcht, man könne ihm sein Exemplar der *Discorsi* wegnehmen, kommentiert er mit dem Satz: "Er selbst ist es, der dem Andrea nahelegt, das Buch 'zu stehlen'" (BFA 24. S. 243–244. Hier S. 244).

[14] BFA 5. S. 103; Z. 29–34. Ab "ein Völliger Irrtum" Sperrdruck im Original.

gelangt schließlich zu einer eigenen Beurteilung Galileis, die er in dem Turmgleichnis ausdrückt:

> Ich sehe, es ist, als ob ein Turm einstürzte, von ungeheurer Höhe und für unerschütterlich gehalten. Der Lärm des Einsturzes war weit lauter als das Lärmen der Bauleute und der Maschinen während der ganzen Zeit seines Aufbaus und die Staubsäule, die sein Einsturz erzeugte, höher als er selber gewesen war. Aber möglicherweise zeigt es sich, wenn sich der Staub verzieht, daß die zwölf oberen Stockwerke gefallen sind, aber die dreißig unteren noch stehen. Der Bau könnte dann weitergeführt werden. Ist es das, was Sie meinen? Dafür spräche, daß ja die Unstimmigkeiten in unserer Wissenschaft alle noch vorhanden sind, und sie wurden gesichtet. Die Schwierigkeit scheint gewachsen, aber die Notwendigkeit ist ebenfalls größer geworden. Ich bin froh, daß ich hergekommen bin (BFA 5. S. 105; Z. 16–29).

Andrea behält das letzte Wort in der Beurteilung Galileis. Auf seine Frage, ob das Turmgleichnis angemessen ist, antwortet Galilei nicht – nach dem Grundsatz "Qui tacet consentire videtur" ist sein Schweigen als Zustimmung zu deuten. Daß Galilei zu einer ähnlichen Beurteilung wie Andrea gelangen könnte, wird aus einer früher von ihm gemachten Äußerung deutlich: "Sicher, die Physik und die Astronomie vermögen über meinen Fall zur Tagesordnung überzugehen" (BFA 5. S. 100; Z. 23–24). Die deutlichste Trennung zwischen Person und Werk findet sich allerdings in einem Entwurf, den Brecht nicht in die erste Fassung übernahm; hier spricht Galilei zu Andrea:

> Ich will nicht behaupten, daß [ich] nicht der folter wegen, sondern, um meine bücher zu retten und neue zu schreiben, also der lehre wegen, widerrufen und mein gesicht verloren habe, aber wer will das gegenteil behaupten? die folter stand, unter uns, an der falschen stelle. sie sagten: schwöre ab, sonst töten wir dich und vernichten dein werk. da schwur ich ab. hätte es geheißen: wir töten dich, wenn du nicht abschwörst, aber dann soll dein werk leben und ich hätte dann abgeschworen, dann wäre ich sehr verächtlich geworden. aber, natürlich, das werk lebt nicht von dem, was ich schwöre oder abschwöre, es steht auf eigenen beinen. es wendet mir den rücken zu, macht eine wegwerfende oder selbst mitleidige gebärde nach mir und spaziert fort, in vollem sonnenlicht.[15]

Der Zuschauer/Leser steht bei der Beurteilung des Falls Galilei mithin vor dem Problem, ob er auf der Basis des Verhaltens Galilei als listigen Widerstandskämpfer oder auf der Basis der Selbstanklage Galilei als Verräter an der Wissenschaft charakterisieren soll. Der wissenschaftliche Interpret wüßte darüber hinaus gern, ob Brecht selbst in der ersten Fassung der rigoristischen Wissenschaftlerethik von Galileis Selbstanklage oder der am "Praktikabilitätskriterium" orientierten Ethik-Konzeption des Logischen Empirismus zuneigte. Auf der Basis der ersten Fassung von 1939 läßt sich das Problem – zumindest im Rahmen dieses Essays – nicht befriedigend lösen. Damit diese Interpretationsaporie nicht allzu

---

[15] BBA 426/34. Überschrieben "schlußszene".

sehr betrübt, möchte ich auf einen brieflichen Kommentar Karl Korschs zur Erstfassung des *Galilei* aufmerksam machen, der in der Brecht-Forschung nie zitiert wird, obwohl es ein vorzüglicher Text ist, in dem liebevolle Verehrung und beißende Ironie einander kunstvoll die Waage halten. Die Stelle aus dem am 31. Juli 1939 in Seattle geschriebenen Brief lautet:

> Ich will und muß Ihnen zunächst meine Begeisterung mitteilen über den Galilei, den mir Hedda [d.i. Korschs Frau] hierher nachschickte, ich habe ihn erst zweimal gelesen und lese ihn noch einmal, ehe ich mehr dazu schreibe. Ich finde ihn stark und gut – vielleicht zu schwer an Gedanken um als "Spiel" auf der sowieso nicht vorhandenen Bühne die von Ihnen sowieso nicht gewünschten Eindrücke, Erlebnisse, Erschütterungen u. Katharsisse zu erregen. Aber, unter uns, trat in der furchtbaren Traurigkeit am Ende doch etwas wie eine "Katharsis" bei mir auf oder ein. Eine so kolossale Figur rein auf dem Geistigen aufgebaut ist eine schöne Leistung des historischen Materialismus… .[16]

Korsch zumindest scheint die idealistische Ethik in Galileis Selbstverurteilung für die Auffassung des Stückeschreibers gehalten zu haben.

3. Die amerikanische Fassung (1947)

Der amerikanischen Fassung gehen einige Neubewertungen der Galilei-Gestalt in Aufzeichnungen Brechts voraus. In ihnen distanziert sich Brecht von Interpretationen der dänischen Fassung, die das Verhalten Galileis billigen, und er verurteilt Galilei scharf aus drei verschiedenen Gründen:

1. Weil er "der Lebensgefahr wegen die Wahrheit verschweigt".
2. Weil er den sozial revolutionären Fortschritt verraten hat zugunsten des "reinen Fortschritts einer Wissenschaft". In der Konsequenz dieser Auffassung behauptet Brecht, der entscheidende Verrat Galileis geschähe gar nicht in der 12. Szene vor der Inquisition, sondern schon in der 11. Szene. Er schreibt: "Galilei vollzieht ihn, wenn er das Angebot der fortschrittlichen bürgerlichen Klasse, gemacht durch den Eisengießer Vanni, ihn in seinem Kampf gegen die Kirche zu unterstützen, ablehnt und sich darauf beruft, er habe ein unpolitisches wissenschaftliches Werk geschrieben".[17]
3. Weil er durch seinen Verrat dem Mißbrauch der Wissenschaft Tür und Tor geöffnet hat, der in der Atombombe seinen Höhepunkt findet.

Wie diesen Äußerungen deutlich zu entnehmen ist, geht es in der amerikanischen Fassung nicht allein um eine Neubewertung des Verhaltens von Galilei, sondern es geht tendenziell auch um ein neues Stück. Thematischer Kern ist

---

[16] Karl Korsch: Brief (Nr. 28) an Bertolt Brecht 31.7.1939. In: *Jahrbuch Arbeiterbewegung 2: Marxistische Revolutionstheorien*. Hg. von Claudio Pozzoli. Frankfurt am Main: Fischer 1974. S. 233.

[17] Vgl. Bertolt Brecht: *Aufbau einer Rolle. Laughtons Galilei*. BFA 25. S. 7–69. Hier S. 51.

nicht wie 1939 die Frage, wie unter Bedingungen der Repression der wissenschaftliche Fortschritt gerettet werden kann, der mit dem sozialen unproblematisch gleichgesetzt ist, sondern im Vordergrund steht der sozialrevolutionäre Fortschritt selbst, dem die Wissenschaft bei Strafe der Verdammung zu folgen hat. Um Galilei als Verräter des sozialen Fortschritts brandmarken zu können, wandte Brecht in der amerikanischen Fassung im wesentlichen drei Strategien an:

1. Die Reduktion der Wissenschaftler-Rolle Galileis.
2. Die soziale Verortung einiger Figuren des Dramas.
3. Die Psychologisierung, Moralisierung und Kriminalisierung Galileis.

Die Reduktion der Wissenschaftler-Rolle Galileis konnte Brecht mit einigen Strichen realisieren.[18] Als erheblich schwieriger sollte sich die nachträgliche Einfügung eines sozialen Szenarios in die Fassung von 1939 erweisen. Die Figuren dieser Fassung waren einem Schema von Anhängern und Gegnern der Wissenschaft zugeordnet. Wenn es Brecht für die amerikanische Fassung ernst damit war, den Wissenschaftler Galilei in eine *soziale* Entscheidungssituation zu bringen, so hätte er die Konfiguration in ein soziales Szenario verwandeln müssen, in dem Anhänger und Gegner des sozialen Fortschritts einander gegenüberstehen. Diese Umstrukturierung hat Brecht nun aber nicht oder nur sehr inkonsistent vorgenommen.

Um seine These zu untermauern, daß der entscheidende Widerruf Galileis gar nicht "vor der Inquisition", sondern schon in der 11. Szene stattfindet, fügte Brecht eigens die Figur des Eisengießers Vanni (in der Berliner Fassung trägt er den Namen Matti) ein, der Galilei treuherzig seine Hilfe bei der Flucht anbietet und ihm versichert: "Hinter Ihnen stehen die oberitalienischen Städte".[19] Als Figur des Dramas besitzt Vanni indes weder das quantitative noch das qualitative Gewicht, das ausreichen würde, Galilei als sozialen Verräter erscheinen zu lassen. Aber wenn schon Vanni/ Matti es nicht zu garantieren vermag, daß "die oberitalienischen Städte" tatsächlich hinter Galilei stehen und dieser, wie es in der Berliner Fassung heißt, "Freunde in allen Geschäftszweigen" besitzt (BFA 5. S. 264; Z. 31), so hätte der Stückeschreiber diese Verpflichtung auf sich nehmen und zeigen müssen, daß es diese "Freunde" tatsächlich gibt. Das ist aber, läßt man die "bürgerlichen" Repräsentanten des Stücks Revue passieren, nicht der Fall.

Zusammenfassend läßt sich feststellen, daß es Brecht weder in der amerikanischen noch in der Berliner Fassung gelungen ist zu zeigen, daß Galilei eine realistische Alternative zu seinem Widerruf hatte. In beiden

---

[18] Auf die entsprechenden Kürzungen in der 1., 7., 8. und 13. Szene kann ich hier nicht eingehen.

[19] Bertolt Brecht: *Leben des Galilei* [Fassung 1955/56]. BFA 5. S. 188–289. Hier S. 264; Z. 32.

Fassungen befindet sich Galilei in der 11. Szene in einer zugespitzten Entscheidungssituation von größter Ungewißheit. Als Wissenschaftler muß er sich zwischen zwei sozialen Kräften entscheiden, die sich beide nicht für die Wissenschaft interessieren, sondern für deren soziale Folgen. Welche – zwischen Repression und Duldung lavierende – Politik die Kirche gegenüber der Wissenschaft einzunehmen gedenkt, kann Galilei nach dem päpstlichen Dekret vermuten, was aber die Eisengießer und die "oberitalienischen Städte" mit der Wissenschaft vorhaben, kann er nicht wissen. Ist seine Entscheidung für den Widerruf also rational?

Möglicherweise war es die Einsicht in diesen Sachverhalt, die Brecht veranlasste, die Gestalt Galilei moralisch immer tiefer einzuschwärzen, ihn zum Kollaborateur der Kirche, zum fanatischen Hasser der Menschheit zu machen,[20] ihn so tief verkommen zu lassen, daß er als Gestalt die Glaubwürdigkeit verliert und ihm nicht einmal mehr ein Interesse an der Verbreitung der *Discorsi* abzunehmen ist – noch weit weniger aber die philanthropischen Bekenntnisse zum einzigen Ziel der Wissenschaft, "die Mühseligkeit der menschlichen Existenz zu erleichtern" (BFA 5. S. 284; Z. 11–12).

In der Darstellung und Beurteilung von Galileis Verhalten in der 13. Szene der amerikanischen und der Berliner Fassung erweist Brecht sich mithin als rigoroser Moralist – hier ist er am weitesten entfernt von der Ethik-Konzeption, die er zu Beginn der dreißiger Jahre vertrat und die noch für die ersten Entwürfe des Galilei verbindlich war. Diese Ethik-Konzeption nun wird in der amerikanischen Fassung in Abbreviatur noch einmal zitiert, im vierten Teil der 13. Szene, nachdem Andrea die *Discorsi* an sich genommen hat:

ANDREA: You hid the truth from the enemy. In your dealings with the Inquisition, you simply made use of the common sense you brought to physics.
GALILEO: Oh!
ANDREA: We lost our heads. With the crowd at the street corners we said: "He will die, but he will never surrender!" You came back: "I surrendered but I am alive." We cried: "Your hands are stained!" You say: "Better stained than empty."
GALILEO: "Better stained than empty. – New". Sounds realistic. Sounds like me. New science… new ethics… (BFA 5. S. 178; Z. 6–15).

Brecht läßt Galileo diese Ethik-Auffassung jedoch nur zitieren, um sie dann desto kategorischer abzulehnen; Galilei selbst "beweist" in der Analyse seines Falls, "daß das wertvollste Werk niemals den Schaden aufwiegen kann, der durch einen Verrat an der Menschheit entstehen muß".[21] Diese Ablehnung der "neuen Ethik" kommt einem Widerruf Brechts gleich. Während die Wissenschaft Galileis in den frühen Entwürfen (und tendenziell in der ersten Fassung) fortschrittlich an sich war, sich "mit der gesamten Menschheit in einem Boot"

---

[20] Vgl. Bertolt Brecht: *Galilei nach dem Widerruf*. BFA 24. S. 245–246. Hier S. 246.
[21] Brecht: *Galilei, 13* (Anm. 13). S. 244.

befand (BFA 5. S. 102; Z. 24) und bei der erfolgreichen Durchsetzung durch ethische Gebote nicht eingeschränkt war, ist sie in der amerikanischen und der Berliner Fassung permanent vom Verrat bedroht und wird unter den Primat apodiktischer moralischer Sätze gestellt, die einer wissenschaftlichen Prüfung unzugänglich sind.

Zu beantworten bleiben die Fragen, wann und aus welchen Gründen Brecht von seiner Ethik-Konzeption Abstand nahm. Die Frage nach dem Zeitpunkt kann ich beim derzeitigen Forschungsstand gar nicht, und die Frage nach den Gründen nicht viel besser beantworten als Ernst Schumacher im Jahre 1965. Brecht, so Schumacher, war zu Beginn der dreißiger Jahre und noch weit bis ins Dritte Reich hinein jener Vernunftoptimist, als der er sich unter andrem in der November 1937 entstandenen *Rede über die Widerstandskraft der Vernunft* zeigte (BFA 22.1. S. 336–338). Seine Desillusionierung und Enttäuschung über die Niederlage von Vernunft und Wissenschaft im Dritten Reich reichten dann aber derart tief, daß er Galilei gleichsam für sie büßen ließ und auch in seinem späteren Werk die Wissenschaft unter den Primat eherner moralischer Maximen stellte und für die Intellektuellen meist nicht mehr als Verachtung übrig hatte.

Stephen Parker

Brecht and *Sinn und Form*: Generating Cultural Capital in the Cold War

This investigation into Brecht's collaboration with Sinn und Form *offers a fresh perspective upon his position within early GDR and Cold War cultural politics. Brecht's publications in the journal, edited by Peter Huchel under the aegis of the elite German Academy of Arts, contributed substantially to its legendary status as a unique organ representing a progressive vision of German cultural unity. Brecht engaged with the emerging cultural-political orthodoxy in a series of key publications in* Sinn und Form, *as the SED leadership sought to subordinate cultural to political capital. Brecht's position in those stage-managed exchanges was informed by aesthetic considerations, yet the SED leadership was driven in the nationalistic discourse that coloured Socialist Realism by the geopolitical imperative of justifying the GDR's status among the people's democracies of the Eastern Bloc. These radically divergent perspectives, exemplifying the irreconcilable claims of cultural and political capital, spawned major antagonisms and illusions. The position occupied by Brecht and his supporters was relentlessly eroded until, quite improbably, the crisis of 17 June 1953 allowed Brecht to turn the tables. While popular opposition was suppressed, as Brecht re-affirmed his loyalty to the SED leadership, whose revolutionary achievements he continued to praise, Brecht and his supporters asserted the relative autonomy of the Academy and its journal vis-à-vis weakened SED cultural politicians. From 1954 to 1956, Brecht and* Sinn und Form *capitalized upon their enhanced reputations, achieving the legendary status that later repression did nothing to diminish.*

Brecht, the GDR's leading author, and *Sinn und Form*, the state's most prestigious journal, stand out as quite isolated sites for the early GDR's accumulation of cultural capital on the international stage.[1] The collaboration between Brecht

[1] The present essay offers a fresh synthesis of research on Brecht in the early GDR, chiefly within the institutional context of the German Academy of Arts and *Sinn und Form*, which has been undertaken at Manchester in recent years. Principal publications are: Stephen Parker: *Sinn und Form*, Peter Huchel und der 17. Juni: Bertolt Brechts Rettungsaktion. In: *Sinn und Form* 46 (1994). Pp. 738–751; Peter Davies and Stephen Parker: Brecht, SED cultural policy and the issue of authority in the arts: the struggle for control of the German Academy of Arts. In: *Bertolt Brecht: Centenary Essays*. Ed. by Steve Giles and Rodney Livingstone. Amsterdam – Atlanta: Rodopi 1998. Pp. 181–195; Peter Davies: *Divided Loyalties: East German Writers and the Politics of German Division 1945–1953*. Leeds: Maney 2000; Matthew Philpotts: *The Margins of Dictatorship: Assent and Dissent in the Work of Günter Eich and Bertolt Brecht*. Oxford: Lang 2003; *Brecht and German Socialism 1942–1956*. Ed. by Stephen Parker, Matthew Philpotts and Peter Davies. In: *Brecht on Art and Politics*. Ed. by Tom Kuhn and Steve Giles. London: Methuen 2003. Pp. 271–342; Stephen Parker, Peter Davies and Matthew Philpotts: *The Modern Restoration: Re-thinking German Literary History 1930–1960*. Berlin – New York: de Gruyter 2004.

and the journal's first editor, Peter Huchel, contributed much to the legendary reputation that Brecht, Huchel and *Sinn und Form* came to enjoy in the early Cold War. The journal was lauded as a unique organ that embodied a progressive vision of German cultural unity grounded in representative literary excellence, which enabled it to transcend political division. That reputation occluded the journal's heavy dependence on state subsidy and institutional support in its promotion – albeit for a restricted, opinion-forming elite – of what was, of course, the GDR's own policy of German unity. That policy derived ultimately from Stalin's acute concern that Soviet security and claims for reparations would be compromised by a divided Germany.[2] Hence, Stalin's placemen in Germany, the KPD/SED leaders around Walter Ulbricht, were initially required to prioritize the establishment not of revolutionary Marxism-Leninism but of a German "bourgeois" democracy. The policy of unity informed, too, the foundation of the journal's parent organization, the German Academy of Arts, which was promoted by the East Berlin elite as a similarly progressive and representative, all-German successor to the discredited Prussian Academy of Arts.[3] Brecht was the most illustrious member of the Academy. He served on its founding commission and participated keenly in its development, acting as a Vice-President from 1954 until his death.[4] The investigation of Brecht's collaboration with *Sinn und Form* in the context of the Academy, a field relatively under-developed in research on Brecht, permits a fresh perspective upon his position within early GDR cultural politics.

The journal's international success in the 1950s, like that of Brecht's Berliner Ensemble, contrasts with the failure of much that surrounded them in the GDR, not least the ruling SED, which never achieved acceptance amongst the GDR's population nor, for that matter, abroad and was thus faced with a near-permanent crisis of legitimacy. The SED leadership was wholly unsuited to representing a Soviet position that ran counter to its own interest in consolidating power in East Germany on the basis of Marxist-Leninist ideology. Since its legitimacy depended on the accumulation of cultural as well as political capital, from the early 1950s it turned to the only way that it understood in order to make up its severe deficit, exercising a "total" claim in all spheres of activity,

---

[2] See Winfried Loth: *Stalins ungeliebtes Kind: Oder warum Moskau die DDR nicht wollte*. Berlin: Rowohlt 1994.

[3] For the early history of the Academy see *"Die Regierung ruft die Künstler": Dokumente zur Gründung der "Deutschen Akademie der Künste" (DDR) 1945–1953*. Ed. by Petra Uhlmann and Sabine Wolf. Berlin: Henschel 1993. The whole GDR period and unification with the West Berlin Academy of Arts is covered in *Zwischen Diskussion und Disziplin: Dokumente zur Geschichte der Akademie der Künste (Ost) 1945/50–1993*. Ed. by Ulrich Dietzel and Gudrun Geißler. Berlin: Henschel 1997.

[4] Brecht's pieces concerning the Academy and its journal are collected in volume 23 of the BFA.

including the elite cultural institutions, and demonstrating the irreconcilability of the respective claims of cultural and political capital.[5]

The Academy and its journal were not remotely equipped to function in a Marxist-Leninist command structure. Neither Huchel, nor Brecht, nor the Academy's first President, Arnold Zweig, was an SED member, nor did the SED control majorities in key sections and committees. Throughout the 1950s, the SED leadership struggled to impose the "total" claims of political capital on the elite cultural institutions that it had created, as it sought to resolve the profound geopolitical tensions between East and West that had informed the state's foundation. Only the building of the Berlin Wall definitively resolved those tensions. SED cultural policy long remained hamstrung by the competing claims of cultural unity and of a partisan socialism articulated through a rigidly imposed Socialist Realism.[6] Crucially, the latter was required not only as an aesthetic doctrine to support the establishment of socialism but also by "integrationists" around Walter Ulbricht as a tool to legitimize GDR claims for a place among the people's democracies of the Eastern Bloc.[7] In the early 1950s, that was by no means secure in a highly unstable field of power, the contradictions in which spawned radically divergent perspectives – with consequent antagonisms and illusions – amongst the artistic and political elites.

Sinn und Form was founded to establish an international presence for a post-fascist, socialist culture in Berlin. A particular aim was to engage the many Western intellectuals who shared its progressive position and whose support for the journal's agenda of cultural unity depended on its perceived distance from Socialist Realist dogma. The journal's unique stance made *Sinn und Form* highly attractive to its Cold War readership in East and West, and to the Western media, if singularly problematic for SED cultural politicians, since the cultural capital generated by the journal was at odds with key elements of the SED leadership's emerging needs. This cultural capital lent the small-circulation journal a surrogate political function for its GDR readership and the watching West. Brecht's frequent publications in the journal, particularly his contestation of dogmatic, official positions in cultural politics, contributed substantially to the journal's reputation as a quasi-autonomous voice within this turbulent field. The journal's incorporation of such dissent from the emerging orthodoxy fed

---

[5] At this point my argument concerning the irreconcilability of the respective claims of cultural and political capital follows Bourdieu. For a fuller discussion, see Pierre Bourdieu: *The Rules of Art: The Genesis and Structure of the Literary Field*. Trans. by Susan Emanuel. Cambridge: Polity Press 1996.
[6] See Stephen Parker: Peter Huchel und *Sinn und Form*: Die Ostberliner Akademie der Künste und das Problem der einheitlichen deutschen Kultur. In: *Sinn und Form* 44 (1992). Pp. 724–738.
[7] See Davies: *Divided Loyalties* (n. 1) for a sustained discussion of this matter.

the paranoia that beset the SED leadership, fuelling its mistrust of an organ whose success it had a stake in promoting.

The foundation of *Sinn und Form* in 1948–9 was informed by quite conventional, broadly progressive "bourgeois" notions of cultural capital, principally prestige accruing from representative literary quality and humane values. The journal's launch was accompanied by the following publicity statement:

> Mit SINN UND FORM wird eine Literaturzeitschrift vorgelegt, deren Herausgabe nur gerechtfertigt ist, wenn sie – fern von jedem Ästhetizismus – dem Geist der Sprache und der Dichtung dient. Denn nur unter dieser Voraussetzung kann sie eine der wesentlichen und repräsentativen periodisch erscheinenden literarischen Veröffentlichungen in Deutschland werden. Die Auswahl der Beiträge erfolgt in erster Linie nach den Gesichtspunkten, die für eine derartige Umschau stets gegolten haben sollten: all den Stimmen Gehör zu verschaffen, die im Sinne menschlichen und gesellschaftlichen Fortschritts, des Humanismus und der geistigen Vertiefung mit künstlerischen Mitteln das Wort formen oder mit kritischen die literarischen Erscheinungen der deutschen und ausländischen Geisteswelt aus gründlichem Wissen bewerten.[8]

The published statement makes no mention of socialism, foregrounding instead the journal's mission to promote German high literary culture by serving the "Geist der Sprache und der Dichtung".[9] The articulation of a representative aspiration is of a piece with the classicistic balance of the journal's title, which was chosen after Thomas Mann declined Johannes R. Becher's request to release the title of his journal produced in Swiss exile, *Maß und Wert*.[10] *Sinn und Form* derived much in its conception from Becher's obsession with the values and prestige of the German tradition. Becher sought to lay claim to the cultural capital traditionally invested in "Geist" by re-establishing literary taste as a hallmark of post-fascist German socialism, associating *Sinn und Form* with the lineage of prestigious journals showcasing classical modernism such as *Maß und Wert*, Fischer's *Neue Rundschau* and Hofmannsthal's *Neue deutsche Beiträge*.[11]

Huchel later acknowledged that a key factor in his choice as editor by Becher was that he was not an SED member, since such a person would have

---

[8] The document is in the Johannes R. Becher Archive, ref. no. 10614, Stiftung Archiv der Akademie der Künste Berlin-Brandenburg.

[9] For a discussion of the published statement and an earlier draft that refers to socialism, see Uwe Schoor: *Das geheime Journal der Nation*. Berlin: Lang 1992. Pp. 27–29.

[10] For a discussion of Becher's correspondence with Thomas Mann concerning the journal's title, see Stephen Parker: *Peter Huchel: A Literary Life in 20th-Century Germany*. Berne: Lang 1998. P. 264.

[11] For a discussion of that lineage, see Schoor: *Das geheime Journal der Nation* (n. 9). Pp. 31–34.

alienated many readers, particularly in the West.[12] An early reviewer of *Sinn und Form*, Alfred Andersch, characterized Huchel with telling acuity as "eigentlich kein Marxist, sondern ein 'bürgerlicher' Lyriker hohen Ranges, dem wohl am ehesten Absichten zuzutrauen sind, wie sie innerhalb des Nazi-Staates die sogenannte 'Innere Emigration' beherrscht haben".[13] Huchel's successful implementation of Becher's conception, increasingly on his own terms as Becher's hands-on involvement waned, has been aptly characterized by Gustav Seibt as exemplifying a "progressive Restauration", drawing strength from the deeper tradition as well as from classical modernism in the promotion of broadly progressive cultural and political values.[14]

This approach, of course, contrasts markedly with the radical position that Brecht had espoused during the later 1920s and early 1930s, as he adopted a position of revolutionary socialism. Actively embracing the linkage between art and revolutionary politics while proclaiming a relative autonomy for the artist, he had trenchantly opposed the "bourgeois" institutions of literature and theatre with their "sentimental" cultivation of a seemingly apolitical tradition. He set against these things the use value of art disseminated by innovative means and with polemical intent in the class struggle.[15] The envisaged destruction of bourgeois cultural capital was predicated upon its replacement by a new form of revolutionary cultural capital explicitly linked with political capital. Already in the final years of the Weimar Republic, understood by Brecht as a pre-revolutionary situation, his iconoclasm was accompanied by a bold vision of the new cultural institutions required by a socialist society, foremost among them a new theatre.[16] The development of this Epic Theatre would remain central to Brecht's theoretical concerns. It was spawned in the years before 1933 for that coming socialist society. He argued that during the inevitable revolutionary upheavals Epic Theatre was equipped to depict the contradictions between the middle classes and the proletariat as possible solutions were presented to underlying social conflicts. Even though that revolutionary situation did not materialize, Brecht would carry forward his thinking, developing his

[12] For a discussion of Huchel's politically non-aligned position, see Parker: *Peter Huchel: A Literary Life* (n. 10). P. 264.

[13] Alfred Andersch: Marxisten in der Igelstellung. In: *Frankfurter Hefte* 6 (1951). Pp. 208–210. Here p. 208.

[14] Gustav Seibt: Das Prinzip Abstand: Fünfzig Jahre *Sinn und Form*. In: *Sinn und Form* 51 (1999). Pp. 205–218. Here p. 208.

[15] For a discussion of Brecht's trajectory from the 1920s to the 1950s, see Philpotts's chapter on Brecht in Parker, Davies and Philpotts: *The Modern Restoration* (n. 1). Pp. 262–296. My argument at this point draws extensively on Philpotts's chapter.

[16] For the development of Brecht's thinking about a new theatre during the Weimar Republic, see Klaus-Dieter Krabiel: Zum Theater. In: *Brecht Handbuch in fünf Bänden*. Ed. by Jan Knopf. Stuttgart –Weimar: Metzler 2001–2003. Vol. 4. Pp. 34–45. Here pp. 41–42.

conception of Epic Theatre in the very different conditions of exile and the post-war years.[17]

During the years of exile, Brecht's attitude towards the tradition moved some way towards differentiated critical respect. His great plays such as *Leben des Galilei* adopted a more conventional approach in terms of form and character portrayal. Similarly, his publication practice in the Malik *Gesammelte Werke* assumed a more conventional concern with the enhanced reputation and prestige value accruing from the permanence and authority bestowed by such an edition within the established institutions of literature and the theatre. At the same time, in the situation of ideological opposition to liberal democracy and fascism, Brecht continued to represent the position of relative artistic autonomy consistent with his revolutionary politics. In that way, Brecht embodied cultural capital that drew on a revolutionary, partisan Marxism-Leninism as well as the more conventional "bourgeois" notion of prestige.

Yet that position proved much more difficult to sustain following his return to the new German socialist state. Brecht possessed a rare capacity to exploit seemingly unpromising situations, playing off divergent interests, yet the constellation of forces in the early GDR taxed even his ingenuity and energy. His interest in cementing his own reputation was served by the pursuit of artistic excellence in the Academy and its journal. Yet Brecht, of course, brought to bear not only his own prestige but also his own brand of socialist partisanship, characterized by his belief in the use value of art grounded in Marxist-Leninist ideology. In this crucial respect, Brechtian partisanship shared common ground with "integrationist" SED cultural politicians. Brecht, previously the iconoclastic outsider far removed from the exercise of power by dominant elites, became the energetic, self-disciplined insider, as he engaged with his peers within the political and cultural hierarchy in the creation of the new cultural institutions of socialism. The situation appeared to offer genuine opportunities to implement fresh thinking in the way that Brecht had conceived since the 1920s. Yet the situation also created fresh dependencies and fostered fresh illusions, which were exposed as the heteronomous claims of political capital asserted by the SED leadership. And Brecht, like other Academicians, misconstrued the motivation of the "integrationists" around Ulbricht. The relative autonomy that Brecht regarded as the preserve of the politically committed artist within socialist institutions was called into question, and artistic positions shared by Brecht and his supporters were attacked by SED figures, who were driven by geopolitical rather than aesthetic concerns. Brecht maintained the illusion, born of his ideological and institutional dependencies, that he could control a situation that was defined by factors which he understood quite imperfectly.

[17] For a detailed commentary on Brecht's theoretical writings about the theatre, see John White: *Bertolt Brecht's Dramatic Theory*. Rochester (NY): Camden House 2004.

The deeply partisan Brecht was an unlikely bedfellow for Huchel. They had met in Berlin before 1933 but they were not close artistically, temperamentally or politically.[18] Rather, they were thrown together by the demands of the Cold War. From the outset, the leading Academician Brecht treated *Sinn und Form* much as a house journal. Huchel's enormous respect for Brecht both as an artist and as an authority in cultural politics guaranteed that *Sinn und Form* would publish all writings offered by him.[19] Huchel had good reason to defer to Brecht. The latter's authority could afford protection, especially when Huchel was abandoned by the mercurial Becher in 1952–3. Meanwhile, Brecht was safe in the knowledge that he had in *Sinn und Form* a prestigious site within German socialism – at times when others were closed to him – which provided him with his most important platform for reaching readers in the East and the West.[20] Brecht took the journal to places – and conflicts – that, left to his own devices, Huchel would rather have avoided. Brecht's publications added political edge and fuelled controversy amongst readers of the journal, which otherwise ran the risk of an elitist remoteness.

It was a shared desire for recognition and for the (re-)establishment of reputations that predominated at the start of the collaboration. Brecht lent his support to the journal's promotion of excellence, urging his friend Bertold Viertel to contribute his Brecht essay to a *Sinn und Form* that "sehr repräsentativ wird".[21] The launch of *Sinn und Form* was quickly followed by the first Brecht special issue, a landmark event in literary history. In a generous letter to Huchel, Brecht suggested that the issue constituted "eine Art Aufnahmegesuch in die Literatur".[22] Brecht was reintroduced to a German reading public through exile works in each principal genre – poems, *Der kaukasische Kreidekreis*, *Die Geschäfte des Herrn Julius Caesar, Kleines Organon für das Theater –*, accompanied by critical essays by Herbert Ihering, Hans Mayer and Ernst Niekisch, and by a six-page bibliography. *Kleines Organon für das Theater*, completed in 1948 in Switzerland, has a particular importance at this juncture. In advance of his return to Berlin, Brecht brought together his thinking on Epic

---

[18] Huchel later acknowledged of his relationship with Brecht: "Ein Freund war ich ihm wohl nicht". Huchel is quoted by Hans Dieter Schmidt in "Der Fremde geht davon…". Erinnerungen an den Dichter Peter Huchel. In: *Peter Huchel: Materialien*. Ed. by Axel Vieregg. Frankfurt am Main: Suhrkamp 1986. Pp. 299–303. Here p. 301.

[19] For example, reflecting on the Barlach Affair in an open letter to Herbert Lestiboudois in August 1953, Huchel described Brecht as "die Stimme der wirklichen Autorität". The letter is in Peter Huchel: *Gesammelte Werke*. Ed. by Axel Vieregg. 2 vols. Frankfurt am Main: Suhrkamp 1984. Vol 2. Pp. 290–292. Here p. 291.

[20] Werner Mittenzwei points out that *Sinn und Form* became Brecht's "wichtigste literarische Plattform" in the GDR (Werner Mittenzwei: *Das Leben des Bertolt Brecht oder der Umgang mit den Welträtseln*. 2 vols. Berlin: Aufbau 1986. Vol. 2. P. 379).

[21] Bertolt Brecht: Letter to Berthold Viertel 14.12.1948. BFA 29. P. 484.

[22] Bertolt Brecht: Letter to Peter Huchel 1.7.1949. BFA 29. P. 539.

Theatre and its role within a society engaged in revolutionary upheaval. The text locates Brecht firmly within Marxist-Leninist discourse. It demonstrates his intention to adopt a partisan position in support of German socialism from a sophisticated, realist perspective.

The special issue laid the foundations for the journal's own reputation. Surveying the opening issues of *Sinn und Form*, which included work by Lorca and Mayakovsky as well as Bloch on Hegel, Brecht commented further:

> Ich bewundere diese geistreiche und planmäßige Kontribution zum Aufbau und Umbau. Ihre Ansicht, daß dieser *im großen* gemacht werden muß, nach einem *breiten* Plan und durch eine allgemeine Entfaltung der Produktivität im Materiellen und Formalen, tritt überallhin deutlich und erfrischend zutage.[23]

Over the years, work by Brecht was published in almost every second issue of *Sinn und Form*. Following his death, Huchel, in the face of major bureaucratic hurdles, put everything into the second Brecht special issue, including material from the Brecht archive and Walter Nubel's 144-page bibliography, an indispensable tool for the burgeoning Brecht industry that accompanied Brecht's stellar international reputation in the 1960s and 1970s.[24]

Yet Brecht's work never became purely a source of prestige value in the GDR. In the negotiation of political and aesthetic boundaries within the East Berlin cultural elite, material from the Academy's Brecht archive, frequently highly sensitive pieces, was always offered in the first instance to *Sinn und Form*.[25] The journal's assumption of this role, both regarding Brecht and more generally in GDR literary life, contributed to the high levels of interest in *Sinn und Form* in East and West throughout the GDR years.[26]

[23] Ibid. p. 540.

[24] For details of Huchel's interactions with the Academy and the publisher Rütten und Loening concerning the second Brecht special issue, see Parker: *Peter Huchel* (n. 10). Pp. 365–367.

[25] See, for example, the publication of "Die neue Mundart" together with "Lebensmittel zum Zweck" by Gerhard Seidel in: Vom Kauderwelsch und vom Schmalz der Söhne MacCarthys. In: *Sinn und Form* 32 (1980). Pp. 1087–1091.

[26] This required a level of responsibility to be invested in the editor-in-chief that was not granted to other publications in the tightly controlled media of the GDR. For a discussion of the editor-in-chief's position, see Stephen Parker: Der Erkenntniswert von Dokumenten bei der Erforschung der Geschichte von *Sinn und Form* 1949–89. In: *Akten des X. Internationalen Germanistenkongresses Wien 2000*. Vol. 7. Ed. by Helmut Kiesel and Corina Caduff. Bern: Lang 2002. Pp. 33–38. During Wilhelm Girnus's editorship (1964–1981), Brecht was used as a test case in a series of essays by figures such as Werner Mittenzwei and Robert Weimann, which argued for a critical appropriation of the classics. And Huchel derived his own personal use value from Brecht's work when he opened his last issue of *Sinn und Form* in 1962 with Brecht's 1938 *Rede über die Widerstandskraft der Vernunft*. The speech begins: "Angesichts der überaus strengen Maßnahmen, die in den faschistischen Staaten gegenwärtig gegen die Vernunft

During his lifetime, Brecht's regular output in *Sinn und Form* included poetry, drama, essays and speeches, all characterized by a Brechtian partisanship. German unity is a recurrent theme. His open letter *An die Künstler und Schriftsteller Deutschlands*, a call for peace and German re-unification, was clearly directed against Western integration, re-armament and the publication in the Federal Republic of "Schriften und Kunstwerke, welche den Krieg verherrlichen oder als unvermeidbar hinstellen, und [...] welche den Völkerhaß fördern".[27] In speeches and essays such as *Der Friede ist das A und O*, delivered in Moscow on the award of the International Stalin Peace Prize, and *Kann die heutige Welt durch Theater wiedergegeben werden?*, written in response to Friedrich Dürrenmatt, Brecht consistently maintains the position that revolutionary socialism provides a qualitatively superior site over capitalism for change in the interest of social justice and peace. The same position is presented in poems published in early issues such as "Aus allem etwas machen" and "Tschaganak Bersijew oder Die Erziehung der Hirse". They were conceived as gentle pieces of socialist didactics and informed by a clarity and simplicity of expression characteristic of late Brechtian "wisdom", but greeted with derision by some Western critics.[28] Both pieces praise the revolutionary leadership of Mao and Stalin in promoting "das Nützliche". Similarly, one of the "Kinderlieder", "Nachkriegsliedchen", celebrates a peace stretching from Moscow to Beijing in which, "Der Vater baut ein neues Haus. / Die Mutter sucht die Steine aus" (BFA 22. P. 291). The unspoken message behind these poems is that a united, socialist Germany should take its place amongst the people's democracies, the repository of constructive wisdom.

All these publications emphasize Brecht's attachment to the political capital of the SED, his strategic, ideological commitment to the East German state as the site for the realization of German socialism. Many critics have viewed such partisan pieces as little more than tactical manoeuvrings, designed to create space for Brecht's real passion, the theatre. This, however, disregards the underlying consistency of Brecht's ideological position and the extent to which he modified his own theory and practice in the light of the socialist transformation that he was witnessing. Brecht repeatedly urged the publication in *Sinn und*

---

ergriffen werden, dieser ebenso methodischen wie gewalttätigen Maßnahmen, ist es erlaubt, zu fragen, ob die menschliche Vernunft diesem gewaltigen Ansturm überhaupt wird widerstehen können" (BFA 22. Pp. 333–336. Here p. 333). The use of Brecht to provide the scarcely veiled comparison between National Socialism and the GDR was regarded as the ultimate insult by the influential SED figures who had engineered Huchel's departure.

[27] BFA 23. Pp. 155–156. The title used in BFA is "Offener Brief an die deutschen Künstler und Schriftsteller". The piece was widely disseminated, including a reading by Helene Weigel on the radio, and published in: *Sinn und Form* 3 (1951). H. 5. P. 5.

[28] See Jan Knopf: *Brecht Handbuch*. 2 vols. Stuttgart: Metzler 1986. Vol. 2. P. 180.

Form of pieces depicting the revolutionary achievements of the GDR.[29] He continued to evolve his views on realism and re-engaged with the theories of Stanislavsky, overcoming the earlier, well-documented polemical opposition.[30] Much research has viewed Brecht's work in these areas, too, as purely reactive, from a position of tactical expediency or of downright opportunism. That underestimates Brecht's sustained immersion in these closely related issues. It also takes at face value the propagandist discourse of SED cultural politicians, shot through with crude binary oppositions – though, for different reasons, Brecht himself misapprehended that SED discourse.

It is characteristic of the late Brecht's broadly assenting position in GDR socialism that he virtually abandoned his favoured weapons of satire and polemic, adopting a studiedly self-disciplined, conciliatory and constructive manner, as he cultivated "wisdom" within socialism. Brecht's self-discipline is evident in private and public statements. Indeed, he was prepared to acquiesce in SED actions that frequently ran counter to his own stated interests. For example, he repeatedly showed his understanding for crude "sociological" excesses of critics and cultural politicians. While he responded with his own, more sophisticated readings, he went a very long way in excusing their vicious outpourings as the product of extraordinary revolutionary upheavals.

Yet, this attempted rapprochement would never be sufficient for a Party driven by concerns of a quite different order from his own. SED leaders viewed Brecht and his fellow Academicians with an increasingly irritated incomprehension as these privileged figures failed to deliver the required endorsement of the Party's position. As pressure from SED "integrationists" built remorselessly between 1951 and 1953, first in the Formalist Campaign, then following the decision at the Second Party Conference in 1952 to proceed with the Construction of the Foundations of Socialism, Brecht's capacity to accommodate himself was tested to the limit. Brecht placed major contributions with *Sinn und Form* during these years: an extract from *Das Verhör des Lukullus*; *Notizen zur Barlach-Ausstellung*; *Thesen zur Faustus-Diskussion*; *Erwin Strittmatters "Katzgraben"*; and six *Buckower Elegien*. Brecht was instrumentally involved in a further key publication, *Vorschläge der Deutschen Akademie der Künste*, formulated in the context of the "New Course", announced on 9 June, and of 17 June 1953. These important publications chart Brecht's central role in the struggle to maintain a relative autonomy for the artistic elite in those turbulent years. It was a struggle that could never be won on the terms upon

---

[29] For example, Brecht advocated the publication in *Sinn und Form* of reportage by Friedrich Wolf, Ludwig Renn, Michael Tschesno and KuBa, describing economic and cultural developments. See Philpotts: *The Margins of Dictatorship* (n. 1). Pp. 273–274.
[30] For a discussion of Brecht's study of Stanislavsky in the context of Brecht's production of Strittmatter's *Katzgraben*, see Philpotts: Ibid. pp. 264–267.

which Brecht and his associates were engaging. The SED's sustained offensive was designed simply to subordinate cultural capital to political capital in pressing the GDR's integration within the Eastern Bloc. Academicians' protestations were dismissed as at best special pleading, at worst treason.

The gulf that would presently open up can be traced back to Brecht's first productions following his return to Berlin. His production of *Mutter Courage* and his adaptation of Lenz's *Der Hofmeister* were hailed as great critical successes, yet their "negativity" in the portrayal of character and of German history was frowned upon. With these productions, Brecht initiated his critical investigation into the unhappy course of German history that reached its nadir in National Socialism. Brecht's attempt to engage with this fraught legacy ran counter to "integrationists'" search for uplifting stories from German history, represented by positive heroes in the manner of Socialist Realism, that could support the GDR's claims for a place among the people's democracies.

The SED codified the binary oppositions of cultural policy in support of its geopolitical interests when it launched the Formalism Campaign in March 1951. At the time, Brecht acquiesced in the SED's use of a nationalistic discourse redolent of Nazism.[31] Precisely what sins Formalism engendered was spelled out as follows:

> Das wichtigste Merkmal des Formalismus besteht in dem Bestreben, unter dem Vorwand oder auch der irrigen Absicht, etwas "vollkommen Neues" zu entwickeln, den völligen Bruch mit dem klassischen Kulturerbe zu vollziehen. Das führt zur Entwurzelung der nationalen Kultur, zur Zerstörung des Nationalbewußtseins, fördert den Kosmopolitismus und bedeutet damit eine direkte Unterstützung der Kriegspolitik des amerikanischen Imperialismus.[32]

In stark opposition to unpatriotic Formalism, Socialist Realism, underpinned by the teleology of the materialist dialectic that was embodied in positive heroes, provides the means for GDR art to further SED interests.

---

[31] On 25 July 1953, when pressure on him had eased considerably, Brecht would complain in these terms to Wilhelm Girnus, who reported the matter to Walter Ulbricht in a letter on 27 July. For further details see Werner Hecht: *Brecht Chronik 1898–1956*. Frankfurt am Main: Suhrkamp 1997. Pp. 1070–1071. The SED's discourse echoes both Nazi anti-Semitism and the anti-Semitism that was sweeping through the Eastern Bloc in the early 1950s. For a discussion of the latter see Jeffrey Herf: *Divided Memory: The Nazi Past in the Two Germanys*. Cambridge (MA) – London: Harvard University Press 1997, especially chapter 5: Purging "Cosmopolitanism": The Jewish Question in East Germany, 1949–1956. Pp. 106–161.

[32] Hans Lauter: Der Kampf gegen den Formalismus in der Kunst und Literatur, für eine fortschrittliche deutsche Kultur. In: Christoph Kleßmann: *Die doppelte Staatsgründung: Deutsche Geschichte 1945–1955*. 4th ed. Göttingen: Vandenhoeck & Ruprecht 1986. Pp. 527–531. Here p. 529.

Brecht's collaborative production with Paul Dessau of the opera *Das Verhör des Lukullus* was subjected to a concerted attack by SED politicians, who held it up as a prime example of Formalism.[33] Brecht indicates in his responses a readiness to accept restrictions on artistic freedom as the price to be paid during a time of revolutionary upheaval: "Was die Absetzung des *Lukullus* angeht: Es ist vorauszusehen, daß bei allen Umwälzungen von solchem Ausmaß die Künste selbst da in Schwierigkeiten kommen, wo sie führend mitwirken".[34] Similarly: "Diktatur des Proletariats ist deshalb keine günstige Periode für die Kunst. Im Vordergrund steht die Politik, die gesellschaftlichen Tendenzen sind oft sogar kunstfeindlich, beschneiden (wegen Diktaturnotwendigkeit) freie Entfaltung, auch der Kunst".[35] Brecht took this approach into discussions with Wilhelm Pieck, which flattered Brecht's self-image as a *Realpolitiker* and resulted in changes to his libretto that brought out more explicitly their shared anti-imperialist, anti-capitalist position.[36] On that basis, the SED Politburo permitted further productions and Brecht could maintain that, for all the furore in the West over his seeming abdication of artistic autonomy and, with that, of the claims of cultural capital, "In Wirklichkeit sind Erscheinungen wie die Formalismus-Realismus-Debatte ohne Kenntnis der großen Umwälzungen nicht zu verstehen und also auch nicht zu beurteilen".[37]

Undoubtedly, Brecht viewed these exchanges as part of the same process which saw him review his relationship with Stanislavsky and realism. The SED's "total" claim, driving the binary opposition between Formalism and Socialist Realism, has served to obscure Brecht's common ground with the Party on realism.[38] Clearly, Brecht's own writings and statements consistently resist the reductionist reading that follows from the binary opposition with its coercive intention. In post-war essays on Formalism, Brecht continued to attack prestige value imputed to art that privileged form at the expense of content. As Philpotts puts it: "Brecht's interest in formal innovation in the GDR stems from a need to represent the new subject matter of post-war German socialism, and as such it is in Brecht's terms a realist undertaking".[39]

---

[33] For an extensive documentation, see Joachim Lucchesi: *Das Verhör in der Oper: Die Debatte um die Aufführung "Das Verhör des Lukullus" von Bertolt Brecht und Paul Dessau.* Berlin: BasisDruck 1993.

[34] Bertolt Brecht: *Journal* 25.3.1951. BFA. 27. P. 318.

[35] Käthe Rülicke's note of Brecht's conversation with Hermann Scherchen on 18 March 1951 is in Lucchesi: *Das Verhör in der Oper* (n. 33). P. 178.

[36] See Davies: *Divided Loyalties* (n. 1). Pp. 193–209. Especially p. 206.

[37] Brecht's letter of 18 January 1952 to the West German artist Günther Strupp is in BFA 30. P. 107.

[38] For a detailed discussion, see Parker, Davies and Philpotts: *The Modern Restoration* (n. 1). Pp. 282–285.

[39] See ibid. p. 286.

Yet the Party leadership's anxieties over what most regarded as the talented Brecht's disruptive wrong-headedness, as he failed to accept their position, led to further measures that were intended to curb his influence. Wilhelm Girnus was directed by the Politburo "mit Bert Brecht eine ständige politische Arbeit durchzuführen und ihm Hilfe zu leisten".[40] Brecht was targeted in a press campaign that attacked productions such as his adaptation of Goethe's *Urfaust*. An analysis of the Academy's achievements undertaken by the SED's Cultural Department notes: "Die Brechtsche Art, Theater zu spielen, herrscht vor [...] Genossin Rodenberg [...] sagte hierzu: 'Brecht ist gut, doch darf er keine Schule machen. Dieser Sektion muß neues marxistisches Blut zugeführt werden' ".[41]

In a journal entry of 1 February 1952, Brecht again shows his readiness to find common ground, this time in the controversy surrounding the Academy's Barlach exhibition, which was subjected to crude attacks in the East Berlin press by Girnus and Kurt Magritz:

> Die Barlachausstellung der Akademie der Künste wurde in der *Täglichen Rundschau* und im *Neuen Deutschland* heftig angegriffen, so daß die wenigen verbliebenen Künstler in Lethargie geworfen wurden. Ich machte mir Notizen dazu, die Werte und das Exemplarische des Werks konkret ins Licht zu setzen gegen eine völlig abstrakte Vernichtung mit gesellschaftskritischen Waffen. Stellte dabei fest, wie richtig, d.h. richtunggebend die gesellschaftskritischen Argumente selbst in den schwächsten und stümperhaftesten Händen bleiben, und schrieb die Notizen entsprechend (BFA 27. Pp. 329–330).

Brecht adopts the discourse of "sociological" criticism in his *Notizen zur Barlach-Ausstellung*, which appeared in *Sinn und Form* after Girnus had declined to publish them in *Neues Deutschland*.[42] Brecht argues that Barlach's *Buchleser* is "realistischer" than Rodin's *Thinker*. Yet, in language reminiscent of SED art criticism, he dismisses other pieces by Barlach as a "Deformierung der Wirklichkeit".[43] At the same time, he frames his criticisms of Barlach within statements which re-affirm Barlach's artistic greatness. In this way, he seeks to demonstrate a differentiated approach to art criticism, which, he makes clear, is absent in the blanket criticisms articulated in abstract terms by Girnus and Magritz. The piece concludes: "Eine abstrakte Kritik führt nicht zu einer realistischen Kunst".[44] From a position of broad assent to SED rule and its achievements in establishing socialism in Germany, Brecht articulates here a specific dissenting position, namely that GDR art criticism could not remain

---

[40] Minutes of the meeting of the Politburo on 2 May 1951. See: Lucchesi: *Das Verhör in der Oper* (n. 33). Pp. 220–221.

[41] See Uhlmann and Wolf (eds.): *"Die Regierung ruft die Künstler"* (n. 3). P. 171.

[42] For details see BFA 23. Pp. 511–514. Here p. 513.

[43] For a detailed discussion upon which the present section draws, see Parker, Davies, Philpotts: *The Modern Restoration* (n. 1). Pp. 286–287.

[44] Bertolt Brecht: *Notizen zur Barlach-Ausstellung*. BFA 23. Pp. 198–202. Here p. 202.

on the level of abstraction but must engage with individual works of art. It was the dissent that was registered among readers and the SED leadership. Huchel later captured succinctly the official reaction to the publication: "Damals galt in der DDR die Parole: Wer für Barlach ist, unterstützt den amerikanischen Imperialismus. Also wurde ich zu Becher zitiert, der mich beschimpfte".[45] In this case, the SED's thorough-going politicization of art through the "total" claim of its binary thinking fostered the public perception of Brechtian dissent in Huchel's *Sinn und Form*, the site for the assertion of artistic autonomy in the defence of cultural capital.

Matters escalated when the SED proceeded with the Construction of the Foundations of Socialism. This was intended by the "integrationists" to put an end to the "compromises" that had bedevilled the fledgling state and its institutions. It imposed greater demands on the economy, which the population was not equipped to meet, and moved matters on to a much more radical plane in the arts. Events were set in train from the autumn of 1952 that were designed to transform the Academy and its journal into fully functioning instruments of cultural policy. Brecht acquiesced in the initial stages of this process, as Becher replaced Arnold Zweig as President of the Academy and Alexander Abusch was unconstitutionally elevated to membership of the Academy and, simultaneously, to the key position of Secretary of the Literature Section. Abusch employed his organizational skills to set in train a series of events designed to force the adoption of official cultural policy upon recalcitrant members. The topics chosen for discussion brought into a single focus the closely related problems of Brecht and the Academy.

Abusch ensured that in April 1953 the Academy would be the venue for the First German Stanislavsky Conference. Under the aegis not of the Academy but of the Staatliche Kommission für Kunstangelegenheiten, the conference was to be dedicated to the question "Wie können wir uns die Methode Stanislawskis aneignen?". Stanislavsky's theories of drama had, of course, been used in the Soviet Union in the 1930s as a model for Socialist Realism in the attack on the avant-garde. In the GDR, they were being promoted as a model for drama in opposition to Brecht's theories. It was well-known that Brecht himself had polemicized against Stanislavsky in the 1930s. The conference was thus to be an "Auseinandersetzung mit dem Brecht-Theater".[46] The situation was one in which, in the wake of the Slánský trial in Czechoslovakia, an atmosphere of totalitarian terror was beginning to take hold in East Berlin.[47] Indeed, "the

---

[45] Peter Huchel: *Gegen den Strom. Interview mit Hansjakob Stehle*. In: Huchel: *Gesammelte Werke* (n. 19). Vol 2. Pp. 373–382. Here p. 374.
[46] Mittenzwei: *Das Leben des Bertolt Brecht* (n. 20). Vol. 2. P. 447.
[47] Davies: *Divided Loyalties* (n. 1). P. 96.

campaign of vilification in the build-up to [the] conference [...] risked becoming theater's equivalent of a show trial".[48]

Brecht had good reason to see the existence of the Berliner Ensemble as directly threatened. He and Helene Weigel proceeded with extreme caution. They countered the unrelenting anti-Brecht tone of the conference with conciliatory statements that were born not simply of tactical expediency but of a sustained interrogation of the value of Stanislavsky for Brecht in the German socialist state.[49] This belies the view, fuelled by the manoeuvrings of Abusch and associates employing crude binary oppositions, that for Brecht in the early 1950s a radical disjunction continued unaltered between Stanislavsky and him.[50] At the same time, while he was by no means unprepared, Brecht seemingly continued to believe that an open discussion of aesthetics, coupled with his continuing support for GDR socialism, was what was required.

Brecht's re-appraisal of Stanislavsky was "one of the last occasions on which Brecht substantially re-thought his theoretical position".[51] For some time, Brecht had been reviewing the value of Slanislavsky for his own theory and practice as he collaborated with Erwin Strittmatter in the production of *Katzgraben*, Strittmatter's comedy of GDR rural life. As early as 1951 Brecht had produced a series of notes addressing the question of "Was unter anderem vom Theater Stanislawskis gelernt werden kann" (BFA 23. Pp. 167–168). A further series of texts was produced along similar lines from February to May 1953 when rehearsals for *Katzgraben* took place at the same time as preparations for the Stanislavsky Conference (see BFA 23. Pp. 224–236). Rehearsals were accompanied by the accumulation of very extensive rehearsal notes, the *Katzgraben-Notate*. Werner Hecht notes of their forthcoming, full publication in the *Große kommentierte Berliner und Frankfurter Ausgabe*: "So kann vielleicht erst jetzt mit der ersten Veröffentlichung des ursprünglichen Textkonvoluts das wirkliche Ausmaß des echten Interesses an dem System Stanislawskis erkannt werden".[52]

[48] White: *Bertolt Brecht's Dramatic Theory* (n. 17). Pp. 2–3.
[49] Weigel read the text that Brecht had prepared. It is published as: *Rede für die Stanislawski-Konferenz*. BFA 23. Pp. 234–236.
[50] This, in turn, encouraged the dismissal of the view held by some GDR academics that a rapprochement had taken place between the two as no more than "eine Erfindung der DDR-Brecht-Forschung". See Knopf: *Brecht Handbuch* (1986) (n. 28). Vol. 1. P. 466. In the new edition of the *Brecht Handbuch*, Joachim Lucchesi argues that in 1953 Brecht made merely tactical concessions, whilst maintaining "grundsätzliche Gegenpositionen" to Stanislavsky. See Joachim Lucchesi: Zum Theater. In: *Brecht Handbuch* (2003) (n. 16).Vol. 4. Pp. 310–316. Here p. 311.
[51] White: *Bertolt Brecht's Dramatic Theory* (n. 17). P. 1.
[52] Werner Hecht: Grund der Empörung über eine "ganz unerträgliche Behandlung": Brechts Stanislawski-Studium 1953. In: *Maske und Kothurn* 33 (1987) No. 3/4. Pp. 75–87. Here p. 87, quoted by Philpotts: *The Margins of Dictatorship* (n. 1) P. 278.

The *Katzgraben-Notate* were followed by Brecht's essay, *Erwin Strittmatters "Katzgraben"*, which was published in *Sinn und Form* when pressure on Brecht had eased later in 1953 and which was clearly therefore not a mere tactical concession. The record of the collaboration demonstrates Brecht's view that the representation of revolutionary change within GDR socialism required dramatic techniques – among them the depiction of positive heroes and "Gestalten [...] voller Individualität, mit köstlichen Einzelzügen" – that differed fundamentally from the stereotypes depicted by means of the *Verfremdungseffekt* in order to expose the mendacity of bourgeois society.[53] The essay positions Brecht firmly within not only Marxism-Leninism but also, more specifically, within the discourse of SED achievements, which he had repeatedly urged *Sinn und Form* to represent: "*Katzgraben* ist meines Wissens das erste Stück, das den modernen Klassenkampf auf dem Dorf auf die deutsche Bühne bringt. Es zeigt Großbauer, Mittelbauer, Kleinbauer und Parteisekretär nach der Vertreibung der Junker in der Deutschen Demokratischen Republik" (ibid.). Similarly, Brecht concludes that the play, "zieht den Zuschauer mächtig in den großen Prozeß der produktiven Umwandlung des Dorfes, angetrieben durch den Dynamo der sozialistischen Partei der Deutschen Demokratischen Republik. Es erfüllt ihn mit dem Geist des kühnen Fortschreitens" (BFA 24. P. 441).

The Stanislavsky Conference ended without any definitive resolution: rather, it was an element in the continuing campaign by an SED leadership determined to demonstrate its capacity to impose its orthodoxy on the cultural elite. The pressure on Brecht and his fellow Academicians intensified. The publication in *Sinn und Form* of an extract from Hanns Eisler's libretto *Johann Faustus* and Ernst Fischer's laudatory essay *Doktor Faustus und der deutsche Bauernkrieg* had been seized upon by Abusch to demonstrate Huchel's severe lack of editorial judgement and the false conception of "deutsche Misere" shared by Eisler and Fischer.[54] Eisler's depiction of the failure of German intellectuals to support the peasant uprisings is clearly intended as a critique of German intellectuals who opposed the GDR's progressive national mission. Given Eisler's undoubted support for SED rule, the escalating vehemence of the attacks in the spring of 1953 only makes sense in the context of the regime's insecurity in the light of Stalin's death and Beria's "New Course", which left Moscow's support for the GDR even less certain as Beria considered jettisoning the GDR.

---

[53] Bertolt Brecht: *Erwin Strittmatters "Katzgraben"*. BFA 24. Pp. 437–441. Here p. 437.
[54] For a detailed discussion of Abusch's actions see Parker: *Sinn und Form*, Peter Huchel und der 17. Juni (n. 1). Pp. 741–743. It was well-known that Eisler and Brecht shared that conception and that Eisler had consulted his friend in the composition of his text. For Brecht's notes of their discussions see BFA 27. P. 333.

In the Academy, Becher abandoned Huchel to the humiliation of ritual self-criticism and dismissal from his post, while Abusch orchestrated the "Mittwoch-Gesellschaften", a sequence of exchanges about Eisler's *Faustus* between, on the one hand, Eisler, Brecht and their supporters and, on the other, Abusch, Girnus and other SED figures. The exchanges were intended to force acceptance of the "integrationists" orthodoxy.[55] Abusch, who had organized majorities for the anti-Eisler camp, led the first discussion on 13 May with a paper entitled: *Faust – Held oder Renegat in der deutschen Nationalliteratur?* This subsequently appeared in *Sinn und Form* alongside Brecht's *Thesen zur Faustus-Diskussion*. In his paper, Abusch puts the "integrationists" case, contesting the view that German intellectuals had betrayed progressive national forces and holding up the example of Goethe's Faust as "ein großer positiver Held des klassischen Nationaldramas", thus as an antecedent of Socialist Realism.[56] Girnus, equally exercised by the question of national legitimacy, followed with the charge that Eisler was actually mounting an attack on the GDR, adding, in nakedly threatening fashion, "hier kommt bei Hanns Eisler eine Fremdheit gegenüber dem deutschen Volk, gegenüber den nationalen Traditionen des deutschen Volkes, gegenüber seiner Geschichte zum Ausdruck".[57] The responses of Brecht and his supporters show that they did not fully understand the game that was being played out with them. Their defensiveness betokens their anxiety as they cautiously deployed arguments informed by their aesthetic sensibility, not by concerns over national security.

Not only did they misconstrue the real terms of debate; they did not appreciate just how fragile the SED leadership's hold on power was. Lack of support from Moscow, mirrored by negligible and ebbing popular support in the GDR, was crystallizing into conflicts in the leadership and challenges to Ulbricht's authority, which would be laid bare in June. For all Brecht's self-image as a *Realpolitiker*, his ideological and institutional dependencies prevented him from contemplating any broader alliance of intellectuals with members of the political elite that could have generated genuine change, though it must be said that figures such as Zaisser and Herrnstadt, who were supported by Beria in criticisms of Ulbricht's leadership, would not have been suitable bedfellows.

The second "Mittwoch-Gesellschaft" on 27 May continued to parallel political developments. That day, taking a cue from Abusch's paper, Johanna

[55] Transcriptions of the "Mittwoch-Gesellschaften" are collected in: *Die Debatte um Eislers "Johann Faustus": Eine Dokumentation*. Ed. by Hans Bunge. Berlin: BasisDruck 1991. For more detailed analyses of the exchanges, see Davies and Parker: Brecht, SED cultural policy and the issue of authority in the arts (n. 1). Pp. 187–193; and Davies: *Divided Loyalties* (n. 1). Pp. 210–245.
[56] Alexander Abusch: Faust – Held oder Renegat in der deutschen Nationalliteratur? In: *Sinn und Form* 4 (1953). No. 3/4. Pp. 179–194. Here p. 185.
[57] Bunge (ed.): *Die Debatte um Eislers "Johann Faustus"* (n. 55). P. 71.

Rudolph attacked Brecht's *Urfaust* in *Neues Deutschland*, with Ulbricht himself following up the attack in a speech.[58] The atmosphere was unremittingly hostile as Brecht cautiously presented his *Thesen zur Faustus-Diskussion*. As ever, he sought to establish common ground, adopting a broadly assenting position and tempering his support for Eisler's text with elements of criticism of Eisler and Fischer, as well as of Eisler's critics. By citing concrete examples, he again sought to overcome blanket abstractions. Yet there was no prospect of common ground being established as long as Brecht and Eisler maintained their critical perspective on the German tradition, which "integrationists" by now ritualistically dismissed as treasonable.

Faced with the third "Mittwoch-Gesellschaft" on 10 June, pressure on Brecht and his supporters to recant was acute. Yet the pressure on the SED leadership from other quarters was by now even greater. Under instructions from Moscow, on 9 June the SED Politburo hurriedly announced its own "New Course", admitting mistakes and withdrawing elements of economic policy introduced after the Second Party Conference.[59] This volte-face caused consternation among Party workers, who had struggled to implement the earlier line. The impact is apparent already at the third "Mittwoch-Gesellschaft". Non-SED Academicians around Brecht, particularly Arnold Zweig, find their voices, while Brecht himself adopts the central role in presenting his revised *Thesen* and challenging the crude assertions of Abusch's supporters. Girnus's certainties start to look less secure. As the SED group loses ground, Becher as chair finally offers some protection to Eisler, hypocritically criticizing Girnus and Walter Besenbruch, where previously he had lent them his support.

The position that Abusch had been building, seemingly inexorably, within the cultural elite since the autumn of 1952 was beginning to unravel. That had everything to do with the GDR's political situation, particularly its relationship with Moscow, rather than with the perceived strength of Brecht's arguments *per se*. Quite improbably, Brecht and his supporters in the cultural elite were able to turn the tables, as the extreme weakness of the SED leadership was radically exposed by the events of 17 June. The events shattered the SED's precarious authority, creating the opportunity for Brecht and his supporters to press their case for changes in the Academy. Brecht seized the opportunity, taking the leading role in a series of emergency meetings.[60] At a Plenary on 26 June, Brecht and Eisler exacted revenge on Abusch and Friedrich Wolf for their

[58] See Johanna Rudolph: Weitere Bemerkungen zum "Faust"-Problem. In: *Neues Deutschland* 27.5.1953. Reprinted in: Bunge: *Die Debatte um Eislers "Johann Faustus"* (n. 55). Pp. 117–126. Details of Ulbricht's speech are given in Deborah Vietor-Engländer: *Faust in der DDR*. Frankfurt am Main: Lang 1987. P. 154.
[59] See Mary Fulbrook: *Anatomy of a Dictatorship: Inside the GDR 1949–1989*. Oxford: Oxford University Press 1995. P. 181.
[60] For a detailed discussion see Parker: *Peter Huchel* (n. 10). Pp. 331–336.

sustained assault on Huchel and *Sinn und Form*. The evident fragility of Ulbricht's position meant that the opportunity existed to press the case for changes on a much broader basis. Yet Brecht was not remotely interested in questioning the SED's fundamental legitimacy. At a time when he was negotiating with Grotewohl for the Berliner Ensemble to take over the Theater am Schiffbauerdamm, his focus was on the re-assertion of the claims of elite cultural capital within the given framework of SED rule.[61] Indeed, in his letters of 17 June to Ulbricht, Semenov and Grotewohl, he went out of his way to demonstrate his loyal support for the SED, the Soviet Union and the GDR (BFA 30. Pp. 178–179). This set the limits for any criticisms of the SED leadership.

The Plenary of 26 June also discussed the *Vorschläge der Deutschen Akademie der Künste*, which Brecht had been instrumentally involved in formulating and which subsequently appeared in *Sinn und Form*.[62] The major issue in the Academy's proposals to the GDR government is the re-establishment of the principle that artistic and editorial responsibility should rest with artists, editors and their organizations, not with the interfering administrative organs of the state.[63] Brecht sought thereby not institutional independence for the arts but a relative autonomy, which, he now asserted, had been eroded by the meddling bureaucrats of organizations like the Staatliche Kommission für Kunstangelegenheiten.

As Brecht cast off previously tight self-discipline, bureaucrats and Party hacks became the butt of a rekindled, scathing satire in poems such as "Das Amt für Literatur" (BFA 15. Pp. 267–268) and "Nicht feststellbare Fehler der Kunstkommission" (BFA 15. P. 268). In those organs and in others in the GDR, Brecht identifies residues of fascism as the principal danger besetting German socialism, which the SED had failed to tackle. The traumatic vision of a resurgent National Socialism informs much of Brecht's writing from the summer of 1953, questioning the GDR's claim to be the home of antifascism but occluding the equally troubling question of the SED's right to rule. Among the *Buckower Elegien* that were published in *Sinn und Form* in late 1953 are verses in which the weight of reaction continues to dominate youthful energy. "Heißer Tag", for example, depicts:

Eine dicke Nonne, dick gekleidet. Vor ihr
Ein ältlicher Mensch im Schwimmanzug, wahrscheinlich ein Priester.

[61] Brecht's letter to Grotewohl of 15 June 1953 is in BFA 30. Pp. 177–178. Following his discussion with Brecht on 25 July 1953, Girnus wrote to Ulbricht, recommending that Brecht should be granted his theatre. The letter is discussed by Hecht in *Brecht Chronik* (n. 31). P. 1071.

[62] Brecht's draft (BFA 23. Pp. 253–255) shows the extent of his involvement. The text was published in *Neues Deutschland* on 12 July 1953.

[63] Brecht made the point in stronger terms in: Kulturpolitik und Akademie der Künste. In: *Neues Deutschland* 13.8.1953. Cf. BFA 23. Pp. 256–260.

An der Ruderbank, aus vollen Kräften rudernd
Ein Kind. Wie in alten Zeiten! denke ich
Wie in alten Zeiten![64]

Similarly, "Gewohnheiten, noch immer" ends: "Der preußische Adler / Den Jungen hackt er / Das Futter in die Mäulchen" (BFA 12. P. 307). The sixth elegy, "Bei der Lektüre eines sowjetischen Buches" (BFA 12. Pp. 308–309), points the way forward, as Soviet workers re-channel the waters of the Volga, providing fresh irrigation to grow more crops.

In case Brecht's public statements concerning the Academy should leave anyone in the West in any doubt over his continuing support for the SED dictatorship, he wrote "Nicht so gemeint", a scathing satire on Western perceptions of the events in the Academy as a victory for freedom of expression. The poem associates such a view with an ideology of freedom-for-all that would re-instate fascist barbarism: "Der Brandstifter, der die Benzinflasche schleppt, / Nähert sich feixend / Der Akademie der Künste" (BFA 15. P. 270).

The Academy's self-assertion led to changes, principally the creation of the Ministry of Culture, which occupied Becher and Abusch for some time as SED cultural politicians licked their wounds, leaving the Academy and its journal to their own devices. Brecht and his fellow Academicians ensured that the Academy and *Sinn und Form* re-gained freedom for manoeuvre internally and externally. Yet that freedom for the elite was, of course, simultaneously suppressed among the general population in the GDR.

In subsequent discussions concerning publication policy for *Sinn und Form*, Brecht reiterated his partisan commitment to GDR socialism: "Wir brauchen Beiträge, die die großen historischen Errungenschaften der DDR beschreiben, so daß die Leute in Westdeutschland und in der DDR sie wirklich als sachlich aufnehmen und verstehen können. Die Fakten sind überwältigend".[65] In addition to securing the immediate future of the Academy and *Sinn und Form* on his terms, Brecht was now granted the Theater am Schiffbauerdamm as the home for the Berliner Ensemble. Brecht and his supporters could now capitalize upon the enhanced authority with which he had emerged from the struggles of the early 1950s. In the years until Brecht's death in August 1956, Brecht and *Sinn und Form* seized the opportunity to showcase work that cemented their legendary reputations, consolidating the cultural capital that exists today. Huchel identified the double issue 5/6 in 1954 as the consummate expression of the journal's all-German mission.[66] Touring productions of the Berliner Ensemble

---

[64] BFA 12. P. 308. Some of the elegies that remained unpublished such as "Der Einarmige im Gehölz" (BFA 12. P. 312) and "Vor acht Jahren" (BFA 12. P. 314) deal with the same issue.

[65] Quoted in Parker: *Sinn und Form*, Peter Huchel und der 17 Juni 1953 (n. 1). P. 749.

[66] For further discussion, see Parker: *Peter Huchel* (n. 10). Pp. 348–349.

were greeted with rapture in Vienna, Paris and London. These productions paved the way for Brecht's stellar posthumous reputation.

Brecht's early death meant that he was spared the further severe test of his belief system following Soviet repression in Hungary. In the GDR, the years 1954–6 were revealed to be no more than an interlude, as the SED leadership resumed the painful process of subsuming cultural life within the given political imperative of the GDR's integration among the people's democracies. Following the aborted rescue of his friend Georg Lukács from captivity in Hungary, Becher renounced his belief in socialism.[67] Abusch, who joined Ulbricht in humiliating the terminally ill Becher, renewed the struggle in the only way he knew: by privileging partisan Socialist Realism above German cultural unity and forcing change on the Academy and *Sinn und Form*. Abusch's "successes" however did nothing to diminish the legendary status of Brecht and *Sinn und Form*, forged in the epic struggles of the early 1950s.

[67] Becher's renunciation of socialism was published as "Selbstzensur" in: *Sinn und Form* 40 (1988). Pp. 543–551.

David Midgley

"Zwei Hände Erde": Brecht on Mortality

Brecht's works display a more widespread fascination with death than might be expected of a self-avowedly political writer. Indeed, Brecht himself seems to have consciously resisted that fascination from the moment when he became more consciously political, as may be seen from the prefatory note he wrote for the Badener Lehrstück *when it was published in 1930. This article notes the dramatic function that the prospect of particular deaths has in Brecht's plays from that time onwards, but since Brecht's treatment of death would be altogether too large a topic for a short paper, it focuses more specifically on the theme of mortality in his poetry. It discusses the influence of his religious education and of baroque poetic models on his early poetry, and the disillusionment with religious tradition and the compensating emphasis on the finitude of human existence and the appeal of earthly pleasures that is manifest in his poems from 1916 onwards. By contrast, it also examines the emphasis that is to be found in much of his writing from 1933 onwards on the senses in which war threatens whole human cultures, as well as individual lives, with extinction. Finally it considers the poem "Verwisch die Spuren!" (1926), which has from time to time been submitted to reductive interpretations of both a political and a psychoanalytical nature, but in which the complexities and ambiguities of Brecht's attitudes to mortality present themselves in a concentrated form.*

The prefatory note that Brecht wrote for the *Badener Lehrstück vom Einverständnis* when it was first published in 1930 contains a striking reflection on the prominence given to the subject of dying in that text: "dem Sterben ist im Vergleich zu seinem doch wohl nur geringen Gebrauchswert zuviel Gewicht beigemessen" (BFA 3. P. 26). This statement, which is offered in justification of the view that the script is "unfinished" ("unfertig"), is striking for a number of reasons. In its immediate context it expresses an evaluation of the effectiveness of the text as a *Lehrstück*, which is to say as an exposition and examination of an ethical issue:[1] to what extent and on what grounds are those who imperil their own lives in pursuit of personal distinction entitled to expect the sympathy and assistance of a human community whose interests are not served by their endeavours? The criterion of "Gebrauchswert" points beyond that immediate context, however, to the stern utilitarianism that Brecht had come to apply to social and cultural issues in the later 1920s, prominent examples of which are the presentation of human identity as definable by the uses to which it is put in *Mann ist Mann* (1926) and the position Brecht adopted when judging a poetry

---

[1] See Klaus-Dieter Krabiel: *Brechts Lehrstücke: Entstehung und Entwicklung eines Spieltyps*. Stuttgart: Metzler 1993. See also David Midgley: *Writing Weimar. Critical Realism in German Literature, 1918–1933*. Oxford: Oxford University Press 2000. Pp. 128–33, with further references.

competition for the journal *Die literarische Welt* in 1927.[2] The dominant sense of his comment on the *Badener Lehrstück* is that the subject of dying is of little use to a human community that is concerned with the issues of how to go on living and of how to establish appropriate precepts by which to live. Death, by implication, is merely the termination of life, and the experience of dying can have little direct bearing on the concerns of the living.[3] For that reason, Brecht's prefatory note argues, the attention given to the subject of dying in the *Badener Lehrstück* is disproportionate to the issues with which the text should primarily be concerned; or rather, Brecht's statement uses the rhetoric of persuasion – "doch wohl nur" – to suggest that *if* the matter is considered with utilitarian criteria in mind, then the weight that has been given to the subject in the text itself is inappropriate.

In practice, the references to death in the *Badener Lehrstück* take a number of different forms. There is firstly the threat of death which prompts the call for help from the stranded pilot and his team of engineers (the "Monteure"). Secondly there are the images of death that are shown to the audience in illustration of the point that people are in general reluctant to help one another: more specifically, these images show "wie in unserer Zeit Menschen von Menschen abgeschlachtet werden" (BFA 3. P. 30). Thirdly there is the advice offered in the form of parabolic "Kommentartexte" on how to adjust to the necessity of death,[4] and it is here that the question of how to prepare oneself for the prospect of physical death becomes difficult to disentangle from a metaphorical implication of the verb "sterben".[5] From this point in the text onwards, the professed *inability* of the stranded group to "die" becomes a metaphorical indicator of their resistance to radical change and the possibility of renewal; and when the chorus ultimately appeal to the "Monteure" with the words, "Richtet euch also sterbend / Nicht nach dem Tod. / Sondern übernehmt von uns den Auftrag / Wieder aufzubauen unser Flugzeug" (BFA 3. P. 45), it is a form of moral rebirth that is implied. By comparison with the other *Lehrstücke* of the period 1929–1930, where the ethical question posed is sharply focused on the justification for sacrificing an individual human life for a communal cause, the *Badener Lehrstück* displays not only a more insistent, but also a more diffuse preoccupation with

---

[2] On the latter, see Midgley: *Writing Weimar* (n.1). Pp. 82–87.

[3] It was for precisely this reason that Brecht had firmly rejected the extensive depiction of the death of the protagonist in Arnold Zweig's novel *Der Streit um den Sergeanten Grischa* (1927): see Bertolt Brecht: *"Der Streit um den Sergeanten Grischa" von Arnold Zweig*. BFA 21. S. 249.

[4] See for instance the text in the *Badener Lehrstück* on how the "thinker" overcame the storm (BFA 3. Pp. 37–38).

[5] See Reiner Steinweg: *Das Badener Lehrstück vom Einverständnis* – Mystik, Religionsersatz oder Parodie? In: *Text und Kritik. Sonderband Bertolt Brecht II*. München 1973. Pp. 109–130. Esp. pp. 120–128.

the question of what it means to die. The use of "sterben" as a metaphor for radical transformation may reflect something of Brecht's fascination with the works of Alfred Döblin during the 1920s, where the thematic linking of death and rebirth is common; and there may be a sense in which his self-critical statement, "dem Sterben ist im Vergleich zu seinem doch wohl nur geringen Gebrauchswert zuviel Gewicht beigemessen" can be viewed as a repudiation of that fascination.[6] But there are also good reasons for viewing that statement as a repudiation of a broader fascination with death that had been a frequent feature of Brecht's own earlier writings.

In the context of Brecht's writing career as a whole, indeed, the statement seems to mark something of a turning point in his treatment of the subject. When we look beyond 1930 to the later plays, then from the execution of Pawel Wlassow in *Die Mutter* to the deaths of Mutter Courage's children and the threats of death invoked in *Das Leben des Galilei* and *Der kaukasische Kreidekreis*, it seems generally to be the case that death plays a subordinate role in the presentation of more prominent issues: the prospect of death – one's own or another's – is evoked in order to bring a particular dramatic intensity to the exploration of the life of the central figure and the purposes for which it is being lived. Before 1930, by contrast, death had been an insistent theme in a wide variety of contexts, which range from the bravado of Baal and the burlesque mock-execution of Galy Gay in *Mann ist Mann* to the macabre scenarios evoked in some parts of the *Hauspostille*. Indeed, Brecht's earliest surviving poems, written in 1913 when he was only fifteen, display the formative influence of his Protestant school education precisely in the strength of their preoccupation with the theme of death;[7] they include an evocation of the Baroque *memento mori* ("Der Mönch". BFA 13. P. 19), references to the vanity of human exploits in the face of death ("Sommer" and "Opfere!". BFA 13. Pp. 8 and 16–17) and a reflection in Latin on the notion of death as victor ("Victor Mors". BFA 13. Pp. 17–18). Since there is not room here for a discussion of the full range of Brecht's approaches to the theme, I shall focus instead on a few key aspects that can be recognized from his poetry as characteristic of an early phase on the one hand, a later phase on the other, and a problematic phase in the transition between the two, to which the *Badener Lehrstück* arguably belongs. I use the term "mortality" rather than "death" in my subtitle because my emphasis will be on Brecht's perspectives on the finiteness of human existence and on how these are modulated

---

[6] See Werner Stauffacher: Alfred Döblin und Bert Brecht. Zwischen *Berlin Alexanderplatz* und dem *Badener Lehrstück vom Einverständnis*. In: *Germanisch-romanische Monatsschrift* 26 (1976). Pp. 466–470.

[7] For a recent assessment of the formative influence of Brecht's Protestant schooling, see Hans-Harald Müller and Tom Kindt: *Brechts frühe Lyrik. Brecht, Gott, die Natur und die Liebe*. München 2002. Pp. 21–27.

in the course of his career. The historicity of his treatment of the subject is important, I think, not because our knowledge of the life of the historical author should necessarily dominate our interpretation of the works, but because the works themselves stand in a manifest relation to historical circumstances, as the author himself expressly noted in his later years.[8] What I want to highlight in Brecht's treatment of the theme of mortality, therefore, is the articulation of attitudes to death in the context of particular life circumstances.

A manifest preoccupation with the question of mortality is not only a common feature of Brecht's early works, it is also one that has enabled Brecht scholars to establish an underlying consistency within the apparently wild profusion of his early writings. What this research has established is that the poems he wrote between 1916 and 1922, and which make up the bulk of the *Hauspostille* (1927), reflect his radical disillusionment with the religious tradition in which he had been brought up, and constitute an emphatic endorsement of the sensual experiences that life has to offer.[9] It is in these poems that we find a strong emphasis on the materiality of human existence, whether in the form of the pursuit of appetites ("Orges Gesang", "Choral vom Manne Baal", the "Mahagonnygesänge") or of the dissolution of the flesh and its reincorporation into the realm of nature ("Das Schiff", "Vom ertrunkenen Mädchen", "Von des Cortez Leuten"). The hedonism that we frequently find expressed in these poems is the obverse of the nihilism: we inhabit a cold universe that is bereft of meaning and indifferent to our fate, therefore we should resolve to live life to the full. Moreover, this outlook is particularly apparent in those poems which parody ecclesiastical idioms – hymns, psalms, and liturgies. It is as if the ecclesiastical forms have been hollowed out and refilled with an unabashed celebration of the material world; the "heavens" are empty, and our lives are circumscribed by the "sky" that we (think we can) see.[10] The sense in which the expressive power of Brecht's early poetry was in fact largely derived from this refractory use of Christian models was fully recognized in 1931 by the Catholic theologian Karl Thieme, and accepted by him as a challenge to reflect on serious moral and theological issues: it was in Brecht's radical secularism, he argued, that contemporary Christianity

---

[8] See especially Bertolt Brecht: *Arbeitsjournal 1938 bis 1942*. Frankfurt am Main: Suhrkamp 1973. Pp. 22–23.

[9] See especially Peter Paul Schwarz: *Brechts frühe Lyrik, 1914–1922. Nihilismus als Werkzusammenhang der frühen Lyrik Brechts*. Bonn: Bouvier 1971. See also Horst Jesse: *Die Lyrik Bertolt Brechts von 1914–1956 unter besonderer Berücksichtigung der "ars vivendi" angesichts der Todesbedrohungen*. Frankfurt am Main: Lang 1994; Müller and Kindt: *Brechts frühe Lyrik* (n. 7). Pp. 28–35.

[10] See Bernhard Blume: Motive der frühen Lyrik Bertolt Brechts. II: Der Himmel der Enttäuschten. In: *Monatshefte* 57 (1965). Pp. 273–281.

could find an estimable opponent.[11] The explicit inversion of a Christian attitude to mortality can be seen, for example, in "Großer Dankchoral", which mimics a famous Reformation hymn and urges us to praise night and darkness as well as all living creatures, insisting that there will be no record of our lives by which we shall be judged in the hereafter: "Lobet von Herzen das schlechte Gedächtnis des Himmels! […] Es kommet nicht auf euch an / Und ihr könnt unbesorgt sterben" (BFA 11. P. 77).[12]

The pronounced sense of transience and the ultimate meaninglessness of human existence that run through these early poems manifest themselves in a variety of emotional contexts. At one extreme it gives rise to gestures of a chillingly cynical and dismissive nature, as in "Vom armen B.B.": "Wir wissen, daß wir Vorläufige sind / Und nach uns wird kommen: nichts Nennenswertes" (BFA 11. P. 120). At the other extreme it can elicit lyrical meditations remarkable for their poignancy and tenderness, as in "Erinnerung an die Marie A." (BFA 11. Pp. 92–93), which has its metaphysical as well as its material dimension,[13] or in the "Terzinen über die Liebe" (1928), verses that were later also distributed between the lovers in *Aufstieg und Fall der Stadt Mahagonny*, and which present love as a necessary illusion that arises from the very experience of transience:

Sieh jene Kraniche in großem Bogen!
Die Wolken, welche ihnen beigegeben
Zogen mit ihnen schon, als sie entflogen

Aus einem Leben in ein andres Leben.
[…]
Ihr fragt, wie lange sind sie schon beisammen?
Seit kurzem. Und wann werden sie sich trennen? Bald.
So scheint die Liebe Liebenden ein Halt (BFA 14. Pp. 15–16; see also BFA 2. Pp. 364–365).

The indissoluble connection that the young Brecht saw between the love of life and the awareness of its finitude is perhaps nowhere more clearly expressed than in "Von der Freundlichkeit der Welt" (1922). Here the entire course of a

[11] Karl Thieme: Des Teufels Gebetbuch? Eine Auseinandersetzung mit dem Werke Bertolt Brechts. In: *Hochland* 29 (1931–32). I. Pp. 397–413.

[12] The recent interpretation of the reference to "das schlechte Gedächtnis des Himmels" by Franck Hofmann as emblematic of a supposed "art of forgetting" arbitrarily isolates the phrase from its context and thereby loses sight of the implications of the travesty of liturgical utterance (Franck Hofmann: Literatur des Vergessens. Brechts Strategien für Städtebewohner und die Kritik der Erinnerung. In: *Germanica* 33 (2003). Pp. 79–96).

[13] See Hans-Harald Müller, Tom Kindt and Robert Habeck: Love – Not – Memory. An Interpretation of "Remembering Marie A." In: *Empedocles' Shoe. Essays on Brecht's Poetry*. Ed. by Tom Kuhn and Karen Leeder. London: Methuen 2002. Pp. 56–70.

human life is reduced to a brief, bleak sketch of its key stages: birth, education, lamentation, and death. We come into the world weak, vulnerable, and unwanted; the world owes us nothing, and the "friendliness" it shows us is of a purely perfunctory kind:

1
Auf die Erde voller kaltem Wind
Kamt ihr alle als ein nacktes Kind
Frierend lagt ihr ohne alle Hab
Als ein Weib euch eine Windel gab.

2
Keiner schrie euch, ihr wart nicht begehrt
Und man holte euch nicht im Gefährt.
Hier auf Erden wart ihr unbekannt
Als ein Mann euch einst nahm an der Hand.

3
Und die Welt, die ist euch gar nichts schuld:
Keiner hält euch, wenn ihr gehen wollt.
Vielen, Kinder, wart ihr vielleicht gleich.
Viele aber weinten über euch.

4
Von der Erde voller kaltem Wind
Geht ihr all bedeckt mit Schorf und Grind.
Fast ein jeder hat die Welt geliebt
Wenn man ihm zwei Hände Erde gibt (BFA 11. P. 68).

This poem has been recognized to be related, again, to a specific Christian tradition, that of the Baroque *contemptus mundi* literature.[14] But whereas that tradition had emphasized the futility of living a life contrary to God, the teachings of the Church or the certainty of death, and had presented the promise of salvation as dependent upon a rejection of earthly existence, Brecht's poem reflects on the character of a life that is emptied of such reassurance. In his reworking of the theme, the dialectical relationship between *love* of this world and the *knowledge* of ultimate extinction is made explicit in the final stanza through the evocation of a simple funeral rite: "Fast ein jeder hat die Welt geliebt / Wenn man ihm zwei Hände Erde gibt". The two handfuls of earth that betoken burial, interment, the termination of a life, are what trigger the protestation of love, and it is precisely that sardonic closing sentiment that epitomizes the fundamentally materialist view of human existence that Brecht had adopted in the course of

---

[14] See Carl Pietzcker: *Die Lyrik des jungen Brecht*. Frankfurt am Main: Suhrkamp 1974. Pp. 40–41.

the First World War.[15] It is also as an emblem of this underlying materialism that I use the phrase in my title.

At the same time, "Von der Freundlichkeit der Welt" also provides a clear marker of the relationship between the earlier and the later phase in Brecht's treatment of the theme of mortality, which is again a relationship of inversion. It was in direct reaction against the bleak scenario of this poem that Brecht was to compose a "Gegenlied" in 1956, where the emphasis is on the political struggles that are needed to overcome the inhospitability of the world and make it a better, friendlier place:

> Besser scheint's uns doch, aufzubegehren
> Und auf keine kleinste Freude zu verzichten
> Und die Leidenstifter kräftig abzuwehren
> Und die Welt uns endlich häuslich einzurichten! (BFA 15. P. 296).

At some point between these two dates – probably as early as 1933, as the *Berliner und Frankfurter Ausgabe* indicates[16] – Brecht also fell to thinking about his own epitaph. In the spirit of Horace,[17] for whom he maintained a life-long admiration, and with the addition of what has often been interpreted as a degree of false modesty, Brecht emphasizes the contribution to collective endeavour for which he would like to be remembered:

> Ich benötige keinen Grabstein, aber
> Wenn ihr einen für mich benötigt
> Wünschte ich, es stünde darauf:
> Er hat Vorschläge gemacht. Wir
> Haben sie angenommen.
> Durch eine solche Inschrift wären
> Wir alle geehrt.[18]

This turn in Brecht's treatment of his own mortality – from emphatic hedonism to the retrospective evaluation of what a life has amounted to – was undoubtedly reinforced by the advent of National Socialism and the experiences of exile.

---

[15] Sigmund Freud had also noted how the prevalence of death was eliciting an affirmation of life, in an essay of 1915: "Der Tod läßt sich nicht mehr verleugnen […]. Das Leben ist freilich wieder interessant geworden, es hat seinen vollen Inhalt wiederbekommen" (Sigmund Freud: *Zeitgemäßes über Krieg und Tod*. In: Sigmund Freud: *Studienausgabe*. Ed. by Alexander Mitscherlich, Angela Richards and James Strachey. Vol. IX. Frankfurt am Main: Fischer 1974. Pp. 33–60. Here p. 51).

[16] See Walter Hinck: *Ausgewählte Gedichte Brechts mit Interpretationen*. Frankfurt am Main: Suhrkamp 1978. P. 152.

[17] See Philip Thomson: "Exegi Monumentum": The Fame of Bertolt Brecht. In: *The German Quarterly* 53 (1980). Pp. 337–347.

[18] Bertolt Brecht: Ich benötige keinen Grabstein. BFA 14. Pp. 191–192.

One obvious factor that contributes to this change is the impact of the deaths of particular victims of Nazi persecution, whom Brecht commemorates in his poetry. Two of these deaths – that of Walter Benjamin while trying to escape from Nazi-occupied France in 1940,[19] and that of Margarete Steffin, who succumbed to tuberculosis on the journey through the Soviet Union in 1941[20] – clearly had a profound personal significance for him. A third, that of the prominent pacifist and former editor of *Die Weltbühne*, Carl von Ossietzky, who died in 1938 of the injuries inflicted on him in captivity, elicited a more public response and a political gesture: his death will not have been in vain, Brecht comments in the *Svendborger Gedichte*, if it can be shown that he was not standing alone.[21]

Reflection on what his own life has come to signify, and on the role he might be seen as playing in the struggles of the times, is also a manifest theme of the *Svendborger Gedichte*, particularly in the concluding poem he composed for the collection in 1938, "An die Nachgeborenen", where the central section takes the form of a meditation on what has come to pass during the speaker's life and how that life has been spent. Each of the four stanzas of this section ends with a couplet that carries a distinct biblical echo: "So verging meine Zeit / Die auf Erden mir gegeben war" (BFA 12. Pp. 86–87).

Jochen Vogt, in a recent article, has noted the new emphasis on the cultivation of collective memory that comes into Brecht's poetry during his years in exile, and he illustrates the point from the "Chroniken" of the *Svendborger Gedichte* (BFA 12. Pp. 29–46).[22] The practice of making collective memory visible is important to the communist cause as celebrated in "Die unbesiegliche Inschrift" and "Die Teppichweber von Kujan Bulak ehren Lenin"; and in "Die Legende von der Entstehung des Buches Taoteking auf dem Wege des Laotse in die Emigration" it is the writing down of the philosopher's knowledge that ensures its endurance. Closely linked to this concern with the preservation of memory, as Vogt also notes, is the fear of what might be forgotten. In "Besuch bei den verbannten Dichtern" (BFA 12. Pp. 35–36), Brecht imagines Dante encountering both the well-known and the unknown banned poets on his journey through Hell, and foregrounds the notion that the worst fate that can befall a poet is that his works are altogether forgotten by posterity. In other poems of

[19] See Bertolt Brecht: *Zum Freitod des Flüchtlings W.B.* BFA 15. P. 48.
[20] See Bertolt Brecht: *Nach dem Tod meiner Mitarbeiterin M.S.* BFA 15. P. 45.
[21] Bertolt Brecht: Auf den Tod eines Kämpfers für den Frieden. BFA 12. P. 50.
[22] Jochen Vogt: *Damnatio memoriae* und "Werke von langer Dauer". Zwei ästhetische Grenzwerte in Brechts Exillyrik. In: *Ästhetiken des Exils*. Ed. by Helga Schreckenberger. Amsterdam: Rodopi 2003. Pp. 300–317 (Amsterdamer Beiträge zur neueren Germanistik. Vol. 54). Cf. also Anthony Phelan: Figures of Memory in the "Chroniken". In: *Brecht's Poetry of Political Exile*. Ed. by Ronald Speirs. Cambridge: Cambridge University Press 2000. Pp. 172–189.

the mid-1930s, too, Brecht reflects on the parallel between his own situation and that of banished poets of past ages[23] or on the fact that in the circumstances of exile poetry acquires a stronger bond with the past and the future than with the present,[24] and such thoughts are patently related to his awareness that the aims of the Nazi regime posed a threat to civilization and to the whole cultural heritage of Europe, as Benjamin noted in his record of the conversations he had with Brecht in Svendborg in 1938.[25] This awareness clearly weighed heavily with Brecht at the time he was putting together the *Svendborger Gedichte* for publication,[26] and it is largely for this reason that the theme of mortality now comes to be linked in his poetry with the question of what will endure beyond the Nazi terror.

Brecht's attitude to this question of what will be passed on to posterity can again be seen to undergo some significant changes in the course of the 1930s. Between 1929 and 1931 he worked at a poem entitled "Über die Bauart langdauernder Werke" (BFA 14. Pp. 34–38), which contains reflections on how works can be said to last only as long as they command input or effort ("Mühe").[27] There the emphasis was on making an impact in the present and on the question of whether the aspiration to create works that will last – and to be remembered for them – might actually detract from the present purpose for which they are being written:

Wer sich an die Ungeborenen wendet
Tut oft nichts für die Geburt.
Er kämpft nicht und will doch den Sieg.
Er sieht keinen Feind
Außer dem Vergessen (BFA 14. P. 38).

When Brecht reflects in exile on his own role as a poet, by contrast, he is weighing up a different kind of dialectical tension: that between the desire to contribute something special to the sum of human culture and the recognition that the individual voice may not be of any special consequence in the outcome of historical struggles. In 1936, in the poem which has been anthologized under the title "Warum soll mein Name genannt werden?" (BFA 14. Pp. 320–321), he again foregrounds the doctrines of utility and humanity for which he ostensibly wishes to be remembered ("Weil ich das Nützliche rühmte […]", "Weil ich für die Menschen war […]"), but also urges the view that there is no compelling reason

---

[23] Bertolt Brecht: Die Auswanderung der Dichter. BFA 14. P. 256.
[24] Bertolt Brecht: "Gedichte im Exil". BFA 14. Pp. 311–312.
[25] Walter Benjamin: Tagebuchnotizen 1938. WBGS VI. Pp. 532–539. Here p. 539.
[26] See David Midgley: Svendborg 1938: A Historical Sketch. In: Speirs (ed.): *Brecht's Poetry* (n. 22). Pp. 16–28. Here p. 23.
[27] See Vogt: *Damnatio* (n. 22). Pp. 315–317.

why he in particular should be remembered for these things while there are many others who show much the same commitment. At a later date he also articulates the guilt of the survivor who has outlived many of his friends in "Ich, der Überlebende" (BFA 12. P. 125): "heute nacht im Traum / Hörte ich diese Freunde von mir sagen: 'Die Stärkeren überleben' / Und ich haßte mich". The self-hatred, by implication, is generated by the awareness that it is not by strength, but rather by good fortune and the instinct for self-preservation, that the speaker has survived.

The late poem from the *Buckower Elegien*, "Beim Lesen des Horaz" (1953/54), for all its lapidary simplicity, encapsulates the profound sense of connection between the loss of lives and the concern for endurance that is forged out of Brecht's experiences in exile. The image of the "Sintflut" with which it begins is not as out of place as it might seem in a poem that alludes to the writings of a classical Latin author, because the cultural memory of Noah's Flood is apparent in the poetry of Ovid, if not directly in that of Horace.[28] That image is, moreover, very close in implication to Brecht's evocation of the flood as a political metaphor in section III of "An die Nachgeborenen", which begins with the words, "Ihr, die ihr auftauchen werdet aus der Flut / In der wir untergegangen sind [...]" (BFA 12. P. 87). The context there is an appeal to those who will have survived – or more precisely, will have resurfaced from – the flood that is about to engulf Europe for sympathy and understanding towards the attitudes and the character of the writing to be found in the *Svendborger Gedichte*. "Beim Lesen des Horaz", by contrast, looks back at the catastrophe and provides a more specific perspective on the notion of survival:

> Selbst die Sintflut
> Dauerte nicht ewig.
> Einmal verrannen
> Die schwarzen Gewässer.
> Freilich, wie wenige
> Dauerten länger! (BFA 12. P. 315).

The poem by Horace that is generally accepted as having provided the stimulus for this particular crystallization of Brecht's thinking is an ode which links the flooding of the Tiber in 27 BC and the experience of recent strife with the new hope attaching to the accession of Octavian as Caesar Augustus who, it is hoped, will lead Rome successfully against its foes.[29] In the last two lines, Brecht directly echoes lines from Horace's ode which refer to the thinning of

---

[28] See Marion Lausberg: Brechts Lyrik und die Antike. In: *Brechts Lyrik – neue Deutungen*. Ed. by Helmut Koopmann. Würzburg: Königshausen & Neumann 1999. Pp. 163–198. Here p. 193.

[29] See Horace: *Odes I*. Ed. by David West. Oxford: Oxford University Press 1995. Pp. 8–15. Here p. 10; ll. 49–52.

the ranks of the young as a result of the faults of their elders: "audiet pugnas vitio parentum / rara iuventus".[30] But the emphasis in Brecht's version is not just on surviving ("überleben"), but on enduring over time: "Freilich, wie wenige / Dauerten länger!". It is that emphasis that takes the poem beyond a merely elegiac reflection on the lives lost in a cataclysmic episode. The question to be asked once the waters have finally subsided is not so much who has survived, but what has emerged that will prove of lasting value. It is in this sense that the themes of mortality, the preservation of cultural goods, and the concern for passing on something that will endure, which had occupied Brecht intensively in exile, might be said to coalesce in "Beim Lesen des Horaz".

My final example – the problematic case that falls between the early and the late phases in Brecht's treatment of mortality – is the opening poem of the collection *Aus einem Lesebuch für Städtebewohner* (1930). This poem actually dates from 1926, it has frequently been anthologized under the title "Verwisch die Spuren!", and it continues to excite scholarly interest because of the complexity of the tensions and ambiguities it contains. The poem bears a certain trace of the earlier, hedonistic phase, particularly in the injunction, at the beginning of the third stanza, to live as if there is no tomorrow – "Iß das Fleisch, das da ist! Spare nicht!" – but the dominant concern in this instance appears to be with the self-discipline that is needed for life in the city. This is the impression created by the series of injunctions – to separate off from all companions, to treat your own parents as strangers, to keep on the move, and to disclaim any thoughts that might be ascribed to you – which are set out in stanzas one to four. What complicates the task of interpretation, however, as well as marking this poem out as different from those that are concerned with what might live on after the death of the individual, is the final stanza, in which the logic of "eliminating the traces" is pursued to the extreme of self-effacement even in death:

Sorge, wenn du zu sterben gedenkst
Daß kein Grabmal steht und verrät, wo du liegst
Mit einer deutlichen Schrift, die dich anzeigt
Und dem Jahr deines Todes, das dich überführt!
Noch einmal:
Verwisch die Spuren! (BFA 11. P. 157).

The earliest extant version of this poem ends with a line in parenthesis ("Das wurde mir gesagt") which sets the whole sequence of statements at a certain distance, and thereby invites a degree of sceptical reflection on their content. It is not without consequence for the present discussion that, at the very time when he was concerning himself with the question of what he had bequeathed

---

[30] Ibid. p. 8; ll. 23–24.

to posterity (in the *Svendborger Gedichte*) and was simultaneously preparing his earlier poetry for publication in the *Gesammelte Werke* of 1938, Brecht changed the last word of that parenthesis from "gesagt" to "gelehrt" (BFA 11. P. 350). The effect of this change is to depersonalize the process of instruction that the poem ostensibly conveys, leaving only one moment of personal "speaking" remaining in line 17 ("Ich sage dir: / Verwisch die Spuren!"). In this way, the over-all character of the series of statements is arguably changed, from a set of instructions passed on from one individual to another into a series of conclusions drawn from experience: this is what life in the city has taught me. Either way, the injunction to self-effacement in death presents a challenge to any attempt to extract a consistent line of argument from the poem.

If we begin with the notion that the poem is constructing guidelines on how to live and survive in the city, then we are confronted at the end by the contradiction of an apparent endorsement of death and oblivion. Whereas the earlier Brecht could be seen to be cultivating an *ars vivendi* (Horst Jesse)[31] in response to the knowledge of the ultimate inescapability of death, this looks like a conscious and deliberate retreat from life into death signalled by the choice of verb: "Sorge, wenn du zu sterben *gedenkst* [...]". This aspect creates a particular difficulty for interpreting the poem in political terms, as Benjamin tried to do in the circumstances of exile,[32] and that difficulty was highlighted by Hans-Thiess Lehmann in 1992, albeit without explicit reference to Benjamin's commentary on the poem: "Keine realistische Deutung wäre angesichts der hohen Abstraktion des Textes haltbar (etwa die, es gelte, Genossen einer konspirativen Arbeit, Angehörige oder Freunde noch durch die Anonymität des Todes zu schützen)".[33] Down as far as stanza four the poem might be viewed as a set of instructions on how to avoid capture and incrimination, but then any notion of effective political intervention is contradicted in stanza five by the erasure of any trace of the individual's position in history: there should be no gravestone, and no inscription with the year of your death, which would incriminate you – as if any trace of your having lived would have an incriminating effect.

This apparent intimation of an impulse to expunge the guilt of personal existence altogether has attracted particular interest since 1990 from those who were aiming to establish a new image of Brecht and his writings by asserting the priority of psychoanalytical over Marxist perspectives. Lehmann's article, which appeared in a volume of the *Brecht Yearbook* entitled *The Other Brecht*, is a leading example of this approach. He takes the evidence of the final stanza

---

[31] See Jesse: *Die Lyrik Bertolt Brechts* (n. 9).
[32] Walter Benjamin: *Zu dem "Lesebuch für Städtebewohner"*. WBGS II.2. Pp. 555–560. Here pp. 555–557.
[33] Hans-Thiess Lehmann: Schlaglichter auf den anderen Brecht. In: *The Other Brecht*. Ed. by Marc Silberman et als.. Madison (WI): University of Wisconsin Press 1992. pp. 1–13. Here p. 10 (The Brecht Yearbook 17).

of this poem, together with the emphatic repudiation of the parents in the second stanza, as the basis for a reading in which the injunctions expressed in the five stanzas are viewed as a form of self-address – "Es geht um ein Ich als Du"[34] – and the final line in parenthesis is seen as signalling a radical division in the psychoanalytical subject that is presented via the text: "es [bleibt] ein immer anderer, der – in der Klammer sprechend – das Gesagte als ein ihm Diktiertes anzeigt und so eine absolute Spaltung der Intention treibt".[35] If we adopt this line of reasoning, then perhaps there are indeed some suggestive intimations of an unconscious motivating force to be recognized in the poem, an impulse that pushes the argument beyond self-concealment as a survival tactic, displays signs of what might be interpreted as panic ("Öffne, o öffne die Tür nicht [...]"; "Zeige, o zeige dein Gesicht nicht [...]"), and culminates in stanza five in a manifest desire for self-obliteration.[36] But to read the poem in this way, as the symptomatic expression of a (divided) subjectivity at work in its generation, is to downplay the references to external, social experience contained in the preceding stanzas, as well as the manifest rhetorical effects built into the text, to which I have drawn attention elsewhere.[37]

Discussion of this poem at the London conference in February 2006 brought forth a number of further possible starting points for interpreting it. One was to view the opening stanza ("Trenne dich von deinen Kameraden auf dem Bahnhof [...]") as representing a moment of existential decision from which all else followed; but this suggestion does not adequately account for the effect of the final parenthesis, in either version of the poem, which is to indicate that the sentiments communicated in the five stanzas originate from outside the subjectivity, and thus the decision-making capacity, of the first-person speaker. An alternative view was that a stable basis for interpretation might be sought precisely in the distancing effect of the closing parenthesis ("Das wurde mir gesagt / gelehrt"), considering it as an enactment of the principle of denial previously advocated in line 20: "Findest du deinen Gedanken bei einem andern: verleugne ihn". But there is no precise consistency even between these two elements in the poem: saying that the sentiments you have just expressed originated elsewhere is not the same thing as denying thoughts that you have previously expressed yourself. A third suggestion was that the injunction to obliterate one's traces, which is issued in relation to each of the five life circumstances evoked in the poem, could be seen as the consistent expression of a

---

[34] Ibid.
[35] Ibid. p. 11.
[36] See Helmut Lethen: *Verhaltenslehren der Kälte*. Frankfurt am Main: Suhrkamp 1994. P. 173: "Das Ich ergreift die Flucht nach vorn – wo der Tod wartet".
[37] David Midgley: The Poet in Berlin: Brecht's City Poetry of the 1920s. In: Kuhn and Leeder (eds.): *Empedocles' Shoe* (n. 13). Pp. 89–106. Esp. pp. 98–104.

philosophical precept to live obscurely – which would bring the overall purport of the poem close to the response to danger that is advocated in the "Kommentartexte" of the *Badener Lehrstück*, namely to reduce one's profile, not to seek to stand out from the crowd, and to survive the storm in one's "kleinste[r] Größe" (BFA 3. P. 38). The self-effacement that this attitude would seem to entail was contradicted, however, by those who detected an air of extravagance, of vainglory even, in the manner in which each piece of advice to the newcomer to the city was set out, taking the elaboration of each life situation to an extreme and giving the poem as a whole a certain swagger. In the light of this observation it might be said that the *memento mori* theme, which had long been a part of Brecht's poetic repertoire, here provides not only the obvious ultimate destination of human existence, but also the ultimate challenge for the posture adopted by the ostensible speaker in the poem: when you come to face the prospect of death, this is how you should do that too. But this in turn raises the question of the potentially ironic light in which that posturing is itself placed by the sequence of situations envisaged in the five stanzas: to what extent is the obliteration of all traces in fact appropriate to each of the life circumstances evoked?

When I have discussed this poem previously in the context of the examination of life circumstances and behavioural responses in the city that Brecht was conducting in the poems he later collected under the title *Aus einem Lesebuch für Städtebewohner*, I have suggested that we might think of it as developing two competing themes that run on "parallel tracks": one, I argued, was private and intimate and took the logic of self-effacement to an extreme, while the other was public and practical and focused on survival in adverse circumstances.[38] In this view, the refrain – "Verwisch die Spuren!" – might be said to hold the two themes together by providing a plausible watchword for each of these attitudes, albeit with a different connotation in either case. Having considered the poem afresh alongside Brecht's treatment of mortality at other times of his life, it seems to me necessary to develop a more complex view of the effects with which the poem works. In that broader context we might say that this poem has not yet detached itself from the characteristic impulses of the early poetry: it resorts to heightened emotive effects in its disillusioning evocation of social connections and their severance, it treats the *memento mori* theme as worthy of contemplation in its own right as the ultimate destination of human existence, and it betrays something of the impulse to outrage conventional expectations precisely in its treatment of that motif from Christian tradition. By the same token, it is not yet subject to the stricture that we find Brecht applying so tersely to the *Badener Lehrstück* in the same volume of the *Versuche* in which the *Lesebuch* poems were published in 1930: in the poem, as in the

---

[38] Ibid. p. 103–104.

Badener Lehrstück, the issue of mortality has not yet been placed under the perspective of "Gebrauchswert". What can be said about the poem in positive terms is that it represents a complex and provocative thought experiment in which each of a number of elements serves to expose the implications or the limitations of another. The reader is required to ponder the relationship of tension between the *memento mori* aspect and the survival tactics, between the intimations of emotional impulses and the aspect of instruction, between the prospect of ultimate oblivion and the possibility of eventual self-assertion. That way of reading the poem seems to me much more satisfactory than trying to resolve the contradictions in favour of any single tendency, and it would be consistent with the emphasis on the "oblique" mode of argument that Philip Brady showed to be characteristic of the *Lesebuch* collection as a whole.[39]

The treatment of the mortality theme that we find here, then, does not provide a straightforward justification for a psychoanalytical reading of the poem, nor does it straightforwardly invalidate the intimation of survival tactics that we find in other elements of the poem. What it does show is the recurrence of a prevalent motif from Brecht's earlier writings which is being used here in conjunction with other elements to provoke reflection through a discomforting interplay of opposing themes and impulses.

[39] Philip V. Brady: *Aus einem Lesebuch für Städtebewohner*: On a Brecht Essay in Obliqueness. In: *German Life and Letters* 26 (1972). Pp. 160–172.

Karen Leeder

"Des toten Dichters gedenkend": Remembering Brecht in Contemporary German Poetry

Fifty years after the poet's death, this essay addresses German poetry written "after Brecht". After examining the different forms of reception in general terms, it focuses on three categories of poems: poems about Brecht himself, those that take on the legacy and those that are inspired by the Brechtian gesture. Surprisingly perhaps, since the demise of the state which Brecht had been seen to legitimize, very many poems have focused on the biographical premise. Poems published since 1989/90 are then analyzed which present the fascinating or vilified person Brecht in context and in conversation with other contemporaries, especially the women around him. I shall also be looking at the many letters or telegrams addressed directly to Brecht from posterity, and finally at the poems which deal with his death – and the ways in which he might be remembered.

It is odd to think that half a century has passed since the death of Bertolt Brecht: partly because he is in so many ways the epitome of the "modern" poet; and partly because his voice is so much a part of the grammar of our times, that it seems he cannot have been gone so long. It is not just that Brecht's poems are still read, nor that they are influential – though they are certainly both of these – but that his poetry has found a further afterlife in the work of the poets who have come after him.

The poems I am going to discuss here give just a taste of a vast reception, which is perhaps unparalleled in any age or language. That Brecht should have acted as a focus for so many poems suggests though that something more has been going on than a simple reading of his work. It has to do with Brecht as a figure as well. His personal charisma, his radical politics, his wayward behaviour, his desire to rip up any rule books and change art and the world, all have contributed to a kind of mythical aura which has engendered reworkings of his life in novels, films and plays. Whether "loving Brecht" (the title of Elaine Feinstein's 1992 novel), or hating him – as in that deeply flawed "Brecht-buster", John Fuegi's *Life and Lies of Bertolt Brecht* of 1994 – the magnetism of the figure still fascinates.[1] As always, it is the details which catch the eye: the haircut, the cigar, the "klug und kahl" demeanour (Thomas Brasch).[2] But the contradictions too, both real and of biographical anecdote, have since become

---

[1] Elaine Feinstein: *Loving Brecht*. London: Hutchinson 1992; John Fuegi: *The Life and Lies of Bertolt Brecht*. London: Harper Collins 1992. See also Jacques-Pierre Amette: *La Maîtresse de Brecht*. Paris: Albin Michel 2003.

[2] Thomas Brasch: Im Garten Eden, Hollywood genannt. In: *Der schöne 27. September. Gedichte*. Frankfurt am Main: Suhrkamp 1980. P. 17.

also part of the legend: the young man who could publish a pornographic son-net under the name of the venerable (and despised) antagonist Thomas Mann, the silk shirts under the worker's jacket, the comradeship and faithlessness in the same breath.

This extraordinary reception, though, also has to do with Brecht's unique diction. Brecht was a superb lyric poet who profoundly distrusted the lyric mode. Nature and love are at the centre of his work and yet he wrote with a con-viction that it was largely illegitimate in times like his to derive poetry from such experiences. That he managed to articulate this contradiction has much to do with "List" – Brecht's word – a project which also became a philosophy of survival for him in the Third Reich.[3] He created an immediately recognizable voice: low-key, simple, but without being arch or sentimental. And it is striking how persuasively that diction infects many of those who come after. Moreover, he is also a poet's poet – in the best sense of the phrase. Although he was a writer urgently concerned with the dark times he lived in, very many of his poems are also themselves about poetry. For that reason those who have come after have felt themselves called on to respond both to their own times and to the demands of poetry.

And finally: the longevity and variety of Brecht's afterlife make sense because Brecht's own poetry is so centrally concerned with the issue of recep-tion. Very many of his poems are explicitly concerned with the way posterity will read and judge the poet and his times – most notably of course the celebrated poem, "An die Nachgeborenen" (BFA 12. Pp. 85–87). Indeed, a whole matrix of symbols of survival and forgetting, memorialization and inscription runs through his work, as Siegrid Thielking has persuasively teased out in her article "L'homme statue? Brechts Inschriften im Kontext von Denkmalsdiskurs und Erinnerungspolitik".[4] This was a very real issue for Brecht, who fled the book-burnings of Nazi Germany on the day after Hitler's accession to power. He sim-ply did not know whether he or his work would survive. His friend and lover Ruth Berlau recalls him asking her to learn his poems off by heart, so that they at least would last.[5] But from an early age Brecht famously also liked to situate himself in a long line of famous poets. Hans Otto Münsterer, for example, tells an anecdote about him standing as a self-styled Friedrich von Schiller in the

---

[3] See Bertolt Brecht: *Fünf Schwierigkeiten beim Schreiben der Wahrheit.* BFA 22. Pp. 74–89.

[4] Siegrid Thielking: L'homme statue? Brechts Inschriften im Kontext von Denkmalsdiskurs und Erinnerungspolitik. In: *Brecht 100<=>2000.* Ed. by John Rouse, Marc Silberman and Florian Vaßen. Madison (WI): University of Wisconsin Press 1999. Pp. 54–67 (The Brecht Yearbook 24).

[5] Ruth Berlau: *Brechts Lai-Tu. Erinnerungen und Notate.* Ed. by Hans Bunge. Darmstadt – Neuwied: Luchterhand 1987.

niche outside an Augsburg theatre where the statues of poets had been removed for the First World War.[6] And of course he lived to see himself become an uncomfortable "classic" in the founding years of the East German State, to which he returned after the end of Hitler's War.

This interest in reception is important because it is also part of Brecht's larger political and aesthetic understanding. The principles of a pragmatic and critical reception are paramount for him. That he aspired to similar forms of reception for himself is suggested by a late poem "Ich benötige keinen Grabstein" in which he suggests a suitable form for his own epitaph:

Er hat Vorschläge gemacht. Wir
Haben sie angenommen.
Durch eine solche Inschrift wären
Wir alle geehrt.[7]

Volker Braun laments in his poem "Zu Brecht, Die Wahrheit einigt": "Wir haben ihn nicht angenommen, nur / Gewisse Termini und die Frisur".[8] In fact his "suggestions" are taken up by many in a spirit of identification, irony, argument and downright contradiction that Brecht would have appreciated as a properly disrespectful – but honourable – legacy.

Any list of poems responding to Brecht reads like a "Who's Who" of modern German literature.[9] It is perhaps to be expected that many of these poems should have been written by writers who knew Brecht personally or had come directly from his sphere of influence. Indeed for some, such as Martin Pohl, the younger poet whom Brecht supported when he was in prison, Heinz Kahlau, B.K. Tragelehn, Peter Hacks or Günter Kunert, the figure casts a sometimes uncomfortably long shadow:

Sein hingebuckelter Grabstein
Auf der Chausseestraße 126
Im Nordwesten von Berlin, jener deutschen,
Jener flachen, ausgedehnten Provinzstadt,
Einen so furchtbar langen Schatten wirft er.[10]

---

[6] Hans Otto Münsterer: The Young Brecht. Ed. and trans. by Karen Leeder and Tom Kuhn. London: Libris 1992. P. 36.

[7] BFA 14. Pp. 191–192. Compare the article by Peter Hutchinson in this volume.

[8] Volker Braun: Zu Brecht, Die Wahrheit einigt. In: Volker Braun: Texte in zeitlicher Folge. Vol. 5. Pp. 72–73.

[9] Many of the poems discussed here are taken up in one or other of the anthologies, "O Chicago! O Widerspruch!": Hundert Gedichte auf Brecht. Ed. by Karen Leeder and Erdmut Wizisla. Leipzig: Transit 2006 and After Brecht: A Celebration. Ed. by Karen Leeder. Manchester: Carcanet 2006.

[10] Peter Hacks: Brecht. From the sequence Briefe. In: Sinn und Form 15 (1963). Pp. 204–205. Other poems in the sequence are addressed to Karl Marx and Georg Büchner.

But other writers too, like Heiner Müller, Volker Braun, Karl Mickel and Wolf Biermann, come back to Brecht again and again as a kind of touchstone in their poetic careers.

More interesting in a way is the fact that this kind of influence extends beyond the sphere of a shared political commitment where one might expect to see writers wrestling with Brecht's legacy. It is perhaps strange, for example, that the hermetic poet of the Holocaust Paul Celan should turn to the Marxist believer in historical progress, and even more so that his diction should be infected by that of Brecht; or that the "grande dame" of Austrian poetry, Friederike Mayröcker, with her surreal reflections on nature and age should borrow the "intonation" of Brecht to express her own grief at the loss of a loved one: "an EJ im Tonfall von BB".[11]

Equally, after the fall of the Berlin Wall, Brecht has been taken up, not only as one might expect by writers sympathetic to his communist ideals, or who lived through the socialist reality they inspired, but also by younger poets who never knew him and who do not share his political convictions. It is clear that, especially in the ruined landscapes of the East after 1990, with Chancellor Kohl's promises of economic upturn ringing hollowly in their ears, new generations of writers have felt a profound affinity with Brecht's sentiments and tone. Annett Gröschner's 1997 poem "Blühende Landschaften" for example borrows from the eighth poem of the *Lesebuch für Städtebewohner*: "Laßt eure Träume fahren" (BFA 11. Pp. 163–164).

> Schäbige schatten ziehst du noch immer
> Wie eine trümmerfrau fort aus dem schlick
> Wozu die anstrengung? was deine mutter
> Dir auf den weg gab kannst du vergessen
> Was hier gebraucht wird sind ballerinen
> Keine matrosin in arbeiterschuhn[12]

Despite the many and repeated claims, then, that Brecht is without real resonance in the contemporary world, his poems remain a constant source of reference to a wide variety of successors, with work from all periods of his life and all styles being taken up.[13]

---

[11] Paul Celan: Ein Blatt, baumlos (July 1968). First published in: *Von den Nachgeborenen. Dichtungen auf Bertolt Brecht*. Ed. by Jürgen P. Wallmann. Zürich: Verlag der Arche 1970. P. 9. Friederike Mayröcker: an EJ im Tonfall von BB (October 2005). First published in Leeder and Wizisla (eds.): *O Chicago!* (n. 9). P. 63.

[12] Annett Gröschner: Blühende Landschaften. In: *drive b: brecht 100. Arbeitsbuch/Sourcebook*. Ed. by Marc Silberman. Berlin: Theater der Zeit 1997. P. 160.

[13] The phrase "Ein Gespräch über Bäume" is a case in point. Compare my "B.B.s spät gedenkend": Reading Brecht in the 1980s and 1990s. In: Rouse et als. (eds.): *Brecht 100–2000* (n. 4). Pp. 111–129.

Some poems though, some phrases even, seem to work as a particular irritant for posterity. The great hymn to posterity, "An die Nachgeborenen", is a case in point, with an extraordinarily sustained reception.[14] Indeed the phrase "Ein Gespräch über Bäume" has arguably become overused to the point of becoming divorced from any sense of its original use. Other poems, or lines, seem to have particular moments of greater or lesser significance. As I will argue below, the poem "Vom armen B.B." (BFA 11. P. 119) is one that seems to have had a special currency during recent years. On the other hand, a poem like "Der Radwechsel" (BFA 12. P. 310) – with its central lines " Ich bin nicht gern, wo ich herkomme. / Ich bin nicht gern, wo ich hinfahre" – seems calculated to resonate at almost any historical juncture. Karl Mickel's "Radwechsel" of 1992 is simply one of the most recent adaptations.[15] Written in 1992, this poem shifts Brecht's observation on the beginnings of the GDR to its demise:

Gewechselt sind Schaltung und Laufräder
Der Rahmen stammt her aus dem vorigen Leben
Der eingerittene Sattel, das Licht.

So fahre ich fort.

Kastanien poltern und Eicheln prasseln
Bucheckern knistern im Sprung.
Das Hundchen am Weltrand schlägt an

Alongside those that cite Brecht directly, there are many poems that borrow or reinvent his diction. Here too the legacy can emerge in sometimes not altogether expected places. One of the most striking descriptions of this kind of reception is to be found in Bob Dylan's *Chronicles*.[16] Dylan recalls a production of various Brecht songs at a local theatre and the almost physical blow the singer felt on first hearing a performance of the "Song of Pirate Jenny": "Within a few minutes I felt like I hadn't slept or tasted food for about thirty hours".[17] Later, having worked on the song, "unzipped it" as he says, he found the structures revealed: "Everything was fastened to the wall with a heavy bracket, but you

---

[14] See Karen Leeder: Those born later read Brecht: The reception of Brecht's "An die Nachgeborenen". In: *Brecht's Poetry of Political Exile*. Ed. by Ronald Speirs. Cambridge: Cambridge University Press 2000. Pp. 211–240.

[15] Karl Mickel: Radwechsel (1992). In: Karl Mickel: *Geisterstunde*, originally Selbstverlag 1999. Reprinted as Göttingen: Wallstein 2004. P. 93. See also, for example, Yaak Karsunke: Matti wechselt das Rad. In: *Tintenfisch* 1 (1968). P. 67; Fitzgerald Kusz: Gegenlied zu Brechts "Radwechsel". In: *Jahrbuch der Lyrik* 2003. Ed. by Christoph Buchwald and Michael Krüger. München: Beck 2004. P. 121.

[16] Bob Dylan: *Chronicles*. London: Simon and Schuster 2004. Vol. 1

[17] Ibid. p. 273.

couldn't see what the sum total of all the parts were [*sic*], not unless you stood way back and waited 'til the end. It was like the Picasso painting *Guernica*".[18] One might naturally make a casual link between Brecht and Dylan, charismatic and passionate singer-poets of the Left. But it is unlikely that the Brechtian origins of songs like "Lonesome Death of Hattie Carroll", "Only a Pawn in Their Game", or "A Hard Rain's A-Gonna Fall" would have come to light without Dylan's express acknowledgement. "If I hadn't gone to the Theatre de Lys and heard the ballad 'Pirate Jenny' ", he writes, "it might not have dawned on me to write them, that songs like these could be written".[19] This kind of account is illuminating for what it says more broadly about the possibilities of Brecht's influence, not only in German poetry, in that it has allowed poets to do things they could not have done without him, it has created aesthetic possibilities. An account of the poetry written after Brecht in this sense would simply be too large to contemplate.[20]

Instead, since the marked interest in Brecht's person is one of the most fascinating aspects of the recent reception, I will focus in the remainder of this essay on poems published since 1989/90 which deal with this aspect in different contexts. Of course many of these poems are simultaneously attempts to respond to Brecht's legacy; they cite and respond to Brecht's work; and they are inspired more or less specifically by his aesthetic. The categories are by no means absolute. But it does appear that, since the demise of the state with which Brecht was most closely identified, the person has once more been uncovered, or released for reassessment.

From the beginning, of course, poets have sought to capture a "Portrait des B.B."[21] Many poems focus, for example, on the physiognomy of the poet; others again on his "Lebensreise";[22] his houses; his relationship with Helene Weigel; his relations with other poets. All stages of his life are represented, from the childhood reminiscences of his friend Hans Otto Münsterer, to his flight with "Augsburg auf den Sohlen" and the long period of exile,[23] before the return to the divided Germany and his troubled relationship with the GDR authorities. Friends, lovers, compatriots, enemies all write to salute or take issue with him: from the intimate greetings of Ruth Berlau's "Ich ging, dir ein Blatt zu holen",

---

[18] Ibid. p. 275.
[19] Ibid. p. 287.
[20] For examples see Leeder and Wizisla (eds.): *O Chicago!* (n. 9). Pp. 83–103. On Brecht's reception in English, see Karen Leeder: "After Brecht": The reception of Brecht's poetry in English. In: *Empedocles' Shoe: Essays on Brecht's poetry.* Ed. by Tom Kuhn and Karen Leeder. London: Methuen 2002. Pp. 231–256.
[21] Heinz Kahlau: Portrait des B.B. (1955). In: Heinz Kahlau: *Probe. Gedichte.* Berlin: Volk und Welt 1957. P. 12.
[22] B.K. Tragelehn: Lebensreise meines Lehrers. In: B.K. Tragelehn: *NÖSPL. Gedichte 1956–1991.* Frankfurt am Main: Stroemfeld/Roter Stern 1996. P. 16.
[23] Ibid.

which concludes with the words "Jeg elsker dig", to a celebration on a grand
rhetorical scale "Du Dichter Prophet Meister" (Albert von Rohden) or the more
circumspect "Schwierigkeiten im Verkehr mit dem Dichter Bertolt Brecht
(1944)" by Hans Sahl.[24]

Temporal distance from the poet himself does not seem to have diminished
this desire to address his person or his life. On the contrary, it is noteworthy to
what extent writers since the fall of the Berlin Wall, and in particular after the centenary of Brecht's birth, have tended to return to the biography and the fascination with, or vilification of, the private and public figure. In 1998 Fredric
Jameson combined an insistence on the plurality of actual and "virtual Brechts"
that were generating debate with a plea for an understanding of the profound
contemporaneity of the work.[25] And it is clear that sometimes at least, Brecht as
"Legende" (Daniel Call), or "Figur" (Kerstin Specht), has become exemplary
in a political context. As Specht puts it in a piece about "Brecht und die Enkel":
"Der Dichter als Mensch. Ein Lehrstück".[26]

To be sure, this interest in Brecht does not necessarily have any implications
for the perceived relevance of his legacy. It could simply reflect a glib or totemic
fascination with the icon and nothing more. This inevitably raises the question
of Brecht's "classicism". For to be a "classic" as Max Frisch understood and
Brecht feared, is potentially to be fêted, but also neutralized, surrounded by the
totems of recognition, but also silenced and reduced to "durchschlagende
Wirkungslosigkeit".[27] And so it is that many (especially) recent poems cite the
"dunklen Anzug" and "erforderte […] Miene" (Kunert), the flowers and wreaths
that signal with official acceptance and veneration, a second greater death:
"Nun ist er Klassiker und ist begraben" (Volker Braun).[28] Exemplary in this respect
is the poem by Günter Kunert, "Vom Dorotheenstädtischen Friedhof" (1993),

---

[24] Ruth Berlau: Ich ging Dir ein Blatt zu holen (December 1955). BFA 15. P. 494. The
final phrase means "I love you" in Danish; Albert von Rohden: Bertolt Brecht. In:
Albert von Rohden: *Excelsior. Gedichte*. Göttingen: Selbstverlag 1968. P. 93; Hans Sahl:
Schwierigkeiten im Verkehr mit dem Dichter Bertolt Brecht (1944). In: Hans Sahl: *Wir
sind die Letzten. Der Maulwurf. Gedichte*. 2nd ed. Frankfurt am Main: Luchterhand
1991. P. 125.

[25] Fredric Jameson: *Brecht and Method*. London – New York: Verso 1998. P. 5.

[26] Kirsten Specht: Brecht und die Enkel. In: *Die deutsche Bühne* 69 (1998) H. 2. Pp.
34–37. Here p. 34 and p. 35 respectively.

[27] This much-cited comment was made by Max Frisch at a theatre conference in
Frankfurt of 1964, "Der Autor und das Theater". In: Max Frisch: *Gesammelte Werke in
zeitlicher Folge*. Ed. by Hans Mayer and Walter Schmitz. Frankfurt am Main:
Suhrkamp 1976. Vol. 10. Pp. 339–354. Here p. 342.

[28] Günter Kunert: Vom Dorotheenstädtischen Friedhof. In: Günter Kunert: *Gedichte*.
Ed. by Franz Josef Görz. Stuttgart: Reclam 1993. P. 43; Peter Dempf: Gstanzl zum
Hundersten in a-Moll. In: *Satyr* 2 (February 1998). P. 17; Braun: Zu Brecht (n. 8).

which makes this point about Brecht, but broadens the scope of its complaint: poetry itself is powerless.

> Auf den Friedhöfen der toten Dichter
> triumphiert die Macht
> über die Ohnmacht des Wortes[29]

The double referent is signalled by "das erbärmliche Geschrei welker Blätter / unter den Sohlen" ("Blätter" being here both leaves underfoot and papers). But the warning is emphatically neither heard nor heeded.[30] The visitors "like you", ignorant and uncomplaining, simply make their way as instructed "zum zugewiesenen Platz" – a play both on the grave to which they are directed, but also on their knowing, and keeping, their place.[31]

Günter Kunert, a poet who has written a large number of poems referring to Brecht during his long writing career, seems to offer a bitter denunciation of his person and his tactics from the perspective of October 2006 in a poem entitled "Schlechter Rat":[32]

> Der Dichter öffnet seinen Mund,
> uns mitzuteilen, was gesund
> und einfach wäre: Das Lavieren.
> Ach, Brecht, wir wollen uns nicht zieren
> und sagen: Dabei kommt nichts raus.
> Nicht Fisch noch Fleisch – so geht das aus.
> Und kostet auch noch Selbstvertrauen:
> Deshalb auf keinen Dichter bauen!

In a remarkably similar mood, Jan Koneffke's "Falsche Moral" is dedicated to "dem verrufenen B.B.":

> Von diesem Leben ließ er sich nicht lumpen
> und rauchte seinen Tabak bis zum Stumpen

---

[29] Kunert: Vom Dorotheenstädtischen Friedhof (n. 28).

[30] Compare Michael Wüstefeld: Staatsmänner und Dichter (zum Achtzigsten von B. B.). In: *Der neue Zwiebelmarkt*. Ed. by Wolfgang Sellin and Manfred Wolter. Berlin: Eulenspiegel 1988. P. 194.

[31] I offer a sustained analysis of poems about Brecht's death in: Karen Leeder: "Nachwort zu Brechts Tod": The Afterlife of a Classic in Modern German Poetry. In: *Brecht and Death*. Ed. by Jürgen Hillesheim, Mathias Mayer and Stephen Brockmann. Madison (WI): The University of Wisconsin Press 2007. Pp. 335–356 (The Brecht Yearbook 32).

[32] Günter Kunert: Schlechter Rat. (October 2005). First published in Leeder and Wizisla (eds.): *O Chicago!* (n. 9). P. 18.

es bleibt halt wahr man kratzt an der Kultur
und findet wieder: gierige Natur

und was am Schluß von einer Lippe sinkt
das ist ein kalter Rest der stinkt[33]

Both poems seem to take Brecht to task, but also to signal a larger crisis of confidence in the poet. Kunert's final line, "Deshalb auf keinen Dichter bauen!" is inevitably in part ironic too, given that the injunction comes in a poem. However, it recalls his own reassessment of the status of writing after 1989, and in particular of the writer's "Sturz vom Sockel".[34] Koneffke, on the other hand, seems to be tapping into the vitalist and materialist ethos of Brecht's early poetry – "gierige Natur" – but the conclusion (while ostensibly about the cigar) also touches on the value of the legacy: "ein kalter Rest der stinkt".

Several poems place Brecht in context and in conversation with his contemporaries, to illustrate a larger political or aesthetic point. In Albert Ostermaier's "abseitsfalle oder: brecht passt zu benn", Brecht commends to the poet Gottfried Benn the healing gravity of football.[35] In the World Cup year, this casts an ironic perspective on the rivalry between Brecht and the West German poet Benn, who, with his dark, highly rhetorical, "monologic" poetry represented in almost every respect the complete opposite of Brecht. In his GDR years Brecht had devoted a pointed verse to Benn, "Beim Anhören von Versen / Des todessüchtigen Benn", in which he notes on the faces of the workers an expression that "kostbarer war / Als das Lächeln der Mona Lisa" (BFA 15. P. 300). Ostermaier's poem is explicitly a (comic) dialogue between the poets at a personal level (their voices are represented by different typefaces), but also a dialogue with their work. An other-worldly Benn, complaining about his isolation (*"ich empfinde nur leere"*) and sceptical about the banality of football, contrasts with the pragmatic and cynical Brecht, who has an eye to the bigger picture: "das ist anschauungsunterricht / für revolutionäre". Yet there are other issues at stake: "fussball lehrt eine masse in der möglichkeitsform / denken", claims Brecht, and both poets and their afterlife are subject to the larger changes of history:

[…] man
erfährt dass sich in sekunden was verändern
lässt das ist mehr als die geschichte lehrt

---

[33] Jan Koneffke: Falsche Moral. (December 2005). First published in Leeder and Wizisla (eds.): *O Chicago!* (n. 9). P. 19.

[34] Günter Kunert: *Der Sturz vom Sockel. Feststellungen und Widersprüche.* München: Hanser 1992.

[35] Albert Ostermaier: abseitsfalle oder: brecht passt zu benn. In: Poems after Brecht. Ed. and trans. by Karen Leeder. In: *Modern Poetry in Translation.* 3rd Series No. 6 (2006). Pp. 5–32. Here pp. 30–31.

Ostermaier also takes up Brecht's so-called "Hollywoodelegien" (BFA 12. Pp. 115–116), famously set to music by Hanns Eisler, in his sequence of "repeat *hollywoodelegie*" poems.[36] Brecht, struggling in exile to become a script writer, saw Hollywood as a kind of hell, and everyone there as prostitutes selling their souls.[37] B. K. Tragelehn also refers implicitly to these poems in his "B und F in H", which situates a dialogue between Brecht and Lion Feuchtwanger in front of the Villa Aurora in Pacific Palisades, California:

Zwei Freunde auf einer Steinbank
Fremdkörper from Bavaria Germany
Warten.

Statt I sagns Ei hier, statt Ei sagns Egg
Statt Egg sagns Koaner, und statt Koaner sagns
Nobaddi.

Das Haus vor dem sie sitzen heißt *Aurora*
Aber die Sonne geht ab in das Wasser
Pacific

Um wieder aufzutreten muß sie erst
Rund um die Erde und dann über den Berg.
Warten.[38]

Though this is not stated, the poem refers to the famous photo of the pair by Ruth Berlau of 1947, and simultaneously echoes the fourth of Walter Benjamin's *Thesen über den Begriff der Geschichte*.[39] This text insists on "die rohen und materiellen Dinge": food and clothing, taken up here in the exiles' conversation. Nevertheless the fine and spiritual things are also present in the struggle – "als Zuversicht, als Humor als List, als Unentwegtheit" – reaching back into the past. This thesis counts on such qualities acting as a motivating and hopeful force in history: "wie Blumen ihr Haupt nach der Sonne wenden, so strebt kraft eines Heliotropismus geheimer Art das *Gewesene* der Sonne sich zuzuwenden, die am Himmel der Geschichte im Aufgehen ist". The poem responds by taking up the trope of the rising sun and by paralleling the personal waiting room of exile with the larger parenthesis of history. Though the villa is called "Aurora", the sun is lost at evening time in the waters of the Pacific, bringing darkness. One is reminded of Brecht's characterization of fascism as "die finsteren Zeiten". Yet the sun will rise again – despite its evident struggle – and, implicitly, fascism

[36] Ibid. p. 32.
[37] See Bertolt Brecht: *Nachdenkend, wie ich höre, über die Hölle*. BFA 15. P. 46.
[38] September 2005. First published in Leeder and Wizisla (eds.): *O Chicago!* (n. 9). P. 32.
[39] WBGS I.2. Pp. 691–701. Here p. 694. I am grateful to Erdmut Wizisla for pointing this out to me.

too will be defeated. Those who remain must wait. Moreover, the poem also responds to Benjamin in a further way. Benjamin urges the historical materialist to be aware of and learn from this "diese unscheinbarste von allen Veränderungen". Accordingly, the poem tracks the humdrum linguistic transformations of exile. The slippage here, though humorous, is not insignificant. However, the emphasis is on the attentive response, the resistance, which must be employed in times of darkness and waiting – perhaps also in these dark times after 1990.

Berlau herself, together with others of the women around Brecht, appears in numerous poems. In line with, and drawing on, the feminist interest in the women who collaborated with Brecht during his lifetime, several poets focus on Brecht's relations with his co-workers and lovers.[40] Ulrike Draesner gives voice to Brecht's long-time Danish collaborator in a fascinating set of eight poems first read in London in 2006: "synger med fuld styrke – zu Bert Brecht und Ruth Berlau".[41] This exquisite sequence of imagined exchanges between the two writers, by turns lyrical or songlike, and brutal, traces the stations of their relationship between 1933 and 1942, in a mix of Danish and German. A final poem, "herzzange", focuses on Ruth Berlau in Berlin in autumn 1973, shortly before her death as a lonely and embittered alcoholic.[42] It begins playfully:

hat eine zuviel b im schrank
batikrock blazer gar eine boa
zum abschlecken einen mit
grünem fell hinter den ohren
augen wie windleuchten
ja, so einen hund!

However the implied naïvety gives way to a final bleak observation that combines the facts of Berlau's miscarriage with the subsequent eclipse of her creative efforts.

fuck. es habe erdig
gerochen das hemd
silbern (wie ruhm) (wie
rufe) das blutige rutschen
später in ihrer hand

In the poem "Grüß Gott" Karin Kiwus explores the moving circumstances of Brecht's flight from the Soviet Union in 1941 leaving behind another collaborator,

---

[40] Important in this respect are books by Sabine Kebir, especially *Ein akzeptabler Mann? Streit um Brechts Partnerbeziehungen*. Berlin: Der Morgen 1989.

[41] The reading took place at the Poetry International Festival, in the Queen Elizabeth Hall, London, on the 27 September 2006. A selection of the poems commissioned for this event were published in Leeder (ed.): Poems after Brecht (n. 35).

[42] Also published in Leeder and Wizisla (eds.): *O Chicago!* (n. 9). P. 103. See also Berlau: *Brechts Lai-Tu* (n. 5) or Sabine Kebir: *Mein Herz liegt neben der Schreibmaschine: Ruth Berlaus Leben vor, mit und nach Bertolt Brecht*. Algiers: Lalla Moulati 2006.

Margarete Steffin, who would die of illness before she could follow him into exile.[43] Brecht wrote over thirty poems for Steffin, quite apart from the *Steffinsche Sammlung*, and her death affected him badly.[44] Kiwus draws on some of these to imagine the journey of "der Klassiker am Mittwoch / dem vierten Juni 1941, gegen drei Uhr / nachmittags im transsibirischen Express" and a potential conversation between Brecht and his lover. Brecht's sentiment and guilt is ironically set against the reality of what he is doing: "und es ist nicht wahr / daß es Freunde geben muß, über die man / fahren kann mit einem Tausendtonnengüterzug". The poem finishes with Brecht's shame and Steffin's imagined efforts "eifrig wie immer ihm einen Trost [zu erfinden]". However, there is also a further reference, in that the title of Kiwus's poem, "Grüß Gott", is part of the acrostic smuggled as a greeting into Steffin's own sonnet with the motto, "Als der Klassiker am Montag, / dem siebenten Oktober 1935 / es verließ, weinte Dänemark", and, famously, the code word used between the lovers.[45] The greeting echoes beyond the poem.

Very many poems address the poet directly. Indeed there is a tradition of poems in the form of letters or telegrams to Brecht that could furnish material for an essay in itself.[46] Many of them, it is true, address Brecht in order to reject him. The poet Bert Papenfuß sends a poetic missive which addresses the poet with his given name of "Eugen Berthold", a name swiftly abandoned when Brecht reinvented himself as a cool, metropolitan poet. Papenfuß begins "Lieber Eugen" and signs off "Dein Bert". In between he makes no bones about his position:

Lieber Eugen,

    Du wurdest nun mal
ein privilegiertes Arschloch mit Kebsweib,

---

[43] Karin Kiwus: Grüß Gott. In: Leeder and Wizisla (eds.): *O Chicago!* (n. 9). P. 30.

[44] BFA 12. Pp. 92–100. On Steffin more generally see *Focus: Margarete Steffin*. Ed. by Marc Silberman, Roswitha Mueller, Antony Tatlow and Carl Weber. Madison (WI): University of Wisconsin Press 1994 (The Brecht Yearbook 19).

[45] This poem is also known as: Geliebter hast Du denn nicht gelesen. See: Bertolt-Brecht-Archive BBA 209/40. This appeared as a poem by Brecht in Bertolt Brecht: *Gesammelte Werke in 20 Bänden*. Frankfurt am Main: Suhrkamp 1967. Vol. 9. P. 549. By the time of the *Große kommentierte Berliner und Frankfurter Ausgabe*, it had been reclassified as a poem by Steffin and accordingly it appears in: Margarete Steffin: *Konfutse versteht nichts von Frauen. Texte*. Ed. by Inge Gellert. Berlin: Rowohlt 1991. P. 206. Kiwus uses other quotations from this poem in her own text. On the "unauffällig Wort" that Brecht and Steffin used as a code and the relationship in general see: Heidrun Loeper: Sonette. Englische Sonette. In: *Brecht Handbuch in fünf Bänden*. Ed. by Jan Knopf. Stuttgart – Weimar: Metzler 2001–2003. Vol. 2. Pp. 224–237.

[46] See for example Habib Bektaş: Brief an Bert Brecht. In: *In einem guten Land braucht's keine Tugenden: Dreißig Autoren schreiben*. Ed. by Habib Bektaş and Werner Steffen. Erlangen: Aleph 1984. Pp. 129–131; Franz Hodjak: telegramm ins jenseits. An Bertolt

Landhaus und Chauffeur, kamst nachlaut, neuklug
und autoritär daher wie eine Werkausgabe auf Stelzen.[47]

Nevertheless, the abrasive reappraisal of the man, the GDR he left behind, and
the state that subsumed it – "Staatseigentum stagnierte, das Volk sah seinem /
Eigentum in der Röhre nach" – makes deft use of Brecht's own work in various
places. It offers a commentary of sorts on Brecht's poetry from a present-day
perspective. For example, the line " 'Ein anderes Volk' ist natürlich auch keine
Lösung" cites Brecht's own poem "Die Lösung" (BFA 12. P. 310) and suggests
that the abuse of the people by government continues unabated. The final strophe contains a further example.

Zurechtgefickt und autoritär gestrickt
wehrt man sich minder gewitzt,
indem man zusammenstaucht
und dicke Zigarren raucht.

Rauchen ist Abwehr – "es kommt nichts nachher".

The quotation from Brecht's "Vom armen B.B." (BFA 11. P. 119) has a double,
perhaps triple, frame of reference. It functions within the poem as a response to
Brecht's own dilemma, but it seems also to point beyond that to a dystopian post-
1990 reality, and finally to signal the end of the reception of Brecht himself.

A poem by another poet from the former GDR, Thomas Martin: "nachbrecht
(wie man mit toten redet)", goes even further.[48] It offers a sustained response
to Brecht's "An die Nachgeborenen", repeating the bitter refrain: "nichts ist
euch vergeben worden, ihr toten". Hope has been buried with the dead and if a
"screaming" is heard from underground, the generation of the present chooses
to silence it themselves.

[…] dann sagen wir:
hört, sie können nicht sterben, noch das pfahl müssen wir
daß sie still sind, ins herz ihnen treiben.
und tuns.

The poem offers a radical rejection of Brecht and the notion of something to be
passed on: "botschaft […]. wir haben da keine". Nevertheless, it is interesting

Brecht. In: Franz Hodjak: *flieder im ohr. Gedichte.* Bucharest: Kriterion 1983. P. 75. There
is a lively tradition of dialogue with Brecht in Romanian German poetry. See Peter Motzan:
Von der Aneignung zur Abwendung: Der intertextuelle Dialog der rumäniendeutschen
Lyrik mit Bertolt Brecht. In: *Budapester Beiträge zur Germanistik* 34 (1999). Pp. 139–165.
[47] Bert Papenfuß: Lieber Eugen. In: Leeder (ed.): Poems after Brecht (n. 35). Pp. 27–28.
[48] Thomas Martin: nachbrecht (wie man mit toten redet). In: *Sklaven* 42 (November
1997). P. 2. The manuscript version has no subtitle.

to note once again, that rejection is addressed to the poet himself and through a counterpoint to one of his most famous poems. The final strophe suggests that beyond fame or betrayal there is simply the oblivion of irrelevance:

was zu vergeben ist, ist längst vergessen
ihr toten. was wir auch tun, jeder schritt
geht über euch; so vorübergehend geht vorüber
unsre zeit, die zu bleiben wir uns nehmen.

This leads quite naturally into a few final reflections on a set of poems, all from the period since 1989, which are united in the overwhelming sense of a Brecht who no longer speaks to posterity and a posterity which does not want to hear.

"B.B.s spät gedenkend"

Der große Dichter
im Stahlsarg unter dem Stein
und im Nirgendwo. Kein
lesender Arbeiter stellt noch
eine Frage: Es gibt ja
keine Antworten mehr.
Der arme reiche Dichter
in enger Erde
aufersteht täglich zum Dienst
als Objekt.
Umgeben von lauter Verrätern
aus Liebe oder
sonstiger Bedürftigkeit
hast du deine Wahl
getroffen: Keine Nachrichten
mehr an Nachgeborene.[49]

This poem by Günter Kunert, from the beginning of 1992, portrays Brecht as dead: literally and metaphorically. He has become a monument, an object, which has first been robbed of its contradictions, and then of its socialist premise. Now even final traces of his vision have vanished. The mood of the poem is elegiac for the failure of Brecht's vision, but there is also a larger sense of loss, which might be understood to be the result of a more profound crisis. The line "Es gibt ja / keine Antworten mehr" responds implicitly to a time in which there are no questions ("Fragen eines lesenden Arbeiters". BFA 12. P. 20). But it seems also to belong to an age in which not only socialism, but also reason and literature, have lost the power even to diagnose social ills, let alone remedy

[49] See Madison *Brecht Then and Now*. Ed. by John Willett. Wisconsin (MI): University of Wisconsin Press 1995. P. 31 (The Brecht Yearbook 20).

them. Kunert's scepticism is not final however, and in another poem of two years later he seems, nevertheless, to project some form of perhaps ambivalent regeneration. In "Des toten Dichters gedenkend" Brecht is once again pictured as a lonely relic of history, "[s]päter Gesandter von Zeiten, / die ich nicht erfuhr", whose context has abandoned him: "sein Land aber welkte indessen dahin / und verstarb ihm".[50]

> […] Er hat seinen letzten Irrtum
> gut vorbereitet: Die Unsterblichkeit
> im Blechsarg in berlinischer Erde.
> Aber manchmal auferstehen
> die Toten erneut
> mit fremder Miene und falscher Stimme
> wie jede Wiederkehr sich gewöhnlich vollzieht.

If Brecht's final mistake is ironically dubbed "immortality" this poem nevertheless insists interestingly on the notion of a revenant Brecht, even if that Brecht and his voice are almost unrecognizable.

It is not uncommon to find Brecht in recent poems as a trace, a disembodied voice, pointing to another context. Heinz Czechowski's "Ein Orkan des Vergessens" of 1998, for example, takes up the wind of Brecht's "Vom armen B.B.", coupled perhaps with an echo of Benjamin's "Engel der Geschichte", again from the *Thesen über den Begriff der Geschichte*, as a force of final confusion and destruction.[51]

> Ein Orkan des Vergessens
> Fegt durch die Zeit. Er schleudert
> Meine Papiere ins Nichts.

The poem calls on "das große Gedicht des kleinen B.B., das alles vorwegnahm" and although he cites "An die Nachgeborenen" explicitly elsewhere in the poem, Czechowski is surely thinking of "Vom armen B.B." This is indicated by that fact that when the poem concludes by turning to one of Czechowski's recurrent motifs, the destruction of Dresden, it introduces it with a quotation from the Brecht poem that suggests this is symptomatic of a larger destruction.

> Bleiben
> Wird davon nur

---

[50] Kunert: Des toten Dichters gedenkend. In: Günter Kunert: *Mein Golem*. München – Wien: Hanser 1996. P. 34.
[51] Walter Benjamin: Über den Begriff der Geschichte, These IX. WBGS 1.2. Pp. 691–704. Heinz Czechowski: Ein Orkan des Vergessens. In: Heinz Czechowski: *Mein westfälischer Frieden. Ein Zyklus 1996–1998*. Köln: Nyland 1998. Pp. 50–51.

Der Bericht der alten Bomberpilotin
Vom Anflug auf meine Heimatstadt,
Die endgültig und für immer
Im Feuer versank.

The return to the final part of "Vom armen B.B." is something of a leitmotif in recent work dedicated to Brecht and nowhere more than in Volker Braun's 1990 poem "O Chicago! O Widerspruch!" of May 1990.[52]

Brecht, ist Ihnen die Zigarre ausgegangen?
Bei den Erdbeben, die wir hervorriefen
In den auf Sand gebauten Staaten.
Der Sozialismus geht, und Johnny Walker kommt.
Ich kann ihn nicht an den Gedanken festhalten
Die ohnehin ausfallen. Die warmen Straßen
Des Oktober sind die kalten Wege
Der Wirtschaft, Horatio. Ich schiebe den Gum in die Backe
Es ist gekommen, das nicht Nennenswerte.

This poem offers a kind of post-apocalyptic response to Brecht's vision of future disaster. As such it is invested with all the "Bitterkeit" that the lyric subject in Brecht's poem was determined to avoid. The earthquake has come; the arrival of the "nicht Nennenswerte" implies the final erasure of the "leichtes Geschlechte", the "Vorläufige", of Brecht's poem. But if Brecht's poem offered a nihilistic vision on an existential scale, Braun counters it with a political one. Capitalism is the place of post-historical banality. Taking up the famous quotation from Act I, Scene 2 of Shakespeare's *Hamlet* – "Thrift, thrift, Horatio! The funeral baked-meats / Did coldly furnish for the marriage tables" – , Braun cunningly offsets the warm streets of past hopes with the cold paths of present reality.[53]

Heiner Müller, himself a "classic" of the GDR, goes further. In one of the many late texts in which he takes up Brecht, he identifies himself with Brecht's disappearance.[54]

Aber von mir werden sie sagen Er
Hat Vorschläge gemacht Wir haben sie
Nicht angenommen Warum sollten wir
Und das soll stehn auf meinem Grabstein und
Die Vögel sollen darauf scheißen und

---

[52] Volker Braun: O Chicago! O Widerspruch!. In: Braun: *Texte in zeitlicher Folge* (n. 8). Vol. 10. P. 51.

[53] On this poem see also Reinhold Grimm: Around and After the "Wende": Five Representative Poems. In: *Neohelicon* 28 (2001). No. 1. Pp. 195–211.

[54] From Heiner Müller: *Germania 3: Gespenster am toten Mann*. In: Heiner Müller: *Werke*.Frankfurt am Main: Suhrkamp 2002. Vol. 5. P. 288.

Das Gras soll wachsen über meinen Namen
Der auf dem Grabstein steht Vergessen sein
Will ich von allen eine Spur im Sand.

Apparently acquiescing in his own oblivion, the lyric subject of Müller's poem voices lines from Brecht's "Ich benötige keinen Grabstein" for himself and offers the answers of the disaffected present. And, in a final return to the starting point of this essay, the lyric subject asks that his grave stone be one dedicated to forgetting. Of course this poem gains an added poignancy from our knowledge of Müller's own final illness, during which this was written, and also of his own monument in the "Dorotheenstadtfriedhof", designed to disappear into rust. But, characteristically for Müller, it also gains added irony when one remembers that, in transforming Brecht's words Müller is in fact not obliterating himself, but inserting himself in a tradition which lives on both by responding to Brecht, and by looking forward to its own posterity. It can perhaps be likened to the gesture of the photograph of the author being torn up in his play *Die Hamletmaschine*.

Since 1990, then, it would seem that the desire to portray or to address Brecht is as strong as ever, if not, indeed, more so. On the one hand, it might look as if Brecht the person should now be able to re-emerge from behind the legend of what he represents. Nevertheless, it is noteworthy that even while addressing themselves to his relationships or the stations of his life, poets are also still addressing him in exemplary fashion. He is still being used to explore questions of politics or aesthetics, and the role of poetry more broadly. To be sure, while some, especially younger, poets have discovered the power of his work for their own times, many poems, especially by older poets who have seen his hopes fail, are written in a spirit of rejection, criticism or disappointment. They proclaim the metaphorical death of the legacy along with the literal death of the poet. A strange kind of presence in absence is in operation – as well as a slightly quirky strand in a tradition of "poetry of mourning": something that has attracted increased critical attention in recent years.[55] Yet it is clear that while poets set about the outward business of forgetting, they are still addressing, citing and responding to the work in complex ways. Like Müller with that "Spur im Sand", the poems are also exercises in remembering, signs which remains against the odds, to make absence legible.

[55] See for example Jahan Ramazani: *Poetry of Mourning: The Modern Elegy from Hardy to Heaney*. Chicago – London: University of Chicago Press 1994.

Martin Brady

Brecht in Brechtian Cinema

This essay examines an aspect of Brechtian cinema which has been passed over by scholarship to date: the direct quotation of Brecht in Brechtian films as a signal of allegiance to a particular kind of anti-illusionistic, politically engaged filmmaking. Focusing on selected films of Jean-Luc Godard, Alexander Kluge and Jean-Marie Straub/Danièle Huillet, the function and significance of these quotations and expropriations is considered. A shift from aesthetic to political allegiance can be dated to around 1968, culminating in two overtly polemical films from 1972: Godard's Tout va bien *and Straub-Huillet's* Einleitung zu Arnold Schoenbergs Begleitmusik für eine Lichtspielscene. *In conclusion it is noted that a "double gesture" – the adoption of a Brechtian critical method and the direct citation of the author – goes hand-in-hand with an overtly didactic approach; and this means that these examples of "hardline" Brechtian filmmaking are also primers of one kind or another.*

1

In recent years both Brecht's involvement with and his influence on film have begun to receive the critical attention they deserve. Wolfgang Gersch's landmark book *Film bei Brecht*, published in 1975, remains the standard work in charting Brecht's own turbulent relationship with the film industry – from his productive collaborations with Karl Valentin (*Mysterien eines Frisiersalons*, 1923) and Slatan Dudow (*Kuhle Wampe oder Wem gehört die Welt?*, 1932) through the *Dreigroschenprozeß* to the frustrations in Hollywood (with Fritz Lang) and the GDR (with Wolfgang Staudte).[1]

Brechtian cinema has also been examined in numerous articles and essays, although a comprehensive study remains to be written.[2] Of particular note here are a number of detailed and searching studies of the filmmakers whose work is most frequently labelled "Brechtian" – co-directors Jean-Marie Straub

---

[1] Wolfgang Gersch: *Film bei Brecht: Bertolt Brechts praktische und theoretische Auseinandersetzung mit Film*. Berlin: Henschel 1975. The issue of *Screen* devoted to "Brecht and Revolutionary Cinema" also played an important role in stimulating debate about Brechtian film (*Screen* 15 (1974). No. 2. Pp. 4–128). See also note 10 below.

[2] See, for example, Roswitha Mueller: Brecht the realist, and New German Cinema. In: *Framework* 25 (1984). Pp. 42–51; Sylvia Harvey: Whose Brecht? Memories for the Eighties: A Critical Recovery. In: *Screen* 23 (1982). No. 1. Pp. 45–59; Martin Brady: Brecht and Film. In: *The Cambridge Companion to Brecht*. Ed. by Peter Thomson and Glendyr Sacks. Cambridge – New York: Cambridge University Press 2006. Pp. 297–317.

and Danièle Huillet.[3] Indeed the first of their two Brecht adaptations, *Geschichtsunterricht* (1972) based on *Die Geschäfte des Herrn Julius Caesar*, has probably been the subject of more critical study than any other single Brechtian film.[4]

2

What has undoubtedly made *Geschichtsunterricht* a canonical film is the simple fact that it is as Brechtian in its style as it is in its source material; it is, according to Karsten Witte, "jener Film in der langen Reihe mißglückter Brechtverfilmungen, die Brechts Vorstellungen [...] am nächsten kommt".[5] Martin Walsh, in a stimulating analysis, concludes that "just as Brecht liberates us from the normative image of Caesar, so Straub-Huillet free us from the visual/aural chains of cinematic illusionism" – "it is a pity [Brecht] never lived to see *History Lessons*".[6] *Geschichtsunterricht* is in many ways, and consciously at that, the model Brechtian film, and it served for some years as a yardstick against which other leftist "counter-cinema" films were measured.

Its much-vaunted antagonism to "visual pleasure and narrative cinema"[7] highlights an important characteristic of Brechtian film which distinguishes it profoundly from Brecht's own Epic Theatre and, in the case of *Kuhle Wampe*, his Epic Cinema. Brechtian cinema, during its prime in the '60s and '70s, was generally cerebral, experimental and, despite protestations to the contrary by its

---

[3] These include: Richard Roud: *Jean-Marie Straub*. London: Secker and Warburg in association with the British Film Institute 1971; Martin Walsh: *The Brechtian Aspect of Radical Cinema*. London: BFI Publishing 1981; Barton Byg: *Landscapes of Resistance: The German Films of Danièle Huillet and Jean-Marie Straub*. Berkeley – Los Angeles – London: University of California Press 1995.

[4] See especially: Gilberto Perez: The Modernist Cinema: The History Lessons of Straub and Huillet. In: *The Cinema of Jean-Marie Straub and Daniele Huillet [sic]*. Ed. by Jonathan Rosenbaum. New York: The Public Theatre 1982. Pp. 9–14; Maureen Turim: Textuality and Theatricality in Brecht and Straub-Huillet: *History Lessons* (1972). In: *German Film and Literature: Adaptations and Transformations*. Ed. by Eric Rentschler. New York – London: Methuen 1986. Pp. 231–245. See also the second Brecht issue of *Screen* 16 (1975/76) No. 4. Other films of Straub-Huillet that have received particular attention include the *Billard um halbzehn* adaptation *Nicht versöhnt oder Es hilft nur Gewalt wo Gewalt herrscht* (1965), the Schönberg film *Moses und Aron* (1975) and *Klassenverhältnisse* (1983), their adaptation of Kafka's *Der Verschollene*.

[5] Karsten Witte: Jean-Marie Straub/Danièle Huillet: Kommentierte Filmografie. In: *Herzog/Kluge/Straub*. Ed. by Peter W. Jansen and Wolfram Schütte. München – Wien: Hanser 1976. P. 194.

[6] Walsh: *The Brechtian Aspect of Radical Cinema* (n. 3). P. 71 and p. 61.

[7] The debates about Brechtian cinema in *Screen* magazine coincided productively with the controversy following the publication of Laura Mulvey's seminal article "Visual Pleasure and Narrative Cinema" in: *Screen* 16 (1975). No. 3. Nr. 3. Pp. 6–18.

adherents, distinctly highbrow. It tended to engage, as Thomas Elsaesser puts it, in "rethinking the question of pleasure and spectacle, developing filmic modes of spectatorial distanciation, and exploring the politics of a representational form such as cinema".[8] Roswitha Mueller has pointed out that in the battle against cinematic illusionism a filmmaker like Godard was able to marshal an arsenal of devices:

> the play with contradictory elements, the stylized, emblematic use of codes, an emphasis on the autonomy of separate and heterogeneous elements, the interruption of the cinematic flow by the written word and by visual, auditory, or verbal commentary; there is the transgression of genre divisions, mixing fictional, documentary, and cinéma vérité approaches in the same film. And finally [...] a complex web of cross-references and quotations taken from literary, visual, and auditory sources.[9]

All of these weapons have been employed, at one time or another, by the German and French filmmakers whose films I will be discussing here: Jean-Luc Godard, Alexander Kluge, Jean-Marie Straub and Danièle Huillet. Together they constitute what might be termed the "hardcore" of political modernist cinema – the Brechtian faction of Peter Wollen's famous "Two Avant-Gardes".[10]

3

As indicated above, the films of these hardcore directors have been the object of detailed analysis, and it is not the intention of this essay to add to this substantial body of scholarship. I will also not be examining the characteristics of Brechtian film *per se*, adaptations (Brechtian or otherwise) of his texts, or the phenomenon of "post-Brechtian cinema", that is the deployment of Brechtian devices in films which no longer adhere to the principles or ideology of leftist political modernism.[11]

Rather, the aim is to examine the phenomenon of which Straub-Huillet's *Geschichtsunterricht* is, perhaps, the paradigmatic text – the appropriation of

---

[8] Thomas Elsaesser: From anti-illusionism to hyper-realism: Bertolt Brecht and contemporary film. In: *Re-interpreting Brecht: His Influence on Contemporary Drama and Film.* Ed. by Pia Kleber and Colin Visser. Cambridge: Cambridge University Press 1990. Pp. 170–185. Here p. 170.

[9] Roswitha Mueller: *Bertolt Brecht and the Theory of Media.* Lincoln (NE) – London: University of Nebraska Press 1989. P. 105.

[10] Peter Wollen: The Two Avant-Gardes. In: Peter Wollen: *Readings and Writings: Semiotic Counter-Strategies.* London: Verso and NLB 1982. Pp. 92–104.

[11] The films of Straub-Huillet aside, there are very few adaptations of Brecht's plays that would qualify as Brechtian in the sense in which the term has now come to be accepted. This certainly applies to the various Berliner Ensemble recordings of Brecht productions. Examples of "post-Brechtian" films include Michael Verhoeven's *Das schreckliche Mädchen* (1988) and Lars von Trier's *Dogville* (2003).

Brecht's own words as a gesture (or gest) of allegiance to a particular kind of critical, self-reflexive, anti-illusionistic auteurism: the quoting of Brecht in Brechtian film. This phenomenon has not, to date, been examined in any of the studies of Brechtian film.[12]

The aim of this brief survey is also, and obviously, not to be comprehensive, but simply to identify instances of a tendency to allude to Brecht – if only in passing – as a sign of fidelity. It is for this reason also that I restrict myself to those filmmakers who are already universally held to be Brechtian, and who have, at one time or another, expressed an allegiance to Brecht's critical method.

4

Exemplary in the present context is the citation – recitation indeed – of a Brecht poem in Godard's early film Le Mépris (1963). This famous scene, appropriately enough set in a cinema, has the ageing Fritz Lang declaim (in French) Brecht's 1942 poem Hollywood to an uncomprehending Brigitte Bardot – delivering BB to BB so-to-speak. This brief episode is typically Godardian, indeed typical of Brechtian cinema, in its erudite set of allusions. Lang's rather melancholy tone is, for the knowledgeable spectator at least, poignantly at odds with the historically verifiable fact of the two men's acrimonious parting of the ways over Hangmen Also Die (1942). Brecht's admission of his sell-out in peddling lies in the Hollywood marketplace is put into the mouth of a former adversary, who – not least in referring to Brecht by name – is positioned somewhat uncomfortably between his role as "Fritz Lang" the fictional director of The Odyssey in Godard's story, and the cinematic legend Fritz Lang outside it. That Godard's allegiance at this time is to Brecht's anti-illusionism, rather than the kind of historical costume-drama being shot by the fictional Lang, goes almost without saying. Godard's interest in Lang and his films is also well documented, however, from the hour-long dialogue in eight parts with the ageing director in 1967, Le dinosaure et le bébé,[13] through to Histoire(s) du cinéma (1989–1998).[14]

[12] To cite an example: it comes as something of a surprise to note that in the substantial collection of essays Forever Godard (ed. by Michael Temple, James S. Williams, Michael Witt. London: Black Dog 2004) there is, if the index is to be trusted, no mention of Brecht in any of the contributions.

[13] Released on DVD by Criterion in 2002 as an extra on their two-disc set of Contempt.

[14] In Chapter 1A Lang's Die Nibelungen is juxtaposed with quotations from, amongst others, Bresson, Chaplin and Fassbinder (Lili Marleen). See: Leslie Hill: "A form that thinks": Godard, Blanchot, Citation. In: Temple et als. (eds.): Forever Godard (n. 12). Pp. 396–416. Here p. 412.

5

Le Mépris is a symptom of what Bernard Dort in 1960 had characterized in *Cahiers du Cinéma* as a "Brecht epidemic" in the French New Wave.[15] During this outbreak Brecht becomes a shorthand for the kind of "breaks with illusionism, with the unified plot and its compelling identificatory structure" catalogued by Roswitha Mueller.[16] Godard himself, for example, claimed that "Brecht is serious" and, more specifically, that *Vivre sa vie* (*It's My Life/My Life to Live*, 1962) was a "Brechtian" film.[17] As Stephen Heath concludes in his *Screen* article surveying Godard's output through to the mid-'70s, "the reference to Brecht often seems to play the major theoretical role for Godard – more so than, say, the reference to Vertov".[18]

Godard begins one of the masterpieces of this period, *Deux ou trois choses que je sais d'elle* (1967), with an epigraphic reference to "Père Brecht". Following the opening titles and four brief shots of modern Paris (the "elle" of the title), the film opens with a close-up of a woman high up on a tower block whilst a voice-over narration (whispered, very recognizably, by Godard himself) introduces her as the actress Marina Vlady, "d'origine russe", and describes her appearance. Her first words, directly to camera, are: "Oui, parler comme des citations de vérité. C'est le Père Brecht qui disait ça. Que les acteurs doivent citer". The voice-over then informs us that she is turning her head to the right, which we can plainly see, adding that "ça n'a pas d'importance". This is followed by a cut and a reframing of Vlady. This time Godard introduces her as Juliette Janson, the character she plays in the film (again, however, "d'origine russe"). This time she turns her head to the left, and again we are told that "ça n'a pas d'importance".

Subsequently, throughout the film, Vlady does indeed speak flatly, as if reciting a text which is not her own. This was in fact the case, as she was fed her text by Godard, line by line, during the shoot. What we have here is a straightforward, and lightheartedly signalled reference to one of the most famous dicta of Epic Theatre: "Das *Zitieren*. Anstatt den Eindruck hervorrufen zu wollen, er improvisiere, soll der Schauspieler lieber zeigen, was die

---

[15] Bernard Dort: Towards a Brechtian Criticism of Cinema. In: *Cahiers du Cinéma 2. 1960–1969: New Wave, New Cinema, Re-evaluating Hollywood*. Ed. by Jim Hiller. London: Routledge Kegan Paul/BFI 1986. Pp. 236–247. Here p. 236. For a detailed account of the reception of Brecht in French film criticism of this period see: George Lellis: *Bertolt Brecht, Cahiers du Cinéma and Contemporary Film Theory*. Epping: Bowker 1982.

[16] Mueller: *Bertolt Brecht and the Theory of Media* (n. 9). P. 105.

[17] Quoted in: *Godard on Godard*. Ed. by Jean Narboni and Tom Milne. New York: Da Capo 1986. Pp. 192 and 187.

[18] Stephen Heath: From Brecht to Film: Theses, Problems (on *History Lessons* and *Dear Summer Sister*). In: *Screen* 16 (1975/76). No. 4. Pp. 34–45. Here p. 34.

Wahrheit ist: er zitiert".[19] It is this axiom which Straub-Huillet had already quoted verbatim as an epigraph to *Nicht versöhnt*, their adaptation of Heinrich Böll's *Billard um halbzehn*.[20]

6

Towards the end of his pre-'68 appropriation of Brecht, Godard begins to be more explicit about his political affiliation with the writer. This is particularly evident in what is perhaps the most iconic reference to Brecht in any Godard film, indeed in any Brechtian film: the blackboard scene in *La Chinoise* (1967). This film, one of Godard's last before his rejection of "bourgeois" filmmaking and his establishment, with Jean-Pierre Gorin, of the activist film-making collective Groupe Dziga Vertov, is an agitational "comedy thriller" which tells the story of a group of young people who set up a Maoist cell in Paris to discuss Marxism and to translate revolutionary theory into practice. There are at least five explicit references to Brecht in the film: he is, for example, lauded, along with Shakespeare, as a dramatist of "un vrai théâtre", a Strehler production of Brecht in Milan is singled out for particular praise (via Althusser), and the early film pioneer Georges Méliès is lauded as a "Brechtian" director. In the "blackboard scene", finally, a role-call of canonical writers, including Dumas, Sartre, Sophocles, Voltaire, Albee, Cocteau, Aeschylus, Goethe, Pinter, Feydeau, Schiller, Chekhov, Duras, Goldoni, Marlowe, Giraudoux, Corneille, Calderon, Claudel, Genet and Racine, is erased one-by-one with a damp cloth, leaving "Brecht" standing alone and proud at the centre of a tabula rasa of Western culture.

In *La Chinoise* Brecht is exalted as a revolutionary dramatist and ever-present as an inspiration for the film's *mise-en-scène* (with its titles, fragmentation, songs, commentaries and so on). Here, more perhaps than in any other film by Godard, we have a correspondence of aesthetic appropriation and political allegiance.

7

It is only with Godard's Marxist Groupe Dziga Vertov films, though, from 1968 to 1972, that Brecht texts are themselves appropriated as direct source material.

---

[19] Bertolt Brecht: *Anweisungen an die Schauspieler*. BFA 22. Pp. 667–668. Here p. 668.
[20] Cross referencing between Brechtian films would make another interesting, if rather erudite, object of study. Godard has on a number of occasions, for example, cited Straub-Huillet: there is a comic reference to their first *Empedokles* film (*Der Tod des Empedokles oder: Wenn dann der Erde Grün von neuem euch erglänzt*, 1986) in *Hélas pour moi* (1993), and – more recently still – the final line of their third Schönberg adaptation, *Von heute auf morgen* (1997), "Mama, was sind das, moderne Menschen?", is heard on the soundtrack of *The Old Place* (1999), co-directed by Godard and Anne-Marie Miéville.

These include the *Buch der Wendungen (Me-Ti)* which, according to Julia Lesage (who discussed Brecht with Godard in 1973), "provided the sound track for both *Pravda* and *Vladimir and Rosa*".[21] However, given the current unavailability of the earlier Groupe Dziga Vertov films,[22] I shall restrict my comments here to the final and most well-known Godard/Gorin collaboration, *Tout va bien* (1972), "starring" Jane Fonda as a reporter and Yves Montand as a disillusioned auteurist filmmaker who has resorted to shooting commercials for a living.

This story of a strike in a meat factory, during the course of which the workers take the boss captive, *Tout va bien* is at times almost doctrinally Epic in its staging, with a remarkable set in which the factory building is opened up along the length of its fourth wall so that action in adjacent rooms, both horizontally and vertically, can be viewed simultaneously, often in tableau form. The resulting composition is strikingly reminiscent of the 1927 Piscator-Bühne production of *Hoppla, wir leben!*.[23] Again, as in *La Chinoise* and elsewhere, Godard musters a full range of *V-Effekte*: fragmented narrative, titles, lacunae, songs, mechanical delivery, address to camera, inserts of documentary footage, voice-over commentary. It comes as no surprise, therefore, that at one point Montand, reflecting – as Godard's mouthpiece – on the current crisis of political cinema, claims that he has rediscovered methods that Brecht had come up with forty years previously: "Vous avez lu la préface qu'il a écrit pour *Mahagonny*? C'est fantastique, non?".[24] Towards the end of the film, still tormented with self-doubt,

[21] Julia Lesage: Godard and Gorin's Left Politics, 1967–72. In: *Jump Cut* 28 (1983). Pp. 51–58. Here p. 54. Examination of the scripts to these films, published in *Cahiers du Cinèma*, would suggest that this claim is exaggerated. Lesage also wrote a PhD dissertation on "The Films of Jean-Luc Godard and Their Use of Brechtian Dramatic Theory" (Indiana University: unpublished 1976). Lesage's substantial essay on Godard and Gorin is one of a series of articles on Brechtian cinema published in *Jump Cut*. These include: Alan Lovell: Epic Theatre and Counter-Cinema's Principles. In: *Jump Cut* 27 (1982). Pp. 64–68; Alan Lovell: Epic Theatre and Counter Cinema. In: *Jump Cut* 28 (1983). Pp. 49–51.

[22] All of Godard's films both long and short – at the time over 80 – were screened in Summer 2001 at the National Film Theatre and Tate Modern. Unfortunately the lesser known have not been seen again since in Britain. Similarly, many of Straub-Huillet's films have not been in distribution in recent years. Kluge has also been poorly served by distribution in this country, and some of his films – like the later works of Straub-Huillet – are still awaiting their first screenings. Aside from a number of Japanese DVD releases, the films of Straub-Huillet are unavailable commercially. Kluge's cinema and television work is being released on DVD (with English subtitles) by Edition filmmuseum.

[23] Alan Lovell also sees parallels to Joan Littlewood and Roger Planchon. Lovell: Epic Theatre and Counter Cinema (n. 21). P. 49.

[24] In the light of this reference *Cahiers du Cinéma* published a translation of the entire text in 1972: Bertolt Brecht: Notes sur l'opéra *Grandeur et décadence de la ville de Mahagonny*. In: *Cahiers du Cinéma* 238/239 (1972). Pp. 28–32. The French translation of the title of the Brecht/Weill piece suggests there may be an allusion to it in Godard's 1986 film *Grandeur et décadence d'un petit commerce de cinema* (a.k.a. *Chantons en choeur*).

he proclaims his aim as a filmmaker to be "trouver des formes nouvelles pour un contenu nouveau" – a neat resumé of the programme of Brechtian film-making at the time. In the film's concluding voice-over there is also a striking parallel to Brecht's *Buch der Wendungen*.

As Fonda and Montand are reunited in a café in Paris, four years after the events of 1968, the commentary tells us that "on dira simplement que lui et elle, ils ont commencé à se penser historiquement. Puisse chacun être son propre historien. […] Alors ils vivra avec plus de soin et d'exigence". In " Über die historische Selbstbetrachtung" Me-Ti recommends "dem einzelnen nach vielem Nachdenken, sich selber ebenso wie die Klassen und großen Menschengruppen historisch zu betrachten und sich historisch zu benehmen".[25] Without wishing to identify a specific, direct source for Godard's and Gorin's script here, the affinity with Brecht is manifest. In an interview with *Le Monde*, Gorin described the film's interweaving of fiction and "reality" as a new kind of realism: "but it's neither critical realism nor socialist realism […] we've gone into a new type of realism, closer to Brechtian theory".[26] What is notable, again, is that the film both employs Brecht's didactic method and signals the fact explicitly.

8

Tout va bien and its pendant *Letter to Jane* (1972) – a sustained assault on Jane Fonda which, in its deconstruction of press photography, bears more than a passing resemblance to the *Kriegsfibel* – mark a decisive turning point in Godard's career, after which he moves away from polemical, agitational film-making to a more reflective, detached and at times melancholic approach. As a footnote to what has been said above, it is therefore perhaps surprising that here too, after 1972, we find a further reference to Brecht, albeit a passing one. In episode 2A of Godard/Miéville's 6-part experimental television series *Six fois deux – sur et sous la communication*, entitled "Leçons des choses", Godard's lugubrious voice-over ruminates over the relationship between objects, images, nomination and the issue of change. As he consumes his one-hundred-and-twenty-third cup of coffee, Godard recalls, and accurately paraphrases, Brecht's poem "Der Radwechsel" (BFA 12. P. 310). The contemplative, aphoristic tone of some of Brecht's later poetry, in particular the *Buckower Elegien*, corresponds very closely to the spirit of the video collaborations of Godard and Miéville, making this allusion to Brecht yet another signal of kinship, albeit one of maturity and reflection rather than of revolutionary zeal.

---

[25] Bertolt Brecht: *Buch der Wendungen*. BFA 18. Pp. 45–194. Here p. 188.
[26] Quoted in Lesage: Godard and Gorin (n. 21). P. 55. The interview, with Martin Evan, was published in *Le Monde* on 27 April 1972 (p. 17). Lesage concludes that at this time it was "Gorin who strove to bring out the films' explicitly Brechtian element" (ibid. p. 54).

9

In the debut feature film of Alexander Kluge, author of the *Oberhausener Manifest* and often dubbed the "Godard of the New German Cinema", a comparably aphoristic text is used to witty effect. *Abschied von gestern* (1966) is unmistakably Brechtian in its structure, narrative, montage, performances and in a panoply of estrangement devices (again titles, fragmentation, commentary, inserts, the dialectical employment of music, direct address to camera and the like). The scene in which the Brecht text appears is, conversely, a relatively straightforward and lighthearted one. The film's protagonist, homeless and unemployed GDR-refugee Anita G., played by Kluge's sister Alexandra, has been taken in by the pompous politician Pichota (Günther Mack). He attempts to better (and seduce) her by introducing her to the delights of Nietzsche, Verdi's *Don Carlos* and, in this instance, Brecht's *Keunergeschichten*: "Wenn Pichota ihr schon nicht helfen kann, will er sie wenigstens erziehen" we are told in an intertitle. Adopting the role of patient teacher, he encourages her to unravel the paradox of Brecht's infamous "Wenn Herr K einen Menschen liebte", the anecdote which has on occasion been (mis)used to demonstrate Brecht's supposed "Parteidisziplin und Inhumanität", even in matters of the heart.[27] Like many a student before and since, she is unable to get her head round Brecht's riddle, and her embarrassment is palpable. The film critic Enno Patalas also seems to have had trouble interpreting Keuner's notion of reciprocal productivity in anything other than doctrinaire terms, as his commentary on this scene in a very perceptive review of the film demonstrates:

> Wenn Alexandra-Anita auf die Keunergeschichte, die Mack-Pichota ihr erzählt, so reagiert, wie sie das tut, so äußert sich darin eine andere, weniger utopische Humanität als die Brechts. Brecht wird dialektisch korrigiert durch Alexandra-Anita, die sich dagegen wehrt, daß man einen Menschen, den man liebt, nach einem selbst-verfertigten Entwurf modeln solle. Genau genommen, wird damit nicht Brecht, nichtmal Herr K., korrigiert, sondern der bundesdeutsche Ministerialrat, der die Keunerthese sich zur eigenen macht; wie er sie liest, deutschen Idealismus in der Stimme, offenbart sich die Inhumanität eines zur Ideologie verkommenen Engagements. [...] So korrigiert die Szene die Keunergeschichte doppelt: durch die praktische Menschlichkeit, die die Darstellerin der Anita, und durch die Erziehung der deutschen Schauspielschule, die der Darsteller des Pichota offenbart.[28]

What is striking here is the attention paid to this short scene by Patalas – it takes up a disproportionately large part of his review; the reference to Brecht,

---

[27] Cf. Jan Knopf: *Brecht-Handbuch: Lyrik, Prosa, Schriften*. Stuttgart: Metzler 1986. P. 320.
[28] Enno Patalas: Abschied von gestern (Anita G.). In: *Filmkritik* 10 (1966). H. 11. Pp. 623–625. Here Pp. 624–625.

with its comic solemnity, is clearly taken as an invitation to grapple with the status of the master himself a decade after his death. Irrespective of how the scene in *Abschied von gestern* is interpreted, and it is apparent that Patalas is himself uncertain as to whether Kluge is taking Brecht to task or not, there is a clear parallel here to Godard: again we have the "double gesture" – the Brechtian *mise-en-scène* of the film as a whole and the direct citation of the author. It is this double gest(ure) which was to become axiomatic in the work of Jean-Marie Straub and Danièle Huillet.

10

Nicht versöhnt oder Es hilft nur Gewalt wo Gewalt herrscht (1965) is Straub-Huillet's second film, and their first to cite Brecht, opening as it does with the lines from the *Anweisungen an die Schauspieler* quoted above. The film's unwieldy title is, of course, also an allusion to Brecht – to Johanna Dark's final speech in *Die heilige Johanna der Schlachthöfe*, in which she famously asserts that "Es hilft nur Gewalt, wo Gewalt herrscht, und / Es helfen nur Menschen wo Menschen sind".[29] Whilst there is no connection drawn in Böll's novel between his protagonist Johanna and Brecht's Johanna Dark (or indeed Die heilige Johanna), there is a neatness to the parallel which Straub-Huillet exploit in politicizing the novel and translating it into a call for revolutionary action – "es lebe das Dynamit" as Johanna's grandson puts it towards the end of the film.[30]

It is perhaps the performance of the non-professional actress Martha Ständner as the gun-toting Johanna which is also the most explicitly "citational". On Straub-Huillet's instructions, Ständner – a neighbour who had never acted on film before – takes Brecht's dictum entirely literally, and delivers her lines in a flatly monotonous tone which Gilles Deleuze characterizes as a "schizophrenic" speech-act "placed cross-wise over all the visual images it crosses".[31] In an interview with Geoffrey Nowell-Smith, Straub refers to the Brechtian quality of Ständner's performance: "sometimes it becomes an epic text in the Brechtian sense, like with the old lady".[32]

It is worth noting in passing that there are other, less explicit Brecht sources in *Nicht versöhnt*; for example, the huddle of scheming politicians against which Johanna's symbolic act of violence is directed was suggested, according

---

[29] Bertolt Brecht: *Die heilige Johanna der Schlachthöfe*. BFA 3. Pp.137–234. Here p. 224.
[30] For a discussion of the significance of Brecht's play for Straub-Huillet, see Byg: *Landscapes of Resistance* (n. 3). Pp. 24–25.
[31] Gilles Deleuze: *Cinema 2: The Time-Image*. London – New York: Continuum 2005. P. 244.
[32] Geoffrey Nowell-Smith: After *Othon*, before *History Lessons*: Geoffrey Nowell-Smith talks to Jean-Marie Straub and Danièle Huillet. In: *Enthusiasm* 1 (1975). Pp. 26–31. Here p. 26.

to Straub, by the gangsters in *Arturo Ui*.[33] Moreover, although there are indeed no direct Brecht sources for the pendant to *Nicht versöhnt*, their debut short *Machorka-Muff* (1962), an adaptation of Böll's short story *Hauptstädtisches Journal*, Straub did evoke him in a text accompanying that film: "What does it mean to make films in Germany, or rather, to make films against that stupidity, depravity, and that mental laziness which, as Brecht remarked, are so characteristic of this country".[34]

Critics were quick to spot the indebtedness to Brecht in Straub-Huillet's films, an allegiance consolidated over time by their adaptations of the Julius Caesar novel and, in 1992, of Brecht's *Antigone*.[35] Their approach remains, as Kaes puts it in reference to the incorporation of documentary archive footage in *Nicht versöhnt*, "in keeping with Brecht's theory of the epic theatre".[36]

11

The final film that I wish to consider in the context of what I have termed the "double gesture" of allegiance to Brecht, is Straub-Huillet's most overtly propagandistic film, *Einleitung zu Arnold Schoenbergs Begleitmusik zu einer Lichtspielscene* (1972). Commissioned by Südwestfunk as a "setting" of Schoenberg's score (which is heard in its entirety on the soundtrack), it is a 16-minute short combining texts by Schoenberg and Brecht with on-screen commentary from Straub, documentary archive footage (of B-52 bombers dropping bombs on Vietnam), photographs (of Schoenberg, of a painted self-portrait of the composer, and of the dead French communards of 1871) and newspaper clippings (reporting the acquittal of two concentration camp architects) into an indictment of imperialism in general and the American involvement in Vietnam in particular.

Schoenberg's text, which takes up the majority of the film, is taken from the famous letters of 20 April and 4 May 1923 to Kandinsky, in which he accuses the painter, in no uncertain terms, of anti-Semitism. The much shorter Brecht text is a quotation from *Fünf Schwierigkeiten beim Schreiben der Wahrheit*,

---

[33] Michel Delahaye: Entretien avec J.-M. Straub. In: *Cahiers du Cinéma* 180 (1966). Pp. 52–57. Here p. 55. In an interview in 1966 Straub listed an adaptation of Brecht's *Die Maßnahme* amongst their future film projects (Jean-Marie Straub: Gespräch mit Jean-Marie Straub. In: *Filmstudio* 48 (1966). Pp. 2–10. Here p. 10).

[34] Quoted in Roud: *Jean-Marie Straub* (n. 3). P. 29.

[35] The film's full title is *Die Antigone des Sophocles nach der hölderlinschen Übertragung für die Bühne bearbeitet von Brecht 1948 (Suhrkamp Verlag)*. As an adaptation of a full Brecht text this film also falls outside the scope of this discussion. For a stimulating analysis of the film see Byg: *Landscapes of Resistance* (n. 3). Pp. 215–232. He notes, in passing, that "Straub has recently distanced himself somewhat from the Brecht quotation at the outset of *Not Reconciled*" (ibid. p. 224).

[36] Anton Kaes: *From "Hitler" to "Heimat": The Return of History as Film*. Cambridge (MA) – London: Harvard University Press 1989. P. 119.

published in December 1934 in the journal *Unsere Zeit*; the extracts are from the third section, "Die Kunst, die Wahrheit handhabbar zu machen als eine Waffe".[37] Both the Schoenberg and Brecht texts are read to camera in a recording studio of Südwestfunk (by Günter Peter Straschek and Peter Nestler respectively), although the first sentence of Brecht's remarks on the relationship between fascism and capitalism is spoken by Danièle Huillet, directly to camera, in a domestic interior. Unusually for Straub-Huillet, but in line with the didactic tone of this "agitational"[38] film, the author is named:

> Aber, fragt Brecht,[39] wie will nun jemand die Wahrheit über den Faschismus sagen, gegen den er ist, wenn er nichts gegen den Kapitalismus sagen will, der ihn hervorbringt. Wie soll da seine Wahrheit praktikabel ausfallen?

Brecht's text serves a dual purpose. It not only functions as an indictment of American aggression in Vietnam, immediately followed as it is by the B-52s, but also serves, within the rhetorical structure of the film itself, to justify the controversial juxtaposition of US imperialism and National Socialism which follows on from the recitation by Nestler. Accordingly, in line with Brecht's subtitle, "truth" is a weapon, and so is the film: "Der Text von Schönberg und der Text von Brecht sind eingeschlossen in die Bewegung des Films, aus der sich die Kritik, die der Film darstellt, entfaltet".[40] As Barton Byg puts it, "the process of quoting merges with the process of filmmaking".[41]

12

Brecht's fondness for quotation, together with the rather more controversial activity of plagiarism, is well documented – "Wie man weiß, gehört meiner

---

[37] For the Brecht text see BFA 22. P. 78. The script to the film appeared in *Filmkritik*, 17 (1973) H. 2. Pp. 80–87. There is a single cut in the passage – the words "Sie sind zufriedenzustellen, wenn der Metzger die Hände wäscht, bevor er das Fleisch aufträgt" are omitted – and this coincides with a change in framing of Nestler from shot 16 to 17.

[38] In interview Straub explained his own presence as narrator in the film as follows: "And because it was so aggressive and went to the limits and we wanted to make an agitational film for the first time, I wanted the responsibility to be clear, that it is us who make it, as persons, and that it is not coming out of the air. And I wanted to be the announcer. I thought it would be better to have one who speaks German badly, with bad accent and pronunciation, so one doesn't have the usual announcer-German at the beginning, so I thought that could be better if I did it and besides, I am the man who made the film". Andi Engel, Danièle Huillet and Jean-Marie Straub: Andi Engel talks to Jean-Marie Straub, and Danièle Huillet is there too. In: *Enthusiasm* 1 (1975). Pp. 1–25. Here p. 19.

[39] Whilst speaking she strokes a cat sitting on her knee. See Serge Daney: Un tombeau pour l'œil. In: *Cahiers du Cinéma* 258/259 (1975). Pp. 27–35. Here p. 29.

[40] Peter Nau: Drohende Gefahr, Angst, Katastrophe. In: *Filmkritik* 22 (1978). H. 3. Pp. 138–145. Here p. 143.

[41] Byg: *Landscapes of Resistance* (n. 3). P. 161.

Ansicht nach die Plagiierkunst zum Handwerk des Schriftstellers" (BFA 21.1.
P. 399). "Gerade die Neuerer", he claims elsewhere, "werden Expropriierungen
vornehmen, Plagiate begehen",[42] and the eighth of the "Ziele der Gesellschaft
der Dialektiker" is the "Bereitstellung der Zitate. Lehre des Zitierens".[43] In the
spirit of the master, the Brechtian filmmakers of the French and German New
Waves discussed here are enthusiastic expropriators, experts in what Kluge and
Oskar Negt term "Zitatkunst".[44]

As noted at the outset of this essay, the impact of Brecht's dramatic theory on
auteurist film – on its *mise-en-scène*, vertical and horizontal montage, hetero-
geneity of material and register, performances, delivery and so forth – is well
recognized. Indeed it might be argued that this is where Brecht's most fertile
legacy is to be found; Joachim Ruckhäberle was, I believe, right to ask
"ob nicht Brecht über Godard folgenreicher für den Film geworden ist als letzten
Endes für das Theater".[45]

The present discussion has deliberately concentrated on direct quotations
from and references to Brecht in films by the so-called "hardliners" of
Brechtian cinema. The more lightweight "Brechtian style"[46] of filmmaking –
of, say, Michael Verhoeven's *Das schreckliche Mädchen* (1990) or Jutta
Brückner's biopic *Bertolt Brecht – Liebe, Revolution und andere gefährliche
Sachen* (1998) – has been passed over, as have mainstream adaptations of his

[42] Bertolt Brecht: *Plagiate*. BFA 21.1. Pp. 404–405. Here p. 404.
[43] Bertolt Brecht: *Ziele der Gesellschaft der Dialektiker*. BFA 21. Pp. 536–537. Here
p. 537.
[44] Alexander Kluge and Oskar Negt: *Geschichte und Eigensinn*. Frankfurt am Main:
Zweitausendeins 1981. P. 1283. Their tome indeed ends with a (studiously footnoted)
quotation, Brecht's "Ginge da ein Wind" epigraph from the *Buckower Elegien* (BFA 12.
P. 310). On quotation in Straub-Huillet see Martin Brady: *Du Tag, wann wirst du sein…
Quotation, Emancipation and Dissonance in Straub-Huillet's Der Bräutigam, die
Komödiantin und der Zuhälter*. In: *German Life and Letters* 53 (2000). No. 3. Pp.
281–302. The Situationist writer and filmmaker Guy Debord, whose tract *La Société du
Spectacle* is itself cited in Godard's *Le Gai savoir* (1968), is perhaps the most famous
proponent of plagiarism as a political programme, pursued under the motto (itself lifted
from Isidore Ducasse); "Le plagiat est nécessaire. Le progrès l'implique". See: Guy
Debord, *La Société du Spectacle*. Paris: Éditions Gérard Lebovici 1987. P. 160. In the
early Situationist manifesto "Methods of Détournement" Debord and Gil J. Wolman
cite Brecht as an ally thanks to his willingness to make "some cuts in the classics of the theatre in order to make the performances more educative". See: Guy Debord and Gil J.
Wolman: Methods of Détournement. In: *Situationist International Anthology*. Ed. by
Ken Knabb. Berkeley: Bureau of Public Secrets 1981. Pp. 8–14. Here p. 9.
[45] Hans-Joachim Ruckhäberle: Antigone. In: *Politics – Poetics: das buch zur docu-
menta X*. Ostfildern: Cantz 1997. Pp. 250–251. Here p. 251.
[46] See: James Ryan: Verhoeven on *Nasty Girl*: "It's not possible to forget". In: *The
Hollywood Reporter* 7.11.1990.

texts. Concentrating on Godard, Kluge and Straub-Huillet, it has been possible
to identify a phenomenon which has gone unnoticed in studies of Brechtian
cinema – the "double gesture" of a Brechtian critical method and direct citation
of the author himself as a token of allegiance to critical, self-reflexive, anti-
illusionistic, authored film-making. Used in this way, Brecht's texts – be they
epigraphs or more substantial citations – serve as "Kommentartexte"; in all the
examples cited the context is, in one way or another, a didactic one – either an
on-screen character (in Godard's case frequently a woman) or the audience
itself is being instructed, aesthetically and politically. Serge Daney, in an article entitled "La thérrorisé (pédagogie godardienne)", notes the importance of
"schooling" in Godard's films: "L'école est par excellence le lieu où le maître
n'a pas à dire d'où lui viennent son savoir ni ses certitudes"; *Tout va bien* he
describes as "la leçon de Brecht sur le 'rôle des intellectuels dans la révolu-
tion'".[47] True Brechtian films, and specifically those which invoke "Père
Brecht" directly, are, it would seem, not only history lessons, but also primers.

---

[47] Serge Daney: La thérrorisé (pédagogie godardienne). In: *Cahiers du Cinéma* 262/263
(1976). Pp. 32–39. Here p. 35.

Godela Weiss-Sussex

"A Ridiculous Thing to Do": Yvonne Kapp and Brecht in Translation[1]

This essay considers the work of Yvonne Kapp, who acted as translator of Brecht texts and as advisor on translations of his work used in Britain, both for the Methuen edition and for theatre performances. As well as reassessing the extent and importance of Kapp's particular contribution to the understanding of Brecht's work in Britain, the essay is concerned more widely with highlighting principles of translation that emerge in Kapp's discussion of her own and of other translators' work, which have significantly influenced Brecht's legacy. The precedence given to the performability and "tone" of a text over a more precise rendering of the original words used reflects Brecht's own emphasis on the expression of Gestus *and attitude.*

Translations play an important part in determining an author's legacy. In the case of Brecht, a number of conflicting concepts of his legacy have jockeyed for position, as his works have been published and performed in numerous different translations and adaptations, some stressing the political aspects of the texts, some the didactic, some the theatricality, and some the versatility of the language used. In Britain, one particular edition, the Methuen series, has predominantly influenced the reception of Brecht's work. This essay investigates the contribution of Yvonne Kapp to the shaping of the Methuen series, and thereby of the dominant legacy of Brecht's works in Britain.

Looking down the list of translators whose texts have been included in the Methuen series, you find some illustrious names: W.H. Auden, Michael Hamburger, Ralph Manheim, John Willett, Arthur Waley, Marc Silberman, Tom Kuhn. And once, only once, as translator of the *Kalendergeschichten*, the name Yvonne Kapp appears. Kapp, born in London in 1903, had studied at King's College, London, then worked as a freelance journalist and as a writer of fiction. Her first novel *Nobody Asked You* (1932), which no publisher had wanted to touch and which she had then published under her own steam, had been highly successful, and three more had followed. She had joined the Communist Party and worked with refugees from the Spanish civil war, from Hitler's Germany and from occupied Czechoslovakia. Through her refugee work, she had met Margaret Mynatt, or Bianca Minotti, as she was known in

---

[1] My thanks go to Bill Abbey for bringing to my attention and facilitating access to the letters and typescripts held in the Yvonne Kapp/Margaret Mynatt collection in the library of the Institute of Germanic & Romance Studies (IGRS), University of London, on which this chapter is mainly based. References to the correspondences between Yvonne Kapp, Elisabeth Hauptmann and Helene Weigel are by names and date.

1920s Berlin, where, as a close friend of Elisabeth Hauptmann, she had belonged to the Brecht circle. Mynatt and Kapp had co-authored a book on *British Policy and the Refugees (1933–1941)*[2] and shared their lives from 1938 until Mynatt's death in 1977.

Kapp had worked as speech writer and researcher for the Amalgamated Engineering Union, then for the Medical Research Council; and – before turning her hand to writing Eleanor Marx's biography (the first volume of which was published to great acclaim when Kapp was 69 years old) – she translated, among other things, the prose texts from Brecht's *Kalendergeschichten*.

Kapp herself, when looking back on her life, allocated only minimal importance to her translation work, although it occupied most of her time from 1953 until the early 1960s. If she is remembered today, it is generally not for this, but for her book on Eleanor Marx and for her work in refugee aid. In an interview given to Sally Alexander in the late 1980s, she not only omits any reference to her work on Brecht, but explains how, after her dismissal from the Medical Research Council,[3] "[…] instead of going back to writing as I should have done, I made the mistake of agreeing to do a translation from the French and this led from one translation to another. And I got stuck in this… like doing crossword puzzles". And then she adds, for good measure: "Translating is not real at all. It's a ridiculous thing to do".[4]

In her autobiography, *Time Will Tell*, she claims: "I started translating more or less by accident and came to wish that I had never done so. In fact, with two exceptions, I got nothing out of this experience, but acute financial anxiety, for the work was abominably underpaid".[5] However, one of the two exceptions to which she refers here was Brecht's *Kalendergeschichten* volume. The *Tales*, as

---

[2] The volume, originally written in 1940, was edited and complemented by a foreword by Charmian Brinson and published by Cass (London) in 1997.

[3] Kapp's work at the Medical Research Council involved carrying out job satisfaction interviews in factories, work she disliked, mainly because of what she perceived to be the patronizing role she had to play in this. Eventually, she got permission to start her own project: to investigate health and safety provisions in West Ham, the London district with the "highest number of accidents, both fatal and non-fatal" (Yvonne Kapp: *Time Will Tell*. London: Verso 2003. P. 266). The report on this project was not only never published, but also cost her her job, for "it was frowned upon by my chiefs" (ibid. p. 267). Elsewhere, however, she gives a different reason for her dismissal, attributing it to a "report on the silliness of the job satisfaction enquiry at Vauxhall's" (Sally Alexander: Yvonne Kapp Talking with Sally Alexander. In: *Writing Lives. Conversations Between Women Writers*. Ed. by Mary Chamberlain. London: Virago 1988. Pp. 99–117. Here p. 116).

[4] Alexander: Yvonne Kapp (n. 3). P. 116.

[5] Kapp: *Time Will Tell* (n. 3). P. 268. Further on she writes about translating as "this pursuit, which had the teasing appeal of crossword puzzles and was as pointless" (ibid.).

she puts it "gave me a fresh and valuable understanding of the possibilities of the German language".[6]

Kapp's involvement in Brecht translation work started in 1957, when Elisabeth Hauptmann suggested that she try her hand at the prose texts from the *Kalendergeschichten*.[7] On receiving Kapp's attempts at the first two stories, Hauptmann's verdict is very positive: "I like them very much", she writes, and: "I have the impression that you are fully aware of the various differences (I do not mean the words) between the two languages".[8] She does not elaborate here, but elsewhere she refers to the required "flow" or, indeed, "lack of flow" of the language, the rhythm, and the attitude behind certain phrases or passages, which Kapp successfully captures.

In September 1958, having seen all of Kapp's translated stories, Hauptmann expands on her initial comments:

> I thought your translations very congenial and more than adequate as to meaning. As far as I can judge the language you have found the proper "tone", that is you found a simple style that avoided fake simplicity and fake naiveté as well as medieval mannerisms. I guess you really found something adequate to Brecht's simple and classical Bavarian language with its special "gestus" – and it's hard for me to formulate – a sort of eternal classic up-to-dateness.[9]

The correspondence between Hauptmann and Kapp makes clear that, in her concern for authenticity, Kapp relied on Hauptmann's advice and judgement. In a letter of 10 March 1958, for instance, she asks: "How to translate the title 'Kalendergeschichten': Are they Tales from the Almanack? Are they Everyday Stories? Are they Stories for Today and Tomorrow? What had Brecht in mind in so naming them? Only you can tell me".

As is evident in her earnest deferral to Hauptmann's advice, Kapp saw herself as a conscientious guardian of Brecht's work. The term she used for herself in this context is that of "literary conscience".[10] As such a guardian, she took a

---

[6] Ibid. The second exception was the translation of the correspondence between Friedrich Engels and Karl Marx's daughter Laura and her husband Paul Lafargue. This work aroused her interest in Eleanor Marx and eventually led her to write her biography.

[7] From a letter from Elisabeth Hauptmann to Kapp of 26 April 1957, it is clear that Yvonne's sample translation met with approval from the Methuen series editors. Hauptmann, hinting at some previous difficulties with the Methuen translations, is very positive about the envisaged collaboration: "I guess that *we* could more easily come to a basic understanding about how Brecht should be translated". In Kapp's letter to Hauptmann of 24 October 1957, she mentions that no decision had been taken by Methuen yet. Kapp worries that, not belonging to "some mutual back-scratching stable", she might not get the contract.

[8] Hauptmann to Kapp 7.2.1958.

[9] Hauptmann to Kapp 25.9.1959.

[10] Kapp to Hauptmann 23.1.1959.

stand when John Willett suggested cutting some material out of the *Kalendergeschichten* and inserting instead some other additional texts for the English publication. Kapp, worried by this, reported the matter to Hauptmann (4.9.1958), who, as might be expected, took a very strong position against the suggestion: "It is absolutely not permissible to change the selection of this volume", she writes categorically.[11]

Kapp then took Hauptmann's protest to the Methuen General Editor, John Cullen. Initially, she was frustrated by her lack of influence, not only in this particular matter, but with regard to advice on Brecht translations and editions in general: "But I can do damn-all except 'suggest' to Methuen's: John Willett is the accepted Brecht authority in this country and the acknowledged adviser to Methuen's – more is the pity".[12] But gradually, she made herself heard: in January 1959, she told Hauptmann that Cullen was now "willing to accept my views rather than Willett's".[13] And she was strongly supported by the two women in Berlin. Only two weeks later, Hauptmann reports: "I wrote to Mr. Suhrkamp to transmit to Mr. Cullen Helli's wish to have you on the Brecht translation project in a leading capacity", adding that she had done so twice before.[14] As a consequence, Kapp came to share – or perhaps rather to rival – Willett's position as an advisor with Methuen. Her position was never formalized, but her influence became significant, as shown by the great number of translation projects with which she became associated. Indeed, at a meeting between Kapp and Willett in early 1960, Willett told Kapp "that he was supposed to have charge of the Brecht translations for Methuen's, but that Suhrkamp had stopped it"[15] – a remark that is more than a little curious, seeing that Willett edited, or at least co-edited the majority of the Methuen Brecht series texts. If Suhrkamp did indeed oppose Willett's involvement, the resistance cannot have been sustained for long.

In the same year in which she became involved with the Methuen translations, Kapp additionally took on, again on Helene Weigel's request – and mediated through the literary agent Suzanne Czech – an advisory function regarding

---

[11] Hauptmann to Kapp 25.9.1958.
[12] Kapp to Hauptmann 2.11.1958. Indeed, as Geoffrey Strachan, Methuen's Plays Editor, reports, Cullen, together with Willett and Ralph Manheim as editor translators, had been laying plans for an English Brecht edition since about the time of Brecht's death in 1956 (see http://highway49.library.yale.edu/arthurwangphotos/popups/alpha/cullen.html).
[13] Kapp to Hauptmann 23.1.1959. Kapp is referring here to her suggestion to ask a poet, for instance W.H. Auden, to do the translations of the *Kalendergeschichten* poems rather than using the translation by Marc Blitzstein favoured by Willett.
[14] Hauptmann to Kapp 9.2.1959.
[15] Kapp to Hauptmann 27.1.1960.

all English Brecht translations used for theatrical productions. The bulk of Kapp's advisory work on Brecht falls into the period of three years: 1959 to 1961; and from her very detailed accounts, we know that she vetted the work of thirty-three translators, on twenty of Brecht's works, between November 1958 and December 1961.[16] At that point, in December 1961, Stefan Brecht took over the vetting of translations to be used for performances of Brecht's work. This, as Kapp points out in a letter to Hauptmann, "of course knocks the bottom out of the arrangement made by Helli with Suzanne Czech, which was that all versions sent in for possible theatrical production should go through my hands […]".[17] She expresses concern that Stefan Brecht might not work with the same care, attention to detail and sense of responsibility as she has done for the past three years.

As far as her position with Methuen's goes, the fact that her authority was never clearly set out, as she was never "an authorised editor", but always "just a sort of casual publishers' reader",[18] led to some frustration on her part, as a few translations that she would not have approved, slipped past her. Most notable among these is the *Dreigroschenoper* translation by Vesey and Bentley that appeared in 1960 in the first volume of the Methuen Brecht series, and at which she proclaims herself to be appalled and "horrified", dismissing it as "clumsy and lifeless and weak".[19]

It is clear that Kapp had very strong opinions on the translations she vetted; but how qualified was she to make these judgements? It is worth recalling Elisabeth Hauptmann's verdicts on Kapp's prose translations. Hauptmann highlighted Kapp's success in conveying, through her English text, the tone of

---

[16] Yvonne Kapp: *Record of Brecht Translation Vetted*, typescript, IGRS.

[17] Kapp to Hauptmann 5.12.1961. On 20 February 1962, she confirms: "I have nothing further to do with the translations that are used here – this is all in Stefan's hands now; […]".

[18] Kapp to Hauptmann 28.11.1960.

[19] John Willett claims not to have seen this translation before publication either, and Kapp writes in clear frustration to Hauptmann: "I only wish there were some way of being absolutely certain that nothing gets published here which hasn't been properly and thoroughly vetted by someone (though I still can't understand how it comes about that Willett, the advisor par excellence, was not consulted)" (Kapp to Hauptmann 28.11.60). Another incident is worth reporting in this context: having invested a lot of work into Vesey's translation of *Das Leben des Galilei*, Kapp was still unhappy with the final version. She was able to take out mistakes, misinterpretations and the occasional "howler", but finds that he has not accepted her stylistic alterations. She comes to the conclusion that "unless the translator is prepared to work with an authorised editor – not just a sort of casual publishers' reader, which is what Methuen's expect one to be – and every controversial point is hammered out jointly, there is no way of getting round it" (Kapp to Hauptmann 2.12.1959).

a passage, an aspect singled out by Brecht, in 1944, as the "main consideration for any translator".[20]

Furthermore, Hauptmann commended Kapp's ability to render the rhythm and its irregularity, where needed; the simplicity and "classic up-to-dateness" of Brecht's prose; and, most importantly, her capacity to express the underlying attitude of a particular text passage, its *Gestus*. Kapp thus transmits, in Hauptmann's opinion at least, the singularity of Brecht's texts.

A look at Kapp's translation of one of the *Kalendergeschichten* stories, *Der hilflose Knabe*, may exemplify her style. In the original text, Brecht gives his Herr Keuner the poetic, heightened, slightly sententious voice of a story-teller; syntactic inversion and participle constructions characterize the first sentence of his short tale: "Einen vor sich hinweinenden Jungen fragte ein Vorübergehender nach dem Grund seines Kummers" (BFA 18. P. 438). Kapp is clearly very aware of this "rhetorical expansiveness" that, as Morley points out, has to be considered a very Brechtian device.[21] As required by the structures of the English language, she turns the first participle construction into a relative clause, but renders the complexity and heightened tone of the sentence: "A passer-by asked a boy who was crying what was the cause of his unhappiness".[22] The affinity to Brecht's text achieved here becomes even clearer when we compare Kapp's text to a recent translation by Martin Chalmers, which contains a simplified and somewhat flattened version of this sentence: "A boy was crying to himself and a passerby asked what was wrong".[23]

The closeness in spirit of Kapp's translation to Brecht's text is evident also in her rendering of the story's ending. Brecht heightens the sense of surprise by increasing the speed of his climactic ending through the use of brevity and ellipsis: " 'Dann gib auch den her.' Nahm ihm den letzten Groschen aus der Hand und ging unbekümmert weiter". Kapp's and Chalmers's respective translations read as follows:

> "Then hand over the other one too." He took the last *groschen* out of his hand and walked on without turning a hair.
>
> (Kapp)

---

[20] Bertolt Brecht: Letter to Ferdinand Reyher, quoted after Michael Morley: Negotiating Meanings: Thoughts on Brecht and Translation. In: *A Bertolt Brecht Reference Companion*. Ed. by Siegfried Mews. Westport (CT) 1997. Pp. 321–338. Here p. 336.
[21] Morley: Negotiating Meanings (n. 20). P. 326. He is referring to Brenton's translation of *Leben des Galilei*.
[22] Bertolt Brecht: *The Helpless Boy*. In: Bertolt Brecht: *Tales from the Calendar*. The prose translated by Yvonne Kapp. The verse translated by Michael Hamburger. London: Methuen & Co. 1961. P. 112.
[23] Bertolt Brecht: *The Helpless Boy*. In: Bertolt Brecht: *Stories of Mr. Keuner*. Translated from the German and with an afterword by Martin Chalmers. San Francisco: City Lights. 2001. P. 16.

"Then give me that one as well", said the man and took the second dime out of the boy's hand and walked away unconcerned.

(Chalmers)

Chalmers slows down the rhythm of the passage through the repeated use of "and" as well as the unnecessary addition "said the man" and thus considerably reduces its effect. Kapp not only avoids this, but further supports the *Gestus* of the man described here by her use of the perfectly suited idiom "without turning a hair".

There is another passage in the two translations of this story which epitomizes the two translators' different approaches. Where Kapp translates the original "'Nein,' schluchzte der Junge" simply but effectively with "'No,' sobbed the boy", Chalmers (quite unnecessarily) expands on Brecht's text: "'No,' sobbed the boy and looked at the man with new hope. Because he was smiling". Unlike Chalmers, Kapp trusts Brecht's writing and sees no need to insert additions or interpretations into a text that affects the reader precisely because of its lapidary brevity and the gaps it leaves. Her work complies with Benjamin's stipulations for a good translation: "Die wahre Übersetzung ist durchscheinend, sie verdeckt nicht das Original, steht ihm nicht im Licht, sondern läßt die reine Sprache, wie verstärkt durch ihr eigenes Medium, nur um so voller aufs Original fallen".[24]

Kapp's awareness of the particular quality of Brecht's prose is also evident in her own comments on the translation process. In a letter to Hauptmann from 29 December 1959 she writes:

That's one of the odd and surprising things about these Brecht translations: their formidable difficulties lie in reaching a very precise understanding of the overtones and undertones of word and phrase and rhythm, the current of humour or anger which slows or hastens them, the exact impact of a dialect – or a biblical – word. But once that understanding has been reached, the extraordinary fact is that the English language lends itself most flexibly to those purposes.

From her judgements on other translators' renderings of Brecht's dramatic works, we can glean an even more acute understanding of the issues involved – and of Kapp's personal priorities. Of Vesey's *Galileo*, she writes:

It is extremely accurate and faithful. It is also rather heavy-handed and, I think, lifeless. This is a great problem: on the one hand, it is necessary to have perfectly accurate texts which stick close to the original (though they do not have to be uninspired); on the other hand, one needs a version which could spring to life on the stage, as this could not do.[25]

---

[24] Walter Benjamin: *Die Aufgabe des Übersetzers*. WBGS IV. 1. Pp. 9–21. Here p. 18.
[25] Kapp to Hauptmann 1.9.1959. In response, Hauptmann suggests that Kapp should work as Vesey's advisor (21.10.1959). The suggestion was taken up, the collaboration was started straight away and, as is clear from subsequent letters, cost her many, many (unpaid) hours.

The two criteria emphasized here are closeness to the original and the theatrical quality or, to put it more precisely, the theatrical potential of the translation. This second criterion is a central, recurring concern of Kapp's. In another letter to Hauptmann, she claims that, "perfection being out of reach", the published plays "should be faithful enough to enable a gifted and imaginative producer to use them" and that if "a playable text is thus evolved in practice, then that text should replace the earlier published versions"(27.1.1960). In its humility, this understanding of translation sounds very much akin to Ortega y Gasset's formulation, that "translation is not the work, but a path toward the work", "an apparatus, a technical device that brings us closer to the work without ever trying to repeat or replace it".[26]

Kapp thus gives preference to the performability of a text and to the practitioner's approach, over the "dry" work of the translator. In an article on Brecht, which she published in *Marxism Today* in 1962, Kapp crystallizes this attitude with the sweeping generalization that "all translations of Brecht are bad". "But the important thing", she continues, "is that not all performances of Brecht plays are bad. Firstly, because they were not written to be read but to be acted; secondly, because if ever an inspired producer of Brecht should appear in this country he would restore what is inevitably lost in the printed word […]".[27]

This idea, that the best translation is one born out of performance, echoes Brecht's idea of "Theaterspielen als Methode der Übersetzung" – a method he used in his collaboration with Charles Laughton on the *Galileo* translation. In a position where the actor spoke no German and the writer had inadequate English, Brecht reports: "Wir waren gezwungen, zu machen, was sprachlich besser bewanderte Übersetzer ja ebenfalls machen sollten: Gesten übersetzen".[28]

If a *Gestus*, in Brecht's usage, signifies a particular attitude of the speaker or writer, then the language transporting these attitudes, *gestic* language, is the core of Brechtian language. Referring to the poet Kin-jeh, Brecht writes in his *Buch der Wendungen*: "[…] er brachte nur Haltungen in Sätze und ließ durch die Sätze immer die Haltungen durchscheinen. Eine solche Sprache nannte er gestisch, weil sie nur ein Ausdruck für die Gesten der Menschen war".[29]

The expression of attitude is thus closely related to the verbalization of gesture. The performative aspect of language could not be stressed in any clearer way. It is only logical that an adequate translation of this kind of language must

[26] José Ortega y Gasset: *The Misery and the Splendor of Translation*. In: *Theories of Translation*. Ed. by Rainer Schulte and John Biguenet. Chicago – London 1992. Pp. 93–112. Here p. 109.

[27] Yvonne Kapp: Some Reflections on Brecht. In: *Marxism Today* 6 (1962). No. 2. Pp. 49–53. Here p. 53.

[28] Bertolt Brecht: Vorwort. In: Bertolt Brecht: *Aufbau einer Rolle. Laughtons Galilei*. BFA 25. P. 12.

[29] Bertolt Brecht: *Über die gestische Sprache in der Literatur*. BFA 18. Pp. 78–79.

itself be performance- rather than text-based. The actor/translator goes further than the playwright in this approach: Brecht speaks, in reference to Laughton's work on *Galileo*, of the "Verschleiß des Textes" in the performance (BFA 25. P. 12). What results from this destruction of the original text is a transformation that is freed from the original's specific form and conveys, in crystallized form, "das Verhalten der Sprechenden zueinander" and, in the case of the monologues (which Brecht calls "Arien"), den "Gestus des Stückeschreibers", or as he specifies when writing about the translation of poetry, "die Gedanken und [...] Haltung des Dichters".[30]

In her concern to find a congenial transformation of Brecht's texts, one that, above all, preserves the *Gestus* of a character or a scene, Kapp was strikingly aware of the need to achieve a balance between showing too much respect for the original, and too little sensitivity towards it. The first tendency she finds in John Berger's *Messingkauf* poems, which she reviewed in April 1959. She summarizes his translation as an "honest, workmanlike job", "done with great – almost, perhaps, too much – respect". As a consequence, the translated poems "lack the humour and humanity of the original. [...] the richness and warmth of the rolling, leisurely, intimate rhythms are lost and the didactic element strikes a much sharper note".[31] Berger has, in Kapp's view, given too much reverence to the text and has not carried the necessary act of destruction and transformation far enough, which alone ensures the "Wandlung und Erneuerung des Lebendigen", that constitutes, to quote Benjamin's definition, the "Fortleben" of the original.[32] For, very similarly to Brecht's understanding of translation as performance related, Benjamin's definition of the task of the translator is to find "diejenige Intention auf die Sprache, in die übersetzt wird, [...] von der aus in ihr das Echo des Originals erweckt wird".[33]

At the other end of the spectrum stands insufficient regard for the original text. Such an over-confident and over-bearing stance Kapp sees exemplified in Alfred Kreymborg's translation of *Schweyk*. As she writes to Helene Weigel on 11 August 1959, "the language is unnatural, stilted and quite un-English". Now, this might be an attempt by the translator to make his text "transparent" ("durchscheinend") in Benjamin's sense. But Kapp's second accusation is more serious: "[...] where the original uses slightly comical and dialectical expressions, the Kreymborg version simply ignores them and struggles on in its own laboured, clanking language". And finally, she accuses Kreymborg of having twisted "the opening verses [...] out of all recognition to arrive at some sort of rhyme". In short, her verdict is clear: the text is "totally unacceptable as a translation".[34]

[30] Bertolt Brecht: *Die Übersetzbarkeit von Gedichten*. BFA 22. P. 132.
[31] Kapp to Hauptmann 30.4.1959.
[32] Benjamin: *Die Aufgabe des Übersetzers* (n. 24). P. 12.
[33] Ibid. p. 16.
[34] It does not help either that "there are many detectable instances of a misunderstanding so complete that I do not think his knowledge of the language [German] can be trusted".

Yvonne Kapp was not one to mince her words. In fact, the formulation that Eric Hobsbawm used in her obituary comes to mind: "tough as oxhide and a professional to her fingertips".[35] And professional indeed is the insight that sums up her attitude to the work of the translator:

> All one can look to is an honest and sensitive rendering in which the translator does not try to interpose himself between the original text and his own version, does not claim special insights into Brecht's material, or spirit messages as to his intentions; […].[36]

While working in her advisory capacity, Kapp also contemplated undertaking further Brecht translations herself. The two most important of these projects, which, however, did not come to fruition, concerned *Furcht und Elend des Dritten Reiches*[37] and *Mutter Courage und ihre Kinder*. This latter project had initially been suggested by John Cullen.[38] The first draft of a scene that Kapp produced met with the approval of both Hauptmannn and Weigel. The latter commends Kapp's sample as "lebendig, sehr Brecht entsprechend" and, though mentioning room for improvement, particularly likes it for being "theater-mäßig gut, sprechbar und spielbar".[39] Hauptmann, who sends her reactions in the same letter, is slightly more reserved, but overall very positive, too: "[…] und das Beste ist", she points out, "sie bleibt im Ton".

Kapp was so committed to this project that she planned to spend a little inheritance from her mother on it. She hoped to produce no less than "the, so to speak, 'definitive' text for the theatre and for publications in the future".[40] In October 1961, however, Cullen decided to use Bentley's translation in preference to Kapp's.[41] This seems to have taken the wind out of Kapp's sails. Financial problems create another obstacle and, though she still mentioned the translation as a pending project in a letter to Hauptmann two months later (5.12.1961), she was eventually unable to complete the work.

This episode is interesting not only because we realize how much Kapp has come to be involved in this "ridiculous thing", but also because it gives us a

---

[35] Eric Hobsbawm: Yvonne Kapp. In: *The Guardian* 29.6.1999. (Yvonne Kapp had died on 22 June.)

[36] Kapp to Hauptmann 21.9.1960.

[37] This is mentioned in Kapp's letter to Weigel of 15 March 1960; also in her letter to Hauptmann of 21 March 1960. But the idea is not followed up, with Weigel assuming that Kapp is working on the translation. The matter is raised again in November that year. Kapp is still interested, but as far as I am aware, the translation was never completed.

[38] See Kapp to Hauptmann 13.7.1959.

[39] Hauptmann and Weigel to Kapp 14.7.1961.

[40] Kapp to Weigel 19.7.1961.

[41] See Kapp to Weigel 31.10.1961.

glimpse of the vagaries of a translator's life. In the case of Kapp, who acted both as translator and as "literary conscience" (as the representative of the Brecht estate in London), it was not only a case of having to be wary of rival translators, but also of keeping an eye on Brecht scholars and interpreters. On the whole, she was very suspicious of any non-Weigel- or Hauptmann-vetted commentators. On 5 February 1959, she writes to Hauptmann: "There is another book on Brecht coming out by a man called Martin Esslin. [...] This chap, whom we've met, has some very special 'theory' about Brecht and his work. I have not been able to understand it [...]". Ten months later, however, having read the book, she has not only understood Esslin's angle, but has come to violently disagree with this "most venomous stuff".[42] Even years later, when lecturing on Brecht – first in local Marxist circles, then also to students, for example at Goldsmith's College in 1967 –,[43] she takes a special delight in "exploding Esslin, Gray & Co.", as she confesses in a letter to Helene Weigel from 20 July 1961.

Then there is John Willett. In his article on Brecht and Willett in *The Brecht Yearbook* 28, Tom Kuhn writes: "We sense his hand over the entire enterprise of Brecht in English".[44] This is an impression that Kapp clearly shares, though she is not nearly as appreciative of this "guiding hand" as Kuhn is:

> I think now that J.W. is really incapable of understanding any single important aspect of Brecht's work, he just cannot, and he's going to do a lot of harm before he's finished. [...] It is beastly to think that he is in a position to decide what shall go into the published translations here.[45]

She is clearly writing here as the London guardian of Brecht's work, trying to safeguard his intentions. Willett was freer in his handling of Brecht's legacy and so was bound to arouse her ire. Apart from this difference in approach, the disagreements between Kapp and Willett were based on political rather than artistic differences. Where the two colleagues express their ideas on translation, their principles are very similar indeed. In his short essay "Some Factors in Translating Brecht" from 1967, for instance, Willett cites rhyme, metre, form and the expression of an "equivalent vitality" as essential points to be considered, and it is highly unlikely that Kapp would have taken issue with this list of priorities.[46] However, as a committed Communist, Kapp cared deeply

---

[42] Kapp to Hauptmann 29.12.1959.

[43] See Kapp's typescript: *Talk on Brecht to Students at Goldsmith's College* (7.2.1967), IGRS.

[44] Tom Kuhn: Brecht and Willett: Getting the gest. In: *Friends, Colleagues, Collaborators*. Ed. by Stephen Brockmann. Madison (WI): University of Wisconsin Press 2003. Pp. 261–273. Here p. 262 (The Brecht Yearbook 28).

[45] Kapp to Hauptmann 2.11.1958.

[46] John Willett: Some Factors in Translating Brecht [1967]. In: John Willett: *Brecht in Context. Comparative Approaches*. London: Methuen. 1984. Pp. 242–245.

about the political and ideological impact of Brecht's work, an aspect that Willett, whose main interest was in its dramatic and literary quality, tended to disregard.[47]

In the later years of their collaboration, Kapp warmed to Willett, even though she still claimed that he "always gets his *facts* right, but never expresses an *opinion* with which I feel in agreement".[48] Only when she had ceased her involvement in the Brecht work, did a friendship develop between them. In a very warm-hearted letter of 1984, for instance, she advises Willett on his contribution to the Brecht *Year Book* on Women and Politics (though not without including a longish list of corrections!).[49]

The Methuen *Tales from the Calendar* with Kapp's translation of the prose texts was finally published on 16 November 1961.[50] A review appeared in the *Guardian* of 24 November 1961, written by Martin Esslin, of all people. He turned out to be far more gracious about her work than she was about his – and, in his verdict, sums up Kapp's achievement as a sensitive, conscientious and congenial Brecht translator: "The translation of these prose pieces (by Miss Yvonne Kapp) is admirable and really captures Brecht's lapidary and laconic style [...]".[51]

---

[47] This becomes evident, for instance, in Kapp's very damning comments on Willett's BBC radio programme of 1st November 1958 on Brecht. She calls Willett "a cheat" and claims: "A programme of this sort – a Piefke voice reading out Brecht's words in the first person and translated poems in quite incomprehensible English – unexplained references to works neither explained or exemplified [...] a lot of trivial stuff about the use of this or that poem or theme in some other guise at some later date – such a programme – and with a whole splendid hour at his disposal – can be of interest to no one" (Kapp to Hauptmann 2.11.1958).

[48] Kapp to Hauptmann 27.1.1960. In this letter, she refers to his "views and interpretations", but also to his "poor ear and what he regards as permissible 'freedoms' ", which are "often highly objectionable" to her.

[49] See Kapp to Willett 16.5.1984.

[50] The publication of the volume had been held up, mainly because it had proved difficult to find a congenial translator for the poems included in the volume. In a letter dated 21.9.1960, Kapp writes to Hauptmann: "[...] many people have been tried. Some – like Auden – refused; others – like Michael Hamburger, who is a very skilful poet, – have such an alien attitude to Brecht that it would be better if they did not do it; Willett's attempts are terribly clumsy and so, at last, I am to have a shot. I don't like it. I always refused to do it, but it's no use am sofa [*sic*] zu sitzen and übel zu nehmen over everyone else's efforts [...]". However, two months later, having read Hamburger's translations, Kapp admits that "he has made a very good job of these poems ON THE WHOLE" (Kapp to Hauptmann 11.11.1960).

[51] Martin Esslin: Unholy Simplicity. In: *The Guardian* 24.11.1961.

Robert Gillett

Iconoclast or Acolyte? GG Plays BB

It is often claimed that Günter Grass's play Die Plebejer proben den Aufstand *is an attack on Bertolt Brecht. By constructing the play as a historical tragedy and assimilating it to Shakespeare's* Coriolanus, *critics read it as an indictment of a very particular intellectual and his failure, at the crucial moment, to match his actions to his words. The thesis put forward here, on the contrary, is that in this play Grass has used eminently Brechtian means in order to convey as precisely as theatre allows the nature of the very real dilemma facing his protagonist. Pursuing this thesis entails taking a careful look at the nature of Brechtian theatre and the possibilities it offers for staging an uprising.*

The 16th of January 1966 saw the first performance, at the Schiller-Theater in West Berlin, of an eagerly awaited new play. Its 38-year-old author had burst onto the scene some seven years previously with a *succès de scandale* which turned out to be one of the most significant events in the literary history of the Federal Republic; but he had achieved only modest recognition as a playwright. In the intervening period he had become more directly involved in politics than is usually thought fitting for an intellectual. If literary gossip is to be believed, his new play had brought sweat to the brow of an influential publisher even before it was staged.[1] And its first night is chiefly remembered for the premeditated spontaneous condemnation of one member of the audience, who at the fall of the curtain loudly proclaimed: "Gott, war das schlecht".[2]

Needless to say, in the charged atmosphere of Cold War Berlin, this remark can scarcely be said to constitute a dispassionate aesthetic judgement. On the contrary, it was a direct expression of political prejudice and to that extent symptomatic. Thus alongside the irritated dismissals in the East German press, we find in certain right-leaning sections of the Western media an equally unsubstantiated adulation.[3] Given that the play is set in the Eastern half of the city in which it was first put on, such reactions are understandable. Slightly more surprising, though, is the question around which so many of them tend to crystallize: the question of the extent to which, and the mode in which, the play can be said to depict Bert Brecht.

---

[1] See Stephan Schlak: Zappelei. Hast du Originalgeräusche? In: *Berliner Zeitung* 16.6.2003.
[2] See Joachim Kaiser: Die Theaterstücke des Günter Grass. In: *Text und Kritik* 1/1a. 5th ed. (June 1978). Pp. 118–132. Here p. 124.
[3] Cf. the anonymous review in *Der Spiegel* 20 (1966). Nr. 5. Pp. 81–87. Here p. 81: "*Neues Deutschland* nannte es ein idiotisches Stück. *Bild* posaunte: Graß gelang der große Wurf".

The name of that playwright is noticeably absent from the play in question. The chief protagonist of Günter Grass's *Die Plebejer proben den Aufstand* is called simply "Der Chef".[4] On the one hand this leaves the author free disingenuously to deny the identification.[5] On the other it cannot but encourage those critics who are inclined to treat the play as the dramatic equivalent of a *roman à clef*. Hence the tireless tendency in certain sections of the secondary literature to ring the changes on the assertion that "we all know the play is *really* about Brecht".[6] And it cannot be denied that Grass's play contains a veritable plethora of allusions to the life and work of the famous founder of the Berliner Ensemble.[7]

A similarly tightly woven net of allusions enables those in the know to identify without difficulty the unspecified date on which the play is set. The death of Stalin significantly sets the year.[8] The season is mentioned when the "Chef" sets about

[4] The edition used here (referred to simply by page number) is that of the Aufbau Verlag (Günter Grass: *Die Plebejer proben den Aufstand. Ein deutsches Trauerspiel*. Mit einem Essay und einem Gespräch. Berlin – Weimar 1990). This not only includes many of the notes from the Luchterhand edition (Günter Grass: *Werkausgabe in zehn Bänden*. Ed. by Volker Neuhaus. Darmstadt – Neuwied: 1987. Vol. 8: *Theaterspiele*. Ed. by Angelika Hille-Sandvoss), but conveniently also contains Grass's essay *Vor- und Nachgeschichte der Tragödie des Coriolanus von Livius und Plutarch über Shakespeare bis zu Brecht und mir*, and the discussion he had about the play with Berlin schoolchildren on 23.3.1968.
[5] Thus Brookes and Fraenkel quote a quotation from the programme of the RSC production in which Grass insists: "I did not intend to write [...] about [...] Brecht" (H.F. Brookes and C.E. Fraenkel: Introduction. In: *Günter Grass: Die Plebejer proben den Aufstand*. Ed. by H.F. Brookes and C.E. Fraenkel. London: Heinemann 1971. Pp. vii–xlii. Here p. xix).
[6] Joachim Kaiser, for example, is ironic: "Der Chef – er hat Brechts Biographie hinter, Brecht-Zitate in und Brechts Theater um sich, so dass man geradezu versucht sein könnte, ihn für eine Art Brecht zu halten" (Joachim Kaiser: Grass überfordert seinen Hamlet. *Die Plebejer proben den Aufstand* in München. In: *Süddeutsche Zeitung* 27.4.1967); Friedrich Liebl is impatient: "Im Mittelpunkt des Stückes steht eine für jeden nur halbwegs Eingeweihten als Bert Brecht erkennbare Gestalt" (Friedrich Liebl: Ein Wallenstein der Revolution. *Die Plebejer proben den Aufstand* von Günter Grass. Uraufführung im Schillertheater. In: *Die Welt* 17.1.1966); Theodor Pelster is pedagogically straightforward: "Die Anspielungen auf Brecht sind zu deutlich, als dass man sie übersehen könnte" (Theodor Pelster: *Günter Grass. Literaturwissen für Schule und Studium*. Stuttgart: Reclam 1999. P. 46); and Andrzej Wirth is blunt to the point of overstatement: "Grass's protagonist is unmistakably Brecht" (Andrzej Wirth: Günter Grass and the Dilemma of Documentary Drama. In: *A Günter Grass Symposium*. Ed. by A. Leslie Willson. Austin and London: University of Texas Press 1971. Pp. 18–31. Here p. 24).
[7] For a full account of such allusions, see Manfred Kux: *Moderne Dichterdramen. Dichter, Dichtung und Politik in Theaterstücken von Günter Grass, Tankred Dorst, Peter Weiss und Gaston Salvatore*. Köln – Wien: Böhlau 1980. Pp. 28–31; see also Ralf Sudau: *Werkbearbeitung, Dichterfiguren. Traditionsaneignung am Beispiel der deutschen Gegenwartsliteratur*. Tübingen: Niemeyer 1985. P. 171.
[8] See p. 13, p. 21, as well as Brookes and Fraenkel (eds.): *Die Plebejer* (n. 5). P. 142.

satisfying his incorrigible curiosity with the help of the building workers (p. 22). The day of the week – the famously wet Wednesday – is twice insisted upon, once when Podulla uses it to qualify the "Chef's" holiday atmosphere (p. 40) and once when the "Steinträger" rather pathetically lays claim to it (p. 52). And the date is the subject of a bitter irony whereby the "Chef" proleptically measures out Grass's own hindsight in a scathing attack on West German indifference (p. 83). These hints, combined with numerous detailed references to the events for which the date is remembered, make it abundantly clear, despite the author's protestations to the contrary, that the action of the play takes place on the 17th of June 1953.[9]

There is broad consensus to the effect that the role played by the Brecht figure on that date is a rather inglorious one. He is seen as arrogant[10] and out of touch,[11] sedate[12] and disorientated,[13] cowardly[14] and opportunistic,[15] an aesthete[16] and a traitor.[17] He shamelessly exploits others for his own ends and refuses his help to those who ask for it.[18] He is so bound up in his own concerns that he fails to seize the moment and misses the march of history.[19] In short: he

[9] In the Aufbau edition, the title given to the discussion with the Berlin schoolchildren is: "Ich hatte nicht die Absicht, den 17. Juni zu dramatisieren" (pp. 113–122).

[10] Gertrud Bauer Pickar: Silberpappeln und Saatkartoffeln. The Interaction of Art and Reality in Grass' *Die Plebejer proben den Aufstand*. In: *Theatrum Mundi. Essays on German Drama and German Literature Dedicated to Harold Lenz on his Seventieth Birthday, September 11, 1978*. Ed. by Edward R. Haymes. Munich: Fink 1980. P. 201.

[11] Martin Brunkhorst: *Shakespeares "Coriolanus" in deutscher Bearbeitung. Sieben Beispiele zum literarästhetischen Problem der Umsetzung und Vermittlung Shakespeares*. Berlin – New York: de Gruyter 1973. P. 142: "Dem utopischen Idealismus des Dichters […] ist die […] Direktheit des Volkes fremd und unzugänglich".

[12] James Redmond speaks of "tired conservatism" (James Redmond: Günter Grass and "Der Fall Brecht". In: *Modern Language Quarterly* 32 (1971). P. 394, while Bauer Pickar uses the word "jaded" (Silberpappeln und Saatkartoffeln (n. 10). P. 211).

[13] Wirth: Grass and Documentary Drama (n. 6). P. 23: "The Boss was a *Versager* […] a Hamletic victim of his own theorems which confused his insights of reality".

[14] Jost Nolte uses the phrase "der eitle Zauderer" (Jost Nolte: *Die Plebejer proben den Aufstand*. In: *Die Welt* 6.1.1968. Reprinted in: *Von Buch zu Buch. Günter Grass in der Kritik. Eine Dokumentation*. Ed. by Gert Loschütz. Neuwied – Berlin: Luchterhand 1968. P. 160).

[15] Josef Mühlberger: *Grass contra Brecht*. In: *Welt und Wort* 21 (1966). Nr. 2. P. 45: "Grass rechnet hart mit Bert Brecht als Opportunisten ab".

[16] Richard Lawson: *Günter Grass*. New York: Ungar 1985. P. 15

[17] Kaiser: Die Theaterstücke des Günter Grass (n. 2). P. 125: "Illoyaler kann man sich kaum benehmen".

[18] Hellmuth Karasek: Stück vom Stückeschreiber. Die Berliner Aufführung des Brecht-Dramas von Günter Grass. In: *Stuttgarter Zeitung* 17.1.1966: "Anstatt den Streikenden zu helfen, […] mißbraucht er ihre Revolution für seine Probenarbeiten".

[19] Alan Frank Keele: *Understanding Günter Grass*. Columbia: University of South Carolina Press 1988. P. 204: "Brecht […] missed an irretrievable historic opportunity to change the world".

leaves undone such things as he ought to have done, before going on to do such things as he ought not to have done (or vice versa, depending on the perspective). Hence it is scarcely surprising that *Die Plebejer* should be widely regarded as an anti-Brecht play,[20] or that those close to the master should have taken umbrage at it.[21]

At the same time, there is no shortage of critics who are keen to insist that this view of the play is entirely misguided.[22] Taking their cue from the author, they firmly deny that the play is ultimately about Brecht at all. For them, this central figure is merely an interchangeable instance.[23] The real concerns of Grass's play are much wider. They have to do with the relationship between art and reality,[24] or intellectuals and politics,[25] or Germans and the Revolution.[26] So far from being an ad hominem attack, *Die Plebejer* abstracts from the historical Brecht to produce something altogether more universal. Eschewing the merely local identifications of the *roman à clef,* such critics assimilate the play to a form they see as at once worthier and more Brechtian: the parable.[27]

And it is perfectly true that the historical Bertolt Brecht did not react to the embryonic uprising in the way Grass imputes to the "Chef".[28] (Indeed Helene Weigel, who is supposed to be the model for the Volumnia figure, was not even in Berlin at the time.[29]) While there is some confusion about which play was actually scheduled for rehearsal on that particular Wednesday, there is no doubt

[20] Irène Leonard: *Günter Grass.* Edinburgh: Oliver and Boyd 1974. P. 61: "Critics have on the whole labelled *The Plebeians* [...] an anti-Brecht play".

[21] Sudau cites what he calls: "gereizte, ja gehässige Reaktionen ehemaliger Mitarbeiter Brechts" (Sudau: *Werkbearbeitung* (n. 7). P. 173).

[22] Hanspeter Brode speaks of a "Mißverständnis" (Hanspeter Brode: *Günter Grass.* München: Beck 1979. P. 137); Manfred Jurgensen of a "Missdeutung" (Manfred Jurgensen: *Über Günter Grass. Untersuchungen zur sprachbildlichen Rollenfunktion.* Bern – München: Franke 1974. P. 134).

[23] Brode: *Günter Grass* (n. 22). P. 38: "Brecht [wäre] prinzipiell auch austauschbar".

[24] Cf. Bauer Pickar's title (n. 10).

[25] Friedrich Berger: Es lohnt doch, mit Grass den Aufstand zu proben. In: *Kölner Stadtanzeiger* 16.1.1967. Reprinted in: Loschütz (ed.): *Von Buch zu Buch* (n. 14). P. 156: "Hier [...] wird [...] die Tragödie [dargestellt], die 'Der Intellektuelle und die politische Wirklichkeit' heißt".

[26] Andrea Ring and Dirk Engelhardt: Theater. In: *Blech getrommelt. Günter Grass in der Kritik.* Ed. by Heinz Ludwig Arnold. Göttingen: Steidl 1997. P. 62: "Es gehe um 'das gebrochene Verhältnis der Deutschen zur Revolution'".

[27] Hellmuth Karasek: Beispiele für das Theater 1966. In: *Jahresring* (1966/67). P. 355: "Das Dokumentarspiel mündet hier wieder in die Parabel".

[28] See Thomas Brown: Brecht and the 17th of June, 1953. In: *Monatshefte* 63 (1971). Pp. 48–55.

[29] G.G.: Brecht und der 17. Juni 1953. Wie war es wirklich? Ein historischer Nachtrag zu Günter Grass' neuem Schauspiel. In: *Der Tagesspiegel* 23.1.1966.

that it was not Brecht's *Coriolan*.[30] Rather than demonstrating his despicable aestheticism by rehearsing through the revolt, Brecht actually interrupted his theatre work and gave precedence to politics. Views of what he was actually attempting to do again tend to diverge along party lines. But it seems to have been motivated more by a not implausible assessment of the situation and its dangers than by quixotic reminiscences of scenes from his past dramas. And his lack of success was due less to personal vacillation than to endemic powerlessness. To that extent, it is only fair to conclude that the play is really not about Brecht.

Much depends, of course, on how much the author actually knew. In this respect the lecture Grass gave to mark the 400th anniversary of Shakespeare's birth proves instructive. Written barely two years before the premiere of *Die Plebejer*, this text contains the bare bones of the play and does much to explain the circumstances of its conception. And in it Grass royally declares: "Wir wissen, daß Bertolt Brecht, während der Aufstand in Ost-Berlin und jenen Provinzen lief, die die Staatsbezeichnung DDR zusammenfaßt, seine Probenarbeit nicht unterbrochen hat. Doch probte er nicht *Coriolanus*, sondern Strittmatters *Katzgraben*" (p. 110). This shows not only how unreliable Grass's information was, but also what use he chose to make of it. Invoking no less a precedent than Shakespeare and Sir Walter Raleigh, he insists on his right to manipulate historical facts in the interests of theatrical truth. And in the process he makes of his *Plebejer* not a "Schlüsselstück", but a "Historienstück" (ibid).

Thus just as in Schiller's *Maria Stuart* Elizabeth and the audience know where they are because the historical castle of Fotheringhay is mentioned by name, so the use of Brechtiana in the Grass likewise serves as a guide to orientation. And just as Schiller's characters have little or nothing to do with their historical counterparts, so the Brecht of Grass's play is not the Brecht we know from photographs or biographies. At the same time, just as the psychological plausibility and dramatic effectiveness of Schiller's queens is ultimately bound up with their status and individuality as queens, so it is not a matter of indifference that the character of the "Chef" should be so elaborately identifiable as Brecht. On the contrary, it is precisely because in his persona and in his work he encapsulates the particular dialectic of revolutionary drama that he is given such a crucial role to play in the rehearsal of the uprising.

After all, the starting point for Grass's play was not a moral reflection about the behaviour of Bert Brecht on the 17th of June, and still less an abstract argument about the role of the intellectual in the revolution. It was the extrapolation into an unhistorical, theatrical scenario of the realization that, in or around the

---

[30] Brown notes that: "The work schedule on this day called for rehearsals of Brecht's adaptation of Molière's *Don Juan* [...] and for a rehearsal made necessary by the recasting of Kleist's *Der zerbrochene Krug*" (Brown: Brecht and the 17th of June (n. 28). P. 49). Elsewhere it is widely assumed that he was working on Strittmatter's *Katzgraben*.

year of the uprising, Brecht had been struggling with the question of how to make effective revolutionaries out of Shakespeare's plebeians, and that, like the East German workers, he had failed (p. 110). It is not for nothing that the play begins, after a command that establishes the theatrical nature of its setting, with the question: "Warum ändern wir Shakespeare?" (p. 7). In Act IV, Scene 5, the aftermath begins with the lapidary realization by the same character that: "Er hat das Stück abgesetzt" (p. 80). What happens in between is a dialectic of possibility and impossibility, ability and inability, which is not accidentally but programmatically coextensive with the raising and the dashing of the hopes of the revolution. And the sober conclusion is that the East German workers are no more able to change their spots than the Romano-Jacobean underclass of Shakespeare's *Coriolanus*.

A number of critics, admittedly, have used the Shakespearean intertext as grist for quite a different windmill. Inspired by the presence on stage of an effigy of Coriolanus, and leaning heavily on a periphrastically retracted remark by Podulla and an angry repudiation by the "Chef" himself, they have devoted extraordinary energy to the business of establishing parallels between Coriolanus and the "Chef".[31] Given that Coriolanus is not one of the more sympathetic of Shakespeare's characters, it should come as no surprise that a number of the negative traits attributed at one remove to Brecht should have their origin in this practice. The accusation of arrogance, for example, is explicitly associated in the play with a reference to Shakespeare's text; so it doesn't take much to conclude, as Noel Thomas does, that "the Boss shares Coriolanus's arrogance".[32] But then Gertrud Bauer Pickar goes one fictitious step further and adds "elitism" to the formula. "The *Chef*", she says, "shares with Coriolanus a feeling of distaste when he believes he must demonstrate his loyalty to the rabble".[33] Thomas though can trump even this, suggesting by implication that the "Chef" "countenances the resurrection of Stalin" and allowing himself the following poisonous parallelism: "Coriolanus's integrity as a soldier destroys his humanity. The Boss's preoccupation with aesthetic considerations is detrimental to his credibility as a social and political being and cuts asunder his bonds with his fellow citizens".[34]

---

[31] See Brunkhorst: *Shakespeares "Coriolanus" in deutscher Bearbeitung* (n. 11); Heinz Ide: Die Geschichte und ihre Dramatiker. Coriolan als Thema für Shakespeare, Brecht und Grass. In: *Beihefte zum Jahrbuch der schlesischen Friedrich-Wilhelms-Universität zu Breslau, VII. Symbola Hans Jessen Oblata*. Würzburg: Holzner 1967. Pp. 134–143; Noel Thomas: Shakespeare's *Coriolanus* and Grass's *Die Plebejer proben den Aufstand* – a Comparison. In: *New German Studies* 5 (1977). Pp. 169–184.

[32] Thomas: *Coriolanus* and *Die Plebejer* (n. 31). P. 172.

[33] Bauer Pickar: Silberpappeln und Saatkartoffeln (n. 10). P. 201.

[34] Thomas: *Coriolanus* and *Die Plebejer* (n. 31). Pp. 177 and 179.

In fairness, Thomas does seem to be dimly aware of how grotesque this comparison is. Earlier in his article, after a mention of the "colossal destructiveness" of Coriolanus, he goes so far as to admit that "to mention such quotations perhaps seems inappropriate when seeking to establish the relationship between Shakespeare's *Coriolanus* and *Die Plebejer proben den Aufstand*, for everybody knows that the Boss alias Brecht was not a God of war, nor had he even been a soldier".[35] His disingenuous formulation, though, not only massively underplays Brecht's passionate opposition to war and hence the utter incommensurability of the comparison with Coriolanus; it also, in its use of the past tense, wilfully ignores the significance in the play itself of the workers' past experience of war and the "Chef's" justified fear of it. In the process he not only suppresses a plausible possible motivation for the "Chef's" hesitancy – he also radically misreads the kind of play he is dealing with.

Coriolanus, after all, is an almost archetypal tragic hero. In him the Aristotelian proscription of greatness is fulfilled in an exemplary manner. And the connection between his status and his fate is so compelling that this object lesson in cathartic causality has been regarded as unsuitable for performance on a democratic stage.[36] Any comparison of Coriolanus with the "Chef" therefore risks tarring the latter with the same brush. In particular, it will involve imputing to the "Chef" (and by extension to Brecht[37]) equivalents of those aspects of the character of Coriolanus that led to his downfall. This in turn entails attributing to the "Chef" approximately the same political and personal importance as accrued to the Roman general. And the absurd disproportion that results provides a useful yardstick by which to measure the distance which separates Grass's play from Shakespeare's.

Thus the reason for making Brecht a "Chef" in the first place is precisely to ironize his greatness. After all, the point at issue in the "Chef's" adaptation of *Coriolanus* has to do with the question of status. And his own designation bespeaks nothing if not his position. In both cases, moreover, reference is made to expendability. In the first scene, Lithenner insists: "Der Chef will zeigen, daß Coriolan zu ersetzen ist" (p. 7). Four scenes from the end, the same words are poisonously applied to the "Chef" himself. "Auch du", spits the humiliated state poet just before his final exit, "bist zu ersetzen" (p. 82). What we have here is a dialectic of "Entbehrlichkeit" which might have come straight out of the mouth of Brecht's Herr Keuner, but which here takes on altogether more sinister overtones. The point is underlined when the "Chef" slips into his own discussion of

---

[35] Ibid. p. 171.

[36] Cf. Dirk Grathoff: Dichtung versus Politik: Brechts *Coriolan* aus Günter Grassens Sicht. In: *Brecht Heute* 1 (1971). P. 169.

[37] Ide: Die Geschichte und ihre Dramatiker (n. 31). P. 123: "Bei Grass heißt Coriolan Bert Brecht".

the subject the words "O Personenkult" (p. 9). In a play in which both the death of Stalin and his resurrection are referred to, and in which a worker cannot resist mutilating the dictator *in effigie*, it is not hard to discern what is meant. By the same token it seems to me that, *pace* Ide, the primary referent of the words "Koloß, nicht abzutragen" is not the alter ego of an artist.[38] On the contrary, it is precisely the implicit equation of Coriolanus with Stalin (which is anyway rather more plausible then the identification with Brecht) that gives the "Chef's" attempted adaptation of the character its piquancy. In acknowledging the failure of the enterprise, then, one of the points the "Chef" is making concerns the failure to replace the "Personenkult" with genuine democracy. In that sense, the fact that the workers seek his help at all is symptomatic. And to take them at their word would only have aggravated the symptoms.[39]

In this connection, it is significant that the term Grass uses in his subtitle is not "Tragödie", but "Trauerspiel". Unsurprisingly, many critics, especially theatre critics for whom matters of genre are naturally paramount, have been greatly exercised by this designation. Comparisons are drawn with Hebbel (the original "deutsch"), with Lessing ("bürgerlich") and with Hochhuth ("christlich").[40] Together with the adjective of nationality, the specifically German word is taken to refer on the one hand to a home-grown genre and on the other to forms of historical specificity. The doublet which gave Reich-Ranicki his title thus re-echoes through the criticism until it attains the status almost of orthodoxy: "Ein deutsches Trauerspiel über ein deutsches Trauerspiel".[41] Yet in as far as the political debacle is seen as typically or generically German, it necessarily lacks the element of individuality needed to constitute a German tragedy. Hence Grass's insistence in his interview with Thomas Brown that: "Im Gegensatz zur Tragödie, wo es den tragischen Einzelfall gibt, gibt es im Trauerspiel das schuldhafte und verstrickte Verhalten von mehreren".[42] One cannot help wondering

---

[38] Ibid. p. 136; cf. Brunkhorst: *Shakespeares "Coriolanus" in deutscher Bearbeitung* (n. 11). P. 155.

[39] Ann L. Mason: *The Sceptical Muse. A Study of Günter Grass' Conception of the Artist*. Bern: Herbert Lang 1974. P. 102: "The workers' attitude appears fatally similar to what Brecht was trying to deflate [...], a kind of hero-worship".

[40] Volker Klotz: Ein deutsches Trauerspiel. In: *Frankfurter Rundschau* 17.1.1966. Reprinted in Loschütz (ed.): *Von Buch zu Buch* (n. 14). Pp. 132–135. Here p. 132; Brunkhorst: *Shakespeares "Coriolanus" in deutscher Bearbeitung* (n. 11). P. 145; Kux: *Moderne Dichterdramen* (n. 7). P. 82.

[41] Marcel Reich-Ranicki: Trauerspiel von einem deutschen Trauerspiel. Günter Grass, Bertolt Brecht und der 17. Juni. *Die Plebejer proben den Aufstand* in Berlin uraufgeführt. In *Die Zeit* 21.1.1966. Reprinted in: Marcel Reich-Ranicki: *Günter Grass. Aufsätze*. Zürich: Ammann 1992. Pp. 67–75.

[42] Thomas Brown: *Die Plebejer* and Brecht: An Interview with Günter Grass. In: *Monatshefte* 65 (1973). P. 10.

therefore on what authority Martin Brunkhorst feels justified in concluding: "Es geht Grass um die Tragik des Individuums".[43]

This uncertainty over genre is symptomatic of the failure in certain sections of the criticism to pay due attention to matters of dramatic form and function. Nowhere is this more obvious than in the treatment of the references to Coriolanus. For although it is perfectly true that the "Chef" is compared by various members of his entourage to Shakespeare's hero, the allusions are motivated in each case by the very particular agendas (the "Verstrickungen") of those making them; they are ironized and repudiated by the "Chef" himself; and they apply not to his character, but to the role he is forced to play. It is only by disregarding this that certain of the charges against the "Chef" can be made to stick. In particular, the view of the "Chef" as an incorrigible aesthete is arrived at by taking the words "was bist du doch für ein mieser Ästhet", spoken in anger by a heavily ironized impetuous lickspittle turncoat (p. 38), and repeating it as if it contained some privileged truth about the "Chef".

Another source of apparently privileged truth about the "Chef" which the critics draw on at their peril and almost always to the detriment of Bert Brecht is Grass's Shakespeare lecture. Here, in the sketch of the play which it is claimed he has not yet written, Grass does indeed describe his future hero in terms which pre-echo the reproach of his future heroine: "Was immer passiert, alles wird ihm zur Szene; [...] alles wird ihm zur ästhetischen Frage: eine ungetrübte Theaternatur" (p. 112). Now it is not hard to see in this a further justification for the second half of Noel Thomas's deleterious comparison. But it is virtually impossible to apply these words to the historical figure of Brecht.[44] And even their applicability to the central character of the finished play is questionable. True, the "Chef" does make remarks which sound, or can be made to sound, as if he is merely gathering booty for his theatre work. At the beginning of Act I, Scene 7, for example, he says: "Es wäre gelacht, wenn sich dieser Vormittag nicht retten ließe" (p. 21). When he is persuaded to return to the stage between Acts I and II, his act of relenting is couched in the following terms: "Aber bitte... bitte... mögen sie sich ausplaudern, doch nicht ohne Gewinn für uns" (p. 29). And at the end of the second act he gloats: "Das nenn ich Beute! Lief das Band?" (p. 49). Indeed, he even allows himself the much-quoted rhyme: "Die Massen wird man auseinandertreiben; /dies Material jedoch wird bleiben" (ibid.). Yet the sense of the ironic reference to the wasted morning turns on the politically existential question of the death of Stalin, on

[43] Brunkhorst: Shakespeares "Coriolanus" in deutscher Bearbeitung (n. 11). P. 146.
[44] Cf. Hilde Spiel: Die Plebejer an der Burg. Zur Grass-Premiere am Burgtheather. In: Frankfurter Allgemeine Zeitung 19/20.5.1966: "Man mag ihn als jesuitischen Marxisten, als pragmatischen Moralisten, als sozialbewußten Außenseiter sehen, nur eines war er nicht: jene 'ungetrübte Theaternatur' als die Grass seine Hauptfigur bezeichnet".

the subject of which the "Chef" is concerned to conduct a Brechtian "Versuch". Equally, apart from its dramatically tainted status as a reluctant concession, the remark about extracting advantage is immediately preceded by a reference to a debate in which the "Chef" quite rightly predicts his own vindication. And the "Material" refers to the short-lived triumph over Kosanke.

For the "Chef" and for the audience, this symbolic rubbishing of the state poet really is the only positive thing to come out of the revolution. It is hard to see where such a piece of Falstaffian comedy might fit in the unusually tight construction of Shakespeare's *Coriolanus*. Conversely, given its status as an obvious surrogate, and the emotional impact of its threatening counterpart, the structural significance of this scene in the architecture of Grass's play is unmistakable. And the effect of the "Chef's" sardonic commentary is ironically to underline the fact. Thus, far from doing the work certain critics demand of them, and nailing the Brechtian "Chef" as an unreconstructed aesthete, each of these quotations from the finished play also points to his political perspicuity; relativizes the ill-considered remarks of Grass's Shakespeare lecture by an act of deliberate citation; and binds that citation in to a piece of theatre in which the theatre reflects on itself.

To be sure, a number of critics, resisting the temptation to attribute the "Chef's" actions to Coriolanian intransigence, have been prepared to countenance the possibility that they may be motivated by political, rather than merely aesthetic, considerations.[45] This does not mean, however, that the "Chef" is either exonerated or freed from tragedy – far from it. Equally, the difference in tone between the play and the lecture has not escaped notice[46] – although this too has been twisted into a reproach against the former as well as the latter.[47] And of course the possibility of turning against Grass himself certain barbs originally meant for either Brecht or the "Chef" has been gleefully seized upon.[48] Intradiegetic ironies, however, are almost completely overlooked. The genuine dilemma facing the "Chef" – namely how to survive in an extremely

[45] G. Aichinger: Der geprobte Aufstand. Enttäuschende Grass-Uraufführung im Berliner Schiller-Theater. In: *Rheinischer Merkur* 21.1.1966: "Brecht vollzog die Ablehnung nicht aus ästhetischen Gründen, sondern aus politischen, weil er, der moskautreue Kommunist, Ulbricht nicht in den Rücken fallen wollte".

[46] Keith Miles: *Günter Grass*. London: Vision 1979. P. 150; Mason: *The Sceptical Muse* (n. 39). P. 110.

[47] W. Gordon Cunliffe: *Günter Grass*. New York: Twayne 1969: "The workers, apparently not reduced to the helpless stupidity they display in Grass' play [...]". Michael Hollington: *Günter Grass: The Writer in a Pluralist Society*. London – Boston: Marion Boyars 1980. P. 116: "Unfortunately traces of the tone of the speech survive into the play itself".

[48] g.g.: Kritisch Ferngesehen: *Die Plebejer proben den Aufstand*. In: *Marbacher Zeitung* 28.4.1970: "Dabei schlägt der Vorwurf, den Grass Brecht macht, auf ihn selbst zurück".

dangerous situation in which private political convictions come up against intractable power – is reduced to a crude moral imperative that is far more completely at odds with the complexities of the situation than could ever be said of Grass's protagonist. (That this moral imperative is given expression in secondary texts by the author of the play does not make it any more persuasive.) And rather than taking seriously the title of *Die Plebejer proben den Aufstand* and examining carefully the relationship between the rehearsal which can be represented on the stage and the uprising which cannot, critics have a tendency to identify in this eminently self-referential play something they are pleased to call "reality"[49] – which is then implausibly distinguished from and privileged over the theatre.[50]

That certain of these aporias are familiar from (largely outdated) Brecht criticism is suggestive. The perceived disjunction between theory and practice, for example, is reminiscent of the infamous but influential thesis of Martin Esslin;[51] and in Brecht's case too has been used to criticize the plays. The distortion of a difficult choice into a simple fault, supported at need by uncontextualized pronouncements from protagonists and author, regularly bedevils accounts of the third scene of *Mutter Courage und ihre Kinder*.[52] And Brecht's subtle and contrapuntal use of tragedy in that play is often dismissed out of hand on the basis of faulty foreknowledge of Epic Theatre.[53] The failings for which Brecht's Galileo has been criticized, both within the various versions of the play and beyond them, have been repeatedly accredited to the play's author,

---

[49] Wirth: Grass and Documentary Drama (n. 6). P. 27: "Grass unintentionally represents the reality of the Uprising". Ute Brandes: *Günter Grass*. Berlin: Colloquium 1998. P. 46: "Vor der Wirklichkeit versagt er jedoch". Cunliffe: *Günter Grass* (n. 47). P. 128: "Real life shows that it can compete with the theater".

[50] Contrast: Dieter Hildebrandt: Brecht und der Rasen. In: *Frankfurter Allgemeine Zeitung* 17.1.1966. Reprinted in: Loschütz (ed.): *Von Buch zu Buch* (n. 14). Pp. 140–144. Here P. 140: "Nur auf den ersten Blick kann cs also so sich ansehen, als werde da einfach dic Realität gegen das Theater gesetzt".

[51] Martin Esslin: *Brecht. A Choice of Evils. A Critical Study of the Man, His Work, and His Opinions*. London: Eyre and Spottiswoode [1959] 1971. P. 207: "The truth of a great poet's intuitive insight has transcended the author's conscious understanding of what he is doing".

[52] Ronald Speirs sums up (and repudiates) this view when he writes: "The fates of Swiss Cheese and Kattrin *can* be drawn into the moral pattern of guilt and punishment by seeing them as victims of their mother's guilt, for she haggles so long over the sale of her wagon that she fails to save Swiss Cheese from execution". (Ronald Speirs: *Bertolt Brecht*. Basingstoke: Macmillan 1987. Pp. 98–99).

[53] Thus Ronald Gray, who notes that "Brecht did not want a sense of tragedy" says of "the structure of the play as a whole": "In its total effect, it is oddly without impact, a series of moments and *coups de theatre* without coherence" (Ronald Gray: *Brecht the Dramatist*. Cambridge: Cambridge University Press 1976. P. 136 and p. 126).

and with a comparable gesture of accusatory triumph.[54] While the ability to disregard what ought to be obvious wherever it contravenes established orthodoxy was a besetting trait of Brecht scholarship long before it came to be applied to Grass.

Especially given the ostensible subject of Grass's play, it is tempting to wonder to what extent these common failings can be grounded in a comparable dramaturgy. And it cannot be denied that many accounts of *Die Plebejer* are shot through with terminology that is familiar from the Brechtian context.[55] Significantly following Grass's own lead, a good number of critics are apt to see in his "Trauerspiel" an example of "dialektisches Theater". The term "episch", too, which is so indelibly associated with the author of the Notes on *Mahagonny*, is regularly used to characterize the techniques of Günter Grass. In the same connection the distinction between "didactic" and "demonstrative" theatre, which is so central to the work of the Master, is also discussed in respect of the Rehearsal Play. The related vocabulary of the "Modell" likewise serves as an aid to understanding Grass as well as Brecht. The term "Verfremdung" also gets bandied about a good deal. And Ann Mason's coinage of the "Lehrstück about Lehrstücke" is the tip of an iceberg.[56]

A number of critics even mention Brecht texts by name. Reich-Ranicki for example is uncomfortably reminded of the *Dreigroschenoper*.[57] Others, possibly following his lead, recall the *Kreidekreis* in the same connection. Given the relatively explicit nature of Grass's allusions, it was only to be expected that critics would make a point of picking up the references to *Mutter Courage und ihre Kinder* and *Trommeln in der Nacht*. But more covert allusions – to *Mahagonny* for example, or *Die Maßnahme,* are also duly explicated. References to *Der gute Mensch von Sezuan* and even *Das Verhör des Lukullus* seem to be rooted more in the critic's expertise than in actual intertextual relations. But the importance of the *Leben des Galilei* for Grass's play has been underlined more than once. François Bondy even puts "Galilée" into the title of his review.[58] And to his eternal credit, Ralf Sudau devotes two of his twenty pages to a comparison of that play with Grass's.

[54] See Michael Morley: *Brecht. A Study.* London: Heinemann 1977. P. 50: "The sensualist and the scientist [...], these [...] qualities in the character of Galileo [are only] apparently contradictory because both for the character and the author they are really part of the same basic impulse".
[55] Cf. Ludwig Plankolb: Mit Brechts Mitteln überführt Grass hier Brecht. In: *Oberösterreichische Nachrichten* 18.5.1966, quoted in Arnold (ed.): *Blech getrommelt* (n. 26). P. 268.
[56] Mason: *The Sceptical Muse* (n. 39). P. 111.
[57] Reich-Ranicki: Trauerspiel (n. 41). P. 74.
[58] François Bondy: Le théâtre à Berlin. Günter Grass et son Brecht – Coriolan – Galilée. In: *Preuves* 181 (March 1966). Pp. 68–70.

Unfortunately but significantly, the banner under which he does so is emblazoned with "Desavouierung".[59] By much the same token, Theodor Pelster, having duly juggled with terms such as "Lehrstück" and "dialektisches Theater" insists: "Wenn es in eine Tradition gestellt werden soll, so wird man weit eher auf Georg Büchner und sein Drama *Dantons Tod* verweisen als auf Brecht und seine Theatertheorien".[60] Elsewhere in the criticism it is widely assumed that what Grass was trying to do in this play was to dislodge Brecht from his pedestal.[61] Applied specifically to matters of dramatic technique, this would mean that Grass was trying either to repudiate Brecht, or to go beyond him, or to outdo him on his own terrain.

Either way, although some critics did hail Grass as Brecht's successor, in the opinion of the majority the relative flop of the opening night was a nemesis fitting the hubris of the whole enterprise. In particular, three scenes in *Die Plebejer* called forth the uncomprehending condemnation of the critics. The relative stasis of the second act led them to complain of boredom.[62] The scene of the attempted hanging in Act III was deprecated as an error of judgement.[63] And the heroics of the hairdresser towards the end of that act were regarded as intolerably melodramatic.[64] In all three instances, the critics are able to support their judgements with quotations from the play itself. Thus at the end of the second act, Volumnia herself complains that "Der Aufstand tritt auf der Stelle" (p. 49). As he is about to be hanged, the "Chef" comments wrily: "Diese Art Dramatik habe ich immer gehasst" (p. 59). And of the voluble "Friseuse" the "Chef" admits: "Fast fürchte ich, sie ist von mir" (p. 70).

By her own admission, the character this character is modelling herself on is "die Kattrin auf dem Dach" (ibid.). Just in case anyone missed it, the notes helpfully point out that this is an "Anspielung auf Brecht: *Mutter Courage*" (p. 127). In other words what is happening here is that a specific kind of dramaturgy is being used quite explicitly to characterize and explain the reaction of the "Chef" to a particular phase of the uprising. And the dramaturgy in question is derived not from Büchner, not from Schiller, but – *mirabile dictu* – from Brecht. Of course there is a certain rueful irony in the "fast fürchte ich". Unquestionably the identification of the hairdresser with the dumb drummer is awkward and slightly absurd. It is even suggested that there might be something uneducated and improper about it. But the arguments she puts forward

[59] Sudau: *Werkbearbeitung* (n. 7). Pp. 184–186.
[60] Pelster: *Günter Grass* (n. 6). P. 50.
[61] Hollington: *Günter Grass* (n. 47). P. 115; Wirth: Grass and Documentary Drama (n. 6). P. 22.
[62] Ring and Engelhardt: Theater (n. 26). P. 60: "Gelangweilt hat sich nicht nur Luft".
[63] Ibid. p. 61
[64] Hildebrandt: Brecht und der Rasen (n. 50). P. 141: "An dieser Stelle ist mit Grass das Pathos […] einigermaßen durchgegangen".

about the ways in which individuals may be able to oppose the superior might of armies are perfectly plausible. And the hope we invest in the possibility that she might prove to be right is precisely comparable to the hope that is riding on Kattrin when she refuses to stop her drumming. Indeed, just as in Brecht's play the young peasant becomes the legitimizing spokesman for that hope, so in the Grass it is not only the "Chef" who makes to follow the "Friseuse", but the entire company.[65]

In the Grass that hope is immediately dashed when the path of progress is blocked by the cynicism of the returning Volumnia. And the abrupt sense of disappointment that arises as a result is powerfully expressed by means of dramatic register. After the iambic exaltation appropriate to the high drama of the conflict between rebels and tanks, the "Friseuse" reverts to prose and expresses her disillusion in a line which can easily be imagined as Berlin dialect: "Das war eine kurze Verlobung" (p. 72). Given its position at the end of the third act, this parting remark can be seen to sum up the "Aufstand" as a whole. And that in turn suggests that Grass is knowingly using different kinds of drama precisely in order to evoke in the theatre-goer the complex feelings associated with the various stages of the unfolding revolution. That discomfiture is one of those feelings is proof not of ineptitude, then, but of mastery.

A careful consideration of the hanging scene confirms this impression. Reich-Ranicki, whose view of the play as a whole is expressed in the words: "mit solchen Mitteln läßt sich den Ereignissen vom 17. Juni nicht beikommen" finds the scene comical.[66] The fact that the "Putzer", just before he goes to search Brecht's theatre for something that will serve as a gallows, says "Können vor Lachen" (p. 58), strongly suggests that this is not contrary to, but perfectly in accordance with the intentions of the author. More perceptive critics, though, who are better attuned to the bitterness and irony of the scene, are reminded, when they metaphorically follow the "Putzer", not like Reich-Ranicki, of the *Dreigroschenoper*, but of *Der kaukasische Kreidekreis*. Just as in Grass's play repeated mention is made of the crucial reaction of the "Volkspolizisten" to the unfolding revolt (pp. 24, 63–65, 68), so in Brecht's the near-hanging and subsequent appointment of Azdak exemplify the ambiguous importance of the forces of order.[67] Where in Brecht the unpredictability of the "Panzerreiter" is shockingly underlined by the actual violence of the "Ballspiel" that precedes the second attempted hanging, so in *Die Plebejer* the pantomime execution is endowed with a chilling realism because it occurs at the behest of the tribune figures, Wiebe and Damaschke, who are quick to denounce others when the

---

[65] P. 71. Cf. Bertolt Brecht: *Mutter Courage und ihre Kinder*. BFA 6. Pp. 6–86. Here p. 83.
[66] Reich-Ranicki: Trauerspiel von einem deutschen Trauerspiel (n. 41). Pp. 73–74.
[67] Bertolt Brecht: *Der kaukasische Kreidekreis*. BFA 8. Pp. 7–191. Here pp. 153–157.

going gets tough. As in the Brecht, the charge levelled at the "Chef" is prefigured in the Grass by an act of exculpatory self-accusation. And because Brecht's Azdak is almost strung up because he missed the moment when the uprising was put down, so Grass is able through the intertextual reference to mark the moment when a similar change begins to occur in Berlin.

Here again, then, the theatrical means Grass employs, so far from being inadequate to the task of representing the uprising, enable him with subtlety and precision to chart its course, and to characterize its stages in all their excitement, bathos, tawdry horror and banality. That it was Grass's intention to mark out the rhythm of the revolution in this way becomes clear from the remark that closes Act II. Here, at the centre of the play, before the audience is released from a state of stalemate into the interval, Volumnia remarks: "Der Aufstand tritt auf der Stelle" (p. 49). The word "Aufstand" of course is used not only in the title of Grass's play, but also in that of the book by Stefan Brant about the 17th of June 1953 which Grass confessedly used as a source for it (p. 123).[68] So the stasis certain critics complain of, together with the difficulty of finding meaningful things for the workers to do in the theatre and the strong sense that they should be doing something constructive outside it, all contribute to create a sense of an uprising that has stalled. The effect is produced – and it is hard to know how else it might be produced – using a specifically theatrical awkwardness which, if in this instance not explicitly Brechtian, nonetheless owes a great deal to Brecht's theatre and constitutes Grass's play as a Brechtian "Modell".

In one respect, admittedly, this "Modell" goes against everything we have learned about Brechtian theatre. Instead of an epic variety of time and place, Grass's play adheres strictly to the Aristotelian unities. In respect of time, for example, it is significant that the "Chef's" first action is to demand more light, and his last is to release the lighting technician (p. 9, p. 85). The mid-point of the play, moreover, is marked as midday (p. 49). For the entire duration of the play we are confined to the interior of a theatre, while much of the action takes place off stage and is conveyed to us by means of "Botenberichte". And the unity of action is guaranteed by the concentration on the uprising itself, each stage of which – the original demands, the reinforcements, the pause, the escalation, the brief desperate exhilaration and the terrible weary aftermath – is carefully reproduced.

Significantly, however, they are not reproduced as straightforward action, but as its opposite: as inaction, as pantomime, as histrionics – that is, as self-conscious theatre.[69] Similarly, by drawing attention to the lighting effects,

[68] The reference is to: Stefan Brant and Klaus Bolling: *Der Aufstand. Vorgeschichte, Geschichte und Deutung des 17. Juni 1953*. Stuttgart: Steingruben 1954.
[69] Cf. W.G. Cunliffe: Grass and the Denial of Drama. In: *A Günter Grass Symposium*. Ed. by A. Leslie Willson. Austin: University of Texas Press 1971. Pp. 60–70. Richard Lawson: *Günter Grass* (n. 16) speaks of "dramas of retardation" (p. 13).

Grass disables traditional explanations for the unity of time and is hence in a position to underline the facticity of the one day celebrated in the West as the day of the revolution. And by making us claustrophobically aware of the theatricality of the theatre, he achieves something like an inside-out effect whereby every exit becomes an entrance and every entrance a retreat. To that extent, Grass's punctilious observance of the rules of classical theatre is not only ironic and therefore constitutes a comment on the nature of theatre itself, it is also a direct reversal and thus makes it possible literally to bring into the theatre important aspects of the event with which he is concerned.

Moreover, just as the Epic format of Brecht's *Mutter Courage* enabled him to repeat, for demonstrative purposes, a scenario which in its rhythm and its emotional impact has much to do with tragedy, so Grass's classical tragic form enfolds a significantly five-fold repetition of the same demonstrative demand. (That the sixth request, the one to which the "Chef" so nearly accedes, is of quite a different order, is rarely remarked upon.) Reduced to its crudest form, the essence of the demand is that the writer should write. In each case, the demand is politically motivated and what is required of the writer is political writing. What is at stake therefore is the relationship between the writer and politics. In this sense, the disposition of the demands and the response to them is particularly significant. It is noticeable for example that of the five requests, three come from the workers and two from the representative of the State. To the former the writer is bound by bonds of sympathy and long-standing ideology. To the latter he is indebted for financial support. Thus the pairing in itself is dialectical. So far from resolving the dialectic, though, the play pointedly subordinates it to a (classical) parallel structure of climax and aftermath. Both sides use threats to raise the stakes. And while neither actually makes good the threat, the "Chef" is left with regard to both in a position of barely tolerable awkwardness.

This kind of unresolved dialectic is a trade mark of Brechtian theatre. The anguished outcry of Shen Te at the end of *Der gute Mensch von Sezuan* is perhaps the most explicit example of it.[70] (And the subversive device of the "dei in machinam" is of course comparably classical.) For our purposes, though, the clearest parallel is surely the ending (or endings) of the *Leben des Galilei*. It is true that the final scene of the border crossing is present in the Grass only in the form of allusions and intertextual references.[71] But the last line of the "Chef", stolen as it is from one of the *Buckower Elegien*, perfectly summarizes the attitude adopted by Galileo in the final encounter with Andrea Sarti, and bespeaks a closely parallel predicament (p. 85; cf. BFA 5. Pp. 280–285). Just as in the Brecht the evidence of the *Discorsi* shows that Galileo is at least right enough to keep the argument alive, so in the Grass the "Chef's" assessment of the

[70] Bertolt Brecht: *Der gute Mensch von Sezuan*. BFA 6. Pp. 175–281. Here p. 278.
[71] Bertolt Brecht: *Leben des Galilei*. BFA 5. Pp. 7–289. Here pp. 109 and 288, Grass: *Plebejer*. P. 84.

situation turns out to be accurate but not persuasive. In the Brecht as in the Grass the question is raised as to whether others could have done what Galileo did (BFA 5. Pp. 99 and 282). And just as Brecht's Andrea undergoes a change of heart with regard to Galileo, so Grass's Volumnia, having previously been vitriolic about the "Chef's" cunning, ends up acknowledging its usefulness (BFA 5. P. 281; cf. Grass: *Plebejer*. P. 85).

For Grass as for Brecht, the opposite of this "List" is heroism. It is no accident that the celebrated exchange on the subject from Brecht's play has its equivalent in a characteristic culinary mixed metaphor of Grass's: "Wo ich hinblicke: Teigkneter, die aus mir einen rasselnden Helden backen wollen" (p. 27; cf. BFA 5. Pp. 93 and 274). In both cases, what is at stake is compounded of greatness and danger. Thus the oleaginous commendation of the cardinal in Brecht's play is dripping with menace (BFA 5. Pp. 61 and 240). And the "Chef" hints at a comparable nexus when he insists: "Meine Größe und mein Name besitzen zu Hause einen Arbeitstisch, von dem aus […] ein hübscher Friedhof beobachtet werden kann" (p. 19). Although what awaits him might not be torture or burning, the position in which the "Chef" finds himself is still very perilous. On what seems to be a simple request there might actually hang his theatre, his freedom, and possibly even his life. The point is underlined by the continuous presence on stage of the (eminently Brechtian) mannequin which, by representing Coriolanus, alludes to Stalinism. Admittedly, in both cases there is some suggestion that that very greatness may offer a protection of sorts. Just as in the Brecht we know – but Galileo doesn't – that the authorities are prepared only to show him the instruments (BFA 5. P. 270), so in the Grass we are aware without being told that Brecht's own Austrian passport and Western publisher may possibly but not necessarily relativize the danger the "Chef" is in. But in both cases even the taking of the risk is repudiated in a way the audience is led reluctantly to approve of. This too of course is a trade-mark of Brecht's. In *Der kaukasische Kreidekreis*, for example, Azdak likewise insists: "Ich mach keinem den Helden" (BFA 8. Pp. 91 and 184). And in *Maßnahmen gegen die Gewalt* the point of the parable is to recommend playing a long game (BFA 18. Pp. 13–14). Thus the "Chef's" similar refusal of the role offered him can be seen as contributing to his authentic characterization as an avatar of the playwright Brecht.

In terms of the history of serious theatre, of course, such a position is counterintuitive, if not downright cussed. And that is another reason why, in Grass as in Brecht, complicated games are played with the genre of tragedy. As the title indicates, *Leben des Galilei* is concerned with a particular individual. Like the "Chef", that individual manages to avoid your classic melodramatic demise. But like the "Chef" he is left at the end isolated and remorseful. Quite whether we are meant to feel sorry for either at this point is equally unclear. Comparable uncertainty also surrounds the question of the attribution of guilt. But there is no doubt that the process which landed each protagonist in this predicament is one in which we have – and are meant to have – considerable emotional investment. In both cases, indeed, that investment is encouraged and directed by the same pair of dramatic devices: by timing and by the provision of spokesmen.

In Brecht's *Leben des Galilei*, an important repeated motif is that of the literal missing of the bus. It occurs when Florence is threatened by the plague (BFA 5. Pp. 46 and 225) and it crucially determines the actual arrest (BFA 5. P. 267). In Grass's *Plebejer* its metaphorical equivalent forms the substance of the (slightly embarrassing) monologue of self-reproach that closes the third act – most notably in the lines: "Ich hab mir meine Finger, zehn, / Vom Zögern schwer vergolden lassen. –" (p. 72). And just as the "Friseuse" by reverting to prose was able to summarize the nature of the revolt from the perspective of the disappointed "Volk", so the pat tetrameters and quasi-religious imagery of this speech give us the poet's summary of the proceedings and his role in them. The effect is to remind us of the extent to which the previous acts have indeed been largely dominated by the dramaturgy of "Zögern". At the same time, just as the critical scene in *Galileo* has us holding our breath to the rhythm of a bell that rings a fraction late, so in Act I of *Die Plebejer* the tension of Scenes 7 and 8 is pointed by their constitution as a bet, underlined by the device of deliberate distraction, incorporated in the interventions of a mason and measured out at its climax in the three stage directions "er will abgehen", "er will gehen" and "er geht ab" (p. 27). The sequence ends moreover with the reference to half-baked heroism that so explicitly resonates with the Brecht.

In the Brecht, what is at stake in the decision is exemplified by the contrasted presence on stage of the assertive scientist Sarti and the gently praying daughter Virginia, although the latter only really comes into her own once the recantation has happened. In the Grass, where the agon is presented as a common assault on a Brechtian-Leninist mountain, the difficulty of the dilemma is underlined by the (prophetic) mention of Russian tanks, emergency exits and elegies (pp. 24–25 and 27). And the effect, as in the Brecht, is to make us temporarily aware of the overhasty nature of our assumptions. The bitterness which, in the Brecht, befalls Andrea Sarti when these assumptions are violently disrupted is later shared in the Grass by Volumnia and Podulla (pp. 38–39, 75–76; cf. BFA 5. Pp. 93 and 274). But the impatience which also partly characterizes Sarti's thought and actions becomes the defining trait of Grass's "Maurer".

It is also of course the fatal failing of the "junge Genosse" in Brecht's *Die Maßnahme*.[72] In that play the central protagonist, driven by pity, anger, disgust, and an impetuousness compounded of all of these, four times flouts the instructions of the Party. Grass's quixotic mason first vents his rage on the image of Stalin;

---

[72] BFA 3. Pp. 73–125. Here pp. 73–98 or 99–125.

then on the basis of groundless suspicion gets embroiled in a brawl; then violently disrupts the rehearsal on the plausible grounds that in post-war Berlin there are no lawns worth preserving; and finally indulges in a senseless act of heroism and does himself serious damage (pp. 23, 30, 42, 63–66). As in the Brecht we are in each case led both to understand the reasons for, and to deprecate, his actions. For just as the "junge Genosse" is at once "einverstanden" and useful (BFA 3. Pp. 116 and 124) so this same "Maurer" picks up the "Chef's" reference to tanks, grudgingly understands the implied need for a second assault on the peak, helps to direct the reconstruction of the early stages of the uprising and willingly contributes to the supply of information about its background (pp. 24, 27, 32, 36). The understandable and excessive nature of his frustration is underlined when the "Putzer", in gently admonishing him, gives him a name ("ist nun genug, Karl", p. 23), and when Erwin tactfully turns off the tape recorder which might otherwise have gathered the evidence against him (p. 24). Thus what Grass is doing to one of the iconic figures of the "Aufstand" is to bind him in to a "Lehrstück" structure that is recognizably derived from Brecht.

In the process, Grass is able to make two important points about the nature of the uprising. The first, laid in the mouth of the mason, concerns the attitude of the intellectuals to the workers' revolt (p. 34). And the second, exemplified by his behaviour, concerns the nature of the revolt itself. In this latter respect, a comparison with *Mutter Courage* is instructive. In the fourth scene of that play, the scene of the "große Kapitulation", the behaviour of the "junger Soldat" ("kommt randalierend")[73] is directly comparable to the symbolic violence proffered by the "Maurer" against the dead Stalin. In the Brecht, the fact that the young man's justified anger proves insufficiently sustainable is underlined when, in a characteristically Brechtian *Gestus* he sits down. Grass, by taking over precisely this *Gestus*, albeit not without irony and immediately after the mason has once again sought to assert himself, is able to indicate that the anger of the East Berlin workers is likewise only "ein kurzer".[74]

At the end of the scene, Mutter Courage herself likewise capitulates and refuses to pursue her complaint. Similarly, in *Der kaukasische Kreidekreis* Azdak, as part of his resolutely anti-heroic stance, repeatedly pays over-obsequious lip-service to those in authority. Grass's "Chef" too, when he scents real danger, abruptly changes his behaviour. Thus Wiebe and Damaschke are greeted "mit überraschendem Charme" (p. 56). And when Kosanke utters veiled threats against his assistants, it is said of the previously recalcitrant "Chef" that he "erkennt die Situation, geht liebenswürdig auf Kosanke zu" (p. 77). Indeed shortly afterwards, what started out as an eye-to-eye conflict

---

[73] BFA 6. P. 46.
[74] BFA 6. P. 50; cf. Grass: *Plebejer*. P. 32.

with the powerful hack is deflected into the sphere of literary allusion, where we can follow but Kosanke can't (p. 79).

The reference is to Shakespeare. And while as we have seen this is a connection which has greatly exercised the critics, the significance of using a Shakespearean intertext in the first place at least partly escapes them. Here too it is the theatre of Brecht that helps to illuminate what Grass is up to. In *Der Aufstieg des Arturo Ui* (BFA 7. Pp. 7–115) Brecht uses a Roman play by Shakespeare on the subject of a putsch in order to illuminate and distanciate his portrayal of Hitler's rise to power. In *Die Plebejer proben den Aufstand* Grass uses a Roman play by Shakespeare concerned with the overthrow of a powerful autocrat in a merely titular democracy in order to enrich his depiction of an uprising which included among its declared aims the unseating of Walter Ulbricht and the institution of free and fair elections. As in the Brecht, part of the purpose of Grass's play – and it is a purpose explicitly aired in the play itself – is to correct tendentious misapprehensions about a relatively recent historical event that is identified only indirectly in the text. To this end both authors use a series of characters whose names have been changed, but whose historical counterparts are relatively obvious to those in the know. The parallels are underlined in both cases by a series of more or less easily decodable allusions. And the Grass, like the Brecht, is written in a form of verse whose demonstrative inappropriateness becomes especially clear when it is reintroduced into its original context in the form of grotesque citation.

Admittedly, the scale is different. (And in this context it is significant that, whereas Brecht triumphantly sustains the pentametric pulse, Grass's verse repeatedly falls short, thus approximating to German models and even doggerel.) Yet the kind of *Verfremdung* implied by the use of historical hindsight, allegory and sub-Shakespearean verse is still patently parallel. And so too is the insistent irony of proportion. For just as Brecht uses all the theatrical means at his disposal in order to take Hitler down from the mythical level to that of banality, so Grass uses his theatre in order to resist respective attempts at aggrandizing the protest. To that extent, the ruthlessness of Ui is the equivalent as well as the opposite of the docility of the workers. And respective attempts to characterize either as the national hamartia of the "deutsches Trauerspiel" are held up to the same deliberate ridicule.

In Grass's play, the means by which this happens is eminently and explicitly Brechtian. Thus even before news of the uprising has reached the theatre, the "Chef" includes in his inventory of possible aesthetic reactions to such an event: "Lehrstück machen. Publikum klüger machen! Hier! Mit geschulten Volkstribünen den Plebejern zeigen: Wie macht man Revolution, wie macht man keine. – Oder Neues von heute?" (pp. 13–14). In Act II, Scene 3, the crucial word "zeigen" recurs specifically with reference to "heute", when the "Chef" says: "Ich zeige euch, was ihr draußen macht" (p. 40). Significantly the means by which he does so involves the pair of assistants whose position within the republic of the theatre is not unlike that of tribunes, and whose "schooling" is alluded to in the line "Litthenner, zeig, was du gelernt hast" (ibid.). The upshot is a demonstrative piece of theatre featuring a "Plebejerchor" on the one hand and on the other "die Arbeiter mit Transparenten" (p. 42). And what is thus demonstrated is a demonstration: "Sie beginnen ihren Umzug, der im Verlauf der Szene […] mehr und mehr in Verwirrung gerät" (ibid.). Of course there is an element of parody about the scene; and it is perfectly natural that the workers, whose uprising is here subjected to a literal *reductio ad absurdum*, should subsequently need instruction in the art of invective. At another level, though, that invective is itself an expression of confusion. And in Act III, Scene 6 this same disorientation comes in from outside and finds expression in the intercut descriptions of two histrionic plebeians (p. 67).

What is here ironically reversed over three of Grass's four acts is the relationship between description and enactment that is the quintessence of Epic Theatre. From the point of view of the play's genesis, it is also the quintessence of Grass's entire undertaking. The task he had set himself, after all, involved conveying by theatrical means the substance and the implications of an event he had himself seen from a distance and read about in (illustrated) narrative prose. One of the ways in which he achieves this within the play is by attributing the descriptions to a variety of actual participants or other witnesses, who then, in the manner of Brecht's "Straßenszene", proceed to a dramatic illustration of what they have seen or experienced.[75] Thus in Act I, Scene 7, a piece of a Roman column is symbolically roped in to allow the "Putzer" to re-enact the elevated address of Hanne the hodman (pp. 22–23.) In Act II, Scene 3, the same "Putzer" takes on the role of minister Selbmann and is driven from his pedestal by a hodman who, because he identifies himself in the first person by his profession but not by his name, may or may not be the eponymous Hanne (pp. 35–36). In Act III the scene with the hanging is immediately preceded by the narrative line "In Halle hängen sie Spitzel auf" (p. 57), and the description of the action with the flag is shot through with elements of accompanying theatricality – as when the "Friseuse", re-enacting her upward gaze towards the Brandenburg Gate on the line "von oben", suddenly becomes aware of the stage, which thus comes to stand in for the distance between the action on the arch and those watching below (p. 63). And in Act IV, Scene 4, Kosanke's account of his own performance quickly becomes a repetition of that performance, whose hollow theatricality is underlined by the combination of silence and brief applause which greets its conclusion (pp. 77–78).

---

[75] See Urs Jenny: Grass probt den Aufstand. In: Loschütz (ed.): *Von Buch zu Buch* (n. 14). Pp. 135–140. Here p. 137.

Not the least of many ironies surrounding this act of rehashed demagogy concerns its alleged spontaneity. Thus the "Chef" responds to the false modesty of Kosanke's "ich habe gesprochen" with the line: "Wie? Einfach so? Das könnte ich nicht" (p. 77). This not only underlines the thoughtlessness of Kosanke's sloganizing, contrasting it with the caution of the "Chef" – it also ties in with the *leitmotif* of the "Probe" that runs through the play and helps to give it its title. Thus it is specifically to Kosanke that the "Chef" expatiates on the need for rehearsal, concluding his list of examples with the line "den Aufstand der Plebejer muß man proben" (p. 47). In the theatrical coup that follows it is Kosanke who gets consigned to the dustbin of history. At the same time, the language employed by the State poet is shown to be hackneyed by repeated practising before he even opens his mouth. Indeed, early in the second act the interchangeable rhetoric of denunciation leads to a brawl that is first deprecated with the word "Spontaneitäten" (p. 30) and then ironically elevated to the level of art by factitious repetition.

The double point at issue here concerns a distrust of unbridled emotion on the one hand and received wisdom on the other. And this difficult dialectic of freedom and ideology informs Grass's play at every level. It is not for nothing that the "Chef", in refusing to take the revolt seriously, insists on its spontaneity and qualifies it as "ungeprobte Zappelei" (p. 17). Yet it is equally no accident that the phrase with which he dismisses Volumnia's inauthentic account of the uprising is "Geprobt, jedes Wort" (p. 18). That this dialectic is central to Brecht's theatre is evident in particular from *Die Maßnahme*, which as we have seen is an important point of reference for *Die Plebejer*. It is therefore entirely appropriate that the "Chef's" apparently spontaneous bid for freedom is expressed through intertexts that recall the anarchist youth of his model – notably *Baal* –, and that the dashing of the utopian dream is expressed through the clash of Expressionist unrealism and the documentarity of the "Flugblatt". At the same time, the awkwardness of this moment is underlined not only because the scene is the culmination of what I would call the *Maßnahme* sequence and because it explicitly takes its inspiration from *Mutter Courage*, but also because, as the presence of the tanks indicates, it so clearly flies in the face of what the audience has been taught to regard as reasonable. Moreover, the attitude of the "Friseuse" towards the "Chef", that naïveté which is literally able to work (apparent) wonders, clearly refers to similar scenes in *Die heilige Johanna von den Schlachthöfen* (BFA 3. Pp. 127–234), and hence enables the "Chef" to come into his own as a captain of industry. In its citationality and in its counter-intuitive timing, then, as well as in its simultaneous evocation and disavowal of heroic emotion, this scene can be read as a classic instance of Brechtian *Verfremdung*.

Exactly the same can be said of the scene's dialectical counterpart, in which the equally referential sybaritic wisdom of the "Chef" constitutes an infuriatingly reasonable impediment to the revolutionary ardour so inappropriately projected onto the gentle rebels by the actress Volumnia. Here too the attitude of the "Chef" is explained through allusions to an early work of his inspiration. Even his enjoyment of the proffered coffee has an equivalent in the milk and geese of *Galileo*. The gesture with which the "Friseuse" acknowledges the presence around her of a theatre is precisely prefigured in the light that blinds the "Polier" on his first entrance. The play that makes the mannequin of Coriolanus into a "Dingsymbol" is likewise comparable to the business surrounding the flag. And the way in which the "Chef" and Volumnia express their "Familiendrama" in a stichomythia of inverted invective not only prefigures the similarly terse exchange between the "Chef" and the hairdresser. It also clearly recalls both the battle of the proverbs from *Der kaukasische Kreidekreis* and the Villon ballades of the *Dreigroschenoper* and therefore emphasizes with the use of virtual quotation its status as a paradigmatic example of that technique of estranged acting that Brecht called "das Zitieren" (BFA 22.2. Pp. 650–651).

In the light of this, the very many allusions to Brecht texts in Grass's play can be seen less as the keys to a "Schlüsseldrama" than as indications of the kind of play we are dealing with. It is not a realistic drama, but a self-consciously theatrical one. It is not a drama of character, but of situation, not a "Tragödie", but a "Trauerspiel" with elements of liberating comedy. It is not a didactic drama, in that it does not deliver ready-made judgements.[76] Rather it provides a model in which the changing roles available to the intellectual in a revolution – mouthpiece, traitor, doomed champion and elegist – are successively suggested and rejected in such a way as to chart the course of the uprising itself.[77] It is not a heroic drama, not even a drama of failed heroism; rather it is a drama in which the very notion of heroism is dialectically deconstructed. It neither lays claim to historical authenticity like documentary drama nor to ahistorical or posthistorical antinomianism like the Theatre of the Absurd. Instead it uses an invented but perfectly plausible "Einfall" to elaborate a multiple allegory whose very *mise en abyme* is able to capture the combination of personal responsibility and futile inevitability – the "schuldbewußte Anklage" – of historical drama.

In its structure, the play combines an Aristotelian tautness with an anti-Aristotelian multiplicity of modes; a dialectic of thesis, antithesis and aftermath; an architecture of double arch and buttress; and the constant of a five-fold repetition. In its styles it confronts grandeur and bathos, Shakespeare and "Berliner Schnauze", "Oh-Mensch"-Expressionism with the "Neue Sachlichkeit" of

---

[76] Mason: *The Sceptical Muse* (n. 39). Pp. 97–98: "The didactic surface masks a network of conflicts which offer no clear solution".
[77] Cf. Cunliffe: Grass and the Denial of Drama (n. 69). P. 69: "The Director plays a series or [sic] roles, from the hardened revolutionary to Hamlet".

political expediency, Falstaffian farce and Beckettian disintegration, narrative and demonstration, "Straßenszene" and "Lehrstück". In its gestures it continually insists on its own constructedness, its status as a citational patchwork, its practised inauthenticity. And its use of *Verfremdung* is so thoroughgoing as to have bamboozled certain sections of the critical community completely. In other words Günter Grass's *Die Plebejer proben den Aufstand* is neither about nor against Brecht, neither a disavowal nor a portrait. As I hope to have shown, it is, quite simply and down to the smallest detail, a Brechtian play. And as such, it is a perfect vehicle for conveying the behaviour of a "Chef" on a celebrated wet Wednesday.

Authors in this Volume

Martin Brady teaches film history at King's College London. He has published articles and chapters on German and French film (Jean-Marie Straub/Danièle Huillet, Michael Haneke, Robert Bresson, experimental and Brechtian film, literary adaptation, GDR documentary film, Kafka and film, Adorno and film, and the Hitler film *Downfall*), music (Arnold Schönberg), literature (Paul Celan), and Jewish exile architects. He is the translator of Victor Klemperer's *LTI*, co-translator (with Helen Hughes) of Alexander Kluge's *Stores of Cinema*. He is also active as an artist and filmmaker. He is currently working on a book on Brutalist architecture.

Steve Giles is Professor of German Studies and Critical Theory at the University of Nottingham. He has published widely on Brecht, modern drama, and critical theory. His most recent Brecht publication is a new edition and translation of *Rise and Fall of the City of Mahagonny* (2007).

Robert Gillett is Senior Lecturer in German at Queen Mary, University of London. He works on modern German and Austrian literature, and gay and queer literature and film, with a special focus on Hubert Fichte. He has been teaching Brecht and Grass to productively sceptical students for a decade or so, and was the organizer, with Martin Swales, of the workshop with which the then Institute of Germanic Studies marked the Brecht centenary.

Peter Hutchinson is Reader in German in the University of Cambridge and Director of Studies in Modern Languages at Trinity Hall. He has published widely on aspects of German literature from the eighteenth century to the present day (especially on the period since 1945), written several pieces on Brecht, and has edited a number of studies of German literature.

Frank Krause is Senior Lecturer in German at the Department of English and Comparative Literature, Goldsmiths College (University of London). His most recent publications include: *Literarischer Expressionismus* (2008); *France and German Expressionism* (ed.; 2008); *Klangbewußter Expressionismus. Moderne Techniken des rituellen Ausdrucks* (2006); *Georg Kaiser and Modernity* (ed.; 2005); *Sakralisierung unerlöster Subjektivität. Zur Problemgeschichte des zivilisations- und kulturkritischen Expressionismus* (2000).

Tom Kuhn is Faculty Lecturer in Twentieth-Century German Literature at the University of Oxford and a Fellow of St Hugh's College. Recent publications have been on Brecht and his contemporaries in German drama and poetry. The co-edited volume *Brecht on Art and Politics* appeared in 2003. Current projects include a study of Brecht and the pictorial. He is series editor of the Methuen Drama Brecht edition with A&C Black.

Karen Leeder is Reader in German at the University of Oxford, and Fellow and Tutor in German at New College, Oxford. She has published widely on modern German literature, especially poetry, including: *"Flaschenpost": German Poetry and the Long Twentieth Century* and *"Schaltstelle": Neue deutsche Lyrik im Dialog* (both 2007). She has published extensively on Brecht, including: *The Young Brecht* (1992) and *Empedocles' Shoe. Essays on Brecht's Poetry* (2002), both with Tom Kuhn, and *O Chicago! O Widerspruch! Hundert Gedichte auf Brecht* (2006) with Erdmut Wizisla. She has also translated work by a number of German writers into English, including, most recently: *After Brecht: A Celebration* (2006).

David Midgley studied German and French at Oxford (BA 1971; DPhil 1975), and did his early research on the life and works of Arnold Zweig. He has been a member of the German Department at Cambridge University and a Fellow of St John's College, Cambridge, since 1980, and he now holds the post of University Reader in German Literature and Culture. He has published widely on German literature of the period 1890–1945, with a particular emphasis on Brecht and Döblin, and his latest book, *Writing Weimar* (2000), is a broad-based study of the literature of the Weimar Republic in relation to its social and cultural context.

Hans-Harald Müller: Professor für Neuere deutsche Literatur an der Universität Hamburg, Gastprofessuren in St. Louis, Johannesburg, Cambridge (St. John's College) und Rostock. Forschungs- und Publikationsschwerpunkte: Theorie und Geschichte der Literaturwissenschaft, Literatur des 19. und 20. Jahrhunderts. Herausgeber der Werke von Theodor Plievier und Leo Perutz.

Klaus-Detlef Müller: Professor für Neuere deutsche Literaturwissenschaft an der Universität Tübingen. Zahlreiche Publikationen zu Brecht, u.a.: *Die Funktion der Geschichte im Werk Bertolt Brechts* (1967, [2]1972), *Bertolt Brecht. Kommentar zur erzählenden Prosa* (München 1980), *Bertolt Brecht. Epoche-Werk-Wirkung* (Hg.; 1985). Außerdem: *Studien zur literarischen Autobiographie der Goethezeit* (1976), *Franz Kafka. Romane* (2007). Mitherausgeber von *Bertolt Brecht: Werke. Große kommentierte Berliner und Frankfurter Ausgabe* (1988–2000) und *Johann Wolfgang Goethe: Sämtliche Werke* (1985ff.).

Stephen Parker is Professor of German and Head of the School of Languages, Linguistics and Cultures at the University of Manchester. Fellowships include: John Rylands Research Institute (1991–2); and Alexander von Humboldt Foundation,

Free University Berlin (1993–4). In 2000–4, he was Director of the AHRC project, The Modern Restoration. Essays on the history of *Sinn und Form* appeared in *Sinn und Form* in 1992, 1994 and 1999. Book publications include: *Peter Huchel: A Literary Life in 20th-Century Germany* (1998); *The Modern Restoration: Re-thinking German Literary History 1930–1960* (with Peter Davies and Matthew Philpotts; 2004); and *Sinn und Form: Anatomy of a Literary Journal* (with Peter Davies and Matthew Philpotts; forthcoming). His next project is a new literary biography of Brecht.

Michael Patterson studied in Berlin and Oxford, where he wrote a doctoral thesis on modern German drama. He taught German at Queen's University, Belfast, Theatre Studies at universities in England and Wales and Northern Ireland, and is now Emeritus Professor at De Montfort University Leicester. He has published six books and many articles on German theatre, including *German Theatre Today* (1976), *The Revolution in German Theatre 1900–1933* (1981), *The First German Theatre* (1990), and *German Theatre: A Bibliography* (1996). His most recent publication, *The Oxford Dictionary of Plays*, has recently appeared in revised paperback as *The Oxford Guide to Plays*.

Ernest Schonfield is Lecturer in German and Comparative Literature at King's College London. He has taught at St Peter's College, Oxford and University College London, and published essays on Thomas Mann, James Joyce and Hubert Fichte. His first book, *Art and its Uses in Thomas Mann's "Felix Krull"*, is due to be published in spring 2008.

Ronald Speirs is Head of the School of Humanities and Professor of German in the University of Birmingham, specializing in German literature from 1870 to the present day. He has written or edited three books on Brecht, one on Kafka and one on Thomas Mann, co-edited volumes on Fascism and European Literature and Germany's Two Unifications, and edited and translated work by Max Weber and Friedrich Nietzsche.

Marielle Sutherland completed her undergraduate studies at The Queen's College, Oxford and her postgraduate studies at UCL. Her PhD dissertation, entitled *Refiguring Death: The Poetics of Transience in the Poetry of Rainer Maria Rilke*, was published in 2006. She has also published on Rolf Dieter Brinkmann and Peter Handke. In 2005 she was the Third Prize Winner in the John Dryden Translation Competition, and her translation of Catrin Barnsteiner's short story *Verglüht* appears in *Comparative Critical Studies* 2007. She was Lecturer in German Studies at Oxford Brookes from 2004 to 2007 and is currently training to be a teacher in London.

Martin Swales studied at the Universities of Cambridge and Birmingham before going on to teach German at the Universities of Birmingham and Toronto, at King's College London and University College London where he is Emeritus Professor of German. He has published widely on German literature from the early eighteenth century onwards – particularly on Goethe, Stifter, Schnitzler, Thomas Mann, on the German "Novelle", the German "Bildungsroman", and on German Realism.

Andrew Webber is Reader in Modern German and Comparative Culture at the University of Cambridge and a Fellow of Churchill College. Both his last book, *The European Avant-garde: 1900–1940* (2004), and his forthcoming study, *Berlin in the Twentieth Century: A Cultural Topography* (2008), include discussion of Brecht.

Godela Weiss-Sussex is Senior Lecturer in Modern German Literature at the Institute of Germanic & Romance Studies, University of London. Her main research interests lie in the culture and literature of the nineteenth and twentieth centuries, in particular: the representation of the city in literature and the visual arts, and the works of German-Jewish writers. Her publications include: *Berlin. Kultur und Metropole in den zwanziger und seit den neunziger Jahren* (ed., with Ulrike Zitzlsperger; 2007), *Urban Mindscapes of Europe* (ed., with Franco Bianchini; 2006), *Georg Hermann. Deutsch-jüdischer Schriftsteller und Journalist, 1871–1943* (ed.; 2004), and *Metropolitan Chronicles. Georg Hermann's Berlin Novels 1897 to 1912* (2000).

Ann White is Senior Lecturer in German and Head of German at Royal Holloway, University of London. She is the author of *Names and Nomenclature in Goethe's "Faust"* (1980), co-editor of an edition of Thomas Mann's *Tonio Kröger* (1996) and has published articles on the work of H. G. Adler, Jurek Becker, Brecht, Chamisso, Hesse, Kafka, Thomas Mann, and K. P. Moritz.

John J. White is Emeritus Professor of German and Comparative Literature and Visiting Senior Research Fellow in German, King's College London. He is the author of *Mythology in the Modern Novel* (1971), *Literary Futurism: Aspects of the First Avant-Garde* (1990), *Brecht's "Leben des Galilei"* (1996) and *Bertolt Brecht's Dramatic Theory* (2004). He has published widely in the fields of modern German fiction, drama, comparative literature and literary semiotics.

Erdmut Wizisla ist Leiter des Bertolt-Brecht-Archivs und Leiter des Walter Benjamin Archivs, beide Akademie der Künste, Berlin. Buchveröffentlichungen (u. a.): *Benjamins Begriffe* (Hg., zus. mit Michael Opitz; 2000), *Benjamin und Brecht. Die Geschichte einer Freundschaft* (2004), *Bertolt Brecht: Geschichten*

vom Herrn Keuner. Zürcher Fassung (Hg.; 2004), *"O Chicago! O Widerspruch!"*.
Hundert Gedichte auf Bertolt Brecht (Hg., zus. mit Karen Leeder; 2006),
Arendt und Benjamin (Hg., zus. mit Detlev Schöttker; 2006), *Walter Benjamins
Archive. Bilder, Texte und Zeichen* (Hg., zus. mit Ursula Marx, Gudrun Schwarz
u. Michael Schwarz; 2006), *Die Bibliothek Bertolt Brechts. Ein kommentiertes
Verzeichnis* (Hg., zus. mit Helgrid Streidt u. Heidrun Loeper; 2007).

Ulrike Zitzlsperger is Senior Lecturer at the University of Exeter. Her main
research interests lie in the culture and literature of the sixteenth and twentieth
centuries. Among her publications are numerous articles on Berlin culture
(including literature, architecture and event culture) in the twentieth century, in
particular in the 1920s and 1990s. Her most recent books are *Vienna Meets Berlin:
Culture in the Metropolis 1918–1938* (ed., with John Warren; 2005) and *Berlin.
Kultur und Metropole in den zwanziger und seit den neunziger Jahren* (ed.,
with Godela Weiss-Sussex; 2007).

Index

Works by Brecht

Persons other than Brecht

G. HÄNTZSCHEL / U. LEUSCHNER / S. HANUSCHEK (HG.)
TREIBHAUS

Jahrbuch für die Literatur der fünfziger Jahre
**Band 3 · 2007: Der Zweite Weltkrieg in erzählenden Texten
zwischen 1945 und 1965**
herausgegeben von Jürgen EGYPTIEN

2007, 249 Seiten, kt.,
26,– EUR

ISBN: 978-3-89129-893-0

Jürgen EGYPTIEN: Erzählende Literatur über den Zweiten Weltkrieg aus dem Zeitraum 1945 bis 1965. Einleitende Bemerkungen zu Forschung, Gegenstand und Perspektiven • Hans-Edwin FRIEDRICH: „Ihr Geist und ihr Körper hatten sich an die Angst gewöhnt". Wahrnehmung des Krieges in Wolfgang Otts Roman *Haie und kleine Fische* (1956) • Sabine ZELGER: Wider die Macht des autorisierten Blicks. Die Arbeit am Wissen in Alexander Kluges *Schlachtbeschreibung* und Heimrad Bäckers *nachschrift* • Günter HÄNTZSCHEL: Der Zweite Weltkrieg in Anthologien der DDR • Elke KASPER: „Ich wünschte, wir kämen durch". Der Kriegsroman in der DDR • Jürgen EGYPTIEN: Figurenkonzeptionen im Kriegsroman. Die Darstellung von Anhängern, Mitläufern und Gegnern des Nationalsozialismus in Gert Ledigs *Vergeltung*, Michael Horbachs *Die verratenen Söhne*, Harry Thürks *Die Stunde der toten Augen* und Manfred Gregors *Die Brücke* • Raffaele LOUIS: Gleichnisse vom verlorenen Sinn. Georg Hensels *Nachtfahrt*, Jens Rehns *Feuer im Schnee*, Werner Warsinskys *Kimmerische Fahrt* und Herbert Zands *Letzte Ausfahrt* • Zygmunt MIELCZAREK: Hugo Hartung: *Der Himmel war unten*. Bericht eines Überlebenden • Heinz SCHUMACHER: „Ein Ausschnitt aus der Berliner Wirklichkeit jener Tage". Anmerkungen zu Gregor von Rezzoris Roman *Oedipus siegt bei Stalingrad* – unter besonderer Berücksichtigung des Phänomens der Intertextualität • Andreas WEBER: Soldaten als Schriftsteller. Über drei österreichische Kriegsromane • Jürgen EGYPTIEN / Raffaele LOUIS: 100 Kriegsromane und -erzählungen des Zeitraums 1945 bis 1965. Eine kommentierte Synopse ihrer Publikationsgeschichte

Das Interesse an der literarischen Entwicklung beider deutscher Staaten sowie der deutschsprachigen Literatur in den Nachbarländern von der Nachkriegszeit bis zu den 60er Jahren ist sichtbar gewachsen. Das Jahrbuch möchte der literaturwissenschaftlichen Beschäftigung mit diesem Zeitraum ein gemeinsames Publikationsforum bieten.

Ebenfalls lieferbar:
Band 1 · 2005: Wolfgang Koeppen & Alfred Doeblin. Topographien der literarischen Moderne
ISBN 978-3-89129-889-3 · 273 Seiten, kt. · 26,– EUR
Band 2 · 2006: Wolfgang Koeppen 1906–1996
ISBN 978-3-89129-880-0 · 306 Seiten, kt. · 26,– EUR

IUDICIUM Verlag GmbH
Postfach 701067 • D-81310 München • Hans-Grässel-Weg 13 • D-81375 München
Tel. +49 (0)89 718747 • Fax +49 (0)89 7142039 • info@iudicium.de
Bestellungen richten Sie bitte an Ihre Buchhandlung oder an den Verlag.
Das Gesamtverzeichnis finden Sie im Internet unter www.iudicium.de

The St Gall Passion Play

Music and Performance

Peter Macardle

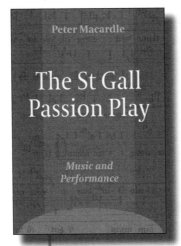

The early-fourteenth-century *St Gall Passion Play* comes from the Central Rhineland. Unfortunately its music (over one hundred Latin and German chants) is given in the manuscript only as brief incipits, without any musical notation. This interdisciplinary study reconstructs the musical stratum of the play. It is the first full-scale musical reconstruction of a large German Passion play in recent times, using the latest available scholarly data in drama, liturgy and music. It draws conclusions about performance practice and forces, and offers a sound basis for an authentic performance of the play. The study applies musical and liturgical data to the problem of localizing the play (the first time this has been systematically attempted), and assesses how applicable this might be to other plays. It presents a detailed study of the distinctive medieval liturgical uses of three German dioceses, Mainz, Speyer and Worms. The comparative approach suggests how the music of other plays might be reconstructed and understood, and shows that a better understanding of the music of medieval drama has much to teach us about other aspects of the genre. The book should be of interest to literary scholars, theatre historians, musicologists, liturgical scholars, and those involved in the performance of early drama.

Amsterdam/New York, NY,
2007 460 pp.
(Ludus 10)
Bound € 92 / US$ 138
ISBN: 9789042023468

USA/Canada:
295 North Michigan Avenue - Suite 1B, Kenilworth, NJ 07033, USA. Call Toll-free (US only): 1-800-225-3998
All other countries:
Tijnmuiden 7, 1046 AK Amsterdam, The Netherlands
Tel. +31-20-611 48 21 Fax +31-20-447 29 79
Please note that the exchange rate is subject to fluctuations

Names of Nihil

Arvydas Šliogeris
Translated from Lithuanian by Robertas Beinartas
Preface by Leonidas Donskis

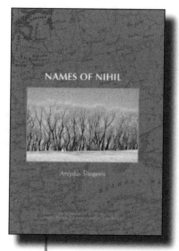

In this book, probably for the first time in Western philosophy, an attempt has been made to point out and systematically explicate the problem scope of the Nothing (which is called Nihil in the book) and to try to explain the springhead of the excessive negativity, inherent only in the human being, or in other words, the springhead of the human's natural nihilism. Nihilism is treated here not as a posture, pose, or an ideological attitude, but as the spread of the human metaphysical nucleus, of Nihil. Nihilistic annihilation, manifesting itself as the road of the naming of Nihil and of the production of thingly crystals (artificial world) as a result of that naming, usually is called "history". Names of Nihil (language phenomena), being the antithesis of Nihil, falsify and cover up Nihil itself, turning it into "supreme" being, e.g. into "the One", "God", "Substance", "Matter", "Spirit", *ad infinitum*. This book should be interesting not only to philosophers or humanitarians, but also to all those who concern themselves with the total human condition.

Amsterdam/New York, NY, 2008 X-136 pp.
(On the Boundary of Two Worlds: Identity, Freedom, and Moral Imagination in the Baltics 14)
Paper € 30 / US$ 45
ISBN: 9789042024021

USA/Canada:
295 North Michigan Avenue - Suite 1B, Kenilworth, NJ 07033, USA. Call Toll-free (US only): 1-800-225-3998
All other countries:
Tijnmuiden 7, 1046 AK Amsterdam, The Netherlands
Tel. +31-20-611 48 21 Fax +31-20-447 29 79
Please note that the exchange rate is subject to fluctuations